WORLD EDIBLE NUTS ECONOMY

About the Author

Shri S.P. Malhotra has long and extensive experience in dealing with agricultural and horticultural commodities, having worked in the Planning Commission, Government of India, and as an FAO Agricultural Planning Advisor in developing countries. He had worked for almost thirty years as a Senior Economist (Commodity Specialist) at the FAO Headquarters, Rome. On behalf of the FAO had organized International Workshops on Horticulture and Tree Nut Crops for Asia, Africa and Latin American regions. Since his retirement from FAO in 1995, he has worked as a consultant/advisor for the World Bank, IFAD and FAO. He has to his credit a large number of research papers and publications. His book on *Livestock Economy in India*, authored jointly with Dr. P.C. Bansil, has been published by CBS Publications and Distributors in 2006 and his latest comprehensive publication on *Indian Fisheries and Aquaculture in a Globalizing Economy* jointly authored with Dr. V.R.P. Sinha, has been published by Narendra Publishing House, Delhi, in 2007.

WORLD EDIBLE NUTS ECONOMY

S.P. Malhotra
Former Senior Commodity Specialist
Food and Agriculture Organization, Rome

CONCEPT PUBLISHING COMPANY, NEW DELHI-110059

ISBN 13-978-81-8069-561-2
ISBN 10-81-8069-561-1

First Published 2008

Published and Printed by
Ashok Kumar Mittal
Concept Publishing Company
A/15-16, Commercial Block, Mohan Garden
New Delhi-110059 (INDIA)

Phones : 25351460, 25351794
Fax : 091-11-25357103
Email : publishing@conceptpub.com

This book is dedicated to my fun loving
grand children Kieran, Monica, Selina
Jay and Arun
who insisted that I should play with them rather
than devote time to Nutty Issues
discussed in this book

PREFACE

The original idea of undertaking a study on edible nuts was initiated in the year 2002 by my esteemed colleague Dr. M.L. Dewan, former senior officer with FAO and founder Chairman and Trustee of HIMCON. He is keenly interested to expand area under walnut, almond and other nuts in Uttaranchal (Now called Uttrakhand). For this he and his team have undertaken a number of studies for sustainable development of the state. They have also been distributing walnut and almond seedlings imported from USA among farmers in the state. Following Dr. Dewan' several meetings with the Chief Minister of the State and the Secretary Horticulture Development, it was proposed to conduct a techno-economic feasibility study on expansion of walnut production in Uttrakhand. The Government of Uttrakhand is keen to promote cultivation of nut trees in the state. The author of the present book, who was involved from the start with the project proposal, continued to work and expanded the scope of the study to deal with the World Edible Nuts Economy. The author's four years labour is reflected in this book.

Edible nuts are used by mankind for food, edible oils, spices, condiments or beverages. They have been an important source of food from prehistoric times and are among the most nutritionally concentrated of human foods, high in protein, oil, energy, minerals and vitamins. Nine major tree nuts of the world may be listed in the order of their importance in terms of production and consumption. These are cashew, almond, walnut, chestnut, pecan, pistachio, Brazil nut, hazelnut and macadamia. Cashew, Brazil nut and macadamia are highly valued nut crops adapted to the tropics. The rest have different climatic requirements and are produced in the sub-tropics and temperate zones. All these nine edible nuts are covered in this book.

The main objective of the study on World Edible Nuts Economy is to review the present status, problems and future prospects for each of nine major world edible nuts. It presents a comprehensive review of different aspects for each of these nuts. Aspects covered include History and Origin of different nuts, agronomic, climatic and cultural aspects, review of world demand supply and international trade followed by country case studies. The book addresses the potential of major world edible nuts. Problems of each of the nine major edible nuts are identified and suitable recommendations and suggestions made to address these problems.

The international trade in edible tree nuts is substantial and one in which developing countries participate fully. However, the current performance of tree nut crops especially in the developing producing countries is far below the inherent potential of respective nut crops. Productivity levels in most developing countries leave much to be desired. There are wide disparities between actual yields obtained and yields achieved by the researchers within the country and also among those in the developed countries. Unfortunately, in most developing countries crop husbandry practices are either absent or poorly applied. With the application of modern agro-techniques and use of superior germplasm, products and productivity of nut trees can be substantially increased. All these issues and problems are discussed in respective individual nut chapter.

Attempt has also made to project import demand with suitable suggestions on how the producing countries can take advantage of the projected future expansion in import demand. The book also analyzes the impact of policies got implemented forcibly by multilateral agencies such as World Bank and the IMF under their Special Adjustment Programmes. The example is the banning exports of cashew kernels by Mozambique based on recommendations of the IBRD and IMF. Some of these policies have disastrous economic consequences on the economy of the developing countries concerned.

Growing of edible nut trees offer several advantages. They could apart from providing valuable nut fruits, serve several purposes, such as afforestation, soil conservation and protection by preventing soil erosion from wind and rain in environmentally vulnerable areas. Some of the nut trees such as cashewnut can be grown on poor or barren soil. Some other nut crops are tolerant to drought conditions and provide hedge against crop failure. Moreover, cashew tree ability to grow on poor soil and to be inter-cropped with food or medicinal crops makes it most suitable for small farmers. In India cashew is being considered as a candidate for rehabilitation of wasteland. In Indonesia cashew growing was originally started for afforestation programme, particularly in areas which are infertile or experienced dry climatic conditions. In China a large-scale tree nut-growing scheme has been undertaken for conservation and diversification of agriculture along with for the poverty elevation. Similarly, hazelnuts in Turkey are grown on soils, which are unsuitable for other crops. Also in high rainfall mountainous area hazelnut prevented soil erosion.

The book consists of 22 Chapters. It is divided into three parts. The first parts contain the introductory chapter, which provides overview of the eight major edible nuts followed by eleven chapters on walnut economy. In the second section five chapters are devoted to Cashewnuts and in the third section eight chapters discuss other edible nuts. The detailed list of chapters is as follows:

PART I : WALNUTS

(1) Introduction: An Overview. (2) History of the Walnut – A Tough Nut to Crack. (3) The Origin of the Walnut. (4) Agronomic Requirements for Establishing an Orchard and Producing Walnut. (5) World Walnut Economy. (6) Countries Case Study. (7) India Walnut Economy. (8) Long Term Prospects for World and Indian Walnut Economy. (9) Economics of Walnut Production in Uttrakhand and Himachal Pradesh.

PART II : CASHEWNUTS

(10) Cashew—*Anacardium occidental.* (11) World Cashewnut Economy. (12) Cashewnut Sector in Major Asian Producing Countries. (13) Cashew Industry in Other Asian Countries. (14) Cashewnut farming in African Countries.

PART III : OTHER MAJOR EDIBLE NUTS

(15) World Almond Economy. (16) World Pistachio Economy. (17) World Hazelnut Economy. (18) World Chestnut Economy. (19) World Macadamia Nut Economy. (20) Macadamia Nut Industry in the USA. (21) World Pecan Nut Economy. (22) World Brazil Nut Economy.

The book is based on professional long experience in the field of the author and on exhaustive review of the available literature and analysis of primary and secondary data on different edible nuts collected from authoritative national and international sources. The information is quite comprehensive, covering all-important areas. It is hoped that the book will stimulate action at all levels to help achieve the full potential of nut tree sectors in India and in other countries. The book should be useful to students, political leaders, planners, policy makers, executives, research workers and teachers.

S.P. Malhotra

ACKNOWLEDGEMENTS

Special thanks are due to Dr. M. L. Dewan who initiated the whole process and encouraged me to undertake this difficult venture. I have benefited from advice, comments and suggestions, on various aspects, given generously by him and a number of officials and experts in the horticulture sector, both in official departments and private sector. Some of them have also provided a valuable data on different tree nut crops. I have drawn extensively from the scientific writings of many experts, which are cited in this book. I have received cooperation and inspiration from a large number of people, official agencies and the industry. It is impossible to acknowledge the assistance of all those who have contributed to the book. However, my grateful thanks to Ms. Kyle Cummingam and Khaliaka Meardry, of USDA, Foreign Agriculture Service, Horticultural and Tropical Service, for their technical advise on world nut economy and trade and supplying up-to-date data.

Thanks are also due to Shri K. Krishna Pillai, Chairman, Cashew Export Promotion Council of India, Cochin, for useful suggestions and supply of relevant material and data. I would also like to convey my thanks to Sarvashri S.D. Kumar and K. Kumar, Department of Fruit Breeding and Genetic Resources; Dr. Y.S. Parmar University of Horticulture and Forestry, Nauni-Solan (HP), for providing insight into present status and problems of walnut cultivation in India. I am also indebted to Dr. M.L. Sharma and Dr. R.S. Tripathi, Agricultural Economic Division, G.B. Pant University of Agriculture and Technology, Hill Campus, Ranichauri, Tehri Garhwal, Uttrakhand, for their technical comments and suggestions. Shri Gunjan V. Jain, Proprietor of one of the large walnuts exporting companies (V.C.K.Nuts) in Jammu provided useful data on the economics of walnut production in Jammu and Kashmir State. These are included in this book.

I would like to express my sincere thanks to the Libertarians and the staff of the UK Trade and Investment Information Centre, Ministry of Foreign Trade, London (England) for allowing me to access the trade data on edible nuts, for various years on their network from Global Trade Atlas. During the personal visit by the author the Librarian, Economics

Department, California University, Berkeley, made available lot of useful material on the USA and world edible economy. I appreciate very much their kind help.

The data and technical material provided by several individuals and authorities have been of immense help, as can be judged from innumerable sources quoted in various chapters of the book. Thanks are also due to Mr. Pratap Narain, Retired Senior Statistician, FAO, for his valuable suggestions and comments.

My life partner (Swarn) provided me the sustenance, succour, support and inspiration throughout without which I would not have been able to complete this work. I shall ever remain grateful to her.

Last but not the least, I am grateful to Shri Ashok Kumar Mittal, of Concept Publishing Company, New Delhi, for bring out the book in its present form and that too within minimum possible time.

S.P. Malhotra

CONTENTS

1

INTRODUCTION
AN OVERVIEW

Edible nuts are used by mankind for food, edible oils, spices, condiments or beverages. They have been an important food source from pre-historic times and are among the most nutritionally concentrated of human foods, high in protein, oil, energy, minerals and vitamins. Nine major tree nuts of the world may be listed in the order of their importance in terms of production and consumption. These are cashew, almond, walnut, chestnut, pecan, pistachio, Brazil nut, hazelnut and macadamia. Cashew, Brazil nut and macadamia are highly valued nut cropped adapted to the tropics. The rest have different climatic requirements and are produced in the sub-tropics and temperate zones. Nuts used solely for spices or condiments have been largely excluded since they are used sparingly, to flavour food and not as a food; traditionally they are considered separately from edible nuts. Nuts which are largely used as commercial sources of edible oil are also not discussed in any great detail since they are already adequately dealt with in the literature for instance the oil palms *Elaeis guienensis*. World production of major edible nuts increased by almost 65 per cent over fourteen years, from 5.06 million tonnes in 1990 to 8.33 million tonnes in 2004 (Table 1.1).

WHAT ARE EDIBLE NUTS

The botanical use of the term "nut" refers to an indehiscent fruit that is usually shed as a 1–seeded unit. It is formed from more than one carpel but only one seed develops, the rest abort. The pericarp is usually lignified and is often partially or completely surrounded by a "cupule". True nuts include the hazelnuts, *Corylus* spp. (Corylaceae), and from the Fagaceae, beechnuts, *Fagus* spp. and acorns, *Quercus* spp. The term is also loosely applied to any woody fruit or seed, such as the walnut (drupe of *Juglans* spp., Juglandaceae), Brazil nut (seed of *Bertholletia excelsa*, Lecythidaceae) or peanut (indehiscent legume of *Arachis hypogea*,

Table 1.1: World Production of Major Edible Nuts (in Tonnes)

Edible Nuts	*Average 1990-92*	*2000*	*2001*	*2002*	*2003*	*2004*	*Average 2002-04*	*% Share*
Cashew Nuts	824,957	1,662,143	1,621,011	1,882,489	2,088,839	2,291,543	2,087,623.7	25.1
Almonds	1,286,756	1,467,339	1,551,603	1,851,468	1,665,536	1,530,271	1,682,425.0	20.2
Walnuts	914,450	1,242,739	1,264,083	1,356,407	1,489,132	1,472,329	1,439,289.3	17.3
Chestnuts	601,390	954,552	945,506	1,029,462	1,111,650	1,122,244	1,087,785.3	13.1
Filberts/Hazel Nuts	610,194	679,641	882,604	834,944	688,332	680,580	734,618.7	8.8
Pistachio	316,977	568,838	293,787	517,974	515,310	549,837	527,707.0	6.3
Brazil Nut	61,891	75,156	72,217	71,149	72,270	72,450	71,956.3	0.9
Miscellaneous	445,240	620,186	720,172	648,326	741,133	697,148	695,535.7	8.4
Total	5,061,855	7,270,594	7,350,983	8,192,219	8,372,202	8,416,402	8,326,941.0	100.0

Source: Prepared based on FAO STAT Database: December 2005.

Leguminosae subfamily Papilionoideae). It is even incorrectly applied in the vernacular names to non-fruiting bodies, such as the root tubers of the pignut or earthnut *Conopodium majus* (Umbelliferae) and *Cyperus esculentus* (Cyperaceae), although in the latter case the root tubers are eaten as a form of dessert nut. A further complication is that the seeds of several members of the Cucurbitaceae and the sunflower, *Helianthus annuus* (Compositae) are eaten as dessert nuts and are included in the literature on edible nuts yet they are always referred to both botanically and in the vernacular as seeds.

Nuts are hard-shelled fruits, or the edible kernels of fleshy drupes or berries, or seeds that are traditionally referred to as nuts. The first two categories of nuts are the fruits of trees or shrubs, the third include some herbs. Since the value of some nuts as food is relative to what better alternatives are available, there are obvious grey areas regarding whether the nut is to be regarded as edible or not and an arbitrary decision has been made as to whether a species should or should not be included. Some 542 species of edible "nuts" have been listed in FAO publication Edible Nuts, 1995.[1] However, in this book detailed information is given only for nine major edible nuts.

Nutritional Value

Most edible "nuts" contain concentrated food reserves for future generations of plants and provide valuable sources of energy, protein, oils, minerals and vitamins suitable for human consumption. Others have their food reserves in the form of starch instead of protein, including chestnuts - *Castanea* spp., acorns - *Quercus* spp., water chestnuts - *Trapa* spp., ye-eb - *Cordeauxia edulis*, Bambara groundnuts - *Vigna subterranea* and lotus seeds *Nelumbo* spp. While *Pinus* spp. is protein rich, some members of the Gymnospermae such as *Ginkgo biloba* and *Araucaria* spp. also have starchy food reserves.[2]

Nuts have a reputation for being indigestible, especially if eaten in large quantities or poorly masticated. They are generally a highly concentrated food but low in water and fibre content and consequently require thorough mastication if they are to be properly digested, and are preferably eaten with other foods. They have the additional value in that their fats are, in the main, highly unsaturated and are consequently beneficial in that they do not raise blood cholesterol. Peanuts (*Arachis hypogea*), sunflower seeds (*Helianthus annuus*), souari nuts (*Caryocar nuciferum*) and soynut (*Glycine max*) are specifically mentioned in this context.[3] The nutritional value for different major edible nuts is given in respective chapters in this book.

Harvesting

The harvesting of nuts from arborescent species is often of fallen nuts and as such is generally a prolonged, laborious and wasteful process since fruits do not necessarily all ripen within a short period. Picking fallen fruits is time consuming, especially in rough terrain and, depending on the time lapse between consecutive harvestings, can lead to rapid deterioration as well as losses to predators. Plantations can improve efficiency by providing better accessibility and easier harvesting conditions and, provided they are large enough, lead to mechanized harvesting by the use of ground harvesters and/or tree shakers. Mechanization is becoming increasingly important in North America where labour costs are particularly high.

Processing and Storage

This discussion is limited to the major nuts, where appropriate techniques and equipment have been developed. By dealing with processing and storage in general terms it is hoped that research worker will obtain ideas for dealing with similar problems in the less-known and little researched species.

Many dessert nuts loose their palatability or otherwise deteriorate if not properly dried or cured after collection or are badly stored, especially those with a high oil content. Among the major nuts walnuts and chestnuts are among the more perishable while pistachios and almonds are among the better keepers.

In-shell nuts are best stored at low temperatures. While rancidity is the main problem with shelled nuts, the kernels also have the ability to acquire off-flavours from the environment, such as tobacco and paint. Apart from rancidity, deterioration during long storage can be difficult to determine and aflatoxins can be present even when there is no obvious presence of moulds.[4]

Dehusking

Modern packaging and marketing is increasingly demanding kernels ready for immediate use, both in the home and confectionery trade. Hand processing is being replaced more and more by mechanization for providing a marketable product, especially where large-scale production is concerned.

Most tree nuts are enveloped in a fleshy or fibrous outer covering or husk which may or may not remain attached to the nut as it ripens and falls to the ground, as is the case for such important commercial nuts as the walnut, pecan, almond and macadamia. In some varieties of walnut and almond the ripe nut readily separates from the husk of their own accord; a few nuts, termed "sticktights" remain attached to their husks, the proportion depending on the cultivar. A poor or dry season may increase the number of sticktights.

The husk has to be removed either mechanically or by hand before nuts can be dried, shelled or otherwise processed. Walnuts especially must be dehusked as soon as they are collected, otherwise the colour and quality of the kernel will be progressively adversely affected the longer the husks remain.[5]

Washing

Nuts gathered from the ground are frequently soiled or dirty, especially after rain, so that washing is necessary in order to make the product more attractive for the market. Again, hand washing in tubs or machine-washing in cylindrical drums may be carried out. Any staining or discolouration is not affected by the washing and is removed at a later stage during bleaching.[6]

Drying and Dehydrating

Artificially produced heat and forced draughts are now increasingly replacing sun-drying for the drying or "curing" of nuts, especially by large-scale commercial producers. Outputs range from 1-7 tonnes for a drying time of 12-24 hours at, in the case of walnuts, not more than 43°C. Such mechanical dryers are not only independent of the weather but also give a more thorough and uniform drying of the nuts and, in the case of walnuts, result in less splitting. In America mechanical drying has been found to increase packing-house efficiency by stabilizing the delivery rate from the growers and to aid marketing by providing an earlier product. The investment costs do not exceed the high labour cost of sun drying.

Sun drying is still largely practised by small producers, particularly with almonds in the producing countries of Europe. It requires a high labour input to spread the nuts out on sheets or in trays, stirring frequently to ensure uniform drying, and also to provide protection at night or in the event of rain. Drying is completed when the kernels can be heard to rattle in the shells or can be broken rather than bent with the fingers. Drying may require only 2-3 days with continuous hot sun or take 2-3 weeks in inclement weather. Similarly, chestnuts in southern Europe were traditionally sun-dried or dried over a wood fire in a specially constructed kiln. A slow process, it may take several weeks and a heavy fuel input to achieve, although the smoke is reputed to have a beneficial effect in inhibiting subsequent fungal infestation but the process results in the loss of the fresh chestnut flavour and the chestnuts may even acquire a disagreeable one. The curing is complete when the shells may be easily separated from the kernels. Modern, mobile mechanical dryers now provide a faster and more uniform drying with a greater economy in fuel.[7]

Bleaching

Some nuts intended for marketing in-shell may have their appearance enhanced by bleaching to remove stains due to sun scorch and disease; walnuts are frequently thus treated by immersion for 1-2 minutes in a bleaching solution.

Sulphur dioxide or burning sulphur may be used, particularly for almonds that have been blemished during harvesting or drying, but this is practised less so now than in the past. Good quality almonds that have been quickly sun dried are already of an attractive appearance, require no bleaching. Over bleaching can give the shells a sickly white appearance and is liable to soften them and flavour the kernels; too little causes irregular bleaching.

Pecans can be considerably improved by removing the outer rough layer and polishing, a process, which, if required, makes the nuts more responsive to bleaching and drying. The outer layer may be removed by steel brushes or by the use of revolving drums containing coarse sand. Bleaching is effected by dipping the nuts for 4 minutes in, for example, sodium hypochlorite containing 2 per cent active chlorine. Various dyes may be used to colour the polished and bleached nuts an attractive brown or reddish brown.

Grading

Mechanical graders, such as a perforated revolving cylinder, are commonly used to sort nuts into various sizes, the smaller nuts being the first to fall. Pecan nuts, due to their ovoid or oblong shape, require special graders consisting of variously spaced rollers.

Imperfect, faulty or broken nuts may be removed by hand as the nuts pass along a continuous belt. A suction machine may also be used to lift blank or imperfectly filled nuts over a trap while the heavier nuts pass on. The low specific gravity of Grade 1 macadamia kernels allows them to be removed by floatation in ordinary water. Grade 2 may be removed using 30 g of salt in 1 litre of water, with Grade 3 sinking to the bottom. The nuts are then thoroughly dried.[8]

Storage

Most nuts can be satisfactorily stored for several months provided they are kept cool and dry. Many nuts are stored in the shell for longer periods but there is now a trend towards the cold storage of shelled nuts or kernels. Although requiring more space, the best results are obtained by storing in moisture proof containers after thorough dehydration. Cold storage in open receptacles can result in an uptake of odours such as ammonia, a loss of colour, flavour and texture and the possible development of rancidity. Cold storage in vacuumized containers or the use of inert gases appears to offer little advantage over cold storage for a similar period.

Commercial cold storage is general practice with the pecan. Better prices can be obtained by holding the nuts in store for some time after harvesting and the higher prices more than offset the cost of storage. It may also be profitable to hold a portion of a heavy crop in store in the expectation that the following crop will be smaller and the price higher.

Freshly gathered chestnuts have high moisture content and consequently prone to fungal attack. Stored in small heaps or shallow layers in an airy store walled on three sides and periodically turned over, they will keep perfectly for up to 3 months or longer. If stored too dry or in a single layer the kernels will shrivel and become hard. The onset of mould, as well as harmful grubs and insects, during storage may be prevented by immersing the fresh chestnuts in a solution of a fungicide for 48 hours. Gas treatment in autoclaves has been effectively used in France; chestnuts have also been successfully held in cold storage. Chestnuts placed in layers of sand and kept cool keep well and retain their germinability but may become less palatable. Cobnuts are sometimes stored in sawdust, which helps to prevent shrivelling.[9]

Cracking

The mechanical cracking of nuts is becoming increasingly important; nevertheless, large quantities of some kernels are still extracted laboriously by hand in some countries, such as the cashew in India and the almond in the Middle East. Mechanical cracking is faster but usually results in a higher percentage of broken kernels, which, fortunately, usually finds a ready outlet in the confectionery trade.

Power-driven, self-feeding nut-cracking machines require grading for size before being fed to the cracking jaws or rollers with special shaking devices to separate the kernels from the broken shells. The kernels may still have to pass along a continuous belt for broken kernels and other debris to be removed by hand.

Individual pecan nuts are commonly picked up in cups on an endless chain passing through a hoppere of graded nuts. Each nut passes to a slot where a piston-like rod exerts pressure at the end of the nut and cracks it, the shells and kernels then being released to a receptacle below. Very dry pecans often shatter badly with this treatment; prior wetting can reduce this problem, the kernels being redried after shelling.

The varying differences in the thickness and texture of the macadamia shell has created problems in the development of a suitable machine for cracking the shell without damaging the brittle kernel as there is less than 0.4 mm clearance between the two. The current vice-like design employs the principle of the nut being held between two blunt movable wedges.

Special cracking machines are also used for pine nuts where the demand is almost entirely for kernels. The tough leathery shell of the cashew is overcome by preliminary roasting, thus making the shell brittle and responsive to cracking, as well as lessening the danger of blistering from the caustic oils in the fruit. The roasting is usually done by hand, placing small quantities of kernels in an open iron pan over a small circular earthenware furnace. Care is required to avoid overcooking or charring of the kernels, while with undercooking, the shell remains tough. Attempts at using roasting ovens have been unsuccessful, resulting in discoloured kernels. Shelling is by hand; in southwestern India a wooden mallet and a flat stone is used to crack the shell, after which the kernel is sometimes removed with a wire prong. The kernels are then spread out on wire gauze trays in a hot-air room under controlled temperature in order to loosen the pink or reddish-brown skin before removal and also to remove any excess moisture.

The oyster nut cannot be cracked in the ordinary way due to its tough, leathery, fibrous shell. However, the shell is easy to cut and a slit is made around the edge of the disc-shaped nut with a knife.

A Chinese method of cracking hard-shelled nuts is to heat them in burning straw and then cool rapidly with cold water.

The shells, which were formerly regarded as a waste product for fuel, now have a number of industrial usages. Cleaned and ground to a fine powder, the shells of walnuts, coconuts, Brazil nuts and almonds have been used as an extender or filler in the manufacture of certain plastics and synthetic adhesives and is often considered superior to the softwood flours commonly used. The coarser grades of walnut shell powder have been utilized as cleaners and finishers in the fur, metal, tinplate and other industries; other uses are in linoleum, jointless flooring, and as a carrier for horticultural insecticides.[10]

Cooking and Salting

Some nuts are traditionally eaten cooked and salted. Peanuts and chestnuts are normally cooked before eating, while almonds are preferred roasted or toasted and salted, likewise the macadamia nut. Cooking definitely reduces the terebinthine or turpentine flavour in pine nuts.

The large, plump grades are used for roasted or toasted almonds; roasting or cooking in oil is said to produce the best flavour. A common method of salting is by immersion in a strong brine solution before allowing the almonds to drain and dry.

In Hawaii macadamia nuts are preferred cooked and salted, either by roasting in an oven or immersion in a vat of hot oil, the latter method is the preferred commercial method as it gives the nut an attractive gold-brown colour. Refined coconut oil is generally used and, because the hot oil tends to corrode many of the commoner metals, the vats are made of monel metal, stainless steel or glass. Excess oil is removed centrifugally and the nuts laid out to cool on wire mesh trays, being salted while they are still luke warm, using a 15 per cent solution of gum arabic or a special oil to enable the salt grains to adhere more readily to the nut. As the cooked nuts tend to be hygroscopic, they are vacuum packed as soon as they are cool.

Cashew nuts are always marketed cooked as the roasting procedure to render the shell more easily removable automatically cooks the kernel. The risk of contact with the caustic sap in the fresh fruit is also removed.[11]

Economics and Marketing

Successful marketing may be defined as identifying what the consumer requires or can be educated to require and to supply that requirement at a profit. The marketing process, however, is customer orientated inasmuch as production is designed to meet the customer's needs. Like other food crops, nuts have a limited "marketing life". The production to marketing chain can be extremely complex, ranging through harvesting techniques, grading and sorting, packaging, transport, storage, processing, curing, distribution and selling. Furthermore, as markets develop, from rural markets to urban chain stores, the consumer become more and more demanding in their requirements and, as a consequence, increase pressures upon the various sectors in the marketing chain.

The local market in a rural community may initially represent the surplus in production to household requirements. Population growth and urbanization accompanied by a proportionate decrease in agrarian activities encourages increased production that has to be met either through cultivation or more intensive harvesting from the wild. The marketing process develops further through regional and national markets to the international. The further along the chain the more stringent are the consumer's requirements, with increasing emphasis on quality and constancy of supply. Local and regional markets are less valuable and may be expected to handle cheaper and lower quality nuts than would be acceptable by international markets. The majority of tropical tree nuts are not yet well represented on the international market. Of the nine major edible tree nuts it is noticeable that only the Brazil nut and macadamia are from the tropics, while only one out of seven minor tree nuts and all 22 potential tree nuts are from the tropics or sub-tropics.

Nuts are largely tree crops and as such the production schedule will be long-term, requiring careful selection of cultivars and, in some cases, rootstocks. Initial investment may be high, with no return until the trees come into bearing. Labour requirements may be high for short periods in the year for pruning, harvesting and immediate post-harvest treatments and low for the rest of the year. High labour costs may be offset by increased mechanization, as in the North American nut plantations.

Quality is obviously of prime importance and good quality nuts can readily be spoiled, especially during harvesting and immediate post-harvest operations. The initial processing can result in broken or discoloured nuts unsuitable for the dessert nut trade. It is important, therefore, that producers should have ready access to other outlets, such as the food, oil and other industries.

Regularity and continuity of supply is important, especially for the international markets. Failure to comply will undoubtedly favour the importation of alternatives. A buoyant and profitable market can quickly change through oversupply or a sub-standard produce. Expansion in production must balance the market if prices are not to be depressed. However, nuts are a good candidate for marketing as "added value products" through processing, roasting, salting, etc., and have an excellent potential in the West for the health food market.[12]

The disposable world production of dessert nuts is shown in Table 1.1. These figures obviously do not show internal consumption. The general trend is towards increased production. In the league marketing tables almonds are the major product, pistachios have the fastest expansion rate while the trend for the Brazil nut shows a steadily declining production due to deforestation and a chaotic marketing system.

The world disposable production of nuts primarily grown as a commercial source of edible oils is shown in Table 1.2. The proportion used directly for food is not known. While the utilization of a few selected nuts by the developed world is reasonably well documented, there are no figures available for the remainder of the 520 edible nut-producing species. Their value within the rural community is largely based on anecdotal evidence. However, the following oil nuts are also not covered in this book.

Table 1.2: Disposable World Production of Oil Nuts and Their Products

('000 tonnes)

	1991-1993	*2001*	*2002*	*2003*	*2004*
Coconuts					
In-Shell	43,407	51,999	52,756	54,043	54,708
Copra	4,340	5,200	5,300	5,404	5,480
Groundnuts (in-shell)	23,943	34,958	36,239	35,895	36,492
Palm kernels	3,969	6,700	7,100	7,700	8,000
Sunflower seeds	21,841	26,433	20,343	24,534	27,795

Source: FAO, STAT DATA Base, March 2006.

Nuts in the Rural Economy

The most obvious value of edible nuts is their contribution as a concentrated food to the diet and, in some cases, as a source of edible oils. The major and minor nuts also have an important commercial value as dessert nuts.

In many of the developing countries, especially in the tropics and sub-tropics, nuts are often available during the dry season or winter months when fresh vegetables are not always readily available. They can also have the additional advantage in that they are not bulky and can usually be readily stored. The arborescent nut producers may have other advantages too, as providers of fuel, timber, fibre, medicines, browse, etc., plus their role in conserving the soil against wind and water erosion, providing shade and shelter, etc., as well as being aesthetically pleasing. The nut-producing herbs, i.e., groundnuts, etc., take their place in the agricultural rotation and, in the case of legumes, contribute to soil fertility.

The large-scale commercial production of nuts for the dessert and edible oil industries is well documented. However, the role of edible nuts in the rural economy is less clear. This is partly due to the confusion in the literature in defining what is an edible nut and as a consequence classifying them with edible fruits, plus a paucity of information regarding their utilization. Like other economic plants, the value of edible nuts, whether they are used for food or edible oil, is relative to what other alternatives are available. This, in turn, creates a problem in ordering the potential for development. A well-written account of a single species by an enthusiastic author tends to mask the value of other species.

The work by Okafor and co-workers in the Nigerian forests on the utilization and improvement of indigenous woody food plants may be taken as an example of how to maximize the forest resource within the forest, homesteads and farmland.[13] Elite trees favoured by local inhabitants were selected and various vegetative propagation techniques investigated, including budding. Budded trees of *Irvingia gabonensis* and *Treculia africana* produced viable fruits in 3.5 and 4 years respectively. An additional benefit in the case of the latter species, a tree up to 35 m tall, was that the reduction in fruiting height from budding eliminated the serious danger from the globular fruits falling and injuring passers-by; the fruits can be up to 50 cm in diameter and weigh up to 15 kg. Perhaps rather surprisingly, the reduced risk resulted in an increase in popularity rating.

Taxonomic investigations into the range of variation within a species can also be rewarding. The recognition of two variants within *Irvingia gabonensis* with different flowering seasons, var. *gabonensis* fruiting in the rainy season from April to September, and var. *excelsa* in the dry season from December to March has encouraged rational selections to be made for extending seasonal availability.

Conservation and Utilization of Genetic Resources

The requirements for the development, improvement and conservation of edible nut producing species are similar to the requirements for other species. Information is required on distribution and reproductive biology, including flowering and fruiting patterns, pollination mechanisms and pollinators, seed dispersal, viability, predation, nature of the breeding system, breeding and propagation techniques, pests and diseases, etc.

There are two conflicting interests involved. Efficient production resulting in a low cost product is mainly obtainable from plantations where the emphasis is on selection of genetic uniformity for ease of management and productivity. Small-scale, usually peasant production mainly makes use of wild resources or less rigorously selected cultivars and may even prefer an absence of uniformity in, for example, ripening in order to obtain a better spread in availability of mature fruit. Furthermore, peasant farming systems often protect useful trees during any land clearance operation while commercial farming systems tend to favour total land clearance with consequential loss of any genetic variability.

Wild resources often have the disadvantage in that the required species occurs sporadically in the surrounding vegetation. Whereas tree crops provide an excellent method of soil conservation, small-scale production can often have the additional advantage of making efficient use of difficult terrain. However, the demand for reliable quantities of a cheap, high quality product is placing increasing pressure on the small-scale producer and favouring the development of large-scale plantations, especially of Old World temperate species introduced to North America. The often-sporadic occurrence of a desirable edible nut-producing species in, for example, the rain forest, means that it can have a disproportionately low value as an economic species in any land clearance or reafforestation schemes. The Brazil nut population is an example of such a threatened species. Problems in maintaining an environment outside the rain forest that is suitable for its pollinator makes the establishment of *ex situ* conservation and commercial plantations difficult.

Although not strictly the result of selection, the canker forming bark disease caused by the fungus *Cryphonectria parasitica* syn. *Endothia parasitica* that first appeared in the New York in the 1890s was probably introduced from Orient with some Asiatic chestnut planting stock. The American chestnut, *Castanea dentata*, was subsequently almost completely destroyed over its entire natural range in the Appalachian mountains.[14] The moral of the above example is that there is always the possibility of a devastating fungal or virus infestation affecting plantation crops through poor crop sanitation coupled with uniform genetic susceptibility, and places increasing emphasis on the preservation of genetic diversity.

Plant conservation may be *in situ* or *ex situ*, the latter in gene or seed banks or *in vitro*. The simplest method is *in situ*, by maintaining breeding populations within their natural environment through the establishment of reserves. Several reserves will obviously be required for widely distributed species. Pressures on land use, especially if only a few conserved species are involved within a reserve can make such reserves politically undesirable. *Ex situ* conservation in gene banks, involving either botanical gardens or research establishments, depending on the land available, enables small numbers of a species to be grown under cultivation. They are expensive to maintain, do not offer safe long-term storage and there can be problems in preventing cross fertilization and maintaining genetic purity. Several fruits, including *Prunus* are normally conserved vegetatively in the form of clones, thereby conserving gene combinations that would be lost through sexual reproduction.

Seed banks are widely used for the long-term storage of orthodox seeds. However, many woody species that produce large seeds, e.g., *Castanea* spp., *Theobroma* spp., *Artocarpus* spp., *Nephelium lappaceum,* etc., are recalcitrant and any drying increases their rate of deterioration. Furthermore, most tropical recalcitrant species will suffer from chilling injury if the temperature of the seed bank falls below 10-15°C. Even under optimum conditions, longevity of recalcitrant seeds seldom exceed a few weeks or months. Unsuitable for storage in seed banks, they require *in vitro* conservation. The latter primarily involves the use of slow growth and cryo-preservation in liquid nitrogen to store germplasm.

Overview of the Edible Nut Trade

Hazelnuts, groundnuts (peanuts), almonds, and cashewnuts dominate the international trade, with other varieties, such as coconut (desiccated), walnuts, macadamia nuts and pecan nuts, also of significance. All these products are to a large extent substitutable in their end uses, and can be consumed directly as "cocktail" nuts or in mixed ingredient snacks, or as food ingredients in the confectionery and bakery trade.

Most edible nuts of inferior quality can be crushed to produce oil and oil cake/oil meal or used directly for non-human consumption as birdfeed. The major nuts entering world trade are presented in Table 1.3. Among the major edible nuts covered in this book, almonds with 59 per cent share, hold the first position in terms of volume, while Brazil nuts,

Table 1.3: Edible Nuts Exports by Major Producing Countries (volume shelled in tonnes) in 2003

Edible Nuts	*Major Exporting Countries*	*World Total*	*% Share (2) of (3)*	*% Share in Total Nuts*	*Major Exporting Countries*
(1)	(2)	(3)	(4)	(5)	(6)
Hazelnuts	146,942	202,762	72.47	7.23	Switzerland, Italy
Groundnuts	757,576	1,067,506	70.97	38.05	U.S.A., India, Argentina
Almonds	205,756	348,626	59.02	12.43	U.S.A., Spain
Cashew	140,115	253,269	55.32	9.03	India, Brazil
Walnut	42,567	92,393	46.07	3.29	U.S.A., China
Coconut	53,213	244,093	21.80	8.70	Philippines, Sri Lanka
Brazil Nuts	19,594	24,093	81.33	0.86	Brazil, Bolivia, Peru
Pistachios	208,716	268,442	77.75	9.57	Iran, U.S.A., Spain
Chestnuts	155,510	232,000	67.03	8.27	China, Italy, Korea Rep.
Macadamia	58,952	72,000	81.88	2.57	Australia, South Africa, Guatemala
Total	1,788,941	2,805,184	63.77	100.00	

Source: *FAO STAT Database*, November, 2005.

at around 0.86 per cent, are a relatively minor constituent of the world edible nut trade. International edible nut prices are primarily influenced by supply and demand factors and there is an absence of commodity exchanges, auctions and futures markets to act as price determinant points. The trade is purely in the physical commodities without futures exchanges. The potential for high prices tends to be limited due to the substitutability of alternative edible nuts in their end products.

International Trade in Edible Nuts

Table 1.4 shows world exports of major edible nuts for selected years. The international trade in edible tree nuts is substantial and one in which developing countries participates fully. World exports of edible nuts (fresh and dried) amounted to US$ 5.2 billion in 2004, according to the FAO Database. The share of the developing countries, consistently high during recent years, was 56 per cent in 2004. World exports of five major edible nuts for which trade data are available from the FAO database, increased from an average of US$ 2.78 billion during 1990-92 to US $ 5.21 billion during the last three years, representing over 6 per cent annual growth. The export performance of various edible nuts varied over the period under review.

Table 1.4: World Exports of Major Edible Nuts: Selected Years

(*US$ '000*)

Edible Nuts	*Average 1990-92*	*2000*	*2001*	*2002*	*2003*	*2004*	*Average 2002-04*	*% share*
Almond	53,773	138,500	133,789	143,113	217,538	254,113	204,921	3.94
Shelled	543,385	742,804	783,450	1,033,628	1,221,308	1,586,583	1,280,506	24.60
Sub-Total	597,158	881,304	917,239	2,093,980	1,438,846	1,840,696	1,485,427	28.53
Pistachios	457,749	536,930	610,840	695,840	963,513	941,565	866,973	16.65
Cashewnuts	94,874	294,178	227,732	251,159	223,893	350,340	275,131	5.29
Shelled	464,500	883,625	720,144	814,625	888,089	1,280,181	994,298	19.10
Sub-Total	559,374	1,177,803	947,876	1,065,784	1,111,982	1,630,521	1,269,429	24.39
Hazelnuts	22,183	42,533	45,333	47,888	42,500	54,810	48,399	0.93
Shelled	516,857	516,666	594,033	494,262	599,993	951,955	682,070	13.10
Sub-Total	539,020	559,199	639,366	542,150	642,493	1,006,765	730,469	14.03
Walnuts	131,562	189,825	165,421	170,779	190,614	257,095	206,163	3.96
Shelled	135,339	230,749	258,156	288,681	343,885	426,574	353,107	6.78
Sub-Tctal	266,901	420,574	423,577	459,460	534,499	683,669	559,270	10.74
Chest Nuts	232,714	233,450	206,209	199,670	232,022	212,070	214,587	4.12
Brazil Nuts	117,141	19,930	11,010	12,220	12,946	16,992	14,052	0.27
Shelled	11,385	61,026	40,825	45,684	58,073	92,795	65,564	1.26
Sub-Total	128,526	80,956	51,835	57,904	71,019	109,787	79,616	1.53
Total Exports	2,781,442	3,890,216	3,796,942	4,197,549	4,994,374	6,425,093	5,205,672	100.00

Source: FAO STAT Databases, March, 2006.

It is becoming more and more difficult for developing countries to maintain their comparatively strong presence in the main markets. There are two major reasons for this: increasingly strict phytosanitary and other quality restrictions and demands, and the tendency of the some developed countries to protect their own nut industries.

Some countries of the European (EU) rank among the largest importing markets for edible nuts. Germany (first), France (fourth), Italy (fifth), United Kingdom (sixth) and Spain (seventh). Measures by the Union to encourage higher self-sufficiency are affecting imports from non-EU sources, including developing countries. These measures are leading to increased competition and a shift in demand from the types of nuts produced by the latter countries to those produced within the Union.

There is thus more than ever a need for developing countries to improve their export marketing knowledge, and their ability to plan and adapt their production to the requirements of their markets.

This study is intended to meet this need. It aims to provide developing countries with up-to-date information on growing conditions, market and market prospects for nuts in the major exporting and importing countries. For developing countries the tropical nuts are of special interest. Apart from the tropical nuts, pistachio nut and other nuts although not considered as tropical nuts, are also covered because of their success in several main markets.

Major information such as climatic requirement, soil requirement, propagation including seed and vegetative propagation, planting time, training and pruning, manuring, time of flower and fruit setting, diseases and insect pest management for each of nuts is given in the text. Attempt has also been made to analyze world production, international trade, and demand/supply for major producing and consuming countries of each of the nut covered in this book.

The author felt there was the need for a comprehensive volume on World edible nut economy, as the available material for this sector is rather limited and scattered. Attempt has been made in this volume to bring together material on all aspects for each of the major edible nut at one place. It is hoped that it would as a useful reference material for planning, policy formulation, as well as for academic, research and extension workers, especially for horticulturists and orchardists.

Efforts Under Way to Promote Edible Nuts Cultivation in India

Production of major edible nuts in developing countries has been gathering more attention over the last few decades. Governments and NGOs are advocating the development of production of major edible nuts such as walnut, cashewnut, pistachio etc. Some of these edible nuts are important and promising sectors for many developing countries. Also in India, which is the leading cashewnut producing country and is one of the important exporters of walnut kernels, increasing attention is being paid by the State Horticultural Departments and the NGO to promote planting of edible nuts in new areas and/or expand areas in the current producing states.

Since 1983 Trees for Life (TFL), a voluntary organization, has been working in India to find out ways and means to bring about a fruit revolution of the magnitude of the Green Revolution in the country. For this it has distributed a large number of fruit and forest trees among the farmers in several parts of the country. Trees for Life Himalayan Programme is being carried out under the leadership of Dr. M.L. Dewan, an eminent Soil Scientist and Watershed Management Expert with experience of nearly half a century in developing countries and with Food and Agriculture Organization of the United Nations. Trees for Life Himalayan Programme has sponsored many eco-development schemes for tree plantings and protection in Uttrakhand. One of these schemes that achieved great degree of success has been bringing walnut and other nut seeds from the Banihal area in Jammu and Kashmir, and planted in Uttrakhand. Additionally, sweet chestnuts from Pithoragarh have been tried in many areas in the state. Also under the programme seedlings of walnut and almond have been imported from Tom Burchell Nursery in California, USA, and distributed among farmers in Central Himalayas, Universities and NGOs and to a Tissue Culture Lab in Shimla. The Chairman of an NGO, The Agrigene International, as a Micro propagators and consultant, has done wonderful work.

However, it was felt that farmers and orchardists lacked knowledge and experience in growing not only about these nut fruits but others also. To overcome this problem a team of three experts consisting of Dr. M.L. Dewan, Prof. M.C. Nautiyal and Dr. V.K. Sah, brought out a comprehensive and very useful book in 1992 on "Nut Fruits for the Himalayas." It deals with the following 11 tree nuts:

1. Walnuts; 2. Almond; 3. Chestnut; 4. Hazelnut; 5. Pecannut; 6. Pistachio Nut; 7. Chilgoza Pine Nut; 8. Apricot; 9. Cherua; 10. Macadamia Nut; and 11. Minor and multi-purpose nuts suitable for the Himalayas.

A detailed information such as Climatic and Soil Requirements, Propagation including seed and vegetative propagation, Planting Time, Training and Pruning, Manuring, Time of Flower and Fruit setting, Diseases and Insect Pest Management for each of the nuts is given in the book. This book published by Concept Publishing Company, New Delhi, serves as a useful guide for farmers of Central Himalayas, Himachal Pradesh and even Jammu and Kashmir.

In Uttrakhand under the TFL Himalayas operations conducted a training programme in Winter 1990-91 for proper planting of walnuts, almonds and chestnuts. It is reported that the walnuts and other nut trees have performed well in nurseries and large numbers in various parts of Central Himalayas and they have been planted in suitable places.

REFERENCES

1. Wickens, G.E: *Edible Nuts: Non-wood Forest Products*: 1995.
2. Melville, R. (1947): The Nutritive Value of Nuts: Chemistry and Industry: 22, pp. 304-306.
3. Howes, 1948; Rosengarten, 1984, *op. cit.*
4. Matz, S.A. (1984): *Snack Food Technology*: Ed. 2: The AVI Publishing Company Inc., Westpoint, Connecticut.
5. Howes, F.N. (1948): *Nuts, Their Production and Everyday Use,* Faber and Faber, London.
   Menninger, E.A. (1977): *Edible Nuts of the World*: Horticultural Books Inc., Stuart, Florida.
   Rosengarten, F. (1984): *The Book of Edible Nuts*, Walker and Company, New York.
6. *Ibid.* (all references mentioned above.)
7. Howes, 1948; Menninger, 1977; and Rosengarten, 1984: *op. cit.*
8. *Ibid.*
9. *Ibid.*
10. Howes, F.N. (1948): *Nuts: Their Production and Everyday Use*, Faber and Faber, London.
    Menninger, E.A. (1977): *Edible Nuts of the World*: Horticultural Books Inc., Stuart, Florida.
    Rosengarten, F. (1984): *The Book of Edible Nuts*, Walker and Company, New York.
11. *Ibid cit.* all the references mentioned above.
12. Meadley, J. (1989): *The Commercial Implications of New Crops*: In. Wickens, G.E., Haw, N. and Day, P. (Eds), pp. 23-28: and Honess, H. (1993): The Regional and International Market and Prices for Tropical Fruits and Nuts in Asia, In: Anthony, K., de Groot and Haq, N. (Eds.) pp. 19-30.

13. Okafor, J.C. (1978): *Development of Forest Tree Crops for Food Supplies in Nigeria*; *Forest Ecology and Management*: 1; pp. 235-247, and Okafor, J.C. (1980): *Edible Indigenous Woody Plants in the Rural Economy in the Nigerian Forest Zone: Forest Ecology and Management*: 3. pp. 45-55 and Okafor, J.C. and Lamb, A. (1994): *Fruit Trees: Diversity and Conservation Strategies*: In Leakey, R.R.B. and Newton A.C. (Eds.), pp. 34-41.
14. Rosengarten, F. (1984) *op. cit*, and Holliday P. (1989): *A Divisionary of Plant Pathology*.

Part I
WALNUT

2

HISTORY OF THE WALNUT

A TOUGH NUT TO CRACK

HISTORY

Walnuts are one of the oldest tree foods known to men. Ancient history dates back walnuts to 7000 BC. Though many historians pinpoint Persia as the country of the walnut's origin, confusion persists because archaeological remains of walnuts were found as far eastward as the Himalayas and to the distant west and northwest of Persia into Turkey, Italy, and Switzerland as well. The oldest archaeological site where walnuts were unearthed is in the Shanidar caves in northern Iraq. Following that find, at a considerable distance from Persia, evidence of walnuts was discovered in a Mesolithic dunghill in Switzerland.

During the New Stone Age or Neolithic period, items found in Switzerland's Lake District included walnuts. The Neolithic period began in Southwest Asia from about 8000 BC and expanded throughout Europe between 6000 to 2000 BC. Travelling slightly eastward, archaeologists delicately brushed away layers of dirt in Perigord, France, from Peyrat to Terrasson, to uncover petrified roasted shells of walnuts from the Neolithic period.

Walnuts are referred to as Persian walnuts. In ancient Persia, only royalty was privy to the pleasure of devouring the walnut, the fruit referred to as the Royal Walnut. Mesopotamia, the area that is now modern Iraq, boasted of walnut groves in the famed Hanging Gardens of Babylon about 2000 BC. As testimony, Chaldeans left clay tablet inscriptions that accounted for these orchards. These were the earliest written records mentioning walnuts. Thus, the walnut is often known as the "Persian Walnut". Likewise, the "English Walnut" refers to the English merchant marines whose ships once transported the product for trade to ports around the world.

Slightly later, about 1795 BC, Hammurabi, the 6th king of the 1st dynasty of Babylon, set down a code of laws known as the Code of Hammurabi. These laws were inscribed on black diorite pillars and categorized by subject. Mention of walnuts was included in the section on laws governing food.

In the Song of Solomon 6:11 of the Old Testament, King Solomon is quoted, "I went down into the garden of nuts to see the fruit of the valley." These words refer to walnut groves flourishing and producing abundantly.

The first cultivation of walnuts is attributed to the ancient Greeks, but it may have actually been the Persians who first cultivated a superior variety. The walnuts growing in Greece were small and didn't produce a significant quantity of oil. When the Greeks encountered the larger Persian walnuts, they began to improve their variety by cultivation. The ancient Greeks utilized the walnut not only for food, but also as a medicine and a dye for the hair, wool, and cloth.

About one hundred years after the Greeks were commonly using walnuts, the Romans discovered their merits and were willing to pay dearly for the luxury of serving them along with fruits for dessert. In the ruins of Pompeii whole, unshelled walnuts were among the foods on the table at the Temple of Isis on that fateful day of August 24, CE 79 when Mount Vesuvius erupted.

Though written records of the walnuts arrival in Kashmir are absent, walnuts were an established presence and, from there, may have journeyed to China during the Han dynasty, some time between 206 BC and 220 CE.

Since trading existed long before written records, merchants, explorers, and conquerors were credited with bringing the walnut from the Mediterranean into Europe, possibly during the third century BC. Some historians question this theory because of archaeological evidence discovered in Switzerland centuries earlier.

It is possible that during the last Glacial Period, known as the Pleistocene era, walnut trees disappeared from the frozen earth of the Northern European countries. After that era, barbarian invaders and Greek and Roman conquerors brought the trees from their homelands into Europe.

In spite of the frequency with which walnuts are referred to as English walnuts, they didn't really penetrate the English soul until after World War I when they became a commercial enterprise. Though the English climate didn't provide the most ideal conditions for growing walnuts, some trees survived nonetheless. In fact it is believed that the concept English walnut came to be used as walnuts were carried as a common trade items by English ships throughout Mediterranean.

The first mention of the walnut's arrival in the British Isles appeared in the Encyclopaedia Britannica dated 1567. However, walnuts were only acceptable served at the end of a meal along with pork and Stilton cheese. In contrast, the French went nuts over the walnut. Early cultivation began there during the fourth century. Charlemagne, eighth to ninth century, ordered his gardeners to plant walnut trees on his extensive properties. Walnuts were so highly regarded that during the eleventh century, the French peasants were expected to tithe walnuts to the church.

From Medieval times up until the end of the 18th century, Europeans were blanching, crushing, and soaking walnuts and almonds to create rich, nutritious milk, a common household staple. While the poor dined on the wild walnuts, the rich were able to afford the larger, more expensive, cultivated variety.

Toward the end of the 17th century, walnuts along with chestnuts became important staples in France. During the famine of 1663 the poor consumed their walnuts and then resorted to grinding up the shells along with acorns to create coarse, unpalatable bread.

In Second World War when families living in the small villages of Perigord, a region in the southern part of France, had little to eat, they turned to their walnut groves for a source of protein.

Walnuts have been spread to the far corners of the world trade item. The outer shell provided a natural protective layer helping to maintain the quality of the nut. Walnuts were seen in some of the earliest European trade fairs, such as Leipzig and Hanover. The listing for walnuts was found on cargo manifests of many ships between the old and the new world. Eventually walnuts travelled from the Mediterranean area to European countries and finally to the new World. Today the nut trade continues to be a well established, ordered, and structured business.

The Black Walnut, a Native of North America

Native American Indians enjoyed the pleasures and health benefits of the black walnut well before European explorers arrived. The upper Great Lakes region provides archaeological evidence of walnut consumption dating back to 2000 BC. Along with eating the walnut itself, the Indians used the sap of the walnut tree in their food preparation.

Wherever the black walnut grows, there is limestone in the soil, a good sign of fertile soil. The early Pennsylvania Dutch made a point of selecting properties that had a stand of sturdy black walnut trees on the land, assuring them of rich soil.

The early colonists carried seeds of the English walnut to the New World and planted them diligently where they settled in Massachusetts and Virginia. However, the trees did not adapt to their new climate and didn't even survive long enough to bear fruit. Black walnuts, however, were plentiful and soon became a valued ingredient in biscuits and confectionary.

Walnuts in California, U.S.A.

In the early 1800s Spanish Franciscan monks established missions along the California coast. Part of their teachings included the cultivation of food plants and trees in the areas surrounding the missions. One area that eventually became the city of Walnut, California, was home to the San Gabriel Mission named for the Gabrielino Indians, originally of Shoshone origin. Many acres of walnut trees, originally brought from Spain, were planted here and became known as "mission walnuts". These first walnut trees produced small nuts with very hard shells.

During the first half of the 1800s, land grants of several acres were issued, and ranchos were established. Walnut groves became well established on these land grants by the 1870s in Southern California near Santa Barbara. In 1867 Joseph Sexton, a horticulturist, initiated California's first commercial walnut enterprise when he planted a grove of English walnuts in Goleta, a small town in Santa Barbara County. Within a few years, 65 per cent of all fertile land in this region was planted with Sexton's English walnuts.

In spite of this early success, by the late 1930s the commercial walnut business was destined to move northward to Stockton, California, where improved irrigation, better pest control, ideal climate, and rich soil were more conducive to larger yields. The California walnut has found its ideal home in the centre of the state, an area that produces 99 per cent of the commercial United States walnut supply. On the global market, California produces two-thirds of the world's supply of walnuts. Other countries that grow commercial walnuts include India, Turkey, China, Russia, Greece, Italy and France.

Though the first walnuts to arrive in the United States came from Spain in the early 1800s, the French contributed many of their varieties during the latter part of the nineteenth century.

Walnuts Featured in World Cuisines

Creative cooks and chefs of many countries have eagerly adopted walnuts and incorporated them into a multitude of dishes from soups to desserts and even dessert cordials. Baklava, a well-known delicacy served throughout the Middle East, is a rich dessert made of alternate layers of buttered filo dough and ground walnuts. A final topping of sweet-spiced syrup is poured over the top and allowed to soak in for several hours before the baklava is cut into diamond shapes and served.

Though we are most familiar with fully mature walnuts, green walnuts, completely edible but quite sour, are an ideal ingredient for pickles, jams, and marmalades. During the seventeenth and eighteenth centuries, many English cookbooks touted an abundance of recipes for pickling both black and green walnuts. In the Middle East, sweet syrup is used to preserve half-ripe walnuts, a process that takes several weeks before the delicious confections are ready to eat. In Italy, walnuts are sometimes added to the pine nuts in the preparation of pesto, a thick basil and olive oil sauce served over pasta. The French enjoy their Walnut Soup and relish sauces made of walnuts, garlic and oil, while the Persians favour a dish called Fesenjen made of poultry or meat, walnuts, and pomegranate juice.

The ancient Persians made a paste of ground walnuts and used it to thicken soups and stews. During the middle Ages this handy technique was introduced into Europe. Before the colonists arrived in America, the Narragansett Indians of the Eastern United States also pounded the black walnut into a paste to thicken their soups and vegetable stews.

During the fourteenth century, walnuts appeared on the dessert list at a French royal banquet. The walnuts for this occasion were preserved in a spiced honey mixture that was stirred once a week for several weeks in preparation for the event.

Naming the Walnut

The origin of the word nut is derived from the Latin word ***nux*** referring to the fruit inside the shell, the nut kernel itself. The walnut tree's formal botanical name, ***Juglans regia***, comes from the Romans. The word ***juglans***, from the Latin, means "the acorn of Jupiter," while ***regia*** refers to royalty. We could actually translate its Latin name to mean "the royal acorn of Jupiter."

Another Roman version, ***Jovis glans***, though not its botanical name, is translated as the royal nut of Jove, another name for Jupiter who is the highest god in Roman mythology. Yet another Roman name for the walnut, ***Nux juglandes***, translates as "the nut of Jupiter." Because the walnut shell has an appearance reminiscent of the human brain, the Afghanistani word for walnut is ***charmarghz*** or "four brains" in their language.

From Teutonic roots comes the German ***Wallnuss*** or ***Welsche Nuss.*** Since many words of our English language came from the German, it's quite apparent how the word ***wallnuss*** could have easily evolved into "walnut".

Folklore

The Romans associated the walnut with the Juno, the Roman goddess of women and marriage and the wife of Jupiter. This association led to the unique wedding practice of throwing walnuts at the bride and groom as a symbol of fertility. Women often carried walnuts to promote fertility. There is a legend that presumes walnuts were one of the gifts presented to Jesus by the three wise men.

English merchant sailors transported walnuts across the globe during medieval times. Walnuts became so associated with the English that they were often called English walnuts, a name that is still used today.

One custom in Poitou, France is to have the bride and groom dance around the city's gigantic walnut tree. The villagers believe that by participating in this dance the bride will produce an abundance of milk for her baby.

In the French countryside, it was tradition to hang a bag of walnuts from the ceiling beam in the kitchen to represent abundance. Walnuts also represented longevity. Some young men in the French countryside believed the walnut tree to possess aphrodisiac powers and attempted to sneak a leaf into the shoe of a young woman they admired.

Along with some items of amusing folklore, the walnut tree holds a few dark superstitions. In seventeenth century Italy there was a walnut tree, the Tree of Benevento that was believed to be the place where witches gathered. According to a legend, the Bishop removed the tree, roots and all, but another witch-haunted tree grew where the original stood.

Another legend warns it is unlucky to plant walnut trees too close to a stable because it might bring illness and death to the animals. Even travellers along the road were warned not to choose the walnut tree as a refuge for the night, fearing they may become ill.

Superstitions and fears also surrounded the shade of the walnut tree. A passage in Pliny's writings states that the shadow of the walnut tree dulled the brain. He also considered the walnut tree a nuisance wherever it was planted. Another superstition warns that one should not try to grow anything near the walnut tree, because it contains evil or poison.

The medieval Doctrine of Signatures stated that because the shape of the walnut resembled the brain, the nut would be beneficial for all ailments associated with the head and brain, including headaches. Later, toward the end of the fourteenth century, walnuts were thought to cause headaches.

One superstition held that if a walnut were dropped into the lap of a person suspected of being a witch, she would be unable to rise from a sitting position as long as the walnut remained in her lap.

AGRONOMY FOR GROWING WALNUT

Walnuts belong to a family that includes the pecan and hickory pecan. There are three main varieties of walnut trees, the most familiar variety being ***Juglans regia***, known as the Persian or English walnut. For the past two centuries its main growing region has been North America, specifically California. Southeastern Europe also grows many varieties of the English walnut, which is also cultivated from Turkey to the Himalayas and even reaching into China. This variety grows to a height of 40 to 60 feet high and has a lifespan of about 60 years or more.

Juglans nigra, or the Black Walnut, grows mainly in the Eastern and Central United States, from New England to Minnesota and Nebraska, and south to the Gulf of Mexico. The black walnut can grow to a height of 150 feet, with the nuts bearing a more rounded shape. Though the tree is grown mainly for lumber, there is a minor industry in harvesting the nuts because of their distinctive, rich, and oily flavour that is valued for baking, candy making, and preparing black walnut ice cream. The black walnut tree is known to be a centenarian, living for 100 years or longer.

Juglans cinerea refers to the Butternut, or white walnut, that is also in the same family and grows in the Eastern United States as well. The butternut tree averages about 30 to 50 feet in height and bears an oval or egg-shaped nut. Considered the hardiest of the walnut trees, its lifespan varies from 50 to 75 years. In some varieties of the Butternut, the bruised leaves and the husks are aromatic.

The walnut consists of three distinct parts. The edible portion, known as the kernel or fruit of the nut, is actually the seed of the walnut tree. It has two lobes. The inner part of the lobe is ivory coloured and is covered by a thin brown skin that is firmly attached.

The shell, called the endocarp, is a very hard material made up of two distinct halves firmly sealed together. The shell is light brown in colour and has an appearance reminiscent of the convolutions of the human brain. An inedible, thin, cellulose-like membrane separates the two lobes of the walnut inside the shell.

The husk, called the pericarp, covers the shell with a soft, fleshy, green skin that protects the walnut. When fully mature the husk is about two inches in diameter. Not commonly known, is that the very immature green husk is edible. At this stage the shell and the nut have not hardened and both are also edible, though they taste quite sour.

All walnut trees are deciduous and grow well in temperate zones if sheltered from extreme cold and strong wind. They thrive best in deep, fertile soil free of alkali and should not be planted closer than 60 to 70 feet apart. The trees will grow easily on mountainsides up to an altitude of 3,000 ft.

Walnut groves must be irrigated frequently because the trees require an abundance of water to produce nut kernels that are moist and well developed. However, it is also necessary to provide good drainage. Deep watering in the winter is important. In Europe the trees grow to a height of 60 to 85 feet with a typical trunk circumference of 3 feet. One farmer recorded a circumference of 16 feet in a farmers' almanac. In the United States walnut trees can grow to a height of 20 feet in 6 to 8 years and finally, reach about 90 to 100 feet when mature.

Those superstitions about not being able to grow anything in the soil surrounding the walnut tree actually have truth and reason to back them up. The tree's roots tend to secrete juglone, a poisonous substance, into the soil that actually poisons some plants growing near the trees. Horticulturists recommend not planting tomatoes, rhododendrons and azaleas within 80 feet of any walnut tree.

Each tree produces both male and female flowers that bloom in April and May, about the same time the leaves begin to appear. Though the trees self-pollinate, most growers will plant one or two other varieties in the grove for optimum cross-pollination.

In the United States, California's Sacramento Valley is the centre of walnut production, whereas in France, Perigord is known for its abundance of walnut groves that were thriving well before1657. Throughout Europe the two varieties of walnut are the ***Juglans regia,*** the familiar commercial walnut, and the black walnut, ***Juglans nigra.*** The English walnuts reach maturity in the early fall when the husks split open. The black walnut and the butternut also mature in the fall season.

Before the age of mechanization, the traditional September harvesting of walnuts consisted of shaking the trees by hand using long hooked poles to knock the nuts to the ground where they could be easily gathered. Today, the trees are shaken by machine, while another machine uses vacuum suction to collect the fallen nuts.

Commercial hot-air dehydrators with blower fans circulate warm air to reduce the moisture of the walnuts to between 12 and 20 per cent to preserve their shelf life. In past centuries, walnuts were simply left on drying racks away from the sun until they were properly dried.

Medicinal Benefits of the Walnut

In Perigord region of southern France the long-standing traditional diet is very high in fried foods, rich meats, and fatty pâtés. Yet, the people suffer fewer heart attacks than Americans. At first medical experts explained this phenomenon by attributing this miracle to the red wine they drink. Red wine is known for its superior antioxidants to protect the heart. Yet, the residents of this region didn't drink any more red wine than those in other parts of Europe. Closer examination revealed that their daily green salads were dressed with walnut oil and chopped walnuts, helping to lower their levels of LDL and overall cholesterol in the bloodstream.

A study published in the *American Journal of Clinical Nutrition* in May 1994, showed that those whose diets included nuts, either walnuts or almonds, were able to lower their LDL cholesterol by 9 to 10 per cent. Another study that appeared in the *Journal of the American Dietetic Association*, July 1995, found that walnuts could also diminish the extent of heart damage after a heart attack.

From ancient times through the nineteenth century herbalists prescribed the walnut, the bark, the roots, and the leaves as an astringent, a laxative, a purgative to induce vomiting, a styptic to stop bleeding, a vermifuge to expel worms or parasites, and a hepatic to tone the liver. The walnut served to induce sweating, cure diarrhoea, soothe sore gums and skin diseases, cure herpes, and relieve inflamed tonsils.

The nut itself was used to prevent weight gain, calm hysteria, eliminate morning sickness, and to strengthen one's constitution. The hulls were boiled and used to treat head and body lice, herpes, intestinal parasites and worms, skin diseases, and liver ailments. The leaf was decocted to cure boils, eczema, hives, ulcers, and sores.

Even the walnut oil was employed as a medicinal aid. It was first diluted before it was used to treat colic, dandruff, dry hair, gangrene, and open wounds, while the green rind of the walnut was used to treat ringworm.

Uses of the Walnut Tree

The walnut tree has provided the creative entrepreneur many opportunities.

The wood of the tree is exceptionally hard, making it ideal for fine furniture, wall panelling, musical instruments, sculpting, and woodcarving. The walnut wood has found its way into the kitchen in the form of plates and spoons, while the farmer employed the wood for animal yokes and water jugs. Even wooden shoes were formed from the walnut tree. During war times the Europeans made gunstocks from the firm wood of the walnut tree. During First World War, the hardy wood of the black walnut was used for making airplane propellers.

In past times walnut shells served many purposes as well. Pliny suggests crushing them finely to use for filling dental cavities. Imagine shaving with the edge of heated walnut shells instead of a razor. King Louis XI's barber engaged in this practice because he thought it would prevent nicks. To prevent bread from sticking, bakers would spread powdered walnut shells on the base of their ovens.

More recently, finely powdered walnut shells served many commercial industries. The powder was employed as a polish for metals used in the aeronautical industry and as face powder in the cosmetics field. Oil riggers use the powdered shells to sharpen their drills. NASA has even put powdered walnut shells to use as thermal insulation in rocket nose cones. Apparently, the powder can withstand extreme temperatures without carbonising.

The French have created a fine liqueur with walnut husks as its base, but leave it to the Italians to create ***Nocino,*** a renowned cordial made from green walnuts. The recipe originated in Modena, where the unripe walnuts are picked on the Festival Day of St. John on 24 June. The walnuts are cracked, steeped in alcohol for two months, and then filtered to remove any debris before the cordial is sipped with gusto.

In past centuries people discovered that all parts of the walnut could be processed to create colours and dyes. Furniture makers and finishers use the husks to create a rich walnut stain. Women developed a beauty secret to enhance their appearance, a hair dye made from the walnut hulls. Scribes made rich brown ink from walnut hulls. Since prehistoric times weavers extracted a rich dark brown dye from walnut juice, while they used the green husks to make a yellow dye. They also boiled the bark to extract a deep brown dye used for colouring wool.

Walnut Oil

Though the walnut oil was used for many purposes, the first pressing of the walnut kernel was highly prized by chefs for its lightness and delicate flavour. High in polyunsaturated, walnut oil is also rich in gamma-tocopherol, a form of Vitamin E considered nutritionally superior. Since it is so high in antioxidants, the gamma-tocopherol protects the oil from becoming rancid quickly.

In France during the eighteenth century, before walnuts were pressed into oil, they were stored for two to three months to cure. To extract walnut oil, the nuts were first crushed into a paste. The most highly valued oils were achieved by heating the paste delicately to bring out the best flavour of the nuts. Next, the nuts were pressed to extract the oil. Oil could also be extracted from walnuts without heating, but heating was preferred, resulting in exceptional flavour. It takes about four pounds (approximately 2 kilograms) of nuts to press out a scant quart (a litre) of oil.

Aside from the delicacies of the table, walnut oil served rather diverse purposes. The ancient Egyptians used the oil in the embalming of their mummies. Parts of Europe where walnuts were plentiful used a lower quality of the oil to light their oil lamps. In nineteenth century France walnut oil was used in the church as holy oil.

European artists favoured walnut oil as a paint medium to be mixed with pigment. In fact, many of the French impressionists preferred it to poppy and linseed oils that actually surpassed it in quality. The paintings of Monet, Pissaro, and Cezanne carry traces of walnut oil as shown by chemical analysis.

Nutritional Benefits

Nuts are a highly concentrated form of excellent nutrition; however, it's important to stress that they ought to be eaten in moderation. Because walnuts, like other nuts, are high in fats, it's important to note they are also high in calories.

While one-fourth cup of raw, unsalted walnuts contains 180 calories, be aware they contain 18 grams of fat, 1.5 grams saturated. The fat in walnuts is mostly polyunsaturated. If you are watching the fat, you can calculate your fat intake by dividing the 77 per cent of calories from fat by the180 calories to learn that a one-fourth cup serving contains 43 per cent fat. That percentage may sound high, but it should not discourage a healthy person from gaining nutritional benefits from eating walnuts in small quantities. Walnuts are rich in protein, providing 7 grams for that same one-fourth cup, 2 grams of fiber, and only 7 grams of carbohydrates. Walnuts can be considered a super food because they contain a full complement of vitamins, including B_1, B_2, B_3, B_5, B_6 and folic acid. They also contain a wealth of minerals, such as iron, magnesium, potassium, and zinc.

Walnuts contain Vitamin E—alpha, beta, delta and gamma-tocopherol, making it exceptionally high in antioxidants. Nutritionists tell us that Omega 3 fatty acids are found in only a few plant food sources, yet are essential to a healthy body. In a 2,000-calorie diet, 3 tablespoons of walnuts will provide our daily requirement of these Omega 3 fatty acids.

Using Walnut Oil

All vegetable oils are high in calories, and all should be used sparingly. Walnut oil contains 260 calories per ounce. One tablespoon contains 120 calories and 14 grams of fat. Use small amounts as a salad dressing or drizzle delicately over steamed vegetables.

Purchasing, Storing and Preparing Walnuts

Since walnuts are harvested in early autumn, usually in September, the freshest nuts are purchased during the autumn season. If kept in their shells, they can keep for six to eight months without spoiling. For longer storage, pack them in heavy plastic bags and store them in the freezer.

Cracking

Removing English walnuts from their husks and shells is rarely a problem. Almost any nutcracker will do. Though they are seldom used today, a nut pick can be quite handy for pulling the walnut out from its shell.

Chopping

Chopping nuts can be done in the food processor using the pulse-chop method. If you only have a few nuts to chop, simply break them up by hand. If you want coarsely ground walnuts, use a nut mill, an item that may be available in kitchen shops.

3

THE ORIGIN OF THE WALNUT

According to some authors the walnut originated when Bacchus, the Greek god of wine and ecstasy, fell in love with Carya, the youngest of three daughters of Dion, king of Laconia[1]. When the jealous elder sisters endeavoured to prevent the two lovers from meeting, Bacchus turned them into stones and, for reasons clear only to a god, transformed his beloved into a walnut tree. However, in recent times most observers have suggested the crop has more mundane origin.

Fossil evidence indicates ancestral forms of walnut once grew in extensive portions of Europe, Asia, and North America, reaching as far north as Alaska. Subsequent changes in climate, particularly glaciation during the most recent ice age, altered the geographical distribution. Further evolutionary adaptations led to the emergence of about 20 modern walnut species, which compose the genus *Juglans.*

All walnut species are native to temperate or sub-tropical climates and are deciduous trees with chambered piths, aromatic compound leaves, and woody-shelled nuts. All have 32 diploid chromosomes and many, but not all, are capable of hybridizing with each other. Most walnut species are highly regarded for their timber and all produce edible nuts, although their size and extractability differ considerably. Other genera in the walnut family Juglandaceae) include the *Carya* (pecans and hickories) and the *Pterocarya* (wingnuts).

The Butter Nut

The various walnut species are grouped taxonomically into four sections. The first of these, Section Trachycaryon contains only a single species, the butternut (J. *cinerea).* Also known as the white walnut or oil nut, the butternut is native to eastern North America and can be distinguished from other North American walnuts by its elongated two-chambered nuts and by the conspicuously four-ribbed husks that do not split at maturity. Nuts are borne in clusters on long stalks. Butternut will tolerate a high water table and is the most cold hardy of North American walnut. The kernels are large and, in good varieties, can be cracked out in halves. A few cultivars have been selected from native seedlings but no significant commercial nut production has developed.

East Asian Species

The three species belonging to Section Cardiocaryon, all of which are native to eastern Asia, appear to be closely related to the butternut. Like the butternut, they produce two-chambered nuts with indehiscent husks and nuts. Nuts are borne in clusters of 5 to 25 each. The most cold hardy of this group is the Manchurian walnut U. *mandshurica,* native to north-eastern China and Korea. Its nuts are difficult to extract and the trees are used primarily for timber and furniture. The Japanese walnut U. *ailantifolia,* also typically bears nuts that are difficult to crack, but seedling variants containing more easily extracted heart-shaped kernels, known as heartnuts, have been propagated as cultivars. The Chinese walnut U. *cathayens,* is very similar to the Manchurian walnut but is adapted to the warmer conditions of southeastern China, where it has limited use as a rootstock.

Black Walnut Species

The Northern California black walnut U. *hindsii,* has long played an important role in the California walnut industry as a rootstock or rootstock parent. At the time of European settlement, this species was found in only a few small groves in Northern California but has since been widely planted both in orchards and as a shade tree. Nuts are sometimes collected for market. The wood, particularly if it exhibits a desirable grain pattern, can command a good price. The Southern California black walnut U. *californica,* is a shrubby tree native to riparian areas of coastal Southern California. It has not been widely utilized as a rootstock because of its purported susceptibility to root diseases. Its rather small original range has been further reduced by agriculture and human habitation.

Two black walnut trees, the Arizona black walnut U. *major,* and the Texas black walnut U. *microcarpa,* are native to the southwestern United States. They have been used only as rootstocks on arid or salty sites. Early settlers who brought seed from the Southwest planted Arizona black walnut trees in California. The Texas black walnut is a rather small tree with very small nuts.

Several additional black walnut species are native to Latin America.

Most of these are poorly described either taxonomically or horticulturally. Some are native to relatively inaccessible temperate or semi-tropical mountainous regions; some are thought to be endangered by deforestation. The nuts and wood of some are used in their native habitat, but none have been developed commercially.

Persian Walnut Species

The commercially valuable Persian walnut, also called English walnut U. *regia,* along with several closely related species or geographical variants, compose the last group, Section Juglans. This group is characterized by four-chambered nuts with hulls that dehisce and separate from the shells at maturity.

The Persian walnut appears to have evolved in the mountain chains of central Asia, which extend from Turkey to Iran through southern portions of what used to be the USSR to western China and the eastern Himalayas. However, millennia of transport in commerce, widespread naturalization from cultivated trees, and extensive deforestation throughout much of the region make precise determination of the species' native range impossible.

The Persian Walnut in Central Asia

In the mountains of the Central Asian republics of Kyrgyzstan, Tadjikistan, and Uzbekistan and at the extreme western border of China, wild Persian walnut forests still exist. Here walnut trees are a natural component of extensive wild fruit forests. In a few locations walnut trees dominate the canopy, forming densely shaded nearly pure stands, but more commonly walnut trees are mingled with wild apple, apricot, pear, almond, myrobalan plum; and grape. Many of the wild walnut forests of this region have been exploited commercially as "forest orchards" but heavy harvesting and grazing limit regeneration and threaten their long-term survival.

Persian walnuts from central Asia are of interest both for their high frequency of lateral bearing and for the extreme precocity, or early bearing age, seedlings often exhibit. These are valuable, but generally rare, traits among walnut seedling trees. For example, the lateral-bearing trait in California cultivars has been derived almost entirely from a single seedling, Payne. Material collected from the mountains of central Asia in what used to be the Soviet Union and in western Xinjiang Province of China has been an important source of these traits for both Soviet and Chinese walnut breeding programmes. Trees from this area are also noted for their unusual cluster bearing, multiple blooming, and heavy yields.

The Persian Walnut of China

With the exception of the extreme western mountains and perhaps part of Tibet, few, if any, wild Persian walnuts exist in China. The species is probably not native to the area. Tradition holds that Zhang Qian introduced walnut trees into China during the Han dynasty, 2000 years ago. At the request of the emperor, Zhang Qian explored the western territories of China and introduced a number of new crops. Some archaeological finds suggest Persian walnut may have been widespread in China as many as 6000 to 7000 years ago, but most observers agree that it was introduced to central and eastern China within the last several thousand years, probably through caravan commerce along the ancient silk routes. The Manregian variety, used as a rootstock in the Pacific Northwest, is derived from seed originally collected in the early 1900s in northeastern China by the great plant explorer Frank Meyers. The sigillata walnut (J. *sigillata)* is a very vigorous walnut variant, perhaps a separate species, from southern China. It is adapted to warm climates and long growing seasons and has been developed commercially in Yunnan Province. Other Chinese selections are known to exhibit extremely thin shells pink kernels, and unusual bearing habits.

The Persian Walnut of the Himalayas

In the Himalayas, Persian walnut trees are most densely distributed in the Western Himalayan regions near Kashmir, but they are indigenous from northern Pakistan east through India and Nepal and as far north as northern Burma and the temperate river valleys of Tibet. They are most commonly found among the foothills and at temperate elevations, where they grow, on disturbed forest sites or on well-drained river bottom soils, in association with a variety of coniferous and broad-leaved forest species.

Walnut trees have long been cultivated in this region, particularly in and near Kashmir. Propagation has been principally from seed, so even cultivated trees exhibit considerable variation. Trees are roughly grouped into the relatively thin-shelled *kaghazi* types, which bear nuts of commercial value, and a second "wild" type. The wild type bears small, very hard nuts and is used mainly as a source of animal fodder. Some observers have suggested the *kaghazi* types derive from the improved types Europeans introduced back into the native range during the colonial period. Probably, however, the *kaghazi* type simply reflects a long period of seedling selections by local growers.

The Persian Walnut of Southwest Asia

Persian walnut trees are also native to the mountainous terrain of northern Afghanistan, Iran, southern Turkmeniya, and eastern Turkey and perhaps to more extensive portions of southwest Asia, including the Trans-Caucasus region. The common name "Persian walnut" acknowledges the walnut's long identification with this area. The ancient Greeks are thought to have first developed their fondness for walnuts during their travels and trade with the neighbouring Persian Empire.

The heritage of several California cultivars can be traced to this region. The parent tree of Eureka was grown from seed reputedly shipped from Iran, and PI 159568, a parent of Sunland and Serr, was grown from seed collected in Afghanistan.

THE WALNUT OF EUROPE AND WORLDWIDE CULTIVATION

The origin of the wild walnut trees found today in the forests of southeastern Europe is a matter of long-standing dispute. Pollen collections by paleontologists demonstrate that the appearance and spread of walnut in the region closely coincides with the establishment of early Greek settlements. This suggests that the bulk of the wild walnut trees now common in the Balkans and much of Turkey most likely derive from nuts introduced from Iran and eastern Turkey by Greek commerce and expansion several thousand years ago. Pliny, the Roman historian, supports this view. He stated that the walnut was originally sent to Greece by Persian kings. Others have argued that small remnant populations of walnut survived the last glacial period in southern Europe and that these native trees then spread to disturbed sites created in the existing forest by early European settlements. A few pollen records as many as 5000 years old and the existence of walnut trees in a few apparently undisturbed pre-glacial forests support the view that some walnut trees survived the last ice age.

Greek and Roman conquest and settlement later extended the cultivation of walnut into North Africa, Western Europe, and as far north as England. The English word *walnut* is a clue that the crop was introduced into England. The name is either a corruption of *Gaul nut* or derived from the Anglo-Saxon word *wealh,* meaning foreign. The term English *walnut* is derived not from its origin, but probably from its widespread transport in English merchant ships. The generic name *juglans* stems from the Roman appellation jovis *glans* meaning Jupiter's nut or, more loosely, nut of the gods.

Roman records of walnuts date to at least the time of Tiberius, and intact walnuts have been recovered from the ruins of Pompeii. In addition to their culinary value, walnuts were valued by the Romans for both medicinal and magical purposes. Romans considered walnuts capable of producing fecundity and began the Mediterranean custom of ceremoniously throwing walnuts at weddings. In some parts of Italy a three-chambered walnut in one's pocket is still considered excellent protection from witches and lightning. Placing one under a chair is said to prevent a witch from rising and can be, therefore, an excellent witch-detection device.

During ancient and medieval times walnuts were used to treat baldness, toothache, headache, rabies, and ringworm. Pliny, the Roman scholar, suggested, "Chewing a nut while fasting is a sovereign remedy against the bite of a mad dog." The Doctrine of Signatures, central to European herbal medicine in the sixteenth and seventeenth centuries, held that plant parts physically resemble the parts of the human body to which they can be usefully applied. The walnut was considered a representation of the human head; the kernel resembled the brain. Therefore, walnut husk was ground and prescribed for head wounds, and eating walnuts was a recommended treatment for the mentally ill. Interestingly, as it turns out, modern biochemists have found that walnut kernels contain very high concentrations of serotonin, a compound important for transmitting signals between neurons in the human brain.

Over the years, European horticulturists have selected a number of walnut variants with weeping growth habit, red kernels, and unusual leaf forms. One very late-leafing tree grew in an English churchyard and leafed out annually, it was said, on the Feast of St. Barnabas 11 June. This was considered miraculous, and cuttings of the tree commanded a high price from King James, Queen Anne, and other notables of the day.

Although early efforts at walnut grafting were doubtlessly undertaken in many countries, horticulturists in France were the first to successfully graft on a routine basis. Their success at grafting facilitated cultivar development and laid the foundation for modern walnut cultivation. Spanish introductions to Latin America, importations by American horticulturists from Thomas Jefferson to Felix Gillet, and the establishment of orchards in New Zealand, Australia, and South Africa have completed the walnuts' conversion into a truly global crop.

REFERENCE

1. See Charles A. Leslie and Gale Mcgranahan: *The Origin of Walnut*.

4

AGRONOMIC REQUIREMENTS FOR ESTABLISHING AN ORCHARD AND PRODUCING WALNUT

Distribution and Ecology

Walnut (*Juglans Regia*) is widely cultivated, extending from Balkan peninsula, Turkey to the Himalayas at altitudes up to 3,000 metres; and is often naturalized. Currently walnut trees are grown in 45 countries in the world. The major walnut producing countries include China, USA, Turkey, Iran, France, India, Romania, Ukraine, and Yugoslavia, FR. World production of walnut has increased from 844,000 tonnes in 1983 to 1,491,439 tonnes in 2005.[1] Total area under walnut is estimated at about 647,000 hectares, with world average yield of 2.31 tonnes per hectare.

Description and Varieties

There are two major commercial species of walnuts: The English walnut, which originated in Persia, and the black walnut, which is native to the US. Virtually all walnuts sold commercially in the US are of the English variety. The term "English" applied to the Persian nut is a misnomer. The name "English walnut" refers to the English merchant marines whose ships transported the product for trade around the world. Walnut is a monoecious, deciduous, aromatic tree growing to the height 30 m tall and its leaves alternate, pinnate, leaflets 7-9. Male catkins on twigs of previous year's growth, female flowers few, on twigs of current year's growth. Fruit is a large, subglobose, indehiscent drupe 4-5 cm in diameter; stone ovoid, acute, wrinkled, and easily splitting. The walnut edible, two parted kernels of the nut are of great commercial value, particularly, the Persian walnut (*Julgan regia*), more particularly known as English walnut. The English walnut is cultivated for commercial use in many parts of the world.

The most important Native American species of walnut is the Black walnut (*Julgan Nigra*). The Black walnut grows naturally in riverbottom land throughout eastern United States to the height up to 150 feet (48 metres) and yields the most valuable North American hardwood.

A large number of walnut varieties are grown all over the world. The varieties are mostly country specific and the main commercial varieties cultivated in the world are shown in Table 4.1.

Table 4.1: Main Commercial Walnut Varieties

Origin	*Name of Variety*	*Origin*	*Name of Variety*
India	Lake English, Drainovksy, Gobind, Eureka, Placentia Wilson, Franqueffe Kashmir, Budded Opex Caulchry	USA	Payne, Hartley, Chandler, Eureka
France	Franqueffe, Mayaffe, Parisienne	Italy	Chandler, Franquette, Parisienne

Cultivation and Cultural Practices

Establishment Cultural Practices

Site Preparation: Clearing of land where walnut trees are to be planted: Land preparation with deep subsoil or slip ploughing the soil profile is required in order to break up any underlying hardpan or layered soils which would affect root and water penetration.

Planting: Planting the orchard starts by making trees sites with a small nursery stake then holes are dug, trees planted, and staked. New trees are topped soon after planting so that trunk development is encouraged. Beginning in the sixth year half of the orchard is pruned and the remaining trees are pruned the next year.

Soil, climate and irrigation requirements: The successful cultivation of the Persian Walnut requires a temperate climate, a rich well drained soil and readily available irrigation facilities. In the United States walnut trees are irrigated at regular intervals throughout the growing season and once again just prior to harvesting to hasten the opening of the nut husks.[2] In Jammu & Kashmir state, which produces bulk of walnut in the country, the crop is mainly rainfed, though farmers who have access to irrigation facilities irrigate the crop at least twice and once again prior to harvesting, to facilitate the opening of the nut husk. Walnut trees are grown in orchards. The trees bear fruit 5 to 7 years after planting and can continue to produce walnut for as long as a century, though its economic life is taken as 40 years.

Frost Protection: Use of mechanical aids or irrigation water for frost protection may be required. For English walnut, however, cover crop management during the spring blossom period March-April provides this defence.

Pest Management: During the developmental years, pest and disease control are minimal, except for controlling mites beginning the first year and worm starting the sixth years. Walnut blight, a major disease, is caused by a bacterium, which infects fruit and young shoots. Affected fruit can drop from the tree or produce shrunken or stained kernels. Chemical (copper) spray may be needed to control walnut blight beginning the fourth year.

Two major insect pests, navel orangeworm and codling moth, are managed with chemical (Guthion and Lorsban) treatment. Both insects can cause major damage to nuts in different stages of development.

Production Cultural Practices

Cultural practices for the production of English walnut vary from grower to grower and region to region.

Prunning: There are many pruning strategies for walnut trees. Each is dependent on several factors such as walnut variety and planting density. Prunning should be carried out in winter months.

Fertilization: Tree nitrogen status is determined by leaf analysis. Based on the sampling analysis, nitrogen and or other fertilizers would need to be applied.

Weed Control: Weeds in mature orchards are controlled with the same combination of chemical and cultural (mowing) practices as one being established. Pre-emergent weeds are controlled in the tree row during the autumn by a strip spray of residual herbicide. Persistent weeds that cannot be controlled by the autumn residual spray may need three spot sprays of a contact herbicide. Control of vegetation in January and February will provide needed frost protection.

Insect and Disease Management: Several insect and disease pests may need to be treated each year. Codling moth is the most significant insect pest or early blooming varieties. Multiple generations occur and are controlled based on careful monitoring of the population.

Harvest: Walnuts mature when hull become easily separable from the shell; the hull normally opening while fruit still attached to the tree. Harvest starts in the fourth or fifth year after the orchard is planted depending on variety. The walnuts are either hand harvested or mechanically harvested. Mature walnut orchards are harvested twice. The first pick usually collects 80 per cent of the nuts. The second pick harvests the remaining walnuts about a week or two later. Mechanical harvesting begins by shaking the tree trunk or branches to drop the nuts. The sweeper windrows the walnuts into the middle on the orchard row so that the mechanical harvester can pick them up to dump into field trailers. The walnuts are hauled from the field to a dehydrator for drying. After drying, the walnuts are sold to trader or processors.

On large walnut plantation older plantings tend to be of large trees and harvesting is carried out by mechanical shaking of the branches using slings attached to a cable and tractor-driven eccentric. Approximately 80 per cent of the nuts can thus be removed from the tree; with care, tree shakers may also be used. For smaller trees the shake and catch method may be used. Nuts may be caught in sheets or mechanically windrowed and collected by a machine with which the leaves and trash are separated, the harvested crop consisting of a mixture of hulled and unhulled walnuts. Prior land preparation to remove weeds and obstacles will speed up the harvest operations.

Yields: As noted above, English walnuts most often begin bearing an economic crop in the fourth year after planting. Typical annual yields for English varieties are measured in clean, dry, in shell tonnes per hectare and are shown in Table below: These yields are from the fourth year of orchard establishment to maturity.

Table 4.2: Walnut Annual Yield

Year	*Yield (Tonne/hectare)*
4	0.37
5	0.86
6	1.85
7	4.32
8+	4.94

Average yield for California walnut ranges from about 2.2 tonnes per ha to 6.7 tonnes. Yields obtained by Chilean walnut producers range from around 1.2 tonnes per hectare to approximately 4 tonnes of in-shell walnuts at full production. In Chile the maximum-yield stage normally starts at 16 years after planting. In Italy the average yield is over 3 tonnes and in France it is 2.1 tonnes per hectare while yields in other producing countries are undoubtedly lower: In India the current yield is 1.03 tonnes and for China it is 1.9 tonnes per hectare.

Planting Technique

Walnuts grown in orchards in California and southern Europe have generally been propagated by budding and grafting of cultivars on rootstock of various species of Juglans. The rootstocks generally used in the state of California include Northern California Black, Paradox hybrid and English walnut. Both varieties and rootstocks vary in susceptibility to diseases, nematodes and insect pests. Unlike many of the other deciduous tree crops, walnut trees like other nut trees experience alternate bearing cycles. Normally, one bumper crop is followed by a decline in production in the subsequent year. There are over 30 varieties of commercially produced walnuts, hybrids of English (Persian) walnut. Varieties have been developed for various characteristics such as:

- Early harvest, late harvest
- Thick shell, thin shell
- High walnut meat content
- Pest tolerance, etc.

Soil, Water and Fertilizer Requirements

With respect of soil requirements, walnuts are probably the most exacting of orchard crops. They do best on fertile, deep, well drained, non-stratified loamy soils. Walnuts produce good commercial crops with irrigation. Both in the US and Chile all commercial walnut orchards are planted on irrigated land. However, in Chile, only an estimated 60 per cent of the planted area has modern irrigation system. But in Jammu and Kashmir walnut crop is raised under rainfed conditions in rocky terrain. The tree bears fruit 5 to7 years after planting and can continue to produce walnuts for as long as a century, though generally economic life of walnut orchard is taken as 40 years. Nut size ranges from 24 mm to 32 mm.

Although in Chile, India and Turkey almost all walnut trees currently in production originated from seeds, budding and grafting of new and improved varieties, many of which are from the US, has increased in recent years. In China older walnut producing areas are scattered throughout the country and are mainly Persian variety walnut. However, over the last several years, black walnut varieties from the United States have been planted successfully in South China. The black walnut varieties have often been grafted to help the seedlings to adapt better to the terrain and weather conditions. In fact as a part of its agricultural restructuring, China's State Forestry Administration has introduced a pilot programme called Cropland Conversion to Forest and Grassland in the year 2000. The programme allows a maximum of 20 per cent of the converted area to be for economic trees (e.g. walnut, pecan and other nut or fruit bearing trees). In some areas, walnut seedlings could comprise 5 to 10 per cent of the total converted area. In the first year of its operation in 2000, a total of 983,600 hectares were converted.[3] The programme provides cash, grain, and seedling subsidies and farmers cannot grow other crops. Walnut and other nut bearing trees are considered a more attractive alternative because they require less management and nut can be stored and distributed easily with little damage. Farmers, specialists and government officials view walnut production as an ecological and economic alternative to cropland agriculture. In general, the programme has been well received, though there have been a few operational difficulties; including management.

Walnut production is considered a form of poverty alleviation in China. Seedling stock is inexpensive and farmers can plant a few trees on their land with little overhead and management costs. In walnut areas that are not part of the conversion programme, farmers often grow food and cash crops between trees. Several provincial forestry station specialists report that walnuts being bearing nuts 3 years after seedlings are transplanted. However, the specialists also report that it may take 7 to 8 years after transplanting before walnut production is significant.

In China traditional walnut production is from walnut trees that grow wild on sparsely treed mountain slopes and valleys from walnut trees that were planted in small clusters (1 or 2 trees) around farm houses. Specialists and government officials are encouraging an expansion of walnut planting by increasing and greater planting density in part of arid western China as a means of protecting against wind erosion. In addition, walnut and other nut bearing trees are considered a good way to control water erosion on sloped or terraced lands in the South. The result is that total planting acreage is increasing and is becoming more concentrated. The State Forestry Administration has recommended a tree planting density of 1 tree per 22 square metres (equivalent to 450 trees per hectare). Not all areas, however, adhere to the national guidelines. For example, recommended density in arid parts of Shanxi is 1 tree forestry for every 12 square metres. In fertile area of Shanxi, recommended density is even greater at 1 tree for every 6 square metre. In Sichuan, a mountainous province with a very wet climate, planting density may be farther apart. Late blossoming tree density is recommended to be 1 tree for every 30 square metres while early blossoming varieties are recommended to be 1 tree for every 20 square metres. The goal in choosing different densities for early and late blossoming varieties is to protect against natural disasters like frosts or prolonged cold weather.

The yield and nut size depends considerably on the weather conditions. For instance favourable weather during flowering and fruiting stage, e.g. in April-May in Jammu and Kashmir State can boost yield and nut size, while dry weather during June-July leads to shrinkage in nut size. Similarly, hailstorm can cause considerable damage.

Quality of in-shell Nut: The parameters considered for quality of in-shell nut are:

- Thinness of the shell
- Appearance
- Shell colour
- Texture
- Shape
- Size
- Weight

Kernel Quality: Shell thickness and structure are the most important determinant of per cent kernel and nut crackability. The highest quality walnuts have a thin outer shell with no internal convolutions protruding into the nutmeat. The inner shell partition between kernel halves should be very thin to allow easy removal of kernel pieces. Most thin-shelled walnut cultivars yield over 50 per cent kernel. In the Persian walnut the heritability for shell thickness is high.

Kernel quality and plumpness is strongly influenced by tree care and harvesting practices, but with tree receiving optimum care, wide differences in kernel quality still exist between cultivars. High quality walnuts have light coloured kernels with an absence of kernel veins. Dark coloured or strongly veined kernels are associated with rancidity by consumers. Kernel colour and venation are under a moderate level of genetic control in Persian Walnut. The bases for determining the quality of kernel are:

- Whole or broken
- Colour
- Size

Post-Harvest Treatments

Walnuts contain as high as 35 per cent moisture when harvested. They should be hulled, washed and dried as quickly as possible to 8 per cent moisture or less and graded. Shelled walnuts quickly darken and develop rancidity under unfavourable conditions; maximum stability is achieved at ca. 3 per cent moisture. Contamination by ammonia during storage can cause severe damage.

Production and Consumption/Utilization

Immature walnuts are pickled and the ripe walnuts eaten as a dessert nut; they are also widely used in baking and confectionery. In the Himalayan region in India walnuts are an important item in the diet. The kernels yield ca. 50 per cent of clear sweet oil, the first pressing, known as virgin oil, is largely used for culinary purposes. Extraction is carried out 2 to 3 months after harvesting, earlier the kernel contains a sort of emulsive milk, and if extracted later the oil is less sweet and possibly rancid. Pounded walnuts and walnut oil is the basis of the delicious Caucasians dish "charkasîya".

Nutritional Value

On dry weight basis walnuts contain approximately 15 per cent protein, 64 per cent fat and 16 per cent carbohydrates (Table 4.3). Although the vitamin C content of mature walnut kernels is low, that of immature green fruit is exceptionally high, as for walnuts used for pickling. However, the vitamin is destroyed where the method of pickling turns the nuts black. They should remain green, or white if the centres only are used. With a 7:1 ratio of polyunsaturated to saturated fat, walnuts are one of the highest naturally occurring sources of polyunsaturated fats. Polyunsaturated fats are an important source of essential fatty acids (EFAs), which we must get from the food we eat. Walnuts are a good non-fish source of alpha-linolenic acid, a key EFA from which omega-3 fatty acids are derived.

Table 4.3: Food Value of Walnut (per 100 grams of Edible Portion)

Calories (Kcal)	65	Moisture (g)	3.5
Protein (g)	14.90	Calcium (mg)	10
Fat (g)	64	Phosphorus	35
Carbohydrates (g)	15.80	Iron (mg)	31
Thiamine (mg)	0.33	Niacin (mg)	0.9
Riboflavin (mg)	0.1	Fiber (%)	15.80
Vitamins (mg)	1.50		

Eating a handful of walnuts a day may lower blood cholesterol level. The research study conducted at Loma Linda University in the U.S.A. and reported in 1993 in the *New England Journal of Medicine* determined that walnuts were beneficial in reducing blood cholesterol levels and protecting against heart disease. Researcher at Loma Linda University found that when men with normal cholesterol values were given walnuts instead of food high is saturated fat and, when calorie levels were held constant, their blood cholesterol levels dropped by more than 12 per cent and their LDL, or bad cholesterol, lowered by more than 16 per cent.

A follow-up study, conducted by Loma Linda University and the Hospital Clinic of Barcelona, was published in the 4 April 2000 issue of the Annals of Internal Medicine. The Barcelona study showed that men and women, with high cholesterol who ate a healthy Mediterranean diet had even further reduction in cholesterol and heart disease risk when walnuts were substituted for some of the foods and fat in the traditional diet. Total cholesterol was lowered by 4.1 per cent and LDL cholesterol by 5.9 per cent more than the typical Mediterranean diet.

Walnuts contain no cholesterol and are an important source of dietary fiber and protein. They are also a good source of many vitamins and minerals including potassium, magnesium, phosphorus, copper, zinc, vitamin B6 and vitamin E. Plant-based foods, including nuts, are natural sources of photochemical and antioxidants.[4]

By-Product

The second pressing of seed oil, known as fire drawn, is used as a salad oil or as a drying oil for use in paints, printing ink, and manufacture of soap. Residual cake is used for feeding livestock. The husk is the source of a dark brown dye used for darkens hair. The sap is the source of sugar in the Caucasus. Large shells are made into trinket boxes. Shells are also used as filler for external plywood glue, plastics, hard rubber products, asphalt roofing material, firebricks, tiles, and stuffing in toys. Shells reduced to dust are used as insecticides and as an abrasive for cleaning jet aircraft engines. The timber is highly valued for cabinetwork and gunstocks. Various parts are used medicinally as an alternative laxative and detergent.

Walnuts are Used from Tree to Shell

- Walnuts are sold in the shell or as kernels out of the shell
- Non-producing trees are used for wood for furniture, gun stocks
- Heavily burled walnut wood is highly prized for veneer for furniture
- dashboards of luxury cars
- Shells are burnt by a walnut handler to produce heat and generate electricity
- Shell are being used by a Japanese tyre manufacture to improve the grip of their tyres
- Shells are ground and used as an industrial abrasive
- Walnut meat is pressed for walnut oil

Risk in Producing and Marketing Walnut

The risk associated with producing and marketing walnuts should not be minimized. Risk is caused by various sources of uncertainty which include production, price, and financial. Examples of these include unfavourable weather at crucial stage, insect damage, and a decrease in price or increase in interest rates. Due to the risk involved, access to a market is crucial. A market channel should be determined before walnut orchards are planted and brought into production.

Discussion

Among various edible nuts, walnut grown in temperate zones is the most important one. It is available round the year in one or another country throughout the world because of its durability and long shelf life. A popular dessert nut whose production has increased significantly from an average of about 817 thousand tonnes 1980-82 to 1.48 million tonnes average annual output during 2003-05. The consumption of walnut is increasing due to being labelled as a health food and due to the position of nuts at the base of the Mediterranean diet pyramid. The gourmet trade in salad oil and pickled walnuts currently monopolized by France and the United Kingdom could be developed in other producing countries. Demand for walnut is expected increase at a higher rate than in the past, especially in the developing countries due to rising income and population and use of walnut in ice cream, bakery, and food preparations following the establishment of ventures in these fields by the multinational corporations in developing countries. These aspects are discussed in the next chapter.

REFERENCES

1. FAOSTAT: *Database*, April 2006.
2. *Collier's Encyclopaedia,* Macmillan Educational Company: 1991 Edition, Vol. 23, p. 224.
3. USDA FAS Agricultural Attachés Report: *China: People's Republic of: Tree Nuts Annual 2002*, Global Agriculture Information Network (GIAN) Report: CH2038: dated 28.2.2002.
4. University of California: *Walnut Industry Fact Sheet.*

5

WORLD WALNUT ECONOMY

Production

For carrying out review of the world walnut economy there are two sources of the time series data. The Food and Agriculture Organization collects data on area, production and yield of walnut for all the countries and world total. It also compiles and publishes walnut trade data. The USDA, Horticulture & Tropical Products Division collects and publishes reports on Walnut Situation and Outlook in Selected Countries. Their reports cover six major countries, i.e. China, USA, Turkey, India, France and Italy. Data in these country reports prepared by the USDA Agriculture's Attaches cover area, production, exports, imports and domestic consumption.

Based on the FAO data, world production of walnut is estimated at 1.49 million tonnes in 2005, from an area of 646 thousand hectares. The world average yield is 2.31 tonnes per hectares. China is the largest producer of walnut with an annual average production of about 410,000 tonnes during the last three years, followed by U.S.A. (about 300,000 tonnes), Iran (150,000 tonnes), Turkey (130,000 tonnes), Ukraine (80,000 tonnes) and India (32,000 tonnes). However, average yields of Romania (12.50 tonnes/hectare) and Pakistan (10 tonnes) are rather high. Nevertheless, the area under walnut in these countries is quite low and their production is around 15,000 tonnes each (Table 5.1).

The trend in walnut production for 17 major producing countries and world total, based on three years average for the 1980-82 and 2003-05, is summarized in Table 5.2. During the last two decades and half world production of walnut has increased by about 81 per cent, i.e. by 2.5 per cent per annum. China appears to have recorded faster growth than other countries, 5.6 per cent per annum. China has about 186,000 hectares of land under walnut production. The production increased as more bearing acreage planted earlier became commercially viable. Improvements in tree nut management also resulted in production increases. Production would continue to increase as planting acreage is expanding and

Table 5.1: World Walnut Area, Production and Yield: 1999-2001

Country	Area (000 Hectares)			Production (000 Tonnes)			Yield (Tonne/Ha)		
	1995	2000	2005	1995	2000	2005	1995	2000	2005
World	552.9	556.3	646.7	1,060.4	1188.4	1,491.6	1.92	2.14	2.31
China	150.0	168.0	186.0	230.7	300.0	420.0	1.54	1.79	2.26
U.S.A.	78.0	69.0	87.0	212.3	216.8	308.4	2.72	3.01	3.54
Iran	32.3	50.0	65.0	119.2	140.0	150.0	3.69	2.80	2.30
Turkey	57.5	58.3	70.0	110.0	122.0	133.0	1.91	2.09	1.90
Ukraine	20.0	28.0	28.0	76.1	50.0	70.0	3.80	1.79	2.50
India	28.8	30.2	30.8	25.0	31.0	31.5	0.87	1.03	1.02
France	14.6	13.6	16.5	21.9	27.8	30.0	1.50	2.04	1.82
Romania	2.5	2.4	2.0	22.8	25.0	15.5	7.75	10.53	12.50
Macedonia	1.3	2.4	2.4	4.0	3.7	3.7	2.15	1.68	1.54
Greece	15.5	15.0	15.0	22.7	22.1	21.5	1.47	1.47	1.43
Pakistan	1.8	1.7	1.4	18.0	18.0	14.0	10.00	10.31	10.00
Georgia	5.0	7.5	7.0	10.0	15.5	12.0	2.00	2.07	1.71
Austria	5.0	5.0	6.0	13.4	17.1	17.7	3.42	3.42	2.95
Germany	5.1	4.5	4.5	13.8	14.5	16.9	2.70	3.22	3.75
Chile	6.8	7.8	9.2	9.8	11.3	15.0	1.44	1.46	1.63
Belarus	4.0	4.5	5.0	9.0	12.0	12.0	2.25	2.67	2.40
Italy	4.3	4.0	4.0	10.6	12.0	16.0	2.46	3.00	4.00
Morocco	7.5	5.5	4.6	3.3	6.5	1.5	0.44	1.18	0.33
Russian Federation	16.0	14.0	14.0	7.5	12.0	14.0	0.47	0.86	1.00
Spain	2.3	3.0	7.5	8.1	10.0	22.0	3.52	3.33	2.93

Source: Compiled from FAO STAT Database, April 2006.

planting density is increasing. Other favourable factors include introduction of new techniques, improved varieties and better inputs. Production in Chile rose by 4 per cent per annum following modernization of production technology and tree varieties. The Chilean walnut industry is well established and expanding its production and planted area. New Plantings are offsetting the conversion of older orchards for residential and commercial purposes. The prices received by walnut producers and the declines of values in alternative tree crops have also caused the area planted for walnuts to increase. The new orchards are often planted with improved-yield varieties. The yield, which was an 1.4 tonne in 1980-82, is projected to increase to 1.6 tonnes per hectare in the year 2005. All the orchards are irrigated and the industry is heavily export-driven, as roughly 85 per cent of domestic supply is shipped to foreign consumers. Domestic consumption is primarily a function of the export market. If the export market is poor, domestic consumption of walnut in Chile rises due to the availability and low prices of walnuts. The increased walnut production is expected to boost its exports in the future.

Table 5.2: Walnut Production in Selected Countries

Country	*Production (000 tonnes)*		*Index 2003-05 over 1980-82*	*% Share in Total Production*	
	1980-82	*2003-05*		*1980-82*	*2003-05*
1. Argentina	8,200	9,000	109.8	1.0	0.6
2. Austria	8,622	18,603	215.8	1.1	1.3
3. Chile	5,608	14,333	255.6	0.7	1.0
4. China	109,667	409,510	373.4	13.4	27.7
5. France	27,933	26,549	95.0	3.4	1.8
6. Greece	24,764	20,720	83.7	3.0	1.4
7. India	18,333	32,167	175.5	2.2	2.2
8. Iran	123,990	150,000	121.0	15.2	10.1
9. Italy	45,200	15,333	33.9	5.5	1.0
10. Mexico	5,084	19,000	373.7	0.6	1.3
11. Pakistan	16,078	13,985	87.0	2.0	0.9
12. Romania	37,452	27,309	72.9	4.6	1.9
13. Russian Fed.	62,667	13,167	21.0	7.7	0.9
14. Spain	8,413	19,039	226.3	14.9	1.2
15. Turkey	121,333	129,667	106.9	14.9	8.8
16. Ukraine[1]		79,884		–	5.4
17. U.S.A.	198,373	299,673	151.1	24.3	20.3
18. Sub-Total	712,517		182.2	87.2	87.7
19. Others	104,321	182,168	176.6	12.8	12.3
20. World Total	816,838	1,480,107	181.2	100.0	100.0

1. included in Russian Federation.

Source: FAO STAT Database, April 2006.

India's walnut output rose by only 2.3 per cent per annum during the last two decades and half, despite lack of proper maintenance of existing trees because of the continued civil unrest in the Kashmir valley, the traditional walnut growing areas. In fact walnut trees in some areas have been cut for firewood. The increase in production reflected higher harvested area as more trees in new non-traditional areas in Jammu came into bearing stage. Production in France, which is the largest producer of walnuts in Europe, remained also constant during the period under review. A small increase in the Grenoble areas seems to have been offset by lower production in other areas. France, despite large importer, is net exporter of walnuts with most exports going to European countries. Most of the French imports are of shelled walnuts, mostly from Moldova, India and Hungary. The market for high-end walnuts is mainly dominated by domestic production. The French food processing industry offers the best market potential for Indian walnuts in shelled nuts and pieces. The rise in popularity of walnuts as a snack also presents an opportunity for Indian walnuts in consumer serving-size packages.

Production in the United States increased by about 51 per cent during the last two and half decades, i.e. over 1.7 per cent per annum. The United State is the leading exporter of in-shell and shelled walnuts, accounting for 54 per cent and 47 per cent of global trade, respectively. Output in Mexico rose by more than three times from rather low base. By contrast, production declined in Italy, which was in the past a leader in the walnut production in terms of both domestic crop size and volume exported to international markets. However, over time Italy gradually lost its position, as minimal replacement planting occurred to compensate for the large number of trees cut to profit from the sale of the lumber. As a result, the surviving walnut trees in Italy are very old and have low yields. The only commercial crop still harvested is the "Sorrento" variety produced mainly in the area around Naples. Crop volumes range between 10, 000 and 15,000 tonnes depending on weather conditions. Non-replacement of orchards, (except for a few in northern Italy) keeps domestic production from meeting the growing domestic demand, thus favouring imports. Production also declined in a number of other countries, such as Greece, Pakistan, Russian Federation and Romania as farmers substituted their walnut areas with other more remunerative horticultural crops.

Walnuts grow naturally throughout most of Turkey and in the past, they were generally not cultivated but simply harvested from natural forests. However, during the last two decades, increasing demand and prices have made walnut cultivation more attractive, leading to increased investment in the sector. The Horticulture Research Institute (HRI) in Yalova is the leading walnut research facility in Turkey and has developed nine standard varieties with higher yields. In addition to the HRI, several private companies have begun commercial propagation of improved walnut. Production of walnuts in Turkey is, therefore, expected to increase during the next 5 years or so, as the number of trees shifted to better varieties reach bearing stage and as more trees are planted.

Walnut Consumption

Information on domestic consumption is available only from the USDA Foreign Agriculture Service Reports on Walnut Situation and Outlook in Selected countries. From the available sources an attempt has been made in Table 5.3 to present three years average estimates for 1995-1997 and 2003-2005 on domestic consumption for the six major producing countries.

Global Consumption during the nine years period is estimated to have increased by 49 per cent, representing an annual growth rate of 3.5 per cent.[1] Consumption increased in almost all countries during this period, though with different rates of growth. Among various countries, EU is the largest consumer entity of walnuts. Germany and the United Kingdom are the leading importers of walnuts. Nuts are used for a number of purposes in these countries, mostly as ingredients in food products. Nuts are also popular as snacks, particularly during the year-end holiday season. To satisfy domestic demand, UK and Germany imports significant quantities of many kinds of nuts, including walnuts, almonds, hazelnuts/ filberts and pistachio. Walnuts have garnered some popularity as an ingredient in chocolate confectionery, backed foods and ice cream.

Table 5.3: Walnut Domestic Consumption in Major Producing Countries

(*in Tonnes*)

Country	*1995*	*1996*	*1997*	*Average*	*2003*	*2004*	*2005*	*Average*	*% Increase 2003-05 over 1995-97*
Chile	1,570	1,690	1,700	1,653	2,000	2,000	2,000	2,000	2.40
China	191,393	188,050	217,946	199,130	302,092	329,458	351,300	327,617	64.52
U.S.A.	46,651	39,832	45,194	43,892	61,778	66,051	73,140	66,990	52.62
Turkey	110,029	115,500	115,934	113,821	149,864	156,827	154,634	153,775	35.10
India	11,000	12,000	13,200	12,067	17,000	18,000	18,500	17,833	47.78
France	20,370	18,500	18,500	19,140	20,063	21,327	19,500	20,297	6.04
Italy	27,042	26,500	30,227	27,923	29,470	33,994	36,600	33,355	19.45
Total	408,055	402,072	442,701	418,548	582,267	627,657	655,674	621,867	48.58

Source: These estimates are based mainly on the USDA Agricultural Attaché's Annual Tree Nuts Country Reports.

China is one of the largest walnut consuming countries in the world. Increasing production and stable exports in China indicate that its domestic consumption is increasing. According to the USDA data, consumption rose by around 6 per cent per annum from 1995-1997 to 2003-2005. Chinese consumers prefer in-shell nuts that can be cracked by hand. They are considered to be cleaner and they are cheaper than processed nuts. Walnut demand is often highest during the Chinese lunar New Year in late winter or early spring. Walnut demand is also high during China's mid-Autumn festival in late September. Walnut demand during the mid-Autumn festival is met with fresh walnuts supplied by domestic growers.

Chinese consider walnuts to be a health food good for human brain, hair, and kidneys. Most often walnuts are consumed fresh or dried but there is also consumption of walnuts as a processed snack food. Processed walnuts are coated in honey or sugar and sesame seeds. Use of dried walnuts in the baking and confectionary industry is growing. It is now much more common to see walnuts baked into breads, rolls, biscuits and cakes. Walnuts are also ground into powder for porridge or processed into milk like product. In some rural areas, walnuts are also crushed for oil. Packaged walnut consumption seems to be higher in large cities like Beijing, Shanghai, and Guangzhou. Consumers in other large cities, such as provincial capitals and coastal cities, also tend to have a higher purchasing power for processed and packaged nuts. According to processors and traders, bulk bin walnut sales in large inland cities and provincial counties surpass sales of packaged nuts.

Turkey follows China in walnut consumption. Its domestic utilization has increased by 33 per cent over the last nine years and averaged 154,000 tonnes per annum during 2003-05. The United States, which is also one of the major walnut consuming country, registered 52 per cent growth during the review period. Its annual average domestic consumption of walnut is estimated at about 67,000 tonnes during 2003-05.

In *France* walnuts are consumed as such for snacking or home cooking, or in by-products, such as walnut oil, or shelled walnuts used aś ingredient in the pastry, bakery and cheese industries. French households are estimated to purchase proximately 7,000-9,000 tonnes of in-shelled walnut (including 2,000 tonnes of fresh walnuts and 7, 000 tonnes of dried walnut), and 6,000 tonnes shelled walnut per year. Most of the French south-eastern section (roughly 75%) is for the in-sell walnut market, while more than half of the south-western section goes to the shelled walnut market segment. Overall, large grades are for the in-shell walnut market and smaller grades are for the shelled walnut market. The French per capita consumption of walnuts is 150 grams of in-shell walnuts and 200 grams of shelled walnuts per year. In-shell walnuts are consumed during the late autumn and winter. However, there is no seasonality for shelled walnut consumption.

Walnut consumption in France according to various studies conducted by the French Fruits and Vegetables Technical Institute (CTIFL) has been relatively stable for several years, at around 18,000 tonnes. Walnut imports in France is estimated at 13,000 tonnes, compared to its exports of 22,000 tonnes each year.

In Italy also domestic consumption is increasing rapidly, while its production of walnuts continues to decline due to declining acreage and lower productivity of domestic supplies. Italy imports around 19,000 tonnes of walnut each year, bulk of which are supplied by the United States in-shell form, with small quantities exported by France and eastern European countries. In Italy walnut consumption is tied to cold weather in the minds of the Italian with 70 to 80 per cent of total consumption (mainly in-shell) taking place from late November and mid-January. This reflects the Italian love of capping off a good meal with freshly shelled walnuts, especially around the Christmas period. However, in recent years the consumption of walnuts has expanded through the spring. Italian consumption increased by more than 4 per cent per annum and is currently exceeds 33,000 tonnes. Domestic consumption in Turkey is increasing by over 3.5 per cent per year, with total consumption approaching 154,000 tonnes. Increase reflects higher demand due to population growth and higher per capita income. The farmers use around 50 per cent of the walnut crop for home consumption and the remainder is marketed. Most of the marketed walnuts are consumed whole, with only a limited amount being processed.

Consumption in *India* increased by more than 4 per cent per annum. Demand for walnut like many other countries has been supported by the growth in the Indian economy and expanding middle class. Consumption is seasonal occurring mostly during the winter festival season from September through January. The relatively low prices favoured the substitution of walnuts for other nuts such as almond, cashews and pistachio, in traditional Indian dishes, snack foods and for confectionary purposes. Prospects for future growth in demand, which are discussed in detail in Chapter 8, will depend on the performance of the economy, price of competing nuts, e.g. almond and consumer preference.

Finally, in *Chile* domestic utilization of walnuts is rather limited. It rose from 1,653 tonnes during 1995-97 to 2,000 tonnes during the last three years.

INTERNATIONAL TRADE

World Exports

World exports of walnut in-shell during the last three years averaged 113,087 tonnes per year[2], valued at US$ 206 million. Global annual exports of walnut shelled averaged 100.5 thousand tonnes, worth about US$ 353 million. Annual total export value of walnut in-shelled and walnut kernels comes to US$ 559 million. Of the total, walnut in-shell accounted for around 37 per cent of annual export earnings while walnut kernels contributed the remaining 63 per cent.

World exports of walnut in-shell increased from about 79,000 tonnes in 1995 to over 129,115 tonnes in 2004 (Table 5.4). This represented a 5 per cent annual increase during the last ten years. The major walnut in-shell exporting countries include USA, which exported over 43 per cent of the world total in 2004, followed by Mexico (with 21% share), France (14 %), Chile (about 4 %) and Ukraine with/3 per cent share (Table 5.5). In addition exports from China, Moldova, Bulgaria and Netherlands accounted for (1-2% each of the world total). India exports only limited quantities of walnut in-shell ranging 500-1000 tonnes. Volume of exports increased for all major countries, except the U.S.A., China and Moldova. The unit value of exports varies considerably. France and Chile unit value was 12 per cent higher than the U.S.A. and 14 per cent higher than the weighted average for all the countries. The performance of the major exporters is discussed later on in this chapter.

Table 5.4: World Exports of Walnut In-shell and Shelled

Year	*Walnut In-shell*			*Walnut Kernels*		
	Tonnes	*Value US$ 1000*	*Unit value US$/Tonne*	*Tonnes*	*Value US$ 1000*	*Unit value US$/Tonne*
1990	77,239	140,873	1823.86	33,447	109,025	3259.64
1995	78,573	155,754	1982.28	50,056	186,045	3716.74
2000	106,564	189,825	1781.13	72,567	230,749	3179.80
2001	95,027	165,421	1740.78	74,873	258,156	3447.92
2002	102,549	170,779	1665.34	89,117	288,681	3239.35
2003	107,596	190,614	1771.57	95,305	343,885	3608.26
2004	129,115	257,095	1991.21	117,088	426,574	3643.19

Source: FAO STAT Database, April 2006.

Table 5.5: Exports of Walnut in-shell (Quantities in Tonnes): 2000–2004

Exports	*Years*					*Average in Last 3 years*	*% Share in World Total*
	2000	2001	2002	2003	2004		
World	106,564	95,027	102,549	107,596	129,115	113,086.7	100.00
Argentina	0	0	70	59	219	116.0	0.10
Austria	176	251	314	599	527	480.0	0.42
Belgium	487	818	1,965	1,762	1,870	1,865.7	1.65
Bulgaria	2,880	1,086	1,240	2,077	4,593	2,636.7	2.33
Chile	3,631	4,540	3,904	4,351	4,343	4,199.3	3.71
China	1,875	1,120	1,811	1,116	1,069	1,332.0	1.18
Hong Kong	876	56	576	125	103	268.0	0.24
France	16,852	16,638	16,486	12,784	18,945	16,071.7	14.21
Germany	1,282	754	1,012	1,099	1,284	1,131.7	1.00
Hungary	556	499	718	772	635	708.3	0.63
India	597	987	655	300	257	404.0	0.36
Iran	21	36	33	48	149	76.7	0.07
Italy	1,369	604	448	276	526	416.7	0.37
Japan	2	11	0	3	14	5.7	0.01
Mexico	20,304	12,527	18,344	22,789	29,738	23,623.7	20.89
Moldova, Rep.	188	281	925	437	2,071	1,144.3	1.01
Netherlands	1,772	2,206	687	2,103	3,026	1,938.7	1.71
Pakistan	154	92	254	121	489	288.0	0.25
Romania	506	172	397	545	3,939	1,627.0	1.44
Russian Federation	3	16	1	13	21	11.7	0.01
Spain	281	667	475	673	578	575.3	0.51
Ukraine	0	766	2,620	2,116	5,898	3,544.7	3.13
U.S.A.	50,612	49,391	48,061	52,035	47,360	49,152.0	43.46
Uzbekistan	969	990	869	421	420	570.0	0.50

Source: FAOSTAT Database, April 2006.

Exports of walnuts in-shell rose from 106.6 thousand tonnes in 2000 to 129.1 thousand tonnes in 2004. The value of exports of walnuts in-shell increased from US$ 189 million in 2000 to US$ 257 million in 2004, registering about 6.5 per cent annual increase. Of the total foreign exchange of US$ 257 million, USA earned about 44 per cent, followed by Mexico with 25 per cent share, Hong Kong with 14 per cent share, and Chile 4 per cent. A number of other countries accounted for 1-2 per cent of world export value (Table 5.6).

Table 5.6: Exports of Walnut In-shell: Value US$ 1,000

	Years					*Average in*	*% Share in*
	2000	*2001*	*2002*	*2003*	*2004*	*Last 3 years*	*World Total*
World	189,149	165,544	170,779	190,614	257,095	206,162.7	100.00
Argentina	0	0	118	121	496	245.0	0.12
Austria	329	499	644	1,075	529	749.3	0.36
Bulgaria	900	756	645	1,254	3,004	1634.3	0.79
Chile	7,930	9,664	6,234	8,205	10,406	8281.7	4.02
China	2,183	1,333	2,053	1,369	1,081	1501.0	0.73
Hong Kong	1,308	97	387	124	148	219.7	0.11
France	32,978	33,118	30,143	24,483	33,225	29283.7	14.20
Germany	2,688	1,581	2,361	2,620	3,369	2783.3	1.35
Hungary	822	869	1,482	1,814	1,579	1625.0	0.79
India	1,716	3,443	1,871	601	182	884.7	0.43
Iran	18	25	32	46	131	69.7	0.03
Italy	2,021	1,188	1,048	828	1,471	1115.7	0.54
Japan	4	16	0	5	18	7.7	0.00
Mexico	38,608	15,049	27,673	41,844	84,074	51197.0	24.83
Moldova Rep.	158	218	490	330	1,105	641.7	0.31
Netherlands	1,804	4,299	1,524	4,642	9,331	5165.7	2.51
Pakistan	178	80	169	100	381	216.7	0.11
Romania	345	135	272	413	2,215	966.7	0.47
Russian Fed.	2	39	1	6	27	11.3	0.01
Spain	614	1,297	1,105	2,064	2,148	1772.3	0.86
Ukraine	0	575	1,886	1,694	3,685	2421.7	1.17
USA	91,993	87,639	85,680	91,946	92,471	90032.3	43.67
Uzbekistan	644	830	466	214	226	302.0	0.15

Source: FAO STAT Database: April 2006.

World exports of Walnut Kernels are shown in Tables 5.7. According to the FAO estimates world exports of walnut kernels totalled 76,649 tonnes in the year 2004, worth US$ 257.5 million. The leading countries participating in the world trade are USA (34%), Romania (11%), Mexico (9%), China (8%), Moldova (8.5%) and India (5%). Other countries that export walnut kernels include France, Mexico, Chile and Austria.

Table 5.7: World Exports of Walnut Shelled: 2000 – 2004: Quantities in Tonnes

	Years					Average in Last 3 years	% Share in World Total
	2000	2001	2002	2003	2004		
World	72,567	74,873	89,117	95,305	117,088	100503	100.00
Austria	1,569	1,940	2,117	1,365	1,040	1507	0.89
Belgium	56	198	1,407	1,132	1,189	1243	1.02
Brazil	368	314	503	521	579	534	0.49
Bulgaria	984	941	831	1,180	1,729	1247	1.48
Chile	2,369	3,084	2,450	2,831	3,224	2835	2.75
China	7,810	9,376	6,722	8,518	9,894	8378	8.45
Hong Kong	251	219	55	126	111	97	0.09
France	2,722	2,679	2,545	2,328	2,667	2513	2.28
Germany	288	332	438	789	1,022	750	0.87
Greece	91	161	431	913	1,041	795	0.89
Hungary	1,275	1,415	1,147	719	703	856	0.60
India	7,145	6,415	6,976	6,001	5,417	6131	4.63
Italy	176	191	282	330	367	326	0.31
Mexico	3,506	2,332	6,137	7,929	10,121	8062	8.64
Moldova, Rep.	6,055	6,533	9,619	9,127	10,930	9892	9.33
Netherlands	352	273	240	431	967	546	0.83
Romania	6,457	7,019	6,817	8,368	13,143	9443	11.22
Slovakia	630	519	782	848	586	739	0.50
Spain	318	360	380	464	610	485	0.52
Turkey	297	513	131	232	339	234	0.29
Ukraine	0	3,164	6,761	7,181	8,597	7513	7.34
UK	130	116	68	217	334	206	0.29
USA	23,271	24,660	29,955	31,218	39,385	33519	33.64
Uzbekistan	2,499	930	762	1,032	1,835	1210	1.57

Source: FAO STAT Database, April 2006.

World Imports

The details of the world imports of the walnut in-shell and shelled are given hereunder. *The world imports of walnut in-shell* increased from about 70.9 thousand tonnes in 1990 to 118.4 thousand tonnes in 2004.

Volume increased by 67 per cent, and value rose by 65 per cent from about US$ 132 million to US$ 218 million. Imports of walnut shelled rose almost five folds from 33.4 thousand tonnes in 1990 to 106.6 thousand tonnes. Their value increased from US$ 116 million to US$ 392 million. The total increase comes to 236 per cent during fifteen years. Both in the case of walnut in-shell and walnut kernels, the unit value registered declining trends (Table 5.8).

Table 5.8: Imports of Walnuts: Selected Years

Year	Walnut In-shell			Walnut Kernels		
	Tonnes	Value US$ 1000	Unit value US$/Tonne	Tonnes	Value US$ 1000	Unit value US$/Tonne
1990	70,917	132,583	1870.0	33,405	116,416	3485.0
1995	68,310	145,891	2135.7	47,476	192,652	4057.9
2000	88,027	159,094	1807.3	65,872	217,700	3304.9
2001	78,527	141,727	1848.2	75,404	262,393	3479.8
2002	95,031	139,240	1465.2	82,465	285,156	3457.9
2003	90,055	156,173	1734.2	91,222	327,582	3591.0
2004	118,369	218,135	1842.8	106,638	391,976	3675.8

Source: FAO STAT Database: April 2006.

As discussed above, world imports of walnut in-shell rose from 88 thousand tonnes in 2000 to 118 thousand tonnes in 2004. The major importing countries are Mexico with more than 17 per cent share of the world imports in 2004 (Table 5.9).High imports in this country is because of cheap processing of whole nuts sent by some of the US firms which are then re-exported to the USA. The next major importing country is Spain, which accounted for 17 per cent of global imports. This was followed by Germany with almost 15 per cent share, Italy (13 % share), Turkey (7%), Netherlands (4%) and Moldova (3.7%).

World Imports of Walnut Shelled: The total worldwide import of walnut shelled (i.e. kernels) is 106, 638 tonnes in the year 2004, valued at about US$ 392 million. Japan is the largest importer of walnut kernels importing 10,050 tonnes in 2004, followed by Germany which imported 10,405 tonnes: Turkey (imported 9,084 tonnes), Spain (imported 5410 tonnes), U.K (imported 4,393 tonnes) and Greece (imported 4,076 tonnes). The respective share of these countries in world total were Japan: 9.96 per cent, Germany: 9.76 per cent, Turkey: 8 52 per cent, Spain 5.07 per cent: U.K: 4.12 per cent and Greece: 3.82 per cent (Table 5.10).

Table 5.9: Walnut In-shell Imports: Quantities in Tonnes

	Years					*Average in Last 3 years*	*% Share in World Total*
	2000	*2001*	*2002*	*2003*	*2004*		
World	88,027	78,527	95,031	90,807	118,369	101,402	100.00
Albania	225	428	760	828	864	817	0.73
Algeria	0	50	199	130	241	190	0.20
Argentina	1,020	989	205	359	0	188	0.00
Australia	283	240	260	148	183	197	0.15
Austria	401	534	533	550	190	424	0.16
Belgium	1,707	1,612	2,233	1,636	2,325	2065	1.96
Brazil	2,295	2,268	1,683	1,535	1,973	1730	1.67
Canada	1,726	1,653	2,012	2,109	1,642	1921	1.39
Chile	160	304	141	292	571	335	0.48
China	848	531	1,081	248	277	535	0.23
Hong Kong	872	70	727	401	172	433	0.15
Denmark	452	471	448	440	327	405	0.28
Ecuador	175	144	173	146	191	170	0.16
Egypt	406	198	561	305	305	390	0.26
France	883	326	314	1,555	390	753	0.33
Germany	12,160	9,875	12,078	11,683	17,372	13711	14.68
Greece	74	239	493	688	407	529	0.34
Israel	522	425	464	480	494	479	0.42
Italy	10,027	12,367	10,754	14,507	15,216	13492	12.85
Japan	261	241	313	88	114	172	0.10
Korea, Republic	146	104	185	267	133	195	0.11
Lebanon	797	979	581	452	204	412	0.17
Lithuania	132	111	103	192	119	138	0.10
Mexico	9,678	6,925	11,217	11,343	20,351	14304	17.19
Moldova, Rep	1,115	1,699	2,390	2,548	4,427	3122	3.74
Netherlands	3,314	4,085	3,584	4,437	4,904	4308	4.14
Norway	334	324	306	276	402	328	0.34
Poland	233	423	325	340	294	320	0.25
Portugal	1,495	1,216	765	1,215	941	974	0.79
Russian Fed.	4,368	4,714	2,022	3,111	3,861	2998	3.26
Saudi Arabia	424	223	313	352	89	251	0.08
Slovakia	48	0	130	182	327	213	0.28
Spain	20,547	17,755	27,720	18,954	20,229	22301	17.09
Sweden	460	380	398	480	485	454	0.41
Switzerland	869	879	823	763	723	770	0.61
Turkey	4,210	988	3,140	3,381	8,697	5073	7.35
UAE	0	0	354	215	578	382	0.49
United Kingdom	2,060	1,785	1,706	1,934	1,823	1821	1.54
Uruguay	116	139	81	95	71	82	0.06
Venezuela	862	1,035	398	341	559	433	0.47

Source: FAO STAT Database: April 2006

Table 5.10: Walnut Shelled Imports: (Quantities in Tonnes)

	Years					Average in Last 3 years	% Share in World total
	2000	2001	2002	2003	2004		
World	65,872	75,404	82,465	91,222	106,638	93,442	100.00
Argentina	814	801	74	344	45	154	0.04
Australia	2,569	2,263	2,440	2,786	3,008	2,745	2.82
Austria	2,691	2,594	3,269	2,552	2,584	2,802	2.42
Belgium	1,106	776	2,417	2,090	1,830	2,112	1.72
Bosnia and Herz	0	0	0	1,187	1,096	761	1.03
Brazil	687	1,072	899	758	1,263	973	1.18
Canada	4,145	6,034	4,654	4,921	4,914	4,830	4.61
China	1,090	910	1,127	1,765	2,546	1,813	2.39
Hong Kong SAR	564	524	470	490	352	437	0.33
Croatia	668	733	1,103	1,211	1,154	1,156	1.08
Czech Republic	258	333	530	405	421	452	0.39
Denmark	422	486	447	458	518	474	0.49
Equador	79	165	228	280	249	252	0.23
Egypt	432	335	662	493	476	544	0.45
France	6,436	6,622	6,434	6,122	8,503	7,020	7.97
Germany	6,501	6,563	7,078	8,060	10,405	8,514	9.76
Greece	2,111	3,888	5,524	4,742	4,076	4,781	3.82
Hungary	943	709	872	629	782	761	0.73
Israel	2,760	4,621	2,365	3,149	2,709	2,741	2.54
Italy	1,414	1,832	1,651	2,235	2,731	2,206	2.56
Japan	9,404	8,846	9,935	9,595	10,620	10,050	9.96
Jordan	872	704	851	1,132	534	839	0.50
Korea, Republic	977	885	1,362	1,838	3,487	2,229	3.27
Latvia	82	164	145	218	195	186	0.18
Lebanon	732	1,281	1,136	1,217	890	1,081	0.83
Lithuania	178	229	229	360	341	310	0.32
Mexico	732	1,185	1,337	1,936	1,637	1,637	1.54
Moldova, Republic	209	462	647	210	114	324	0.11
Morocco	17	38	212	412	166	263	0.16
Netherlands	1,311	1,517	1,385	1,364	2,740	1,830	2.57
Norway	520	741	818	1,294	1,840	1,317	1.73
Russian Federation	477	1,684	1,029	1,740	2,788	1,852	2.61
Serbia and Monten	0	60	360	447	426	411	0.40
Singapore	223	270	276	268	256	267	0.24
Slovakia	145	0	371	586	863	607	0.81
Slovenia	73	931	1,064	1,038	852	985	0.80

(*Contd.*)

(Contd.)

	Years					Average in Last 3 years	% Share in World total
	2000	2001	2002	2003	2004		
South Africa	74	111	74	176	263	171	0.25
Spain	3,032	3,588	3,556	4,385	5,410	4,450	5.07
Sweden	210	243	291	328	481	367	0.45
Switzerland	1,344	1,256	1,474	1,394	1,421	1,430	1.33
Syria	2,421	1,805	1,500	2,257	3,023	2,260	2.83
Turkey	1,428	1,250	5,279	6,527	9,084	6,963	8.52
UAE	0	0	572	493	631	565	0.59
United Kingdom	3,057	3,290	3,115	3,771	4,393	3,760	4.12
USA	133	468	37	71	142	83	0.13
Uruguay	122	124	64	83	82	76	0.08
Venezuela	196	257	122	131	167	140	0.16

Source: FAO STAT Database, April 2006.

India's Share in World Trade

India exports both walnuts in-shell as well as kernel. However, its share in the world market for walnut in-shell is negligible, as it has consistently increased exports of shelled walnut. India's total exports of walnut in-shell and kernel account for 5.4 per cent of world exports in 2004. Spain is the largest importer of Indian walnuts, importing 1426 tonnes of shelled walnut in 2004 and 367 tonnes of walnut in-shell in 2003, but nil in 2004. The value of import was US$ 4.91 million. The total imports of Indian walnut, kernels and in-shell, in this market has increased slightly during the last three years. Germany imports of walnut kernels from India increased from 99 tonnes in 1998-99 to 562 tonnes in 2004 while imports of walnut in-shell rose from 81 tonnes to 161 tonnes in 2002 but was nil in 2004. Imports especially of walnut kernels increased tremendously in other EU countries such as France, UK, Greece, Denmark, during the last three years. Indian exporters were also able to increase exports of walnut kernel to Australia from 70 tonnes in 1998-99 to about 279 tonnes in 2002 but declined to 100 tonnes in 2004. Other important markets include Egypt, Switzerland and UAE.

Table 5.11: Production, Exports, Imports and Domestic Consumption in Selected Countries

(Average 2003-2005 MY): (In Tonnes)

Country Marketing Year[1]	*Production*	*Exports*		*Imports*	*Domestic Consumption*		*Share in Total Exports (%)*
		Total	*% Share of output*		*Total*	*% Share in Production*	
1. China	357,667	32,583	10.9	2,533	327,617	91.6	15.2
2. U.S.A.	299,673	132,890	44.3	275	167,058	55.7	62.2
3. Turkey	129,667	596	4.6	22,463	151,534	116.9	0.3
4. India	32,167	15,000	46.6	—	17,167	53.3	7.0
5. France	26,549	21,664	81.6	13,202	18,796	70.8	10.1
6. Chile	14,334	11,100	77.4	518	3,752	26.2	5.2
7. Total	860,057	213,833	24.9	38,991	685,924	79.80	100.0

1. Marketing year China, France and India: October-September: USA August-July: Turkey and Italy: September-August: Chile March-February.

Source: USDA FAS Online: Horticultural & Tropical Products Division: Walnut Situation and Outlook in Selected Countries: 2002-03 Report, and Global Trade Atlas, 2005.

World exports of walnuts are estimated to be around 20 per cent of the total production[3]. Among major exporting countries, the respective shares differ considerably. China utilizes 92 per cent of its production for domestic consumption, compared to 56 per cent in the U.S.A. In the case of India during the last three years exports constituted around 47 per cent of its production. By contrast Chile exported almost 77 per cent of production while France exports constituted about 82 per cent of its domestic production. However, it also imports large quantities. Among the five major producing countries Turkey and China also import large quantities of walnuts.

Export Performance of Competitor Countries

There seems to be keen competition among the major walnut exporting countries, viz. the United States, France, Moldova, Chile and India, especially in large importing countries such as EU, Turkey, Italy and Spain. India also face strong competition from Ukraine and Hungry. Eastern European countries are supplying a greater share of nut exports to Europe. In fact Moldova has become France's leading supplier of shelled walnuts. Not only labour costs (which is major factor in price competitiveness of shelled walnuts) in Moldova are low, but shipments are much faster than from India or China. Importers don't need to carry stocks to meet customers demand. The quality of the Moldavian walnuts also suits French users' requirements regarding size, colour and taste. However, India appears to be increasing its market share in some countries such as Australia, and a few countries in the Middle East. Attempt is made below to present information on walnut exports by destinations for the major exporting countries and three importing countries. This can provide an indication of the current markets for Indian competitors in the international trade and serve as guide for India to explore new markets.

Some exporting countries enjoy preferential treatment such as Chile for Latin American Integration Association and France in EU. Chile mainly exports in-shell walnuts to the Latin American market and the European Union (EU). The most important markets in Latin America are Latin American Integration Association (ALADI) member countries where Chile has a tariff advantage over other exporting countries. Brazil is the *largest Chilean export* market both for in-shell and shelled walnuts, far surpassing any other market. Argentina is the second largest market for both in-shell and shelled walnut. Exports from Chile are highly dependent upon Brazilian demand and prices. Only small quantities of the highest-quality nuts are exported to Europe, mainly to Germany.

Yearly export variations are the consequence of production changes. Increased exports from Chile are expected in the coming years, which will reflect the expansion in production and better quality as improved orchards begin to bear fruit. Chile has only a small import market, mainly coming from the United States, due to an increase in demand for higher quality fruit.

India supplied 9 per cent of the total exports of the major countries. Walnuts exports depend largely on domestic prices and export demand. Exports vary considerably from one year to the next. For instance in 2000-01 exports rose to a record 18,460 tonnes but declined to 15,350 tonnes in 2003 and 14,400 tonnes in 2004 (Table 5.12). The major export destinations were the Spain, Germany, Egypt, France, the United Kingdom, Greece, the Netherlands and France. During the last two years exports were shipped to three new counties, viz. Egypt Arab Republic, Australia and Argentina. More than 95 per cent are exported as kernels (40 per cent light halves; 20 per cent amber halves/broken; and the balance as broken).

Table 5.12: Walnut Exports of India and Chile by Destinations
(in Tonnes In-shell basis)

India			*Chile*		
Exports to	*2003-04*	*2004-05*	*Exports to*	*CY 2003*	*CY 2004*
Spain	4490 (14.2)	4125 (21.2)	Brazil	2668 (21.9)	2360 (22.3)
Germany	1800 (11.5)	2290 (12.4)	Italy	2662 (21.8)	2348. (22.2)
France	1630 (29.3)	2073 (11.2)	Spain	1473 (12.1)	1885 (17.8)
U.K.	1300 (14.2)	1712 (9.3)	Germany	1453 (11.9)	1263 (11.9)
Greece	815 (10.8)	1504 (8.1)	Portugal	1146 (9.4)	998 (9.4)
Egypt Arab Rep.	—	1085 (5.9)	Argentina	1060 (5.6)	—
Netherlands	570 (4.8)	820 (4.4)	Netherlands	310 (2.5)	558 (5.3)
Italy	420 (3.6)	515 (2.8)	Ecuador	196 (1.6)	122 (1.1)
U.S.A.	195 (2.0)	140 (2.4)	Uruguay	111 (0.9)	—
Australia	—	360 (2.0)	Switzerland	666 (5.6)	343 (3.2)
Sub-Total	8574 (72.7)	15079 (79.8)	Sub-Total	11745 (96.4)	10149 (96.3)
Others	3226 (27.3)	3731 (20.2	Others	4542 (3.6)	418 (3.7)
Grand Total	15350 (100.0)	144400 (100.0)	Grand Total	12187 (100.0)	10575 (100.0)

Note: Figures in brackets are percentage share in the total.

Source: Global Trade Atlas, 2005.

France accounted for over 10 per cent of total exports of the major producing countries. It is a net exporter of walnuts principally to EU member states and Switzerland. French and US walnuts compete for these countries based on the respective prices and the U.S. dollar and Euro exchange rate. Italy, Germany and Spain are France's leading export markets. In 2003-04 as US walnuts were sold at significantly lower prices than French walnuts in Europe, prices for French walnuts declined and were lower than in 2002-03.

French exports and imports of walnut during the last two years are shown in Table 5.13. During the last two years the United States lost its rank as France's leading supplier of in-shell walnuts, replaced by Moldova and Austria, whereas Moldova also provided the bulk of shelled imports.

France imports walnuts in-shell, though in certain years and in limited quantities. However, it imports large quantities of shelled walnuts. The supplier of in-shell walnuts is the United States, while Moldova is the leading supplier of shelled walnuts. Quantities imported during the past two years averaged 2 tonnes of in-shell walnuts and 5,730 tonnes of shelled walnuts. These quantities come to equivalent of 13,416 tonnes of walnut in-shell basis.

Italy is one of the large and growing markets for walnut imports. With domestic production not able to meet the growing domestic demand,

Table 5.13: French Walnut Export-Import Matrix 2004 and 2005: (in Tonnes)

Country	Exports In-Shell basis		Country	Imports In-shell basis	
	2004	2005		2004	2005
1. Germany	5302 (28.3)	6428 (28.9)	1. Moldova	8924 (57.6)	7169 (54.5
2. Spain	3933 (21.0)	4355 (19.6)	2. Ukraine	1740 11.2)	1762 (13.4)
3. Italy	931 (5.0)	2593 (11.7)	3. China	630 (4.1))	370 (2.8)
4. Switzerland	1382 (7.4)	1634 (7.3)	4. India	572 (3.7)	1176 (13.4)
5. Portugal	806 (4.3)	919 (4.1)	5. Romania	368 (2.4)	0 0
6. Moldova	3468 (18.5)	3529 (15.9)	6. Hungary	569 (3.8)	300 (2.2)
7. Belgium	771 (4.1)	865 (3.9)	7. Spain	301 (1.9)	465 (3.5)
8. Denmark	523 (2.8)	535 (2.4)	8. Italy	266 (1.7)	330 (2.5)
9. Netherlands	337 (1.8)	386 (1.8)	9. Svakia	348 (2.2)	208 (1.6)
9. Others	1300 (6.9)	995 (4.5)	10. Other	1748 (11.3)	1572 (11.7)
10. Total	18753 (100.0)	13,848 (100.0)	11. Total	15493 (100.0)	13144 (100.0)

Note: Figures in brackets are per cent share in the total: Source: Global Trade Atlas, 2005.

it has to import large quantities. Italian consumption of in-shell walnuts has increased over 18 per cent to 40,000 tonnes (3 years averaged over 2003-05). While consumption fluctuates with domestic production (mainly as a reflection of price), there is potential for continued increase in consumption through effective marketing activities. Excluding relatively small quantities from France and Eastern Europe, most of Italy's imports are US in-shell walnuts, which accounted for 77-79 per cent of total shipments in the past two years (Table 5.14). As regards imports of shelled walnuts, the US supplies less than 17 per cent of total imports, while large quantities are imported form other countries. Italy exports of walnut are rather limited. Italy's exports of walnut in-shell totalled 277 tonnes in 2003 and 524 tonnes in 2004. It did not export any quantity of shelled walnuts during these two years.

Table 5.14: Italy: Walnut Imports and Exports (in Tonnes)

Country	Imports In-shell Walnuts		Country	Imports shelled Walnuts	
	2003	2004		2003	2004
1. U.S.	11,176 (76.5)	12043 (79.1)	1. Total E.U.	90 (4.0)	643 (23.5)
2. France	613 (4.2)	818 (5.3)	2. Romania	156 (6.9)	72 (2.6)
3. Germany	489 (3.3)	242 (1.5)	3. U.S.	380 (16.9)	72 (2.6)
4. Other E.U.	45 (0.3)	30 (0.2)	4. Chile	75 (5.5)	20 (1.9)
5. Chile	1452 (9.9)	1010 (6.6)	5. India	40 (1.8)	40 (1.5)
6. Romania	71 (0.5)	89 (0.6)	6. Other	1016 (45.3)	828 (30.3)
7. Bulgaria	243 (1.7)	237 (1.6)	7. Grand Total	2245 (100.0)	2731 (100.0)
8. Others	524 (3.6)	747 (4.9)			
9. Grand Total	14613 (100.0)	15216 (100.0)			

Source: Global Trade Atlas, 2005.

China's walnut exports continue to increase. However, as a percentage of production, walnut exports have been stable. Its annual exports currently total over 26,000 tonnes (Table 5.15). It exports walnuts in-shell, shelled and packaged walnut kernels. Chinese industry sources believe that China's walnut exports will depend on its ability to produce highly processed and high value walnut products. These products will most likely be targeted at markets in Asia and Europe because of price will be too high for most domestic consumers. Chinese walnut are loosing ground in the international markets where Eastern European countries specially Moldova, are supplying greater share. China's top five walnut exports markets in 2004 were UK (7346 tonnes), Japan (5569 tonnes), Canada (2253 tonnes), Germany (2296 tonnes) and Viet nam (1373 tonnes). China also imports walnuts, which averaged 2070 tonnes during the last two years. Lower domestic production and rising domestic demand in 2003 increased imports to a record 2669 tonnes in 2004. In addition rising international demand for shelled and processed walnuts helped increase China's imports for processing walnuts that were later re-exported to other countries.

Table 5.15: China: Walnut Exports and Imports

Exports of Walnut In-shell Basis (in Tonnes)			*Import Trade Matrix (In Tonnes)*		
Country	*2003*	*2004*	*Country*	*2003*	*2004*
1. UK	4775 (19.4)	7346 (26.6)	1. U.S.	1398 (95.2)	2588 (97.33)
2. Japan	4075 (16.5)	20.2 (20.2)	2. Russia	47 (3.2)	0 0
3. Germany	3213 (13.0)	2296 (8.3)	3. South Africa	8 (0.5)	8 (3.2)
4. Canada	2700 (10.9)	2253 (8.2)	4. Japan	9 (0.6)	9 (0.2)
5. N. Korea	2211 (9.0)	1273 (4.6)	5. Peru	4 (0.3)	—
6. Hong Kong	1614 (6.5)	962 (3.5)	6. Australia	—	5 (0.2)
7. Australia	1270 (5.I)	1050 (3.8)			
8. France	833 (3.4)	—			
9. Vietnam	—	1373 (5.0)			
10. Taiwan	508 (2.1)	725 (2.6)			
11. Others	2829 (11.5)	3977 (14.4)			
Total	24666.(100.0)	17624 (100.0)			

Note: Figures in brackets are percentage to the total.

Source: Global Trade Atlas, 2005.

Turkey is a net importer of walnuts. During the last two years period average imports totalled around 25,530 tonnes annually, representing 16.9 per cent of annual consumption of about 151,500 tonnes. Most imports are inexpensive, lower quality nuts from neighbouring countries. High quality domestic nuts, not more than 800 tonnes, are usually exported each year (Table 5.16).

Table 5.16: Turkey: Walnut Imports and Exports: (In-shell basis: Tonnes)[4]

Imports In-shell Basis			*Exports of Walnuts In-shell Basis*		
Country	*2003*	*2004*	*Country*	*2003*	*2004*
1. Uzbekistan	3856 (19.6)	2400 (7.7)	1. Egypt	0 0	102 (12.1)
2. Kyrgyzstan	3064 (15.6)	2150 (6.9)	2. Cyprus	17 (2.8)	30 (3.6)
3. Ukraine	4330 (22.0)	1347 (4.3)	3. Germany	13 (202)	25 3.0
4. Bulgaria	1264 (6.4)	3646 (11.8)	4. France	3 (0.5)	88 (10.4)
5. Romania	3850 (19.6)	14332 (45.7)	5. Australia	0 0	197 (23.3)
6. Moldova	1370 (7.0)	1159 (3.7)	6. Greece	2 (0.5)	2 (0.2)
7. Afghanistan	308 (1.5)	53 (1.3)	7. US	17 (2.8)	75 (8.9)
8. Others	885 (4.5)	4045 (12.9)	8. UAE	2 (0.5)	55 (6.5)
9.Total	19700 (100.0)	31351 (100.0)	9. Others	543 (91.0)	271 (32.1)
			10. Total	597 100.0)	845 (100.0)
11. Georgia	—	34 (0.8)	11. United. Arab. Em.	10 (2.7)	33 (2.6)
12. U.A.Em.	—	1,635 (39.7)	12. Syria	—	295 (23.0)
13. Others	21 (0.6)	157 (3.8)	13. Others	39 (10.3)	227 (17.7)
14. Total	3,427 (100.0)	4,113 (100.0)	14. Total	376 (100.0)	1,284 (100.0)

Note: Figures in brackets are per cent share in the total.

United States of America

The United States is a large net exporter of walnuts.It supplied over 44 per cent of total exports during the last three years. Nevertheless, its exports fluctuate considerably depending on the price competition with other suppliers, quality and world demand. During the last three years its exports averaged 133,000 tonnes. Exports have also responded well due to the support from the Market Access Programme (MAP) as well as publicity following the publication of several health studies showing health benefits of walnut consumption. The top export destinations in 2004 were Spain, Japan, Germany, Italy, Canada, Israel and Netherlands. The EU member countries together received about 54 per cent of exports, while Japan and Canada accounted for 18 per cent and 7 per cent of total walnut shipments from the United States exports and Mexico about 3 per cent. Exports to MAP targeted countries such as Canada, Germany, Italy, Israel, Japan and Korea are expected to grow from 5 to 20 per cent over the next five years. The United States also imports small quantities of walnuts mainly from Moldova, Turkey, China. Imports during the last two years were 491 tonnes in 2003 and 1154 tonnes in 2004.

Germany is a leading importer of walnut (Table 5.17). The analyse of its pattern of consumption, level of imports, leading suppliers, how walnuts are imported, import tariffs etc. in this important and growing market can serve as a useful guide for India and other major walnut producing countries. Nuts are used for a number of purposes in Germany, mostly as ingredients in food products. Nuts are also popular as snacks, particularly during the year-end holiday season. To satisfy domestic demand, Germany imports significant quantities of many kinds of nuts, including walnut, almonds, hazelnut/filberts and pistachio.

Walnuts are mostly consumed in-shell during the year-end holiday season; consumption of in-shell walnuts outside the end of the year holidays is relatively limited. Shelled walnuts are mostly used as ingredients in a variety of food products and, to a relatively limited extent, for snack use. Walnuts have garnered some popularity as an ingredient in chocolate confectionery, baked foods and ice cream. There is growing demand for shelled walnuts.

During the year-end holidays, in-shell walnuts are available for sale in most major retail food outlets and outdoor sales stands. Shelled walnuts are usually for sale throughout the year at major retail food outlets. Much of the shelled product is sold in retail food outlets for home cooking and backing or is sold to the food processing industry for use as an ingredient. Shelled walnut competes with a number of other nuts, particularly hazelnuts and almonds.

As domestic production is very limited, Germany imports virtually all its domestic requirements. In 2004 Germany's imports amounted to about 42,000 tonnes of walnut in-shell basis. About 40 per cent of walnut imports consisted of in-shell nuts and the remaining 60 per cent was shelled product. The United States is the leading supplier of walnut (accounting for about 50% of total imports), followed by France (about 14 per cent). India supplied less than 4 per cent of total imports. Germany is the third export market for US walnuts after Japan and Spain.

In Germany most walnuts are imported in bulk (mostly during October through December) by national companies that focus on the importation of nuts and possibly a variety of similar products, e.g. dried fruit. These companies repack the imported walnuts for resale or sell in bulk to retailers or German food processors. There are some U.S. companies with branded, consumer-packaged walnuts available in the German market. Good prospects exist for Indian shelled walnut exports to Germany. Large quantities of Germany's imports of walnut will continue to be used to meet in-shell nuts demand for the year-end holidays. There are also opportunities for increased sales of shelled nuts for snacks, as ingredients for the food processing industry and for home backing use. However, competition from major suppliers will remain strong.

Import Tariffs: Effective 1 July 1998, EU/German import tariffs for imports from non-EU member countries are 5.3 per cent for in-shell and 6.1 per cent for shelled raw nuts (not prepared/preserved). Walnuts from France enter duty free since it is a EU member state.

Table 5.17: Germany: Walnut Import Matrix

	Walnut Shelled (in Tonnes)			*Walnut In-shell (in Tonnes)*	
Imports from	*2003*	*2004*	*Imports from*	*2003*	*2004*
1. USA	2182 (26.9)	3732 (35.9)	1. U.S.A.	5987 (50.8)	11804 (67.9)
2. France	1261 (15.5)	1156 (11.1)	2. France	3079 (26.1)	3354 (18.9)
3. India	695 (8.5)	676 (6.5)	3. Chile	640 (5.4)	312 (1.8)
4. Chile	380 (4.7)	523 (5.0)	4. Belgium	552 (4.7)	1 (neg.)
5. Moldova	492 (6.0)	706 (6.8)	5. Netherlands	1037 (8.8)	1311 (7.4)
7. Belgium	1172 (14.4)	1087 (10.4)	6. Romania	0 0	1 (neg.)
8. Netherlands	89 ((1.1)	1066 (10.2)	7. Italy	25 (0.2)	8 (neg.)
9. Greece	203 (2.5)	387 (3.7)	8. Moldova	49 (0.4)	39 (0.2)
10. Others	1659	1072 (10.3)	9. Hungary	124 (1.1)	291 (1.6)
11. Total	8133 (100.0)	10405 (100.0)	10. Other	288 (2.4)	641 (3.6)
			11.Total	11781 (100.0)	17372 (100.0)

Source: Global Trade Atlas, 2005.

Concluding Remarks

The analysis presented above indicates that although walnut international market is widely dispersed, the major importing areas and countries are rather small. The EU member countries are by far the largest importers of walnut, though other countries are also importing increasing quantities. Exports destinations for major walnut producing countries indicate the respective areas of their operations. Future prospects for walnut international trade are highly dependent on their ability to maintain and expand market access, ensure fair competition and level the international playing field for major producers and exporters. The World Trade Organization (WTO) and the future trade negotiations should help to ensure these.

REFERENCES

1. In the absence of data for all countries it is assumed that the pattern of consumption in the seven major countries covered by the USDA Foreign Agriculture Service holds good for the world as a whole.
2. The data on walnut shelled has been converted on the bases of 53 per cent of the weight in-shell. Export of walnut shelled totalled 68,114 tonnes in 1999 and 76,649 tonnes in 2001.

3. If we assume that around 20 per cent of world production is traded internationally, average world exports of walnut during the last three years comes to 240,000 tonnes, compared to average exports for the six countries was 170.4 thousand tonnes. Thus exports of six major countries constituted 71 per cent of the total exports.
4. Data for all the tables included in this chapter have been taken from (i) FAO STAT Database; (ii) Global Trade Atlas, 2004 and 2005; (iii) from US Agricultural Attaché Annual Tree Nuts Reports for the respective countries; and (iv) from the USDA Annual and Semi-Annual Reports Walnut Situation and Outlook in selected countries.

6

COUNTRIES CASE STUDY

INTRODUCTION

Walnut is produced in more than fifty countries, of which 20 are developing countries. Currently the ten major walnuts producing countries include China, US, Iran, Turkey Ukraine, France, India, Greece, Italy and Chile. These countries accounted for 79.1 per cent of the total world production in 2005. Their respective shares are China 28.2 per cent, USA 20.7 per cent, Iran 10.1, Turkey 8.9 per cent, Ukraine 4.7 per cent, India 2.1 per cent, France 2.0 per cent, Greece 1.4 per cent, Italy 1.1 per cent, and Chile 0.1 per cent.

World walnut production has undergone significant changes over the last two decades. Total walnut production increased from 795.4 thousand tonnes in 1980 to 1,491.6 thousand tonnes in 2005.[1] The annual growth comes to 2.6 per cent. Production expanded by 11 per cent from 1980 to 1990 and by 14 per cent from 1990 to 2000 and by 25.5 per cent during the last five years.

This chapter reviews the performance of the major walnut producing countries. The main topics covered include area and production, use of input, consumption, trade, stocks, National walnut policy and marketing. Their performance in international trade is reviewed in Chapter 5.

CHINA'S WALNUT ECONOMY

Production

China produces approximate 28.2 per cent of all commercial walnuts worldwide, but accounts for 6 per cent of world exports. In China tree nut production is considered to be an important part of China's Poverty Alleviation Programme. In addition, China continues to implement the

Sloped Land Conversion Programme (SLCP) that allows for tree nut plantings in economic and ecological forests. By 2012, China's SFA intends to have a total walnut planting area of 1.41 million hectares: (970,000 hectares of newly planted trees and 440,000 hectares of trees improved through grafting). The SFA admits, however, that the goal may not be achieved.

Chinese tree nut production increased steadily as acreage planted over the last several years began bearing nuts. Growers continue to increase planted tree nut acreage as this fits into China's goal of retiring land for economic and ecological tree crops. In addition, as scientific advances allow for improved matching of a variety of tree nuts with the more suitable terrains, tree nut production is likely to become more efficient, diversified, and profitable for growers who are able to increase tree planting density.

In China walnut production had steadily increased as trees planted in the 1990s have begun bearing walnuts. Production rose from 128 thousand tonnes in 1984 to 420 thousand tonnes in 2005. Table 6.1 shows production by Province. There was a sharp decline in output in 2001 due to inclement weather in some provinces within western China in addition to the alternate bearing cycle of walnut trees. The unusually cold weather during spring bloom adversely affected several growing regions, which resulted in a sharp decline in output. However, output recovered in the last two years. China's forestry specialists attribute increased walnut production in recent years to increased bearing acreage and improved weather conditions. In addition, many of the walnut trees are improved varieties that have been grafted and adapted to growing regions in an improved, more scientific manner. These improved varieties can be planted more densely than traditional ones and produce nuts earlier and maintain commercial production over a longer period. FAO data indicates walnut planting area and production were over one million hectares and 420,000 metric tonnes (MT). Provincial tree nut specialists, however, indicate the actual volume of walnuts reaching market was likely below 420,000 MT.

Chinese walnut planting area consists not only of commercial groves, but also traditional walnut planting acreage comprised of trees growing wild in large numbers over mountainous areas and trees that grow in small numbers around rural homes.

Table 6.1: China: Walnut Production by Province, 1993 to 2003: (Volume: Metric Tonnes)

Province	*1993*	*1996*	*1997*	*1998*	*1999*	*2000*	*2001*	*2002*	*2003**
Yunnan	48,730	55,448	58,709	57,168	60,452	68,788	68,568	74,664	61,200
Shanxi	21,277	34,236	37,376	40,365	39,724	46,988	40,215	39,382	38,400
Sichuan	17,732	27,720	23,409	28,711	23,842	32,095	32,744	70,534	65,000
Hebei	14,057	21,742	27,905	29,441	30,365	30,102	28,761	30,613	30,200
Henan	12,220	13,534	12,898	12,248	13,428	17,143	13,387	15,271	13,000
Xinjiang	6,490	6,695	7,213	8,362	15,779	11,523	11,727	12,987	11,800
Shaanxi	30,419	30,433	26,222	32,519	33,340	34,498	10,596	34,779	33,300
Others	41,234	20,025	27,517	27,481	37,230	37,777	46,349	61,944	67,000
Total	192,159	237,989	249,834	265,121	274,246	309,875	252,347	340,174	320,000

* 2003 Total production data is estimated by China's State Forestry Administration 1996-2003.

Source: National Statistics Bureau.

Indications are that tree nut specialists have increased extension efforts to encourage growers to plant walnut trees more commercially; such as in rows between grain or vegetable crops and along sloped lands being reclaimed under the SLCP (see Policy). As this happen, commercial plantings increased and occupy a larger share of total planted area. In addition, the planting density was expected to increase as trees in commercial groves are planted closer together.

The State Statistical Bureau and the State Forestry Administration are faced with a problem that many growers do not report their production data or planting acreage. It appears most growers produce a small volume of walnuts and the growers may not feel obligated to report their production. When considered using an individual grower-by-grower basis, production is not noticeable. However, when multiplied by the vastness of overall growers, there is room for large discrepancies in production data. Also, production data collection is difficult since many growers consume nuts on the farm; both fresh and crushed for home cooking oil. In addition, growers have little incentive to report large production as they could be assessed a specialty product agricultural tax. According to provincial officials, the tax is collected, but in practice, the effective tax rate is lower than what is reported. One of the reasons for the lower collection rate is that many programmes have been launched or publicized in the last several years to lower the tax burden of Chinese growers and farmers in order to allow them to remain on the farm and compete in the global agricultural market.

Chinese forestry/walnut production specialists categorize traditional walnut production into two growing areas: North and South. Specialists indicate northern walnuts are from Persian variety walnut trees, whereas, traditional southern walnuts are from black walnut trees. Specialists elaborate there are five primary mountain ranges within China where walnut production is most suitable. These mountain ranges are the: Yungui Mountainous Area Plateau (Yunnan and Guizhou), Qingba Mountainous Area (Sichuan and Shaanxi), Taihang Mountainous Area (Henan, Hebei, and Shaanxi), Luliang Mountainous Area (Shanxi), and Yanshan Mountainous Area (Hebei and Beijing).

According to tree nut specialists, seedling stock from the following varieties performed well in research trials: Chandler, Chico, Franquette, Hartley, Serr, and Vina. These varieties are being used in central and northern parts of China. The varieties are suitable for several reasons, including; nut production, ecological or climactic attributes, and growers do not need to compensate for new-plant variety protection. Specialists continue to experiment with walnut grafting to produce more walnuts per tree, larger and more uniform walnuts, thin shell walnut varieties, larger kernel walnuts, lighter coloured walnut kernels, shorter trees for easier harvesting, trees with greater drought resistance, and trees that will pollinate at different times. Currently, the Walnut Research Institute under the State Forestry Administration recommends over 50 walnut tree varieties. Of these, 16 are strongly encouraged, but provincial forestry research institutes are able to recommend other varieties that are most suitable for the local conditions.

In Yunnan, southwestern China, improved varieties are crossbred from northern and southern walnut stock (J. Regia and J. Sigillata; respectively). After being crossbred, the improved seedlings are often grafted or top grafted with other walnut tree varieties that are suitable for the ecological demands of the region.

Nearly one-fourth of China's reported walnut production occurs West and North of Yunnan's provincial capital Yunnan. The main growing areas (Dali, Baoshan, Lijiang, and Chuxiong) are located in mountainous areas that have clay soils, cool to mild temperatures, and a long rainy season lasting several months as well as a dry season. Yunnan's provincial forestry bureau officials indicate 2001 walnut production was over 68,000 metric tonnes (MT) and 2002 and 2003 production increased over 2001 but did not surpass 80,000 MT. It appears much of Yunnan's production is consumed within China as local nuts have thinner shells allowing for in-shell sale and in-home shelling. Many of the thicker shelled nuts from the region are normally crushed for oil.

In Xinjiang, North-western China, specialists report the area has a long history of J. Regia walnut production; especially in the Kashgar, Hotan, and Aksu districts. The province continues planting walnut trees under the SLCP and has walnut bearing acreage of 12.1 thousand hectares. These specialists also indicate that unlike southern varieties, the alternate bearing cycle of northern walnut trees is minimal to non-existent. Currently, the specialists report that although there are 26 varieties of walnut trees planted in the province, only nine are considered suitable for the region due to their cold tolerance and stable nut bearing. Xinjiang encounters significant temperature extremes ranging from –40 in winter to 40 degrees centigrade in summer. Despite the long production history, specialists are still researching the most suitable cold tolerant varieties and exploring the planting or expansion of other trees in the province such as Pistachio, Chestnut, and Almond trees.

Although walnut-planting acreage in the central provinces of Shanxi, Shaanxi, and Hebei is not as large as some other provinces, growers in the mountainous regions of these three areas have been able to plant or graft high yielding walnut trees in high density. During each of the last several years, these three provinces accounted for around 30 per cent of China's walnut production. Also, since these provinces do not suffer from dramatic climate extremes, walnut production from the region is often from early arrival varieties. It appears growers appreciate the walnuts as an early arrival crop, but will abstain from planting greater acreage to tree nuts. This is chiefly due to the fact that growers see better profit prospects from producing certain fruit crops, including; cherries, dates, kiwis, apples, and grapes.

Wholesale Price Information[2]

The China tree nut market, as it pertains to processors and distributors, remains price sensitive and thereby a barrier for some high quality tree nuts. There appears to be a good market for bakers and confectioners in need of high quality and consistently sized products with no foreign matter. Table 6.2 shows walnut wholesale prices in selected regions in 2004 and 2005.

Prices

Domestic walnut prices rose further in 2004 on continued domestic demand and export opportunities. Record high farm gate prices in MY 2004 ranged from 15 to 18 RMB per kilo, compared to 10-12 RMB per kilo in 2003. Domestic prices during Chinese New Year 2004 were up more than 60 per cent over the same period of the previous year. Walnut processors also reported that export prices have been rising. Given strong market demand, walnut prices remained high in MY 2005 despite a good harvest. The import prices of almost all nuts increased dramatically in MY 2004 on tight world supply. For example, the average import price of in-shell almonds doubled in 2004 to reach US$2.59 per kilo from US$1.29 in 2003, according to China Customs statistics.

Consumption

According to tree nut specialists in Yunnan, about 70 per cent of the provincial walnut production meets exceptional or good quality grades. Of the exceptional and good quality nuts, specialists report about 80 per cent is traded to other provincial or overseas markets. The remaining 20 per cent of these nuts are given simple processing such as cracking,

Table 6.2: China Walnut Wholesale Market Prices in Selected regions

	Monthly and quarterly average prices in US$ per Kilogram: (RMB 8.205 = US$ 1)						
	North	Northeast	Central	Sourth	Southwest	West	China
2004							
January	0.96	1.11	1.03	N/A	1.57	1.09	1.04
February	1.01	1.37	1.51	N.A.	1.39	N.A.	1.23
March	1.12	1.23	1.07	N.A.	1.15	N.A.	1.13
Average Q1	1.03	1.24	1.20	N.A.	1.33	1.09	1.13
April	1.03	1.26	1.05	N.A.	1.94	N.A.	1.13
May	1.02	1.21	1.09	N.A.	1.94	N.A.	1.19
June	1.09	0.97	1.09	N.A.	1.94	N.A.	1.25
Average Q2	1.05	1.19	1.07	N.A.	1.94	N.A.	1.32
July	1.09	1.45	1.09	N.A.	2.06	N.A.	1.32
August	1.11	1.15	1.09	N.A.	1.94	0.32	1.15
September	1.00	1.36	1.06	N.A.	1.94	0.43	1.08
Average Q3	1.06	1.32	1.08	N.A.	1.97	0.40	1.17
October	1.26	1.14	1.09	2.42	1.81	0.44	1.26
November	1.24	1.25	1.29	N.A.	1.39	N.A.	1.26
December	1.19	N.A.	1.27	1.45	1.45	N.A.	1.26
Avg. 2004	1.10	1.24	1.14	1.94	1.50	0.44	1.26
2005							
January	1.39	1.45	1.23	N.A.	N.A.	N.A.	1.37
February	1.56	1.45	1.27	9.62	1.94	N.A.	2.76
March	1.34	1.33	1.27	N.A.	1.94	N.A.	1.38
Average Q1	1.43	1.41	1.26	9.62	1.94	N.A.	1.84
April	1.32	N.A.	1.45	1.94	1.94	N.A.	1.53
May	1.48	N.A.	1.51	N.A.	1.94	N.A.	1.52
June	1.40	1.21	1.09	N.A.	N.A.	N.A.	1.30
Average Q2	1.40	1.21	1.09	N.A.	N.A.	N.A.	1.48
Avg. 2005	1.42	1.38	1.32	7.06	1.94	N.A.	1.67

Source: USDA Agriculture Attaché's China Annual Tree Nut Report, 2005.

shelling, or in-shell flavouring/seasoning. Of the 30 per cent of provincial production that falls outside of these grades, most is crushed for oil (home cooking walnut oil and consumer retail walnut oil). Smaller portions are processed into beverage drinks, powders, food additives, and pharmaceuticals/traditional Chinese medicines.

Xinjiang tree nut specialists report nearly all of the walnuts and other tree nuts produced in the province are for fresh consumption. Some of the nuts, however, they report do undergo some simple processing such as cracking, roasting, or seasoning. Furthermore, they report that although there is some interest in using tree nuts as a food additive and value added product, at present, there is not enough supply for the processing industry to take an interest in developing facilities. And, without such processing facilities, the specialists report that growers will not plant more trees or try to better manage current trees.

While many nuts are consumed fresh in Shanxi, Shaanxi, and Hebei, reports indicate most walnut exports originate from nuts produced in these provinces. As well as a highly developed shelling, seasoning, and packaging industry for walnuts and other tree nuts in these areas, there are also facilities that supply walnut oil to retailers throughout the country. In addition to walnut oil, many of these processors supply walnut and nut powders and pharmaceuticals such as digestive aids derived from tree nuts and capsules containing walnut oil to retail outlets nationwide.

Chinese consumers tend to prefer in-shell nuts that can be cracked by hand. The nuts are considered more sanitary and have the added consumer benefit that the nuts are a little less expensive than shelled or processed nuts. Walnut demand is often highest during the Chinese lunar New Year in late winter or early spring. Demand for walnuts is also high during China's mid-Autumn festival in late September that is met by fresh domestic nuts.

Consumption of packaged and processed walnut and other tree nut products seems to be greater in large cities like Beijing, Shanghai, and Guangzhou. However, consumers in China's emerging city markets are trying to catch-up with these larger cities trends and are consuming walnuts and other tree nuts as a snack food purchase from retailers in greater frequency. The growth of overall sales in retail stores and hypermarkets *versus* traditional Chinese markets is not, however without growing pains. In 2002 a major retailer ran into dispute with a municipal nut association that represents several different nut processors. The dispute centred on slotting fees for processed and packaged tree nuts that, in the end, was resolved by an announcement from the retailer to lower fees.

According to processors and traders, bulk bin walnut and other nut sales in large inland cities and provincial county seats surpass sales of packaged nuts. In addition, consumption of packaged and flavoured walnuts has been increasing. In spite of this, some processors see the market stagnating and are looking to replicate successful sales strategies from other markets. Thus, many processors are trying to combine other flavourings or coatings with nuts (e.g. coconut, honey, sesame, or brown sugar) in order to further segment the market and reach more snack food consumers.

As China's baking industry has developed, many bakers and confectionary shops are using walnuts and other tree nuts as an ingredient in breads, cookies, cakes, and muffins. Bakeries in retail stores, hotels, as well as in private bakeries and bakery chains almost always have walnuts and tree nuts added to some of their breads and baked goods. Shops report the items retail very well and one retailer with an in-store bakery reports banana bread with walnuts is the leading bakery sales item in the store; which routinely gets more than 6,000 customers a day. Another national retailer reports their franchised store locations around the country have a strong interest receiving training on how to use other nuts in bakery items or at least information and recipes about bakery items that contain walnuts and tree nuts.

Domestic consumption of walnuts is estimated to have increased from about 95 thousand tonnes in 1984-85 to 295 thousand tonnes in 2002-03. The increase was 80 per cent during the decade 1984-85 to 1994-95 and 73 per cent from 1994-95 to 2002-03. Domestic consumption increased further during the last two years, reaching 391,000 tonnes in 2005 (Table 6.3).

Table 6.3: China: Walnut Production, Supply and Disposal in China: 1995 - 2005

(*Area in hectares: Trees in thousand numbers; other data in Metric tonnes*)

Item	*1995*	*2001*	*2002*	*2003*	*2004*	*2005*
Area Planted		666000	890000	916750	935000	1009800
Area Harvested		400000	750000	779000	790000	858000
Production	219000	252347	340000	320000	360000	388000
Imports	95	939	1409	1782	2438	2800
Total Supply	219095	253286	341583	321782	362438	390800
Exports	45000	15806	21906	21000	32980	39500
Domestic Consumption	200040	237480	319677	300782	329458	351300
Total Distribution	260040	253286	341583	321782	362438	390800

Source: US Agriculture Attaché's Tree Nuts Annual Reports: Various issues.

Trade—Walnuts

Imports

Over the past several years, China imported a lot of in-shell walnuts while its imports of shelled walnuts were few. In the past, in-shell nut imports were sold to retail stores, wholesale markets, and processors that shelled the nuts for the food ingredient sector or for re-export. Imports are influenced by domestic production and increasing domestic demand. In addition, rising international demand for shelled and processed walnuts helped increase China's imports for processing walnut that are later re-exported to other countries.

Demand for in-shell walnuts has grown in recent years. This is in large part due to increased processing capacity by existing processors in South China that re-exported packaged in-shell nuts, shelled nuts, and seasoned nuts to other countries in Asia, Europe, Latin America, Australia, North America and elsewhere.

Processing operations prefer US or third country nuts for a variety of reasons. One reason is that nut size is more uniform than most Chinese walnuts thereby making walnut cracking or shelling much easier. In addition quality is often more uniform. Another reason is that in coastal cities it continues to be easier to order a shipment of US or third country walnuts for delivery than to coordinate delivery from several domestic growers and suppliers from inland China.

Consumer preference affects imports too. (For consumption preferences, see Consumption section above).

Indications are that increased imports of shelled nuts stems from greater awareness of using high-quality walnuts in the bakery sector along with increased affordability of shelled walnuts due to lower Chinese import tariffs. In addition, it seems that certain attributes of Chinese in-shell walnut quality has improved and there is less need for imported in-shell nuts featuring the same type attributes. Total imports increased from 95 tonnes in 1995 to 2800 tonnes in 2005.

Exports

Exports of walnuts from China have declined in recent years. Exports rose from 33 thousand tonnes in 1984-85 to about 55 thousand tonnes in 1984-86 but declined in the next three years and recovered in 1992-93. During 2001 to 2003 exports have continued declining trend. However, these recovered during the last two years. Total walnut exports averaged 36.2 thousand tonnes. As a percentage of domestic production, exports declined from 31 per cent in 1988-89 to less than four per cent during the last two years.

The most often reason is increased domestic demand has eroded

China price competitiveness. Chinese sources believe that China's walnut exports depend on its ability to produce highly processed and high value walnut products. These products are targeted at markets in Asia and Europe because the price is too high for most domestic consumers.

Chinese traders report that eastern European countries are supplying a greater share of walnut exports to Europe. Meanwhile, India also seems to have increased its market share in Australia. The result is that China's tree nuts are loosing ground on the international market. Chinese trading companies feel that international walnut consumption is increasing by around one per cent a year. These companies do not want to be excluded from what is considered a stable and growing market.

The top export destinations for in-shell walnuts for the marketing year 2004-05 were regional neighbours and middle-Eastern nations; e.g. North Korea, Lebanon, South Korea, the United Arab Emirates, Vietnam, Hong Kong and Algeria. Most in-shell exports to northeast Asian countries were from the northern ports of Dalian Qingdao, Tianjin and Changchun. Trade for middle-eastern and Southeast Asian countries originated from Shenzhen. Huangpu, and Kunming. Chinese traders do not anticipate export competition from American or other country suppliers because Chinese nuts are cheaper, have shorter trade routes, and enjoy consumer familiarity with the products.

US WALNUT ECONOMY

USA is the second largest walnut producing country in the world. Its total production in 2005 was 308.4 thousand tonnes, about 26 per cent of the world output. California is the main producer of English walnuts in the United States and produces 99 per cent of the nation's walnuts. There are two species of walnuts, the English (*Juglans regia*), which originated in Persia, and the black walnut, which is native to the United States.

The Sacramento and San Joaquin Valleys of California are the largest production areas. Acreage is well distributed throughout these regions. The coastal valleys in the counties of Santa Barbara, San Luis Obispo, Monterey, and San Benito also have significant production. Unique areas in the Sierra Foothills and Lake County also have some walnut production.

Crop Profile for Walnuts in California

California produces 99 per cent of the walnuts grown in the United States and 25 per cent of the world's production.

Bearing walnut area in California in 2004 totalled 87,854 hectares with an additional 3,700 hectares of non-bearing trees.

From 1999-02 California's average production was 125,042 tons. In 2004-05 walnut output was 147,700 tonnes valued at $438.75 million.

Over 40 per cent of the California walnut crop is currently being exported.

Thirty-five per cent of the crop is marketed in-shell.

The California walnut industry is made up of more than 5000 walnut growers and about 55 walnut processors. A federal marketing order is in place for walnuts, which established the Walnut Marketing Board and regulates that all walnuts be inspected and certified as meeting strict USDA specifications.

Harvesting

Harvested from September to November, there are 37 varieties of walnuts commercially grown in California. All of which are hybrids of the English walnut. The Northern California black walnut is primarily used as the rootstock for English walnut cultivars. The black walnut is of high flavour, but due to its hard shell and poor hulling characteristics it is not grown commercially for nut production. The Eastern American Black walnut is grown east of the Rocky Mountains primarily for wood and veneer. Out of the all the varieties, four varieties (Chandler, Harley, Payne and Serr) account for over 80 per cent of total production. A limited number of California walnut growers produce certified organic walnuts.

Post-Harvest

Dried walnuts are fumigated after harvest with methyl bromide primarily for control of codling moth, navel orangeworm, and storage pests. Control of these insects is critical to maintain markets that demand insect-free walnuts. Some countries like Japan require fumigation of walnuts with methyl bromide prior to export to control pests (e.g., codling moth) that could be present. An alternative to methyl bromide is phosphine, but unfortunately it has the significant disadvantages of a longer treatment time (4 to 10 days or more as compared to 3 to 12 hours for methyl bromide resulting in costly delays in overseas shipments) and reduced activity at lower temperatures that can be a significant problem in the fall when walnuts are harvested. In addition, it has demonstrated resistance problems for some pests. Phosphine also costs twice as much as methyl bromide.

Production

Table 6.4 shows time series data on area, production and yield of walnut in the USA. It also indicates the season-average grower price and value of walnut output in California from 1977 to 2004. During the last two decades annual average production increased by more than three and half times, from 76.4 thousand tonnes during 1980-82 to 303.4 thousand tonnes during the last

Table 6.4: USA: Walnut Bearing Area, Yield, Production, Grower's Price

Years	Bearing Area (Hectares)	Yield/hec. (Tonnes)	Production (Tonnes)	Grower Price US$/Tonnes	Total Value 1000 US$
1977	71,377	0.99	70,728	659	71,377
1978	73,441	0.80	58,753	1184	73,441
1979	72,551	1.05	76,508	770	72,551
1980	72,834	1.00	72,834	851	72,834
1981	70,891	1.17	83,135	922	70,891
1982	72,065	1.19	85,823	927	72,065
1983	71,255	1.03	73,198	574	71,255
1984	72,065	1.09	78,616	664	72,065
1985	72,470	1.11	80,375	725	72,470
1986	72,874	0.91	66,250	982	72,874
1987	71,255	1.27	90,688	895	71,255
1988	71,660	1.07	76,872	838	71,660
1989	72,470	1.16	84,328	973	72,470
1990	73,279	1.14	83,272	945	73,279
1991	73,279	1.30	95,263	964	73,279
1992	72,065	1.04	74,685	1282	72,065
1993	74,899	1.28	96,007	1264	74,899
1994	76,518	1.12	85,561	936	76,518
1995	78,138	1.10	85,951	1273	78,138
1996	77,733	0.98	76,319	1436	77,733
1997	78,138	1.26	98,738	1300	78,138
1998	78,138	1.07	83,820	955	78,138
1999	77,328	1.35	104,041	886	77,328
2000	80,972	2.68	217,251	1,240	296,360
2001	82,591	3.36	277,245	1,120	341,600
2002	85,020	3.02	256,338	1,170	329,940
2003	86,235	3.44	296,334	1,160	378,180
2004	87,854	4.07	357,536	1,350	438,700

Source: USDA Fruit and Tree Nut Year Book 2005.

three years. Better yields contributed the bulk of the increase, while increased area contributed only 15 per cent to higher output. However, production has fluctuated over the years due to the alternate bearing cycles of walnut trees. Harvests were particularly low at 77,000 tonnes in 1996 and 1998.

Area under walnut has been increasing. In 1977, walnut trees were grown on 71.4 thousand hectares. By 2004, area had risen by about 21 per cent to 87.93 thousand hectares. Yield per hectare has improved from 0.99 tonnes to 4.07 tonnes during this period.

Consumption

Per capita consumption of walnut has changed little during the 1990s, decreasing slightly from 0.23 kg., per person in 1990 to 0.17 kg per person in 2001 and increased to 0.25 kg in 2004. However, total domestic utilization increased from 48.8 thousand tonnes in 1977-78 to 73.1 thousand tonnes in 2004-05 (Table 6.5).

Exports

The United States is the leading exporting country for both shelled and in-shell walnuts, with more than a 40 per cent share of exports among the countries in the GTA database. Total shelled walnut exports for the United States came to $152 million in 2004-05. Traditional markets for U.S. shelled walnuts —Japan, Spain, Canada, and Germany—have continued to grow at a steady pace. Expansion of smaller markets—mostly European and South American—accounted for most of the export growth. Total export sales of US in-shell walnuts for 2004-05 were $92 million. The European Union (EU) is the primary market for US in-shell walnuts, and US export levels fluctuate with changes in EU walnut production. For 2005-06, US walnut exports in-shell bases are forecast to be 145,000 tonnes.

The United States is a net exporter of walnuts with California being the only walnut exporting US state. Exports have increased considerably during the last two decades or so. Total exports (Shelled basis weight) rose from 16.3 thousand tonnes in 1977-78 to 62.8 thousand tonnes in 2004-05.

Througnout the 1990s, in-shell walnuts were the most important walnut export product of the United States. In 1989, two-thirds of the exports were in-shell walnuts. However, by 2001, shelled walnuts had a higher export value than in-shell walnuts. Shelled walnut exports consistently increased in value from $34.3 million in 1989 to $152 million in 2004.

Table 6.5: U.S.A.: Walnut Production, Supply and Distribution (In-shelled Basis[1]): 1977-78 – 2003-04

(*In tonnes*)

Year[2]	*Utilized Production*	*Loss and exempt*[3]	*Marketable Production*[4]	*Import*[5]	*Beginning Stocks*[6]	*Total Supply*[7]	*Ending Stocks*[6]	*Exports*[5]	*Consumption*	
									Total	*Per Capita Kgs.*
1977-78	64,490	168	64,322	67	10,149	74,538	9,462	16,292	48,784	0.22
1978-79	50,234	157	50,078	484	9,462	60,024	10,874	11,409	37,741	0.17
1979-80	68,466	296	68,169	146	10,874	79,189	18,308	17,223	43,659	0.19
1980-81	66,639	338	66,301	4	18,308	84,612	13,767	19,292	51,553	0.23
1981-82	82,034	365	81,670	4	13,767	95,441	17,270	23,678	54,492	0.24
1982-83	82,674	353	82,320	136	17,270	99,726	32,382	17,649	49,696	0.21
1983-84	65,533	1,370	64,163	35	32,382	96,580	25,644	15,734	55,202	0.24
1984-85	61,017	286	60,731	143	25,644	86,518	19,214	15,662	51,642	0.22
1985-86	76,195	348	75,847	58	19,214	95,119	23,711	18,972	52,437	0.22
1986-87	64,397	358	64,039	1,207	23,711	88,956	12,882	22,407	53,667	0.22
1987-88	92,767	376	92,391	214	12,882	105,487	27,239	26,829	51,419	0.21
1988-89	78,706	377	78,330	84	27,239	105,652	21,943	27,654	56,056	0.23
1989-90	89,330	390	88,940	65	21,943	110,948	24,633	35,404	50,910	0.20
1990-91	82,537	364	82,174	43	24,633	106,849	22,151	32,955	51,744	0.20
1991-92	96,014	371	95,643	37	22,151	117,831	25,311	40,107	52,414	0.20
1992-93	76,783	378	76,405	3,657	25,311	105,372	16,908	34,105	54,360	0.21
1993-94	98,574	379	98,195	541	16,908	115,644	33,175	37,865	44,604	0.17
1994-95	91,261	393	90,868	320	33,175	124,363	25,879	45,280	53,204	0.20
1995-96	89,894	384	89,509	1,049	25,879	116,437	25,120	44,666	46,651	0.17
1996-97	77,467	372	77,095	2,643	25,120	104,857	18,337	46,688	39,832	0.15

(*Contd.*)

(*Contd.*)

1997-98	100,610	374	100,236	129	18,337	118,703	30,728	42,780	45,194	0.16
1998-99	85,383	376	85,007	71	30,728	115,807	27,019	41,287	47,500	0.17
1999-00	108,129	382	107,747	82	27,022	134,851	28,815	41,291	64,746	0.23
2000-01	93,117	390	92,727	168	28,815	121,711	21,008	44,448	56,255	0.20
2001-02	117,071	384	116,687	92	21,008	137,787	36,366	47,009	54,413	0.19
2002-03	110,892	393	110,499	88	36,366	146,953	33,372	51,803	61,778	0.21
2003-04[8]	127,013	390	126,623	169	33,372	160,165	37,339	56,778	66,051	0.23
2004-05	128,345	395	127,950	381	37,339	174,670	30,581	62,768	73,139	0.25

[1] Conversion factors from in-shell to shelled bases varies from year to year for production, stocks and exports and were 0.41 in 1996-97, 1997-98 and 1998-99, 0.42 in 1999-2000, 0.43 in 2000-01, 0.42 in 2001-02 and 0.43 for 2002-03 to 2004-05.

For imports, the conversion factor was a constant 0.35.

[2] Season beginning 1 August.

[3] Edible and non-commercial usage.

[4] Utilized production minus loss and exempt.

[5] Bureau of Census. U.S. Department of Commerce.

[6] Walnut Marketing Board.

[7] Marketable production plus imports and beginning stocks.

[8] Preliminary estimates.

Source: USDA: Fruit and Tree Nut Year Book 2005.

Walnut exports to Canada were valued at $18.2 million in 2003 and have more than quadrupled since 1989. From 1989 to 1990, total value of walnuts exported to Canada doubled to $8.8 million. Exports averaged $11.9 million during the 1990s. In 2003, exports jumped to $20.8 million, with shelled walnuts making up 79 per cent of the export value. In 1989, the value of exports was almost equally made up of shelled and in-shell walnut shipments. In-shell walnuts in 2003 were slightly higher than in 1989.

Trade with Mexico has fluctuated during the post-NAFTA era. US walnut exports to Mexico were relatively low until 1993, the year before NAFTA, when they surged to $1.8 million. Exports were $5.7 million in 1998 and peaked a year later at almost $15 million. In 2004, walnut exports to Mexico amounted to $1.7 million. The majority of exports in 2004 consisted of shelled walnuts.

Imports

USA also imports walnuts though the quantities vary considerably. When domestic production declines walnut imports are large. However, during the last decade the volume of imports declined from 3.4 thousand tonnes during 1995-96-1997-98 to 116 tonnes during the last three years. In 2004, the total shelled walnut imports into the United States were valued at $435,000, down from $1.7 million in 2001, and came mainly from Brazil, China and the Ukraine. Walnuts in-shell were imported from Canada and only a small quantity of in-shell walnuts (valued at $6,000) entered from Mexico.

Tariff Rates and Policy Changes Resulting from NAFTA

The United States charges seven cents per kilogram on in-shell walnut imports and 26.5 cents per kilogram on shelled walnut imports from countries with which the United States maintain normal trade relations. Trade partners without normal trade status with the United States face tariffs of 11 cents per kilogram and 33.1 cents per kilogram for shipments of in-shell and shelled walnuts into the United States.

Canada did not impose a tariff before signing the Canadian-US Free Trade Agreement (CUSTA) in 1988. Before NAFTA became effective in 1994, Mexico imposed a tariff of 20 per cent on walnut imports from the United States. The Mexican tariff was eliminated immediately upon NAFTA's implementation.

The US tariffs for imports from Canada were eliminated over 5 years in the case of in-shell walnuts and over 10 years in the case of shelled walnuts. The tariffs for imports from Mexico were eliminated upon NAFTA's implementation in 1994.

Prices

When taking into account inflation and adjusting for 1996 dollars, California walnut prices in 2004 at $1,350 per ton were higher than at $1,285 in 1989. However, prices fluctuated strongly during the last decade, ranging from $1,580 per ton in 1996 to $846 per ton in 1999.

FRENCH WALNUT ECONOMY

Production

France is the leading European producer of walnuts, with roughly 25 per cent of total European production. It is also a net exporter of walnut. Average annual walnut production increased from 22.5 thousand tonnes during 1995-96–1997-98 to 26.5 thousand tonnes during the last three years. French production suffered from two consecutive short crops in 2003 and 2004, due to severe drought in 2003, but recovered in 2005. In addition, the French trade balance is hurting from the stiff price competitiveness of US product on the European market, chiefly due to the dollar's relative weakness to the euro.

Regional Production

Walnut production is concentrated in south-western and the south-eastern regions of France. These two regions traditionally provide the bulk of the domestic crop, and virtually all of the country's walnut exports. Most of the production in other French regions is sold locally or used for on-farm consumption.

There are now 2 appellations of origins (AOC) labels for high quality walnuts in France: "noix de Grenoble" and "noix du Périgord". Nuts marketed under these appellations are grown in delimited zones: "Noix de Grenoble" is grown in the south-eastern producing regions of France; and "Noix du Périgord" is grown in southwestern France.[3]

The southwest districts, Dordogne, Correze, Lot and Lot & Garonne, produce about 43 per cent of French walnut production while the southeast districts, Isere and Drome produce about 51 per cent (40 per cent alone comes from the Isere district). About 80 per cent of walnut crop in the Southeast was marketed under the "Grenoble walnut" appellation of origin. Only walnuts grown in a designated area (80 per cent of which is in the Isere district, and 20 per cent in the Drome district) and which meet specific variety, size and quality standards, can benefit from the "Grenoble walnut" appellation.

The total area planted to walnuts in France rose from 17,719 hectares to 20,400 hectares in 2005. Of the total area, about 75 per cent are for commercial orchards. The increase in planted area relative to 1993 is mostly due to an adjustment by the French Min Ag in the area estimate for non-bearing trees or trees harvested for on-farm consumption. However, the increase in commercial orchards (up 3 per cent from 1993) reflects the start of production by trees planted in the mid-1980s; planted area increased to 19,230 hectares.

Yields

The average walnut yield increased from 1200 kg per ha, during 1995-1998 to 1750 kg, during the last three years, up 45 per cent. The highest average walnut yield is obtained in the Lot et Garonne district in south-western France, with 3,800 kg/ha.

Walnut Varieties

The "Franquette" variety of walnut accounts for more than 80 per cent of the total French walnut production. Its nearest challenger, the "Marbot" variety, now accounts for only seven per cent of the French walnut production. The French Walnut Technical Institute developed new varieties like "Lara" which came into production by the year 2000. The most interesting characteristic of the new varieties is their high kernel yield (weight of kernels divided by the weight of the in-shell nuts) which, at 52 to 55 per cent, is much higher than the yields of other varieties ("Franquette": 41 to 48 per cent, "Marbot": 41 to 47 per cent). Their cultivation could increase the competitiveness of the French walnut shelling industry.

Domestic Consumption

Walnut consumption in France falls into three categories: snacking and home cooking, by-products (oils), and shelled walnuts used as ingredients in the pastry, bakery and cheese industries.

French households are estimated to purchase approximately 7,000-9,000 MT of in-shell walnuts (including 2,000 MT of fresh walnuts and 7,000 MT of dried walnuts), and 6,000 MT shelled walnuts per year.

Most of the south-eastern production (roughly 75 per cent) is for the in-shell walnut market, while more than half of the south-western production goes to the shelled walnut market segment. Overall, large grades are for the in-shell walnut market, while smaller grades are for the shelled walnut market.

The French per capita consumption of walnuts is 150 grams for in-shell walnuts and 200 grams for shelled walnuts. In-shell walnuts are mainly consumed in the fall and in winter (mainly November and December). There is no seasonality for shelled walnut consumption. Total annual domestic consumption is over 20 thousand tonnes. Table 6.6 shows production, supply and disposal of walnuts for selected years.

Table 6.6: France: Walnut Production, Supply and Disposal for Selected Years

(Area in Hectares: Trees in 1000 numbers; other data Metric tonnes)

	1993-94	*2002-03*	*2003-04*	*2004-05 Forecast*
Area Planted	16852	20200	20200	20200
Area Harvested	12602	15600	15600	15600
Bearing Trees	1260	1600	1600	1600
Non-Bearing Trees	425	450	450	450
Total Trees	1685	2050	2050	2050
Beginning Stocks	0	0	0	0
Production	18900	24000	28000	30000
Imports	7000	15490	13000	12000
Total Supply	30050	39490	41000	42000
Exports	11850	18750	20000	21000
Domestic Consumption	18200	20740	21000	21000
Total Distribution	30050	39490	41000	42000

Source: USDA Agriculture Attaché's France: Annual Tree Nut Report 2005.

Trade

France is a net exporter of walnuts, and exports principally to EU member states and Switzerland. French and US walnuts compete in these markets. As indicated in Chapter 5, Tables 5.5 and 5.9, France mainly exports in-shell walnuts and principally imports shelled walnuts.

Annual average exports increased from 12.8 thousand tonnes during 1995-96 and 1997-98 to 22.7 thousand tonnes during 200-01 to 2002-03. In MY 2003-04, French exports of walnuts decreased by 15 per cent, due to the lower availability and lower quality (mainly smaller grade nuts) than in the previous year, as French walnut harvest was negatively affected by drought in 2003. In MY 2003-04, French walnuts also faced increased competition from California product, which benefited from the lower Dollar to Euro exchange rate. Market shares for French walnuts in Spain and Germany have declined, to the benefit of US product. However, exports recovered somewhat in 2004-05. Unfortunately quantitative data on France walnut exports and imports for the year 2004-05 are not available in the Global Trade Atlas.

Annual average imports of walnut increased from 9.5 thousand tonnes to 12.7 thousand tonnes during 1995-96 to 2002-03. In 2003/04, reduced French domestic production led to higher imports of shelled walnuts from Moldova and Ukraine. Imports from the United States also significantly increased but remained limited, and mainly consisted of in-shell walnuts. Walnut imports totalled 15.5 thousand tonnes in 2003-04, compared to 14.1 thousand tonnes the previous year. Trade matrix for selected years is show in the following tables:

Table 6.7: French Exports of In-Shell Walnuts, MT, Product Weight

Countries	*1993-94*	*MY 01-02*	*MY 02-03*	*MY 03-04*	*2004-05*
Total	4,971	17,118	17,291	13,779	15,185
Spain	641	5,416	5,759	3,548	3,880
Germany	1,444	4,100	4,782	3,527	3,636
Italy	0	2,908	1,627	851	1,526
Moldova	0	1,356	1,945	2,115	3,701
Portugal	1,069	1,159	1,059	859	651
Belgium		605	456	463	551
Switzerland	516	501	487	443	404

Table 6.8: French Imports of in-shell Walnuts, MT, Product Weight

Countries	*1993-94*	*MY 01-02*	*MY 02-03*	*MY 2003-04*
Total	2,219	293	1,170	849
U.S.	1,848	194	195	459
Spain	0	54	637	17
Netherlands	40	6	16	226
Italy	24	13	209	28

Table 6.9: French Exports of Shelled Walnuts, MT, Product Weight

Countries	*1993-94*	*MY 01-02*	*MY 02-03*	*MY 2003-04*
Total	2,749	2,568	2,440	2,490
U.S.	3	0	0	0
Germany	1,311	953	1,050	967
Switzerland	588	558	475	468
Spain	84	224	161	111
Netherlands	219	186	125	153
Portugal	0	157	96	62
Belgium	0	152	167	169
Denmark	0	104	128	135

Table 6.10: French Imports of Shelled Walnuts, MT, Product Weight

Countries	*1993-94*	*MY 01-02*	*MY 02-03*	*MY 03-04*
Total	3,569	6,200	6,467	7,322
U.S.	233	0	95	40
Moldova	0	3,666	4,119	4,451
India	871	870	444	286
Hungary	636	402	226	298
Greece	0	144	75	104
China	1150	111	317	315
Ukraine	0	212	488	870
Poland	99	148	101	46
Romania	191	151	75	184

Source: French Custom Data for Shelled and In-Shell Trade.

Policy

The French Fruits and Vegetable Board (ONIFLHOR) is the French Ministry of Agriculture agency responsible for distributing EU and GoF funds to the French fruit, vegetable and flower sectors. French walnut growers do not receive direct payments for growing walnuts, but they do benefit from programmes run through Producer Organizations (POs).

Over the past few years, the 11 walnut/hazelnut/almond POs used GoF and European funds to form POs. In addition, working capital insurance to partially pay storing, packaging and sorting was provided to growers until 2001.

From 1992 to 2003, 26 million euros were provided to French POs specializing in walnut/hazelnut and almond production under the "programme for improving quality and marketing" (improving orchards, renewing equipment, getting technical assistance). This amount included 1.5 million euros paid in 2003, 0.275 million euros from the GoF and remainder from the EU budget.

Marketing

While the in-shell large grade, high quality and high-priced walnut market segment is dominated by domestically-grown walnuts sold under the origin logos "Moix du Périgord" and "Noix de Grenoble", the shelled walnut and the walnut pieces market segments offer the best opportunities for US walnuts.

The 6,000 MT of shelled walnuts annually purchased by French households are principally sold by supermarket chains as a cooking ingredient more than as a snacking product. The market for snacking products has increased significantly over the past few years. Developing consumer-oriented packages (small size, easy to open and close) of shelled walnuts, as snacks would certainly help increase sales of shelled walnuts on the French market.

CHILE WALNUT ECONOMY

Production

Walnut production rose from 5,200 tonnes in 1980 to 13,200 tonnes in 2002. During the next three years industry sources indicated that walnut production expanded further, as the weather has been generally favourable. The quality of production has also improved. Additionally, as many producers have been adopting improved technologies like pruning and drip irrigation, total production is expected to expand further in the coming years as yield increases. Producers also are expected to continue to replace aging orchards with improved varieties, increase grafting of their lowest-yielding trees, and expand planted areas. Thus, the long-term forecast is that production will continue to expand. This forecast assumes normal weather conditions.

Crop Area

Although walnuts are planted from the Third Region (Copiapo) down to the Ninth Region (Temuco), over 90 per cent of this crop is planted in the central areas, specifically Region Five (San Felipe-Los Andes), the Metropolitan Region (Santiago) and Region Six (Rancagua). The two main factors for the overall increase in planted area (Table 6.11) are a continuous deterioration in the profitability of alternative fruit crops and the relatively good prices obtained by walnut producers.

Inputs

All commercial walnut orchards are planted on irrigated land. However, only an estimated 60 per cent of the planted area has modern irrigation systems. As a result, when there is not enough water supplied from wells, rivers and streams flowing from the Andes Mountains, water availability becomes an important factor limiting production, mainly in Regions V and VI, where output can be affected significantly. The average orchard size is 10 to 15 hectares, which is double the size of orchards in France and half the size of orchards in the U.S.

Table 6.11: Chile—Walnut Planted Area Production and Exports

Years	*Planted Area (Ha)*	*Production (MT)*	*Exports (MT)*
1995	6,980	9,800	8,665
1996	7,000	8,800	8,277
1997	7,480	10,950	8,880
1998	7,250	9,955	8,114
1999	7,015	12,000	8,503
2000	7,165	10,000	6,582
2001	7,200	11,800	9,551
2002	7,250	12,400	8,890
2003	7,808	13,800	12,187
2004	7,856	12,400	10,791
2005	8,255	13,800	12,787
2006[1]	8,500	17,700	16,668
2008[2]	9,850	18,000	16,600

[1] Estimated, [2] Forecast

Source. US Agricultural Attaché's Chile Tree Nuts Annual Reports; various years.

Although a large percentage of walnut trees in production in Chile originated from seeds, budding and grafting of new and improved varieties like Serr and Chandler has increased in recent years.

Increasing labour costs are an important factor affecting walnut production and processing. Chile has a competitive quality advantage in shelled walnuts, since almost all shelled walnuts are hand-cracked. Although the premium Chile obtains from this quality advantage has thus far continued to encourage hand-shelling; increased labour costs may mean that Chile could lose this advantage in coming years.

Consumption

As with most other Chilean fruits, domestic walnut consumption is a residual of the export market. If international prices are low, exports fall off and domestic consumption increases as the larger supply drives domestic prices down. However, domestic demand does not drive consumption or determine market prices. In fact the domestic consumption has declined from 2570 tonnes in 1991-92 to 1770 tonnes in 2002-03, and is estimated at around 2000 tonnes during the last three years. This is largely because of the expanding export markets. Table 6.12 shows supply utilization of walnut in the country for the last five years.

Trade

Chile's exports of walnut almost doubled from 5,680 tonnes in 1991-92 to 11,500 tonnes in 2002-03. Tables 6.13 and 6.14 show Chile's walnut exports to major destinations during the last five years. Chile mainly exports in-shell walnuts to the Latin American Market and the European Union (EU). The most important markets in Latin America are MERCOSUR member countries where Chile has a tariff advantage over other exporting countries. Exports are highly dependent upon Brazilian demand and prices. Only small volumes of the highest quality nuts which meet the often demand size and grade specifications of customers, such as Germany, are exported to Europe. As a result of a deterioration of Chile's main Latin American markets for walnuts, export companies have increased their marketing efforts in the European Union. As a result, the EU accounts for more than 65 per cent of total exports, up from 33 per cent in 2000. Export to the EU are expected to keep expanding as a result of the Chile-EU Free Trade Agreement, which lowered tariffs on Chilean in shell and shelled walnuts to zero in 2003.

Table 6.12: Chile Walnut Supply Utilization Pattern

(Area in hectares: Trees in 1000 Nos. and other data in Metric Tonnes)

Item	*2001*	*2002*	*2003*	*2004*	*2005 (Forecast)*
Area Planted	7250	7769	7856	8255	8500
Area Harvested	5400	5600	5680	5870	5950
Bearing Trees	524	545	636	669	678
Non-Bearing Trees	181	210	261	286	305
Total Trees	705	755	897	955	983
Beginning Stocks	139	260	494	412	412
Production	12400	12500	12500	14200	1550
Imports	141	450	518	400	400
Total Supply	12680	132104	13512	15012	16312
Exports	10570	11000	11100	12600	13900
Domestic Consumption	1850	1720	2000	2000	2000
Ending Stocks	260	494	412	412	412
Total Distribution	12680	12910	13512	15012	16312

Source: US Agriculture Attaché's Chile: Tree Nuts, Annual Reports various years.

As production continues to expand due to an increase in planted area, and improvements in orchards begin to bear fruit, total exports are expected to expand further in the coming years. Exports are expected to increase further in 2005 due to a larger output.

Table 6.13: Chile: Exports of Walnuts In-shell 2001 to 2004 (Tonnes)

Country	2000	2001	2002	2003	2004
Brazil	1749	1984	1705	1270	1091
Argentina	848	751	204	335	0
Italy	352	488	760	1441	1009
Spain	170	136	543	1234	1479
Germany	151	362	279	600	327
Portugal	71	148	223	393	280
Uruguay	91	114	59	78	40
Venezuela	3	2	50	0	22
Netherlands	0	0	20	0	13
Other countries	187	154	245	254	81
Grand Total	3551	4139	4088	5605	4342

Source: Global Trade Atlas, 2005.

Table 6.14: Chile: Exports of Walnuts Shelled: 2000 to 2004 (Tonnes)

Country	2000	2001	2002	2003	2004
Brazil	488	860	752	703	687
Argentina	800	711	67	362	22
Italy	107	151	267	610	678
Spain	0	125	6	119	211
Germany	256	198	259	427	474
Portugal	150	205	290	377	359
Switzerland	256	239	247	333	180
Uruguay	54	49	32	16	4
Netherlands	10	40	189	155	280
Ecuador	27	43	84	51	46
Other countries	77	85	208	160	283
Grand Total	2,225	2,706	2,401	3,295	3,224

Source: Global Trade Atlas, 2005.

Stocks

There are no trade or official statistics available on Chile's average stocks. However, exporters reportedly do not normally carry over stocks.

Policy

There are no specific Government policies regulating or benefiting tree nut production in Chile. The general import duty on walnuts was permanently lowered to 6 per cent in January 2003. The US-Chile Free Trade Agreement lowered duties on US in-shell and shelled walnut to zero as of January 2004. Whereas Chilean exports to the US face a zero duty for in-shell walnuts and pay 13.2 cents per kg. duty for shelled walnuts. This rate will be reduced to zero by 2007.

Marketing

An increasing number of walnut producers are joining Chile Nut Producers association that was created to improve quality and standardize production. Export promotion, mainly in developed countries, is another of Chile Nuts objectives. Members of the association contribute one cent per kilo of walnuts produced for training and marketing activities.

As indicated, Chile Nut's first objective is to standardize and improve the quality of Chilean walnut production, with the goal of creating a quality category called "Chilean Nut". "Chilean Nut" is expected to embody a high international quality standard. Another objective of this organization is to train associated producers in "good agricultural practices", as most of Chile's export markets require high standards of quality. Finally, Chile Nut expects to become an important service organization for walnut producers, generating needed market, price and agricultural practices information that will be available through their web page. With this they hope to improve Chile's marketing position.

Another important activity of this organization is export promotion. For this, a project was presented to ProChile and approved, to co-finance a market study in Europe (Spain, France, Italy and Germany) and Japan during CY2005. This market study project, of which ProChile will provide 50 per cent, would cost US$620,000. It has three stages; development of promotion materials, an access study mission and export training workshops.

ITALIAN WALNUT ECONOMY

Production

According to both FAO data and the US Agricultural Attaché's reports walnut area in Italy had declined considerably since 1987. The decline seems to be due to substitution with other tree crops which more profitable crops. Planted area remains marginal and is not expected to expand in the near future, with the only limited exception of some newly planted orchards in northern Italy. Consequently the total production of walnut has also registered a declining trend. Walnut production declined from 42,800 tonnes in 1980 to 16,000 tonnes (in-shell basis) in 2005. Weather developments in Campania, the leading producing region of the local "Sorrento" variety determines the level and the quality of crop quality.

Consumption

Although still mainly concentrated during the Christmas season, in-shell walnut consumption has recently expanded through the spring. Sales of shelled walnuts, on the other hand, have increased remarkably in the most recent years. While in-shell walnuts are mainly consumed at the end of main meals, shelled walnuts are either eaten directly or as snacks or used by the confectionary industry. Total consumption of walnut increased from16,540 tonnes in 1984-85 to 36,600 tonnes in 2005. Table 6.15 shows walnut production, supply and utilization for selected years.

Table 6.15: Italy: Walnut Production, Supply and Disposal for selected years

(Area in Hectares: Trees in 1000 numbers; other data Metric tonnes)

	1993-94	*1994-95*	*2002-03*	*2003-04*	*2004-05 Forecast*
Area Planted	5,712	5,069	4,600	4,600	4,600
Area Harvested	4,869	4,257	3,900	3,900	3,900
Bearing Trees	0	0	0	0	0
Non-Bearing Trees	0	0	0	0	0
Total Trees	0	0	0	0	0
Beginning Stocks	2,500	1,000	1,000	1,000	1,000
Production	16,000	9,000	20,000	18,000	16,000
Imports	10,654	18,000	14882	20,095	22,044
Total Supply	29,154	28,000	35,878	39,095	39,044
Exports	1,123	800	1,100	1,000	1,000
Domestic Consumption	27,031	26,700	34,778	38,095	38,044
Total Distribution	29,154	28,000	35, 878	39,095	39,044

Source: FAT State Database, April 2005 and USDA Agriculture Attaché's Italy: Tree Nut Annual Reports: Various issues.

Trade

Italy is a net importing country. Its total walnut imports tripled during 1984-85 to 2004-05. Imports depend on domestic production; a relatively large domestic crop causes import to decline, while a good domestic crop results in lower imports. During the last two years Italy imported around 15,000 tonnes of walnut in-shell and about 2,500 tonnes of shelled walnuts (Table 6.16). The United States is the predominant supplier of in-shall, accounting for 72 per cent of Italian imports. However, Chile has recently edged the United States as the main supplier of shelled walnuts. In 2002, Chile surpassed the United States in exports claiming

22 per cent of Italian shelled imports compared to 21 per cent for the United States. Italy exports of walnut in-shell have declined from around 1000 tonnes annually to around 350 tonnes in recent years while it has not exported any quantities of shelled walnuts.

The EU customs duty for in-shell walnuts is fixed at 4 per cent, while that for shelled walnuts is 5.1 per cent. The EU export refund for shipments to third countries is currently 66 euros per metric ton for in-shell walnuts.

Table 6.16: Italy: Walnut Imports selected years (In tonnes)

Imports	*1992*	*1993*	*2003*	*2004*
		In-shell Walnuts		
France	75	60	213	818
Germany	209	82	489	242
Other EU	45	115	148	27
Total EU	329	257	637	269
Chile	200	550	1,452	1,010
US	5,491	7,926	11,176	12,043
Romania			71	89
Bulgaria			243	237
Other non-EU	201	374	184	481
TOTAL	6,221	9,260	14,613	15,216
Exports				
France	33	42	47	261
Belgium	121	144	35	26
Germany	127	238	18	34
UK	104	199	35	87
Spain			47	261
Other EU	5	9	18	14
Total EU	390	632	200	275
Other non-EU	240	125	77	249
TOTAL	630	757	277	524
		Shelled Walnuts		
Total EU	55	122	61	643
Romania	7	30	156	72
US	86	54	380	459
Chile	83	116	563	689
India	0	0	40	40
Others	134	166	1,045	827
Total	365	488	2,245	2,731
Exports				
Total EU	112	115	0	0
Other	13	13	0	0
TOTAL	125	128	0	0

Source: Global Trade Atlas, 2005.

TURKEY WALNUT ECONOMY

Production

Walnuts grow throughout most of Turkey. In the past, they generally were not cultivated but simply harvested from natural forests. However, during the past two decades or so, increased demand (and prices) have made walnut cultivation more attractive and increased resources have been devoted to its cultivation. The Horticultural Research Institute (HRI) in Yalova is the leading walnut research facility in Turkey. As a result, nine standard varieties with higher yields have been developed. Thus far, only a few of these improved varieties have been planted commercially. In addition to the HRI, several private companies have begun commercial propagation of improved walnut varieties.

According to official data, the number of bearing and non-bearing trees has been increasing slowly. Based on this trend and the shift to better varieties, the production is likely to continue increasing steadily as earlier planted trees reach bearing age and more trees are planted. Although official estimates current walnut production at around 120,000 tonnes (in-shell basis at a conversion factor of l: 2.5), most private report lowers figures. The lack of a systematic crop survey and widely divergent estimates make it difficult to accurately estimate the crop. Walnut production has increased from 72,000 tonnes in 1984/85 to 133,000 tonnes in 2005.

Consumption

Per capita consumption appears relatively stable, with long-term increases in aggregate consumption resulting from increased in population. More than fifty per cent of the crops are used for home consumption and the remainder is marketed commercially. Domestic consumption of walnut increased from 66,000 tonnes in 1984/85 to 77,000 tonnes in 2004/05. Most of the commercially marketed walnuts are consumed directly with very little processed. The retail price for shelled walnuts in Ankara are currently about TL 15,000,000 per kilogram compared to TL 8,000.000 in 2003.

WALNUT FARMING IN NEW COUNTRIES

Introduction

Internationally, confidence in walnut production is at an all time high with countries like the USA, China, France, Spain, Turkey and Chile having expanded their industries. South Africa, through its Industrial Development Corporation Ltd., has already completed an economic feasibility study for a proposed 600 hectares project to establish a new walnut industry. The South Africans have budgeted for a yield profile with the first commercial harvest in year 5 and a projected yield of 0.91 tonne ha-1 which will increase to 4.48 t ha-1 in year 10 when the walnut trees reach maturity. In recent years a number of countries have initiated programmes to develop walnut plantations, some of them for increasing their current level of walnuts production and others for walnut timber or for duel purposes i.e. for walnuts and timber. These countries, to name a few, include Australia, UK and New Zealand.

REFERENCES

1. *FAO STAT Database*, April 2005.
2. US$ 1 equals RMB 8.265.
3. *US Agriculture Attachés Tree Nuts Annual Report* (No. FR3040, dated 8/11/03).

7

INDIAN WALNUT ECONOMY

Introduction

Walnut (*Juglans regia L.*) is one of the most important temperate nuts grown in India. It is grown in hilly regions of Arunachal Pradesh, Himachal Pradesh, Uttrakhand and Jammu & Kashmir under rainfed and poor soil conditions in marginal lands. Jammu and Kashmir account for almost entirely (98%) of India's total volume. Other states' produce is marginal and consumed within these states. Walnut tree are mainly scattered trees of seedling origin and not in the form of compact and well laid out orchards. These seedlings trees exhibit extreme variation in tree and nut characters. This variation among seedling population provides an opportunity to select the desirable ones and the efforts have been made by many scientists in this direction since 1978 to 1996.

Walnut trees generally grow along roadsides and riverbanks and areas, which are not suitable for other crops as well as on steep hillsides. In Jammu and Kashmir, the State Horticulture Department, the Agricultural University and the Horticulture Processing and Marketing Corporation provide institutional support for cultivation of fruits and tree nuts. Although most of the walnut crop is concentrated in the southern districts of J & K, production occurs throughout the state. Persian walnut and black walnut, the two most important temperate nuts, are grown in India. Three varieties of walnuts are grown in India; hard shell, medium shell and thin shell (*kaghazi*). In addition to earning foreign exchange, walnut production provides jobs for thousands of families engaged in shelling, lumbering, woodcarving and marketing of the fruit.

Although production is currently concentrated in Jammu and Kashmir state, according to experts, moist coniferous forests of the Eastern and Western Himalayas, Himachal Pradesh, Jammu and Kashmir, hilly regions of North and South, the Eastern hills, Uttrakhand and Arunachal Pradesh are most suitable for the cultivation of walnut. Total area under walnut is estimated at 36,500 hectares with annual production over 33,000 metric tonnes.[1]

Weather

The State of Jammu and Kashmir experiences a range of weather conditions during the growing season, some having a negative impact on crop development. For instance good moisture during the flowering and fruit formation period may be followed by hail in mid-March and at time flood in July. The hail may seriously damage walnut crop in important growing areas. Jammu and Kashmir receives approximately 30 inches of rainfall annually.

Crop Area

Historically, walnut trees grew wild in the northwestern Himalayan belt. New walnut plantings in Jammu region are more structured. However, the Ministry of Agriculture, does not maintain official data on walnut area and production. Actual harvested area is estimated at around 80 per cent of total planted area. The Jammu and Kashmir Horticulture Department brought additional area under walnut cultivation in Jammu and area has increased over time.

Inputs

Most of the walnut area is rainfed. Where canal water is available, farmers provide irrigation 7 to 14 days before harvest. This helps the shucks to open and remain suspended on the trees, dropping clean nuts on the ground. The application of fertilizer is somewhat random, although the Horticulture Department recommends increased applications beginning with 20 grams of nitrogen for a one-year-old tree to 2,000 grams for trees older than 20 years. In practice, phosphatic fertilizer applications vary from 20 grams to 1,500 grams per tree depending on the type of fertilizer. Growers find it difficult to implement the fertilizer recommendations due to lack of irrigation, the large size and old age of many trees and the rocky terrain. Some trees are several centuries old and have attained heights of up to 50 feet and girths of up to 36 feet. Leaf manure is commonly mixed in the nursery beds to improve soil fertility and drainage. Young seedlings are transplanted after 2 to 3 years in the autumn when growth ceases temporarily.

Varieties and Yields

Jammu and Kashmir is a rich source of walnut germ plasma with about 330 types catalogued. Out of this total, about 70 varieties are being propagated. Walnut yields have increased little over the years as producers continue to use traditional rearing practices. Problems include:

- Lack of standard cultivars;
- Poor propagation techniques;
- Problems associated with various pests and diseases;
- Trees are often scattered and very large which complicates normal maintenance.

The normal yield of a walnut tree during its productive life should be 45-50 kgs year. However, the actual yield per bearing trees, as discussed below, is almost half of this level. The current ratio between bearing and non-bearing trees is approximately 80:20 with an estimated total tree population of 1.6 million. Walnuts in Jammu and Kashmir have an average shelling percentage of 40 per cent. Thin shell varieties such as the Basksi variety reach 70 per cent.

Crop Quality

Unfavourable weather conditions early in the season leads to decline in the quality of the crop. On average, about half of India's crop is rated superior quality because of its colour and thin shell. The quality of walnut produced is above average when common pests such as blister mite, stem borer, walnut weevil and aphids do not attack the crop and it is disease free.

Production Policy

The Department of Horticulture provides incentives for bringing new areas under cultivation of dry fruits. The Department's research programme on walnuts consists of surveying local quality strains, and introducing exotic types for growth under local conditions. Continuous attempts are being made to establish sound and successful techniques for budding and grafting walnuts under different conditions. Attempts are being made to dehull walnuts at proper maturity without affecting kernel quality by application of chemicals in the form of dips or sprays. J&K Horticulture Processing and Marketing Corporation looks after post harvest handling, grading and marketing of walnut crop.

Area, Production and Yields

The time series official data on area and production are not available. The only source is the US Agricultural Attaché's India Annual Walnut Reports. However, data in these reports, except for exports, are also mostly guess estimates. The time series data on Indian walnut economy derived from these annual reports for the period 1993 to 2005 are summarized in Table 7.1. It covers area planted, area harvested, number of bearing and non-bearing trees, yield per harvested hectare and per bearing tree[2], total supply and utilization of walnut in terms of domestic consumption, exports and change in stocks. India does not import any walnut.

Since the late 1980s area has expanded to some non-traditional producing regions especially in Jammu state where climatic conditions are similar to those in traditional growing areas. Trees in these areas are increasingly coming into bearing stage, which has resulted in higher production. The total planted area is estimated to have increased by about 4 per cent from 35.2 thousand hectares in 1993 to 36.6 thousand hectares in 2005. The number of trees planted to walnut rose by 21.6 per cent from 1.39 million in 1993 to almost 1.69 million, while the number of bearing trees during the last thirteen years increased by 23.1 per cent from 1.08 million to 1.33 million. Although yield per harvested hectare increased almost by 50 per cent, the yield per bearing trees has increased only marginally from 20 kgs. in 1993 to 25 kgs. in 2005 The current yields are less than half of the average normal yield of between 45-50 kgs./year, during its productive life of a walnut tree.[3] The low yield is partly due to the fact that most of the walnut area lacks irrigation and is dependent on rainfall. The application of fertilizer is somewhat random as growers find it difficult to apply recommended levels due to the large size and old age of many trees and the rocky terrain.

Production of walnut in-shell basis increased from 22 thousand tonnes in 1993 to 32 thousand tonnes, over 45 per cent increase in thirteen years. The annual growth rate comes to 3 per cent. The arrival of commercial volumes from the new production area in Jammu in 1994-95 surprised many in the industry. Production varies from one year to another, as the walnut trees experience alternate bearing cycle. Normally a bumper output in one year is followed by lower crop next year. Moreover, unfavourable weather conditions at the time of blossom and fruit formation during March through May at times adversely affect crop. Walnut production in the Kashmir valley, the traditional walnut growing area, continues to be hampered by civil unrest. Area has not expanded and proper maintenance of existing trees has been neglected over the years. In addition, trees in some areas are being cut for firewood.

Utilization Pattern

Domestic Consumption

Currently domestic consumption of walnut is around 56 per cent of the total output. Ample supplies, anticipated lower prices, the post harvest onset of the festival season spur up consumption. In the domestic market there appears to be keen competition between the price of imported Californian almond and of local walnut. For instance when reduced almond production in the US increases almond prices in India, consumers shift to walnuts and cashews, particularly among poorer consumers. Walnuts are cheaper than other nuts (almonds/cashews/pistachios) and are often the preferred festival nut among lower income groups. Walnut use in the Indian confectionary, chocolates and ice cream industries is on the rise. About 5 per cent of domestic production is consumed in Jammu and Kashmir. Kashmiris also use walnuts as a colouring agent, extracting black and green dyes from the husk.

Current utilization of walnuts for oil extraction (only from rancid nuts) is 3 per cent of annual production. The oil extraction rate varies from 50 per cent to 60 per cent. Major consumers of walnut oil are the soap and cosmetic industries.

The domestic demand for walnut is influenced by several factors such as total supplies, export demand and level of prices *vis-à-vis* other nuts such as almond and cashew. For instance tight supplies, strong export demand and comparatively firm local prices could limit domestic consumption of walnut. Similarly low prices of almonds, due to the large US Crop (the major supplier to India) encourages middle class consumers and some institutional users to shift from walnut to almonds during the winter festival season. Walnut usage by the confectionary and ice-cream industry is expected to continue to increase. Total annual domestic consumption of walnut, which varies considerably, has doubled from 9 thousand tonnes in 1993 to 18 thousand tonnes. The annual rate of growth in domestic consumption comes to 5.5 per cent. Future prospects, discussed in the next chapter, both for domestic consumption and exports appear to be good.

Table 7.1: India: Walnut In-shell basis: Supply/Utilization: selected years

Item	*Unit*	*1993*	*1995*	*2000*	*2001*	*2002*	*2003*	*2004*	*2005*
Area Planted	000 Hectares	35.2	36.0	36.5	36.5	36.5	36.5	36.6	36.6
Area Harvested	000 Hectares	27.5	28.8	30.2	30.2	30.2	30.5	30.8	30.8
Bearing Trees	000 Nos.	1082	1152	1305	1305	1307	1320	1330	1330
Non-bearing Trees	000 Nos.	305	288	255	255	255	255	265	265
Total Trees	000 Nos.	1387	1440	1560	1570	1572	1575	1595	1595
Yield/hectare harvested area	kgs.	800	868	1027	960	1060	1016	1006	1039
Yield/bearing tree	kgs.	20.3	21.7	23.0	22.2	24.5	23.5	23.3	25.4
Beginning Stocks	Tonnes	4,940	5,740	5,270	3,770	4,770	2,550	2200	1800
Production (October/ Sept.)	Tonnes	22,000	25,000	31,000	31,000	32,000	31,000	31000	32000
Total Supply	Tonnes	26,940	30,740	36,270	34,770	36,770	34050	33200	33800
Exports	Tonnes	14,550	16,540	15,500	15,000	17,220	15,500	14400	14000
Domestic Consumption	Tonnes	9,000	11,000	17,000	15,000	16,000	16,500	17,000	18,000
Ending Stock	Tonnes	3,390	3,200	3,770	4,770	3,550	2,050	1,800	1,800
Total Distribution	Tonnes	26,940	30,740	36,270	32,770	36,450	34,050	33,200	33,800

Source: USDA Agriculture Attaché's India: Tree Nut Annual Reports: various issues.

External Trade

Walnut exports from India depend largely on domestic prices; export demand and competition from other suppliers especially from the eastern European countries, e.g. Moldova, Bulgaria, Hungary, and Romania. The world export market is dominated by the United States of America, which supplied over 62 per cent of total exports for the six major countries for which data are available, during the period 2003-05. As regards India's share of global walnut market, Indian average exports of 14,633 tonnes, accounted for only 6.8 per cent of total exports by the six major walnut producing countries (*viz.* China, USA, Turkey, India, France and Chile), during the period 2003-05.

Indian walnut exports declined from 16.54 thousand tonnes in 1995-96 to 13.8 thousand tonnes in 1997-98 and to 9.4 thousand tonnes in 1997-98. However, exports have recovered since then reaching an estimated of 14.4 thousand tonnes in 2004.[4] The decline in exports was due to reduced sales in traditional European markets where Indian walnut face intense competition from eastern European countries particularly from Moldova whose walnut crop precedes India's by a month and from Hungary and the United States. Indian exporters managed to capture some of the markets by lowering export prices. Indian exports of walnut recovered following improved competition due to the decline in Indian Rupees *vis-à-vis* US dollar. The value of Indian rupee compared to US dollar declined by 15 per cent during 2003-04. Exports also increased in 2004 on strong demand from the EU. Major export destinations include Spain, Egypt, France, United Kingdom, Germany, Greece, Netherlands Italy and the United States.

India's nitrogen flush vacuum pack pouches (two pouches of 5 kgs. each in one carton) have become very popular in Europe. According to exporters, the shelf life of "vacuum packed" nuts is 7 to 8 months against the normal pack's life span of 4 months. Indian walnut kernels vacuum packed continue to enjoy a premium of about $150/mt in the world market due to their excellent quality, which results from manual shelling. More than 80 per cent of walnut exports are currently in vacuum-packed pouches and the balance in cardboard cartons with butter lining. Most walnuts are exported from October through March with a bulk shipped during November-January. More than 95 per cent are exported as kernels (40 per cent light halves; 20 per cent amber halves/broken; and the balance as brokens). Exports of shelled walnut increased from 1999 to 2002, but have declined during the last two years. Exports of walnut shelled by destination for the period 1999-2004 are shown in Table 7.2.

Exports of in-shell walnuts are declining as exporters are getting better returns on shelled walnut exports. Exports have declined from 829 tonnes in 1999 to about 218 tonnes in 2004 (Table 7.3). The main markets are Spain, United Kingdom, Germany, Netherlands, Greece, France Italy, Denmark and Egypt.

In India there are no restrictions on walnut exports, and no export subsidies are given. Walnuts, like most other dry fruits and nuts, are allowed to be imported without restrictions under the Open General Licence (OGL), and subject to an effective import duty of 40.4 per cent. Given the high tariffs and strong domestic production, opportunities for imports of walnuts are negligible.

Table 7.2: India: Walnut shelled Exports:1999–2004 (In Tonnes)

Country	*1999*	*2000*	*2001*	*2002*	*2003*	*2004*
Spain	550	1,107	1,658	1,624	1,556	1,426
Germany	875	423	800	786	593	562
France	445	940	541	771	150	235
United Kingdom	594	566	496	628	487	554
Egypt	388	731	495	572	337	330
Greece	446	573	464	809	265	331
Denmark	131	169	316	253	278	265
Netherlands	214	313	266	334	302	398
USA	3	23	227	0	26	0
Australia	56	131	183	279	120	100
Taiwan	25	11	118	167	130	242
Italy	195	124	114	51	35	21
Kuwait	50	55	97	125	132	216
Uruguay	40	59	88	11	41	88
Argentina	30	95	82	0	0	11
New Zealand	43	91	77	107	98	92
Portugal	53	33	75	51	20	31
UAE	72	120	69	74	114	94
Austria	12	0	59	69	55	50
Belgium	11	62	58	58	72	56
Canada	56	27	46	88	58	12
Switzerland	23	55	33	56	105	42
Bahrain	10	24	27	29	20	36
Norway	6	15	20	25	42	31
Sweden	20	22	18	43	34	21
Cyprus	0	48	17	98	36	77
Grand Total	4,419	6,400	6,720	7,418	5,446	5,677

Table 7.3: India: Exports of Walnut In-shell: 1990–2004 (In Tonnes)

Country	*1999*	*2000*	*2001*	*2002*	*2003*	*2004*
Spain	66	132	172	42	94	0
UK	91	45	96	20	83	10
Germany	104	50	95	161	60	0
Netherlands	65	51	61	65	0	0
Greece	43	10	54	70	43	0
France	121	94	10	54	0	0
Italy	86	10	4	0	0	0
Denmark	90	69	0	48	42	0
World total	829	578	762	636	570	218

Source: Global Trade Atlas, 2005.

There seems to be considerable scope to increase exports of walnut not only to the traditional markets but also to the new and emerging markets especially in the near eastern countries. The future growth markets for walnut exports should include China, Korea Republic, Mexico, Egypt, Lebanon, Emirates, Mexico and Chile. India need to increase its walnut production through improved productivity and also through expansion/establishment of new walnut orchards in other states such as Uttrakhand. The traders are experiencing considerable difficulties to get adequate supply of good quality walnuts especially from the Kashmir valley where orchard owners, as mentioned earlier, are unable to take proper care of their orchards due to disturbed conditions in the producing areas. The Horticulture Department of Uttrakhand should take the lead to encourage its farmers in their state to undertake walnut cultivation on commercial scale. For this the Department need to provide some incentives such as seedling subsidy, cash and other concession, which are detailed in another chapter of the study. The Department can in fact take a leaf out of the China's State Forestry Administration Pilot Conversion programme initiated in the year 2000, allowing conversion of the cropland to cultivate economic trees, e.g. walnuts, pecans and other nut or fruit bearing trees. Farmers, specialists and the government officials consider walnut production as an ecological and economic alternative to cropland agriculture.

Walnut Export prices (C&F Europe) and wholesale prices in Srinagar for the last four years are shown in Table 7.4.

Table 7.4: Walnut Prices: 1999-2000 – 2003-04

Price	*Unit*	*1999-2000*	*2000-01*	*2001-02*	*2002-03*	*2003-04*
Export Price (C&F Europe)	US$/ Tonne					
1. Light Halves	-do-	3600-4800	3900	3800-4500	3950-4900	4150-4850
2. Light Broken/ Amber Halves	-do-	2800-3400	2700-3400	2700-3400	2850-3700	2950-3650
3. Amber Broken	-do-	2200-2800	2400-3100	2600-2900	2600-3300	2750-3100
4. Wholesale Price of FAQ Walnut (in-shell) in Srinagar	Rs. /kg.	27-32	30-40	35-45	50-60	48-55

Source: Market sources.

Price Review

The wholesale prices of walnuts (in-shell) in the Delhi market peaked in 1998 and have declined since then. In 2002-03 prices rose by 40 per cent from Rs. 4850 per 100 kgs, to about Rs. 5600 (Table 7.5). The rise seems to be in line with the increase in price of almond but lower than for cashewnut. The wholesale price of walnut kernel in Delhi Market during 2005 was 35 per cent cheaper than for almond kernel prices. The respective average prices were Rs.220 and Rs. 340 per kilogram respectively. Despite the walnut kernel being cheaper as much as 25-30 per cent, almond annual consumption is much higher, around 25,000 tonnes. In fact almonds are widely used in Indian sweetmeats and other food preparations, in addition to consumed directly.

Table 7.5: Monthly Average Wholesale Prices of Walnut In-shell Average Weekend Prices in Delhi Wholesale Market: 1993-2005

(Rs. per 100 kgs.)

Month	Years								
	1993	1995	1997	1999	2000	2001	2003	2004	2005
January	5,000	5,000	8,400	9,000	7,200	7,200	9,400	9,250	11,500
February	5,000	4,750	8,400	8,400	7,200	7,200	8,700	10,000	12,000
March	5,000	4,500	8,400	8,000	7,200	7,200	9,000	10,000	12,000
April	4,750	4,500	9,600	8,000	7,840	7,200	9,000	8,000	10,000
May	5,000	4,875	9,000	8,000	8,000	7,200	9,000	8,000	10,750
June	5,000	4,500	8,000	8,000	7,000	7,200	9,350	8,000	11,500
July	4,400	4,900	8,000	8,000	7,000	7,200	10,000	8,000	11,500
August	4,750	5,000	7,400	8,000	8,000	8,100	11,000	8,000	11,500
September	4,000	5,000	7,000	7,600	8,000	9,000	11,000	8,000	11,000
October	4,000	4,800	9,800	7,730	7,200	9,000	8,000	8,400	13,500
November	6,000	7,250	7,000	8,700	7,200	9,000	8,000	13,000	15,000
December	5,250	7,000	7,280	7,200	7,200	8000	9,000	14,000	15,000
Average	4,846	5,173	8,190	8,053	7,420	7,792	9,287	9,387	12,104

Source: *Economic Times*, New Delhi.

CONSTRAINS AND FUTURE PROPSECTS

Jammu and Kashmir is the principal walnut producing state in India. Despite many constraints, the agro-climatic conditions of Jammu and Kashmir are ideally suited to walnut growth and production. Some of the trees in Jammu and Kashmir state are several centuries old.

Currently walnuts of seedling origin selected from variable population grafted on seedling rootstocks are mainly grown, and no standard cultivars are grown. Some selected seedlings like Govind, Roopa, Ratna, Pratap and Sholding are found in Himachal Pradesh. In the.hills of Uttrakhand Chakrata No. 2, 4, 6, 13 are recommended for cultivation. In Jammu and Kashmir, important selections are Bulbul, Karan, Wossan, Wossan-2, Wossan-3, Wossan-4, Wossan-7, Shalimar-l, Shalimar-2, Shalimar-3, P-1, P-2, P-12, V-I, V-6.

In a paper presented at the IV International Symposium, Sharma and Kumar has dealt with the constraints and opportunities for walnut cultivation in India. Their recommendations are summarized below.[5]

PROBLEMS OF WALNUT CULTIVATION IN INDIA

Lack of Suitable Methods of Propagation and Availability of Adequate Vegetatively Propagated Plant Material

According to these two scientists, the availability of grafted plant material is a major limiting factor in the cultivation of walnut. This is because of low and variable success obtained with different methods of vegetative propagation. Some of the results of these studies are discussed below:

A 50 per cent success was achieved with side tongue grafting. However, the success as high as 85 per cent was obtained with veneer grafting when attempted in the last week of July. In dormant grafting under controlled conditions, it was 72 and 67 per cent with cleft and tongue grafting, respectively. In a study on the effect of plant growth regulators on stooling in walnuts, reported that better response was obtained with *5000* ppm IAA + *10000* ppm IDA + *5000* ppm NAA and *10000* ppm NAA. Another research trial reported that stool shoots treated with IDA+IAA+NAA each at *7500* ppm in Lanoline at incisions above the debarked portion, gave 80 per cent rooting compared with 13.3 per cent in the control. However, two other research workers obtained no success with hardwood cuttings, air layering and mound layering even with the application of growth regulators.[6]

Lack of Clonal Rootstocks

The clonal rootstocks are not available and generally seedlings of the same or related species are used. These seedlings exhibit lot of variation among the plants. Due to hard shell, the seed germination is also a problem in these nuts. The studies conducted in 1981, have indicated that nuts having 0.17 cm thick shell gave 74.50 per cent germination and with 0.35 cm thick shell gave only 33.33 per cent germination.[7] A number of factors such as nut type, size, position of seed, planting depth, soil moisture and temperature and seed treatment influence the germination of seeds. The planting of large nuts at 7 cm depth soil and in vertical position gives better germination and seedling growth.

Lack of Standard Cultivars

A lack of suitable cultivars of walnut in India is one of the serious constrains. The existing plantation is of seedling origin. The produce obtained from these non-descript trees is not uniform and as such production cannot be geared to various market outlets where uniform crop of better quality is in demand. It has been seen that in general; nuts produced from present plantation belong predominantly to thick shell group where shelling per centage is low. Hence, there is a need to identify the suitable trees from native seedling populations or introduce cultivars from other countries, which are suitable for different climatic conditions prevailing in India.

Problem of Re-establishment of Nursery Plant in the Orchard

When nursery plants are planted in the orchard there is very high mortality. This is perhaps due to the tap root system, which is disturbed while uprooting the plant from the nursery. This needs extra care after planting to get better success in the field. Another method of raising seedlings in polythene bags has also been suggested. These seedlings can be grafted while in the bags and later these can be planted at a desired place without any disturbance to the root system.

Specific Climatic Requirements

The climate is a limiting factor in the expansion of walnut cultivation. The high temperature of about 38°C causes sunburning of hulls and shrivelling of kernels resulting sometimes into blank nuts. Severe damage is further aggravated if the humidity is low and temperature exceeds 40°C. If low temperature persists in summer, the filling of nuts is not proper. The cool or short growing season is a limiting factor in walnut production.

Pollination Behaviour of the Species and Lack of Suitable Pollinizers

The walnut tree is monoecious and the problems in pollination and fruits set are due to dichogamy. Dichogamy varies with the age and is more pronounced in young trees. The mature trees have more catkins, which are produced over a longer period and thus may better overlap the female bloom. The climatic conditions also play an important role. The catkins respond more quickly than the female blossoms during warm period. This makes dichogamy more complete in protandrous cultivars. The non-coincidence between the flowering periods of male and female flowers is the major cause for low yields in walnut and to overcome this problem, the scientist Kalmykov (1940) has recommended the top working of branches that bear flowers producing pollen at the required time. The pollen can be used for pollinating the same cultivar or other cultivars at the same location or different locations. Improvement in productivity can be achieved with the planting of suitable pollinizer cultivars or by hanging the catkins of male flowers on trees where the male flowers are not yet mature or have shed pollen but stigmas of female flowers are ready to receive pollen or by dusting the pollen or instead planting of homogenous cultivars.

Lack of Proper Package of Practices for Cultivation

The walnut growers lack any proper technology for taking up walnut cultivation on scientific lines under Indian conditions. This is due to lack of well-planned orchards and no systematic trials have been laid out to study the various aspects of walnut cultivation. The trees are planted mostly on marginal and neglected land and do not receive any fertilizer and irrigation. The trees are not trained and pruned which results in giant sized trees often difficult to manage and create problem for harvesting. Thus, there is a need to standardize techniques to develop low-headed trees of desired size giving optimum production.

Long Juvenile Period

The walnut has long juvenility period and takes about 8 to 10 years to come into fruiting on seedling rootstocks. Due to long juvenility period, the growers are not tempted to plant walnut trees. However, use of less vigorous rootstock may help in reducing the juvenile period.

Harvesting

Harvesting is a problem because of large size of the trees. Use of big sticks causes damage to fruiting limbs, shoots and also involves risk to harvesters. The collection of nuts is cumbersome when plantation is on sloppy land. At present, all operations such as harvesting, dehulling, washing and cleaning of nuts are carried out manually which besides, being time consuming do not give crop of uniform quality and better market standards. In view of great demand for quality nuts and kernels, harvest management warrants greater attention.

Conclusion

There seem to be a good potential for walnut cultivation in India because of its high nutritive value, better export potential, long productive life, hardy nature of trees, non-perishable and longer storage life and high timber value. Keeping in view the scope and problems of walnut cultivation in India the two experts mentioned above have recommended that the following measures need to be initiated:

- Efforts should be made for mopping up indigenous genetic resources.
- Better cultivars should be introduced from West Asia, North Africa, Europe, USA & USSR.
- Research should be strengthened so as to study problems being confronted in various agro-climatic zones and evolve suitable measures.
- More emphasis should be laid on clonal rootstock, varietal improvement, propagation, nutrition, water requirement, pruning and training, harvest management, and insect pest and disease management.
- Research staff should be trained in advanced technologies in countries known for growing quality production of nut crops.

REFERENCES

1. Other estimate put walnut area in India at 67,053 hectares with annual production of 71,758. c.f. Indian Agro-Industry Homepage: Agricultural Commodities: Dry Fruits–Walnut.: Estimates put out by the National Horticulture Board (Area 84,000 hectares and production of 90.8 thousand tonnes) are almost three times higher than suggested by the FAO, and the USDA.

2. The author has calculated yields for harvested area and bearing trees in the table.
3. Yield per hectare of planted area in India is only 0.84 tonnes, compared with 1.60 tonnes for France, 1.65 tonnes for Chile, 3.2 tonnes for Italy and 4.2 tonnes for the U.S.A. China yield is only 0.45 tonnes.
4. Of these exports of walnut shelled averaged were 5,561 tonnes (equivalent to 13,903 tonnes converted at the 1: 25 ratio
5. S.D. Sharma and K. Kumar: Present Status and Problems of Walnut Cultivation in India: Paper presented at the IV International Symposium: ACTA Hort. 544, *ISHA* 2001.
6. Samuel, R. and Sharma, S.D., 1991. Clonal propagation of walnut, *Agric. Scd. Digest*; 11(4): 185-89.
7. Sharma, S.D. and Chauhan, J.S., 1981. Effect of shell thickness on seed germination and growth of seedlings obtained from the nuts of seedling walnuts. *South Indian Hort.* 29(2): 87-89.

8

LONG-TERM PROSPECTS FOR WORLD AND INDIAN WALNUT ECONOMY

Introduction

This chapter is divided into three sections. The first section deals with the long-term prospects for the world walnut economy. That is, however, limited to the production aspect, as information and data on utilization of walnuts are available from the USDA report only for seven selected countries. The second section deals with these aspects for the selected countries. The results of the analysis can serve as a guide to the global situation. However, it is essential to stress that the data on production from FAO and the USDA vary considerably for some countries. Therefore, the production projections based on two sources also vary significantly. There is an urgent need to reconcile the data by the two agencies, i.e. FAO and the USDA. The final section discusses prospects for expanding walnut area and production in two Indian States, viz. Uttrakhand and Himachal Pradesh.

SECTION I

Production Projections

The long-term prospects for the world walnut economy have been analyzed based on the times series data available from two sources. In the first instance, the liner trend in production has been worked out for about 30 countries and the world as a whole. These trend projections were critically examined and refined based on the material available on walnut production and other policies for some the countries concerned. The main objective has been to present consistent long-term projections for the year 2015 and 2020. The walnut production data for the 1993-95, 2003-05, and projections are shown in Table 8.1.

India's share in the world production of walnut has declined slightly from 2.3 per cent during 1993-95 to 2 per cent in 2003-05. However, China's share during this period has increased by almost ten points from 20.4 per cent to 27.7 per cent. It thus became the leading producer of walnuts in the world, surpassing the USA, whose share declined marginally to 20.2 per cent for the period 2003-05.

Production projections have been prepared based on the FAO Time series data for the period from 1990 to 2005. For each country data different equations were fitted and one that gave the consistent and most reliable fit were used to arrive at the projected output. As a first step future output was projected based on the linear trend value for the period 1990 to 2005. Other regression equations used included Logarithmic, and Exponential. It seems more realistic to assume that the future walnut production will continue to follow the trend of the last decade. In fact with the improvement both in the field as well as management practices being implemented in some leading countries, production trend could be even better.

The world walnut production is projected to increase by 2.9 per cent per annum during the period 2003-05 to 2015. This rate of growth is lower than 3.3 per cent registered during the last decade. The projections indicate that the annual rate of growth will slacken further to 2.5 per cent during the period 2015 to 2020. World walnut production in projected to increase from an average of 1.48 million tonnes during 2003-05 to 1.95 million tonnes in 2015 and to about 2.25 million tonnes in 2020. In the case of India, the respective annual growth rates come to 5.6 per cent during both periods.

These rates of growth are lower than what were achieved during the last five years. India needs to increase its production from current level of 35,000 tonnes by over 40 per cent during the next two decades. Although it represents 4.22 per cent increase by annum, this would necessitate not only increase in productivity, which is very low, compared to its competitors, but expansion of area in traditional as well as other states, such as Uttrakhand, which seem to have a suitable agro-climatic conditions. Based on the trend rate of growth in productivity, India's yield would increase from 1 tonne per hectare to 1.8 tonnes of harvested area by the year 2020. The harvested area is 80 per cent of the total area under walnut crop. With the projected yield level a production level of 72,550 tonnes in 2020 would therefore require around 48,400 hectares, compared to 36,500 hectares currently estimated. The current yield per bearing tree in India is 25 kgs. against 40-50 kgs. in other competing

Table 8.1: Walnut Production: Actual and Projections

World/Country	Production (In Tonnes)				Percentage Increase			Percentage Share in World output			
	Actual		Projected								
	1993-95	2003-05	2015	2020	2003-05 over 1993-95	2015 over 2003-05	2020 over 2015	1993-95	2003-05	2015	2020
(1)	(2)	(3)	(4)	(5)	(6)	(7)	(8)	(9)	(10)	(11)	(12)
World	1,072,848	1,480,107	1,954,620	2,247,810	138.0	132.1	115.0	100.0	100.0	100.0	100.0
Argentina	8,500	9,000	11,200	12,280	105.9	124.4	109.6	0.8	0.6	0.6	0.546
Austria	13,598	18,603	22,010	24,290	136.8	118.3	110.4	1.3	1.3	1.1	1.081
Azerbaijan, Republic of	7,667	7,912	9,419	9,880	103.2	119.0	104.9	0.7	0.5	0.5	0.440
Belarus	9,000	12,000	17,481	19,608	133.3	145.7	112.2	0.8	0.8	0.9	0.872
Bosnia and Herzegovina	3,300	3,231	3,669	3,769	97.9	113.5	102.7	0.3	0.2	0.2	0.168
Brazil	3,102	2,000	2,500	3,000	64.5	125.0	120.0	0.3	0.1	0.1	0.133
Bulgaria	12,300	5,010	4,621	4,674	40.7	92.2	101.2	1.1	0.3	0.2	0.208
Chile	9,533	14,333	19,044	21,337	150.3	132.9	112.0	0.9	1.0	1.0	0.949
China	218,888	409,510	576,068	664,105	187.1	140.7	100.0	20.4	27.7	29.5	25.628
Croatia	4,018	3,229	2,303	1,801	80.4	71.3	78.2	0.4	0.2	0.1	0.080
Czech Republic	7,239	3,292	2,500	-2,244	45.5	75.9	-89.8	0.7	0.2	0.1	-0.100
France	22,376	26,549	35,375	38,340	118.6	133.2	108.4	2.1	1.8	1.3	1.706
Georgia	11,333	10,992	12,402	12,193	97.0	112.8	98.3	1.1	0.7	0.5	0.542
Germany	14,867	16,900	21,298	23,233	113.7	126.0	109.1	1.4	1.1	1.1	1.034

(Contd.)

(Contd.)

(1)	(2)	(3)	(4)	(5)	(6)	(7)	(8)	9	(10)	(11)	(12)
Greece	23,458	20,724	18,767	17,755	88.3	90.6	94.6	2.2	1.4	1.0	0.790
Hungary	7,500	6,486	4,767	4,155	86.5	73.5	87.2	0.7	0.4	0.2	0.185
India	25,000	32,167	55,450	72,550	128.7	172.4	130.8	2.3	2.2	2.8	3.228
Iran, Islamic Rep of	115,741	150,000	271,470	311,430	129.6	181.0	114.7	10.8	10.1	13.9	13.855
Italy	11,281	15,333	15,148	15,570	135.9	98.8	102.8	1.1	1.0	0.8	0.693
Kyrgyzstan	3,667	4,667	5,673	6,266	127.3	121.6	110.5	0.3	0.3	0.3	0.279
Macedonia	2,938	3,106	2,781	2,690	105.7	89.5	96.7	0.3	0.2	0.1	0.120
Mexico	416	19,000	25,000	30,000	4571.0	131.6	120.0	0.0	1.3	1.3	1.335
Moldova, Republic of	14,063	17,997	18,450	20,530	128.0	102.5	111.3	1.3	1.2	0.9	0.913
Morocco	2,600	1,500	2,500	3,200	57.7	166.7	128.0	0.2	0.1	0.1	0.142
Pakistan	17,856	13,985	15,700	18,200	78.3	112.3	115.9	1.7	0.9	0.8	0.810
Portugal	3,105	4,570	4,098	4,083	147.2	89.7	99.6	0.3	0.3	0.2	0.182
Romania	24,958	27,309	36,750	39,039	109.4	134.6	106.2	2.3	1.8	1.9	1.737
Russian Federation	7,500	13,167	19,281	22,051	175.6	146.4	114.4	0.7	0.9	1.0	0.981
Serbia and Montenegro	20,309	24,129	21,230	21,376	118.8	88.0	100.7	1.9	1.6	1.1	0.951
Spain	8,370	19,039	24,650	28,433	227.5	129.5	115.3	0.8	1.3	1.3	1.265
Turkey	115,000	129,667	132,404	136,074	112.8	102.1	102.8	10.7	8.8	6.8	6.054
Ukraine	70,178	79,884	70,711	72,851	113.8	88.5	103.0	6.5	5.4	3.6	3.241
United States of America	219,553	299,673	380,000	440,000	136.5	126.8	115.8	20.5	20.2	19.4	19.575

countries. It is essential to increase the productivity per hectare as well as per bearing tree to their normal potential. It is also essential to uproot the old trees and graft the new high yielding varieties and increase the density of tree per hectare in the existing orchards. Even with the higher yields than projected, it would be necessary to bring in more area under walnut production to achieve the projected level of production. Because of scarcity of suitable land in Jammu and Kashmir State, it is essential to expand walnut production to other states, which has suitable agro-climatic conditions.

As regards the competitiveness of walnut production in India *versus* other competing countries, India enjoys the cost advantages in terms of labour, which is rather cheap. For instance, in India the total management cost per hectare of walnut orchards assuming normal practices are followed, comes to US $ 450 against US$ 3,120 estimated for California. However, the difference in productivity per hectare (One tonne in India compared to 4.2 tonnes in California) reduces the cost advantage for India. India's productivity, which is the lowest among the major walnut producing countries, needs to be improved considerably. Fortunately, for this there is a considerable potential which needs to be tapped fully.

Nevertheless, competitiveness analysis of Indian walnut sector presents two deficiencies in relation to other world producers. These include mainly structural deficiencies. Indian walnut orchards are often in mountainous or less-favoured areas, where intensive production cannot be carried out. In addition, US government support such as the Market Access Programmes encourages US farmers to develop more assertive marketing strategies and tactics towards international markets. However, India which has labour-intensive system of walnut production, and technical advances are not easy to implement (mountains or environment deficiencies) low-cost labour in India, as in Turkey, should allow producers to compete with important advantage.

In EU specific market measures to support nut production have been in operation since 1990. General market mechanisms (operational funds) were introduced for all fruit and vegetables since 1996 and are also applicable to nuts. Additional (complementary) support is available through rural development and environmental schemes. To make good the inadequacy of production and marketing facilities for certain nuts in EU, specific measures were introduced in 1989, under a new Title II added to Council Regulation (EEC) No. 1035/72 of 18 May 1972, on common organization of the market in fruit and vegetables. Under this five products including walnut qualified for assistance under these measures.

Under these measures EU provided aid to producer organizations, which have received specific recognition and submitted a plan approved by the competent authority for improving the quality and the marketing of their produce. Aid is granted principally through a quality and marketing improvement plan. The specific aid granted for improvement plans is restricted to a period of 10 years to allow to a shift of financial responsibility on to the producers. The last plans are to finish in 2006-07.

SECTION II

PROJECTIONS FOR CONSUMPTION AND INTERNATIONAL TRADE

Consumption/Utilization Projections

Since the FAO data pertain to production only, projections for domestic consumption have been worked out from the USDA data on supply and distribution of walnuts for the seven major countries. Again the same procedure, described above, for preparing these projections, was adopted. However, much more information on policy and other aspects are available for these seven major countries. This helped to present complete projection covering exports, imports, and domestic consumption for the years 2015-16 and 2020-21. These projections are summarized in Table 8.2.

Domestic Consumption/Utilization

Global domestic consumption of walnut, based on seven countries data, is projected to increase over 3.4 per cent per annum during 2005 to 2015, which is slightly lower rate than 3.9 estimated for the current decade. The annual rate of growth is likely to slacken further to 3 per cent during 2015 to 2020. However, consumption in India, China and Italy is projected to continue increasing at a faster rate than in the past (Table 8.3). India's domestic consumption is anticipated to increase by more than double to 40.2 thousand tonnes by the year 2020. The rapid increase projected in consumption following the opening of the Indian market to branded ice creams, chocolates and processed food manufactured by the multinational corporations and the targeted growth rate of GDP of over 8 per cent during the tenth plan and thereafter. Prospects for further increase in domestic consumption in other major producing countries where utilization of walnut is already high, such as USA, and Turkey are rather limited. In France consumption is anticipated to recover from the decline registered during the last five years.

International Trade in Walnuts

World exports of walnut in-shell are projected to increase from an average of about 113 thousand tonnes during 2002-04 to 170 thousand tonnes in the year 2015 and 205 thousand tonnes in 2020. It represents an annual growth rate of 3.7 per cent over the next decade and half. Global exports of walnut shelled would increase from an average of about 101 thousand tonnes to 210 thousand tonnes in 2015 and 280 thousand tonnes by the year 2020 (Table 8.2). Total exports in terms of walnut in-shell (converted at the ratio of 45 % kernels to in-shell), are forecast to increase from 337 thousand tonnes during 2002-04 to 610 thousand tonnes in 2015 and 827 thousand tonnes in 2020. The annual growth rate is forecast at 5.4 per cent during the projected period. The export performance of exporting countries is likely to vary considerably.

Table 8.2: World Walnut Exports and Imports (In Tonnes)

Item	*Actual Average*		*Projected*		*Growth Rate (Percent/annum)*		
	1992-94	*2002-04*	*2015*	*2020*	*02-04/92-94*	*2015/02-04*	*2020/2015*
Exports							
Walnut In-shell	66,616	116,087	170,000	205,000	5.7	3.3	3.8
Walnut Shelled	51,826	100,503	210,000	280,000	6.8	6.4	6.0
Imports							
Walnut In-shell	66,546	101,495	165,000	200,00	4.3	5.1	4.0
Walnut Shelled	48,401	93,442	193,000	275,00	6.8	7.5	7.5

Global imports of walnut in-shell are projected to increase from 101 thousand tonnes during 2002-04 to 165 thousand tonnes in 2015 and 200 thousand tonnes in 2020. Imports of walnut shelled are anticipated to increase from an average of 93 thousand tonnes to 193 thousand tonnes in 2015 and 275 thousand tonnes in 2020. Total imports of walnut in-shell terms are expected to increase from 307 thousand tonnes during 2002-04 to 594 thousand tonnes in 2015 and 811 thousand tonnes in 2020.The annual rate of growth for world imports of total walnuts expressed in-shell terms, comes to 5.9 per cent. Turkey and Belgium markets for walnut in-shell would continue to expand over the next decade and half at a fast rate, while based on the past trend, Germany is likely to register lower growth rates than in the past. As regards imports of walnut kernels (i.e. shelled), Japan, Germany, France, Canada, UK Austria and Australia

Table 8.3: Walnut Production, Imports, Exports and Domestic Consumption

Item	*1995/96*[1]	*2003/05*	*2015/16*	*2020/21*		*% Increase*	
	In-shell basis in Tonnes				Col.3/Col.2	Col. 4/Col.3	Col.5/Col.4
(1)	(2)	(3)	(4)	(5)	(6)	(7)	(8)
I. India							
1. Production	26,000	31,300	55,450	72,550	120.4	177.2	130.8
2. Exports	15,257	14,633	24,150	32,350	95.9	165.0	134.0
3. Domestic Use	11,067	17,167	31,300	40,200	155.1	182.3	128.4
II. Chile							
1. Production	9,917	14,067	19,044	21,330	141.8	135.4	112.0
2. Exports	8,386	12,530	17,054	19,000	149.4	136.1	111.4
3. Domestic Use	1,479	2,000	1,850	2,330	135.2	92.5	125.9
III. China							
1. Production	226,288	356,000	576,070	664,105	157.3	161.8	115.3
2. Exports	42,797	32,583	40,530	55,600	76.1	124.4	137.2
3. Domestic Use	183,560	327,180	535,540	608,505	178.2	163.7	113.6
IV. France							
1. Production	24,307	27,330	35,500	38,600	112.4	129.9	108.7
2. Imports	9,900	13,497	16,288	17,848	136.3	120.7	109.6
3. Exports	13,133	19,920	27,600	30,500	151.7	138.6	110.5
4. Domestic Use	21,073	20,910	23,500	24,500	99.2	112.4	104.3
V. Italy							
1. Production	12,333	18,000	16,000	15,000	145.9	88.9	93.8

(Contd.)

(*Contd.*)

2. Imports	15,247	19,010	23,600	25,980	124.7	124.1	110.1
3. Exports	1,218	1,100	–	–	90.3		
4. Domestic Use	11,067	35,900	39,600	40,980	324.4	110.3	103.5
VI. Turkey							
1. Production	115,000	130,000	132,400	136,100	113.0	101.8	102.8
2. Imports	839	6,333	13,000	16,150	754.8	205.3	124.2
3. Exports	708	500	1,000	1,200	70.6	200.0	120.0
4. Domestic Use	115,131	135,833	144,400	151,050	897.7	106.3	104.6
VII. USA							
1. Production	203,816	299,673	380,000	440,000	147.0	126.8	115.8
2. Imports	3,240	495	1,200	1,500	15.3	242.4	125.0
3. Exports	108,482	132,830	170,000	185,000	122.4	128.0	108.8
4. Domestic Use	98,574	167,338	211,200	256,500	169.8	126.2	121.4
VIII. Total 7 countries							
1. Production	617,661	876370	1214464	1387685	141.9	138.6	114.3
2. Imports	29,226	39335	54088	61478	134.6	137.5	113.7
3. Exports	189,981	214096	280334	323650	112.7	130.9	115.5
4. Domestic Use	441,951	706328	987390	1124065	159.8	139.8	113.8

[1] Three years averages centred on the year shown.

Source: FAO STAT Data base time series; USDA Walnut Situation and Outlook report for selected countries, various years. Projections prepared by the Author.

would continue to import larger quantities. Import demand in Argentina, Lebanon, Israel, Greece, Switzerland and Syria is likely to increase at a faster rate than in the past. India needs to strengthen its foothold in its conventional markets and expand its presence in the new markets.

Exports: Factors Affecting Indian Walnut Trade Prospects

The outlook for international trade in walnut is shaped by long-term and short-term factors. Some of the underlying long-term factors are the income growth of trading customers and increased market access stemming from trade liberalization. Any deviations from the long-term trend are a result of short-term factors that can intermittently hinder or help trade prospects of producers. Examples of these short-term factors are changes in the US dollar exchange rates in foreign markets and fluctuations in world supplies. Other factors, such as trade barriers and productivity changes from technological innovations may have a long-term or short-term effect.

To a certain extent, production of good crop of walnuts in 2000-01 and devaluation of Indian Rupees *vis-à-vis* US Dollar, pulled down prices for these commodities and, along with good quality, improved the competitiveness in the EU market. However, the Japanese yen had depreciated even before the financial crisis began in Southeast Asia and has adversely affected exports to that country. Despite the weaker Yen, Japanese demand for Indian walnut remains strong. While Southeast Asia is currently a relatively small market for Indian walnut, there is considerable scope to increase exports to these countries, including China, Korea Republic, Japan, Malaysia, Singapore, and the Philippines.

Fluctuations in world supplies also affect the demand for Indian exports. The Indian exports to the global market increases when domestic supplies are large and/or traditional suppliers in the world market experience a decline in production. These supply factors are generally unpredictable, caused in most cases by unusual weather.

A number of barriers, both natural and artificial, diminish export opportunities for Indian producers. Depending on the nature of the barrier, the impacts to Indian exports could either be long-term or short-term. Examples of these barriers include costly transportation of products to far off markets and legal trade barriers such as government protectionist policies. Liberalization of trade through multilateral, bilateral, and/or regional trade agreements are important in relaxing many of these existing legal trade barriers either by tariff reductions or harmonizing technical barriers to trade (TBT).

Technical barriers to trade, such as Phytosanitary requirements and labelling issues, are an example of a legal trade barrier. TBTs are not necessarily associated with developed or developing countries, but rather involve importing countries setting standards of quality or requirements, which potential trade partners must meet. Because the Japanese are very concerned about the spread of fire blight, codling moths, and other crop diseases, their government imposes rigorous and costly import requirements for shipments of agriculture produce. Another example is Brazil's mandatory fumigation at origin requirement for all US walnuts and fruit entering their market, effective June 1997. This requirement was imposed following the detection of Pacific spider mite and thrips in some earlier shipments. Mandatory fumigation-at-origin requirement may dampen prospects for future exports to these foreign markets.

Technological innovations can lead to achieving a larger share of the world market through a competitive advantage—either a higher quality product for the same price, or a lower price for a product of comparable quality. However, these technologies can be exported as well, and so any gains in export market shares may be short lived. The benefits of technology adoption for an exporting country are usually larger with proximity to major export markets. Example of this is Moldova walnut export to EU because of much lower transportation cost than shipment from India and the harvesting of walnut one month before Indian supply become available. India has successfully adopted vacuum packaging technology in walnut kernel, which has extended the shelf life of the produce. However, India needs to improve yields through introduction of better varieties, lower cost of production through improved field management practices and also to expand cultivation of walnut in other states to meet its increasing domestic consumption and for the increased exports.

Prospects in EU: EU is the biggest export market for Indian walnuts. However, India's share in exports to the large walnut importing countries such as France, Germany, Greece, Italy, Netherlands, Spain and the UK remains rather small (less than 9 per cent of their total imports). During the last two years India's exports of walnuts to these countries averaged 10,720 tonnes out of their total imports of 120,000 tonnes. The overall market of the European Union is a differentiated one, with each Member State market having characteristics that merit individual attention. Thus, although export business strategy for Europe is a must, tactics should be adjusted for each country. With approximately 370 million consumers, the EU is one of the world's largest importers of agricultural products, accounting for roughly 20 per cent of total world imports. The EU is the largest market for walnut imports. Consistent with the global trend, the market for consumer food products is a very promising growth area. While the prospects for different products vary from country to country within the EU, tree nuts are selling well in a number of EU countries.

In EU member countries walnuts, almonds, and pistachios are the biggest sellers in agricultural product category, but they face competition from local production in the Mediterranean countries. The walnut market in the EU is seasonal, with most imports occurring in the October-January period. As part of the Uruguay Round results, the EU is gradually cutting the tariff on tree nuts. Exports to the EU have been negatively affected by the continued slump in the European economies, but the long-term prospects remain bright as local economic situations improve. It is essential for India to increase exports to these EU member countries and also supply to the new markets such as Korea Republic, Japan, China and Switzerland. Increased competition from local producers can be expected. Exporters, however, should check on health certification requirements prior to shipment.

Total exports for the seven major producing countries are projected to increase at an annual rate of 3.2 per cent. This would partly reflect a recovery in exports, which declined during the last three years. However, exports from India, based on the present trend, are anticipated to increase by only 2 per cent per annum during the next two decades, compared with about 5 per cent for China, 4 per cent for Chile, and 3.5 per cent for USA. Despite the projected increase, India's share in total exports of seven major countries would decline by 1.5 per cent to 7.5 per cent. However, China and the USA shares are anticipated to increase by two points, to over 16 per cent and 59 per cent respectively. India needs to reverse the projected decline in its share in the total export. For this it is recommended that it should boost its annual exports of walnuts to at least 25,000 tonnes, by strengthening its traditional markets and capturing new markets, particularly in Asia and the Middle East, which offers good prospects.

Concluding Remarks

India needs to more than double its production during the next two decades. It represents a 6 per cent increase by annum. This would necessitate not only increase in productivity but expansion of area in traditional as well as other states which have suitable agro-climatic conditions. India' yield would need to improve by at least thirty per cent.

The yield per bearing tree in India is 25 kgs. against 40-50 kgs. in other competing countries. It is essential to increase the productivity per hectare as well as per bearing tree to their normal potential. It is also important to implement in stages the replanting scheme for old trees in Jammu and Kashmir State, graft the new high yielding varieties and increase the density of tree per hectare in the existing orchards. Even with the higher yields than projected, it would be necessary to bring in an additional 18,400 hectares under walnut production to achieve the projected level of production. This augurs well for expanding walnut production to other state, such as Uttrakhand.

Global domestic consumption of walnut is projected to increase over 2 per cent per annum, the same rate as during the last five years. However, consumption in India, China and Italy is projected to continue increasing at a faster rate than in the past. India's domestic consumption is anticipated to increase by 33 per cent to 40.2 thousand tonnes by the year 2020. Consumption may even increase at a high pace than the projected one following the opening of the Indian market to branded ice creams, chocolates and processed food manufactured by the multinational corporations and if the targeted growth rate of GDP of over 8 per cent during the tenth plan and thereafter is realized.

SECTION III
PROSPECTS FOR WALNUT PRODUCTION IN UTTRAKHAND AND HIMACHAL PRADESH

As discussed in the above section on Long-Term Supply/Demand Projections, total requirements for walnut in India are projected at 55,450 tonnes by the year 2015 and 72,550 thousand tonnes for 2020. Based on the assumption of almost doubling of the yield levels and the trend rate of growth in area, India would need to bring an additional area of about 18,400 hectares under walnut to meet the projected requirements by the year 2020, compared to 36,500 hectares currently estimated under walnut. The current yield per bearing tree in India is 25 kgs. Against 50-60 kgs., in other competing countries. It is essential to increase India's yield. Owing to the scarcity of suitable land in Jammu and Kashmir State, the major walnut producing state in India, it would be essential to expand walnut production to other states, which has suitable agro-climatic conditions. This augurs well for expanding walnut production in other states, such as Uttrakhand and Himachal Pradesh, where currently only small and scattered walnut trees are found.

In India, Persian walnut is mostly grown in Jammu and Kashmir, Himachal Pradesh Uttrakhand and Arunachal Pradesh. Only scanty data are available on area, production and productivity status of walnut in some of these states. Table 8.4 summarizes the available information on walnut in India.

Table 8.4: Area Production and Productivity of Walnut in India

State	*Year*	*Area (Ha)*	*Production (Tonnes)*	*Yield (Tonnes/ha)*
Arunachal Pradesh	1993-94	1450	210	0.14
Himachal Pradesh	1993-94	5362	2206	0.41
	1994-95	5459*	—	—
	1995-96	5538*	—	—
Uttrakhand	1994-95	15900	9222	0.58
Jammu and Kashmir	1994-95	44341	60120	1.36

* Directorate of Horticulture, Himachal Pradesh.

Note: These estimates are rough figures; in fact for Jammu and Kashmir the current walnut production is estimated by the USDA at around only 36,000 tonnes.

Source: National Horticulture Board: Production Year Book 1997: Vol. IV/97, March, 1997.

Uttrakhand and Himachal Pradesh are small hilly states in India. These states have good potential for horticulture development since topographically and agro climatically there are wide range of variations which are suitable for growing large number of horticultural crops. Moreover grain farming is proving unremunerative in comparison to growing horticulture crops in the hilly undulating areas, which are devoid of irrigation facilities. Yet horticulture potential has remained unexploited especially in Uttrakhand although the State Government has been making endeavours for the upliftment of the state. The location specific technologies generated so far, however, had limited applicability. Due to this horticulture could not be established as a major industry. Nevertheless, the economies of Uttrakhand and Himachal Pradesh are largely dependent on the horticultural production especially apples, nut fruits and off-season vegetables and the tourism. The hill zones of the state are one of the most economically backward regions of the country where the crop output level of most of the cereal crops is very low primarily due to lack of water resources, non-application of high yielding technology and lack of basic infrastructure.

Horticultural Crops: Horticulture occupies a very important position in the predominantly agricultural economy of these states. Fruits and vegetable make a valuable contribution to the economies of these states. Tree crops tend to bind the soil and prevent soil erosion, help in maintaining the eco-system, ensure optimum utilization of the marginal and cultivable wastelands and offer better economic returns.

Among various fruit crops grown in these two states, apples are most planted and are commercially the important fruit crop. Among crops, according to some studies walnuts are grown in the Uttrakhand and Himachal Pradesh, though on a very small area which is rather scattered. As in the case of foodgrains, the productivity of the horticultural crops in these states is generally low. The low yields of most crops indicate the potential, which needs to be harnessed. While this offers opportunities for growth in production, income and employment in rural economy of these states, it also poses an immense challenge that needs to be overcome without loosing much time. For meeting the increasing demand for foodgrains and protective food items like fruits, vegetables and milk, it is essential to develop the economy through scientific transformation and modernization of agriculture in these states. Both land and water resources are limited in these states.

With the limited land and water resources in the two states, it is essential to introduce improved integrated intensive holistic farming system. Ecological or organic farming shall bring stability and sustainability to agriculture. It is farming with biological, cultural and natural inputs. Organic farming systems rely on large-scale application of organic or animal, or farmyard manure, compost, crop rotations, crop residues, weeds, legumes in crops rotations, green manuring, off-farm organic wastes, vermiculture or earthworms, mechanical cultivation, biofertilizers, biopesticides and biological control to maintain soil productivity and tilth to supply plant nutrients and to control insects, weeds, other pests and diseases. Under the organic farming system nothing should be wasted in agriculture. Farmers should be advised to utilize even the broken twigs leftover straws and weeds on their farms to increase soil fertility or humus and organic matter as such or via compost or farming yard manure, which is necessary for long-run sustainability of agriculture.

Hi-tech agriculture is composed of significant advances in agriculture in the form of advanced package of practices combining the organic farming system, appropriate farm machinery and implements, green house technology; watershed management technology, the latest outcomes of biodiversity, biotechnology, integrated nutrient supply systems, integrated pest management systems, integrated intensive holistic farming systems, improved irrigation system coupled with improved extension and agricultural marketing systems. Improved integrated intensive holistic farming system model has been developed and adopted by the farmers in Himachal Pradesh.[1]

Production of foodgrains and other crops in Uttrakhand needs to be increased remarkably by the adoption of advanced package of practices. As the experience in the Himachal Pradesh indicates, the average yield of maize, rice and wheat can be increased by more than 2-3 times compared with the existing average yields of farmers in the State. Similarly, the yield of vegetables and fruits can be raised by 3-4 times compared with the existing average yields. This increase would give a quantum jump in income of farmer. The production and income of farmers can be increased further by the adoption of improved cropping systems. For higher production, income and sustainability, foodgrain crops must be inter-cropped with leguminous pulses and oilseeds. The vegetables and vegetable-based cropping systems would give the highest production and income per hectare. The progressive farmers in Himachal Pradesh have already adopted the improved cropping systems. The intensity of cropping of these progressive farmers having average holding of 1.33 hectares increased to as high as 230 per cent, which increased their income substantially. Such a high cropping intensity and farm income is sustainable only through organic farming adopted by the farmers.[2]

The farmers can raise their income further through the adoption of integrated intensive holistic farming system. Farmers should follow a mixed cropping type of farming system. In general, depending on their sources, four farming systems can be recommended, viz. foodgrains-based, dairy-*cum*-poultry based, vegetable-based and horticulture-based. Farmers can also adopt various other farm and non-farm sub-systems (enterprises or activities) as a part of the integrated intensive holistic farming systems to further enhance their income substantially. These system or sub-systems include (i) Foodgrains, oilseeds and other crops; (ii) Vegetable including potato; (iii) Fruits and farm forestry; (iv) Dairying (sale of milk, other products and animals): sheep, goats, poultry and sericulture; (v) Rabbbitry, mushrooms, apiculture and fishery; (vi) Tailoring, photography, carpentry, gold and blacksmithy. Depending on their preferences, resource, manpower and availability of training facilities and market, farmers can take up all of them on a small scale or some of them on a large scale to increase their production and income.

Prospects for Expansion of Walnut Production in Uttrakhand and Himachal Pradesh

As mentioned earlier, walnuts are grown in Uttrakhand and Himachal Pradesh. However, the information about area, production and productivity of walnut is readily available only for Uttrakhand. The district-wise information for the state is summarized in Table 8.5. Trees are rather old and according to the trade sources area and production of walnut in the state have now declined considerably. Most of the produce in Uttrakhand is now being used within the state, with no quantities sold outside the state or for exports.

Table 8.5: Production and Yield per Hectare of Walnut in Uttrakhand

District	Area (Hectares)	Production (Tonnes)	Yield/Tonnes/ Hectare
I. Almora	1900	1120	0.58
2. Nainital	1300	1050	0.81
3. Pithoragarh	1850	1090	0.58
4. Pauri	1650	950	0.57
5. Tehri	1750	950	0.54
6. Chamoli	1950	980	0.51
7. Uttarkashi	951	680	0.72
8. Dehradun	1701	680	O.39
Total	13052	7500	O.57

Source: Tripathi, R.S. and Jagdish Kumar: Nut Fruit Production and Markerking in Hils: G.P. Pant University of Agriculture and Technology. Hill Campus Ranichauri, Tehri-Garhwal: Appendix II, March, 1992.

The fast increase in population in the hills areas in the state has led to (i) reduction in arable land per family; (ii) deepening of poverty; and (iii) massive deforestation. The impact of these factors results in the vicious circle, in that the needs of the burgeoning subsistence population exert increasing pressure on the forest cover leading to massive deforestation, which is the cause of accelerating rate of mass wastage.

In fact the pressure on land, the resource that is rather limited, is increasing immensely. In the past this pressure was partly offset by bringing in the forestland and slopes under cultivation. However, now the opportunity for such expansion no longer exists, and thus individual landholdings are rapidly decreasing, with the average size being less than 1 acre. Nevertheless a large tract of arable land has been rendered as a waste and degraded land due to the negligence and lack of measures to harvest the rainfall through proper small irrigation works. As a result land is no longer able to sustain the growing rural population, and migration from rural to urban areas and other states is increasing. This is particularly the case in the hill areas, where people are moving to the cities like Dehradun and Haridwar in search of employment. At the same time, many people remain in the hill areas, where underemployment and unemployment are rife and at least half the population lives below the poverty line.

In Uttrakhand and Himachal Pradesh there is a considerable amount of wasteland. This consists of forest-degraded area and non-forest degraded land. Culturable wasteland alone is estimated at over 350 thousand hectares for Uttrakhand and 104 thousand hectares in Himachal Pradesh. It constitutes over 25 per cent of the currently total cropped area in Uttrakhand and 10.5 per cent in Himachal Pradesh.[3] Destruction and degradation of forests are taking a heavy toll of soil with essential nutrients in the hilly areas being washed away each year. This seriously affects the economy of the state. The degradation makes land less productive leading to impoverishment of the rural population. It is essential to regenerate degraded forest and wasteland. A programme of generation and restoration of ecosystem will provide productive employment to a large section of rural population. The wasteland can be converted to grow tree and other crops, fodder and fuel. As mentioned above, an Ex-serviceman, Jagat Singh Chaudary has successfully converted wasteland in the hills of Rudraprayag district by planting various species of plants. This experiment needs to be replicated on a large scale.

In fact, the varied agro-climatic zone of the two states combined with generally a diligent peasantry offer good opportunities for producing horticultural products including walnuts. The development of walnut and other horticultural crops will not only help in the creation of employment opportunities and increasing income level of the masses, they will also provide permanent green cover to the soil besides acting as soil binder thereby prevent soil erosion to a considerable extent. Planting of trees also will help in bringing back the nutrients that are actually lost and cannot be used by the field crops as a result of leaching to the deeper zones of the wild. Moreover, the cultivation of walnuts and fruit crops is labour intensive compared to the cultivation of field crops starting from the stage of tree plantation to marketing. Thus the intensive cultivation of walnut tree could serve as a viable alternative strategy for the development of the hill regions. This would at the same time check the migration of the able bodied workforce and provide gainful employment opportunities within the region. Walnut trees seem to have good potential in the "state, which are mostly grown in backyard garden, and no compact orchard exists. The existing walnut trees are of inferior varieties. Productivity can be increased by introduction of superior varieties. Preliminary results indicate that Walnut, Almond and Kiwi fruit, such low volume but high value fruit crops, will be of immense value and there is considerable scope for commercial cultivation at higher altitude of the state. However, for this it is essential to undertake a comprehensive feasibility study on the promotion of walnut tree plantation on commercial scale in the selected districts of the State.

Present Position

Realizing the need for the introduction of new tree crops and the importance of good quality planting material and seeds TFL/HIMCON, a voluntary organization, has during the last couple of years introduced new high value horticultural crops and medicinal plants in the selected hill areas of the state. *Walnut, Kiwi and Almond* are being promoted together with granium, *brahmi*, *aswagandha*, *shatavari*, *kuth* and *kutki*. It seems that walnuts can be successfully grown between the elevations of 1000 to 3000 metres above sea level. Walnut production in the state, as mentioned above, has declined considerably and most of the produce is currently being consumed within the state. However, traders and export are experiencing difficulties to get adequate supplies of walnuts from Jammu and Kashmir to meet increasing demand for exports as well as domestic consumption. They are interested to diversify the source of supplies.

Although a good start seems to have been made to distribute walnut stems among farmers in the Ranichauri area. There is, however, need to carry out a proper feasibility study which should cover soil analysis at the farmer's fields and provide him the proper technical guidance for planting and caring of the plants say upto three years or so. At present the farmer is left to himself and he does not plant walnut tree in a scientific manner. Also most of these farmers are not aware of the type of the walnut stems supplied to them. Walnut orchard, like other tree crop plantation, has a long gestation period. The tree starts bearing fruit after eight years and net economic return accrues to farmer almost after 10 years of planting. This involves a considerable amount of risk by the farmers. It is, therefore, essential to carry out a proper scientific research by the Horticultural Department of the Hill Campus of G.P. Pant University of Agriculture and Technology, on the soil, water and the type of walnut trees which can be grown successfully in different areas of the state, before undertaking a large scale walnut planting campaign in the state. Otherwise, there are chances that the experiments undertaken on trial and error bases may not yield good viable results. This will have in turn a negative impact and would shake the confidence of the farmers to undertake any new venture in the future.

Need for a Feasibility Study

Before initiation of the programme of promoting wide scale walnut planting in Uttrakhand state it is essential to undertake a comprehensive feasibility study in at least two districts of the state. A multi-disciplinary team of experts, working together-particularly economist, and financial/ commodity analysts, together with agronomist, soil scientist, and horticultural/nut tree expert, should carry out the feasibility study.

In Himachal Pradesh the Department of Fruit Breeding & Genetic Resources, Dr. Y.S. Parmar University of Horticulture & Forestry, Nauni-Solan, is engaged in conducting research and promoting planting of walnut and other crops raised from tissue culture. However, very little information is available on the status of the walnut production in Himachal Pradesh.

Attempt has been made in Chapter 9 to work out the economics of walnut production in Uttrakhand and Himachal Pradesh. These analyses are based on the data collected mainly from the secondary sources. The results of the analyses are summarized in Table 9.7. These partial analyses do indicate that investment in the walnut growing in Uttrakhand and Himachal Pradesh is likely to be highly paying. The net returns over costs 'A', 'B' and 'C' in these states are estimated at Rs. 41,080, Rs. 36,710 and Rs.39,073 per hectare per year. The benefit cost ratios are positive and range from 1: 3.93 under cost A, and 1: 2.60 with net cost C. However, these analyses need to be confirmed and there is also need to carry out agronomic study whether walnut tree plantation can successfully be established on commercial scale in the selected districts of the state.

REFERENCES

1. D.S. Thakur, *High-technology agriculture and organic farming in Himachal Pradesh for higher production, income, sustainable agriculture and evergreen revolution: in Indian Farming*; Vol. 47, No. 7, October 1997.
2. D.S. Thakur, *op. cit.*, p. 20.
3. *Source*: Himachal Pradesh: Human Development Report 2002, p. 204 and Uttrakhand: Tripathi, R.S. and Jagdish Kumar Nut Fruit Production and Marketing in Hills: *ibid.*

9

ECONOMICS OF WALNUT PRODUCTION IN UTTRAKHAND AND HIMACHAL PRADESH

Introduction

Economic and Financial analysis provides a framework within which all aspects of a proposed project can be evaluated in a coordinated and systematic manner. Careful project analysis will point up unrealistic or questionable assumptions and indicate ways in which a project can and should be modified to improve its earning capacity or to increase the non-economic or non-quantifiable values, which we expect to gain from it. A project carefully analysed and revised in the light of this analysis has a much-improved chance of being implemented on time and of yielding the benefits we seek. The cost benefit ratio or the rate of return when computed is a useful measure of a project's wealth creating capacity, but it is whole system of evaluation which justified the time and effort devoted to a project analysis and from which comes the payoff in terms of better projects.

Clearly, projects which a state or nation chooses to implement should be a high priority in the development programme of the state and/or the country. The economies of Uttrakhand and Himachal Pradesh are largely dependent on the horticultural production especially apples, nut fruits and off-season vegetables. These states, especially Uttrakhand, are economically backward states in India, where the crop output level is uneconomic for most of the cereals primarily due to non-adoption of modern scientific crop production technology. In this situation walnut, apples and other temperate fruits production offers tremendous scope to raise the income and employment opportunities and to develop fruit based processing industry. Since the inception of the Uttrakhand state a few years ago the State Government has laid increasing emphasis on development of horticulture sector, which has been declared a priority area of development.[1]

Economic Feasibility of Walnut Production

Currently, there is hardly any data available on the economics of walnut production even for the Jammu and Kashmir state, which accounts for almost 90 per cent of the walnut production in the country. Based on data gathered by the author from selected walnut growers in Jammu and Kashmir and from other sources on economics of horticultural crops in Uttrakhand and Himachal Pradesh, an attempt is made in this chapter to work out the economics of walnut production in the two states. The initial cost of walnut orchard establishment include the components of layout, demarcation, terracing, digging of pits, filling of pits, manure and fertilizers application, plant protection, cost of sapling and other miscellaneous expenses to be incurred during the plantation of walnut trees in the orchards. Details of cost components for planting one per hectare under walnut in the fruit belt hill areas in the state are given in Table 9.1. It is estimated that on an average, a sum of Rs. 31,000 are needed for the establishment of per hectare of walnut orchards. Out of the total establishment cost, a lion share is on layout, demarcation and terracing component, cost estimate being Rs. 16,200 per hectare, which constitutes about 58 per cent of the total establishment cost. The manure and fertilizer account for about 10 per cent of the cost, while the expenditure on digging pits for plantation is estimated at 6.5 per cent of the total establishment cost. The cost of the sapling and their transportation also comes to 12.9 per cent of the total cost. The cost of plant protection is estimated to be the least being 1.93 per cent. It is purposely assumed that the use of plant protection chemicals, based on prevailing practice in the Jammu and Kashmir, is not common due to lack of technical knowledge about diseases and their control measures.

Maintenance Cost of Non-Bearing Orchards

The non-bearing stage of walnut orchard is at least 10 years after plantation of the tree. During this stage the major cost components is human labour, fertilizers, plant protection and overhead cost. The physical units of various input components required for the maintenance of per hectare of walnut orchard in non-bearing for the hills fruit belt in the states are given in Table 9.2. On an average, the human labour for the maintenance of walnut

Table 9.1: Cost of Establishing Walnut Orchard per Hectare in Hill Areas in Uttrakhand and Himachal Pradesh

Cost Component	Unit	Cost/Unit (Rs.)	Quantity or Number	Total Cost (Rs.)	% of the Total Cost
Layout, demarcation and terracing	Man-days	120	150	18,000	58.07
Digging Pits	Pit	30	100	3,000	9.68
Filling of Pits	Pit	20	100	2,000	6.45
Manure and Fertilizers	Plant	30	100	3,000	9.68
Plant Protection	Plant	6	100	600	1.93
Cost of Sapling (incld. Transport)	Plant	40	100	4000	12.90
Miscellaneous	Plant	4	100	400	1.29
Total Cost				31,000	100.00

Table 9.2: Physical Inputs Required for Maintenance per Hectare of Walnut Orchard Non-bearing Stage in the Sample Orchards in Uttrakhand and Himachal Pradesh

Input Components	Age of Trees (in Years)							Total	Average Per Year
	1-4	5	6	7	8	9	10		
Family human labour (Days)	600	175	175	175	175	175	175	1650	165
Hired human labour (Days)	240	60	60	60	60	60	60	720	72
Farm Yard manure (Qtls)	40	10	20	30	40	50	60	250	25
Fertilizer (kgs.)	280	100	120	150	180	200	230	1260	126

Table 9.3: Physical Inputs Required for Maintenance per Hectare of Walnut Orchard in the Bearing State in Uttrakhand and Himachal Pradesh

Input	Age of Trees (In Years)						Total	Average per Year
	11	11-15	16-20	21-30	31-40	41 Yrs. & Above		
Family labour (days)	100	130	130	130	130	130	4000	130
Hired human labour (days)	50	50	50	50	50	20	1750	44
Manure (qtls)	70	80	80	90	90	70	3370	84
Fertilizers Nutrients (kgs.)	230	230	250	250	230	200	9430	235

orchard plantation is estimated at 225 days per hectare per year. Out of total human labour requirements 75 per cent can be family labour. The use of farmyard manure (FYM) is estimated at 25 qtls per hectare and of chemical fertilizers at 1.3 qtls per hectare per year.

The details of maintenance cost per hectare of walnut orchard in non-bearing stage are given in Table 9.4. The expenditure on human labour, manure, fertilizers and plant production is assumed nil from 1 to 4 years due to the fact that during the early stage of plantation the inter-crops can cover most of the area under walnut. The advantage of the operations like hoeing, weeding, manuring etc. to be carried out for intercrops will also benefit the walnut area.

The average Cost 'A' for the maintenance of per hectare of walnut orchard in non-bearing stage is estimated at Rs. 6730 per year. Out of the total cost the highest share will be on human labour. The total cost of human labour is reckoned at Rs. 3000 per hectare, out of which 20 per cent will be on hired human labour. The manure and fertilizer is estimated to account for about 28 per cent of the total cost 'A'. The expenditure on plant protection measures is estimated at Rs. 540 per hectare in non-bearing stage of walnut orchard, which will constitute less than 8 per cent of the total cost 'A'.

The cost 'B' for maintenance of per hectare of walnut orchard is estimated at Rs. 13,580 per year. The total establishment cost Rs. 31,000. The rental value of land is estimated at Rs. 3,750 per hectare per year. The total investment on maintenance per hectare of walnut crop is estimated at Rs. 1,35,800, as a cost 'C' upto 10 years of the plantation. Per year net cost 'C' is worked out at Rs. 13,580 per year per hectare for maintenance of the non-bearing walnut trees.

Maintenance Cost of Bearing Orchards

The bearing stage of the walnut trees starts from the age of about 9th year of plantation and continues up to about 50 years. The experience of the walnut orchards in Jammu and Kashmir indicates that after 50 years of plantation the bearing efficiency of walnut trees declines and does not prove economic for further investment. Therefore, in the present study the actual bearing stage of the walnut orchards is considered from 10th to 50th years after plantation and cost and returns have been estimated accordingly.

The main items of the cost for maintenance of bearing orchards are family human labour, hired human labour, manure, fertilizers, plant protection, interest on working capital, establishment cost, rental value of land and marketing costs. The details of estimated physical inputs required for the maintenance of per hectare of walnut, in the bearing stage are given in Table 9.3. The total human labour required is estimated at 174 days per hectare per year during the bearing stage of the orchards. The family human labour is assumed to contribute about 75 per cent of the total labour required during the bearing stage of the orchards and the hired labour the remaining 25 per cent. Hired labour is required *inter alia* for plucking, hulling and cracking of walnuts (See for instance the cost/return analysis for walnut in Jammu and Kashmir state, presented at the end of this chapter). The use of manure and fertilizer is estimated at about 84 qtls, and 235 kgs. per ha per year for the bearing orchards.

The estimated maintenance costs of walnut orchard during non-bearing stage is shown in Table 9.4, while those for bearing stage are given in Table 9.5. The total cost 'C' for maintenance of during the bearing stage, i.e. from 11 to 50 years age, is estimated at Rs. 6,04,700, while costs 'A' are estimated at Rs. 4,54,700 per hectare. Out the total cost 'A', the highest share of investment is likely to be on fertilizers (Rs. 3,450 per hectare per year) followed by human labour (Rs. 3,585) and manure (Rs. 1,645). Combined share of manure and chemical fertilizer is estimated at 45 per cent of the total cost 'A'. Average cost 'C' per hectare during the bearing life of the walnut orchard is estimated at Rs. 15,118 per year. The net cost 'C' comes to Rs. 13,448 per hectare per year after deducting the net returns from the intercropping.

Total Cost per Hectare of Walnut Production

The total cost per hectare of walnut production includes initial cost of establishment, maintenance of trees in non-bearing stage, maintenance of trees in bearing stage and marketing costs. The estimated physical units of inputs required during the non-bearing and bearing stages per hectare of walnut production is given in Table 9.6. The human labour employment on the maintenance of walnut orchard during the bearing and non-bearing stages is estimated at 7472 days per hectare. Out of this 75.6 per cent shall be contributed by the family labour. The family and hired human labour requirement for the maintenance of the orchards is estimated at 113 days and 37.5 days respectively per year per hectare. The use of manure is estimated at 3360 quintals during the whole life of the orchard, while on per hectares it is estimated at 72.4 quintals. The requirement of chemical fertilizer, on an average is estimated at 214 kg. per hectare.

Table 9.4: Estimated Maintenance Cost per Hectare of Walnut in Non-bearing Stage (Rs./Hectare)

Cost Component	*Age of the Trees (Years)*										*Total*	*Average per Year*
	1	*2*	*3*	*4*	*5*	*6*	*7*	*8*	*9*	*10*		
Family Human Labour	—	—	—	—	4000	4000	4000	4000	4000	4000	24000	2400
Hired Human Labour	—	—	—	—	1000	1000	1000	1000	1000	1000	6000	600
Manure	—	—	—	—	200	400	600	800	1000	1200	4200	420
Fertilizers	—	—	—	—	1500	1800	2250	2700	3000	3450	14700	1470
Plant Protection	—	—	—	—	800	800	800	900	1000	1100	5400	540
Depreciation	1000	1000	1000	1000	1000	1000	1000	1000	1000	1000	10000	1000
Interest on Working Capital (10%)	—	—	—	—	500	500	500	500	500	500	3000	300
Cost 'A'	1000	1000	1000	1000	9000	9500	10150	10900	11500	12250	67300	6730
Establishment Cost	31000	—	—	—	—	—	—	—	—	—	31000	3100
Rental Value of Land	3750	3750	3750	3750	3750	3750	3750	3750	3750	3750	37500	3750
Cost 'B'	35750	4750	4750	4750	12750	13250	13900	14650	15250	16000	135800	13580
Cost 'C'	35750	4750	4750	4750	12750	13250	13900	14650	15250	16000	135800	13580
Net Return from intercropping	1200	1300	1300	1300	1400	1500	1500	1300	1200	1100	13100	1310
Net Cost 'C'	34550	3450	3450	3450	11350	11750	12400	13350	14050	14900	122700	12270

Table 9.5: Estimated Maintenance Cost per Hectare of Walnut Orchard in Bearing Stage in Uttrakhand and Himachal Pradesh (Rs./Hectare)

Cost Component	*Age of Trees (Years)*						*Total*	*Average per Year*
	11	*12-15*	*16-20*	*21-30*	*31-40*	*41 Yrs. & over*		
Family Human Labour	2000	2600	2600	2600	2600	2600	103400	2585
Hired Human Labour	1000	1000	1000	1000	1000	1000	40000	1000
Manure	1400	1600	1600	1800	1800	1400	65800	1645
Fertilizers	3450	3450	3750	3750	3450	3000	138000	3450
Plant Protection	1100	1100	1200	1200	1300	1100	47500	1188
Depreciation	1000	1000	1000	1000	1000	1000	40000	1000
Interest on Working Capital (10%)	500	500	500	500	500	500	20000	500
Cost 'A'	10450	11250	11650	11850	11650	10600	454700	11368
Establishment Cost	—	—	—	—	—	—	—	—
Rental Value of Land	3750	3750	3750	3750	3750	3750	15000	3750
Cost 'B'	14200	15000	15400	15600	15400	14350	604700	15118
Cost 'C'	14200	15000	15400	15600	15400	14350	604700	15118
Net Return from intercropping	1250	1350	1550	1860	1830	1550	66800	1640
Net Cost 'C'	12950	13650	13850	13740	13570	12800	537900	13448

Table 9.6: Estimated Physical Inputs Required for Maintenance per Hectare of Walnut Orchard During Non-bearing and Bearing Stage in Uttrakhand and Himachal Pradesh

Input Component	*Unit*	*1-10 Years Age Group*	*11-50 Years Age Group*	*Total for the Whole Life of Orchard*	*Average per Year*
Family Human labour	Days	1650	4000	5650	113.0
Hired Human Labour	Days	72	1750	1822	37.5
Manure	Qtls.	250	3370	3620	72.4
Fertilizers	Kgs.	1260	9430	10,690	213.8

Income and Return from Walnut Orchard

The returns from walnut orchard will be in terms of walnuts and the production of grains, medicinal plants, vegetables and fodder from the intercrops on the proposed orchards. The details of the estimated cost per hectare of walnut production and costs 'A', 'B' and 'C' total cost and net cost 'C' are given in Table 9.7. It also gives the estimated income and return likely to accrue from walnut orchard in Uttrakhand. The average yield of production of walnut is estimated at 1,500 kgs. per hectare, which will be attained in 13th years of plantation, even though the walnut fruit bearing shall start from 10th years onwards. During the first three years, i.e. 10th, 11th and 12th years from planting of walnut trees, average yield per hectare is assumed at 1000 kgs., 1200 kgs., and 1400 kgs. respectively. The price of walnut is assumed at Rs. 40 per kg from 10th to 15th years and thereafter

Table 9.7: Estimated Total Cost 'A', 'B', 'C' and Net Cost 'C' and Cost Benefit Ratio on per Hectare Walnut Production

Input-Component	*1-10 Years Age Group*	*11-50 Years Age Group*	*Total for the Whole Life of the Orchard*	*Average per Year*
	Rs. per hectare			
Costs:				
Family Human Labour	24,000	1,03,400	127400	2548
Hired Human Labour	6,000	40,000	46000	920
Manure	4,200	65,800	70000	1400
Fertilizers	14,700	1,38,000	152700	3054
Plant Protection Measures	5,400	47,500	52900	1058
Depreciation	10,000	40,000	50000	1000
Interest on Working Capital	3,000	20,000	23000	460
Cost A	67,300	4,54,700	5,22,000	10,440
Establishment Cost	31,000	—	31000	620
Rental Value of Land	37,500	1,50,000	187500	3750
Cost B	1,35,800	6,04,700	7,40,500	14,810
Cost C	1,35,800	6,04,700	7,40,500	14,810
Marketing Cost	—	31,830	31,830	637
Total Cost C (incl. Marketing cost)	1,35,800	6,36,530	7,72,330	15,447
Net Returns from Intercropping	13,100	66,800	79,900	1598
Net Cost C	1,22,700	5,69,730	6,92,430	13,849
Gross Income	6000	25,70,000	25,76,000	51,520
Net Return over				
Cost A	(-) 61,300	21,15,300	20,54,000	41,080
Cost B	(-) 1,29,800	19,65,300	18,35,500	36,710
Cost C	(-) 1,29,800	19,33,470	18,03,670	36,073
Benefit Cost Ratio Over	Ratio			
Cost A	—	4.65	3.93	3.93
Cost B	—	3.25	2.48	2.48
Cost C	—	3.20	2.43	2.43
Total Cost C (inc. Market Cost)	—	2.32	2.34	2.34
Net Cost C	—	2.59	2.60	2.60

Rs. 50 per kg. The total walnut production is estimated at 45,500 kg. in the whole life of the orchard. The per year weighted average walnut production for the bearing stage comes to about 1110 kgs. per hectare.

Total gross return based on the farm gate prices of walnut mentioned above is worked out at Rs. 25,70,000, in the whole life of the orchard with an average estimated at Rs 64,250 per year during the bearing stage. Total income from intercropping during the early phase of the walnut orchard is worked out at Rs. 6,000.

The net returns over cost 'A', 'B' and 'C' are estimated at Rs. 21,15,300, Rs. 19,65,300 and Rs. 19,33,470 per hectare, respectively, in the bearing stage of the proposed walnut orchards. On the basis of the assumed annual average yield and the farm-gate price of walnut during the bearing stage, discussed above, for whole life of the walnut orchard the net return over cost 'A', 'B' and 'C', as shown in Table 9.7, works out to be Rs. 20,54,000, Rs.18,35,500, Rs.18,03,670 per hectare, respectively. The net returns over total cost 'C' (including marketing cost) and net income from the intercrops comes to Rs. 18,83,570 per hectare per year.

The gross return from walnut orchard is worked not at Rs. 25,76,000 per hectare during the whole life of the orchard. The gross average return during the bearing stage comes to Rs. 64,250 per year. The highest gross return per hectare per year will accrue between the 16-30 years age of planted trees, when they will achieve their optimum yield of 1500 kgs. The average return during the bearing life of orchards on per rupee investment is estimated at Rs. 2.59 over net cost 'C'. However, on the basis of cost 'A', 'B', 'C' and total cost 'C', this ratio comes to Rs. 4.65, Rs. 3.25, Rs. 3.20 and Rs. 2.32.

The details of the net returns and benefit-cost ratio over various costs during the whole life of the orchard on per hectare walnut production are shown in Table 9.7. The average gross income of the walnut orchard on per hectare production is estimated at Rs. 51,520 per hectare per year. The net returns over cost 'A', 'B' and 'C' during the whole life of the orchard is worked out at Rs. 41,080, Rs. 36,710 and Rs. 36,073, per hectare per year. The benefit cost ratio over 'A', 'B' and 'C' is estimated at Rs. 3.93, Rs. 2.48, and Rs. 2.43 for the whole life of the walnut orchard. The benefit cost ratio over total cost 'C' and net cost 'C' comes to Rs. 2.34 and Rs. 2.60 respectively. These analyses clearly indicate that investment in the walnut growing is highly paying which proves the economic feasibility of the proposed walnut project in the fruit belting growing areas in Uttrakhand and Himachal Pradesh.

Appendix A describes various cost concepts used in the analysis presented above, while Appendix B contains economics of Walnut growing in Jammu and Kashmir state.

APPENDICES

APPENDIX A

Cost Concepts

The various cost concepts such as 'A', 'A1', 'B' and 'C' are used in the cost analysis as well as economics and project appraisal. These concepts are described below. The input items included under each category of cost are indicated below:

Cost 'A': The cost 'A' is a paid out cost which the farmer/orchardists actually pay from their pocket. This includes value of:

(i) hired human labour,
(ii) owned and hired bullock labour,
(iii) owned and hired machinery charges,
(iv) farm produced and purchased seed,
(v) owned and purchased manure,
(vi) fertilizers,
(vii) depreciation of implements and farm buildings.
(viii) irrigation charges,
(ix) land revenue and other taxes,
(x) interest on working capital,
(xi) miscellaneous expenses.

Cost 'A1' includes cost 'A' and the rent paid for leased-in land.

Cost 'B' includes cost 'A1' imputed rental value of owned land (less land revenue) and imputed interest on owned fixed capital (excluding land).

Cost 'C' includes cost 'B' and imputed value of family labour.

Total cost 'C' includes cost 'C' and the marketing cost.

Net cost 'C' is estimated by deducting the net return, received through the field crops grown in the orchards as a intercrops, from the total cost 'C' or including the net loss received from the intercrops.

APPENDIX B

Economic of Walnut Orchard in Jammu and Kashmir

The author has collected the following information from personal sources on the economic of walnut production in Jammu and Kashmir:

The normal practice in Jammu and Kashmir at present is that as soon as the tree starts bearing fruit, the farmer gives the contract for the year at a fixed price around April while the trees start bearing walnut in August/September. The middleman keeps his labour (Watch and ward: about 5 months, plucks the fruit, hulls (Removal of the upper soft portion); he gets the walnut cracked to recover the kernel from the shell.

The middleman takes the cracked Kernel or shell Walnut to the market where the Traders bid for the product and buy the same through the Commission agent. It is the responsibility of the trader to carry out various processes to sell the final product to the wholesaler in India or abroad. Accordingly economic costing has to be examined separately for each of the three stages.

Costing of Walnut Orchard Per Hectare Basis Comprising 100 Trees

Sl. No.	*Item*	*Cost in Rs.*
	Stage I - Former	**Rs. Per Hect (100 trees)**
1.	(a) Planting Material	4,000
	(b) Seed/seedling (intercropping)	
2	*Manuring and watering of walnut orchard First l0 years (@ Rs. 50 per tree per year for l0 years)*	*50,000*
	Stage II - After Fruiting: Middle Man	
3.	Assumed cost of I hectare walnut orchard paid to farmer	45,000
4.	Watch and ward l7 labourers @ Rs. 20 per day	61,200
5.	Plucking (one labourers plucks one tree in one day @ Rs. 20/labour/day	2,000
6.	Hulling—Either allowed to rot on the ground or put in running water (walnut camps)	
7.	Cracking—One person cracks about l0 Kg. @ Rs. 50 per day—150 labours per hectare	7,500
8.	Sub-total	1,15,700
	Stage III - Trade	**Rs. Per Kg.**
9.	Commission agent—Around Rs. 9/- per kg. Total cost shown is worked out by assuming 40 % recovery. The Kernels which come from Srinagar has l0% moisture	9.0
10	Drying cost Rs. 2/- per kg.	2.00
	Loss in weight 7% (on Rs. 200/- per kg).	14.00
	Loss in quality @ Rs. 4/- per kg.	4.00
	Stage I - Former	**Rs. Per Hect (100 trees)**
11.	Sieving -, Separating halves & brokens (halves still contains 30 percent broken	0.1

(*Contd.*)

(Contd.)

Sr. No.	*Item*	*Cost in Rs.*
	Stage I - Former	**Rs. Per Hect (100 trees)**
12	Sorting—Colour and size, wastage, removable of shell pieces or nay other foreign material	0.1
13.	Packing—Volume packing for kernels	
	5 Kgs. Packing	7.00
	1 Kg Packing	10.00
	500 gram packing	13.00
14.	Export—CIF export destination – transport form Jammu to Port, bank charges, terminal handling, shipping, agent's commission, freight, and Government levies	13.00
15	Farmer realization	40.00
16.	Exports price—mostly broken and off grades	170.00
17.	Domestic market realization—only premium—extra light halves	190-200

Total cost of the farmer is around Rs. 54000 per hectare. for 10 years till the plants start bearing fruit. Assuming an average yield of 1500 kg. per hectare, his cost would calculate to Rs. 36 per kg., over a period of 10 years. Really speaking, if planting material is supplied free, other costs of manuring and watering etc. are not of much significance. The current farm gate price is about Rs. 40/- per kg. And this price is likely to increase in the future. The walnut orchardists continue realizing all the money for a period of at last 50 years (even though trees in some areas in the State are l00 years olds) and at the end the period value of wood be another big gain. A tree planted today will bear fruit for two/three generations at practically no cost to the family. Another interesting feature of the walnut economy is that inter cropping of particularly medicinal aromatic plants is being carried out from day one. The loss of the farmer is, therefore, nil in this respect as well. There is no doubt that it involves heavy cost in establishing a new orchard and the grower has to wait for more than ten years before the walnut trees will start bearing fruits.

REFERENCE

1. T.N. Tewari: CM Uttranchal: Statement on his government achievements: in *Hindustan Times,* l2 April, 2005.

Part II
CASHEWNUTS

10

CASHEW—*ANACARDIUM OCCIDENTALE*

Introduction

The Cashew, *Anacardium occidentale* L., is a member of the Anacardiaceae family, allied with mango, pistachio, poison ivy and poison oak. The family contains 73 genera and about 600 species. *Anacardium* contains 8 species, native to tropical America, of which the cashew is by far the most important economically. *Anacardium excelsum*, known as Espavel, is a tall, riparian tree of the tropical dry forest, and produces a nut similar to the cashew, but is not cultivated.

The Anacardiaceae is known for having resinous bark and often-caustic oils in leaves, bark, and fruits. Several species cause some form of dermatitis in humans. It is, therefore, ironic that two of the most delectable nuts and one of the world's major fruit crops come from this family. The cashew industry, in particular, had to overcome severe limitations imposed by caustic oils in the nutshell. Today, the caustic substance that made plant domestication difficult is a valued by-product of cashew nut production.

The Importance of Cashew

Cashew is held in great esteem in many customs and cultures. Its value can be estimated from a question that appeared on the household census in Mozambique that asked whether the house owned any cashew trees.

Cashew is known by many names. In Mozambique, the Maconde tribe refer to it as the "Devil's Nut". It is offered at wedding ceremonies as a token of fertility and is considered by many to have aphrodisiac properties. The cashew tree and its products are known by the various names in different parts of the world[1].

Origin, History of Cultivation

Cashew is native of tropical America, probably originating in equatorial north-eastern Brazil, in the area between the Atlantic rain forest and the Amazon rain forest. The vegetation type of the region is dry forest, savannah woodland or thorn scrub, and includes the almost desert-like Caatinga. Cashew is sometimes referred to as a rainforest species and the nuts are found in products that have a rainforest friendly label or connotation. Although the trees will grow in tropical wet forests, they rarely produce many nuts, and production is far greater in areas with a distinct wet and dry season. It is thus widely cultivated in the tropics with commercial production concentrated in India, Brazil and East Africa. It has a high potential for development in West Africa, where plantations have been quickly developing recently. It occurs in warm and humid climates with 1000-2000 plus mm annual rainfall, from sea level to 1000 m altitude.[2]

The Portuguese introduced cashew to the west coast of India and east Africa in the 16th century, shortly after its discovery in 1578. It was planted in India initially to reduce erosion, and uses for the nut and pseudofruit, the cashew apple, were developed much later. The trees were well adapted to the region, and became naturalized. Trees also became naturalized in Central America and the Caribbean islands. Nut domestication predated the arrival of Europeans to Brazil, although international nut trade did not occur until the 1920s. Native South Americans discovered that roasting nuts in fire would remove the caustic oil, allowing the nut to be cracked and consumed without any ill effects. The roasting practice was either not known or not appreciated outside the native range, and as a result the cashew apple was the first product consumed, with the nut being discarded. Natives also knew of many medicinal uses for the apple juice, bark, and caustic seed oil that were later exploited by Europeans.

India developed more refined methods for removing the caustic shell oil, and this country is given credit for developing the modern nut industry. India led the world in cashew production for many years until just recently, when production in Vietnam surged about 3-fold in a few years. In its native Brazil, cashew nut production ranks in the top 5 of the world, and virtually all cashew apples and juice products come from this country. Preliminary data indicate the cashew nut production surpassed almond in 2003, and thus cashew now claims the title of No. 1 nut crop in the world.

Folklore, Medicinal Properties, Non-Food Usage

Medicinal uses of cashew bark, leaves, and apple juice are plentiful, and were well known prior to recorded history in the native region of Brazil.

Bark teas were used for diarrhea, and the caustic shell oil was used to treat skin infections, warts, worms, and botfly larvae beneath the skin. Teas and fruit juices are known to have antimicrobial, anti-inflammatory, astringent, diuretic, hypoglycemic, and other medicinal properties. The active principles are thought to be tannins, anacardic acid, and cardol. The red apples have higher tannin content than the yellow. Modern uses of shell oil and fruit juice include facial peels and scalp conditioners and shampoos. Clinical studies have documented the anti-inflammatory properties of tannins, and the antimicrobial properties of anacardic acid against several species, including *Escherichia coli* and *Helicobacter pylori.* Leaf extracts show hypoglycemic activity in rodents, and a reduction in artificially induced diabetes. Cashew apples contain up to 5 times the amount of vitamin C as citrus and strawberries, and higher amounts of some minerals than other fruits. Cashew nut shell liquid (CNSL) is sandwiched in a honeycomb layer of tissue between the two walls of the nutshell. Industrial uses include automobile brakes, adhesives, paints and varnishes, insecticides, electrical insulation, and anti-microbial. The shell oil is highly caustic, causing moderate to severe skin irritation. When wood is burned or nuts roasted, contact with or breathing of the fumes can cause skin and eye irritation, inflammation, and poisoning. In addition to CNSL, resins and gums from fruit stems or bark is used as a varnish for books, wood, and flooring to protect from ants and other home-invading insects.

Botanical Description

The cashew tree, *Anacardium occidentale L.*, belongs to the *Anacardiaceae* family of plants, which also includes the mango, the pistachio and the poison ivy. The tree is native to Brazil, but has spread to other parts of tropical South and Central America, Mexico and the West Indies. In the 1600s, Portuguese traders introduced the cashew tree into India and Africa to prevent soil erosion. It is now widely cultivated for its nuts and other products in the coastal regions of South Africa, Madagascar and Tanzania and in South Asia, from Sri Lanka to the Philippines.

The cashew tree is a tropical evergreen, resistant to drought, unexacting as to soil (although it prefers deep, sandy soil), which grows up to 12 metres high and has a symmetrical spread of up to approximately 25 metres. It has leathery oval leaves. Reddish flowers grow in clusters and the pear-shaped fruits, referred to as cashew apples, are red or yellowish in colour. At the end of each fruit is a kidney-shaped ovary, the nut, with a hard double shell (Fig. 10.1). Between the shell and nut is black caustic oil, which is difficult to remove and can be used in varnishes and plastics.

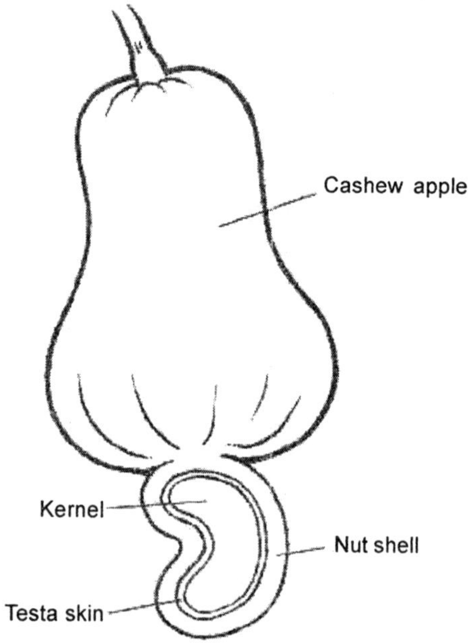

Fig. 10.1: Cashew Fruit

The cashew tree grows with a minimum of attention and is easily cultivated. It is usually found from sea level to an altitude of 1,000 metres (3,000 feet), in regions with annual rainfall as low as 500 mm (20 inches) and as high as 3,750 mm (150 inches). For maximum productivity, good soil and adequate moisture are essential. Optimum conditions include an annual rainfall of at least 889 mm (35 inches) and not more than 3,048 mm (120 inches). The tree has an extensive root system, which helps it to tolerate a wide range of moisture levels and soil types, but commercial production is only advisable in well-drained, sandy loam or red soils. The cashew tree can flourish in the sand of open beaches, but it grows poorly in heavy clay or limestone.

Most cashew trees start bearing fruit in the third or fourth year and are likely to reach their mature yield by the seventh year if conditions are favourable. The average yield of nuts of a mature tree is in the range of 7 to 11 kg per annum. Although the cashew tree is capable of living for 50 to 60 years, most trees produce nuts for about 15 to 20 years.

Plant

Cashew is evergreen shrub or a small to medium tree, generally single-trunked and spreading in habit, up to 40′ in height but generally 10-20′ in cultivation. In older trees, spread may be greater than height, with lower limbs bending to touch the ground. Leaves are thick, prominently veined, oval to spatulate in shape, 6-20 cm 4-15 cm, with blunt tips and entire margins. New foliage contains reddish pigment. Its leaves are simple, leathery. Inflorescence polygamous, with *ca.* 60 hermaphrodite and *ca.* 10 male flowers. Pedicel and receptacle are swollen and fleshy in fruit (cashew apple), thin-skinned, bright yellow, red or scarlet, eventually larger than fruit, 10-20 cm × 4-4 cm. Fruit is obliquely kidney-shaped, 2-3 cm × 1.5-2.5 cm, compressed, grayish-brown; and mesocarp oleaginous; seeds are kidney-shaped with thick cotyledons.[3]

The nutshell has an inner and outer wall, separated by a honeycomb tissue infused with caustic oil. Cracking the nuts fresh results in the oil contaminating the kernel, so nuts are roasted to drive off oils before they are shelled. The nuts are about 22-30 per cent kernel by weight, and kernels are difficult to extract whole compared to other tree nuts.

General Culture

Soils and Climate

Cashews are said to be tolerant of sandy, poor soils where many other crops will not thrive. Soil *p*H is generally on the acidic side, 4.5-6.5. Trees are strongly taprooted and drought tolerant if soils are deep, and can grow in areas receiving only 30-50″ of rain per year. Cashews are especially intolerant of poor soil drainage.

Climatically, cashews prefer hot, tropical lowlands (<3000 ft elevation) with a distinct dry season. High rainfall and humidity favour diseases that destroy the flowers and reduce fruit set. They have no cold tolerance whatsoever, requiring from even in extreme southern Florida.

Cashew tree is fast growing, is drought-resistant and easy to grow under cultivation by direct seeding of germinated seeds—seedlings do not transplant readily. Well-drained friable soils at low altitudes recommended, frost-free with an annual rainfall of 1,000-3,000 mm, preferably with a pronounced dry season of 3-4 months. Cashews can also be grown satisfactorily in semi-arid areas but can show erratic production as a result of relative small variations in rainfall. Trees with a productive life span of 30-40 years, normally bear fruit in third or fourth year and, under favourable conditions, attaining maximum production in *ca.* 7 years. The effectiveness of insect pollination is variable, for example, it has proved satisfactory in Tanzania, artificial pollination is required in India. Fruits mature in 2-3 months.

Botanical Characteristics

Varieties

Cashew seedlings present great variation in growth habit, quality of crop and yield. The tree cross-pollinates freely and this has further contributed to high variability although there are as yet very few named varieties of cashew trees. Generally a distinction is made only between those with yellow or red cashew apples. Tests have indicated that very large nuts usually have inferior kernels, low density and slow germination.[4]

Agricultural Practices, Propagation and Culture Sowing

The cashew tree is usually grown from seeds placed directly in the field, since seedlings do not transplant well due to their delicate root system. Seed nuts should be thoroughly dry, clean and free from insect or fungal attack. Seeds should be stored until the next rainy season before they are planted in the field, unless irrigation facilities are available, or seedlings are raised in polythene bags in a nursery where water is available. After a few months, stored nuts gradually lose their germination capacity.

Seeds should be water tested prior to planting those that sink should be chosen as they have a high success rate and tend to germinate quickly. Seeds should be planted at a depth of about 5 cm. The maximum depth at which a seed should be sown is about 10 cm, depending on the soil conditions. Two or three seeds should be planted together, stem end up, at a slight incline and covered with 5 to 8 cm of soil. Germination usually takes place in 15 to 20 days, although seeds of low density (i.e. those that float in water) may require as long as eight weeks to germinate. Using seeds of high density, from selected trees, considerably increases the chance that some of the seeds at one site will perform well. Two months after sprouting, the two weakest seedlings should be removed from the site, leaving only the strongest one to grow. By planting more than one seed, the occurrence of gaps in a plantation is reduced.[5]

In orchard practice, pits measuring from 30 cm × 30 cm × 30 cm to 60 cm × 60 cm × 60 cm are dug and left to weather for a month or two. They are then filled with soil, which has been mixed with rotting manure about two weeks before seeding. In loose soils of sufficient fertility, the root system of the seedlings develops so quickly that, when growing naturally, root lengths would exceed the size of the planting hole within a few months and therefore, in optimum growing conditions planting holes is not essential.

Advantages of Sowing

- The plant can develop its root system and especially its root tap quickly.
- It is the cheapest method of planting.
- It is the quickest method of planting as one person can plant 400 to 500 sites each day.

Disadvantages of Sowing

- Lower rate of germination.
- Danger of serious damage by animals.
- Less opportunity for selection of seedlings than when planting seedlings that are raised in plastic bags in the nursery.

Seasonal Planting

Cashew seeds should be sown or planted during the rainy season in areas that lack irrigation facilities. The best time for planting is during periods of regular rainfall, so that the soil does not dry out again. If the soil dries out before the germinated seeds have become securely rooted, they may die. The advantage of early planting is that it gives the seedlings more time to develop before the onset of the dry season.

In climates with irregular rainfall and short rainy seasons, the risk of germinated seedlings drying out can be reduced by pre-soaking the seeds before planting, deep sowing (5 to 10 cm) and covering the site with mulching material to reduce evaporation. The mulching material should be carefully selected and any weeds with mature seeds should be removed.

Raising Seedlings in a Nursery

Where it is necessary to raise seedlings in a nursery, the seeds should be sown in containers of a type that can be set in the ground and readily disintegrate. In Cuba, baskets of uva-grass or *cona brava* are used and cut away before setting the plant into the ground. In Jamaica, it has been found that nursery seedlings can be raised in the ground and transplanted with 90 per cent success, providing the plant is taken up with a good ball of soil and the top is cut back by one-third, when it is put into the field. It is recommended that the seedlings be transplanted within a week of emerging, to ensure that the transplantation is successful.[6] Seedlings can also be planted using plastic bags as containers. The seedlings should be lifted into their planting holes in the plastic bags, which are then carefully slit with a sharp knife and removed.

Layering

Ground Layering

The lowest branches of the cashew tree tend to trail on the ground at a distance of several metres from the trunk. Where branches touch the ground, spontaneous rooting may occur. Covering such branches with soil and keeping the area moist encourages rooting, a method which has been used in India for a long time. However, such layers cannot be easily transplanted to other places and the shape of the material tends to produce low trees of spreading habit. The number of layers that can be obtained in this way is also rather low.

Air-Layering

A strip of bark about 0.5 cm wide is removed from either a year-old branch or a pencil-thick shoot (about 1 cm diameter) of the current season, at about 20 to 30 cm from the growing point. The exposed wood is wrapped with twine to prevent the bark from growing over it during the healing process and covered thickly with moist moss, wood shavings or sand. It is then wrapped securely in a sheet of 100 to 150-gauge plastic and the ends are tied tightly to the branch with twine (Fig. 10.2).

After 20 to 30 days, callus is formed at the foot of the layer and 40 to 50 days later, small roots emerge from the callus tissue. After approximately 75 days, there should be adequate root formation (five or more well formed roots measuring 1.0 to 1.5 cm long) to separate the twig from the tree. The part of the twig below the layer is cut about halfway through. One week later, the cut is deepened and a few days later the layer can be removed and transplanted into plastic bags or other containers and hardened off before planting. If the layer is separated from the tree in one cut, the shock will be too great for it to survive. The whole process takes about two and a half months, although the time varies depending upon the period of the year when the layer is being prepared. Layers that are produced early in the rainy season have time to establish themselves and develop a large enough root system to survive the dry season.

Air-layering has been one of the most successful methods of

vegetative propagation in cashew. The method is rather laborious and the cost is relatively high, but the advantages of obtaining a plantation from high yielding, uniform material make these costs extremely worthwhile. A large disadvantage of this method, as with all methods of layering, is the relatively small number of layers that can be produced by one tree per year. It is estimated that from one tree, 80 to 120 successful layers can be obtained. In order to obtain sufficient material for a fairly large plantation, the first generation of air layers should be grown to maturity and only then, from many trees of the same quality, could sufficient material be obtained for later plantings.

Approach-Grafting or Inarching

The technique of approach grafting is relatively easy but labour intensive and like air-layering has to be done in the field. Seedlings to be grown as rootstocks are raised in containers. Once they are 8 to 9 months old, they are cut back to half their height and kept in grass baskets for a month in the shade until new shoots appear. A sheet of 100-gauge plastic to retain moisture replaces the basket and the seedling is joined to a year old branch of the same diameter on a selected tree as described below.

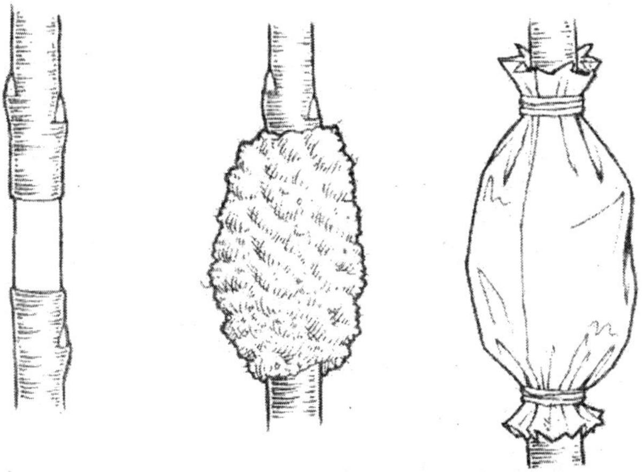

The stem is girdled to induce root formation above the cut.	The girdled stem is covered with damp moss.	Aluminium foil or plastic sheeting is wrapped around the moss and tied at both ends. This cover is removed 2 to 3 months after tying or when the roots can be seen.

Fig. 10.2: Air-Layering

From the stem of the seedling and from the shoot with which it will be united, strips of bark and inner wood, measuring about 5 to 8 cm in length, are removed (Fig. 10.3). Both cut surfaces, which should be of the same size, are bound together with twine and the join is firmly tied with string, binding the seedling stem and the shoot together. In 90 days the union should be complete and the grafted plant is gradually separated from the parent (Fig. 10.4). A "v" cut is made half way through the branch 2 cm below the graft and a similar cut is made in the rootstock 2 cm above the graft. Seven or eight days later the cuts are deepened and after a further period of four days the severing is completed. About 60 per cent take is expected.

Land Preparation

Cashew seedlings are very sensitive to competition with weeds, but in many areas, especially on sloping land, the vegetation should not be removed completely before planting because of the danger of water and wind erosion. In tropical countries with a marked dry season and where the rainy season tends to start with torrential rains, the danger of erosion increases if large areas of land have been cleared.

If the soil is very sandy and subject to strong winds, clearing the land may result in severe wind erosion, which is virtually impossible to stop. In these areas, the land should be cleared in strips, which are perpendicular to the direction of the prevailing winds. Once the cashew trees have developed to such an extent that their rows act as windbreaks, the remaining land can be cleared. Another important reason for leaving strips of natural vegetation is to ensure that the insect population required for pollinating the cashew flowers is maintained.

The removal of tree stumps is an expensive but essential part of the clearing process. The sprouting stumps need to be slashed each year as they compete with the cashew trees and prevent a good view between the rows.

Spacing

To promote maximum development and reduce competition for available moisture, it is recommended that the seedlings be planted 10 to 15 metres apart. This is considered to be the most productive spacing for mature trees. The average yield per hectare will be 700 to 1000 kg. but yields outside these limits are encountered. However, cashew trees are normally planted more closely, which results in overcrowding and they are often intermixed with other trees either in small orchards or in the wild.

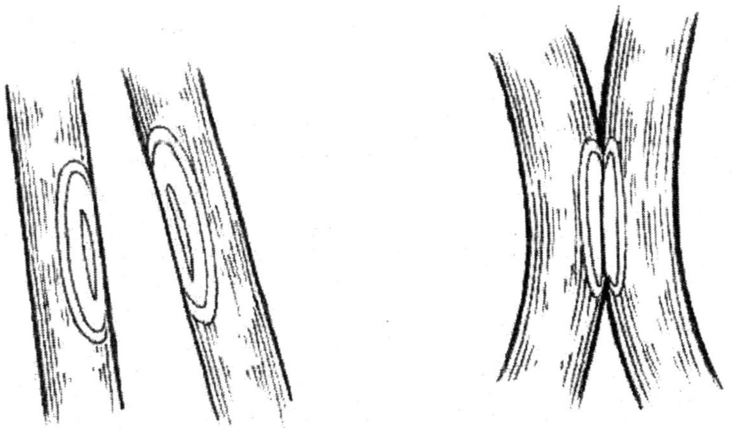

Two independent plants with stems approximately the same size. For example, seedling plants in containers and established plants.	Identical slices of wood and bark (2.5 to 5 cm long) are cut from both stems. The stems are placed closely together.

Fig. 10.3: Inarching

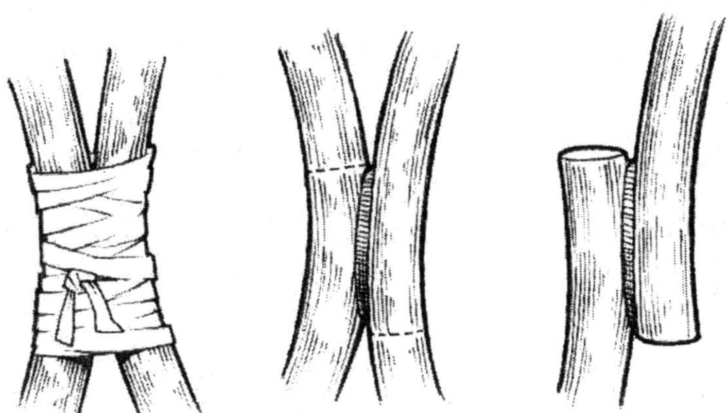

The stems are bound tightly together with string, tape or raffia.	After graft union heals, the stock plant is cut above the union and the scion is cut below the union.

Fig. 10.4: Inarching

Flowers

Cashew flowering is similar to the close relative mango: both male and perfect flowers are borne in the same inflorescence (polygamous). Individual flowers are 1/4″ across, with crimson petals, often striped longitudinally and reflexed. They are borne terminally on panicles, generally at the beginning of the dry season. Flowering may occur over several weeks, and it is not uncommon to have ripening fruit and flowers on the tree at the same time.

Fertilizer Use in Cashew

Smallholder farmers often grow cashew as a casual crop and as a result its fertilizer requirements are overlooked. Also the trees are long standing and are frequently grown in soils that are of poor quality. As each season passes, the soils become more depleted and productivity gradually declines. Yields of trees grown in this way are very much lower than the potential that could be gained if fertilizer was applied.

Experiments have demonstrated that regular application of the major plant nutrients (nitrogen, potassium and phosphorus) is beneficial for healthy trees and increased cashew yields. In addition, application of magnesium to cashew is beneficial.[7] Two separate mixtures of fertilizer, based on the combination of nitrogen (N), phosphorus (P) and potassium (K), have been recommended according to the growth stage of the plant. Young plant mixture is recommended for cashew plants from field planting up to 5 years of age. It contains N:P:K in the ratio of 4:3:2.

For 100 kg. of young plant fertilizer, the following is used:

Compound	*Weight (kg.)*
Urea	38
Rock phosphate	47
Muriate of potash	15

Adult Plant Mixture: This mixture is recommended for cashew plants from 5 years onwards. It contains N:P:K in the ratio of 4:3:4.

For 100 kg. of adult plant fertilizer, the following is used:

Compound	*Weight (kg.)*
Urea	33.5
Rock phosphate	41
Muriate of potash	25.5

Basal Dressing at Planting

Each planting hole should be filled with topsoil mixed with young plant mixture and dolomite and if possible with organic matter. In a hole that measures 60 cm × 60 cm × 60 cm, 250 kg. young plant mixture and 300 kg. Dolomite are required, plus 1 to 2 kg. organic manure. The soil is removed from the hole and mixed with the chemical fertilizer. The hole is then re-filled with the mixture of soil and fertilizer. This should take place before the rains to allow the soil and fertilizer time to settle before the seedlings are planted. If the seedlings are planted directly into the fertilizer, the tender roots may be damaged. To avoid damage, the seedlings should be planted at the beginning of the monsoon or four to six days after refilling the hole.

Rate of Fertilizer Application

During the early stages of growth, it is better if the amount is split and applied in two separate doses at the end of each season, to avoid the heavy rains.

Method of Fertilizer Application

Fertilizer should only be applied after weeding and cleaning the base of the individual trees within a 1 to 2-metre radius, to avoid the competition for nutrients from weeds. In the early years (up to 1.5 year), fertilizer should be broadcast close to the plant, covering an entire full circle up to a distance of 0.5 m from the base of the plant. The fertilizer should be lightly mixed with the soil. As the plant grows older, the area should be gradually extended to reach 1.0 m. Mulching the fertilized area is encouraged, as it is beneficial. With adult plants, the fertilizer should be broadcast in a circular strip (1 to 1.5 m wide) and about 0.5 to 1.0 m away from the base of the tree. The fertilizer should be lightly mixed with the soil.

Time after transplant (years)	*Young plant mixture (g/plant/year)*
1	200
2	350
3	500
4	650
5	800

After five years of age, the rate of application of adult mixture varies with the plant yield.

Average yield/plant (kg/plant/year)	*Adult mixture (kg/plant/year)*
<10	1
10 to 15	1.5
15 to 20	2.0
>20	2.5

Frequency and Timing of Application

Fertilizer should be applied to young plants twice a year at the end of each monsoon rain. It is applied to adult plants annually at the end of the monsoon rains and before flowering. The fertilizer should be applied when the soil is moist, at the end of the monsoon season so as to avoid the heavy rains. Application of fertilizer during the dry season is not advisable, as the nutrients require water to be dissolved and absorbed by the roots.

Pollination

Trees are at least partially self-fruitful, as lone trees can bear many fruit. One study of pollination biology showed no difference in pollen tube growth between self and cross-pollinated flowers, yet final yield was higher when cross-pollinated. In practice, cashews are often grown from seed, and cross-pollination in orchards must occur to a high degree. Another study showed no indication of self-incompatibility, but a low percentage of fruit set (1-18%). Fruit set is highest in flowers that open first, and suggests some type of apical dominance with respect to fruit set, as found in the close relative the pistachio. Fruit set is similar for female and perfect flowers. Various insects, even flies and ants provide pollination.

Fruit

The true botanical fruit is a nut, about 1" long, shaped like a small boxing glove, hanging below a fleshy, swollen peduncle called the cashew apple or pseudofruit. The cashew apple resembles a pear in shape and size, is juicy, fibrous, and astringent tasting. It has thin skin of either yellow or light red colour, and yellow flesh. Fruit are borne singly or in small clusters, and mature in 60-90 days. The nut develops first, followed by the rapid swelling of the cashew apple in the last few weeks.

Diseases

Cashew seedlings can be affected by a number of different diseases. The fungus, *Colletotrichum gloeosporioides,* is one of the most common pathogens in cashew. Initial symptoms show the development of reddish-brown, shiny, water-soaked lesions, followed by resin oozing out onto the affected parts. As the lesions grow, the affected shoots and inflorescences are killed and the leaves become crumpled. The affected nuts and apples decay and shrivel and the flowers turn black and fall off. The trees can be sprayed with various fungicides, including Bordeaux mixture, to control the fungus.

Several diseases that result in the terminal twigs dying off are grouped under the name "die-back" or "pink disease" which is produced by *Glocosporium.* There may be associated pitting of the surface of the nut. This serious disease requires the affected branches to be pruned and sprayed with a 1 per cent Bordeaux mixture or other copper-based fungicides.

Characteristic symptoms of other infections which attack cashew include wilting and withering; the yellowing of the lower leaves; the seedlings turning pale and showing water-soaked girdles of darkened tissue around the stems; or the rotting of the underground portion of the stem. Powdery mildew may appear on young leaves and inflorescences during dry weather.

Pests

Insect pests are a major source of crop loss in all cashew-growing areas of the world. More than 60 species of insects attack the crop during its different stages of growth. These pests include sap-sucking bugs, leaf-chewing caterpillars, beetles, aphids, scales, thrips and some mites. They can cause considerable damage to the tree and the crop by bringing about the death of the floral-flushing shoots, the early abortion of young nuts and loss of yield.

The adult weevil, or borer, is dark grey in colour and about 2 cm long. The larva has a curled whitish body with wrinkled skin and dark brown head. The eggs are laid singly in small holes made by the female in the bark of the trunk or the main branches of the cashew tree. After hatching, the larvae tunnel down just beneath the bark, eating the sapwood. The grubs should be removed as soon as they are detected because they cause gum leakage and will eventually kill the tree. To control the borer, all heavily infested trees should be cut down and the bark should be cut away in places that show signs of weevil attack. Once the wood has dried out sufficiently, it should be burned, to kill all the remaining larvae and eggs. Alternatively, the base of the tree can be sprayed with Malathion and the boreholes filled with the spray.

The tea mosquito bug (*Helopeltis antonii* Sign.) is a common pest found in Sri Lanka, causing up to 30 per cent loss of yield. The adults and nymphs of the species feed on tender shoots and floral branches, as well as on the developing nuts and apples, by piercing and sucking the sap.[8] *Helopeltis* populations increase during the rainy season, reaching a maximum at the end of the rainy season and the beginning of the dry season. This coincides with the emergence of a new flush. Insecticide application should be started when the new flush emerges. The damage caused by *Helopeltis* is of two types. Primary damage, which is seen as brown lesions surrounding the feeding punctures, causes affected leaves and young shoots to turn brown, wither and die. Secondary damage occurs when the puncture holes are infected by secondary pathogens and the whole stem or branch dies back or is affected by blight.

Helopeltis can be controlled by chemical spray. Three applications of a 0.1 per cent mixture of Carbaryl are recommended at flushing, onset of flowering and the fruiting season. However, Carbaryl is indiscriminate and will kill other beneficial insects. Special attention must be paid to the second spray at the onset of flowering, to minimize the effect of insecticide on pollinators. The optimum time to spray is between 0600 hours and 0800 hours and again between 1600 hours and 1900 hours, when the *Helopeltis* bug is active.

A copper fungicide or Bordeaux mixture (1 per cent) can be used to control inflorescence dieback, which may occur. *Helopeltis* damage can be limited by careful cultural practices. The plantation should be kept weed-free to remove alternative hosts of the bug. Removal of non-productive and diseased branches from the trees allows for improved air circulation and solar radiation within the crop canopy and can then reduce the humidity of the canopy. This in turn can reduce the damage caused by the pest.

Thrips are known in many countries to attack cashew leaves, causing a symptom called "silvery leaves". They suck the leaf juices and leave a "scorched" area. Heavy attacks will stunt the growth of young plants but can be controlled by spraying with a 0.05 per cent solution of Malathion.

The caterpillar of the leaf miner attacks young plants by tunnelling through new leaf tissues. The first signs are winding trails on the leaves.

Later the infestation shows as patches of white blisters. The adult is a tiny, silvery-grey moth. The larvae appear red when they are fully-grown and are about 6 mm long. Affected trees should be sprayed with a 0.06 per cent solution of "Folidol E.605" (30 ml in 50 litres of water).

A sporadic leaf-eating caterpillar, which has poisonous stinging hairs, sometimes occurs in swarms and defoliates the cashew tree. It pupates in silky cocoons and the adult moth is large and reddish-brown in colour.

The mealy bug attacks the cashew inflorescence but can be controlled by spraying with a 0.06 per cent solution of "Folidol E.605" (30 ml in 50 litres of water). Among the other pests are leaf webbers, flea beetles, spider mites and scales.

Rodents, such as rats, squirrels and porcupines, may cause serious damage to cashew seedlings, particularly when they emerge above the ground. Cashew apples are sometimes attacked by fruit flies. Monkeys are partial to ripe apples and can cause damage to the cashew trees whilst foraging for the fruit. Bats and parrots also eat cashew apples.

Harvesting

The harvesting and processing of cashew is very labour intensive. After producing clusters of flowers, cashews produce the edible apple and also a nut encased in a heavy shell, which is the true cashew fruit. The cashew tree flowers for two or three months and fruit mature about two months after the bloom. The cashew nut forms first at the end of the stem. Subsequently, the stem swells to form the "apple" with the nut attached externally.

The cashew nut is 2.5 to 4.0 cm (1.0 to 1.5 inches) long and kidney shaped. Its shell is about 5 mm thick, with a soft leathery outer skin and a thin hard inner skin. When fully ripe, it falls to the ground. Harvesting generally involves collecting the nuts once they have dropped to the ground after maturing. Workers scour the area and detach the nut from the fruit. For the nuts to be easily traced, the surface under the tree has to be free from weeds. In some places, the whole area under the tree is swept free of dry leaves. The nuts are generally collected in baskets or sacks. Cashew fruit are generally left to fall to the ground before being collected, as this is an indication that the kernel is mature. If fruit are picked from the trees, the cashew apple will be ripe, but the kernel will still be immature.

The quantity of nuts, which can be harvested, depends upon the yield of the trees. Where many nuts fall together, much less time is required for walking in search of them. On average, each individual can harvest a maximum of 50 kg per day. A very limited number of nuts fall at the beginning of the production season. A peak in the number of nuts falling is gradually attained and production slowly declines. Although activities are labour intensive and time consuming, they are not heavy and women and children can help.

In very dry climates where the topsoil remains dry overnight, nuts can be left under the trees for several weeks without their quality being affected. However, where humidity of the air or soil causes moisture and dew formation, the nuts should be repead at least twice a week. This is not very economical, unless it is carried out on smallholdings with relatively high labour intensity, as there will not be adequate numbers of nuts to harvest sufficient quantities to achieve collection levels of 50 kg per day.[9]

Apples to be used for processing into products such as jam or juices should be picked from the tree before they fall naturally. On falling to the ground, apples may become damaged. Once damaged, the apples may ferment and deteriorate quite rapidly. The riper the apple, the sweeter the taste. It is, therefore, recommended that the apple be picked, as it is about to fall. At this stage the nut is fully-grown for about two weeks and is ripe and ready for harvest.

Apples, which are not within reach of the picker's hands, can be harvested using a small basket or sack attached to a ring at the end of a long stick. Fully ripe apples will drop into the sack when the tree is shaken. Apples that have not matured completely should be cut off with a small knife attached to the stick. The nuts must remain attached to the apple, since some juice may be lost on their removal.

The cashew apple will only keep for 24 hours after it has been picked. Transporting large quantities of apples is difficult for this reason. When stacked in layers, apples may burst and lose their juice because of the weight on top of them.

Drying of the Raw Material

Cashew nuts are dried in the sun for two reasons:

- To reduce the moisture content of the nut.
- To mature the seed in the infrared and ultra-violet rays of the sun.

Cashewnuts should keep for 12 months or more, provided that they are dried to moisture content of eight per cent or below, packed in sealed polythene bags and stored under dry conditions. The moisture content of cashewnuts at harvest is dependent on climatic conditions, moisture content of the soil, on which the nuts have fallen, weed growth density under the tree and the time between nut fall and harvest. High moisture content may cause deterioration of the kernel due to mould or bacterial attack or enzyme action. Drying the nuts immediately after harvesting is essential in preserving their quality, but this process is often neglected.

Sun drying of cashew nuts can be done on specially prepared drying floors or mats made of bamboo or palm leaves. The drying areas should be smooth and slightly sloping, so as to allow rainwater to run off. The cashewnut layer on the drying floor should not be thicker than 10 cm, thus allowing for about 60 kg of nuts per square metre. The nuts should be constantly raked in order to ensure that they all receive the same benefit of the sun's rays and therefore they are dried evenly. The nuts should be heaped together and covered in the evenings. If the nuts are heaped while still warm, they will continue to dry under the cover of a tarpaulin. The nuts should be checked the following morning to ascertain the need for further drying.

Dried nuts should make a rattling sound when falling. Drying may take between one and three days depending upon local climatic conditions. As soon as the nuts are dry, they should be stored and protected from rain.

Storage

Technical requirements for storage are dependent on weather conditions. As cashew nuts are usually produced in climates with a long dry season, simple buildings with concrete floors and walls and roofs of corrugated metal, should provide adequate storage.

Certain prerequisites must be satisfied to ensure safe storage:

1. a waterproof, dry floor;
2. a firm and secure roof;
3. openings in the wall must be protected in order to prevent water from entering the room;
4. headroom must be adequate to allow the bags in a stack to be moved around if large quantities;
5. the store should be easily inspected: there must be sufficient clearance between the wall and the bags, to allow individuals to walk around and check the condition of the stack;
6. the stack must be placed on a raised wooden platform, in order to prevent moisture from being drawn from the floor to the nuts.

Infestation of Harvested Nuts

Raw cashew nuts, stored in sacks, sometimes in the open awaiting shipment and frequently without protection from rain, are subject to infestation through the stem-end. This may go undetected until damage has progressed to the point of heavy loss. Infestation also occurs in the shelled kernels at various stages of handling.

Post-Harvest Handling

The nut is encased in a rock hard shell that is virtually impossible to penetrate after harvest. In order to extract the nut, the whole shell is soaked in water, softened by steaming and carefully air-dried to the final moisture content (9 per cent). Each nut is hand massaged and cracked via a manual process that entails putting the nut against one sharp blade and bringing another blade, which is on a foot powered lever, through the outer shell. The blade on the foot lever is raised by an enthusiastic stomp allowing the outer shell to separate from the nut. The nut inside is carefully picked out of the outer shell using a nut pick.

Processing

Traditionally experienced semi-skilled workers performed the various processing operations manually. This is still the case in India, which is the world's largest producer of cashew kernels. Since the 1960s, various mechanized pieces of equipment have been developed and are available in several countries. The processes that have been mechanized are roasting, cashew nut shell liquid extraction and shelling. For the most part, the cleaning of raw materials and sizing and kernel grading have remained labour intensive manual operations.

There are significant differences in investment requirements, labour skills, health requirements and levels of efficiency between the Indian manual technology and the medium to large-scale mechanical and semi-mechanical operations. In general the Indian processing system involves lower investment and variable costs and achieves far greater efficiency in terms of kernel material yield and the proportion of whole kernels extracted. However, this system requires large numbers of experienced workers who work at unhealthy levels of exposure to CNSL. The mechanized systems are more vulnerable to breakdown due to shortage of spare parts, require large volumes of nuts for efficient operation and operate well below manufacture specifications when strict grading and sizing activities are not in place prior to shelling.[10]

Opportunities for Small-Scale Processors

Cashew processing is a very competitive but also a potentially lucrative activity that can and should be exploited by more small-scale processors. African countries that are in the process of re-building their local cashew processing industry would be well advised to follow the Indian example of small-scale, mainly manual processing operations. There are several good reasons why small-scale producers and processors should get involved in cashew processing, including the following:

- Cashew kernels are a high value luxury commodity with sales growing steadily at an annual rate of 7 per cent, with every expectation that the market will remain strong.
- There is substantial potential to exploit cashew by-products, such as cashew butter, from broken nuts, CNSL for industrial and medicinal purposes and the juice of the cashew apple that can be processed further.
- Cashew is a good crop for small holder farmers. In Mozambique cashew is considered by small holder farmers to be one of their most lucrative crops. It requires few inputs and harvesting does not coincide with peak labour demands for other food crops.[11]
- Thus cashew has the potential to increase the incomes of poor producers, to create employment opportunities during harvesting and processing and to increase exports. However, as with all small-scale processing operations, cashew processing is not without risk or problems. In order for the small-scale processor to succeed, there are certain constraints, which also need to be considered.
- Cashew production is very weather dependent so supply is variable. World prices, although stable on average, are highly volatile in the short-term.
- Luxury goods must be of high quality. In order to compete directly in the world market, a high level of standards, branding and marketing are required.
- Exploitation of by-products requires new technology, which may be expensive or difficult to obtain.
- Production volumes must be sufficient to ensure a consistent supply of raw material.

These constraints are not, however, insurmountable. With good committed support from local governments, introduction of policies that favour rather than hinder the small-scale entrepreneur and back-up from relevant development organizations, cashew processing can be an attractive and viable option for the small-scale processor.

The Way Ahead

Small-scale producers and processors need to establish more direct relationships with the European food industry, which packs and markets cashewnuts. Currently middlemen, brokers and wholesalers who control prices, quality requirements and the volumes sold dominate the world purchasing circuits.[12] Development organizations can be instrumental in bridging the gap between the small-scale processor and the buyer, thus helping the former to succeed. They can offer a range of support services, including the following:

- training in quality assurance and control,
- providing information on available equipment and machinery,
- advice on standards and export legislation,
- providing information on packaging,
- providing access to packaging materials and suppliers,
- advice on marketing.

One area that deserves special attention is the development of value-added products for export. Most exports are in the form of plain kernels in bulk, which are imported by large wholesalers in the consuming countries. These are then re-packaged, either as they are, or after roasting and salting and sold to retailers. Opportunities exist for processors to penetrate these markets, however, they are fraught with difficulties, such as pricing and competition from existing products. The key to opening up new markets or expanding the existing ones is to supply the best quality products at competitive and steady prices. Particular attention to providing goods of consistently high quality is vital and cannot be over-stressed. This requires inputs from various stakeholders in the food processing chain and is a service that can be provided by government and non-government organizations interested in supporting the small-scale food processor.

REFERENCES

1. Andrighetti, L. Bassi, G.F. Capella, P. de Logu, A.M. Deolalikar, A.B. Haeusler, G. Malorgio, G.A. Franca, F.M.C. Rivoira, G. Vannini, L. and Deserti R. (1989). *The World Cashew Economy*, L. Inchiostroblu, Italy.

2. FAO (1982). *Fruit-bearing forest frees*: Forestry Paper No. 34, FAO, Rome: and ITC (1993): Tropical Tree Nuts. Export Opportunities for the Andean Region: International Trade Centre: UNCTAD/GATT, Geneva.
3. Purseglove, J.W. (1987). *Tropical Crops: Dicotyledons.* Longman Scientific and Technical, Harlow, Essex, and Kokwaro, J.O. (1986): *Flora of Tropical East Africa*: *Anacardiaceae*. A.A. Balkema, Rotterdam.
4. Caribbean Technological Consultancy Services (CTCS) Network (1993). *Information Package on Cultivation, Processing and Marketing of Cashews*, St. Michael, Barbados, Caribbean Technological Consultancy Services Network.
5. Ohler, J.G. (1979). *Cashew. Amsterdam*, Department of Agricultural Research.
6. Caribbean Technological Consultancy Services Network, 1993, *op. cit.*
7. Fernandopulle, M.N. (2000). Fertilizer Use in Cashew. *Cashew*: *Bulletin*, 3(1): 1-6.
8. Ranaweera, B. (2000). *Management of Tea Mosquito Bug (Helopeltis antonii) in cashew. Cashew Bulletin*, 3(1): 1-6.
9. Ohler, J.G. (1979). *Cashew. Amsterdam*, Department of Agricultural Research.
10. Jaffee, S. and Morton, J. (1995). *Marketing Africa's High Value Foods: Comparative Economics of an Emergent Private Sector*. The World Bank, Washington, USA.
11. Hanlon, J. (2000). Power without responsibility: the World Bank and Mozambican Cashewnuts. *Review of African Political Economy*, 27(83).
12. Partnership, (1995). Cashew Nuts: Potential in Africa, *Partnership* 18, March/April, 1995.

11

WORLD CASHEWNUT ECONOMY

Introduction

The cashew industry ranks third in the world production of edible nuts with world production in 2005 estimated at about 2.34 million tonnes of nuts-in-shell and an estimated value in excess of US$ 2.5 billion. India and Brazil are the major cashew exporters, with 40 per cent and 31 per cent respectively of world market share. The major importers are the United States (50 per cent), the Netherlands (10 per cent), Germany (4 per cent), Japan (3 per cent) and the United Kingdom (6 per cent).

Cashew kernels are ranked as either the second or third most expensive nut traded in the world. Macadamia nuts are priced higher and pecan nuts can be more costly, if the harvest is poor.

Global Cashew Production

In the early 1970s, the majority of global cashew production (68 per cent of total) took place in African countries, in particular, Mozambique and Tanzania. Over the following thirty years, production trends shifted, with Asian countries emerging as the world leaders in cashew production. In 2002 Vietnam overtook India and since then it became the leading cashew nut producing country. Currently, India commands about 40 per cent of the international cashew market. Other Asian countries, particularly Indonesia, have also expanded their production capacities. Currently, the five main cashew-producing countries are Vietnam, India, Nigeria, Brazil, and Indonesia.

World production of cashew nuts grew rapidly during the 1950s and 1960s, reaching a peak of 624,000 tonnes of raw nuts in 1973. Three countries, India, Mozambique and Tanzania accounted for the majority of this production, while smaller industries had developed in Vietnam, Brazil, Kenya and several other African countries. In 1975 and 1976, there was a sharp decline in world production, which continued into the 1980s. This decline was largely due to decreased production in Mozambique and Tanzania, since production in India during that period remained static.[1] Trends in global and regional production over the last forty-six years are summarized in Annex Table 11.1. During the late 1980s and continuing into the 1990s, production picked up and continued to increase gradually. In 2005, world cashew production exceeded 2.34 million tonnes. Asian and African countries produced 1.46 million and 0.62 million tonnes respectively.

Cashew Production in Africa

Overall cashew production in Africa steadily increased during the 1950s and 1960s, until the mid-1970s when that continent was the prime producer of cashew nuts. The year 1975 was the start of a fifteen-year period of decline in production throughout the continent due to combination boiological, agronomic and socio-political factors. The decline in prices at the end of the 1970s, combined with lower levels of production, dissuaded many farmers from improving cultivation techniques and replanting their cashew plantations.[2]

Since the early 1990s, production has recovered and has continued to increase steadily over the last decade and half. In 2000, Africa accounted for about 38 per cent of world cashew production. However since then its share in the global output has declined and in 2005 the region accounted for 26.4 per cent of world production. The decline in its share reflects a continued sharp increase in Asian countries' production during the last five years, especially in Viet Nam and Indonesia, which boosted up considerably the world production.

Historically, Mozambique and Tanzania were the main cashew-producing countries in Africa, with smaller amounts produced in a number of other countries. During the last five years Nigeria has emerged as a leading producer of cashew nuts in Africa (Tables 11.1 and 11.2).

CASHEW PRODUCTION IN ASIA

Cashew production in Asia currently accounts for about 63 per cent of global production. It has held this prime position for almost twenty years. African countries previously dominated the world cashew market, with Asian cashews accounting for about 30 per cent of the world total.

Table 11.1: Cashew Production in African Countries from 1961 to 2005

(Metric Tonnes)

Country	*2005*	*2000*	*1995*	*1990*	*1985*	*1980*	*1975*	*1970*	*1965*	*1961*
Angola	1,100	1100	900	1,200	1,200	1,200	1,400	1,300	1,000	1,000
Benin	40,000	40,00	15,000	3,000	1,200	1,086	345	627	50	50
Burkina Faso	3,500	3,500	2,500	1,074	645	200				
Cote d Ivoire	90,000	78,000	39,400	7,000	3,500	600	450	300	400	400
Ghana	7,500	7,500	1,000	500						
Guinea-Bissau	81,000	72,725	37,000	30,000	13,000	3,500	2,500	2,500	2,000	2,000
Kenya	10,000	15,500	5,000	7,000	8,500	15,000	21,600	22,200	9,000	3,000
Madagascar	6,500	6,500	6,500	5,300	4,000	3,400	2,900	2,400	1,900	1,600
Mozambique	58,000	57,894	33,423	22,524	25,000	71,100	188,000	184,000	136,000	107,000
Nigeria	213,000	184,000	95,000	30,000	25,000	25,000	25,000	25,000	22,000	7,000
Senegal	4,500	7,000	1,500	500						
Tanzania	100,000	121,200	63,400	17,060	32,750	41,416	115,840	107,445	76,000	50,000
Togo	300	150	750	587						
Total Africa	616,600	593,119	301,373	125,745	114,795	162,502	358,035	345,772	248,350	172,050

Source: FAO STAT Data Base, March, 2006.

Table 11.2: Leading African Producers of Cashew: Percentage of African and Global Production (1961 to 2005)

(In Metric Tonnes)

Year	*2005*	*2000*	*1995*	*1990*	*1985*	*1980*	*1975*	*1970*	*1965*	*1961*
World	2337358	1662011	1127814	606681	520973	464215	563795	511939	386303	287535
Total Africa	618 600	593119	301373	125745	114795	162502	358035	345772	248350	172050
Mozambique	58000	57,894	33423	22524	25000	71100	188000	184000	136000	107000
% of Africa	9.4	9.8	11.1	17.9	21.8	43.8	52.5	53.2	54.8	62.2
% of World	2.5	3.5	3.0	3.7	4.8	15.3	33.3	35.9	35.2	37.2
Tanzania	100000	121200	63400	17060	32750	41416	115840	107445	76000	50000
% Africa	16.2	20.4	21.0	13.6	28.5	25.5	32.4	31.1	30.6	29.1
% Total	4.3	7.3	5.6	2.8	6.3	8.9	20.5	21.0	19.7	17.4
Nigeria	213000	184000	95000	30000	25000	25000	25000	25000	22000	7000
% Africa	34.4	31.0	31.5	23.9	21.8	15.4	7.0	7.2	8.9	4.1
% Total	9.1	11.1	8.4	4.9	4.8	5.4	4.4	4.9	5.7	2.4

Source: FAO STAT Database, March 2006.

India has long been the main cashew producer in Asia, accounting for between 70 and 90 per cent of total Asian production (Table 11.3). During the 1970s and 1980s when African production was on the decline, production in India continued to grow at a steady rate. In recent years production in Viet Nam has expanded considerably and according to the FAO data, in 2002 it became the leading cashew producing country in the world. It accounts for 36 per cent of the global output. Consequently, India's now accounts for only 20 per cent of world cashew production.

During the 1990s, Indonesia and Vietnam emerged as important cashew producing countries within Asia, helping to boost Asia's position as a prime producer. Increased production in these two countries is responsible for reducing India's share of total Asian production from 90 per cent at its peak in the early 1970s to just over 32 per cent today. Production in Thailand, Malaysia and Sri Lanka has increased steadily over the past forty years.

Production in India

For a long time, cashew was not considered to be a serious crop in India. Rather it was grown as a wild crop on land that was unsuitable for other crops. It was frequently grown as a source of fuel or to prevent soil erosion rather than as a cash crop. In India, cashew is produced in the coastal regions of the States of Kerala, Karnataka, Goa, Maharashtra, Andhra Pradesh, Orissa and Tamil Nadu. The State of Kerala accounts for approximately 50 per cent of cashew production in India. Kerala has a centralized procurement system and families do much of the processing on an outworker basis. Although Kerala only accounts for about 25 per cent of the total area under cashew, yields in this state are relatively high when compared to those in other states. Estimated cashew productivity in Kerala is 900 to 950 kg raw cashew nuts per hectare, which is almost double that in the rest of India.

Cashew is predominantly a smallholder crop in India. Small-scale farmers grow about 70 per cent of cashews. The remaining 30 per cent are grown under re-forestation programmes. Cashew yields in India average around 1.5 kg of nuts per tree. In Kerala average cashew yields are about 5 kg per tree, which is substantially less than the potential yield of 10 to 15 kg per tree under optimum conditions. The poor quality of raw cashews has been a long-term problem for the cashew processing industry in India. The main reasons for poor quality are incorrect harvesting techniques, unsatisfactory drying of raw nuts and inadequate storage of dried nuts.

Table 11.3: Cashew Production (tonnes) in Asian Countries from 1961 to 2005

(*In Metric Tonnes*)

Country	*2005*	*2000*	*1995*	*1990*	*1985*	*1980*	*1975*	*1970*	*1965*	*1961*
Bangladesh	10	10	20	80	60	20	10			
China	900	2,000	923	1,000	6,500	6,000	4,800	3,250	2,400	2,000
India	460,000	440,000	321,640	285,590	221,330	180,266	144,254	123,319	100,000	85,000
Indonesia	122,000	118,300	74,995	29,907	21,114	9,074	9,122			
Malaysia	13,000	13,000	13,000	10,000	6,000	5,200	11,200	4,300	3,600	3,600
Sri Lanka	6,200	4,610	13,000	10,000	9,500	8,260	4,330	2,770	8,800	4,240
Thailand	24,000	22,000	18,000	11,850	9,500	4,500	1,800	1,300	800	500
Vietnam	827,000	270,400	52,800	26,000	9,000	5,600	3,500	2,100	700	700
Total Asia	1,453,110	922,399	494,378	374,427	283,004	218,920	179,016	137,039	116,300	96,040

Source: FAO, STAT Database: March 2006.

The number of cashew proccssing units in India has increased rapidly over the last four decades, from 170 in 1959 to over 700 today. Over two-thirds of the processing units are in the State of Kerala, while the remainder are scattered throughout the other producing states. Together these units have a processing capacity of over 800,000 tonnes per year and provide employment to over 500,000 people, 95 per cent of whom are women. Industry is dominated by small-scale, single-owner or family-owned businesses.

Cashew has gained significant economic and social importance in India as a major foreign exchange earner. In 1992 to 1993, India exported 53,436 tonnes of cashew kernels valued at US$160 million. In the same year, a further US $0.8 million was generated through the sale of 4,258 tonnes of cashew nut shell liquid.

In the 1980s and 1990s, India rapidly expanded its cashew production, to become the world's largest producer and now accounts for about 20 per cent of global production. Processing capacity increased more rapidly than production, so Indian imports of raw nuts increased rapidly, reaching 203,000 tonnes in 1996 (of which 41 per cent originated from Tanzania and 13 per cent from Mozambique). In recent years, an increasing number of non-African countries have also supplied raw nuts to India. The decline in African production in the 1970s and 1980s resulted in a rapid decline in imports into India. Alternative supplies of raw nuts were obtained from Vietnam. According to India's 8th Five Years Plan, domestic cashew production was to match processing capacity by the year 2000. However, India continues to import raw cashewnut.

The beginnings of India's international trade in cashews date back to after the First World War. This trade expanded rapidly in the 1920s with the introduction of improved packaging materials for long distance transit. By the start of Second World War, cashew nuts had become the second most important traded dessert nut after almonds and have remained in this position for the last fifty years.[3]

Cashew is the only major plantation crop that is not regulated by an autonomous board. Other plantation crops, such as tea, coffee, cardamom and rubber all have efficient and autonomous boards and as a result have experienced much faster growth in productivity than cashew. Cashew is one of the most neglected plantation crops in India despite its status as a major source of foreign exchange. The international price of Indian cashew kernels has fluctuated widely over the last decade.

Production in Indonesia

Indonesia currently ranks the third largest producer of cashew in Asia. Production has picked up over the decade and half, increasing from 30,000 tonnes in 1990 to 122,000 tonnes in 2005. Some of the Indonesian production is exported to India for processing.

Production in Vietnam

Cashew production in Vietnam has increased quite rapidly over the last decade. Vietnam now accounts for about 57 per cent of total Asian production and is now the largest cashew producing country in Asia. Previously, mostof the raw nuts were exported to India for processing, to make good the shortfall that India experienced when East African supplies dried up. Now, however, Vietnam has about 150 processing plants, with a capacity of 800,000 tonnes of raw nuts. Vietnam has now become an importer of raw nuts from East and West Africa and South East Asia.

Production in Sri Lanka

Sri Lanka has a very small share (around 4 per cent) of the Asian cashew production market. Some of the cashews are processed locally, while the remainders are exported to India for processing.

Production in Australia

Cashew is a crop with good potential for the Australian tropics, particularly in the Northern Territory and Queensland, where agro-climatic conditions are suitable for its production. Australia currently produces about 100 tonnes and imports about 5,000 tonnes of cashew a year. There is potential therefore to increase production to meet domestic demand. The cashew industry in Australia is at an infant stage, with three plantations—one in north Queensland and two in the Northern Territory. Expansion of the industry will necessitate a good supply of high yielding plants.

The Australian government is supporting a large cashew research programme [at the Commonwealth Scientific and Industrial Research Organization (CSIRO)] to develop high yielding hybrids adapted to the local conditions. Australia has no shelling facilities. The raw nut is exported to China for shelling and returned to Australia where it is sold either as raw kernel or further processed into value added goods such as chocolate coated, salted or honey coated nuts.[4]

CASHEW PRODUCTION IN SOUTH AND CENTRAL AMERICA

Brazil is the main cashew producing country in the South and Central American continent. A handful of Central American countries also produce minor quantities of cashewnuts (Table 11.4). Brazil currently holds third place in global production of cashew, after Vietnam and India. Overall, production has tended to increase gradually over the last thirty years, but at times (1988 and 1983 especially) has plummeted, mainly due to periods of drought. Brazil recognized the economic value of cashew cultivation at the beginning of the Second World War, when there was a considerable demand for cashewnut shell liquid for the North American war effort. The expansion of cashew areas began at the end of the 1960s through government incentives and funding. This increase in production allowed Brazil to enter the international market, although actual yields of the crop were low. Cashew cultivation, of which 99 per cent is in the north of the country, is of great economic importance for the states of Ceara, Piaui and Rio Grande de Norte, which are some of the poorest regions. Interruptions in incentives and financial aid, linked with low internal prices and a stagnation of export demands, were the main factors responsible for the decline in the production of cashew. Over the past twenty years, however, cashew production in Brazil has boomed, with producers making the most of the large US market for the kernels.[5]

GLOBAL CASHEW NUT TRADE

International Classification

In order to safeguard and guarantee quality, producers and exporters have introduced quality standards, which must be met by cashew exporters. The ISO 6477 standard was introduced in 1988 in order to unite the Brazilian and Indian classifications and to give one single classification scheme for quality control.

Cashew kernels are selected on the basis of the number per unit weight, of the kernels. They are also classified either as wholes, chips, splits, butts or baby bits, in accordance with the integrity of the kernel. White or ivory kernels are preferred over brown ones. There is a maximum permitted moisture level (both for raw cashews and cashew kernels) and the product must be free from insects, mould, rancidity and extraneous materials. The highest price is paid for better quality kernels of the W180 and W210 grades, which are the largest and heaviest grades.

Table 11.4: Cashew Production in South and Central American Countries, 1961 to 2005

(*Metric Tonnes*)

Country	*2005*	*2000*	*1995*	*1990*	*1985*	*1980*	*1975*	*1970*	*1965*	*1961*
Brazil	251268	138608	164156	99367	115000	75000	20490	20309	13789	9670
Dominican Republic	1000	950	930	930	910	870	810	804	789	775
El Salvador	2600	2530	3000	2098	2162	2208	1702	1700	1600	1500
Honduras	1800	450	400	350						
Mexico	650	650	235	168	1154	316				
Peru	2300	2717								
Total South America	259618	146625	168721	102913	119226	78394	23002	22813	16178	11945

Source: FAO STAT Database, March 2006.

International Trade

Cashews rank first in world production of edible nuts that are traded globally. World trade in edible nuts has experienced relatively rapid growth, averaging about 2.7 per cent per year since the early 1970s and increasing in value from US $1.94 in 1980 to US $2.84 billion in 1990. Export earnings from edible nut rose further to about 6 billion in 2005.[6]

Worldwide, trade in cashews (raw and shelled) totaled US$ 1.63 billion in 2004 and demand is increasing. In 2004 out of the 2.34 million tonnes world supply of raw cashewnuts, 492,467 tonnes were traded on international markets. This constituted 21 per cent of world production. In addition, 299, 218 tonnes of cashewnut kernels were exported in that year. India (60 per cent) and Brazil (31 per cent) are major exporters.

World exports of cashew raw increased almost six fold from 85,366 tonnes in 1990 to 350340 tonnes in 2004. Value of exports rose from US$ 69.2 million to 350.3 million, representing five-fold increase. The smaller increase in value is due to decline in unit value of exports realized during this period (Table 11.5). Global exports of cashewnut shelled increased during the last fifteen years from 116,087 tonnes to 299,218 tonnes, and the value rose from US$ 417,776 to US$ 1,280,181. By contrast, the export unit value in the case of cashewnut shelled registered almost 20 per cent increase, compared to almost 18 per cent decline for raw cashewnut.

The USA which is a major importer of cashew, has a strong influence over the world price, which is fixed in US$ per pound (1 pound = 0.45 kg). The price of W320 grade (320 kernels per pound) over the last 15 years has ranged from US$ 2.73 to US$ 3.18. The 2004 price for W320 grade was US$ 4.30 per lb (US$8.2 per kg) FOB.

International trade in raw cashewnuts has traditionally involved shipments from East Africa to India. India was the first country to build up a processing industry, but domestic production has long been insufficient to meet the requirements of the country's hundreds of small and medium-scale processing outlets. The imports from East Africa generally took place from December to May, which complimented the national harvest from May through to July. Thus, the Indian processors were able to operate over a prolonged period without having to maintain large stocks of raw nuts. This trade declined in the early 1980s when East African production reached low levels and Indian importers had problems with access to foreign exchange. Since then, import levels have increased

Table 11.5: World Exports of Cashew Raw and Shelled: 1990-2004

Year	Cashew Raw			Cashewnut Shelled		
	Quantity (Tonnes)	Value (US$ 1,000)	Unit value (US$/ Tonnes)	Quantity (Tonnes)	Value (US$ 1,000)	Unit value (US$/ Tonnes)
1990	85,366	69,216	810.8	116,087	417,776	3598.8
1991	123,526	113,826	921.5	114,604	460,050	4014.3
1992	114,684	101,582	885.8	159,679	515,673	3229.4
1993	128,683	105,727	821.6	159,651	550,965	3451.1
1994	208,467	173,463	832.1	200,067	707,761	3537.6
1995	200,386	178,086	888.7	136,330	637,340	4675.0
1996	212,351	197,710	931.0	137,236	660,075	4809.8
1997	258,678	232,766	889.8	157,838	704,751	4465.0
1998	243,481	285,837	1174.0	155,446	728,291	4685.2
1999	431,563	392,161	908.7	164,311	947,114	5764.2
2000	324,487	294,178	906.6	183,785	883,625	4807.9
2001	355,981	227,732	639.73	186,290	720,144	3865.7
2002	411,385	251,159	610.5	241,788	814,625	3369.2
2003	401,789	223,893	557.2	254,011	888,089	3496.3
2004	492,467	350,340	711.4	299,218	1,280,181	4278.4
Index 004/1990	576.9	506.2	87.7	257.8	306.4	118.9

Source: FAO STAT Database, March 2006.

due to greater supply availability, particularly from South East Asia, Vietnam and Indonesia and Tanzania.[7] Cashews from Tanzania used to command premium prices over other suppliers, but recent years have seen a growing uncertainty about the quality of Tanzanian shipments, resulting in the loss of premium grade.[8]

India has long been the world's largest supplier of cashew kernels with its prices and quality, setting the standards for the industry. In Europe, India has been the preferred supplier, with long standing trading relationships based on confidence in product quality and on fast and regular deliveries. India has more than 150 cashew kernel shippers, many of whom have offices in Europe and the United States. Throughout the 1970s, Mozambique was also a major exporter, but its market share has declined. At the same time, Brazilian exports have expanded. The quality of Brazilian cashews does not match that of Indian cashews. Brazilian nuts however have a comparative advantage in the US market, based on lower transportation costs and the unique larger size of the Brazilian cashewnut. Other suppliers, including Tanzania, Kenya and China, are reputed for producing nuts of irregular quality, which contributes to substantial price discounts (up to 30 per cent), in international markets.

Most cashew kernels exported form India are plain kernels packed in four gallon prime cans, flushed with carbon dioxide and having a net weight of 11.34 kg (25 lb). These cans are encased in cardboard cartons. Global pricing is generally quoted in US dollars per pound or per kilogram of nuts.

The United States is the largest importer of cashew kernels, accounting for almost 50 per cent of world imports. Other importers include the Netherlands (10 per cent), Germany (4 per cent), Japan (3 per cent) and the United Kingdom (6 per cent). The former Soviet Union was previously a major importer of cashew kernels, but with recent economic changes trade to this part of the world has diminished. Other emerging markets include the Middle East, South East Asia and Australia.[9]

Cashew kernels are usually the second or third most expensive nuts traded in the United States. Macadamia nuts are more expensive and pecan nuts can cost more in years when there is a poor harvest. Cashew nuts have a well-established market in the United States with a great variety of end uses. Retail prices vary from about US$4 to US$11 per lb (US$9 to 23 per kg) depending on kernel size and packaging.

The extensive market connections of large exporters from Brazil and

India make it difficult for smaller exporters to make gains in the US market. Importers may appreciate the low prices that small suppliers can offer, but the lack of reliability in quality, tends to make them favour the larger, more reputable suppliers.[10]

Almost all of the world's raw cashewnuts are sent to India for processing, since India has an inexpensive labour force and does not produce adequate quantities of cashews to fulfil its domestic processing capacity. Approximately, 25 to 40 per cent of nuts processed in India originate in foreign countries. India also has a long tradition and good reputation as a high quality processor of cashew. A number of countries, therefore, prefer to export their raw nuts to India for processing rather than to process themselves and produce lower quality kernels.

China also has a high processing capacity and benefits from having an inexpensive labour force. Chinese processed cashews were previously considered inferior to Indian nuts, but with improving standards, the import of raw nuts to China is on the increase.

World prices of cashew kernels vary according to the size, class and composition of the product. W320 (320 kernels per pound weight) is the category in highest demand and is the reference point for pricing. International prices for cashew kernels are influenced by the behaviour of market operators. There is no fixed market price and the market is speculative.

Cashew quality is of utmost importance. High quality is a major criterion for success on the world market. India and Brazil have worked hard to ensure high quality of the processed kernels. India's cashew industry was the first to use quality control for improvement of performance. Quality control is administered via the Cashew Export Promotion Council (CEPC).

GLOBAL CASHEW IMPORT DEMAND

Cashews are a premium nut in developed countries. They contain 10-20 per cent less fat than other nuts, most of it unsaturated, which is preferred by health conscious consumers. Imports of cashew kernels by developed countries have grown 7.1 per cent a year during the last decade. The largest consumer market is the United States, with a 45 per cent share of world imports during the 1990s (Table 11.6). The six importers shown in Table 11.6 account for 75 per cent of the world imports. During the 1990s imports of cashew kernels grew by 12.0 per cent in the European Union, 5.6 per cent in the United States, and 2.6 per cent in Japans. The large differential in per capita consumption of Japan and most European countries compared with the United States suggests considerable opportunity for increasing demand in Japan and Europe. In the United States cashews had a 23 per cent share of tree nut consumption during 1995–99 (compared with 16 per cent in the 1980s) and the highest average price among major nuts. Cashews compete most directly in the United States with almonds, which have a slightly larger market share and lower prices. Other major nuts and their share of the US market during the 1995–99 include pecans (20 per cent) and walnuts (19 per cent).

Table 11.6: Cashew Imports and Per Capita Consumption

	Imports				*Per Capita Consumption (Grams/Year)*	
	Tonnes		*Percentage of World Total*		*1980-99*	*1990-99*
	1980-99	*1990-99*	*1980-99*	*1990-99*		
United States	38,353	58,358	64	45	161	227
France	4,119	14,051	7	11	14	51
Netherlands*	2,209	7,428	4	6	152	479
Germany	2,392	7,339	4	6	30	90
United Kingdom	3,116	5,767	5	4	55	98
Japan	2,847	5,591	5	4	23	45
World	59,901	130,480				

* Per capita consumption may be overstated because of re-export to other European countries.

Source: Calculated by the author from FAO STAT.

Import demand equations were econometrically estimated for major importing countries using annual data for 1978–98 (Table 11.7). The functional form used to estimate demand provides constant elasticities. The weighted average income elasticity of demand for the six countries was 1.88, the weighted average own-price elasticity was 0–.58, and the weighted average cross-price elasticity with almonds was 0.19. The income elasticity of import demand for all countries was positive and statistically significant at the 1 per cent level. The price elasticity of import demand was negative in all equations. It was significant at the 1 per cent level for the United States, Netherlands, Germany, and the United Kingdom; at the 5 per cent level for France; and statistically insignificant at the 10 per cent

Table 11.7: Import Demand Equations for Cashews in Major Importing Countries

Country	Constant	Income	P–Cashews	P–Almonds	Adjusted R 2	Durbin–Watson Test	Augmented Dickey–Fuller Test
United States	−9.43***	1.06***	−0.36***	−0.08	0.84	1.64	−3.60
	(−2.88)	(3.62)	(−2.95)	(−0.78)			
France	−81.69***	6.51***	−0.59**	1.36***	0.89	1.02	−3.10
	(−14.20)	(6.01)	(−2.34)	(3.78)			
Netherlands	−40.69***	2.94***	−1.44***	0.87***	0.90	1.37	−317
	(−6.22)	(7.09)	(−5.36)	(3.45)			
Germany	−34.71***	3.23***	−1.32***	0.74**	0.87	1.59	−4.38
	(−3.72)	(4.00)	(5.04)	(2.31)			
United Kingdom	−19.43***	1.97***	−0.39***	−0.16*	0.93	1.71	−4.05
	(−9.05)	(9.01)	(−3.27)	(−1.75)			
Japan	−32.00**	1.95***	−0.19	0.23	0.49	1.11	−3.73
	(−2.81)	(2.88)	(−0.82)	(0.69)			

* Significant at the 10 per cent level. ** Significant at the 5 per cent level. *** Significant at the 1 per cent level.

Note: The model used to estimate cashew kernel demand for each country was: Log (Qt)=Â0 + B1Log (Yt) + B2Log (Pt)+B3Log (PAt) + ?t. Where Qt is net per capita cashew kernel imports in year t and is assumed to equal consumption, Yt is real per capita GDP, Pt is real cashew import prices PAt is real almond import prices, and ? denotes the error term. The equations were estimated using ordinary least squares on annual data from 1978 to 1998. The numbers in parentheses denote t-ratios.

Source: Estimated by the author.

level for Japan. The overall level of explanatory power of the estimated equations was good, with the adjusted R2 ranging from 0.84 to 0.93 for all countries except Japan (which was 0.49). Serial correlation was present in some of the estimated equations, but not severe according to the Dickey-Fuller tests. The individual country equations were used to project world cashew demand to 2020 (Table 11.7). The projections are for slower demand growth than during the last decade because of slower projected real per capita income growth. However, if world income growth during the 1998-2020 periods were equal to growth during the 1990-98 periods, demand growth would continue at the same rate. World imports are projected to grow 4.6 per cent over the 1998–2020 period compared with 7.1 per cent during the 1990s. Real cashew prices were assumed to remain constant over the forecast period (the base case), and thus the slower growth is due mostly to projected slower income growth. Slightly slower population growth rates also contribute to the reduced demand growth.

The relatively high price elasticity of demand for cashews in Europe suggests considerable opportunity for increasing demand through price competition. Therefore, as an alternative to the base case demand projection, the 2020 projection was also made under the assumption that real cashew kernel prices declined by 25 per cent over the 1998–2020 period. Under this alternative world cashew kernel demand would grow by 5.9 per cent a year over the forecast period, and cashew demand would increase to 431,795 tonnes by 2020 compared 403,390 tonnes with 4.6 per cent growth under the base case (Table 11.8).

Table 11.8: Projected Cashew Kernel Import Demand to 2020

Country or Region	*Demand in 1998*	*Real Per capita GDP Growth Rate 1998-2020 (Per cent)*	*Population growth 1998-2020 (Per cent)*	*Elasticity*		*Growth 1998-2020 (Per cent)*
				Price Income (Per cent)	*Demand In 2020 (Tonnes)*	
France	6,250	2.58	0.24	–.59 6.51	59,688	10.80
Germany	12,454	3.01	–0.22	–.32 3.23	40,702	5.51
Japan	5,532	2.29	–0.03	–.19 1.95	13,168	4.01
Netherlands	10,667	2.94	0.25	–1.44 2.94	48,506	7.15
UK	6,604	2.58	0.02	–.39 1.97	17,690	4.56
USA	70,368	2.41	0.69	–0.36 1.06	142,806	3.24
Sub-total	111,875				322,560	4.64
Rest of World	28,000				80,823	4.64
World	139,844				403,390	4.64

Note: The average annual growth rate for the sub-total of six countries from 1998 to 2010 is applied to the rest of the world to obtain world demand. Real prices of cashews are assumed constant over the forecast period.

Source: Real per capita GDP and population growth rates are from the World Bank (2001). Elasticities are from Table 11.7.

Global Supply

Cashews are a highly profitable crop. They can be intercropped with food crops such as cassava. Cashew trees are drought-tolerant and thus provide a hedge against annual crop failure. They have been called the poor man's crop and the rich man's food. These attributes have contributed to the rapid growth of global cashew supplies, including a recovery of production in Africa and expansion in Asia. India and Brazil are the largest producers and exporters of cashew kernels, but Vietnam has emerged in the last decade to become a major producer and exporter. Production in Sub-Saharan Africa has increased rapidly during the 1990s. Most African producers export raw cashews to India for processing, with only Mozambique processing significant quantities of cashews domestically.

The projected increase in import demand for cashew kernels augurs well for the cashew nut producing developing countries, such as Vietnam, India, Brazil, Tanzania, and other African and Latin American Countries. In Africa Tanzania is a large producer and exporter of raw cashew nuts, accounting for an average of 44 per cent of exports from Sub-Saharan Africa and 28 per cent of global raw nut exports during 1990–98. Despite this, Tanzania has little power to set prices because of the increasing production of neighbouring countries and the limited processing capacity. Tanzania will probably provide a smaller share of total exports from Sub-Saharan Africa in the future because of the expansion of other producers. It is unlikely that Tanzania will have significant market power in the future, and any attempt to exert market power would probably encourage competitors to increase production and increase their market share.

The relatively large share of Tanzanian exports in world raw cashew exports naturally leads to the question of whether there is a case for an optimal export tax. The justification for an optimal export tax is based on the argument that the exporting country can increase its total welfare (the sum of producer surplus and government revenue) by imposing a tax on exports when it faces a downward sloping demand curve for its commodity. The determinants of the optimal export tax are the price elasticity of demand for the commodity, the elasticity of supply in the exporting country and its competitors, and temporal issues such as the social discount rate.

Global Price Prospects

The near-term outlook for cashew prices is not good because of the large supply increases in both Asia and Africa. Tanzania is but one of many countries that increased production during the 1990s. The emergence of Vietnam as a major producer and exporter has contributed to the recent oversupply. In addition, demand growth is very sensitive to economic growth in the United States and Western Europe, and growth in these countries has slowed since mid-2001. Nevertheless, cashew demand is expected to grow about 5.0 per cent a year over the next decade and half, and prices are expected to recover. Over the longer term international prices are not expected to return to the lofty levels of 1999, except in years when one or more major producers suffer a large production shortfall. But prices will likely remain near the average of the 1990s. Compared with most other agricultural commodities, cashews are attractive commodity for small holders in most cashew growing countries. They are one of the best opportunities some of these countries have to export agricultural commodities in the global economy. Few crops offer better demand growth prospects, and Vietnam, India and Tanzania having revealed comparative advantage in production of cashews for export.

ANNEXURE

Annex Table 11.1: Trends in Global Production of Cashewnuts: (1961-2005)

(In Tonnes)

Region/Country	*2005*	*2004*	*2003*	*2002*	*2001*
Africa					
Tanzania	100000	100000	100000	100000	121900
Mozambique	58000	58000	58000	58000	58000
Nigeria	213000	213000	209000	186000	185000
Others	245100	245900	239930	225101	241383
Total	616100	616100	606930	569101	606203
% of World	26.4	26.9	29.1	30.2	37.4
Asia					
India	460000	460000	470600	460000	450000
Indonesia	122000	120000	118300	116000	91200
Vietnam	827000	825696	657600	515200	292800
Others	50210	49560	48950	49387	48413
Total	1459210	1455256	1295450	1140587	882438
% of World	62.4	63.5	62.0	60.6	54.4
South America					
Brazil	251268	182632	183094	164539	127073
Others	9780	9805	7963	8162	5270
Total	270828	192437	186359	172701	132343
% of world	11.5	8.5	8.9	9.2	8.5
World Total	2,337,358	2,265,473	2,095,295	1,884,214	1,622,129

Annex Table 11.1 (Contd.): Trends in Global Production of Cashewnuts: (1961 to 2005)

(*in Tonnes*)

Region/Country	*2000*	*1999*	*1998*	*1997*	*1996*	*1995*	*1994*	*1993*	*1992*	*1991*	*1992*
Africa											
Tanzania	121200	106500	93200	63000	82000	63400	46500	42300	41300	29850	41300
Mozambique	57894	51894	51716	43325	65000	33423	23000	23935	54217	31134	54217
Nigeria	184000	176000	152000	125000	110000	95000	85000	75000	55000	45000	55000
Others	115455	115455	108355	97006	87338	83148	73924	70009	67065	57680	67065
Total	595069	449849	405271	328331	344338	274971	228424	211244	217582	163664	217582
% of World		37.6	37.8	30.4	30.9	29.1	24.6	25.7	27.3	21.1	27.3
Asia											
India	440000	440000	440000	430000	417830	321640	350000	350000	305310	294590	305310
Indonesia	69027	69027	69027	66878	67676	74995	72077	69751	62217	57247	62217
Vietnam	41200	41200	54000	66900	59100	52800	78000	65000	58000	32000	58000
Others	52010	52010	51010	49575	49210	44943	42920	39050	38250	36850	38250
Total	602237	602237	614037	613353	593816	494378	542997	523801	463777	420687	463777
% of World	49.5	50.3	57.3	56.8	53.4	52.4	58.4	63.8	58.2	54.1	58.2
South America											
Brazil	167123	130841	39836	125397	167211	164156	149804	77098	107955	185965	107955
Others	8895	8895	5630	5131	4692	4565	4224	4250	3680	3463	3680
Total	176018	139736	45466	130528	171903	168721	154028	81348	111635	189428	111635
% of World	14.5	11.7	4.2	12.1	15.4	17.9	16.6	9.9	14.0	24.4	14.0
World Total	1,217,210	1,197,822	1,070,774	1,080,212	1,113,057	944,070	929,449	820,393	796,994	777,465	796,994

Annex Table 11.1 (Contd): Trends in Global Production of Cashewnuts: (1961 to 2005)

(in Tonnes)

Region/Country	*1990*	*1989*	*1988*	*1987*	*1986*	*1985*	*1984*	*1983*	*1982*	*1981*
Africa										
Tanzania	17060	19260	22470	18490	19200	32750	38100	33070	43200	64000
Mozambique	22524	50225	45000	35000	30000	25000	20300	35600	61000	71100
Nigeria	30000	25000	25000	25000	25000	25000	25000	25000	25000	25000
Others	56161	63901	44823	39927	38794	32045	39600	21800	25584	26754
Total	125745	158386	137293	118417	112994	114795	123000	115470	154784	186854
% of World	20.7	24.5	22.6	22.6	20.7	22.0	26.0	25.0	31.9	37.8
Asia										
India	285590	274330	260260	245580	234480	221330	210870	201440	195760	185250
Indonesia	29907	27990	23305	24042	22515	21114	19411	18047	16830	11444
Vietnam	26000	8500	8000	12000	10000	9000	8500	7700	7000	6500
Others	32930	34897	41302	39210	36156	31560	30640	22970	23827	22900
Total	374427	345717	332867	320832	303151	283004	269421	250157	243417	226094
% of World	61.7	53.4	54.7	61.2	55.6	54.3	56.9	54.1	50.1	45.8
South America										
Brazil	99367	136130	128080	75000	120000	115000	74000	90000	80000	74000
Others	3546	3655	4179	4202	4339	4226	3105	3520	3108	304
Total	102913	139785	132259	79202	124339	119226	77105	93520	83108	77404
% of World	17.0	21.6	21.7	15.1	22.8	22.9	16.3	20.2	17.1	15.7
World Total	606681	647665	608533	523874	544866	520973	473435	462719	485398	494167

Annex Table 11.1 (Contd.): Trends in Global Production of Cashewnut: (1961 to 2005)

Region/Country	*1980*	*1979*	*1978*	*1977*	*1976*	*1975*	*1974*	*1973*	*1972*	*1971*
Africa										
Tanzania	41416	57128	68478	93285	83637	115840	121704	145080	125559	126409
Mozambique	71100	66000	61000	91500	122000	188000	213400	240000	200000	202000
Nigeria	25000	25000	25000	25000	25000	25000	25000	25000	25000	25000
Others	24986	27560	45500	44160	35660	29195	23747	22658	19356	26450
Total	162502	175688	199978	253945	266297	358035	383851	432738	369915	379859
% of World	35.0	38.4	40.9	48.9	52.5	63.5	65.6	69.3	66.3	68.0
Asia										
India	180266	171817	165323	162457	161536	144254	135451	129766	130000	127223
Indonesia	9074	9764	8799	7370	7176	9122				
Vietnam	5600	4900	4900	4900	4900	3500	3500	3500	3500	3500
Others	23980	23665	25525	23650	23860	22140	21170	14060	11790	12100
Total	218920	210146	204547	198377	197472	179016	160121	147326	145290	142823
% of World	47.2	45.9	41.9	38.2	38.9	31.8	27.4	23.6	26.0	25.6
South America										
Brazil	75000	65000	77000	60000	36800	20490	34901	36936	35000	28602
Others	3394	3068	2892	2552	2522	2512	2650	2587	2543	2548
Total	78394	68068	79892	62552	39322	23002	37551	39523	37543	31150
% of World	16.9	14.9	16.3	12.0	7.7	4.1	6.4	6.3	6.7	5.6
World Total	464215	457696	488657	519629	507544	563795	585246	624348	558142	558846

Annex Table 11.1 (Contd.): Trends in Global Production of Cashewnuts: (1961 to 2005)

Region/Country	*1970*	*1969*	*1968*	*1967*	*1966*	*1965*	*1964*	*1963*	*1962*	*1961*
Africa										
Tanzania	107445	95700	92500	83800	83200	76000	71000	50000	70000	50000
Mozambique	184000	154200	185900	101000	119600	136000	156000	149000	108000	107000
Nigeria	25000	25000	25000	24000	23000	22000	19000	15000	14000	7000
Others	29327	13510	14605	17582	15460	14350	14650	12250	12150	8050
Total	345772	288410	318005	226382	241260	248350	260650	226250	204150	172050
% of world	67.5	63.7	65.8	58.4	63.3	64.3	68.0	64.8	62.8	59.8
Asia										
India	123319	120438	118542	114182	103818	100000	95000	92000	88000	85000
Indonesia										
Vietnam	2100	2100	2100	2100	2100	700	700	700	700	700
Others	11620	10440	13180	12950	13870	15600	9610	7690	9820	10340
Total	137039	132978	133822	129232	119788	116300	105310	100390	98520	96040
% of World	26.8	29.4	27.7	33.3	31.4	30.1	27.5	28.8	30.3	33.4
South America										
Brazil	20309	23443	23683	24181	13677	13789	9643	13621	11987	9670
Others	2504	2510	2466	2471	2427	2389	2334	2327	2238	2275
Total	22813	25953	26149	26652	16104	16178	11977	15948	14225	11945
% of World	4.5	5.7	5.4	6.9	4.2	4.2	3.1	4.6	4.4	4.2
World Total	287,535	324,895	349,088	383,437	386,303	381,318	387,776	483,538	452,676	511,939

REFERENCES

1. Jaffee, S. & Morton, J. (1995). *Marketing Africas High Value Foods: Comparative Experiences of an Emergent Private Sector*, The World Bank, Washington, USA.
2. Andrighetti, L. Bassi, G.F. Capella, P. de Logu, A.M. Deolalikar, A.B. Haeusler, G. Malorgio, G.A. Franca, F.M.C. Rivoira, G. Vannini, L. & Deserti R. (1989). *The World Cashew Economy*, L. Inchiostroblu, Italy.
3. Jaffee, S. & Morton, J. (1995). *Marketing Africa's High Value Foods: Comparative Experiences of an Emergent Private Sector*. The World Bank, Washington, USA
4. O. Farrell, P. Blaikie, S. & Chacko, E. (1998). The New Rural Industries, *A Handbook for Farmers and Investors*. Australia, RIRDC.
5. CDI, (1995). Cashewnuts: Potential in Africa. *Partnership*, 18, pp. 6-7.
6. *FAO STAT Database*: Primary Agricultural Commodities: Foreign Trade Statistics: March 2006.
7. Nayar, K.G. (1995). *Cashew: a crop with unlimited potential. The Cashew*, Jan/March, 1995.
8. Jaffee, S. & Morton, J. (1995). *op. cit.*
9. O. Farrell, P. Blaikie, S. & Chacko, E. (1998). *op. cit.*
10. The Clipper, 1994. US Cashew Kernel Imports Remain Strong, *The Clipper*, 4.

12

CASHEW SECTOR IN MAJOR ASIAN PRODUCING COUNTRIES

Introduction

The cashew nut sector in Asia is reviewed in this and the next chapter. This chapter deals with cashewnut industry in four major producing countries viz. Vietnam, India, Indonesia and Thailand. The next chapter analyzes cashew sector in Sri Lanka, Myanmar, Philippines and China.

CASHEW SECTOR IN VIETNAM

In Vietnam the cashew was introduced in the 19th century. It was originally grown in-home gardens as a shade tree. Cashew has been recognized as an industrial crop since about 10 years ago. Soil and climatic conditions in Quangnam-Danang province and further to the South are considered suitable for cashew production. In 1980, the area under cashew occupied only 30,000 ha. It has since gone up to 282,500 ha by 2005. The total production has increased phenomenally. At present, many provinces in the South including Dongnai, Songbe, Tayninh and Binhthuan are having large extents of cashew plantations in production. According to the FAO data cashew nut area under the crop in Vietnam rose from 195,000 hectares in 1996 to 282,500 hectares in 2005, while production increased from 263,400 to 827,000 tonnes, during this period. FAO seem to have revised its data series for Vietnam arbitrarily and more than doubled production estimates in a single year for the country, i.e. from 292,800 tonnes in 2001 to 515,200 tonnes in 2002, and raised it in the three subsequent years to 657,600 tonnes in 2003, 825,696 tonnes in 2004 and 827,000 tonnes in 2005. Such a marked increase from one year to another seems unrealistic. To make the data consistent FAO need to revise its series for earlier years as well.

Vietnam Becomes the Top Cashew Nut Producing Country

In the early 1980s, the cashew tree was considered as a forest tree or a shade tree for home gardens in Vietnam. Seedlings were mostly used as planting material and little care was given for its culture. As a result, the crop gave very low yields and poor quality nuts. In August 1989 however, the crop was recognized by the government as an industrial crop and came under the Ministry of Agriculture. In 1990, The Vietnam Cashew Tree Association was set up to promote the development of the crop, and since then there has been a rapid increase in the area of production. Table 12.1 shows area production and yield of cashew from 1990 to 2005. Vietnam started cultivation of cashew in a big way and had produced 8.27 lakh tonne of raw nuts in 2005 from an area of 2.92 lakh hectares with a yield of 2,927 kg/ha. It had only 1,000 ha under cashew in 1961 and production of 700 tonnes. From this level, area had gone up to 1.55 lakh ha in 1991 and to 1.99 lakh ha in 2001 and 2.92 lakh ha in 2005. The yield per hectare had also increased from 700 kgs to 1,032 kgs, 1,470 kgs., and 2,927 kgs., respectively during this period, according to FAO statistics.

Table 12.1: Vietnam: Area, Production and Yields of Cashew Nuts: 1990–2005

Year	*Area (Hectares)*	*Production (Metric tonnes)*	*Yield (kgs./hectare)*
1990	140,000	140,000	1000
1991	155,000	160,000	1032
1992	79,000	94,800	1200
1993	122,500	184,400	1522
1994	172,700	208,000	1204
1995	189,400	202,400	1069
1996	194,900	236,400	1213
1997	202,500	267,600	1321
1998	191,800	216,000	1126
1999	143,700	164,800	1147
2000	195,600	270,400	1382
2001	199,200	292,800	1470
2002	240,200	515,200	2145
2003	261,500	657,600	2515
2004	282,300	825,696	2925
2005	292,500	827,000	2927

Source: FAO STAT Databases, March 2006.

Vietnam tops global production with 8.27 lakh tonne followed by India (4.6 lakh tonne), Nigeria (2.13 lakh), Brazil (2.51 lakh) and Tanzania (1.00 lakh) in 2005. At the same time, in area under the crop, Vietnam is at the fourth position with India topping with 7.3 lakh ha and others being

Brazil 6.74 lakh ha, and Nigeria 3.21 lakh ha. Vietnam has become a major competitor for India in the world market with the industry receiving active support from its Government.

Earlier Cashew yields improved marginally, mainly because of inferior germplasm, poor management and aftercare of orchards, which have resulted in low yields. In 1995-1998 about 30,000 ha of cashew trees were cut down and replaced by mango and longan; also other trees in Songbe, Dongnai and Tayninh provinces were chopped due to their unstable yields and low income.[1] However, during the last five to six years yields of cashew have increased considerably reaching about 2.52 tonnes per hectares.

Area and production of cashew nut for selected years by zone/provinces are shown in Table 12.2. As mentioned earlier many provinces

Table 12.2: Area and Production of Cashew in Various Provinces of Vietnam

Zone/Province	Area (In hectares)			Production (Metric Tonnes)		
	1995	1996	2003	1995	1996	2003
1. *Eastern Provinces*	*135.29*	*149.00*	*155.85*	*39.31*	*83.32*	*448.85*
Dongnai	32.99	45.00	47.07	11.40	25.00	134.68
Songbe	77.54	82.00	85.77	16.22	45.00	242.42
Tayninh	7.51	15.00	15.69	7.64	8.40	45.25
Baria-Vungtau	17.25	7.00	7.32	4.05	3.92	21.12
2. *Central Provinces*	*21.12*	*61.00*	*63.81*	*5.26*	*26.70*	*143.83*
Binhthuan	12.98	20.00	20.92	3.90	11.20	60.34
Ninhthuan	0.45	5.00	5.23	0.14	1.75	9.43
Khanhhoa	1.86	4.00	4.18	0.49	1.50	8.08
Phuyen		10.00	10.46		3.50	18.85
Binhdinh	5.86	7.00	7.32	0.67	2.50	13.47
Quangngai	0.27	10.00	10.46	0.06	3.50	18.85
Quang-nam-Danang		5.00	5.23		1.75	9.43
3. *Central Highland Provinces*	*28.44*	*27.00*	*28.24*	*3.93*	*9.50*	*51.18*
Gilai	11.48	10.00	10.46	0.30	3.50	18.85
Kontum		5.00	5.23		1.75	9.43
Daklak	9.63	5.00	5.23	1.88	1.75	9.43
Lamdong	7.34	7.00	7.32	1.75	2.50	13.47
4. *Other Provinces*	*5.70*	*13.00*	*13.60*	*5.18*	*4.55*	*24.51*
Total	187.55	250.00	261.50	50.68	122.07	657.60

Source: (a) Agricultural Statistics: 1994-1995 and 2003-2004.
(b) Donafood, 1996. *Cultural Practices for Cashew Trees*. Agric. Services Department of Dongnai Province.

in the Eastern and Central Provinces including Dongnai, Songbe, Tayninh and Binhthuan are having large extents of cashew plantations in production. According to the latest data available Eastern provinces currently account for 60 per cent of the total area under cashewnuts and they contribute more than 68 per cent of the crop output. The share of the central provinces is 24 per cent in area and 22 per cent in output.

Planting Material

The most popular practice was selecting high yielding trees and using the seeds for planting. This method has led to low yields, as most progenies from such trees were not true to type. However, since 1994, about 46 per cent of new cashew plantations have been planted with selected clones raised vegetatively (Table 12.3). Cleft grafting is recommended for propagation of planting material while the best time for grafting is from May to August.[2]

Table 12.3: Variety Situation and Planting Density of Cashew Plantations

Year	*Varieties (%)*		*Density (trees/ha)*			
	Selected	Unselected	> 400	300-400	200-300	150-200
Prior to 1987	0.0	100.0	67.2	27.8	5.0	–
1988-1990	5.8	92.2	31.0	45.6	15.4	8.0
1991-1993	28.3	71.7	35.3	30.0	23.7	11.0
1994-1996	46.5	53.5	12.3	19.5	52.2	16.0

Source: Bien, P.V. and N.T. Binh, 1997. *Cashew tree technical aspects: Workshop on Cashew Tree Development in Vietnam*, Hanoi.

Establishment of Cashew Orchards

Cashew trees were usually established on degraded soils in the eastern provinces and central coastal provinces of the South. The spacing applied is 10 m × 5 m (200 plants/ha). Before 1990 however, farmers resorted to high density planting as high as 400 trees/ha (Table 12.3). It was the general practice to add organic manure at the rate of 10-20 kg/planting hole.

Care and Management of Cashew Orchards

Most of the cashew growers neither apply fertilizer nor prune their trees. This is mainly because the low and unstable yields from their cashew crop do not encourage them to manage their crop using such inputs. It has been estimated that only 37.7 per cent of the cashew plantations were fertilized while the rest did not receive any fertilizer (Table 12.4). The survey also revealed that the fertilized cashew yielded on average 155 kg more than the unfertilized orchards with an overall yield of 698 kg/ha for the fertilized orchards and 543 kg/ha for the unfertilized, respectively.

Table 12.4: Application of Modern Agro-Techniques for Cashew

Technologies Applied	*Percentage of Farmers' Applying Modern Agro-Techniques*			
	Applied	Yield (kg/ha)	Not Applied	Yield (kg/ha)
Fertilizer	37.7	698	62.3	543
Pruning	56.5	672	43.5	672
Plant Protection	21.7	–	78.3	–

Source: Bien, P.V. and N.T. Binh, 1997. *Cashew Tree Technical Aspects. Workshop on Cashew Tree Development in Vietnam, Hanoi.*

Pests and Diseases

Of the pests that afflict the cashew crop, shoot borer and red bug were recorded as the most serious pests on the crop (Table 12.5). Control measures applied for pests and diseases were practiced only in 2.17 per cent of orchards.

Table 12.5: Pests and Diseases Recorded in Cashew Orchards in Dongnai, 1996

Diseases and Pests	*Percentage of Orchards Showing Infestation*	*Damage Level*
Insects		
Red Bug (*Helopeltis antonii*)	60.5	Serious
Shoot borer (*Alcides* sp.)	92.3	Serious
Stem borer (*Plocaederus ferrugineus, P. obesus*)	23.4	Moderate
Leaf miner (*Acroercops* sp.)	84.3	Serious
Mealy bug (*Coccidae*), Ants	65.8	Moderate
Diseases		
Sooty mold (*Mellol* sp., *Capnodium* sp.)	7.2	Limited
Anthracnose (*Colletotrichum* sp., *Fusarium* sp.)	32.4	Moderate

Source: Bien, P.V. and N.T. Binh, 1997. *Cashew Tree Technical Aspects. Workshop on Cashew Tree Development in Vietnam*, Hanoi.

Rejuvenation of Orchards by Topworking

Although rejuvenation of old trees by topworking with selected high yielding clones has been recommended, this has however, not been widely applied by farmers, despite the fact that production and productivity of cashew can be certainly improved if the method is practiced.[3, 4]

Harvesting of Nuts and Yield

Since the majority of plantations were established with low yielding genetic material and managed poorly, average yields of cashew are as low as 500-600 kg per ha per year. The size of cashew kernels is also below accepted standards and market acceptance is a problem for the producers. However, according to the FAO data yield per hectares have improved from 1000 kgs in 1990 to 2927 kgs. in 2005.

Marketing

Marketing is not been well organized and several companies incorporated in the provinces export most of the cashew kernel. Growers' Cooperatives have not yet been established for the marketing of cashew. There is a keen competition among the private companies for the export of cashew. In accordance with the National policy a single export Agency to handle cashew exports, has been established. This strategy has yet to be ratified by the Central Government. The current practice therefore of exporting processed and unprocessed cashew is bound to continue for some time.

Nearly 90 per cent of cashew kernels produced in Vietnam are exported mainly to Canada, China, USA, Japan and Australia. In 1990, about 24,749 tonnes of cashew kernels were exported. This brought about US$ 15 million of foreign exchange. By 2005, exports have increased to 105,100 tonnes worth about US$ 436 million (Table 12.6). Export price per tonne reached peak of US$ 5965 in 1999, and thereafter it declined reaching US$ 4048 per tonne in 2004. The local market accounts for only about 10 per cent of total production, mainly as snack food and confectionery items such as cashew candy, popular among local consumers in Song Be province.

Potential for Cashew Production Development

Cashew production is projected to increase to 1.92 million tonnes compared to 827,000 tonnes produced in 2005 (Table 12.7).[5] The export value of kernels is likely to increase to US$ 1115 million, compared to around US$ 436 million in 2004. The anticipated average yield is expected to increase to reach 3.2 tonne/ha by then, which the country hopes to achieve through the application of advanced technologies such as use of fertilizer, better cultural practices and high yielding clones raised vegetatively through the adoption of grafting techniques.

Table 12.6: Vietnam: Cashewnut Kernels Exports: 1990 – 2004

Year	*Quantities (Tonnes)*	*Value (US$ 1000)*	*Unit value (US$/tonne)*
1990	24,749	14,917	603
1991	30,700	21,100	687
1992	51,700	41,415	801
1993	47,700	50,000	1048
1994	81,300	114,000	1402
1995	19,800	34,000	1717
1996	16,500	60,000	3636
1997	33,299	133,331	4004
1998	25,700	116,699	4551
1999	18,400	109,748	5964
2000	40,734	191,355	4698
2001	43,672	151,707	3474
2002	62,235	208,996	3358
2003	82,200	276,544	3364
2004	105,100	435,983	4048

Source: FAO STAT Database, March 2006.

Table 12.7: Current Area of Production and Future Projections

Criteria	*1990*	*2004*	*2020*
1. Area harvested (in '000 ha)	140	282	600
2. Average yield (tonnes/ha)	1.0	2.92	3.2
3. Production ('000 tonnes)	140	827	1,921
4. Planned exports (kernel) ('000 tonnes)	25	105	350
Projected export value (million US$)	15	436	1,155
Processing labour force ('000 persons)	60	150	350

Source: Vietnam Cashew Tree Association, 1997 and author's projections.

Constraints in Cashewnut Production Development

The major constraints in the cashew industry are as follows:

Technical Issues

- Lack of improved varieties.
- Agro-ecological areas suitable for cashew are yet to be identified.
- Lack of sufficient high quality planting material.

Policy Aspects

The following policy issues need to be approved by government to support the cashew industry:

- Amount of capital investment required for care and management of existing cashew plantations and for new plantings will be around VN dong 2,500 billion by the year 2020. Another VN dong 500 billion will be required for new processing facilities for cashew.
- A Cashew Tree Research Center should be established to backstop production activities.
- Growers' Cooperatives should be organized for marketing of cashew products.
- Demonstrations and extension programmes should be initiated to assist farmers in topworking old trees so as to attain higher yields.

Concluding Remarks

The cashew crop has demonstrated its adaptability to local growing conditions in Vietnam and has emerged as an important export crop, which at present provides valuable foreign exchange of nearly US$ 436 million per year (2004). This has amply demonstrated its place in the agricultural production system of the country although many policy changes and technical inputs are needed to assist further development of the crop. In order to realize the projected targets of expanding the area under production to 600,000 ha with a yield of 3.2 tonne/ha, intensive research and development efforts are urgently needed. Based on impressive progress made in increasing cashewnut production during the last decade or so, it seems feasible to achieve the higher projected target during the next two decades or so.

CASHEWNUT INDUSTRY IN INDIA

Introduction

Cashew as a marketable commodity has a very important role to play in the liberalized Indian economy. With export earnings of Rs. 13,718 million in 2003-04, cashew ranked as one of the top agricultural export commodities.[6] From the farmers' as well as from the exporters' point of view, the current emphasis that cashew is receiving as a horticultural crop from the research and development front, is a welcome sign. At present, India has a processing capacity of nearly seven hundred thousand tonnes and to meet the raw nut demand, the country depends partially on imports from several African, and in recent years, from Southeast Asian countries. This involves spending considerable foreign exchange. There is an urgent need to increase local production to substitute imported raw material in order to derive the maximum benefits from a strong processing and marketing capability developed over the years by the Indian cashew industry.

Research work on cashew was initiated on a relatively small scale in early 1950s resulting in the development of several production techniques. These efforts were further strengthened when the national research mandate was delegated to the Central Plantation Crops Research Institute (CPCRI), Kasaragode, in 1970, which spearheaded the All India Coordinated Spices and Cashew Improvement Project from 1971. These research activities received further impetus with the implementation of a World Bank aided multi-State Cashew Project in the States of Andhra Pradesh, Kerala, Karnataka and Orissa from 1982-86. A National Research Center for Cashew was established at Puttur to increase the production and productivity of cashew with the mission-mode approach in 1986.

The cashew development component of the combined All India Coordinated Spices and Cashew Improvement Project was de-linked and an independent National Cashew Research project was initiated with the newly established National Research Center (NRC) for the crop at the same time. There are eight research centers and one sub-center at present, located in eight cashew growing States in the country. This can be considered as a milestone in cashew development with firmly established linkages with the Directorate of Cashewnut Development Corporation and other extension agencies, which assisted in the transfer of newly developed production technologies.[7]

Present Status of Cashew Production

Areas of Production

Cashew is grown in the western and eastern coastal areas and further inland in some parts of Karnataka and Madhya Pradesh. During the last fifteen years cashewnut area has increased from 532 thousand hectares in 1990-91 to 770 thousand hectares in 2002-03. Production during this period rose from 295 thousand tonnes to 500 thousand tonnes. The yield per hectares went up from 636 kg/hectare to 760 kgs (Table 12.8).

Table 12.8: All-India Area, Production and Yield of Cashewnut: 1990-91 – 2002-03

Year	Area (000 hec.)	Productive area (000 hec.)	Production (000 Tonnes)	Yield (kgs./hec.)
1990-91	532	464	295	636
1991-92	534	482	305	633
1992-93	560	508	349	687
1993-94	565	57	348	673
1994-95	577	510	322	631
1995-96	635	485	418	862
1996-97	659	515	430	835
1997-98	675	512	360	703
1998-99	706	573	460	803
1999-2000	686	601	520	865
2000-01	720	627	450	710
2001-02	750	666	470	710
2002-03	770	675	500	760

Source: Ministry of Agriculture, Directorate of Economic and Statistics: Agricultural Statistics at a Glance: 2004, p. 99.

Among major cashewnut growing state, Maharashtra state is at the top. With 148,000 ha and a production of 110,000 tonnes, Maharashtra accounts for 19.22 per cent of the area and 22 per cent of production respectively (Table 12.9). The highest productivity is observed in Maharashtra with around one tonne per ha. The high yield in Maharashtra is primarily due to the fact that cashew production is of recent origin and the major part of the plantations have been established with high yielding clonal material. Even the orchards raised from seeds are from selected progenies. The Tenth Five Year Plan target is to produce 700,000 tonnes in the country.

Table 12.9: Area, Production and Productivity of Cashew in India: (2002-03)

States	Area (000 ha)	National % Area	Production (tonnes)	National % Prod.	Productivity (kg/ha)
Maharashtra	148.00	19.22	110.00	22.00	1000
Kerala	100.00	12.99	90.00	18.00	890
Andhra Pradesh	136.00	17.66	90.00	18.00	740
Orissa	120.00	15.58	70.00	14.00	810
Tamil Nadu	92.00	11.95	50.00	10.00	570
Karnataka	92.00	11.95	40.00	8.00	470
Goa	55.00	7.14	30.00	6.00	660
West Bengal	9.00	1.17	8.00	1.60	890
Others	18.00	2.34	12.00	2.40	760
Total	770.00	100.00	500.00	100.00	760

Source: Ministry of Agriculture, Directorate of Economic and Statistics: Agricultural Statistics at a Glance: 2004, p. 100.

Varieties

The National Research Center as well as several Agricultural Universities have released thirty-three cultivars so far. Most of the varieties have a mean yield of 8-10 kg per tree which gives over one tonne per ha. In view of the export potential, however, cultivation is recommended only for such cultivars that have a kernel grade of W-210 to W-240 (210-240 kernels per lb). Cashew cultivar recommendations for different States are given in Table 12.10.

Table 12.10: Cashew Cultivars Recommended for Different States

State	*Cultivars Recommended*	*Progeny*
Karnataka	Selection 1	VTH-107/3
	Selection 2	VTH-40/1
	Ullal 1	8/46 Taliparamba
	Ullal 2	3/67 Guntur
	Ullal 3	5/37 Manjeri
	Ullal 4	2/77 Tuni: Andhra
	UN 50	2/27 Nileshwar
	VRI 1	M-10/4
	VRI 2	M-44/3
	Vengurla 1	Ansur-1
	Vengurla 4	Mid Red x Vetore 56
	Chintamani 1	8/46 Taliparamba
Kerala	Madakkathara 1	BLA-39-4
	Madakkathara 2	NDR 2-1
	K-22-1	22 Kottarakkara
	Dhana	ALGD-1-1 x K 30-1
	Priyanka	BLA-139-1 x K 30-1
Maharashtra and Goa	Vengurla-1	Ansur-1
	Vengurla-4	Mid Red x Vetore-56
	Vengurla-6	Vetore 56 x Ansur-1
Tamil Nadu	VRI-1	M 10/4
	VRI-2	M 44/3
	VRI-3	M 26/2
Andhra Pradesh	BPP-4	EPM 9/8
	BPP-6	T No.56
	BPP-8	T No.1 x T No. 39
Orissa	VRI-2	M 44/3
	Bhubaneshvar-1	Vengurla 36/3
West Bengal	Jhargram-1	T No. 16 of Bapatla
Madhya Pradesh	T No. 40	
	Vengurla 4	Mid Red x Vetore-56

Propagation and Production of Planting Material

A number of propagation methods have been tested for the multiplication of cashew. Air layering was found to be one of the popular methods among growers. This technique, however, produced trees with poor anchorage as the root density was found to be low. It also resulted in poor field establishment and high susceptibility to cyclones and drought conditions. Air layering was therefore found to be unsuitable for commercial exploitation. In the case of mound layering too, the absence of a taproot was found to be a disadvantage. Epicotyl grafting was another method that had limitations due to high mortality at transplanting and incidence of collar-rot at the nursery stage. Softwood grafting developed at the research centers was found to be the most viable method of propagation that was commercially acceptable; it gave a success rate of about 70 per cent. The technique of softwood grafting described below is similar to Epicotyl grafting except the difference in the age of the rootstock.

Forty to sixty-day-old seedlings are used as rootstocks. Two pairs of leaves are retained and the seedlings are decapitated at the softwood apical region. Wedge-grafting is then carried out with a 4-5 cm cleft on the rootstock and with a small portion of the inner surface removed to facilitate a perfect union of the wedge-shaped scion, which has been prepared by shaving a portion of the bark and tissue on either side. The union is then secured by tying with a 15-30 cm polythene strip. The top of the scion is covered with a polythene cap to protect the apical portion of the scion from desiccation. The grafted plants are maintained in a lath or screen house for 8-10 days until sprouts emerge, and then the grafted plants are provided more sunlight and the caps removed. This wedge grafting technique is carried out by using only the softwood tissues of the stock and scion. The following management techniques are important in nursing young grafted plants.

- Grafts need to be watered frequently depending on the season.
- Excess water needs to be drained by providing drainage holes in polybags.
- Shoots on the rootstocks have to be nipped off frequently.
- Polythene wrapping at the union has to be removed about three months after grafting to prevent girdling.
- When the scion leaves turn from brown to green, rootstock leaves have to be removed (approximately 60 days after grafting).
- Flower shoots that sprout during the normal flowering season should be removed at the nursery stage.

- To prevent roots penetrating into the ground, grafted plants should be shifted frequently or placed on thick gauge black polythene sheets.
- Partial shade has to be provided to avoid sun-scorch by placing the grafted plants in a lath/screen house. Direct sunlight should be avoided, as polythene bags tend to perish. Watering on alternate days should be done in summer.
- Regular insecticide sprays need to be given to control leaf-sucking insects.
- When transporting grafted plants, terminal shoots and taproots should be protected.

ESTABLISHMENT OF NEW CASHEW ORCHARDS

Large amount of land is available in Karnataka, Maharashtra and West Bengal for establishing new plantations under the cashew expansion programme. There is also the possibility of expanding cashew cultivation into non-traditional areas in Madhya Pradesh, Bihar, etc.

Selection of Site and Land Development

When selecting land for cashew, soils with salinity/alkalinity or waterlogging should be avoided. Soil depth, slope, course texture, soil fertility and water availability seem to impose very little limitations, as cashew is a hardy crop. For establishing new plantations, land preparation should begin with the first pre-monsoon rains. Land should be cleared of shrub vegetation before digging pits for planting.

Planting Season

Planting of grafted plants is usually carried out during the monsoon season from July-August both in the west coast as well as in the east coast. Orchards should have pits dug to receive grafted plants well in advance of the main monsoon weather.

Spacing and Planting Systems

A spacing of 7.5m × 7.5m or 8m × 8m is recommended for cashew, which gives a tree density of 175 and 156 trees per ha, respectively. High density planting at 4m × 4m giving a tree density of 625 trees per ha in the initial years and subsequently thinning in stages to reach a final spacing of 8m × 8m is also practiced in some areas. This enables higher returns during the initial years and as the canopies grow in volume, alternate trees are removed to achieve the desired final spacing. In level sites however it would be advantageous to plant cashew at a spacing of 10m × 5m which will give a tree density of 200 trees per ha and at the same time providing sufficient space for growers to plant inter-crops during the initial years of establishment.

Planting of Cashew

Pits are usually dug at the onset of the pre-monsoon rains to a size of 60cm × 60cm in light to medium soils. If a hard substrate like laterite is present pits may be 1m × 1m to compensate for the lesser depth of soil. It is preferable to dig pits 15-20 days before planting to expose planting holes to direct sunlight, which can help remove termites and other harmful insects that can damage young plants, if present. When filling, topsoil mixed with compost (5 kg) or poultry manure (2 kg) and 200g of rock phosphate are placed in the pits. Contour planting is usually followed in sloping areas. Standard conservation measures need to be followed on steep lands when establishing cashew plantations.

Young plants are planted in the months of July-August. Most nurseries supply 5-12 month old grafted plants in polybags. At planting, the polythene bag is removed without disturbing the ball of earth and the roots. Care is taken to place the grafted plant in the pits leaving the graft joint at least 5 cm above ground level. Normally the scion is staked to avoid damage from wind and the support should remain up to the third year from planting. Most orchard growers use mulch around the planting hole to suppress weeds and conserve moisture.

Management and Aftercare of Cashew Orchards

Terracing and Bunding

In the western and eastern coastal areas cashew is grown mostly on sloping land. A considerable amount of nutrient leaching and soil erosion is common in such situations.

Growers have been advised to construct terraces and contour pits to conserve runoff water. Studies on the extent of root distribution revealed that 90 per cent of the root system was confined to a radius of 2m and a depth of 1 m. In order to achieve maximum utilization of applied nutrients, fertilizer practices are confined to this part of the root zone. Before the advent of the southwest monsoon in May-June, basins of about 1.5m radius are prepared for 2 year-old trees and subsequently widened to 2m in the third year. Terraces are made by removing the soil from the elevated portion above the tree trunks to create basins of 1.5-2m. Contour drains are also constructed to collect rainwater above the tree line and prevent soil wash from the slopes.

Application of Manures and Fertilizer

Application of 10-15 kg of farmyard manure or compost annually is generally recommended for cashew. In addition, the current fertilizer recommendation is 500g N (1.1 kg urea), 125g P_2O_5 (625g rock phosphate) and 125g K_2O (208g muriate of potash) per tree per year. This has increased production in the All India cashew trials carried out at the research centers. These trials also showed that the cashew responds well to increased N applications up to 750g. Since local NPK fertilizer mixtures do not deliver the required nutrients, application of straight fertilizer is recommended.

Fertilizer is applied annually at the end of the rainy season into a shallow trench at the drip line of trees. It is also recommended that fertilizer be applied in split doses during pre-monsoon (May-June) and post-monsoon (September-October) periods to assure better uptake of nutrients. If a single application is done, the post-monsoon period is more suitable when ground moisture is adequate. One-third of the recommended dose is applied in the first year, two-third of the dose in the second year and the full dose thereafter (Table 12.11).

Table 12.11: Recommended Doses of NPK Fertilizer for Cashew (g/plant)

Year	*Urea (gm)*	*Rock Phosphate (gm)*	*Muriate of Potash*
1	330	200	70
2	660	400	140
3 onwards	1,100	625	208

Based on the results of research conducted by the National Coordinated trials, the following methods of fertilizer application are recommended to cashew growers. In the red loamy soils in low rainfall areas such as the east coast, fertilizers have to be applied and raked into the soil along the drip line of tree canopies. In laterite soils and steep lands of the west coast, fertilizer is applied in circular trenches of about 25 cm width along the drip line of trees. Trenches are filled and mulch is applied to ensure soil moisture retention.

Weeding

Until tree canopies shade out the weeds, weeding is essential around the tree trunks up to a radius of about 2 m. The rest of the orchard requires slashing of under growth at least twice a year. The weeding cycles are generally confined to the pre-monsoon and post-monsoon periods to coincide with the fertilizer application.

Alternatively, weedicides may also be applied after slashing, well in advance of the rainy season if the under growth is too dense. The recommendation is to apply Agrodar-96 (2-4 D) at the rate of 4 ml/litre of water followed by Grammoxone at the rate of 5ml/litre of water. Approximately 400 litres of spray is required to cover one ha. The spraying is repeated in the post-monsoon season if the weed load is heavy.

Mulching

In low rainfall areas, mulching around the base of trees helps in the control of weeds, retention of moisture and modulation of soil temperature, especially in the hot summer months. This becomes an essential operation as cashew is usually planted in very dry areas where other crops are seldom grown. Most growers utilize the slashed weeds to mulch their orchards.

Training and Pruning

During the initial phase of orchard establishment, shoots arising on the rootstock have to be regularly removed to promote better scion growth, particularly in the first year after planting when scion rejection could occur if rootstock shoots are left unchecked. Training of young trees during the first three years is essential to develop uniform canopies. Training in the juvenile phase comprises of removing basal branches and water shoots. The plants are trained to a single stem and branches are allowed to grow about 0.75-1m from ground level. Deformed branches are also removed during the first few years. Since cashew trees tend to spread their canopies and lodge easily, proper staking is also essential. Trees are kept under check by topping off the main stem at a height of 4-5m from ground level. Orchard operations such as terracing, weeding, fertilizer application, nut collection and stem/root borer infestation control can be easily achieved if trees are properly trained. Pruning should be carried out in August-September at least once in three years when unwanted growth is removed to provide adequate sunlight into the canopy. Since fruiting is only encouraged from the third year, de-blossoming has to be carried out as flower clusters appear during the juvenile phase.

Plant Protection

Root and stem borer infestation is usually controlled with swabbing tree trunks with carbaryl (2 %) or using a coal tar/kerosene suspension (1:2). After pruning of trees, a standard practice is to smear all cut surfaces with Bordeaux mixture paste (10 %) to prevent fungal infections and dieback. A 1 per cent Bordeaux spray is also administered if the cut surfaces are small.

More than 60 species of insect pests have been identified in cashew in India. The major pests are the tea mosquito, stem/root borer, leaf minor, leaf and blossom webber and flower thrips. No major diseases that cause economic losses have been reported so far in cashew.

For efficient management of the tea mosquito bug (*Helopeltis antonii*), it is important to check the build up of the pest population on the cashew crop as well as on the alternate hosts such as neem, drumstick, cocoa, guava etc. Tea mosquito bugs can be effectively controlled by three sprays at flushing, flowering and fruiting stages with endosulfan or monocrotophos (0.05 %) for the first and second sprays and carbaryl (0.15 %) for the third spray. In case of severe infestation, it may sometimes lead to dieback caused by a secondary infection of *Botrydiplodia theobromae.* In such instances it will require pruning of the diseased shoots and swabbing of the cut surfaces with 10 per cent Bordeaux paste and spraying the trees with a 1 per cent solution of Bordeaux mixture.

The stem and root borer (*Plocaecderus ferrugineus* L.), is capable of killing cashew trees. In severe cases of injury by this pest, gummosis of the stem and yellowing followed by drying of leaves can occur. The effective control measure is to remove immature stages of the pest and swabbing the trunk and exposed roots with carbaryl (0.2 %) or neem oil (5 %) and application of Sevidol 8G (75g/tree) into the basin around the tree. Prophylactic treatment of swabbing the trunk up to one-meter height with coal tar and kerosene in the ratio of 1:2 twice a year during March and November could also give effective control. The spray schedule indicated for tea mosquito bug will also be effective against the control of other foliage and inflorescence pests.

Cover-Cropping and Inter-Cropping

Popular cover crops for cashew plantations are *Peuraria javanica,*

Calapagonium muconoides and *Centrosema pubescens*, which improve the fertility and moisture balance and help, conserve orchard soils. Cover crop seeds are generally sown with the advent of the monsoons at a seed rate of about 7 kg/ha. On degraded steep lands, cover crops are usually established on seedbeds between tree rows.

Inter-cropping has become popular with the systematic establishment of large-scale orchards. It is practiced in the first few years when there is sufficient space between crop rows with the main objective of deriving some income until the cashew starts giving economic returns. In Andhra Pradesh, popular inter-crops are horsegram, cowpea, groundnut etc. Casuarina is also a tree inter-crop planted at a spacing of 1.5m × 1.5m in cashew orchards in Andhra Pradesh and Orissa. In the west Godavari district of Andhra Pradesh, cashew is grown in combination with casuarina and coconut.

In Kerala and coastal Karnataka, pineapple is grown as a biennial crop in the initial 4-5 years and farmers find it far more profitable than crops such as redgram and cassava. Adopting a two-row system of planting in contour trenches, yields of 15-20 tonnes/ha have been achieved from this inter-crop. The pineapple inter-crop also indirectly benefits the main cashew crop as contour trenches help to conserve water and nutrients. When hedgerow planting at a spacing of 5m × 10m is used, inter-crops of Acacia, casuarina etc. is taken without any ill effects on the main crop. These trees are planted about 3.5 m away from the cashew in two-row plots spaced 1m × 1m apart in the center of crop avenues.

Irrigation and Drainage

Cashew cultivation is generally carried out under rainfed conditions. In homesteads however, it is preferable to give some supplementary irrigation during the warm summer months from January to March. An application of about 200 litres of water per tree every fortnight was found to double cashew yields in trials conducted at the National Research Center at Puttur. In the sandy tracts of the East coast, although frequency and quantity of water applied varies, trees are watered during the summer months. Both in the homesteads and large-scale orchards, cashew is susceptible to waterlogging and proper drainage is essential in low-lying areas.

Harvesting of Nuts and Cashew Yields

Bearing commences after the third year of planting and the trees will be in full production by the tenth year whilst the economic life of a tree is about

20 years. The main harvesting season is from February to May. Most farmers harvest their crop before they drop to prevent pilferage. This very often results in poor quality of the kernels. The optimum stage of harvest is when nuts drop to the ground. High quality nuts are obtained when freshly fallen nuts are separated from the cashew apples and sun dried for 2-3 days to bring down the moisture percentage from about 25 per cent to below 9 per cent. It is very essential to dry the nuts in order to prevent spoilage during storage. The drying process helps to retain flavour and quality of the kernels. When cashew apples are used for processing, harvesting has to be carried out before they drop. A simple test of maturity is to float nuts in water when mature nuts will sink while the immature and unfilled nuts will float. Nuts are usually gathered every week during the harvest season. Cashew apples for the fresh fruit market should be harvested daily.

Normally, about 92 per cent of the trees yield by the third year from planting. The average yield per tree increases from about 2 kg at 3-5 years to 4 kg at 6-10 years and 5-10 kg when trees are 11-15 years of age. Thereafter, trees yield in excess of 10 kg as the trees get older.

Marketing

Raw cashewnuts are a seasonal commodity and the trading season is from March to May. Growers usually supply the primary or village markets where small traders collect and supply the urban markets. The cashew trade is seldom handled by exclusive traders. Usually, those traders who deal with other plantation products also trade in cashew. Due to the highly competitive nature of the cashew trade growers have few marketing problems.

When large quantities are collected by middlemen, the processors enter the marketing chain and make wholesale purchases. Grades and standards for cashew are yet to be introduced in India. Quality is generally determined by appearance and cutting tests that traders employ prior to purchase. The raw cashew nut market involves a large amount of capital where nearly 80 per cent of the produce is transacted within a matter of 35 days. The current value of Indian production is estimated at around Rs. 10,000 million. This capital is made available by industry for procurement and processing operations.

There are no growers' cooperatives or organizations for cashew marketing. In Kerala, however, the government has been involved in the procurement process and supply to large-scale processors. This adversely affected the cashew trade and has now been replaced by a free market policy.

In addition to the local production of nearly 520,000 tonnes, India also imports a considerable quantity of raw nuts from several African and South-east Asian countries to satisfy the national processing capacity of 700,000 tonnes established in the country.

Potential for Cashewnut Production Development

In 1960-61, 228,000 tonnes of raw nuts were processed of which nearly 50 per cent was imported. During the same year, 44,000 tonnes of processed kernels were exported which accounted for 77 per cent of the total kernel output from the industry. The processing output has considerably increased in recent years and in 1995-96 about 640,000 tonnes were processed (Table 12.12), of which 65 per cent raw nuts were obtained from local production. Domestic consumption has also increased considerably from 13,000 tonnes in 1960-61 to 92,000 tonnes in 1995-96, while the country also earned a foreign exchange equivalent of Rs. 12,320 million (US$ 352 million) through the export of cashew kernels and cashewnut shell liquid (CNSL). Export earnings reached a peak in 2002-03 when 129,400 tonnes of kernels were exported with a value of Rs. 20,530 million (US$ 424 million). Exports in 2003-04 totaled 100,300 tonnes worth Rs. 16,970 million (US$ 377 million). With the establishment of new orchards using high yielding vegetatively propagated planting material, the future looks bright for the cashew industry in India.

Table 12.12: Raw Nut Availability, Processing and Export Statistics of India: 1960-60 to 2003-04

(in '000 tonnes)

Year	Domestic Production	Imports	Total Raw Nuts	Kernels	Exports	Domestic Consumption
1960-61	111	118	228	57	44	13
1970-71	177	169	346	87	50	37
1980-81	185	16	201	50	32	18
1990-91	295	83	378	95	49	46
1995-96	418	222	640	160	71	92
2000-01	430	249	679	170	84	86
2001-02	360	162	522	131	92	39
2002-03	500	403	903	228	129	115
2003-04	520	442	962	240	100	119

Source: Ministry of Agriculture: Agricultural Statistics at Glance: 2004, and Ministry of Finance: Economic Survey, various issues.

Constraints in Cashewnut Production Development

A study of the industry carried out in 1985 revealed that most of the plantations were of seedling origin and cashew cultivation was mainly carried out as afforestation and conservation programmes for wastelands rather than an economic venture. Since productivity was not the basic objective of such a programme, the cashew was maintained under highly neglected conditions. Poor soil fertility in cashew growing areas, seedling progenies of nondescript origin and neglect of the crop resulted in low productivity. This was prevalent in most of the cashew growing areas of Karnataka, Goa, Andhra Pradesh, Orissa and Tamil Nadu. Neglected trees established for conservation purposes hardly responded to the application of any inputs. Seedling progenies that were established in Maharashtra, however, showed that these plantations responded to the application of modern inputs developed by research. These seedling progenies were from selected stock and orchards had received better attention from the beginning of their establishment. In order to ensure better productivity, all new plantings are encouraged to use vegetatively propagated material of recommended cultivars and the use of seedlings is completely discouraged.

One of the major thrusts being advocated lately is to rehabilitate existing unthrifty seedling plantations. It may, however, not be profitable to attempt rehabilitation of senile and sparsely populated orchards. The working group responsible for the preparation of the 8th national plans revised yield estimates from 2 tonnes per ha to one ton per ha, mainly having these plantations in view. The cashew nut area reached peak in 1998-99 of 706 thousand hectares and was likely to reach 1 million ha by the turn by the year 2010. Cashew is being considered as a candidate crop for rehabilitation of wastelands by many development planners. The issue is, however, being debated whether more wasteland be brought under cashew or rehabilitation of old orchards be undertaken using elite planting material. Wastelands that are now being considered are far more inferior to those areas, which already have cashew plantations. The cashew crop has contributed in some ways to conserving the soil in the existing orchards. The logical alternative would, therefore, be to utilize existing cashew lands for a development programme using available technologies to reach the required production levels without expanding into any more degraded wastelands.

Concluding Remarks

One of the key factors in favour of expanding the cashew industry in

India is the stable price in the International market compared to other nuts such as almond, hazel nut etc. Nutritionally, cashew also compares well with other tree nut crops. It is a commodity rich in unsaturated fatty acids with high protein and low levels of saturated fats and soluble sugars. Higher levels of polyunsaturated fatty acids, which lower blood cholesterol, are particularly of high nutritional significance. The crop is steadily gaining acceptance in many western markets where consumers are more health conscious.

The elaborate research network and development infrastructure in India is beneficial for the expansion of the cashew industry. Development and introduction of eco-friendly production packages such as organic farming and integrated pest management can provide a further boost to the development of the crop and the cashew industry in the future.

CASHEW NUT INDUSTRY IN INDONESIA

Introduction

Cashew growing in Indonesia was originally meant for afforestation programmes; particularly in those areas that were infertile and experienced dry climatic conditions. Within the last two decades however, expansion in area under cashew was carried out for the economic value of cashew nut kernels rather than for afforestation purposes. There has been a steady increase in cashew growing areas annually, especially in the Eastern part of the country where the climatic conditions are favourable for its production. From an area of 58,000 ha which produced 9000 tonnes in 1975, it increased to 230,000 ha with a total production cf 78,000 tonnes in 1996. Output increased further to 122,000 tonnes in 2005. Unfortunately, the increase in yield has been rather limited. Low productivity of plantations is partly due to the use of unselected germplasm and traditional management practices. As a result, mean yield/ha ranged from 150-250 kg/ha/year.[8]

The volume of cashew exported has been increasing in recent years. In 1978, the country exported 39 thousand tonnes, which increased to 55 thousand tonnes by 1994. The volume of exports decreased to 27 thousand tonnes in 1996, partly due to a steady increase in domestic consumption. In recent years exports of raw cashew have recovered to 56.5 thousand tonnes in 2004. Also Indonesia has started exports of cashewnut kernels. Cashewnuts are mainly exported to India and the USA, and recently, Japan too has become an importer of Indonesian cashew. More than 90 per cent of cashew production is in the hands of small farmers.

Present Status of Cashew Production

Cashew production in Indonesia is mainly confined to the Eastern parts of the country. These areas are characterized by sparse rainfall and a long dry season, which is considered ideal for high productivity of cashew. In order to minimize losses during orchard establishment, timing of the planting to synchronize with the short rains becomes critical. If planting losses occur however, re-planting is carried out the following year.

There are indications that the cashew growing areas are steadily increasing. For example, in 1978 the cashew-harvested area was about over 33,000 ha with a total production of 8,800 tonnes. This increased to 102,744 ha with a production of 23,305 tonnes by 1988, and it rose to 268,000 ha in the year, 2005. Production statistics are presented in Table 12.13. The main growing regions are the provinces of South East Sulawesi (46%), South Sulawesi (23%), East Java (10%), West and East Nusatenggara (4%), Bali (3%) and other minor areas (14%).

Table 12.13: Cashew Production Trends in Indonesia (1978-2005)

Year	*Area (Ha)*	*Production (tonnes)*
1978	33,405	8,800
1983	78,374	18,047
1988	102,744	23,305
1993	168,000	69,751
1996	229,786	77,663
1999	250,000	89,500
2002	260,000	84,200
2003	260,000	118,300
2004	260,000	120,000
2005	268,000	122,000

Source: Usman Daras: Integrated Production Practices of Cashew in Indonesia: *op. cit.* and FAO STAT Database: March 2006.

The increase in production has been largely due to higher area under cashewnuts with only a marginal improvement of crop yields. This is mainly as mentioned above due to the use of unselected planting material and poor management practices followed by growers.

Propagation and Production of Planting Material

The low productivity of Indonesian cashew orchards is a result of the indiscriminate use of unselected and inferior germplasm by growers. No serious selection work has been carried out so far to develop superior clones and farmers have been compelled to use their own planting material. This has now been realized as a major drawback to the development of the cashew industry. Some attempts have been made to improve the situation, which have met with little success. Although the Ministry of Agriculture, Directorate of Extension has recommended several selections from high yielding mother trees identified as seed sources in the main production areas, these improvements in the germplasm status are yet to be realized in any substantial way.

In addition to the above selections identified as bulk populations, some collections of superior germplasm are also available at the Research Institute for Spices and Medicinal Crops, which have been mandated for the improvement of cashew. Seeds of these selections are also available for distribution. The potential productivity of the above bulk populations varies from 900-2,200 kg/ha/year. As the number of trees for each selection is limited, an immediate impact on production cannot be achieved in the short-term, although through a long-term multiplication programme this can be achieved.

There has been little success in the use of clonal material for artificial propagation of cashew. The majority of plantations are therefore being established from seedling progenies. In the future, vegetatively propagated planting material will be used for new areas, once the techniques are developed. Since grafting of clonal selections can be carried out relatively easily, a programme is to be launched to improve the skills of cashew growers in vegetatively propagated planting material production.

Establishment of Cashew Orchards

As mentioned earlier, cashew cultivation is mainly confined to the eastern parts of the country, which have a relatively dry climate. Plantations are established on flat terrain as well as in hilly areas. Since land clearing on hilly slopes is very costly, cashew trees are established with minimum land development. When inter-crops have to be grown in the rainy season, farmers clean their lands, but weeds are allowed to grow in the dry season after the annual crops have been harvested. Potential fire hazards in the dry season discourages weeding and collection of dry vegetation in summer. Torrential rain in the monsoon season also tends to erode hill slopes when the vegetal cover is removed. Since large-scale conservation on hill slopes is considered too expensive, most farmers resort to mini-conservation measures for individual cashew trees.

Land clearing operations and digging pits are carried out 1-2 months before planting. Tree spacing used by farmers varies from 6m × 6m to 10m × 10m or more. For afforestation programmes, the spacing used was generally 4m × 4m with the intention of thinning out later in order to ensure a good ground cover. Due to its widely spreading growth habit, cashew trees perform badly and are less productive at high plant densities. With high competition for water and overcrowding, these plantations become uneconomical. The current practice adopted by farmers, therefore, is to increase the spacing in order to utilize crop avenues for cultivation of inter-crops such as upland rice, maize, cassava etc. Cashew planting is usually carried out in November-December when monsoonal conditions bring regular rains.

Management and Aftercare of Cashew Orchards

In general, cashew receives very little attention as a crop. It is considered more as a forest tree rather than an agricultural crop, since cashew does not seem to require much attention compared to other crops. Therefore, growers incur minimal production costs for maintenance of cashew orchards. In most instances, cashew is a companion crop to various annual inter-crops and economically, is of secondary importance to farmers.

Since cashew is usually grown on marginal lands where farmers face long dry periods without any access to irrigation, it is not only the area of land and resources that is limiting but also the high labour inputs required to grow many annual crops during the short rainy season. Since the family labour is relatively and frequently unemployed, some income from crops like cashew helps to supplement family income and cashew planting and harvesting is often carried out by family labour.

After a few years of weeding and care of the young cashew plants, the trees develop large canopies and the farmers move to other vacant plots to grow annual crops. As cashew trees grow in size, there is less weed competition, care and management problems will diminish except for clean weeding under the canopies to facilitate harvesting. The only orchard operation in the dry season is harvesting and an occasional weeding at the end of the dry season, before the advent of the rainy season. In some instances, mulching and cover cropping are practiced, although these agronomic applications are seldom seen in most cashew orchards. Farmers are often scared of fire hazards when dry plant residue is heaped in cashew plantations in the summer months. Some general fertilizer recommendations for those farmers who wish to apply for their cashew crop are available (Table 12.14).

Table 12.14. General Recommendations for Fertilizer Application in Cashew

(gm/tree/year)

Age (crop year)	*Nitrogen (N)*	*Phosphorus (P_2O_5)*	*Potash (K_2O)*
1	100	80	–
2	200	80	60
3	400	120	120
4	500	130	130
5	700	250	420
6	900	250	420
7	1,000	500	300

Note: The fertilizer is to be applied in two split doses, at the beginning and the end of the rainy season.

Source: Abdullah, A. 1994. Technological packages for cashew development. Upland Farmer Development Project, Directorate-General Estate, Ministry of Agriculture.

As subsistence farming is the dominant land use system in dry and marginal lands where cashew is grown, farmers give much higher priority to their annual food crops such as maize, upland rice, cassava etc. The ability to inter-crop is an important economic factor in determining planting distances for the permanent cashew crop, especially in the eastern part of the country where a limited choice of annual crops are available to farmers. Furthermore, use of fertilizer for annual inter-crops is indirectly beneficial to the main cashew plantations.

Replanting and/or Rejuvenation of Old Cashew Orchards

As previously mentioned, cashew was used mainly in afforestation programmes in the early 1970s. Consequently, the narrow spacing used resulted in severe overcrowding and low productivity as trees advanced in age. Improving yields by thinning plantations failed to attract farmers as it was considered too expensive and labour intensive. This operation was, therefore, more of an academic practice followed in research institutions rather than in farmers' fields. Low yields in cashew have also been attributed to pest and disease incidence. Common pests attacking cashew are *Cricula, Helopeltis,* and diseases such as *Fusarium* and *Pseudomonas.*[9] Losses from pests and diseases have been considered to be substantial although there are no accurate statistics available.

Harvesting and Productivity in Cashew

Time of harvesting varies from region to region, but is usually carried out in the dry season from July to November. In South East Sulawesi, harvesting months are from July to September, whereas orchardists in West and East Nusatenggara harvest their cashew crops from September to November. These differences are mainly due to micro-climatic variations between regions.

The main source of income for growers is the cashew kernel. Other products such as the cashew apple and CNSL are of little importance. In some areas, the cashew apple may be marketed, used for manure or given as livestock feed. The economic value of CNSL is exploited only by a few processing industries that have been established in the country. Statistics on the utilization or marketing of CNSL or the percentage of shelling of nuts by farmers and processors are not available. The main difficulty in shelling of nuts is the high variability in size and resultant quality. Prices of nuts also vary according to different grades of whole and broken kernels.

Marketing

Growers market their produce through local traders and middlemen who collect and supply exporters and processors. Current prices are about US $ 1 per kg of raw nuts and US$ 5-6 for kernels. Prices at farm-level are remunerative and tend to increase every year (Fig. 12.1). Development programmes on cashew growing in the Eastern part of the country therefore, meets ready acceptance by farmers.

Exports of Cashewnuts and Cashew Kernels

Indonesia started exports of cashewnut from 1977 onwards, and of cashew kernels from 1996 onwards. Its exports of cashewnuts increased from the meagre amount of 55 tonnes in 1978 to about 57 thousand tonnes in the year 2004, the last year for which the data are available. Its export earnings from the commodity rose from US$ 205,000 to over US$ 50 million during this period. Export of cashew kernel rose from 680 tonnes in 1996 to 3341 tonnes in 2003, but declined to 2881 tonnes in 2004. By contrast export earnings from cashew kernels rose from US$ 6.57 million to US$ 7.84 million. In the case of cashewnuts the higher export earnings reflected a sharp increase in volume shipped, as the unit value realized declined sharply. The export value per tonne of cashewnuts fell by more than

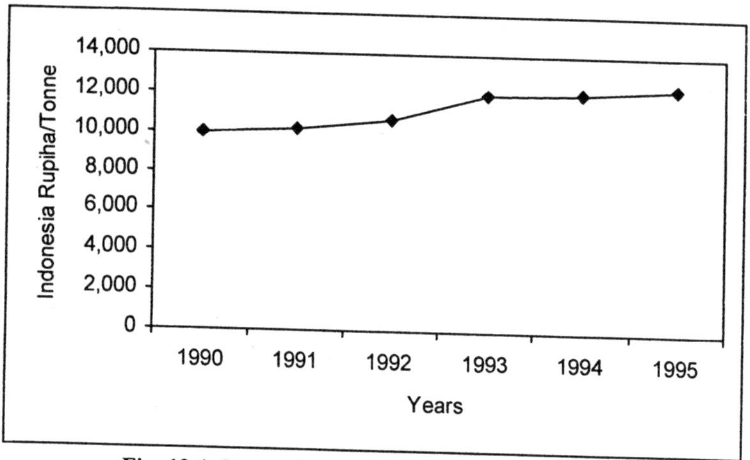

Fig. 12.1: Domestic Price of Cashewnut in Indonesia

five-fold from US 3,727 in 1978 to about US$ 890 in 2004, while for cashew kernel the price per unit declined by more than half, from almost US$ 4,340 in 1996 to US$ 2,722 (Table 12.15).

Potential for Cashew Production Development

Currently the total area under cashew production is estimated at 270,000 ha with a total cashewnuts output of 120,000 tonnes of kernel. The world production of cashew was estimated at 2.34 million tonnes in 2005. Based on these figures Indonesia has contributed over 5 per cent of world production. The role that Indonesia can play in the supply of cashew to world markets will increase in the future. Production statistics show a steady increase in cashew growing area each year. In recent years the cashew programme has been assisted by foreign donor funding from ADB and UNDP.

Land use surveys have shown that more than 15 million ha spread out over 9 provinces in the country are suitable for the expansion of the cashew industry. There does not seem to be any limitations on land availability as seen from the above survey. World cashew prices are also very favourable for the development of the crop in Indonesia.

Constraints to Production Development

There are, however, several constraints that the cashew industry may have to face in the future. There is bound to be increased competition in the international market between the main producing countries and as a

Table 12.15: Exports of Cashewnut and Cashew Kernels from Indonesia

Year	Cashow Nuts			Cashew Kernels		
	Qty. (Tonnes)	Value (US$ 1000)	Unit value (US$/Tonne)	Qty. (Tonnes)	Value (US$ 1000)	Unit value (US$/Tonne)
1978	55	205	3,727.3	Nil	Nil	Nil
1980	367	1673	4,558.6	Nil	Nil	Nil
1985	3,800	4,104	1,080.0	Nil	Nil	Nil
1990	3,218	8,243	2,561.5	Nil	Nil	Nil
1995	28,105	21,308	758.2	Nil	Nil	Nil
1996	27,206	20,800	764.5	680	2,951	4,339.7
1997	15,359	15,386	1,001.8	944	3,766	3,989.4
1998	28,603	28,706	1,003.6	1,684	6,291	3,735.7
1999	31,639	30,774	972.7	2,881	12,733	4,419.6
2000	25,621	22,781	889.2	1,998	8,721	4,367.9
2001	39,546	23,946	605.5	1,539	4,983	3,237.8
2002	50,385	31,213	619.5	1,332	3,597	2,700.5
2003	57,087	36,968	647.6	3,341	6,566	1,965.3
2004	56,491	50,346	891.2	2,881	7,841	2,721.6

Source: FAO STAT Data Base: October; 2005.

result, the prices of cashew may go down. Among other problems facing the local cashew industry are those of a technical nature. Lack of high quality planting material/varieties, variable quality in home-level and small-scale processing enterprises, pest and disease constraints, drought effects, fire hazards and economic instability would be some of the factors that could adversely affect the cashew industry.

Of the 18 processing companies established in the 1980s, only 8 are functioning today. Low production and consequently, the lack of raw material supply are the major causes for their decline. There is strong competition between rawcashew nut exporters and processors. In this situation, farm-gate prices are good, but probably not conducive for development of the processing industry. Some government intervention in developing a price control policy to benefit the producer and the processor is, therefore, essential in the interests of the industry.

CASHEWNUT INDUSTRY IN THAILAND

Introduction

Cashew was introduced to Southern Thailand in 1901 from adjacent areas of Malaysia from where it spread all over the country. The crop began to be considered as having economic importance by 1984 following the government policy to reduce cassava production by substituting with cashew, particularly in the North East. The Cashew Research and Development in the North East Thailand project, partly supported by the EC, was later formulated for the replacement of cassava production. Although cashew forms only a small portion of the national economy, it is increasingly becoming important to growers in the East, in terms of regional economy at present.

Current Status of Production

Area of Production

Thailand ranks as the fourth important cashew producing country in Asia. Since 2002 Vietnam has become the leading producing country, lowering India position to second rank and Indonesia to third rank. Initially, in Thailand major commercial planting areas were concentrated in the South, which were predominantly small-scale enterprises. However, in 1984 a rapid expansion of area took place in the Northeast following the government policy, in agreement with the EC, to reduce cassava production due to an international surplus of the commodity. In addition, a number of extension projects were initiated by the government. Eventually, the area under cashew substantially increased from 22,022 ha in 1983 to 61,748 ha in 1989, with major areas in the Northeast such as Nakhonratchasima, Burirum and Si Sa Ket provinces, and in the South in areas such as Ranong, Songkhla and Pattani provinces.

In 1991 however, cashew production greatly decreased, mainly due to poor fruit setting. Insect infestation and environmental stress may have been responsible for reduced productivity. Consequently, a number of cashew trees, particularly in the North and Northeast have been cut down and many orchards were neglected in 1991-92. Thailand had only 55,407 ha in 1994 with a total production of 58,359 tonnes.[10] Although planting areas in the North and Northeast have declined since 1991, those in the East, particularly in Chon Buri province, continued to increase leading to an expansion of small to medium-sized shelling factories for processing of nuts.

Varieties

Popular cashew varieties grown in Thailand include *Si Sa Ket 60-1* and *Si Sa Ket 60-2,* which are officially recommended by the Department of Agriculture (DOA), and *Sirichai 25* which has been commercially released by a private company. In addition, at the beginning of the national promotion project of cashew, seedlings of the composite variety *Si Sa Ket A* and seedlings of *Maboonkrong* from the private sector were also recommended to growers due to insufficient supply of grafted plants to satisfy growers' requirements.

Si Sa Ket 60-1 and Si Sa Ket 60-2 were developed following clonal selection. They were recommended after results from yield comparison and regional yield trials indicated that they are of good quality in terms of nut and kernel size, and 40 per cent higher yield than unselected local varieties. The average nut yields of Si Sa Ket 60-1 and Si Sa Ket 60-2 at year 11 are about 33.4 kgs. and 25.0 kg per tree and the nut weights are 6.29g and 7.20 g, respectively. Both selected clones have an average about 320 kernels per pound, which is the international market standard grade. Si Sa Ket composite A was derived from 10 selected clones including Si Sa Ket 60-1 and Si Sa Ket 60-2. Sirichai 25 had not been tried in the Northeast before widespread planting began in this region. Early yields of young trees were good but the Si Sa Ket varieties may well have yielded better under the same conditions. Among the improved cashew varieties of Thailand, only the composite Si Sa Ket A has genetic variation so that there is little likelihood of all trees becoming susceptible to a new strain of a disease or pest. The potential yield for selected clones Si Sa Ket 60-1 and Si Sa Ket 60-2 is shown in Table 12.16.

Table 12.16: Average Yield at Si Sa Ket of Recommended DOA Varieties (kg/Tree)

Varieties	*Year 3*	*Year 4*	*Year 7*	*Year 9*	*Year 11*
Si Sa Ket 60-1	1.2	9.8	13.7	15.7	33.4
Si Sa Ket 60-2	1.7	6.9	9.6	10.1	25.0

Yield potential and quality of different cashew varieties were investigated at four different locations. Results showed that the Si Sa Ket varieties were the most promising (Table 12.17).

Propagation and Production of Planting Material

Following the government policy to decrease cassava production by introducing cashew to the farmers, particularly in the Northeast in 1981, the Si Sa Ket Horticultural Research Center of the Horticultural Research Institute (HRI) was responsible for the supply of cashew nut planting material. Both grafted plants and seedlings were produced. The grafted varieties using a modified inarching method included *Si Sa Ket 60-1* and

Table 12.17: Yield and Quality of Different Cashew Varieties at Year 4 (Average of 12 Trees from 4 Locations)

Varieties	*Yield (kg/tree)*	*Nut Weight (g)*	*Kernel Recovery (%)*	*Number of Kernels/lb*
Si Sa Ket 60-1	4.4	6.6	26.7	263
Si Sa Ket 60-2	3.0	7.2	26.0	245
Composite SK-A	2.2	5.9	27.5	279
Sirichai 25	2.5	7.0	28.0	238
Maboonkrong	1.4	6.7	27.4	251
Local	1.4	5.4	28.1	302

Source: Suwit Chaikiattiyos: *Integrated Production Practices of Cashew* in Thailand: Si Sa Ket Horticultural Research Centre, Muang District, Si Sa Ket, Thailand: FAO RAPA Publication: 1998/12, p.62.

Si Sa Ket 60-2 which were released by government agencies. A private company was also involved in cashew extension by supplying grafted plants, namely *Sirichai 25* to growers who obtained bank loans from the Bank of Agriculture and Cooperatives. In most cases, rootstocks were prepared from seeds with high specific gravity since such seeds gave higher percentage of germination.

Propagation by marcotting, budding and from cuttings is also possible, but this is considered too expensive, unreliable and more complex. In grafting, the rootstocks should be 2-4 months old and scions should be 8 to 10 cm long and of pencil thickness. The colour of the scion should be turning from green to brown and the top 4-5 leaves should be dark green indicating proper maturity. A longitudinal cut of 3-4 cm is made on the scion on either side to make a wedge and is inserted into the split on the rootstock and tied with polythene strips. The grafts are kept in the shade for 3 to 4 weeks and later transferred to an open site to allow new vegetative flushes to grow.

Establishment of Cashew Orchards

Cashew can be cultivated on a wide variety of soils in Thailand. However, for realizing better yield potential, sandy loam soils without a hard pan are desirable. Although considered drought tolerant, the tree requires a well-drained soil with substantial moisture available for the root zone if commercial yields are to be attained. This has been confirmed by the rapid expansion of areas in the East where soil moisture content and relative humidity are relatively higher than the North and Northeast. Furthermore, cultivation of cashew in the South over a long time also substantiates the theory that sufficient moisture content assures high yields.

It is strongly recommended that the crop be raised from grafted plants. Recommended spacing is 6m × 6m except those trees grown from seedlings, particularly in the South. Pits are opened to a size of 50 cm × 50 cm × 50 cm and manure is mixed before planting. The planting should be started during the early rains in June to ensure maximum tree survival. After year 8, every other tree in the row may be removed to allow the remaining trees to spread their canopies without inter-row competition.

Care and Management of Cashew Orchards

Cashew trees should be trained to one main stem. After branching begins, training may be practiced to achieve a tree with one leader shoot of 0.5-1.5 m. A major vegetative flush follows the onset of the rainy season in May or June and flowering occurs at the growing tips of terminal shoots within 3-4 months after the period of restricted growth in November and December. Cashew may produce fruit at year 2 or 3 if trees are raised from grafted plants. Light pruning need to be practiced soon after harvesting in April-May in order to allow new vegetative flushes and to get rid of dead wood.

Fertilizer application recommended for cashew is presented in Table 12.18. Irrigation on cashew is not generally practiced in Thailand. However, weeds are controlled at the time of orchard establishment to reduce competition, and to later facilitate harvesting.

In large-scale plantations in the past, inter-cropping was considered fairly important since it provided an income to growers during the initial years. Trials at the Si Sa Ket Horticultural Research Center have indicated that sweet corn, groundnut and vegetables can be profitably grown in the crop avenues during the initial years of orchard establishment.

Table 12.18: Fertilizer Recommendations for Cashew

Year	*Density (trees/ha)*	*Type of Fertilizer*	*Fertilizer Rate (kg/ha)*
1-2	280	12-24-12	140
3-5	280	15-15-15	280
6-8	280	13-13-21	560
8-12	140*	13-13-21	550
12-20	140	13-13-21	550

* Trees in between rows are removed at year 8.

Although cashew has been considered as a hardy crop that can withstand the onslaught of pests and diseases, significant crop losses could be caused by them. Thrips (*Haplothrips* sp.) can suck sap from tender shoots and inflorescence resulting in dieback. The pest can be controlled with Carbosulfan at 30 ml per 20 litres of water or carbaryl at 50 g per 20 litres of water. Tea mosquito bugs (*Helopeltis antonii*) cause severe damage to the tender shoots and inflorescence of the cashew tree, often leading to heavy economic loss of the crop. Both adults and nymphs suck the sap from tender shoots, floral parts, cashew apples and even from immature nuts. The pest can be controlled with either carbaryl at 20 g per 20 litres of water or with cyhalothrin at 10 ml per 20 litres of water. Although insect infestation, particularly thrips and mosquito bugs is reported on both the *Maboonkrong* and DOA varieties, it is significant that the former types are more prone to attack by these pests than the latter varieties. Stem borers (*Plocaederus ferrugineus*) cause damage in the form of small holes in the collar region of the tree trunk, which results in gummosis, yellowing and shedding of leaves, drying of twigs and ultimately, the death of the tree. The pest can be controlled effectively by mechanical removal of the larval stages in the early stages of the infestation. The pest is also controlled by injecting carbaryl or ichlovos into the tunnels. Severely affected trees beyond recovery should be cut and removed from the plantation. Many other insects have been reported including aphids and mango shoot weevils. Control measures using insecticides are possible, but alternating between different chemicals is advisable in order to prevent the build up of resistance.

Damping off of seedlings can occur under wet conditions or due to poor drainage in the nursery. Different fungi including *Fusarium* sp., *Pythium* sp., *Phytophthora palmivora* and *Cylindrocladium scoparium* have been reported as causal organisms. The fungi attack either the root or collar region or both, mainly at the tender seedling stage. Control measures include provision of adequate drainage in the nursery and the use of benalaxyl. Anthracnose (*Colletotrichum gloeosporioides* and *Botryodiplodia* sp.) can infect the panicles by penetrating through the wounds on panicles caused by sucking insects such as thrips. The anthracnose pathogen penetrates the dead tissue. The fungus enters the fruit through the stigma of flowers at the blooming stage. The disease is severe when rainy weather occurs during flowering. Recommended control measures include removal of affected parts and spraying trees with copper oxychloride or mancozeb at 40-50 gm per 20 litres of water.

Topworking of Old Trees

For rejuvenation of old trees, topworking can be done using scions from superior varieties. This is being practiced in most cashew orchards in the South where trees were established from unselected seeds. A two to three fold increase in yield in the third year after topworking has been reported provided proper fertilizer application; regular chemical sprays and weeding operations were practiced.

Harvesting of Nuts and Yield

Mature nuts are manually harvested and collected over a period of 8-10 weeks in the months of March-April. Fruits are usually allowed to drop during the first 4-6 weeks at the beginning of the harvesting season. Nuts can later be picked from the trees. After separation from the apples, nuts are cleaned in water and sun dried for 2-3 days to reduce the moisture content before disposal.

Marketing

In 1990, Thailand exported 5636 tonnes of raw nuts at a value of US$ 3.7 million and 290 tonnes of kernels valued at US$ 335000. Exports have however, greatly decreased since 1993 because of poor productivity, particularly in the North and Northeast. Production now almost equals consumption and there is only a small net export trade. In 1995, export of raw nut and kernel was only 70 and 79 tonnes, respectively. In 2004 exports of cashew nut kernels were 1,183 tonnes worth US$ 1.72 million, while exports of raw cashewnut amounted to 13 tonnes valued at US$ 11,000 (Table 12.19). Any future increases in production may have to find export markets.

The cashewnut shelling industry in Thailand is relatively small. There is only one company (Maboonkrong) operating nut shelling on a large scale. Most cashew nuts produced in the country are sold and sent across to factories in the East for shelling although there are several local factories for each region. Processing starts from sun drying of nuts for 2-3 days. Before shelling nuts are boiled for 2-3 hours. Shelling is done manually by hand and leg operated shelling machines. The kernel is scooped out by means of a sharp needle. On average one operator can shell 1-1.5 kg per hour depending on individual skill. After shelling, kernels are oven-dried at 50°C in a homemade gas oven to reduce the moisture and to loosen the adhering testa. Peeling of the testa is later done by hand. Then kernels are graded into three grades, namely, Jumbo, A and B

Table 12.19: Thailand: Exports of Cashew nut and Cashew Kernels: 1990–2004

	Cashew Nut		Cashew Kernels	
	Quantity (Tonnes)	Value (US$ 1000)	Quantity (Tonnes)	Value (US$ 1000)
1990	5,636	3,782	290	335
1991	2,659	2,151	132	675
1992	3,334	2,682	102	543
1993	860	612	260	400
1994	57	46	81	456
1995	70	28	79	437
1996	5	25	97	529
1997	531	215	189	651
1998	535	891	226	829
1999	214	402	227	721
2000	63	48	176	741
2001	1	2	74	312
2002	27	74	208	900
2003	9	24	697	2,801
2004	13	11	1,183	1,719

Source: FAO STAT Database, March 2006.

grades. Labour costs for shelling, peeling of testa and grading amounts to about Baht 20-25 per kg of finished kernels. Although seed coats and seed testa can be utilized, they offer only marginal returns. Cashew kernels are usually sold to a central market in Bangkok and are then subsequently traded for domestic consumption and export. In addition, particularly in small scale processing in the South, after separating nuts from the fruit, the nuts are roasted to drive off the caustic cashew nut shell liquid (CNSL) and then opened individually using hand shelling machines.

Potential for Cashewnut Production Development

Although cashew is considered to be a low-potential crop as indicated by an obvious decrease in planted area, especially in the North and Northeast, it is increasingly becoming an important commercial crop in the Eastern region. The market price of cashew in this area remains high in comparison to other crops. It has also been found that the productivity of trees in this area is much higher than those grown in the North and Northeast. It is also noteworthy that farmers in the Eastern region have turned to cashew growing instead of sugarcane, which requires very high labour inputs, especially at harvest time.

Major Constraints in Cashew Nut Production Development

During extension of cashew production, the major constraints included insect infestation from thrips, mosquito bugs, stem borers, and disease infection from anthracnose, all of which could be satisfactorily controlled by chemical application. In 1991, dieback of panicles and insect problems became widespread and adversely affected productivity of nuts. In addition, it was evident that trees with satisfactory flowering did not set fruit even if chemical sprays were appropriately applied. It is probable that trees had undergone environmental stress such as an extended drought period resulting in a marked drop in relative humidity and/or higher day temperatures. This affected flowering, fertilization and even fruit growth and development. Since the DOA varieties were mostly early types, they had a better chance of evading drought conditions, in comparison to Maboonkrong varieties. Nonetheless, under certain conditions, the DOA varieties, which were selected for the wetter regions, were less adaptable to long droughts. Starting in 1985, BAAC in conjunction with a commercial company offered a medium term loans to farmers, which resulted in a successful extension effort to increase the management skills of farmers. Using improved varieties, fertilizer and clean cultivation methods, farmers were given the technical knowhow by extension workers who made regular visits. Production inputs were provided in kind by the agency servicing the loan. Despite the fact that there was strong government backstopping for the programme, many farmers were unable to exploit the situation to their advantage due to the poor production skills of workers.

Concluding Remarks

Cashew production in Thailand has declined since 1991 due to poor productivity of crop. Planted area has decreased repadily particularly in the Northeast, whereas in the South the change has only been marginal. In the East however, cashew production has expanded and several shelling factories have been installed which augurs well for the future of this region.

It is possible that cashew production will play a significant role in the regional economy of the East.

Despite the relatively low cost of orchard establishment when seedlings are used, it is recommended that grafted plants be used for new plantations. The recommended varieties available now include Si Sa Ket 60-1 and Si Sa Ket 60-2 released by the DOA. In addition, the agro-techniques recommended should be strictly followed if higher productivity is to be achieved.

Further research on cashew improvement would has to focus on development of better adapted varieties with tolerance/resistance to biotic and abiotic stresses through conventional and non-conventional breeding programmes. Other problems that research need to concentrate would be the physiological causes that affect fruit set. The germplasm thus developed would not only benefit Thailand but the neighboring countries as well.

REFERENCES

1. Nguyen Minh Chau: *Integrated Production Practices for Cashew Nut in Viet Nam*: Director, Long Dinh Fruit Research Center, Long Dinh, Chau Thanh, Tiengiang, Viet Nam. A paper prepared for the FAO Regional Expert Consultation on Integrated Production Practices in Cashew in Asia. 7-9 October, 1997, Bangkok 1998.http://www.fao.org/docrep/005:
2. Donafood, 1996, *Cultural Practices for Cashew Trees*, Agric. Services Department of Dongnai Province.
3. Donafood, 1996, *op. cit.*
4. National Institute of Planning and Projects, 1997. *Orientation for Cashew Tree Development in Vietnam*, Hanoi.
5. Vietnam Cashew Tree Association, 1997, *Present Situation of Cashew Production and Programmes for Cashew Development up to 2010*, Workshop on Cashew Tree Development in Vietnam, Hanoi. This publication gives very conservative projections for cashew nut production by the year 2010.
6. Ministry of Agriculture: Directorate of Economics and Statistics: *Agricultural Statistics at a Glance*: 2004, p. 151.
7. Bhaskara Rao, E.V.V.: *Integrated Production Practices of Cashew in India*: Director National Research for Cashew, Puttar, D.K., Karnataka: Paper Presented at the FAO Asian workshop: http://www.fao.org//docrep/005.
8. Usman Daras: Integrated Production Practices of Cashew in Indonesia: Research Officer, Institute for Spices and Medicinal Crops, Agency for Agricultural Research and Development, Indonesia: *FAO Document.*
9. Tombe, M., *et al.,* 1996. Penelitian jamur Fusarium beresal dari tanaman jambu mente dengan gejala busuk akar. Prosiding Forum Komunikasi Ilmiah Komoditas Jambu Mente. Balai Penelitian Tanaman Rempah dan Obat. 210-217 hal.
10. FAO data on Thailand cashew nut seems to be unreliable based on adhoc guess estimates of the FAO staff. The discussion in this section is, therefore, based on the Suit Chaikiattiyos paper on Integrated Production Practices of Cashew in Thailand: FAO RAPA Publication: 1998/12.

13

CASHEW INDUSTRY IN OTHER ASIAN COUNTRIES

In this chapter the status and prospects for the cashew industry in four smaller Asian cashew producing countries are presented in a summary form. Countries covered include Sri Lanka, Myanmar, the Philippines and China.

CASHEW IN SRI LANKA

In Sri Lanka cashew has become an important cash crop for farmers especially in the dry zone. There is great potential for increased production for the local market as well as for export. The development of the cashew industry in the country is the responsibility of the Sri Lanka Cashew Corporation under the Ministry of Plantation Industries. In the dry zone of the country there are about 2 million ha of agricultural land that is presently undeveloped, and which could be used for cashew production. With increased production from the use of improved varieties and agro-techniques, cashew production is bound to increase, which will enhance local consumption and promote more exports. In 1990 Sri Lanka earned US$ 6.9 million from cashew exports.

Current Status of Cashew Production

Cashew is cultivated in almost all the districts in the country. Cashew is mainly found in home gardens or cultivated in smallholdings. Nurseries are raised by the Sri Lanka Cashew Corporation through selected nurserymen. High density planting is not commonly practiced by local farmers. Banana is a popular inter-crop in many cashew plantations. Cashew is a crop that requires low management as compared to other orchard crops. Rejuvenation by top-working is not generally practiced in cashew orchards in Sri Lanka. Cashew nut harvesting is usually carried out in the months of May-July by gathering fallen nuts.

Production

The FAO time series data indicate a fluctuating trend in output over time. Cashewnut production almost doubled from 1961 to 1965, and declined in the next decade. Production reached a peak in the mid-eighties. Area harvested data are available from 1980 onward. It initially rose marginally but declined subsequently. However, yield of cashewnut has generally declined and remain rather low at less than 250 kgs. per hectares. In 2005 Sri Lanka produced 5,500 tonnes of cashew from harvested area of over 22 thousand hectares. Sri Lanka has a very small share (around 2 to 2.5 per cent) of the Asian cashew production market. Some of the cashews are processed locally, while the remainder is exported to India for processing.

Exports

Sri Lanka cashew kernels are known for their consistently bigger size. Although the main volume of kernels supplied to the world market comes in the small size of 320 counts, over 85 per cent of the Sri Lankan exports consist of the bigger counts of 180, 210 and 240. Nearly 40 per cent of total production is used for local consumption and 60 per cent is exported in bulk packages. In 2004 Sri Lanka exported 100 tonnes of cashew earning Sri Lankan Rs. 47 million. Its exports has declined continually from a peak of 1300 tonnes reached in 1993.

The cost of production of cashew in Sri Lanka is much higher than other countries due to high labour costs, low efficiency and lack of technical know-how in the production of cashew.

Potential for Cashewnut Production Development

The following factors shall contribute to the development potential of the cashew industry:

Compared to other crops, cashew needs minimal inputs and production costs. Due to their chemical composition, cashew kernels have high keeping quality and good storability characteristics.

In the first three years, young cashew plantations can be successfully inter-cropped to provide farmers with supplementary income until the crop gives economic yields. Many subsidy and credit schemes are available for cashew farmers. The Sri Lanka Cashew Corporation, the ADB funded Perennial Crops Development Project, the Southern Development Authority and the Mahaweli Project are government assisted programmes for improvement of crops such as cashew.

Constraints in Cashewnut Production Development

The following are the major constrains that need to be overcome:

- Under-utilization of cashew orchards and losses due to poor post-harvest practices.
- Lack of price support system for cashew.
- Very weak research support for the development of cashew.
- Displacement of large number of cashew growers due to civil unrest.
- High unemployment and low incomes of cashew farmers.

Concluding Remarks

Research and development activities should be strengthened to evolve appropriate technology on breeding, soil testing, disease and pest control, irrigation systems, fertilizer management and post-harvest technology. In view of the increased involvement of women in the cashew industry, more women development programmes should be initiated. The government should seriously consider establishing a price support system to help small-scale cashew farmers.

CASHEW IN MYANMAR

Current Status

In Myanmar cashew is cultivated at present in ten regions, namely, in Kachin State, Kayin State, Sagaing Division, Taninthayi Division, Bago Division, Mon State, Rakhine State, Yangon Division, Shan State and Ayeyarwady Division. The major production areas are Taninthayi Division (4,187 ha), Mon State (4,367 ha) and Yangon Division (2,353 ha). Area under cashew has extended to 17,700 ha with an annual production of 4,500 tonnes in 2005. The high potential areas for cashew production are in Taninthayi Division followed by Mon State. Production of cashew in Sagaing, Rakhine, Kachine and Shan States may be restricted to homesteads along with other tree species to supplement small-farmers' incomes.

Future Prospects

The Government of Myanmar has prepared an ambitious expansion plan for rubber, oil palm and cashew. Of these, the expansion of rubber is progressing satisfactorily with an annual increase of 20,000 ha and cashew has a targeted annual increase of 3,000 ha. The pace of increase for cashew however, is rather slow when compared to rubber

Constraints in Cashewnut Production Development

- By and large, the marketing system for cashew remains undeveloped and unorganized.
- Myanmar Perennial Crop Enterprise (MPCE) should be mandated to provide extension and technological support to cashew growers.
- The present practices, from land preparation to processing of kernels, need major improvements.
- Established cashew varieties of proven yield potential and adapted to different regions should be made available to the farmers.

Concluding Remarks

Of all the areas identified for cashew production, Taninthayi Division has the ideal rainfall and optimum distribution for highest productivity. Cashew production in Sagaing Division, Rakhine, Kachin and Shan States may be confined to homestead-level production only. The national cashew agronomists have made a number of suggestions. Agronomic practices pertaining to land development and orchard establishment should be systematically carried out to ensure the best conditions for cashew orchards. There is scope for development of cashew production in Myanmar although the crop is not, at present, so attractive to farmers as compared to other tree crops like oil palm and rubber. To expand cashew cultivation in the country obviously requires a strong government support and financial help from donor organizations

CASHEW IN THE PHILIPPINES

Cashew (*Anacardium occidentale* L.), locally known as *'kasoy'*, is one of the most important nut crops in the Philippines. In 2004, the Philippines exported 2,223 tonnes of raw cashewnuts valued at US$ 1.38 million.

Current Status

Cashew is grown in most regions of the country mainly as a backyard crop or as a component of many small-scale diversified orchards. Palawan is the leading production center where more than 90 per cent of the 2.6 million bearing trees are found. Other important areas are Llocos Region, Central Luzon, Northern Mindanao and Western Visayas. In these areas, most of the bearing trees are of local origin. However, for new plantings, predominantly in Palawan, the recommended superior varieties such as Mitra, Recto and Fernandez have been planted.

Marketing

Cashew is mainly marketed as raw nut to local traders and processors. Some growers process cashew nuts into roasted splits and whole kernels and sell them directly to consumers, wholesalers or retailers. Some traders go directly to farmers to buy cashew nuts and transport the produce to processors.

Potential for Cashewnut Production Development

The domestic demand for cashew nut alone by the year 2005 is estimated at about 6,720 tonnes. With the 5.4 per cent annual growth rate of world cashew nut exports, the market for the commodity is still enormous.

Constraints in Cashewnut Production Development

Since cashew can assure a good income, considering the range of products it can give from the nut alone, the problems facing the production sector need urgent attention. These include:

- Limited supply of grafted plants of recommended varieties;
- Control of pests and diseases, especially anthracnose during the reproductive phase;
- Low level of knowledge of farmers on production and post-harvest technologies brought about by poor communication links to production areas;
- Lack of financial resources for farmer groups to embark on processing of their crop of nuts and cashew apples.

Concluding Remarks

It is inevitable that cashew production will improve with the availability of vast natural resources available for the development of the crop. The increasing domestic requirements for food confectioneries for the nut alone and eventually for cashew apples can assure a good income for cashew farmers, especially if village-level processing can be developed for the crop. However, the information and the technology application are very important to the cashew industry. Furthermore, research and development in cashew production and post-harvest activities have to be strengthened to offer the new technologies to the cashew industry. The utilization of various by-products will undoubtedly motivate farmers to embark on expanding cashew production.

CASHEW INDUSTRY IN CHINA

China has a cashew cultivation history of about 60 years. The total land area under cashew increased to 13,000 ha in 1979 and has since declined to the present 8,930 ha, which is mainly confined to the coastal areas of the south and southwest Hainan. The soils are poor and infertile in these areas with long dry spells in winter and spring and are generally considered unsuitable for the cultivation of other tropical food crops without irrigation. The cashew trees, however, grow well under such conditions.

The European Community has provided grant in aid for the development of the cashew industry from 1985-1990, through which systematic research was carried out on cashew production technology in Hainan island. These efforts have helped in promoting cashew production in Hainan.

Current Status

Major cashew producing areas are distributed in the coastal areas of Ledong Lingshui, Dongfang and Sanya of Hainan Province. Scattered cultivations are also found in Wanning and Wenchang in Hainan and trial plantings in Xishuangbanna and Gejui in Yunnan Province. Total area under cashew is estimated at 8,930 ha of which 7,650 ha were in production in 2005. Ledong County in Hainan has the largest area under the crop with 4,650 ha, accounting for 54 per cent of the national production followed by Dongfang Changjiang, and Lingshui.

There are no large scale State owned or private nurseries for cashew propagation in Hainan. Most cashew plantations have their own nurseries for production of planting material required for their expansion programmes.

In general, tree density ranges from 120-270 trees/ha for seedlings and 105-150 trees/ha for clones. To achieve better fruit-set, young cashew trees are often trained to provide a better tree form. In young orchards cashew is also intercropped with green manure cover crops and/or short-term annual crops.

Plant Protection Practices

Cashew diseases are of minor importance in China. Pests on the other hand are economically important in cashewnut production. The cashew fruit borer develops large populations during the fruiting season between March and June, mostly attacking the cashew apple, nuts, racemes and tender shoots. Cashew orchards in Hainan mostly comprise unselected seedling trees often giving very low yields.

Harvesting and Productivity of Cashew

The cashew apple is hardly utilized for processing at present. Cashew yields are usually low with maximum annual average yields reaching only about 240 kg/ha (2002-04 average) even in well managed orchards that have reached peak harvests, while about 30 per cent of the orchards yield negligible harvests. Ledong County in Hainan has the largest area under cashew.

Marketing

Cashew is a crop that is freely marketed in China. Cashewnut mills exploit this situation and even import unprocessed nuts from foreign sources for processing and re-export as well as trade in domestic markets. It exports very small quantities of cashewnuts and cashew kernels. Exports of cashewnuts have declined even more sharply.

Imports of cashewnut kernels which increased considerably, from 1,277 tonnes in 1990 to 8,283 tonnes in 2002, declined to 5,018 tonnes in 2004.

Potential for Cashew Nut Production Development

Although there is some potential for cashewnut development, China does not have the optimum climatic regime for expansion of the cashew industry. Expansion of the cashew crop has many socio-economic benefits. Since cashew cultivation does not require intensive production methods or high input costs, it is an ideal crop for impoverished areas.

Constraints in Cashewnut Production Development

Major constraints to cashewnut development in China include climatic, varietal, and management problems including soil fertility maintenance and plant protection problems.

Typhoons often damage cashew trees, as the tree tends to spread and produce weak branches resulting in loss of the crop. A large proportion of the cashew plantations on Hainan Island comprise unselected seedling trees, which are low yielding, and of poor quality. The majority of cashew orchards in Hainan are poorly managed especially at the juvenile stage. Low yields experienced in most cashew plantations that have reached their peak bearing stage can be attributed to improper orchard fertilizer application practices. Cashew production is mainly confined to the southern and south-western coastal areas of Hainan Island. Cashew area has progressively declined during the last 10 years.

Concluding Remarks

Cashew production is mainly confined to the southern and south-western coastal areas of Hainan Island. The majority of plantations have been established with unselected seedling germplasm, which has resulted in low production and productivity. Nevertheless, cashew can be considered as a suitable economic venture for the resource-poor farming communities as well as an environmentally and ecologically stable crop for a sound land-use system for the coastal areas of Hainan Island.

China has an enormous domestic demand for the cashew crop and local production has been unable to keep up with existing market requirements. The country has to overcome the major constraints to cashew nut development discussed above.

Cashew production is not likely to assume any economic importance in the agricultural framework of the country unless a vigorous campaign is carried out to encourage and attract cashew growers through the offer of better varieties, supported by a strong research and extension effort to backstop the industry. It is only such a consolidated effort based on scientific management techniques that can assist farmers to increase production and productivity of the crop.

14

CASHEWNUT FARMING IN AFRICAN COUNTRIES

CASHEW SECTOR IN NIGERIA[1]

Cashew (*Anacardium Occidentale* L.) is a tree crop of considerable economic importance to Nigeria and other tropical countries. Cultivation of cashew started in the early 1950s, through the efforts of the then Eastern Nigeria Agricultural Development. The majority of export quality nuts come from the Western and Eastern parts of the country.

Harvesting

Cashewnut setting begins in the middle of dry season, while harvesting takes place mainly in February or March. In the Eastern and Western parts of the country, where quality cashewnuts are grown, nuts are allowed to drop to the ground before they are collected.

Grading

In the cashew producing areas, the products are graded according to market requirements. The nuts are graded into two categories by visual determination of the grade according to their surface appearance and size. The two grades are:

(i) *Standard Grade Nuts*: They are sound, mature, thoroughly dried nuts, which apparently show no defect or deformity. Their colour is usually light grey or light brown;

(ii) *Under-grade Nuts*: They may have surface blemishes, spots or somewhat tolerable discolouration. The small size nuts are part of this grade.

Processing of Cashewnuts

Nuts can undergo primary and secondary processing. Primary processing is as old as cashew in Nigeria. About 200 to 300 tonnes of primary processed cashew kernels are marketed locally. Secondary processing entails a higher level of transformation, which targets mainly exports markets, and recently the local urban markets too.

Three types of cashew processing are practiced in Nigeria, namely:

(i) *Small Cottage Processing*: This manual processing is carried out by small cottage industries. The quality of cashews obtained through this processing is poor.

(ii) *Processing for Export*: This type of processing emerged mainly after the deregulation of the economy. At present, the six processing plants operating in Nigeria have a total annual processing capacity of 12,000 tonnes. These plants process about 10 per cent of the local production, and some of them contract processing for merchants of nuts and

(iii) *Processing for the Local Market*: This group of processors has gone further to add flavour and taste to the Nigerian cashew nuts.

Development Strategy

In its efforts to increase food production, the Government of Nigeria has initiated various programmes to accelerate food output and to increase the quantity and the quality of export industrial crops. To complement the efforts of the government, other agencies such as state (provincial) governments; international agencies such as USAID, Non-Governmental Organizations and professional groupings are implementing additional programmes to develop the production and the exports of cashewnuts from Nigeria.

National Accelerated Industrial Crops Production Programme (NAICPP)

The aim of the programme was to increase the production of ten industrial crops including cashew. The main thrust of the Cashew NAICPP project was to sensitize farmers to increase the productivity of the crop by using improved planting materials, through application of improved agronomic practices, and use of improved agro-chemicals. Since the start up of this programme, a total of 1.1 million cashew seedlings have been distributed to farmers and about 8,881 hectares of cashew holdings have been covered.

Cashew Development Programme (Under Tree Crop Development Programme)

This Central Government programme aims at:

- Rehabilitating and resuscitating moribund plantations and expansion programme;
- Training of extension staff and farmers;
- Providing and distributing inputs such as seedlings, agro-chemical etc; and
- Quality control at primary (farm) level.

The programme was implemented over a 4-year period (2001-2004) and is based on the following premises:

- That a total of 2,321 hectares of cashew plantation were to be established.
- That the capacity of Cocoa Research Institute of Nigeria (CRIN) would be further strengthened to allow the development and the production of high yielding, disease resistant, Brazilian cashew varieties for distribution to farmers, with a view to double the total annual output.

FAO supported the agricultural development of Nigeria through sponsorship of a TCP on major tree crops, including cashew. Also the United States Development Aid Agency (USAID) through its Tree Crop Programme had chosen 5 agricultural products with export potential in order to assist in the agricultural development of Nigeria. The five products selected are the gum Arabic, sesame seed, ginger, cashew nut and leather products.

Cashew Sector Performance

The Nigerian cashew plantation dates back to 1954, with then 800 hectares in the present Enugu State and 200 hectares in the Western part of Nigeria. According to the estimations of the USAID sustainable tree crop programme, raw cashew production in Nigeria stands at present at some 50,000 tonnes per year, most of the harvested cashew production takes place on plantations and small holdings.

Production

During the past decade, the production of cashewnuts in Nigeria has increased almost six-fold from 30000 tonnes in 1990 to 176,000 tonnes in 1999 and it rose further to 213,000 tonnes in 2005 (Table 14.1).

Table 14.1: Nigeria: Area, Production and Yield of Cashewnut: 1990-2005

Year	Area Harvested (000 Hec.)	Production (000 Tonnes)	Yield (kgs./hec.)	Year	Area Harvested (000 Hec.)	Production (000 Tonnes)	Yield (kgs./hec.)
1990	50	30	600	1998	243	152	625
1991	75	45	600	1999	178	176	633
1992	90	55	611	2000	291	184	632
1993	120	75	625	2001	291	185	636
1994	135	85	630	2002	321	186	579
1995	155	95	613	2003	321	209	651
1996	175	110	629	2004	324	213	657
1997	243	125	514	2005	324	213	657

Source: FAO STAT DATABASE, March, 2005.

Types of Cashew Cultivated

Nigeria produces a limited variety of cashew, consisting mainly of the yellow and red varieties. New, high yielding cashew varieties, with low gestation period and bigger nuts have been introduced, mainly through the present nursery/plant multiplication programme of the national and provincial governments.

The Cocoa Research Institute of Nigeria (CRIN), with mandate to research into cashew, has developed an improved variety of cashew called "Brazilian Jumbo", with nuts maturing within one year, in contrast to the local wild varieties which mature after 5 years.

Main Factors Influencing Production and Harvesting Performance

Like several other cash crops, production of cashewnuts is influenced by various internal and external factors. However, most of the factors influencing production and harvesting of export cashew are external, including:

- Market price of the product.
- Competition amongst the local buying agents.
- Quality.
- Disease, pest and fire outbreaks.

Price plays a major role in the production of cashew. Among climatic factors shortfall in rainfall or sunshine adversely affects the quality of the cashew.

Export Performance

Prior to the Structural Adjustment Programme commenced in 1986, the export of cashewnuts was not given prominence. Very few firms were in the business and the acreage was reduced considerably. However, since 1987 cashewnuts became prominent among the exported commodities. Exports of cashewnuts from Nigeria fluctuated widely, falling from 14,325 tonnes (US$ 4 billion) in 1990, to 12,580 tonnes in 1991. The highest exports were recorded in 1995, when 16,938 tonnes of cashews, worth over US$ 7.4 billion (Table 14.2).

Table 14.2: Exports of Cashewnuts from Nigeria, 1990-2004

Year	*Exports (Tonnes)*	*Value (US$ Billions)*	*Unit Value (US$/Tonne)*
1990	14,235 (11,456)*	4.00	280.6
1991	12,580	4.46	354.5
1992	12,100	5.20	429.6
1993	13,234	6.99	528.2
1994	12,307	2.82	229.0
1995	16,938 (10,020)*	7.42	438.3
1996	12,388	n.a.	n.a.
1997	530	0.25	463.4
1998	13,640	7.02	514.66
1999	13,136	3.41	259.59
2000	15,000 (14,152)*	7.02	467.5
2001	17,500	7.8	445.71
2002	19,056	6.1	320.11
2003	22,006	10.2	463.51

n.a.—Not Available.
* Of which quantities exported to India.

Source: Federal Office of Statistics and the Nigerian Export Promotion Council and FAO Export Trade Data.

Following the increase in the export prices between 1990 and 1995, cashew farmers and exporters started the 1996 crop season with high hopes, but exports that year did not exceed 12,385 tonnes. That year recorded the lowest export of nuts since deregulation in 1986, of only 530 tonnes. This shock made many operators to leave the business with dramatic losses being recorded by farmers, exporters, banks, warehouse keepers, buying agents etc. Nevertheless, only three major operators dominate the market since 1998, namely Olam Nigeria Plc., an Indian-owned Trading House with offices located in Singapore and London;

Premier Agro Oil Nigeria Limited and Century Exports Ltd. Among these Olam Nigeria Plc. exports currently some 60 per cent of the Nigerian cashew. Exporters are highly and increasingly dependent on India, the major destination of Nigerian raw cashew nuts, which are further processed for re-export. Unlike the exports of cashew nuts, the exports of kernels, which form only a small part of total exports, are more diversified, the main export destinations being the United Kingdom, Spain, USA and the Saudi Arabia.

Cashew exports were not significant until the Nigerian economy was deregulated in 1986. During that period, four private companies were exporting cashewnuts, and Enugu plant was the only one to process kernels. A large number of companies and individuals entered the cashew market, with the resultant increase in production and exports. Through the period under review, there were problems related to the low quality nuts, due to poor farm practices, lack of knowledge of proper post-harvest handling and lack of quality control mechanisms. All these led to the rejection of Nigerian cashew in the international markets, or their sale at discounted prices.

Nigerian cashews are packed in 80 kg jute bags, or in polyethylene or polypropylene bags. Processed nuts are exported in metal tins or cartons. Export prices for Nigerian nuts averaged US$ 377 a tonne between 1990 and 1996, and US$ 397 per tonne between 1998 and 2000, ranging however between US$ 200 and US$ 650 per tonne, depending on the quality.

Constraints to Export Development

Production and Harvesting

Nigeria's cashew production is faced with various problems. These include (i) *Old trees*: Before deregulation of the economy, the cashew trees were neglected. (ii) *Deforestation* has been the major problem affecting cashew production. (iii) *Low yield varieties*: Most of the existing cashew tree varieties have low yields, resulting in low productivity. (iv) *Unstable prices*: Prices of both local and international markets impact significantly on production and productivity. (v) *Lack of awareness on the economic importance of cashew*: Cashew apple is more popular in Nigeria than the cashewnut. This practice contributes to about 40 per cent post-harvest losses of cashewnuts. Consumers of cashew apples throw away most of these nuts. The immature nuts have high moisture content and are unfit for export. (vi) *Dominance of smallholdings and of wild cashew varieties*: About 70 per cent cashew nut produced in Nigeria comes from smallholdings and wild strands, where improved varieties are not available. The high proportion of this type of production accounts to a large extent for the low quality of nuts produced in the country. (vii) High Costs of inputs. (viii) *Post harvest losses*: large quantities of cashewnuts are lost due to poor post-harvest handling, inadequate packing, storage, drying procedure, etc.

Processing

The cashew processing companies in the government and the private sector faced several constraints, which are listed below. Most of these constraints also adversely affected export performance:

- Inadequate supply of raw nuts
- Bad quality of exports nuts
- Lack of market
- Post harvest losses
- Unstable prices
- High interest rates

Production and Harvesting

Thus Cashewnut producing sector needs assistance in the following areas: Distribution of improved seedlings and disease resistant cashew varieties to farmers.

Promotion of certified organic cashews may improve the export value of cashew products and open new niche markets to Nigerian exporters. Distribution of improved cashew seedlings and disease resistant cashew varieties to farmers should continue through programmes financed by donor agencies including FAO, IFAD, and CFC. Improved methods of preservation and storage of cashew nuts need urgent attention.

Export Marketing

Currently the Nigerian Export Promotion Council (NEPC) undertakes various activities to promote exports of cashewnuts and kernels. Exporters of cashewnuts and kernels have already participated in exhibitions organized in Egypt, Japan, USA and UK. NEPC provides exporters with Export Promotion Tools, such as product profiles, product catalogues and brochures, posters (on specific products or product groups including cashewnuts) and digital media, such as CD-ROMs and website hosting. The Council provides up-to-date Price Indices and cashew prices on both local and international markets. Many exporters of cashewnuts are beneficiaries. The following are some of the areas that country's cashew sector need to address:

(i) Nigeria's greatest problems in cashew sector are quality control and certification and the organization of trade. India, Brazil, and recently Vietnam acquired leading positions as leaders in production, processing, marketing and quality control of cashew.

(ii) *Market promotion of Nigerian Cashews* in USA, Canada, Europe, Japan, Singapore, Saudi Arabia, etc., would facilitate the access of Nigerian nuts and kernels to these markets. There is a need to sponsor cashew nut officers from Nigerian Export Promotion Council, as well as send produce inspectors to international courses, seminars workshops and conferences, in order to update their knowledge on cashew sector, as well as in trade promotions, quality control, farming practices etc.

(iii) *Increased Usage of Cashews By-products*: There is the need to increase the domestic utilization of cashew by-products and their access to export markets.

Cultivation and collection of cashewnuts are labour intensive, having the capacity to create employment, increase rural earnings and earn foreign exchange. The Scheme is expected to use co-operative societies for export development of specific products, including cashewnuts.

Nigerian cashewnut sector needs assistance in terms of organization and capacity building. *Networking Between Producers*: Networking between the African cashewnut producers and exporters is critical to the success of the export business. Export quality improvement and assurance; Implementation of quality control and *assurance* at all levels of cashew production and marketing chain is urgently required.

CASHEWNUT INDUSTRY IN TANZANIA

Cashews are an important export commodity for Tanzania and an important source of income for small farmers in the southern coastal region. The problems facing cashew sector include defining a more constructive role for the Cashew Board, reversing the decline in export crop quality, assisting farmers with financing input costs, and reducing high taxes on exports. Development of a competitive private sector processing industry would create jobs and reduce dependence on India as the market for raw nuts.

In Tanzania small holders, estimated at 280,000 households, on some 400,000 hectares in mono or mixed-crop production systems predominantly grow cashewnut. The average smallholder cashew farmer occupies about one to two hectarcs of cashew trees, sometimes intercropped with food crops, mainly cassava, grain staples and legumes. Some non-traditional cashew growing regions such as Dodoma, Kigoma and Musoma are planning for cashew planting in the due course.[2]

Cashews are especially important in the southern coastal region, with Mtwara, Lindi, and Ruvuma districts accounting for 80-90 per cent of Tanzania's marketed cashew crop (Table 14.3). Cashewnuts are also important to the national economy, providing 18 per cent of Tanzania's merchandise export earnings in recent years. Cashews are well suited to Tanzania and to production by poor farmers. Production responds to fertilization, but the cashew tree produces some nuts even without the application of purchased inputs. Cashewnuts are consumed as food as well as marketed for export.

Table 14.3: Cashewnut Marketing (Tonnes)

District	*1990-91*	*1995-96*	*1996-97*	*1997-98*	*1998-99*	*1999-2000*	*2000-01*
Mtwara	14,800	49,107	29,627	65,955	67,211	79,935	48,665
Lindi	3,254	11,585	9,160	16,480	14,737	17,652	18,411
Ruvuma	1,338	7,997	5,093	9,237	9,414	13,184	15,022
Pwani	5,732	6,858	4,991	655	4,380	5,910	11,976
D'Salaam	2,830	1,590	7,133	7,341	9,026	3,952	2,289
Tanga	1,622	978	24	116	957	571	907
Mbeya							58
Iringa							100
Mingineyo	221	3,613	7,005	133	716		
Total	**29,868**	**81,729**	**63,033**	**99,915**	**106,442**	**121,207**	**97,428**

Source: Cashew Marketing Board.

Grading

Formal grading of cashewnuts was not introduced until 1965-66, it was carried out when the cooperative societies delivered the nuts to the National Agricultural Products Board warehouses and was aimed at meeting the quality requirements of buyers rather than improving nut quality.[3] Two grades of cashew nuts are distinguished in Tanzania: "Standard" and "Under-grade".

Marketing

Since 1960 there was a large increase in the number of co-operatives and farmer's associations representing cashew producers. In 1962 the Southern Region Cashewnut Board (SRCB) was set up and this took over marketing the whole crop. In 1985, the Tanzania Cashewnut Marketing Board (TCMB) was formed to replace CATA and procurement of nuts was again channelled through Regional Co-operative Unions (RCU) and village primary societies.[4] In 1993, the functions of TCMB were taken over by the Cashewnut Board of Tanzania (CBT).[5]

Marketing Performance

The producer price is a function of many considerations and influences, the most important of which are production cost structure, the international cashew supply and demand dynamics, the domestic market situations, the effectiveness of regulation mechanism and the tax structure on the agricultural sector. The average producer price of cashewnut increased substantially in 1994-95 after the agricultural marketing system was liberalized (Table 14.4).

Table 14.4: Raw Cashewnuts Production, Producer Prices and Export Prices: (1990-91 to 2000-2001)

Year	*Production (000 tonnes)*	*Producer price (Tsh/kg)*	*Export Price (US$/ton)*
1990-91	29.8	110	n.a.
1991-92	41.2	137	n.a.
1992-93	39.3	140	n.a.
1993-94	46.6	177	n.a.
1994-95	63.4	300	n.a.
1995-96	81.7	325	850
1996-97	63.0	315	750
1997-98	99.9	300	850
1998-99	106.4	440	900
1999-2000	121.2	600	1,055
2000-01	122.3	250	600

Source: Cashewnut Board of Tanzania (CBT).

Primary and Secondary Processing

Most of the cashewnut crop is sold for export. Over 95 per cent of the cashewnuts produced in Tanzania are exported in raw form to India and a small proportion goes to small-scale backyard processors. Unfortunately, to a large extent, this situation continued to prevail even when there are 12 large-scale cashewnut processing factories in the country.[6] Currently there are two medium scale cashew nut processors. Mohamed Enterprises processes about 1,500 tonnes of raw nuts while Premier Cashew Industries process 4,000 tonnes annually. Following exports of cashews in raw form for more than ten years, the Government had declared a national policy to encourage local processing of cashew nuts and to discourage exports of raw nuts. In respect of the cashew industry the government had decided to revamp the industry and rehabilitate all cashew nut processing factories so that Tanzania can once again export processed cashew nuts. In order to fully utilize the capacity of processing factories, production of raw cashew nuts has to be increased and be sustained. By not processing cashew nuts, Tanzanian qualify only for one market (raw nuts) instead of distinguished markets for raw nuts, kernels, cashew nut shell liquid (CNSL) and cashew powder found in several other countries. The government through CBT had rehabilitated two factories, namely Masasi and Kibaha processing factories and leased to private investors.

Generally cashew gained economic importance in Tanzania just after Second World War when 7,000 tonnes of raw nuts were exported to India.[7] Ten years later cashew production increased by three folds and in 1960 about 42,000 tonnes of raw nuts was exported. Production reached 121,900 tonnes in 2001 and according to the FAO data has hovered around 100,000 tonnes in recent years (Table 14.5).

Table 14.5: Cashewnut Production Trends, 1945 to 2004 ('000 Tonnes)

Year	Production	Year	Production	Year	Production	Year	Production
1945	145	1961	70.0	1977	57.1	1992	46.6
1946	16	1962	50.0	1978	741.4	1993	63.4
1947	122	1963	71.0	1979	64.0	1994	81.7
1948	n.a.	1964	76.0	1980	64.2	1995	63.4
1949	20	1965	83.2	1980	43.2	1996	81.7
1950	40	1966	83.8	1981	33.1	1997	65.4
1951	60	1967	92.5	1982	38.1	1998	93.2
1952	80	1968	92.5	1983	32.9	1999	106.5
1953	100	1969	95.7	1984	19.2	2000	121.2
1954	120	1970	107 4	1985	18.5.	2001	121.9
1955	140	1971	125.6	1986	22.5	2002	100.0
1956	160	1972	145.1	1987	19.3	2003	100.0
1957	45	1973	110.8	1988	17.1	2004	100.0
1958	55	1974	83.6	1989	29.9		
1959	NA	1975	93.3	1990	41.3		
1960	50.0	1976	68.5	1991	39.3		

Source: 1945 to 1959: Nut Board and 1960 to 2004: FAO STAT Database.

Tanzania government has been taking various measures to revive the cashewnut industry since 1987-88 marketing season. This involved establishment of Cashewnut Production Improvement Pilot Project (CPIPP) in 1987 to 1989. After that, two other programmes, namely the Cashewnut Improvement Programme (CIP 1990 to 1996) and the Cashewnut Research Programme (CRP) were implemented with support from cashew levies.[8] However, liberalization of cashew marketing has contributed significantly in improving the industry through fair market pricing. More than 9.2 millions of neglected cashew trees were reclaimed. Twenty per cent of the total cashew trees were protected from powdery mildew attack by some 24 per cent of all cashew-growing farmers. Farm gate price has risen to about 65 per cent of the export price. Moreover, Cashew research became fully dependent on funding derived from a cashew nut export levy.

Main Factors Influencing Production and Harvesting Performance

Since the 1960s the cashew industry has experienced similar changes in fortunes to those affecting other cash crops in Tanzania over the same period, viz. healthy export industries were stifled by low producer prices and inefficient centralized marketing organizations working under monopolistic conditions. An effective marketing system needs to remain in operation and the farm-gate price of raw nuts must continue to be attractive. Among other factors that influence production and harvesting performance of cashewnut sector includes:

Implementation of a comprehensive cashew research programme covering breeding, pathology, crop protection, agronomy, vegetative propagation and socio-economics and farming systems.

Improving the availability of better planting materials from CDCs, farmers training and establishment of village based nurseries operated by farmers.

Implementation of a comprehensive extension approach, complementing the national extension service that was particularly aimed at cashewnut production promotion.

Market liberalization of the cashew industry, whereby inputs, crop and processing business were privatized with minimum interference from the government.

Future development of cashew industry in Tanzania would depend upon:

(i) Proper management of the Regional Input Funds.
(ii) Widespread adoption of Integrated Cashew Management Package.

(iii) Development of small to medium scale cashew processing technology.
(iv) Funding of cashew research by the industry itself while scaling down other cashew levies not directly contributing to the development of the industry.
(v) Availability of capital and production loans from banks and the development of Savings and Credit Co-operatives (SACCOs) among cashew farmers.

Processing

Ever since the start of the industry, most cashew exports have been raw nuts, which have been shipped to India where there is plentiful, cheap manual processing capacity. The volume of raw nuts exported from Tanzania has followed closely the trend in national production (Table 14.6).

Table 14.6: Raw Cashewnuts Exports to India: 1989-90 to 2000-2001

Year	*Production (Tonnes)*	*Exports (90%) (Tonnes)*	*Export Price (Fob $/tonnes)*	*Total Export Value (US $)*
1989-90	17,059	16,200	750	12,150,000
1990-91	29,846	28,300	850	24,055,000
1991-92	41,238	39,000	800	31,200,000
1992-93	39,323	37,350	600	22,410,000
1993-94	46,603	44,200	750	33,150,000
1994-95	63,403	60,200	800	48,160,000
1995-96	81,729	74,200	850	63,070,000
1996-97	63,034	60,000	750	45,000,000
1997-98	99,916	95,000	800	76,000,000
1998-99	106,442	101,000	900	90,900,00
1999-2000	120,000	119,136	1,039	123,782,304
2000-01	122,283	121,379	708	96,913,812

Source: Cashew Board of Tanzania.

Tanzania gradually moved towards more processing of cashew nuts locally. In 2001, there were two medium scale cashew nut processors. Mohamed Enterprises processed about 1,500 tonnes of raw nuts, while Premier Cashew Industries (established 1998) processed 4,000 tonnes annually. The Government promotion had involved setting incentives for local processors and investors in the cashew nut industry sector. Modern marketing principles have to be applied including branding of products from Tanzania including cashew nuts. Processed kernels are the main commercial product exported from Tanzania. Cashewnut Shell Liquid

(CNSL) was another export product from Tanzania during early 1990s when processing was taking place in the country. There is a great necessity to develop policy instruments to encourage small to medium scale cashew nut processing locally. Medium scale cashew processing technology involving centrifugal decortications should be tried on pilot basis.

Main Factors Influencing the National Processing Performance

Some of the factors influencing the national processing performance are:

1. Low comparative advantage in processing (technology and labour),
2. Low nut production below factory requirement,
3. Low effective demand (difficult in market penetration), and
4. Expensive technology and labour.

The government addressed the situation by encouraging local nut processing and selling or leasing out the existing factories to private traders. Other incentives to encourage local processing include removal of 1 per cent cess to cashewnut destined for local processing; provision of 2 years tax holiday for the acquired factories and some relief on export taxes of kernels are under consideration.

Export Performance

Tanzania exports most of this crop in raw form and looses massive revenue since the largest "profit margins" are found in processing and marketing areas (Table 14.7). During 1980s and 1990s Tanzania exports of raw cashewnut to India rose steadily to about 100,000 tonnes to feed the expanded processing capacity estimated to be 500,000 tonnes per annum.[9]

Quality of Export Performance

Cashew quality is of utmost importance. Currently, the common trade practice is to utilize the US cashew grading system, due to the strong influence that demand from the United States has on the world prices. Cashew producers and Exporters in India and Brazil introduced food quality standards in the late 1980s to ensure product safety and guarantee quality. In Tanzania, Cooperatives served as original buyers in most cases and delivered the nuts to the Cashew Board warehouses in Mtwara. Farmers were required to grade their nuts at farm level before selling to

Table 14.7: Exports of Cashew Kernels, 1972 to 2004

Year	*Export (Tonnes)*	*Export earnings (TSHs 000)*	*Average Price (TSHs/tonne)*	*Average Price FOB (US$/tonne)*
1972	2,902	22,440	7,736	1,081
1973	3,710	32,724	8,820	1,256
1974	4,060	46,736	11,511	1,611
1975	3,999	44,115	11,032	1,416
1976	5,954	76,227	12,803	2,274
1977	3,898	85,301	21,883	1,623
1978	3,635	67,904	18,680	2,423
1979	3,871	83,107	21,469	2,612
1980	5,474	215,009	39,278	4,780
1981	3,961	114,923	29,014	3,503
1982	4,337	123,957	28,576	3,004
1983	2,301	77,192	33,559	2,865
1984	1,694	65,369	38,604	4,217
1985	1,518	58,338	35,410	3,380
1986	0	0	0	0
1987	0	0	0	0
1988	1,014	407,950	402,318	4,252
1989	1,711	816,933	477,459	3,109
1990	1,412	969,187	686,393	3,486
1991	956	976,453	1,021,394	4,477
1992	1,027	1,043,954	1,016,506	3,512
1993	Nil	Nil	Nil	Nil
1994	Nil	Nil	Nil	Nil
1995	Nil	Nil	Nil	Nil
1996	Nil	Nil	Nil	Nil
1997	169			663
1998	2,627			1,544
1999	3,168			999
2000	4,282			1079
2001	816			914
2002	399			1316
2003	1,809			916
2004	892			2663

the cooperatives. Discoloured, pitted, shriveled nuts were not to be mixed with good nuts. The Cashewnut Board of Tanzania in collaboration with SGS Company Limited basically carried nut quality analysis. Pests and diseases play an important role in determining nut quality since they can cause premature nut fall, incomplete nut filling and damage to the nut. Measures are underway to establish a quality control laboratory at the Agricultural Research Institute, Naliendele, Mtwara.

Constraints to Export Development

Production and Harvesting

(i) Devastating effects of Powdery Mildew Disease (PMD) is a major constraint in cashewnut production in the country. It can cause a yield loss ranging between 70 to 100 per cent depending upon phytosanitary measures taken.
(ii) Inadequate use of modern farm inputs.
(iii) There is inadequate coverage in dissemination of research findings due to inadequate and weak extension services, poor infrastructure and inadequate transport facilities.
(iv) Low motivation of farmers due to low producer prices.
(v) *Farmers' knowledge*: Most farmers have limited knowledge not only on technical issues related to cashew growing and processing but also in farm business management.

Processing

Cashewnut processing sector is faced by a number of problems:

(i) Decline of raw nuts output.
(ii) Poor quality of kernels.
(iii) Perception of processing technology.
(iv) High interest rates.
(v) Uneconomic operations.

Export Marketing

The salient factors affecting export marketing of cashewnuts in the country includes:

(i) Few marketing channels.
(ii) Weak Farmer Organizations: Co-operative Unions and farmers primary societies have failed to handle marketing activities.
(iii) Lack of information: Currently, there is no effective marketing information system in cashew industry.

FUTURE PROSPECTS FOR TANZANIAN CASHEW SECTOR

Cashew Industry in Tanzania

Cashew production in Tanzania has made a remarkable recovery since the near collapse of the 1980s. Export earnings from raw cashewnuts rose from less than $4 million in 1990 to $107 million in 1998 (Fig. 14.1). The producer's share of the export price fell to 25 per cent in the 1986-87 season. Cashew factories were operating at a loss, and 9 of 12 factories closed between 1985 and 1990. Local authorities contributed to the problems of the factories by preventing cashew shipments between factories, which would have facilitated processing. Reforms in 1994-95 allowed private sector participation in marketing, which raised the share of f.o.b. prices received by farmers to 60-65 per cent from the 40 per cent paid by the Cashew Marketing Board prior to liberalization. Real producer prices for raw cashewnuts nearly tripled from the mid-1980s to the mid-1990s, due to the devaluation of the exchange rate, the increase in the average export price relative to the international price, and the increased share of the export price received by producers. World market prices remained firm through 1999, but then declined sharply.

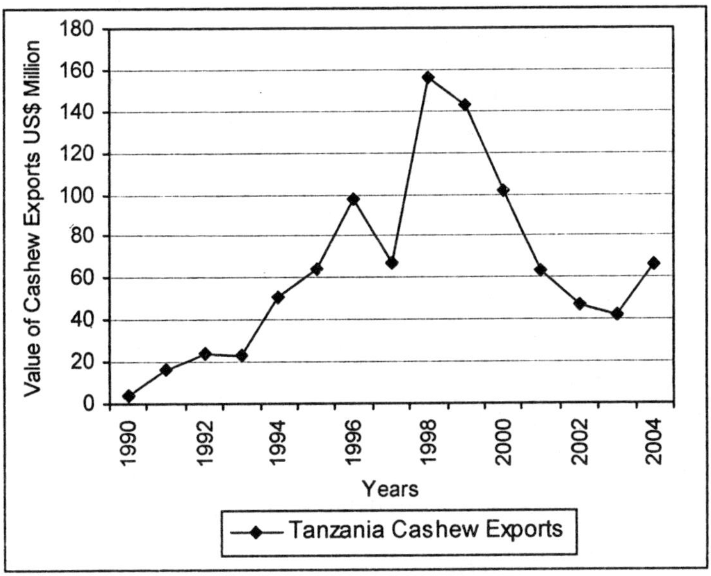

Fig. 14.1: Tanzania Cashew Exports

The future of the cashew sector in Tanzania is threatened by developments since 2000-01 that reflect longer-term issues of cashew-nut marketing and the role of the Cashew Board. The Cashew Board announced an indicative price of 540 Tanzanian shillings (Tsh) a kilogram for standard grade cashewnuts in September 2000. This bolstered farmers' expectations of high prices. The indicative price, unchanged from the price announced in September 1999, did not reflect the decline in the world market price of processed cashew kernels from $3.33 a pound in September 1999 to $2.65 a pound in September 2000. Exporters protested that the indicative price was too high and offered farmers 300-360 Tsh instead. The Cashew Board advised farmers and the primary societies not to sell at less than the indicative price. Meanwhile, the world market price for cashew kernels continued to fall, and in December the Cashew Board revised its indicative price to 435 Tsh a kilogram for standard grade cashews. Farmers were slow to sell their cashewnuts, and many exporters withdrew from the market.

In addition to the above, the Cashew Board unexpectedly announced a regulation, in early September 2000, that exporters of raw cashewnuts must ship these in sisal bags instead of traditional jute bags. The Cashew Board regulation and court case created uncertainty and delayed exporters' purchase of cashewnuts by about two months.

Delayed Marketing Hurt Crop Quality

Marketing in the 2000-01 season was thus delayed by the combination of the Cashew Board's sisal regulation, and above-market indicative price, the Cashew Board's urging farmers to withhold their crop. The delay led to deterioration in the cashewnuts, because farmers did not store them properly. Following harvest, farmers typically sun dry and bag cashew nuts and store them in their houses in polypropylene bags. Exporters in Tanzania then dropped their offer prices for cashews to as low as Tsh. 175 a kilogram. Exporters were no longer purchasing cashew nuts at the farmers' villages. By mid-March 2001 about 90 per cent of the crop had been marketed, but the low quality and the decline in world market prices meant that the cashew nuts fetched prices that were only a third of what farmer's had expected at the start of the season.

Several major issues in the cashew sector were highlighted by events during the 2000-01 marketing season.

Export Quality Deteriorated

The quality of Tanzania's raw cashewnut exports has deteriorated since the marketing liberalization of 1994-95. The average export unit value for Tanzanian raw cashewnuts declined 14.8 per cent from the pre- to post-liberalization period compared with other Sub-Saharan African countries (Fig. 14.2).

Now cashewnuts are purchased and exported without grading and often include nuts that would have been rejected before 1994-95. This has reduced the average export price received for raw cashews. The failure to grade cashew nuts in the villages has several undesirable consequences. It reduces the incentives for farmers to produce high-quality nuts because they receive an average price regardless of quality. Also the unsorted nuts do not store well because wet or rotten nuts contaminate good nuts.

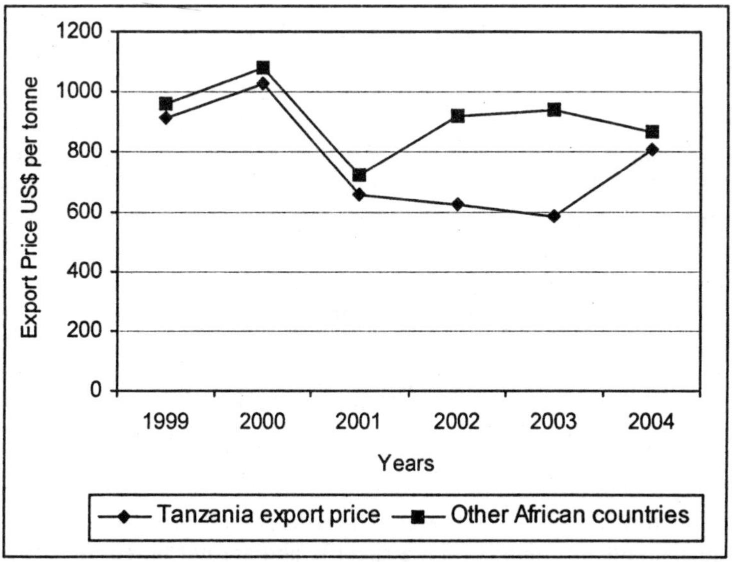

Fig. 14.2: Cashew Export Prices: Tanzanian *versus* Other African Countries

Farmers Unable to Finance Production Costs

The cash costs of inputs and labour required to produce cashews were estimated to be about Tsh 79 a kilogram of raw nuts produced. This was 25 per cent of the Tsh 315 received by farmers for raw cashewnuts during the November-December selling period in the 2000-01 season. However, as world prices declined later in the season and the quality of the cashew nuts deteriorated the cash cost's share of the sale price rose to as much as 40 per cent. The problem of financing production costs is not unique to cashew producers in Tanzania.

Tanzania has a good climate for cashewnut production, especially in the southern coastal region bordering Mozambique.

Lack of Domestic Processing

The lack of a competitive domestic processing industry puts the entire cashew sector in Tanzania at risk of being displaced by other raw cashew nut producers or by a change in policy in India. Processors in Vietnam purchased 3,000 tonnes of raw nuts from Tanzania in 2000-01, but this was a small share of the total crop and there was effectively only one foreign buyer for Tanzania's raw cashewnuts—factories in India that process the cashews for domestic and export markets. This may change in the future if Vietnam becomes a large processor of cashewnuts.

Prospects for reviving the mechanized cashew processing factories in Tanzania are not good while manual processing appears promising. For example, the price of processed cashew kernels exported from India during 1996-98 averaged $5,106 a ton compared with $1,063 a ton for raw nut imports. After two years of operation, a company that began with 40 employees was employing 1,400 workers (mostly women) and processing 5 per cent of Tanzania's raw cashewnut production.

This gave cashew farmers another market for their production, and the factory provides year-around employment for workers.

High Overall Taxes and Rapidly Increasing Local Taxes

Total taxes on cashew producers by the end of 1990s amounted to about 18 per cent of producer prices. Since then producer prices have declined, while total taxes as a share of producer prices have increased substantially as some taxes are specific and are not based on cashew prices. The local tax was Tsh. 100 and traders are required to pay the district taxes before they purchase cashewnuts. Thus, the farm gate price is net of district taxes. For example, in Mtwara some farmers received Tsh. 175 a kilogram for cashews, paid Tsh. 79 a kilogram for cash inputs, and then were taxed Tsh. 100 a kilogram in local taxes and Tsh.38 a kilogram in central taxes.

The Cashew Board's Role Remains Ambiguous

The Cashew Board of Tanzania was created to regulate and promote quality in the marketing and export of raw and processed cashewnuts. The Cashew Industry Economic Development Fund uses two per cent on its operation. This raises concerns that the Cashew Board may be returning to its role of competing with the private sector in cashew marketing.

Government officials and Cashew Board members travelled to cashew importing countries on a marketing promotion mission, again impinging on a private sector responsibility. The Board calculates export prices rather than using exporter records. This encourages overstating export prices in order to inflate export levies. The combined levies of the Cashew Board and the Cashew Industry Economic Development Fund could have exceeded $3 million in 1998, based on reported export revenues—even more if the Cashew Board overstated export revenues.

Defining a More Constructive Role for the Cashew Board

A key concern is the role of the Cashew Board. The producer's prices in the 2000-01 season would have been substantially higher and the marketing more orderly had the Cashew Board not issued the regulation requiring sisal bags for cashew exports (a private sector matter), announced indicative prices that were too high, or urged farmers to withhold their cashews from market. The Cashew Board should not announce indicative prices or regulations that relate to private sector activities.

Reversing the Decline in Export Crop Quality

The deterioration in cashewnut quality and the decline in average export prices relative to those commanded by other countries is largely a problem of the marketing system. Buyers collect nuts from many small producers and then mix them during the collection process. Thus producers with premium grade nuts do not receive higher prices than producers with lower quality nuts. The auction need not be mandatory in order to provide producers who sort and grade nuts with a market that rewards premium grade nuts.

Tanzania has a comparative advantage in cashewnut production. A major concern is the lack of an internationally competitive domestic processing industry in Tanzania. This makes raw nut exporters dependent on India's processing capacity, domestic production, and policies. Resumption of mechanized cashew processing in Tanzania is unlikely but there appears to be significant potential for manual processing of cashews. Domestic processing could have the added advantage of obtaining a better price than is currently obtained from exporting raw nuts to India.

The high estimated price elasticity of demand in European countries provide an incentive for exporters to reduce production costs and increase exports and suggest a high return to research to improve the varieties and production techniques for cashews in Tanzania.

CASHEWNUT INDUSTRY IN KENYA

In Kenya Cashew is among the oldest cash crops. Cashew tree bears fruit after three years, but the first crop do not exceed 4 kg/tree. In Kenya, processing of cashewnuts started in a very small way at Kilifi in 1930, with roasting and cracking the nuts under a mango tree. Mr. W.G. Lilywhite showed small holders how to grow cashew and provided the seed. When the trees began to bear, his vans collected the nuts and farmers were paid in cash. When steamed, the containers were ideal for exporting cashew kernels. Between 1960 and 1963, the processing was taken over by Mitchell Cotts Cashew Limited. They increased processing capacity to 800 tonnes per year. Kenya Cashew Nut Limited commenced operations on 5th August 1975 and started by processing 5 tonnes per day. The cashew crop was marketed through farmers' cooperative societies, traders and agents. The liberalization of marketing of cashewnuts took place in 1997-98. Cashew nut farming in Kenya is a smallholder activity and there are no large plantations. Growing of cashewnuts is confined to the agro ecological zones I, II, III of the Coastal Province of Kenya. A few patches within Mombassa District contain some cashew nut trees that are not really cared for. The main characteristics of cashewnut growing areas in Kenya are shown in Table 14.8.

Table 14.8: Characteristics of Cashewnut Growing Areas in Kenya

Zone	*Rainfall in mm*	*Area in Hectares*	*Tree population Per Hectare*
I	900-1200	18,500	70
II	600-900	7,500	50
III	400-600	5,000	10

Source: Baseline study by M. Rabu, 2001.

Nuts are mainly harvested after natural fall on the ground. Some farmers would harvest the ripe apples still carrying the nut and manually separate them, then dry the nuts on mats or hessian cloth under the sun. The harvesting of cashewnuts starts in October and ends in March. Nearly all the cashew trees are very old, receive very little attention by the owners and are, therefore, characterized by low yields. The baseline study conducted in 2001 revealed that average yield of 47.7 kg/ha, while the average yields per mature tree was 3.2 kg (Table 14.9). The trees are not uniformly distributed and the spacing is very variable. The mean number of cashew trees per acre is six, while the district means are 5, 6 and 8 for Kilifi, Kwale and Malindi respectively. Besides cashew, farmers grow other fruit trees, such as coconut, mangoes and citrus. As stated previously, farmers do not apply any inputs such as fertilizers or products to control pest disease. The pruning of trees is not done. This explains why yields are low and very variable.

Table 14.9: Cashewnut Yields in Kenya, by District

District	*Yield (kg./ha)*	*Yield (kg./tree)*
Kilifi	61.5	3.1
Kwale	24.2	2.1
Malindi	47.0	4.1

Source: Baseline study by M. Rabu 2001.

One factor, which has contributed to lack of serious cashewnut farming apart from poor prices, is the land tenure problem. Most of the currently producing trees are found in the ecological zone I, where the land tenure system has not been clearly defined. Most of the people living in this zone (some of whom have been settled there for over 100 years), are called squatters, and do not yet have title to the land, despite the fact that the original owners can no more be traced. Status of land ownership in Kilifi, Kwale and Malindi Districts is given below:

Districts	*With Title Deeds (%)*	*Without Title Deeds (%)*
Kilifi	80	20
Kwale	45	55
Malindi	24	76

Processing of Cashewnuts

Pan roasting of cashew nuts has always existed in all cashew-growing areas. However, the failure of the Kilifi processing unit led to the proliferation of microprocessors, mainly in Kwale, Kilifi and Malindi districts. The operations are being managed by farmer groups; self-help groups and individuals who used to work at the processing factory. Over the last few years, the Community-Based Organizations (CBOs) have found it difficult to access markets. Their operations face an uncertain future, unless the marketing problems are addressed.

Marketing

Before liberalization of the marketing of raw cashew nuts, the crop was marketed through farmers' cooperative societies, agents and traders' agents and was finally purchased by Kilifi Cashew Limited, the only major processor in the country. The farmer' marketing problems have been made worse by the collapse of the marketing system after liberalization. Cases of mismanaged co-operatives led to farmers being paid late, or denied their dues outright. The farmers have always considered the prices offered for their crop too low compared to their expectations. The fluctuating nature of prices resulted in the discouragement of small holders and the consequent neglect of their cashew orchards.

The liberalization of cashewnut marketing coincided more or less with the closure of the main processing factory, Kenya Cashew Nuts Limited, in 1998. It was expected that the liberalization of cashewnut marketing would allow competition in a buyers' market. The export of unprocessed nuts has obviously exacerbated the potential for establishing a viable export industry within the country.

Current Marketing and Processing

Pricing is a big issue in the cashew sector because of the prevalence of exploitation of farmers, farm prices being set by external forces. Prices vary between KSHs/kg 20 and 30 across the three districts. Marketing of raw nuts is not organized, as there are no viable farmers groups with bargaining power. A small sample survey conducted by Kenya Nut Company Ltd., came up with the figures shown in Table 14.10 for farm gate and rural markets spot prices for raw cashews.

Table 14.10: Raw Cashew Producer Prices by District in 2000-01 (In KSHS/Kg and Us Cents/Kg)

District	*Mean*	*Low*	*High*
Kilifi	24.50 (32)	13.80 (18)	37.30 (48)
Kwale	20.10 (26)	19.00 (24)	29.45 (38)
Malindi	25.70 (33)	21.30 (27)	33.45 (43)

Figures in brackets are US cents/kg. Exchange rate KSHs 78 for one dollar.
Source: Field Survey by Kenya Nut Co. Ltd.

Development Strategy

More than 56 per cent of the inhabitants derive their income from tree crops, of which cashew is among the most important. Cashewnuts grow along the Coastal belt from Lunga Lunga in the south, to Lamu in the North East of the Province, covering Kwale, Kilifi, Malindi and Lamu Districts. The total area under cashewnut cultivation is estimated at 30,921 hectares. The Kenya Government has initiated policy guidance for farmers, community based organizations and private investors, to revive the cashew nut sector. Small scale processing is being encouraged through community based organizations, as they own some trees and some are already processing their crops. Assistance needed include locally fabricated roasting pans as processing technologies to improve on quality. The Government institutions operating in the cashew growing zones, namely the Coast Development Authority and the Kenya Agricultural Research Station in Mtwapa, have commenced some activities in this line.

Sector's Performance

Production

Kenya's production of cashewnut declined from an annual average of 24,000 tonnes/year in 1969-71 (5.9 per cent of world production), to 16,500 tonnes/year (4.2 per cent of world production) in 1979-81 and to 10,008 tonnes in 2000-2005 (4.6 per çent of world output).[10] The factors responsible for the continuing decline are largely associated with the collapse of the marketing system, consequential loss of interest by farmers due to price instability and the lack of production support services. Although cashew represents only one per cent of the total Kenyan agricultural production in value, it is an important crop because it is grown in an areas with few alternative cash crops. Table 14.11 shows cashew area, production and yield of cashew in Kenya from 1990 to 2005.

Table 14.11: Kenya: Cashewnut Area and Production, 1990 to 2004

Year	*Area (hectare)*	*Production (Metric tonnes)*	*Yield (kgs./ hectare)*	*Year*	*Area (hectares)*	*Production (Million)*	*Yield kgs/ hectare*
1990	37,668	22,224	590	1998	30,850	10,986	356
1991	31,952	19,062	597	1999	30,921	14,615	473
1992	32,051	10,363	323	2000	31,250	12,500	400
1993	32,126	19,920	620	2001	31,250	12,500	400
1994	32,272	10,376	322	2002	30,815	10,031	332
1995	32,318	12,802	396	2003	31,060	12,300	396
1996	30,872	10,173	330	2004	31,155	10,250	329
1997	30,898	9,182	297	2005	31,260	10,000	320

J.H.G. WAITHAKA: Assessment of the Situation and Development Prospects for the Cashewnut Sector, 2 July 2002 and FAO STAT DATA Bank, October 2005.

There is room for establishment of new plantations and improvement of existing orchards through a proper management. There is a big potential for expansion of cashew plantations especially in CGEZ III that covers the area beyond 35 kms. People are moving into these areas because land is still cheap. This is an area where natural vegetation is being destroyed and cashew could serve as an agro-forestry species.

Production in Coastal Province is characterized by low productivity per tree and unit area and large fluctuations from year to year. The liberalization of cashewnut marketing was expected to result in increased business confidence among the various stakeholders, including the small holders, traders and small processors, which should have led to dynamic changes in the sector. Price levels are determined elsewhere, without their involvement. The lack of a regulatory body for the cashew sector has made the situation worse. Raw cashewnut marketing is dependent on external marketing forces, mainly emanating from India. At the same time, countries outside traditional regions are expanding their cashew nut crop.

Research and Development

Cashew seeds from selected trees in Matuga were established at Mtwapa in 1958, and a number of improved cashew tree varieties have been released by Kenya Agricultural Research Centre, Coast Province, Mtwapa.

Several diseases and pests attack cashew and cause considerable losses. A study conducted by Oltremare in 2000 in cashew growing areas showed the levels of attack ranged from 50 per cent in Kambe Ribi to 9 per cent in Gede. Considering the low resulting yields obtained, the attack levels might have been even higher. The assessment of powdery mildew infestation revealed that application of fungicides significantly reduced the infestation. Yields were increased by six times over untreated trees, through the application of fungicides.

Ongoing Work

A "Cashew management improvement project" had already been implemented and covered the following activities:

- Identification of high yielding cashew trees in farmer fields,
- Introduction of cashew upgrading techniques in farmer fields, and
- Evaluation of fungicides for control of powdery mildew in Kwale and Malindi Districts.

The main factors influencing production and harvesting performance are:

(i) diseases (mainly mildew);
(ii) the age of trees;
(iii) neglect by farmers;
(iv) drought; and
(v) poor soils, without any addition of fertilizers or proper pruning.

Farmers attribute their lack of interest in cashew cultivation to the high cost of pesticides and fertilizers, low prices of raw nuts, lack of improved, high-yielding varieties and the closure of the processing factory.

Table 14.12 shows the evolution of cashew processing by the Kenya Cashew Nuts Ltd., up to its closure in 1996-97. Since the closure of the factory, procurement figures are difficult to obtain. The data shows that production has been declining. Currently, no cashew products are being processed in Kenya. Microprocessors produce only raw kernels. The reversion to the old technologies, using crude pan roasting techniques, is unable to produce quality products. The main factors influencing the processing performance have been the lack of organization and the prevalence of a chaotic marketing system, characterized by irregular demand and low prices for raw cashew nuts. Small-scale processors can only handle about 10,000 tonnes, which would not meet export quality standards.

Table 14.12: Raw Cashewnuts Processed by Kenya Cashew Nuts Ltd.

Season	*Production (Tonnes)*	*Average Price KSHs/kg.*	*Income Generated (KSHs. 1,000)*	*Income Generated (US$)*
1985-86	11,018	5.50	60,599	776,910
1986-87	7,839	4.50	35,273	452,218
1987-88	12,591	5.50	69,251	887,833
1988-89	2,958	7.00	20,706	265,462
1989-90	2,957	7.00	20,699	265,372
1990-91	8,708	10.00	87,082	111,644
1991-92	9,363	11.00	102,980	1,320,260
1992-93	5,531	11.00	60,845	780,064
1993-94	5,441	14.75	80,260	1,028,974
1994-95	1,859	13.75	25,567	327,728

Source: Kenya Cashew Nuts Ltd. Exchange rate 78 KSHs = one dollar.

Exports

According to the FAO data Kenya continues to export cashewnuts. It also exports cashew kernels, though quantities fluctuated considerably. In recent years exports of cashewnut varied from 5,106 tonnes in 2004 to 37 tonnes in 2002. Exports of cashew shelled reached a peak of 2,821 tonnes valued at US$ 2.51 million in 2004 (Table 14.13). All the nuts processed by Kenya Cashew Nuts Ltd. were exported largely the United Kingdom and to European destinations. Kenya does not produce any cashew nut by-products. In Kenya cashew nut is not considered as a major export crop, despite the potential that has been identified recently.

Table 14.13: Kenya: Exports of Cashewnuts and Cashew Kernels: 1990-2004

Year	Cashew Nuts		Cashew Kernels	
	Quantities (Tonnes)	Value (US$ 1000)	Quantity (Tonnes)	Value (US$ 1000)
1990	48	48	394	1,379
1991	45	209	1,236	5,061
1992	147	423	342	1,052
1993	17	58	44	109
1994	592	1,395	158	548
1995	12	80	81	317
1996	71	241	95	357
1997	36	128	245	986
1998	167	1,624	35	166
1999	1,278	7,904	71	328
2000	511	2,915	87	368
2001	1,004	3,878	48	124
2002	37	100	13	45
2003	633	1,877	63	252
2004	5,106	2,297	2,821	2,505

Source: FAO STAT Database, March, 2006.

Export Marketing

Potential for export contract markets exists, but farmers are not able to produce the quality and quantity to meet the importers' demand. Lack of quality products and inadequate volumes have both impacted negatively on the export marketing potential. Until these factors are resolved, Kenya is unlikely to become a significant cashew nut exporter.

Conclusions

The cashewnut sector in Kenya has been rapidly declining, for reasons ranging from poor crop husbandry, rampant disease spread to endemic levels, to the complete collapse of the marketing system. Some NGOs are assisting farmers in crop husbandry improvement and farm gate marketing of unprocessed nuts. Previously raw nuts were exported to India. However, according to the FAO latest data Kenya exported 2821 tonnes of cashew kernels in 2004, compared to only 63 tonnes in 2003. The potential for cashewnuts production and export from Kenya is not exploited at present and should be examined with a view to attract private sector participation.

CASHEWNUT INDUSTRY IN MOZAMBIQUE

Production in Mozambique

Cashew production has been extremely important to Mozambique throughout much of the 20th century. The Portuguese promoted cashew cultivation during the colonial period and by the 1960s Mozambique had established itself as the world leader in cashew production. Shortly after Mozambique gained independence from Portugal, cashew production went into a long period of decline. Cashew production is still depressed in spite of efforts to revive the sector. In the 1960s, Mozambique accounted for half of the world's cashewnut production and in the mid 1970s it was the leading world producer with 240000 tonnes of raw nut production.

In Mozambique cashewnuts are grown entirely by small-scale farmers and subsistence families, mainly in coastal areas. A 1996-97 survey showed that 26 per cent of all rural families have cashew trees and 16 per cent of rural families have more than ten cashew trees. Even 10 per cent of urban families have cashew trees. The importance of cashew in Mozambique was shown by a question on the 1997 national census, which asked: "Do you have any cashew trees?"

From 1972 onwards, there has been a general decline in cashew production in Mozambique. For example, in 1976 about 21,150 tonnes of processed cashew kernels worth US$33.4 million were exported, and accounting for 23 per cent of export earnings. Cashew remained Mozambique's largest export until 1982, with the majority of the crop going to the United States. Currently, Mozambique only produces less than 3 per cent of the world total, fewer than one million small-scale farmers are involved in cashew production and the processing workforce is less than 1,000. Nevertheless, with the annulment of the policy recommended by the World Bank/IMF, Mozambique has resumed exports of raw cashewnuts and cashew kernels. In 2001 it exported 4700 tonnes of cashew kernels worth US$ 15 million. During 2002-04 exports totaled 631,221 tonnes and 500 tonnes respectively of cashew kernels worth US$ 1.18 million US$ 0.67 million and US$ 1.97 million. Exports of raw cashewnut during these years were 38,447 tonnes, 32,659 tonnes and 39,731 tonnes, valued at US$ 18.7 million, US$ 18.4 million and US$ 28.5 million. Table 14.14 shows time series data on Mozambique cashew production and exports. See also Figure 14.3.

Most of Mozambique's cashew processing factories were opened during the colonial era and then abandoned in the late 1970s. In 1997, there were 15 operational cashew factories, with an installed capacity of 144,000 tonnes of raw nuts but an actual capacity to process 75,000 tonnes of raw nuts per year.

A boom in its cashew processing industry accompanied Mozambique's early success in the production of raw nuts. Mozambique

Table 14.14: Mozambique: Cashew Production and Exports

Year	*Cashewnut Production (000 Tonnes)*	*Exports Cashewnuts*		*Exports Cashew Kernels*	
		000 Tonnes	US$ 1,000	000 Tonnes	US$1,000
1961	107.0	89.6	11,601	2.0	1,800
1964	156.0	141.8	18,364	2.0	1,800
1967	101.0	56.2	10,734	8.2	7,778
1968	185.9	132.9	24,264	11.6	12,643
1971	202.0	53.4	11,788	20.4	23,602
1974	213.4	72.9	17,606	24.8	42,935
1976	122.0	13.8	2,487	21.15	33,400
1977	91.5	0.0	0.0	17.0	45,557
1980	71.1	0.0	0.0	12.2	53,468
1982	61.0	0.0	0.0	16.7	43,607
1987	35.0	0.0	0.0	6.0	31,088
1990	22.5	0.0	0.0	4.3	14,288
1995	33.4	0.0	0.0	2.0	7,000
2000	57.9	0.0	0.0	4.7	15,000
2001	58.0	0.0	0.0	4.7	15,000
2002	58.0	38.4	18,728	0.6	1,179
2003	58.0	32.7	18,399	0.2	671
2004	58.0	39.7	28,473	0.5	1,974

Source: FAO STAT Database, March, 2006.

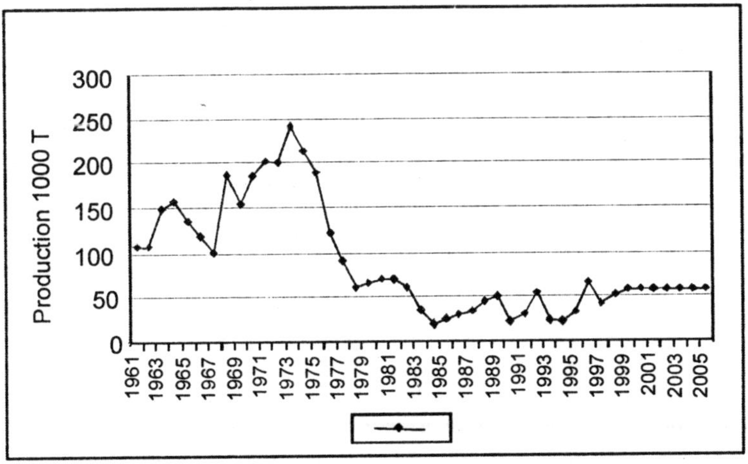

Fig. 14.3: Mozambique Cashew Production: 1961-2005

became the first African country to process cashews on an industrial scale as large, mechanized factories replaced small manual processing systems.[11] The first industrial plant was established in 1950 and two decades later there were 14 processing factories with a total processing capacity of approximately 150,000 tonnes of raw nuts. Processing of cashew peaked in 1973 when 149,800 tonnes of cashew were processed for export. However, since then the industry has declined dramatically and in 1999-2000 Mozambique processed a total of only 8000 tonnes of raw cashew.[12]

In an attempt to stem the decline in processed cashew exports, the Mozambican government banned the export of raw cashew in 1978. Cashew production peaked in 1973 at 240,000 tonnes and since then that level has not been achieved. At the same time, world cashew production increased steadily and by the late seventies Mozambique had lost its dominant position in cashew production to India and Brazil. By 1990, Mozambique produced only 22,106 tonnes, and its share of world raw cashew nut production had dropped to 5 per cent.[13] Since that time, the range of cashew production has become much smaller, fluctuating only between 23,000 and 66,510 tonnes.

Even during its most successful years, the cashew industry in Mozambique has been highly regulated. Prior to independence, the Portuguese government established producer prices and marketing margins throughout the cashew marketing chain.[14] During the post-colonial period, Frelimo (The Front for Liberation of Mozambique) continued to regulate the cashew industry. Around the time raw cashew exports were banned, the State Secretariat of Cashew (SSC), the central body controlling the cashew industry, and Caju de Moçambique, the holding company for the state-owned processing factories, were established.[15]

Producer prices and trading margins continued to be established by the government and—as previously mentioned—a ban on exporting raw cashews was imposed. Relaxation of government control of the cashew sector began in the late 1980s when Mozambique entered into its first structural adjustment programme with the World Bank. While it was not specifically focused on the cashew industry, it covered the cashew sector along with other products and sectors of the economy.

To ensure that the processing factories could remain competitive in the processed cashew market prices for traders and producers were based on the world kernel price and the domestic industry's processing costs rather than the world price for raw cashewnuts. According to Deloitte and Touche the producer price was 50 per cent of the government-established factory gate price. According to Pomerantz the government did not follow this advice and privatized the industry before it liberalized cashew marketing.[16]

In its 1995 Country Assistance Strategy (CAS) Report, the World Bank required Mozambique to liberalize cashew marketing and exporting in order to satisfy the "base case" conditions and qualify for approximately $400 million of loan assistance.[17] In addition to recommending that Mozambique liberalize cashew marketing, the World Bank also recommended as a subsequent step that it privatize the processing industry. According to Pomerantz the government did not follow this advice and privatized the industry before it liberalized cashew marketing.[18]

The World Bank's advice to liberalize Mozambique's cashew industry was based on a 1995 report by Hilmar Hilmarsson, a World Bank consultant.[19] It was assumed that liberalization would increase the producer share of the FOB price to 50-70 per cent and increase cashew production, export value, and farmers' income, as illustrated in Table 14.15.

Mozambique became a member of the Bretton Woods Institutions in 1984. The World Bank's proposed lending programme for FY1996-2000 included low and base scenarios. Liberalizing the cashew industry was a condition for the latter, in which it would receive a loan package of $665 million. Under the former, the loan package would be reduced to $240 million. While the Bank and the government agreed that liberalization and privatization were appropriate, they disagreed on the extent and the time horizon for the liberalization. Table 14.16 illustrates the different proposals, the schedule agreed by the government and the World Bank, and the actual tax rates implemented. Some of the reforms recommended by the World Bank are discussed below.

Table 14.15: Mozambique: Hypothetical Supply Response for Raw Cashewnuts

	Thousand Tonnes	*Export (Million US $)*	*(Millicn US$)*
Producer Price US$ 0.375/kg—Producer Share 50%			
Short Terms	46.6	34.9	17.4
Medium Terms	54.3	40.9	24.5
Long Term	96.7	72.5	36.2
Producer Price US$ 0.45/kg—Producer Share 60%			
Short Terms	49.9	37.4	22.4
Terms	59.9	44.9	29.9
Long Term	114.7	86.0	51.6
Producer Price US$ 0.45/kg—Producer Share 70%			
Short Terms	53.3	39.9	27.9
Medium Terms	65.5	49.1	34.4
Long Term	132.6	99.4	69.6

The Table assumed an initial production of 35,000 tonnes of raw cashewnuts.

Short Term: 1-2 Years, Medium Term is within 5 years, and Long Term is within 10-15 years.

Elasticities for scenario are: 0.15 (short term), 0.25 (medium term), and 0.80 (long term)

Source: World Bank (1995). Mozambique: Impediments to Industrial Sector Recovery. Report No. 13752-MOZ. World Bank, Washington, D.C.

Table 14.16: Schedule of Tax (Proposed and Actual)

Year	*Industry Proposal*	*WB/Industry Negotiated Scheme*	*Actual*
1995-96	25%	20%	20%
1996-97	20%	12%	14%
1998-99	16%	7%	14%
1999-2000	12%	5%	18%
2000-01 and thereafter	8%	0	18%

Source: Margaret McMillan, *et al.*: When Economic Reform Goes Wrong: Cashews in Mozambique, May 2003.

Price Reforms

In 1991-92, the export ban on raw cashewnuts was lifted and limited quantities of raw nuts were allowed to be exported. However, a 60 per cent tax on the difference between the FOB and factory gate prices and a quantitative restriction of 10,000 tonnes were imposed.[20] In 1993-94, the export tax was maintained, but the quantitative restriction was loosened. in both the 1999-2000 and 2000-01 seasons, the export tax was 18 per cent. Producer prices were significantly increased in 1987-88 from 10 Meticais/kg to 105 Meticais/kg. Also at this time, the government announced that a minimum producer price would replace the fixed producer price as the liberalization programme progressed. During the period of the export ban, the government also fixed the "factory gate price" or the price processors paid for their raw nuts. It is quite obvious from Table 14.16 that actual tax on cashew sector differed significantly from those proposed by the industry and the World Bank negotiated levels.

Marketing Reforms

Liberalization of the cashew industry also led to significant changes in the marketing system. According to the then Mozambique Country Economist for the World Bank, Peter Moll, the rationing arrangement for export licences was eliminated. Exporters were, however, still required to be licensed by the State Secretariat of Cashew.[21]

Privatization

Privatization of Caju de Mozambique—the holding company of the state-owned processing factories—began in 1991 when a privatization unit (UTRE) was created within the Ministry of Finance. On James Wolfensohn's first visit to Mozambique in 1997, he was approached by angry industrialists who claimed that the World Bank was responsible for the difficulties the industry was facing to procure raw cashew. Wolfensohn responded by authorizing another study of the cashew industry in Mozambique, which came out in favour of protecting the processing factories for some period of time. Abt Associates performed a third analysis of the processing industry[22] and Jaikishan Desai performed an analysis of cashew farmers.[23]

Economic Evaluation of Liberalisation of Cashew Sector in Mozambique

In a case that has become a cause calibre for the anti-globalization movement; the World Bank prevailed on Mozambique's government in the early 1990s to liberalize the cashew sector and to remove restrictions on exports of raw cashews. The Bank hoped that resources would be allocated more efficiently and the incomes of cashew farmers would be boosted. The policy was met with fierce opposition from the domestic cashew-processing industry, which ironically had just been privatized.

Historically, the cashew sector has constituted a significant part of Mozambique's economy, providing income to several million individuals across the country. In the 1960s, Mozambique produced as much as half of the world's total. Following independence in 1975, the government had banned the export of raw cashew nuts to stimulate domestic processing. Mozambique became the first African country to process cashews on a large scale. By 1980, the country had 14 processing factories.

Following World Bank advice, the government began to loosen restrictions on raw cashew production in the late 1980s. The ban on exporting raw cashews was lifted in 1991-92 and replaced with an export quota and export tax.

Margaret McMillan, Karen Horn, and Dani Rodrik carried a study to evaluate the welfare effects of cashew liberalization on various sections of the society.[24]

To gauge the overall impact of these reforms on the economy of Mozambique, the rough estimates of the net economic-surplus gains associated with these reforms, were computed using observed levels of prices and quantities. In developing these estimates several assumptions were made. For instance to compute the increase in farmer surplus, it was assumed that had the ban remained in place, farmers would have received no more than 20 per cent of the FOB price for raw cashew. At the time the ban was lifted, farmers received approximately 25 per cent of the FOB price and subsequently they were receiving 57 per cent of the FOB price.

The implications of export liberalization were indeed realized. Farm gate prices rose, raw cashew exports increased, and resources were pulled out of cashew processing. However, even under the most favourable assumptions, the magnitude of the benefits generated by these effects were quite small—both in economic terms and in relation to the amount of time and energy that Mozambique's government spent on this question over the years. The efficiency gains generated by the removal of the export restrictions could not have amounted to more than \$6.5 million annually, or about 0.14 per cent of Mozambique GDP. The additional income accruing to the farmers was probably no greater than \$5.13 million, or

$ 5.13 per year for the average cashew-growing household. These are peny amounts for a policy that was a key plank in the World Bank's reform agenda, and that became a serious bone of contention between the Bank and Mozambique, requiring the personal attention of both of their presidents.

Moreover, small as they are, these numbers overstate the benefits involved. The standard gains from the liberalization have to be set against the efficiency losses that have resulted from the idling of processing plants. A large number of workers remained unemployed, perhaps because of the expectation that the liberalization would be eventually reversed. One account claims that 90 per cent of the sector's 11,000 workers were unemployed in 2001. Even if we take a fraction of this number, the loss in real output (equivalently, loss of real income of workers) that is involved is of the order of $ 6.1 million, or 0.12 per cent of GDP. Note that this amount is roughly equivalent to the direct efficiency gain generated by the liberalization. In all likelihood, therefore, the aggregate static gains produced by the liberalization were a wash.

To summarize, the study found that the net effect from the reforms, was a benefit of about $ 6.6 million on an annual basis generated by new efficiencies in the cashew sector. That was largely offset by an estimated $6.1 million loss annually on account of unemployment among the processing industry's 11,000 workers. Rural farmers, meanwhile, did see some benefit, but it only averaged out to between $5 and $6 per year for the average cashew-growing household.

Future Prospects for Cashew Nut in Mozambique

Historically, Mozambique was prohibited by law to export raw (unprocessed) cashewnuts until the capacity of the local processing industry had been met. In the 1960s, however, there was some export of raw nuts to India (then the second largest producer of cashew). In 1992, Mozambique replaced its export ban with an export tax on raw (but not processed) nuts. In April 1995, the government changed the export tax on raw nuts to 25 per cent on sales up to US$ 600 per tonne and 70 per cent thereafter. In 1998 the Government of Mozambique has banned exports of raw cashew nuts.

There are good reasons to believe that cashew has the potential to regain substantial importance for Mozambique and other developing countries because:

- Cashew kernels are a high value luxury commodity with sales growing at a steady rate of 7 per cent per annum in recent years and with every expectation that the market will remain strong,

- Developed countries markets are not controlled, protected or organized into cartels, leaving substantial opportunity for Mozambique and other countries to capture the value added by processing and marketing the kernels,
- There is substantial potential to exploit cashew by-products such as cashew butter from broken nuts, CNSL and the juice of the cashew apple, which has a good flavour and is high in Vitamin C,
- The climate in Mozambique is suitable for growing cashews, and
- Cashew is considered by small-scale producers to be one of their most lucrative crops and the work needed comes at times which do not conflict with peak labour times for food crops. Thus it has the potential to increase earnings, create jobs and increase exports.

Certain Constraints However Need to be Overcome

- Cashew production is weather dependent, therefore supply is variable.

Hazard of policy solutions imposed by multilateral agencies on developing country like Mozambique, have been discussed earlier. This Box text presents lessons learnt from the Mozambique cashew sector.

The Mozambique cashew sector case provides several important lessons that are already being applied in development work around the world. **First** is that imposing conditions on a nation from outside won't work because the people in the government responsible for implementing the reforms won't necessarily believe in them.

Second, though reforms that affect price are important, they are often inadequate without structural measures, such as adding training programmes to give skills to idled workers and changing cashew distribution methods to ensure price increases are kept by farmers, not traders and middlemen. Social factors, political environment, and simple logistic factors—such as whether there are good roads for farmers to transport their crops to market—can also make or break a project.

Third Successful outcomes cannot be achieved by making governments do things they don't want to do. Individual cases like that of Mozambique's cashews make us wiser.

One of the important question is **"Can Mozambique Make the World Bank Pay for Its Mistakes?"**

- World prices, although stable in the long-term, are highly volatile in the short-term.
- Luxury goods must be of high quality. Standards, branding and marketing are required in order for the product to compete directly in the world market.
- New technology is required in order to exploit by-products.
- Production volume must be dramatically increased.

REFERENCES

1. This chapter is based partly on the study carried out on behalf of ITC/ UNCTAD by W. Ezeagu: Nigeria: Assessment of the Situation and Development Prospects for Cashewnut: June 2002: Mr. Ezeagu was the Assistant Chief Trade Promotion Officer, Nigerian Export Promotion Council (NEPC): Abuja, Nigeria.
2. Dr. Sijaona, M.E.R. *Assessment of the Situation and Development Prospects for Cashew Nut Sector in Tanzania: Country Case Study Carried Out on Behalf of ITC/WTO.*
3. Topper, C.P.; P.J. Martin; N. Katinila; L.P Kikoka; R. Lamboll; P.A.L. Masawe and S.H. Shomari (1998). The Historical and Institutional Background of the Tanzanian Cashew Industry. In: *Proceedings of the International Cashew and Coconut Conference; Trees for Life—The Key to Development*: (Topper, C.P.; Caligari, P.D.S; Kullaya, A.K.; Shomari, S.H.; Kasuga, L.J.; Masawe, P.A.L. and Mpunami, A.A., eds.) pp. 76-83, Biohybrids International Ltd., Reading UK.
4. Marketing Development Bureau (1993). *Industry Review of Cashewnuts 1992-93*, Dar es Salaam.
5. Topper, *et al.*, 1998, *op. cit.*
6. Cashewnut Board of Tanzania, *Annual Report 2001.*
7. Northwood, P.J. and Kayumbo, H.Y. (1970). Cashew Nut Production in Tanzania. *World Crops* (UK) 22 (2): 88-91.
8. 1 per cent of the fob price is channelled to Research.
9. Cashew Board of Tanzania, *Annual Report 2001.*
10. *FAO STAT Database*, March 2006.
11. Deloitte and Touche, ILA (Africa) and Deloitte Touch Tohmatsu Sisteconta (1997). *Cashew Marketing Liberalizătion Impact Study.* Government of Mozambique, Maputo.
12. INCAJU (Instituto de Fomento do Caju). (2001). Data obtained from Ana Machalela through e-mail dated July 20, 2001.
13. Desai, Jaikishan (2001a). "*Cashew Production and Marketing in the Smallholder Sector in Mozambique*", 47 Unpublished report for the World Bank.

14. Tarp, Finn (1990). "Prices in Mozambican Agriculture", *Journal of International Development*, Vol. 2, No. 2, 172-208.
15. Nomisma (1994). *The World Cashew Economy*, Edizioni L'inchiostroblu. Oltremare SpA. Bologna, Italy.
16. Pomerantz, Phyllis (2001a). *Personal Interview*, July 3, 2001.
17. World Bank (1995a). *Country Assistance Strategy. Report No. 15067-MOZ*, World Bank, Washington, D.C.
18. Pomerantz, Phyllis. (2001a). *Personal Interview*, July 3, 2001.
19. Arulpragasam Jehan. (2001). *Personal Interview*, July 2, 2001.
20. Desai, Jaikishan (2001). *Cashew Production and Marketing in the Smallholder Sector in Mozambique*. 47 Unpublished Report for the World Bank.
21. *Ibid.*
22. Abt Associates, Inc. (1999). *Assessment of the Status of Competitiveness and Employment in the Cashew Processing Industry in Mozambique*, Abt Associates, Bethesda, Maryland AIM Mozambique.
23. Desai, Jaikishan (2001). *Cashew Production and Marketing in the Smallholder Sector in Mozambique.* 47 Unpublished report for the World Bank.
24. When Economic Reports Goes Wrong: Cashew in Mozambique.

Part III
OTHER MAJOR EDIBLE NUTS

15

WORLD ALMOND ECONOMY

A Historical Reference of the Almond

Almonds had been cultivated for thousands of years before they had an official name. Linnaeus first named the almond Amygdalus communis in the 1750s, which translates roughly to "the common Greek nut". A few years later, Miller classified almond as Prunus dulcis, the name used today, to indicate the sweet ("dulcis") nature of the kernel of the cultivated form. Although primarily a California product today, the cultivated almond traces its origins to the deserts and Lower Mountain slopes of central and southwest Asia. Some of the wild stands of almonds occurred near population centres, and important trade routes, such as the Silk Road that connected central Asia with China, passed through wild almond groves. As almonds travelled with humans, they took root wherever they fell. Wild stands of almonds can be seen along ditch banks and roadways in central California.

By 4000 B.C., almonds were in use in nearly every ancient civilization. Almonds took readily to what is modern-day Iran and Iraq, and the lands surrounding the Mediterranean Sea. The climatic patterns of present-day Israel and Turkey favour almonds: cool, wet winters, mild spring, warm dry summer, and mild fall. Hebrew literature from 2000 B.C. mentions almonds in Canaan, modern-day Israel. Early references from Turkey, Romania and the Baltic peninsula also mention almonds.

The next major migration of almonds took the sweet seed to the Mediterranean countries of Europe. Perhaps some almonds from Persia or Egypt accompanied Alexander the Great's minion's home to Greece. Almonds, as do humans, adapted well to the Mediterranean climate's mild, wet winters and dry, warm summers. However, except for Spain, which is the second-largest almond producer after California, these sources no longer playing an important role in the international trade in almonds. Other small-scale almond producers, most of whom date their almond culture to ancient times, include Sicily, Sardinia, Yugoslavia, Bulgaria, Romania, Israel, Tajikistan, Uzbekistan, the Caucasus, Iran, Syria, Iraq, Afghanistan, Pakistan, India and Australia.

Bible stories make numerous references to almonds as an object of value and symbol of hope. Almond blossoms figured prominently in the design of the ancient Hebrew seven-branched lamp-stand.[1]

Origin, History of Cultivation

Almond and related species are native to the Mediterranean climate region of the Middle East (Pakistan eastward to Syria and Turkey). The almond and its close relative, the peach, probably evolved from the same ancestral species in south-central Asia. The original population of peach/almond progenitor species was separated by the formation of mountain ranges in southern Asia millions of years ago. The resulting climate change allowed almonds to evolve in the arid western part of this region, while peaches evolved in the humid eastern areas of south-central China.

Almonds were domesticated at least by 3000 B.C., and perhaps much earlier since wild almonds have been unearthed in Greek archaeological sites dating to 8000 B.C. In the wild state, most species of almonds are bitter and unpalatable, as they contain the cyanide-releasing compound amygdalin. Presence of amygdalin in almonds is controlled by a single dominant gene, thus a simple mutation would produce non-bitter almonds, and by chance, early farmers found these trees occasionally. Trial and error combined with selection of the best tasting almonds to plant new trees eventually led to the domestication of modern, sweet almonds.

The almond was spread along the shores of the Mediterranean in northern Africa and southern Europe by Egyptians, Greeks, and Romans. Spanish Padres who settled the Mission at Santa Barbara brought it to California in the 1700s. Larger plantings did not occur until the mid-1800s. Around the turn of the century, the industry started in California, due to development of superior cultivars in the late 1800s. Tariffs on almond imports were levied to protect the industry. From then until about 1960, the industry grew at a moderate pace, but acreage and production have increased several-fold since then, making California the world leader in almond production.

Distribution and Ecology

Almond trees naturally occur in the oak forests of Northern Syria, Turkey,

Caucasus, Iran and Iraq. Introduced and widely naturalized in North Africa, Cyprus, Crete, Southern Europe, Afghanistan, Kashmir, California, etc.[2]

Agronomic Background on Almond

TAXONOMY (Classification)

Almonds are members of the Rosaceae (rose) family, along with many other tree fruits such as peaches, apples, pears, plums, cherries, and apricots. Within the genus Prunes, almond is most closely related to the peach, and the two crops share the subgenus Amygdalus. Peach and almond are generally cross and graft compatible, and hybrids of the two are used as rootstocks.

The cultivated almond is placed within the section Eumygdalus, one of five sections that contain 20-25 species of near relatives. The bitter almond (P. *dulcis var. amara*), which is used for its essential oil and as a flavouring, is the only near almond relative of commercial significance.

Cultivars

Dozens of almond cultivars are grown commercially around the world, with different centers of production having unique selections. Some areas of the Middle East continue to use seedlings, sometimes grafting existing trees over to superior local selections. Thus, thousands of cultivars or selections probably exist worldwide, but mainstays of production number fewer than 10 in most regions. The top 10 Almond Cultivars in California are:

1. Nonpareil
2. Carmel
3. Mission (Texas)
4. Merced
5. Price Cluster
6. Ne Plus Ultra
7. Peerless
8. Thompson
9. Butte
10. Monterey

The major California cultivar is 'Nonpareil' (60% acreage), with several of the other cultivars listed above used as pollinizers since almonds are largely self-incompatible. 'Nonpareil' was a chance seedling discovered by A.T. Hatch in 1879 in California. It has retained the number one ranking largely due to its superior nut yield and quality. It has medium sized, smooth, attractive kernels with thin shells giving a very high shelling percentage, 65-70 per cent. However, the thin shell makes it more vulnerable to pests than hard shell cultivars such as 'Peerless'. 'Nonpareil' also tends to be a consistent bearer, giving yields of up to 3000 lbs of kernels per acre.

Botanical Description

Plant

Almond plant is small to medium sized tree with a spreading, open canopy, usually 10-15 feet in commercial orchards. Leaves are linear or slightly ovate, about 3-4 times longer than wide, with acute tips and finely serrate margins. Leaves are 3-5 inches in length, slightly smaller and less folded along the midrib than those of its close relative the peach.

Flowers

Almond flowers are nearly identical to peach and other Prunus flowers in structure, but light pink or white in color, and fragrant. Flowers have 5 petals and sepals, and many elongated stamens; all of these appendages originate from a hypanthium or floral cup, which surrounds the ovary. The ovary is perigynous. Flowers are borne laterally on spurs or short lateral branches, or sometimes laterally on long shoots as in peach, particularly in younger trees. Flowering on basal spurs of 4-6 years old wood gradually declines, since terminals fail to grow out when many flowers per spur set fruit; hence older limbs become unfruitful and are pruned out.

Pollination

Almonds are self-incompatible, and require cross-pollination. A few self-fertile cultivars (e.g., 'Halls Hardy') are available, but are generally inferior in quality. Pollinators (honey bees) are absolutely essential, especially since cool, wet weather can occur at the relatively early blooming period.

Pollinizers are generally planted in separate rows so that nuts can be shake-harvested a row at a time without mixing different cultivars. Since pollination is so critical to fruit set and yield, in some cases two pollinizers are used: one blooming slightly ahead (but overlapping) of the main cultivar, and one slightly after.

Fruit

Fruit is ovoid-ellipsoid, 3-4 cm × 2-2.5 cm (larger in cultivated varieties), splitting at maturity, stone 2.5-3 cm × 1.5-2 cm, pitted, seed ovoid, compressed, *ca.* 1.5-2 cm × 1-1.5 cm. Two races are recognized, sweet almonds grown for their edible nuts and the bitter almonds for oil of bitter almond. Hard and soft-shelled forms are recognized in the former as nut. The entire fruit including the hull is a drupe; however, the hull dries and splits prior to harvest, revealing what appears to be the pit of the fruit. Botanically, this pit with the kernel inside fits the definition of a nut (dry, indehiscent fruit with a hard shell). Fruiting begins in 3-4 years old trees, with maximal production in 6-10 years. Unlike its short-lived cousin the peach, almond trees can produce for 50+ years. Thinning is unnecessary; a high proportion of flowers must set fruit for normal cropping.

General Culture

Soils and Climate

Almonds produce best on deep, loamy, well-drained soils, but will tolerate poor soils, and even drought during the latter portion of fruit development better than most tree crops. In intensive orchards, soils are managed similar to other stone fruits, but less-intensive plantings of the Mediterranean area occur on calcareous, rocky, and droughty soils. Like all Prunus species, almonds are intolerant of wet, poorly drained soil.

The almond is a true Mediterranean tree, requiring mild winters, and long, rain-less, hot summers with low humidity. Rainfall is deleterious anytime during growth; during bloom, it decreases bee activity and therefore fruit set; during fruit development it causes fungal and bacterial diseases; prior to harvest it can cause brown rot or Rhizopus rot of fruits as shucks split. It is no surprise that all of the almonds in the US are grown in California. Realistically, almonds are only suited to the arid western states, particularly California, Arizona, New Mexico, and western Texas. Trees grown in the east will generally succumb to diseases and experience frost damage.

Almonds require only 300-500 chill hours. Almonds bloom in late February in California, and frost is a perennial problem. Open flower hardiness is similar to other tree fruits, with death occurring below 28°F; young fruits may be killed by temperatures as high as 31°F. Frost is a serious limitation in most areas outside of California. Mid-winter hardiness is not as limiting a factor as spring frost damage to blossoms. Almonds routinely survive temperatures in the single digits °F and even lower in some cases. 'Nonpareil' matures in late August/early September in California, after blooming in mid-late February (6 to 7 months).

Cultivation

Most almond cultivars are soft shelled; they are also self-incompatible, consequently plantations require the interpolating of two rows of self-incompatible with a row of cross-compatible cultivars; the keeping of honeybees for pollination is considered an essential part of almond production. Almond trees begin to bear after 3-4 years and reach full productivity in *ca.* 7-8 years. Irrigation is favoured in California.[3]

Propagation

Almonds are budded onto seedling rootstocks so that the integrity of the cultivar is kept intact. Propagation of trees by seed is possible, and practiced in some regions of the Mediterranean. However, tree uniformity is poor in seedling orchards since almonds are self-incompatible and heterozygous as a species. Almonds root poorly from cuttings, as opposed to peach which is easily rooted.

Rootstocks

Peach seedlings ('Lovell', 'Halford', 'Nemaguard', 'Nemared') are the primary rootstocks for almond. Trees on peach seedling stocks are more vigorous and bear earlier than those on almond seedling stocks. Peaches are slightly more tolerant of crown gall, verticillium, oak root rot and Phytophthora than almond.

Almond seedlings are used as rootstocks in less-intensive orchards of the Mediterranean area, where soils are calcareous and irrigation is not available. These trees may tolerate drought better than trees on peach. Peach × Almond hybrids (for example, GF 677, GF 557), are recent introductions, but are now the dominant rootstock for peach and almond in France. These stocks have similar disease response as almond seedlings, but some have been produced with resistance to root-knot nematode and iron deficiency.

Planting Design, Training, Pruning

Trees are planted in rectangular or hexagonal arrangements, with separate rows of pollinizers and main cultivars, usually alternating with each other. Solid rows of pollinizers are used since trees are shake harvested, and this makes it easier to harvest without mixing cultivars. In some orchards, two different pollinizers are used, generally one blooming slightly before and the other slightly after the main cultivar. Spacing must be wide enough to permit movement of harvesting equipment, or about 18 feet. Spacings of 24 × 24 feet are common in California, yielding about 87 trees per acre.

Trees are trained to an open center shape in the first year. Young trees are headed at 3 feet to allow adequate room for trunk shaker attachment. Three scaffolds are selected initially, about 3-6″ apart from each other on the trunk, spaced equidistant when viewed from above. Various degrees of pruning are practiced after the first year, with minimal pruning allowing the most rapid production of bearing area. In subsequent years, scaffolds are trained to fill their allotted spaces in the tree. At maturity, pruning consists of watersprout removal, removal of dead and interfering branches, and limb thinning. Little pruning is needed since so many fruiting points are needed for cropping, and vigour is low in mature trees. Since fruiting spurs live about 5 years, fruiting wood should be renewed every 5 years, or, 20 per cent of the canopy should be pruned back each year to allow new wood to grow and replace the old. In practice, trees can be pruned every other year with no loss of productivity. Under proper management, trees should have many 15-20″ long 1-year-old shoots. These shoots will branch, grow spurs, and become fruiting wood in subsequent years.

The hull splits at maturity, and nuts physically separate from the tree at this point. Trees are harvested when hulls of fruit in the interior of the canopy are open, since these split last. The seed coat turns brown during the drying-out process of maturation. Delay in harvest increases risk of navel orangeworm infestation.

Formerly, almonds were harvested by beating the tree and collecting the falling almonds on canvas sheets. Now they are harvested using mechanical shakers, which can deal with 120 trees per hour; the fallen nuts are then swept into windrows and picked up mechanically for transport to the factory. The use of shake and catch machines lessens the danger of fruits of the more open cultivars coming into contact with the soil, thereby lessening the risk of mould and aflatoxin infestation.[4]

In California, trees are harvested by mechanical tree shakers. Young trees may be damaged by shakers, so are harvested by hand knocking in the first few years. Hand knocking is used in production regions that lack mechanization or are too hilly to accommodate shakers. Nuts are then left to dry on the ground for 1-2 weeks, then swept into windrows for harvesting. In situations where rain, higher humidity, or pest pressure necessitates, nuts are shaken and taken immediately to a processing facility. A mechanical harvester then picks up the windrowed nuts, blowing off extraneous leaves and debris.

Post-Harvest Handling

Fruits may be dried and hulled immediately, or stockpiled for fumigation against Navel Orangeworm after harvest. At the factory the brown, outer, leathery coat (hull) is removed by blanching, which involves placing the almonds in contact with water at 82°C for 3 minutes and either skinning by hand or by a special machine. The almonds are then dried to less than 8 per cent moisture content and stored. Nuts are then dehulled and shelled. The hulls are often sold for livestock feed. In-shell nuts can be stored in bins for weeks or months until final processing. Nuts are then shelled and sorted for size and appearance. Last, nuts are bleached for colour improvement, then salted, roasted, and/or flavoured before packaging.

Airtight containers must be used to prevent moisture pick-up. Although relatively resistant to rancidity the almonds will deteriorate in time. The grading process uses ultra-violet scanners for high-tech colour sorting to separate damaged and foreign matter before mechanical grading. Storage. Almonds can be stored for months either in-shell or shelled if dry, or very long periods when frozen (years). Commercially, nuts for long-term storage are fumigated for navel orange worm and kept at temps below 40°F.

Production and Consumption/Utilization

Worldwide approximately 65-70 per cent of the crop is sold shelled either as natural and retaining the brown skin or blanched, with the skins removed. Almonds can be eaten as a dessert nut either dry roasted or roasted in almond oil and then salted and seasoned. They are also used for baking, confectionery, cereal, dairy or snack formulations; processing may produce blanched whole, slivered, meal, diced, split, sliced or flaked almonds; almond butter is a recent development.[5]

Contribution to Diet

Almonds are the most widely used nut for confectionery items like candy bars, cakes, toppings, etc. Much of the crop is roasted and flavoured or salted and sold in cans; broken and small kernels go to confectionery. Highest prices are received for whole kernels. “A can a week, that’s all we ask”, was the old advertising slogan of the California almond growers. About 99 per cent of almonds in the USA are shelled prior to sale, and 1 per cent sold in-shell. Nutmeats can be sold as whole kernels, or further processed by blanching or slicing.

Nutritional Value

Almonds contain approximately 22 per cent protein, 57.7 per cent digestible fat or oil and 15 per cent carbohydrates. Dietary value, per 100-gram edible portion of almond is shown in Table 15.1.

Table 15.1: Almond Kernel Dietary Value

Water (%)	5	Riboflavin, B2	58
Calories	598	Niacin	19
Protein (%)	19	Vitamin C	0
Fat (%)	54	Calcium	29
Carbohydrates (%)	20	Phosphorus	63
Crude Fiber (%)	2.7	Iron	50
	% of US RDA*	Sodium	—
Vitarnin A	0	Potassium	17
Thiamin, B1	17		

Per cent of recommended daily allowance set by FDA, assuming a 154 lb male adult, 2700 calories per day.

By-Products and Other Uses

The gum exudate may be used as a substitute for gum tragacanth and was formerly exported from Iran via Mumbai to Europe. Almond yields both an essential oil and fixed fatty acid for use in perfumery but frequently adulterated with other oils. The essential oil from the bitter variety is highly toxic due to presence of HCN but with careful preparation yields an agreeable essence for use in perfumery and confectionery. Both bitter and sweet varieties may be grown as ornamentals. The hulls of sweet almonds can be fed to livestock. The shells can be used for roughage in cattle feed or converted into charcoal briquettes.

WORLD ALMOND PRODUCTION

Almonds are regarded as the most important and versatile of all edible tree nuts. They are produced commercially in 44 countries on 1.48 million hectares. Production (in-shell bases) has increased by 9 per cent in the last sixteen years from 1.32 million tonnes in 1990 to 1.62 million tonnes in 2005 (Table 15.2). World production rose steadily from 1 million tonnes in 1979-81 to 1.3 million tonnes in 1992 and fell to 1.2 million tonnes in 1993. Output rose further and averaged 1.69 million tonnes during the last three years. This trend is reflected in North America where production in thousand tonnes was 273, 412 and 735 for 1979-81, 1992 and 2005 respectively. Production in Europe, the largest of the continental scale has decreased steadily from 482,000 tonnes in 1979-81 to 436,000 tonnes in 1993. Spain, the major producer in Europe increased production slightly from 243,000 tonnes in 1979-81 to 279,396 tonnes in 2002, but since then its production declined to 215000 tonnes during the last three years. Italy production has declined markedly, from 174,000 tonnes in 1979-81 to an average of 101,000 tonnes during 2003-2005.

Almond producing countries in current order of importance are USA (California), Spain, Syria, Italy, Iran, Morocco, Greece, Turkey, Libya, and Pakistan. Table 15.3 shows percent share of top ten almond producing countries in the global output. Based on FAO data of average production during the last three year's, the top five producers were the United States at about 739,000 tonnes (44 per cent of the world output), followed by Spain (215,000 tonnes and 13 per cent), Syria (130,000 tonnes and 8 per cent), Italy (about 96,000 tonnes and 6 per cent) and Iran (80,000 tonnes and 5 per cent). Worldwide, yield averages about 1030 kgs/hectare, but can reach 3500-4500 kg. in some countries.

Average world almond production in shelled weight basis increased from 334,000 tonnes during 1992-1996, to 557,160 tonnes during 2001-2005. The 1960s witnessed an increase in USA almond production, which passed from 22 per cent of the world production in the period 1957-61, with a total of 24,000 tonnes of shelled product, to the current 80 per cent, with a production of 442,000 tonnes. During the same period (1957-61), the Mediterranean countries provided 63 per cent of the world production with about 75,000 tonnes of shelled almonds. During 2001-05, their percentage went down to about 20 per cent, with the same production of 110,000 tonnes of shelled product. The increase in the Spanish production, has offset the drop in Italian production although the comparative percentage has decreased. Table 15.4 shows based on relative share of different countries in the world output five-year average almond production (Shelled basis) from 1947-51 to 2002-05.

International Trade

Almond in-shell and shelled are exported and imported. According to the FAO data export volume of almond in-shell increased more than four-fold from 21524 tonnes in 1990 to 104,035 tonnes in 2004 (Table 15.5). The export value rose more than twelve-folds from US$ 19.76 million to US$ 254.11 million during this period (Table 15.6). The higher growth

Table 15.2: World Almond Production 1990-2005 (Tonnes)

	1990	1994	1995	2000	2002	2003	2004	2005
World	1,317,054	1,358,067	1,030,731	1,471,111	1,851,768	1,719,261	1,725,869	1,622,006
USSR	18,000							
Algeria	11,733	19,106	19,869	26,483	32,287	33,234	33,000	33,000
Australia	6,516	9,000	10,056	17,420	10,040	9,554	9,430	9,430
Chile	2,240	2,700	2,800	8,140	9,100	8,800	9,000	9,100
China	17,000	18,000	19,000	17,000	22,000	23,000	24,000	25,000
France	4,200	3,669	3,910	6,936	6,800	6,800	6,800	7,000
Greece	53,394	55,677	57,575	50,956	37,349	33,899	48,200	47,000
Iran	69,866	100,000	79,531	89,637	107,000	80,000	80,000	80,000
Israel	3,335	2,600	3,100	5,068	9,142	4,712	4,201	4,500
Italy	94,970	89,944	90,284	104,755	104,891	91,382	105,245	105,312
Lebanon	13,000	18,000	28,000	24,700	23,000	27,400	27,500	27,500
Libya	33,070	28,000	27,000	26,000	26,000	26,000	25,000	25,000
Macedonia		690	800	800	208	1,478	1,175	1,175
Morocco	57,700	30,700	45,700	65,044	82,400	70,808	70,000	70,000
Pakistan	30,900	45,193	48,996	32,336	26,414	23,688	23,924	23,100
Portugal	18,190	9,819	7,172	27,038	30,850	23,829	13,953	14,000
Spain	250,200	238,200	158,900	225,217	279,396	214,448	224,595	204,500

Table 15.3: Percentage Shares of Top Ten Almond Producing Countries in World Output (Average 2003-2005)

1. USA (44)	6. Morocco (4)
2. Spain (13)	7. Greece (3)
3. Syria (8)	8. Turkey (2)
4. Italy (6)	9. Libya (2)
5. Iran (5)	10. Pakistan (1)

in value is partly due to higher unit export value realized during the period under review. The main exporting countries include U.S. (accounting for over 80 per cent of volume and 85 per cent in value for world exports in 2004), followed by Spain (less than 2 per cent in volume and 4 per cent share in value), Australia (1.97 per cent and 2.82 per cent share) and Syria (1.25 per cent and 0.38 per cent share).

Exports of almond shelled have increased from 200,644 tonnes in 1990 to 349,663 tonnes in 2004. The value rose from US$ 266 million to 1.59 billion. The respective increases come to 74 per cent for volume and 253 per cent for value. Higher per unit value accounted for almost two-thirds of increase in exports value. The USA shipped 73 per cent of the world almond shelled exports in 2004. It was followed by Spain with 9.4 per cent of volume and Germany with 2.1 per cent share (Tables 15.7 and 15.8).

Imports

Imports of almond whole increased from 26,714 tonnes in 1990 to about 60,810 tonnes in 2004 (Table 15.9), registering 13 per cent annual increase. In 2004, the major importing countries were Hungary (with 42.4 per cent share of world imports), followed by Norway (10.5 per cent share and Chile (7.1 per cent share). During the last sixteen years world imports of almond shelled rose from 207,570 tonnes in 1990 to 382,543 tonnes in 2004. The annual increase comes to over 5 per cent. During the last three years, annual average world imports of almond shelled totalled about 356 thousand tonnes, valued at about US$ 1,280 million. The top ten importing countries include Germany (17.5 per cent share in world volume), Spain (16.0 per cent), Italy (7.4 per cent), France (7.2 per cent), Japan (6.8 per cent share), Canada (4.4 per cent), Netherlands and UAE (3.2 per cent each), U.K. (2.7 per cent) and Switzerland (2.1 per cent), (See Table 15.10).

Table 15.4: Almond Production (in Shelled weight) in Major Producing Countries: 1947-2005

Years	USA		Spain		Italy		Morocco		Portugal		Others		Total	
	Tonnes	% share	Tonnes	% share	Tonnes	% share	Tonnes	% share	Tonnes	% share	Tonnes	% share	Tonnes	% share
1947-51	18,500	21.1	22,600	25.7	31,000	35.3	3,200	3.6	3,800	4.3	8,700	10.0	87,800	100.0
1952-56	19,200	24.2	17,600	22.1	27,600	34.7	2,700	3.4	4,300	5.4	8,100	10.2	79,500	100.0
1957-61	24,000	22.0	29,400	26.4	36,400	32.7	4,300	3.9	4,100	3.7	13,200	11.8	111,400	100.0
1962-66	34,300	29.6	28,800	24.8	32,500	28.0	5,000	4.3	2,600	2.2	12,800	11.1	116,000	100.0
1967-71	55,300	39.4	31,200	22.3	30,400	21.7	4,400	3.1	4,800	3.4	14,100	10.1	140,200	100.0
1972-76	90,800	49.5	49,600	27.0	16,800	9.2	3,700	2.0	4,700	2.6	17,800	9.7	183,400	100.0
1977-81	145,000	60.2	47,600	19.8	21,000	8.7	4,600	1.9	2,800	1.2	20,000	8.2	241,000	100.0
1982-86	164,000	60.9	50,400	18.7	17,400	6.5	4,400	1.6	4,100	1.5	29,000	10.8	269,300	100.0
1987-91	245,000	67.9	55,200	15.3	15,600	4.3	6,100	1.7	4,200	1.2	34,400	9.6	360,500	100.0
1992-96	228,000	68.4	52,400	17.7	14,400	4.3	5,600	1.7	3,600	1.1	30,200	6.8	334,200	100.0
1997-2000	314,630	68.5	59,110	12.9	15,900	3.5	8,810	1.9	4,490	1.0	56,470	12.3	459,410	100.0
2001-05	442,160	79.4	40,520	7.3	14,300	2.6	7,050	1.3	7,330	1.3	45,800	8.2	557,160	100.0

Table 15.5: Almond Exports: (Quantities in Tonnes): Selected Years

	Yerars							*% share world total*	
Exports	1990	1993	1995	1998	2000	2003	2004	2004	1995
World	21,524	53,196	35,548	36,341	66,763	94,893	104,035	100.00	100.00
Afghanistan	2,460	737	1,332	3,300				0	3.75
Australia	2	158	7	2,795	793	1,108	2,053	1.97	0.02
Chile	180	108	164	73	605	102	475	0.46	0.46
Hong Kong	27	99	156	592	6,805	1,878	1,070	1.03	0.44
Georgia		547	900	800	800	0	0	0.00	2.53
Iran	1,200	6,585	2,200	828	810	234	156	0.15	6.19
Italy	618	523	834	530	693	754	974	0.94	2.35
Netherlands	113	20	247	121	136	92	98	0.09	0.69
Pakistan	2,061	1,802	736	265	93	14	7	0.01	2.07
Palestine	900	900	900	0	172	50	50	0.05	2.53
Portugal	572	780	868	1,064	1,992	1,014	727	0.70	2.44
Spain	1,310	1,241	1,308	1,743	1,766	2,082	1776	1.71	3.68
Syria	513	23,359	5,184	383	547	3,778	1304	1.25	14.58
Tunisia	231	688	200	281	459	212	393	0.38	0.56
Turkey	105	30	74	177	46	13	9	0.01	0.21
USA	9,014	13,493	18,605	22,531	42,340	73,642	83,604	80.36	52.34

Table: 15.6: Almond Exports Value (US$ 1,000): Selected Years

	1990	1993	1995	1998	2000	2003	2004	2004 (%)	1995 (%)
World	39,461	94,303	83,355	89,699	138,500	217,538	254,113	100.00	100.00
Afghanistan	5,330	800	1,390	4,000	0	0	0	0.00	1.67
Australia	16	727	26	7,115	1,835	3,375	7,162	2.82	0.03
Chile	416	285	551	225	1,481	232	1,609	0.63	0.66
Hong Kong	85	395	429	1,644	15,587	1,566	1,948	0.77	0.51
Georgia		350	750	680	780	0	0	0.00	0.90
Iran	1,400	9,300	7,100	1,293	1,158	376	203	0.08	8.52
Italy	1,434	827	1,364	966	852	1,587	2449	0.96	1.64
Netherlands	391	86	489	507	434	242	293	0.12	0.59
Pakistan	1,369	2,522	1,017	401	134	16	6	0.00	1.22
Palestine, Occ. Tr.	360	360	360	0	197	60	60	0.02	0.43
Portugal	349	616	1,149	1,057	1,229	1,166	985	0.39	1.38
Spain	3,256	4,183	3,455	5,335	4,671	9,084	10,969	4.32	4.14
Syria	716	35,894	15,288	1,011	1,062	2,471	955	0.38	18.34
Tunisia	259	1,074	396	437	513	253	766	0.30	0.48
Turkey	229	26	95	274	108	22	16	0.01	0.11
USA	19,761	32,435	47,002	63,438	103,563	190,452	216,530	85.21	56.39

Source: FAO STAT Database, March 2006.

Table 15.7: Almond (Shelled) Exports Quantities in Tonnes: Selected Years

	Years								*% Share World Total*	
	1990	*1993*	*1995*	*1998*	*2000*	*2002*	*2003*	*2004*	*1995*	*2004*
World	200,644	164,898	274,717	227,047	260,421	360,026	359,265	349,663	100.00	100.00
Australia	59	39	187	0	1,694	1,200	1,061	1,366	0.07	0.39
Belgium	0	0	0	0	1,853	4,311	4,708	4,536	0.00	1.30
Chile	554	1,044	1,390	1,230	2,128	2,228	2,296	3,164	0.51	0.90
China	108	117	29	223	213	477	68	34	0.01	0.01
Hong Kong	145	976	1,497	1,909	5,997	3,746	1,885	930	0.54	0.27
Denmark	43	136	255	520	307	272	145	264	0.09	0.08
France	1,212	1,192	1,269	1,368	2,002	4,773	5,927	5,803	0.46	1.66
Germany	3,516	4,735	5,771	3,582	2,794	3,826	3,893	4,322	2.10	1.24
Greece	2,921	1,737	1,452	677	1,090	589	1,544	3,960	0.53	1.13
Iran	0	0	0	3,123	2,917	21,549	2,162	1,435	0.00	0.41
Italy	1,723	4,490	1,932	921	2,419	3,621	5,628	9,018	0.70	2.58
Morocco	1,308	1,736	1,198	1,684	1,635	1,514	1,869	1,924	0.44	0.55
Netherlands	2,001	1,243	2,025	1,097	1,755	4,187	4,018	3,728	0.74	1.07
Portugal	874	1,270	411	229	244	168	399	291	0.15	0.08
Spain	27,345	36,537	25,903	42,146	38,885	53,860	52,617	40,729	9.43	11.65
Sweden	122	228	88	151	245	169	216	185	0.03	0.05
USA	154,341	105,799	226,592	164,174	190,572	250,130	253,139	257,967	82.48	73.78

Table 15.8: Exports Almond Shelled: Value (US$ 1,000)

	Years								% Share World Total	
	1990	1993	1995	1998	2000	2002	2003	2004	1995	2004
World	622,437	666,582	960,068	938,520	742,804	1,003,628	1,221,308	1,586,583	100.00	100.00
Australia	172	266	1,004	0	4,280	3,634	4,122	6,643	0.10	0.10
Belgium	0	0	0	0	5,642	13,119	17,245	23,005	0.00	0.00
Chile	2,106	4,898	8,121	6,489	7,826	6,741	9,239	16,139	0.85	0.85
China	274	207	89	394	282	446	70	192	0.01	0.01
Hong Kong	501	3,845	6,710	6,638	16,053	5,619	2,823	2,271	0.70	0.70
Denmark	269	892	2,183	3,639	1,383	1,583	1,213	2,223	0.23	0.23
France	4,538	4,887	7,683	6,474	5,814	16,236	23,477	29,926	0.80	0.80
Germany	12,518	19,195	20,697	15,553	9,542	14,159	17,354	24,556	2.16	2.16
Greece	10,576	7,865	8,875	3,292	3,154	2,160	6,537	22,985	0.92	0.92
Iran	0	0	0	6,852	6,595	37,626	6,213	4,185	0.00	0.00
Italy	9,237	20,638	12,569	6,441	8,938	14,758	27,180	55,162	1.31	1.31
Morocco	4,727	4,211	5,493	5,333	3,354	3,916	5,831	8,103	0.57	0.57
Netherlands	7,331	5,342	9,369	5,243	5,605	13,715	15,347	19,915	0.98	0.98
Portugal	2,889	4,722	2,405	1,157	853	632	1,431	1,284	0.25	0.25
Spain	103,707	175,139	151,168	201,594	125,613	186,744	221,954	232,339	15.75	15.75
United States of America	451,120	400,657	704,834	651,429	527,436	681,424	838,666	1,100,196	73.42	73.42

Source: FAO STAT Database: March 2006.

COUNTRY CASE STUDIES

US Almond Industry

The United States is the world's leading producer of almonds, with almost all the production concentrated in California's San Joaquin and Sacramento Valleys. US became the largest almond producer in the late seventies, out producing Spain for the first time in 1977. Following heavy plantings in the late seventies to early eighties, California's production continued to grow rapidly, increasing an average of 23 per cent annually throughout the eighties as the trees planted during the seventies became commercially productive. While continuing to grow, although at a slower pace in the nineties and early 2000s, California's crop accounted for almost half the world's production in 2004.

Although it is the leading producer, the United States has fewer acres in almond production than Spain and Tunisia. US acreage has higher yields than either of these countries, mainly due to higher tree density per acre among its recent plantings. US yields, however, are not as high as some traditional almond producers, such as Syria and the United Arab Emirate.

Economic Significance of Almond Industry

There are more than 6,000 almond growers and 115 almond handlers (processors) in California. Almonds are grown on 550,000 bearing acres. The almond growing region stretches more than 500 miles between Red Bluff and Bakersfield in fertile Central Valley of California. Each almond orchard has at least two varieties of almonds planted within its rows to allow honeybees to pollinate the crop during the early spring bloom. More than 1.2 million beehives are required each year to pollinate California's 550,000 bearing acres of almonds. Almond Growers rent two or more hives per acre to adequately pollinate the 75-120 trees found in each acre.

Almonds are the No. 1 horticultural export for the United States valued at $1.5 billion in 2005 and Almonds are California's No.6 leading agricultural commodity valued at $ 2.25 billion dollars in farm value to California almond growers. California ships 70 per cent of its total crop to more than 80 countries throughout the world.

Table 15.9: Imports of almond: Quantities in Tonnes: Selected Years

Imports—Qty (Mt)	Years								% Share of World Total	
	1990	1993	1995	1998	2000	2002	2003	2004	1995	2004
World	26,714	23,226	25,383	31,449	57,718	62,478	57,814	60,807	100.00	100.00
Austria	47	35	59	24	475	314	433	686	0.23	1.13
Belgium	0	0	0	0	279	240	216	357	0.00	0.59
Belgium-Lux.	198	270	98	154	0	0	0	0	0.39	0.00
Bolivia	0	0	0	0	235	2,047	1,132	5,834	0.00	9.59
Bosnia & Her.	277	272	516	360	275	145	107	165	2.03	0.27
Cambodia	1,454	213	111	125	42	369	756	335	0.44	0.55
Cape Verde	5	100	148	598	2,731	3,522	1,454	512	0.58	0.84
Chile	136	252	251	237	7,839	9,716	7,622	4,321	0.99	7.11
Fiji Islands	992	1,281	1,659	869	1,223	1,345	1,159	1,317	6.54	2.17
Gabon	2,018	922	681	1,427	864	1,055	1,136	1,179	2.68	1.94
Hungary	13,514	12,002	13,664	16,677	24,367	19,089	19,072	25,785	53.83	42.40
India	0	600	1,500	0					5.91	0.00
Iraq	200	93	0	0	284	387	424	426	0.00	0.70
Ireland	1,086	312	460	741	645	1,102	1,497	1,657	1.81	2.73
Italy	11	98	98	108	174	151	123	150	0.39	0.25
Jamaica	94	129	1	315	426	621	337	513	0.00	0.84

(Contd.)

Table 15.9: (*Contd.*)

Imports—Qty (Mt)	*Years*								*% Share of World Total*	
	1990	*1993*	*1995*	*1998*	*2000*	*2002*	*2003*	*2004*	*1995*	*2004*
Kenya	471	464	460	565	585	142	139	181	1.81	0.30
Kuwait	510	15	3	230	39	4,169	3,628	1,079	0.01	1.77
Norway	245	498	728	1,294	7,516	8,420	8,864	6,363	2.87	10.46
Philippines	21	112	4	4	50	195	244	225	0.02	0.37
Qatar		20	0	684	79	32	380	518	0.00	0.85
St Vin/Gren	1,057	1,027	839	1,157	1,050	781	1,395	580	3.31	0.95
Slovakia	35	37	26	11	45	6	53	59	0.10	0.10
Slovenia	82	301	633	2,734	3,034	3,293	1,480	1,793	2.49	2.95
Trinidad and Tobago	0	157	0	185	1,279	30	1,032	1,592	0.00	2.62
Uganda	0	0	0	0	580	1,680	1,556	1,322	0.00	2.17
Ukraine	581	463	467	413	418	512	271	413	1.84	0.68
USA	4	145	2	3	14	30	20	0	0.01	0.00
						Sub-Total		57,524		94.60

Source: FAO STAT Database, March 2006.

Table 15.10: Imports of Shelled Almond: Quantities in Tonnes: Selected Years

Almond Shelled	*Years*								*% Share of World Total*	
	1990	*1993*	*1995*	*1998*	*2000*	*2002*	*2003*	*2004*	*1995*	*2004*
World	207,570	196,525	227,866	226983	278,140	326,129	364,770	382,543	100.00	100.00
Algeria	0	1	6	6	26	1,401	2,160	3,318	0.00	0.87
Argentina	638	1,382	1,316	1,405	1,497	270	705	885	0.58	0.23
Australia	2,449	1,933	1,450	910	551	1,796	3,091	1,646	0.64	0.43
Austria	2,884	3,538	2,566	1,417	1,551	2,812	3,196	2,880	1.13	0.75
Belgium	0	0	0	0	7,528	10,683	11,292	9,412	0.00	2.46
Belgium-Lux	3,489	4,151	5,030	5,821	0	0	0	0	2.21	0.00
Brazil	236	352	625	585	758	607	858	670	0.27	0.18
Bulgaria	0	49	32	68	258	671	892	951	0.01	0.25
Canada	7,276	8,689	7,228	7,440	9,887	12,525	14,497	16,644	3.17	4.35
Chile	0	65	68	359	539	639	793	1,111	0.03	0.29
China	2,542	3,079	2,608	2,336	3,413	4,145	3,642	3,853	1.14	1.01
China, Hong Kong SAR	1,633	1,671	2,741	2,378	10,151	8,970	6,320	4,686	1.20	1.22
Cyprus	204	109	414	97	301	401	232	541	0.18	0.14
Czech Rep		570	506	871	1,447	2,477	2,730	2,099	0.22	0.55
Denmark	3,622	5,836	5,096	5,897	6,645	6,392	7,084	8,261	2.24	2.16
Egypt	366	140	325	697	927	771	980	630	0.14	0.16
Finland	938	983	1,207	833	966	662	844	747	0.53	0.20
France	20,077	20,842	19,505	20,865	24,343	27,849	27,077	27,515	8.56	7.19
Germany	57,416	57,669	55,825	55,327	62,527	61,690	61,239	66,758	24.50	17.45
Greece	3,099	770	1,971	2,012	2,387	5,754	9,079	8,394	0.86	2.19
Hungary	0	198	156	383	511	680	890	850	0.07	0.22
India	1,037	841	1,424	2,763	3,747	2,463	2,443	2,396	0.62	0.63
Israel	1,755	1,970	2,000	2,300	2,273	2,857	2,896	2,011	0.88	0.53
Italy	11,148	6,065	6,831	13,885	14,895	17,978	27,216	28,325	3.00	7.40
Japan	20,508	21.623	22,523	18,795	21,175	27,827	28,735	26,119	9.88	6.83
Jordan	392	193	110	506	983	797	1,133	1,085	0.05	0.28

(Contd.)

Table 15.10: (*Contd.*)

Almond Shelled	*Years*								*% Share of World Total*	
	1990	*1993*	*1995*	*1998*	*2000*	*2002*	*2003*	*2004*	*1995*	*2004*
Korea, Rep.	3,106	5,211	3,849	2,793	4,276	5,400	6,190	5,754	1.69	1.50
Lebanon	520	740	1,640	1,723	1,975	2,092	2,232	1,331	0.72	0.35
Libya	0	0	0	0	0	1	396	373	0.00	0.10
Lithuania		0	92	175	419	616	570	558	0.04	0.15
Malaysia	456	751	660	545	1,052	1,371	1,194	1,268	0.29	0.33
Mexico	2,032	3,281	1,804	2,808	4,149	4,653	5,382	5,144	0.79	1.34
Netherlands	12,624	9,814	9,844	8,477	8,582	10,798	11,970	12,209	4.32	3.19
New Zealand	404	405	425	575	629	761	667	858	0.19	0.22
Norway	2,559	2,474	1,691	2,120	2,382	1,937	2,200	2,124	0.74	0.56
Pakistan	0	880	94	286	268	117	1,080	5,358	0.04	1.40
Poland	200	223	441	757	1,092	1,706	1,894	2,197	0.19	0.57
Portugal	581	789	790	1,272	1,139	1,253	1,542	2,160	0.35	0.56
Russian Fed.		350	2,791	3,267	2,694	5,442	6,913	8,515	1.22	2.23
Saudi Arabia	1,549	903	742	1,114	2,003	1,934	2,467	2,624	0.33	0.69
Singapore	0	0	757	647	861	859	1,066	971	0.33	0.25
Slovakia		0	74	102	207	292	397	392	0.03	0.10
Slovenia		66	31	0	207	83	98	107	0.01	0.03
South Africa	538	417	407	505	668	827	958	1,068	0.18	0.28
Spain	3,796	2,250	16,812	23,233	29,112	40,543	51,446	61,457	7.38	16.07
Sweden	4,979	5,094	4,294	4,090	3,619	3,235	3,628	3,760	1.88	0.98
Switzerland	7,338	7,301	7,543	6,788	7,688	7,623	8,262	7,952	3.31	2.08
Thailand	2	12	76	195	461	488	716	973	0.03	0.25
Tunisia	233	31	866	56	66	1,507	1,661	634	0.38	0.17
Turkey	141	306	178	951	1,621	1,316	971	1,791	0.08	0.47
UAE	4,300	861	5,436	5,200	9,420	13,103	12,034	12,100	2.39	3.16
UK	12,471	8,890	8,981	9,149	9,840	9,633	11,508	10,372	3.94	2.71
USA	23	26	81	27	51	378	768	1,153	0.04	0.30
Venezuela	145	289	229	298	521	428	324	428	0.10	0.11
						Sub-Total		375,418		98.14

Source: FAO STAT Database March 2006.

Almond Acreage Increased Steadily Since the Early 1920s

The number of almond-bearing acreage has increased at an average annual rate of 3.5 per cent since 1919, the first reported almond data by USDA. The number of bearing acres ranged from 35810 in 1920 to 72,210 by 1929, with rapid increases during the first half of the decade. Another big jump in bearing acreage took place during the mid-1960s through the 1970s, when they increased from 117,250 in 1965 to 324,000 in 1979. The number of bearing acres has continued to increase, but at a slower rate since 1980. The number of almond-bearing acres has remained at 550,000 between 2003 and 2005.

Along with the increase in the number of acres producing the commercial almond crop were improvements in production and harvesting technologies that increased yields. Although yields alternate annually, increasing one year and declining the next as part of the alternate-bearing nature of the trees; overall yields increased an average of 12 per cent annually between 1920 and 2003, going from 237 kgs. of nuts per hectare in 1920 to a record-high 2,250 kilograms per hectare in 2002.

Almond Grower Prices Increased along with Production

The increase in bearing acreage and yields brought increases in the size of the almond crop until it reached a record 495,000 tonnes in 2002. At the same time, the prices growers received for their almonds have also been trending upward (Table 15.11). Over the past 35 years, almond production grew at an average annual rate of 14 per cent, while grower prices grew on average 11 per cent annually. During the 1990s, production increased at a more rapid pace than prices. However, since 2000, prices have been increasing 20 per cent annually, while production growth has slowed to an average of 6 per cent a year. US almond output is estimated at 458,130 tonnes in 2004-05. Increasing world demand for US almonds has helped growers maintain high prices even while they have increased the quantity available in the markets.

Domestic and International Demand for US Almonds Continues to Grow

Demand for US almonds has been growing steadily over the past 35 years in both the United States and in international markets, with growth especially robust since the late 1990s. The almond industry has been very successful at increasing worldwide demand for its products, helping to strengthen grower prices while increasing its production.

Table 15.11: Almond Bearing Area, Yield/Hectares, Production (Shelled Basis), Season-average Grower Price and Value in California: 1980-2004

Year	Bearing area	Yield/hectare	Production	Grower Price	Value
	1,000 hectares	Kilograms	(Tonnes)	Centres/kg.	1,000 dollars
1980	132.23	1105.89	146,364	323.40	473,340
1981	132.06	1403.41	185,455	171.60	299,520
1982	137.25	1145.18	157,727	206.80	311,140
1983	145.75	754.47	110,000	228.80	231,920
1984	154.25	1740.23	268,182	170.28	446,134
1985	165.59	1279.91	211,364	176.00	360,640
1986	168.42	674.76	113,636	422.40	461,568
1987	168.83	1773.91	300,000	220.00	648,000
1988	169.64	1583.05	268,182	231.00	600,075
1989	166.40	1336.05	222,727	224.40	480,930
1990	166.40	1807.59	300,000	204.60	597,990
1991	163.97	1358.50	222,727	261.80	564,179
1992	162.35	1538.14	249,091	286.00	691,340
1993	167.21	1336.05	222,727	426.80	930,618
1994	175.30	1908.64	334,091	294.80	965,202
1995	169.23	993.61	168,182	545.60	880,896
1996	173.28	1336.05	231,818	457.60	1,018,368
1997	178.95	1931.09	345,000	343.20	1,160,640
1998	186.23	1266.52	235,87	310.80	703,590
1999	196.36	1924.29	377,85	189.60	687,742
2000	206.48	1544.37	318,88	213.80	666,487
2001	214.57	1754.56	376,49	200.60	740,012
2002	220.65	2240.77	495,42	244.70	1,200,687
2003	222.67	2118.55	471,74	346.10	1,600,144
2004	222.67	2057.43	458,13	487.20	2,200,055

Source: USDA: Tree Nut Year Book: 2005: Table E7.

With the growing demand for almonds by Americans, the share of the crop going for domestic consumption has increased over the past 10 years from about 20 per cent of the crop in 1997-98 to 32 per cent in 2004-05 (Table 15.12). At the same time, export demand has also been growing. The increase in export demand, however, has mostly been met by the increased production, as exports accounted for an average of 60 per cent of the crop in 2004-05, relatively unchanged over the previous decade. US exports of almond rose from about 85,000 tonnes in 1980-81 to 321,970 tonnes in 2004-05.

The international markets during this time, however, have changed. In the mid-1990s, the major market was Germany, followed by Japan and Spain. In the past 2 years, Spain has become the major export market, followed by Germany and India. Other important markets include Italy, France, Canada, the Netherlands, Hong Kong and Belgium.

Table 15.12: US Almond Supply & Utilization: 1980/81 - 2004/2005

Season 1/	Utilized Output 2/	Loss & exempt 3/	Marketable Production 4/	Import 5/	Opening Stocks 4/	Total Supply 6/	Current year Market Res. 7/	Ending Stocks	Exports 4/	Domestic Consumption Total	Domestic Consumption Per capita
	In Tonnes										kgs.
1980-81	146,057	7,648	138,409	32	35,811	174,252	0	46,111	84,790	43,351	0.19
1981-82	185,066	11,281	173,785	18	46,111	219,914	0	73,035	94,297	52,582	0.23
1982-83	157,397	7,366	150,030	259	73,035	223,323	3,003	80,263	80,730	62,330	0.27
1983-84	109,769	9,167	100,602	82	80,263	180,947	3,016	41,106	77,882	61,959	0.26
1984-85	267,619	11,957	255,663	109	41,106	296,878	12,782	102,970	121,009	72,898	0.31
1985-86	210,920	9,525	201,395	209	102,970	304,574	20,139	65,465	150,679	88,430	0.37
1986-87	113,398	6,491	106,907	313	65,465	172,685	0	35,842	78,930	57,914	0.24
1987-88	299,371	11,539	287,832	295	35,842	323,968	51,809	103,371	155,718	64,879	0.27
1988-89	267,619	11,548	256,071	218	103,371	359,660	64,015	122,498	165,094	72,068	0.29
1989-90	222,260	14,891	207,369	112	122,498	329,978	0	92,125	168,167	69,687	0.28
1990-91	299,371	20,071	279,299	60	92,125	371,484	19,550	109,479	177,663	84,342	0.34
1991-92	222,260	12,138	210,123	92	109,479	319,694	572	67,177	181,969	70,548	0.28
1992-93	248,569	12,111	236,458	116	67,177	303,751	0	59,472	174,992	69,286	0.27
1993-94	222,260	9,045	213,216	133	59,472	272,820	0	46,553	155,666	70,602	0.27
1994-95	333,390	17,594	315,796	177	46,553	362,526	27,578	92,918	205,828	63,781	0.24
1995-96	167,829	8,420	159,409	256	92,918	252,583	0	42,093	151,999	58,492	0.22
1996-97	231,332	10,748	220,584	566	42,093	263,243	0	21,903	169,876	71,465	0.26
1997-98	344,277	14,873	329,403	53	21,903	351,359	0	78,007	203,148	70,204	0.26
1998-99	235,868	11,158	224,710	84	78,007	302,800	0	41,655	186,149	74,996	0.27
1999-00	377,842	15,604	362,239	103	41,655	403,996	0	79,764	199,369	124,863	0.45
2000-01	318,875	11,793	307,082	245	79,764	387,091	0	48,655	232,849	105,587	0.37
2001-02	376,482	13,290	363,191	400	48,655	412,246	0	36,706	265,679	109,862	0.38
2002-03	494,416	9,163	482,395	904	36,706	520,005	0	73,502	305,547	140,956	0.49
2003-04	471,736	9,888	458,627	1,473	73,502	533,603	0	67,558	317,014	149,031	0.51
2004-05	458,128	11,437	446,691	3,077	67,558	517,325	0	62,452	321,967	132,906	0.45

1/ Season begins August 1; 2/ National Agricultural Statistics Service, USDA; 3/ Utilized production minus marketable production; 4/ Almond Board of California; 5/ Bureau of Census, US Department of Commerce; 6/ Marketable production plus imports, plus beginning stocks; 7/ Market reserve allocated to domestic consumption, export, or ending stocks.

Source: USDA: Economic Research Service, Fruits and Tree Nut Year Book 2006: Table E-8.

ALMOND FARMING IN SPAIN

Spain accounted for about 13 per cent of the world average production during the last three years (2003-2005). In Spain the most important almond producing provinces include Balearic Islands, Zaragoza, Tarragona, Lleida, Granada, Almeria, Málaga, Alicante, Castellon de la Plana, Valencia, Murcia and Albacete.

The most widely cultivated varieties are 'Marcona' and 'Desmayo Rojoand Largueta', which account for 55 per cent of the Spanish current production. Other cultivated varieties are 'Desmayo Rojo', 'Garrigues', 'Ramillete' and 'Atocha'. In the Balearic Islands cultivars like 'Jordi' and 'Vivot' are grown. In most modern orchards, 'Ferragnes', 'Cristomorto' and 'Ferraduel' have also been planted. Recently Spanish bred cultivars like 'Guara', 'Moncayo', 'Masbovera', 'Glorieta' and 'Francolí' are being planted.

At the moment the Spanish production is only correlated to the large almond planted areas, while the production per hectare is very low. However, in new irrigated orchards, production is very high and competitive with American cropping (1.0-1.2 tonnes/ha of shelled almond).

Various problems affect Spanish almond: non-homogeneous production, low production in dry areas and small farm size. Also, in the new orchards the pollination problem is a strong constraint.

Although Spain is currently the second producer of almond in the world, it is also an important importer with its average annual imports reaching 42,000 tonnes during 2000-04.

Production

In 1966 the almond growing area was about 220,000 ha; in 1970 it increased to about 280,000 ha; in 1975 it was about 440,000 ha and currently it is 620,000 ha. The Ministry of Agriculture, Fisheries and Food in making this estimation also took into account about 10 million isolated trees, which account for 60,000 ha. In 1992 production reached 80,000 tonnes of shelled product and the average related to the last few years (2000-04) was 56,000 tonnes.[6]

According to a last survey crop area is estimated at about 794,000 hectares, a figure much larger than the previous data available. Almond production takes place mainly in regions bordering the Mediterranean, primarily in Andalucia and Valencia. Only about 44,000 hectares are irrigated, so rainfall is crucial to the level of output. Almond production in Spain varies considerably from year to year, depending on weather conditions. During the period 1990 to 2004 the almond production (in-shell basis) ranged from a peak of 388.9 thousand tonnes in 1997 to as low as 86.4 thousand tonnes in 2004, and output recovered to 201 thousand tonnes in 2005-06.[7] Table 15.13 shows In-shell almond production by region in Spain for the last three years:

Table 15.13: Spain: In-Shell Almond Production: 2003-04 to 2005-06

Region	*2003-04*	*2004-05*	*2005-06*	*Increase in 2005-06 over 2004-05*
		Thousand tonnes		*Percentage*
C. Valenciana	55.3	25.6	57.7	225.4
Andalucia	48.0	11.8	42.1	336.7
Aragon	30.4	11.4	34.4	302.0
R. de Murcia	26.9	8.5	8.5	100.0
Cataluna	18.0	8.5	16.8	196.7
Castilla-Mancha	12.3	3.7	18.4	500.1
Baleares	11.4	10.0	12.0	120.0
Extremadura	4.3	3.5	3.5	100.0
La Roja	4.1	1.9	4.5	236.8
All Other	3.7	1.5	3.1	106.7
Total	214.4	86.4	201.0	232.6

Source: MAPYA, AVANCES, June 2005.

Producer prices in 2000 for in-shell almonds averaged 114.95 pesetas per kilogram (94.66 pesetas in 1999) and price ranged from 86.28 to 121.59 pesetas per kilogram, depending on variety, area of production and time of the year. Following a larger crop prices in MY 2001-02 declined.

Consumption

Domestic consumption of almond (shelled) in the country increased by over 22 per cent from 41 thousand tonnes in 2000 to 51,000 tonnes in 2004. The confectionery industry accounts for about 70 to 80 per cent of domestic consumption, and most of the balance is consumed as snacks. The nougat industry is a major consumer of almonds. Nearly all of the industry's consumption occurs in the months before Christmas, since nougat is a traditional holiday treat. As snacks, the main almond items consumed are unblanched roasted almonds and blanched fried almonds. They are mainly marketed in the form of snack packs.

The domestic Marcona variety is generally used for premium brands of almond products like nougat because of its distinctive taste and higher oil content. Domestic almonds are also generally used for snack products, roasted unblanched almonds in particular, because consumers can easily peel them. US almonds are used for most other products. Relative prices generally determine the proportion of domestic and US almonds used in almond-based products.

Due to their uniformity and low breakage, processors for food ingredients, including almond flour, dices and fillets, generally prefer US almonds. A significant proportion of these products are exported. In fact, trade sources estimate that at least half of all US almonds imported into Spain are subsequently re-exported — in one form or another — to other EU countries. US almonds are also generally preferred for the production of sugared almonds.

Almond Exports and Imports

Although Spain is the second top almond producing countries, it imports as well as exports large quantities each year. Generally it is a net exporter of almond. Imports of almond (shelled weight basis) increased from 33,233 tonnes in 1999 to 63,000 tonnes in 2004 and are expected to total 40,000 and 37,000 tonnes in 2005 and 2006 (Table 15.14). Almond exports (in-shelled weight basis) ranged from 42,000 tonnes and 60,000 tonnes (Table 15.15).

Table 15.14: Spain: Almond Imports (Shelled weight basis): 1999-2006

Marketing year	*1999*	*2000*	*2001*	*2002*	*2003*	*2004*	*2005*	*2006*
	Tonnes							
In-Shell	804	1,117	915	576	356	400	250	220
Shelled	32,419	28,038	41,258	48,678	57,988	62,600	39,750	36,780
Total	33,223	29,155	42,183	49,254	58,344	63,000	40,000	37,000

Source: Global Trade Atlas (GTA) till 2003-04, and Author's estimates for the remaining period. The conversion coefficient of 3.30 has been used for In-shell into shelled almonds.

Table 15.15: Spain: Almond Exports (Shelled weight basis): 1999-2006

Marketing year	*1999*	*2000*	*2001*	*2002*	*2003*	*2004*	*2005*	*2006*
	Tonnes							
In-Shell	754	657	845	657	672	600	750	750
Shelled	41,715	44,768	49,832	59,437	44,850	40,400	49,250	50,250
Total	42,469	45,425	50,677	60,094	45,522	41,000	50,000	51,000

Spain almond import and export trade matrix for the last two years is presented in Table 15.16. More than 80 per cent of the imports are from the USA, followed by EU member countries. Small quantities are also imported from Chile and Australia. Almost 95 per cent of the exports are shipped to EU member countries.

Table 15.16: Spain: Almond (Shelled basis) Import and Export Trade Matrix

(*In Tonnes*)

Import Matrix			*Export Matrix*		
Country	*2003*	*2004*	*Country*	*2003*	*2004*
USA	52,309	54,000	U.S.	135	400
France	3178	2500	Germany	16,071	14,000
Italy	939	3000	France	6884	7300
Portugal	584	500	Italy	6421	4000
Germany	350	200	Netherlands	3520	4000
Greece	101	800	Belgium	2766	2500
Other EU-25	309	400	Portugal	1710	1500
Chile	347	600	U.K.	1509	1400
Australia	185	100	Greece	1232	...
Other	42	900	Other EU-25	2902	2400
			Switzerland	1216	1400
			Others	1156	1200
Total	58,344	63,000	Total	45,522	41,000

Source: USDA Agricultures Attaché's Spain Tree Nut Annual Report 2005.

Factors Affecting Imports

Level of imports in Spain is a function of domestic production and Spanish almond/products exports. Regarding the maximum aflatoxin levels set by EC Regulation 466/2001, nuts, including almonds and dried fruit intended for human consumption or as ingredients in foodstuffs, maximum limits allowed are 2 parts per billion (2 PPB), or 2 micrograms/kilogram for aflatoxin B1, and 4 PPB for aflatoxin Bl, B2, Gl and G2 combined.

EC Regulation 466/2001 also determines that nuts and dried fruit with aflatoxin levels up to 5 PPB and 10 PPB may be allowed in, provided the fruit is subject to sorting or another physical treatment before human consumption, or use as ingredient in *foodstuffs.* The sorting or physical treatment applied must lower the aflatoxin levels down to 2 and 4 PPB limits.

The Spanish Ministry of Health (MOH) has a surveillance system in place for imports. When sanitary inspectors detect above-limit aflatoxin presence in almond shipments, the shipment is refused entry, and the MOH places the exporter under "alert," which requires aflatoxin testing of all shipments from the same grower or packer.

MOH requires a minimum of three satisfactory aflatoxin tests before lifting the "alert" on the exporter, or before recommending that the EC lift the EC "alert" on the exporter.

During MY 2004/05, the MOH has placed US exporters under "alert" 19 times for elevated aflatoxin levels. Each exporter's "alert" status remained in effect until at least MOH had tested three shipments with acceptable aflatoxin levels.

The new EC food safety regulation that came into effect on January 1, 2006 (EC 882/2004), leaves Member States to decide if and when imported product, that does not meet EU standards, needs to be destroyed. Spanish almond importers have met with Spanish MOH officials to encourage an administrative approach consistent with current practices. Currently, if an almond shipment is found to have an elevated aflatoxin level and is rejected at port by the Autonomous Regional Government MOH inspectors, or is rejected after attempts to bring it into conformity with EC aflatoxin limits, it can be re-exported or returned to the shipper.

The GOS has developed a Royal Decree (RD) proposing to the EC new labelling requirements for almonds and hazelnuts sold at retail. The GOS notified the EC of a proposed RD, and the EC was to react up to August 24, 2006. The draft RD proposes that packed almond and hazelnuts to be sold at retail must include the following information on the label:

- In case of products from Spain: product grown in Spain and/or Autonomous Community, and/or Province.
- For products from other EU countries: "product of/from (Member State where produced)".
- From other origins: "product of/from (country produced)".

The EC is likely to reject the proposal, because it appears to violate national treatment provisions, including for other Member States.

Production Policy

Spanish tree nut production takes place within the legal framework set by the EU common fruit and vegetables policy. This policy encourages the constitution of Producer Organizations (POs) to concentrate and market production. POs can apply to EU for co-financing of so-called Operational Programmes. These are investment programmes designed to increase producer competitiveness and marketing efficiency.

Up till 2004, tree nut producers were eligible to a special subsidy paid on a hectare basis, subject to presentation of so-called Improvement Plans on farms. This subsidy was set at € 241.50 per hectare, and was co-financed by the EU, MAPYA and the Autonomy Regions. In addition to almonds, this regime applies to hazelnuts, walnuts, pistachios and carob.

In 2005, new dispositions concerning the tree nut subsidy regime, which were approved under the 2003 CAP Reform, came into force. Level of individual farmer subsidy remained unchanged, and subsidy payments continued to be co-financed by the EU, Spanish Central Government and Autonomies.

However, farmers now must apply individually and not through the OP, even if OP membership remains a condition for subsidy access. Further, there is a minimum area restriction for subsidy access, set at 0.2 hectares.

Producer sources have been complaining at this restriction, especially in the Valencia Community, where tree nuts are produced largely in disadvantaged areas. Farmer sources report that areas in producer subsidy applications in 2005 declined 15 per cent in this region relative to previous year levels on account of this restriction. Same sources report that at national level, out of 16,000 ha under Improvement Plans finalized in 2004, only some 2,200 ha were submitted for subsidy in 2005.

According to Spanish Farmer's Organizations, the new policy could lead to a progressive abandon of tree nuts in less productive regions, and are requesting Spanish authorities to negotiate with the EU a change in this disposition.

Spain has a Maximum Guaranteed Area (MGA) for tree nuts of 568,000 hectares, of which 167,000 ha in the Valenciana Community (800,000 hectares in total EU) in over 252,000 farms. This figure includes almonds, hazelnuts, walnuts, pistachios and carobs.

Tariffs

Spanish almond imports are subject to payment of an *ad valorem* duty. Tariffs currently in effect are shown in the table below. Almonds sold in Spain are subject to a 7 per cent VAT (Table 15.17).

Table 15.17: Spain: Almond Import Tariffs

Harmonized Trade Code	Duty (Per cent)	
	2004	2005
0802.11.90 Almond in-shell	5.6 (1)	5.6 (1)
0802.12.90 Almond shelled	3.5 (1)	3.5 (1)

Note: There is a WTO tariff rate quoted for the EU of 90,000 tonnes/year, under which third country almonds can be brought into EU at a 2 per cent tariff.

ALMONDS IN GREECE

Almond cultivation in this country dates back a long time and is traditional; it has only recently been developed in the new areas. The most important varieties are 'Texas', 'Troito' (probably 'Tuono') and 'Retsou'. Lately, the cultivar 'Ferragnes' has also been introduced. The most important area is Crete; new orchards have been planted in Tessalia, also with irrigation. Production in Greece has increased in the last few years and at present is around 12,000 tonnes.

The main areas for traditional almond production in Greece are located in the prefectures of Magnesia, Larisa (Thessaly) and Serres and Kavala (E. Macedonia), where 70 per cent of the national almond tree population is concentrated. Almond production in the country has registered a declining trend since 2001 owing to a continuing loss of some orchards due to uprooting and forest fires, which affected agricultural areas close to forested land. Greek almond producers are reported to be less interested in the almond crop due to the fact that domestic prices are less competitive than imports. Also, the EU Common Market Organization has excluded the almond crop, which means there is no support of any kind for it. Adverse weather in recent years has also discouraged farmers from replacing and/or managing almond orchards in a better way. Aging of the trees is another problem coupled with a lack of labour at harvest. An increase in the cost of labour is reported in most producing regions. Immigrants used to receive 15 euros per day in 1999 and today they are paid 32 euros per day plus insurance. Young Greek farmers do not stay on the farm; they seek jobs in other sectors of the economy such as tourism and services.

Although almond orchards are all irrigated with drip irrigation systems, the unfavourable weather conditions that prevail from time-to-time especially in the main growing areas negatively affect production. For instance in 2003, frost, hail, heavy rains, extreme heat and summer drought caused serious damage to the 2003-04 almond production. Yields vary, with the best size and quality kernels being those of the late blossoming Feragnes variety, which are produced in central Greece and Macedonia. The actual planted area has decreased to approximately 39,000 ha without a drop in yields, which is due to better growing methods and more trees per area unit. Old, non-yielding orchards and aged, scattered trees have been uprooted, or otherwise taken out of a harvesting programme. However, almond crop area in Greece is reported to have now stabilized at a little over 40,000 hectares, including all types of systematically cultivated orchards and a large number of scattered older trees. These older trees are composed of local traditional varieties, which produce periodically and are easily affected by adverse weather. Acreage is expected to increase in the next five years due to increasing demand for almonds, particularly for confectionary use and growing trade activity with the new EU member states.

Domestic Consumption

Greeks are the largest nut consumers in the world. According to trade sources, domestic almond consumption has risen almost 30 per cent in the past ten years and is expected to stabilize somewhere between 22,000-23,000 MT per annum. Greece's consumption of tree nuts is 5.5 kilograms per capita, annually (or over 12 pounds/capita/year). This includes all nut consumption: almonds, pistachios, hazelnuts, walnuts, groundnuts, pecans and other types of nuts. Over 35 per cent percent of the total amount, or 2.0 kilograms (4.4 pounds) per capita represents personal consumption of almonds. One primary reason is that the confectionery sector, ice cream and chocolate industries prefer to use almonds. In an average year, heavy consumption of tree nuts starts in October, peaks in December and January, and declines in April and May. However, consumption increases again in summer when tourists arrive. A quarter of the nuts Greeks consume are in the form of processed "snack packs," eaten directly out of the bag.

Trade sources report that the tree nut consumption increase is recently observed not only in Greece but also all over Europe and worldwide, estimated at 15-20 per cent over the past five years. Trade sources also comment that this change is due to an aggressive US market promotion activity, a better priced product and the fact that new virgin markets were recently developed and became oriented to almond consumption.

Imports/Exports

Greece is a net importer of almond. During the last five years its imports of almond shelled averaged around 9,000 tonnes, while its annual exports averaged 3,500 tonnes. Local production and imported almonds are re-exported to the new markets. Demand in Bulgaria, Poland and Cyprus has increased in recent years and Greek suppliers are satisfying it. Moreover, the opening of other markets (i.e. China and India) has resulted in a higher world demand for almonds and better prices to both farmers and packers/exporters.

Trade in almonds is becoming more significant as both exports and imports are on the rise. According to NSS official data (only available on a calendar year basis), Greek almond exports increased from 1,127 tonnes in 2000 to over 4,100 in CY 2004, which is more than double of CY 2003. The value of exports increased from US$ 3.26 million in 2000 to US $ 19 million in CY 2004, with 50 per cent of the volume destined for Italy and Germany. More than 80 per cent of Greek almonds are sold to the EU-25, with the Balkan countries figuring largely in the remaining 20 per cent. According to trade sources, a large amount of imported almonds are re-exported. In CY 2003, exports exceeded 1,600 MT (valued at € 6.0 million) compared to just under 600 MT in CY 2002 (valued at € 2.0 million) and over 800 MT in CY 2001 (valued at € 2.1 million).

The amount of almond imports into Greece is growing rapidly, reaching 8,650 MT in CY 2004. In CY 2004, the value of imported almonds is reported by the National Statistical Service of Greece (NSS) at €31.6 million, which represents steady growth from € 7.1 million in 2000. Almonds are purchased mostly from the US Purchases from the US in CY 2004 totalled 7,582 MT, the largest volume ever recorded. In CY 2003 almond purchases from US, the main supplier of the Greek market, were valued at € 20.6 million. According to trade sources, import prices of US almonds in the second half of CY 2004 fluctuated at levels just below € 5.0/kg (CIF Basis). In 2005 Greek importers booked shelled almond at import prices between € 6.0-6.5/kg (CIF Basis). This was largely due to increasing world demand after the opening of large international markets (in Asia). US exporters have already sold most of their stocks to satisfy Asian demand. Actual US almond imports into Greece were higher than reported taking into consideration additional amounts that enter from Germany, UK and other EU member states. These US origin amounts are estimated to be somewhere between 300-400 MT per annum.

Import volumes of almonds in the past 2-3 years tended to increase due to the shortage of domestic production and the needs of domestic traders to satisfy clients in the neighbouring Balkan countries. These foreign supplies are primarily used by the confectionery, ice cream and chocolate industries, largely due to a different taste from those that are produced domestically. Domestically produced almonds are primarily consumed as snacks. Almond imports are up significantly and will remain strong in the coming years. The second largest supplier of almonds in CY 2004 and CY 2003 was Spain with more than 500 MT and 2,000 MT, respectively. The value of the US Dollar against the Euro has also positively influenced the quantity of almond imports into Greece from the United States.

Trade sources also report that tree nut imports from the US will continue to be high in the years to come due to enforcement of EU aflatoxin requirements. The aflatoxin certification provided by US exporters has been more accurate than certifications from other origins (mainly from Iran, Syria and Turkey). The GOG Ministry of Agriculture and Public Health Authorities (EFET—Food Control Organization of Greece) require an aflatoxin certification to accompany imports. Since mid-2005 EFET has intensified health controls after a number of samples of both almonds and pistachios were found by the National Chemical Laboratory to contain aflatoxin in excess of limits allowed by the legislation in effect. In these cases, the offending products were discarded and/or withdrawn from the market and high penalties were imposed on the importing firms and food stores. Periodically, EFET samples and tests all kinds of raw, processed and packaged nuts, at various points of sale. Supermarkets are the common venue for this kind of "spot check".

According to relevant EU Regulations (Council Regulation No. 194/97 as amended by Commission Regulation No. 1525/98), it is stipulated that three 10 kg samples must be taken and analyzed when testing bulk raw nuts for aflatoxin. The total aflatoxin content of any of the samples must not exceed 4 mg per kg—that is equivalent to a concentration of 4 ppb for total aflatoxin or 2 ppb for aflatoxin B1 in both the end product and in nuts destined for consumption without any further processing. The Commission also specified firm tolerance limits of 5 mg per kg of aflatoxin B1 and 10 μg per kg of total aflatoxins in raw product. If a higher level is found in any sample, the whole consignment must be rejected.

It has to be noted that Greek tree nut producers, processors and traders regard these limits and regulations as too strict and unrealistic. In their view, the regulations bring no improvement in public health precautions and, by burdening the producers and consumers with high additional costs, are equivalent to a trade barrier both for nut exporters to the EU and EU nut exporters to the rest of the world.

Policy: CAP 2004 Reform Decisions on Tree Nuts

Until 2004, when tree nuts became part of the new CAP reform plans, neither almonds nor pistachios (or other tree nuts) were eligible for the common market organization in the EU (CMO) and did not benefit from the old CAP. In addition, the lack of support from EU Agricultural Support Policies persuaded farmers to uproot productive tree acreage and to convert the land to heavily subsidized arable crops (cotton, corn, sugar beets, industrial tomatoes and durum wheat), supported by such EU Policies for over 25 years.

The main regions for traditional almond production in Greece are the prefectures of Magnesia, Larisa, Serres, Katerini and Kavala, all in Central and Northern Greece. The number of trees has been significantly reduced since the accession of Greece into the EU in 1981. This reduction in orchards occurred when farm prices did not cover producers' fixed costs. Under the new 2004 reform for tree nuts, Greek farmers received approximately 120.75 Euros/hectare in EU support per area unit, provided that the farmer is a member of a farmer group recognized by the EU. GOG Ministry of Agriculture is allowed to offer an equal amount on top of that from the national budget. Farm gate prices are set between farmer groups and traders, according to supply and demand based on quality and variety. The tree nut crops are fully decoupled and no price subsidies are paid to farmers.

Under the new 2004 CAP reform decisions, almonds, pistachios, walnuts, hazelnuts, chestnuts and carobs have become covered products, effective 1st of January 2005. Under this programme, Greek (and all EU) Tree Nut farmers will receive the amount of € 120.75/ha, as income support (based on land surveys of 1999 and 2000). In addition, National governments can offer up to an equal amount of Euros, as an additional support, called a "top-up" payment, from their national budget sources. This support will be paid for a certain acreage cultivated with the above mentioned nuts (guaranteed threshold in hectare), which for Greece is limited to 41,100 Ha. This makes a total annual EU payment for Greek tree nut farmers of around €5.0 million while an equal amount may be paid-out by Greek budget sources. The Greek government has not decided yet the terms of the matching payment to support the tree nut farmers. Reportedly, the Ministry of Agriculture was to proceed with negotiations with farmer groups around the country during the fall of 2004.

The minimum size of an orchard to be eligible for EU and/or GOG payments is one-tenth of a hectare, cultivated only with nut trees (not mixed with other crops). Scattered trees among other crops, orchards that cover less than one-tenth of a hectare, or trees planted in yards and along road verges, are not eligible. Presently, only almonds and pistachios occupy a large enough acreage (which equals 45,122 hectares around the country), to qualify for the new tree nut regime. This means that much of the acreage will not be eligible for

EU support payments nor Greek National payments. According to the Ministry of Agriculture, the total acreage actually cultivated in Greece with nut tree systematic orchards (all tree nuts) is presently estimated at only 3,017 ha (irrigated and satisfying the EU standards for payment eligibility). This means that the EU guaranteed threshold is not fully covered; therefore, there are good prospects for expansion of such crops in Greece. Acreage per individual nut tree can be determined according to demand and can vary from region to region provided that the acreage threshold is not exceeded. Farmers and farmer groups in various regions of Greece, see this as an incentive to restructure their crops and shift from arable crops (i.e. cotton, sugar beets and other) to Tree Nut crops.

EU Member States have the freedom to impose certain terms in order to consider which farmers are eligible for these payments (i.e. members of farm groups). Farmers may apply every year before March 15 by citing information such as: their number of trees, density of trees per orchard, geographical location and size of orchard etc. Payments will be granted after the completion of field inspections that are to be carried out by local Ministry of Agriculture authorities.

Future Prospects

In the past 10 years, Greek farmers have introduced new late-blooming varieties of almonds, particularly Texas-Mission and Feragnes. Later almond blooms mean less risk of damage from spring frost. The newer Feragnes variety has replaced many traditional varieties and has almost entirely replaced the older Texas-Mission variety in certain regions. The quality of Greek almonds is considered excellent. The best quality is used mostly as snack food and/or exported to Western Europe, while second grades are channeled to the confectionary industry.

The new CAP implementation starting in 2006, will certainly affect agricultural land use in Greece. Crops not favoured by the EU subsidy system and subsequently abandoned or significantly reduced, are expected to return if market conditions permit. By 2010, it is expected that a number of farmers will withdraw from once highly EU supported field crops (under the old CAP), and will shift to tree nut cultivation, particularly in areas like Thessaly and Central Macedonia. Almonds are considered a potential alternative for irrigated soils in these areas, due to high demand in the local market and in neighbouring countries. Based on these predictions Greek almond inshell output by the year 2020 may reach 70,000-80,000 MT (i.e. 17,000-20000 tonnes shelled basis). Poor soils in Greece, where unmarketable varieties of tobacco used to be grown, as well as hilly areas where irrigated cotton has been the dominant crop for over 20 years, are suitable for almond production.

ALMONDS IN ITALY

Crop Area

The planted area in Italy as officially reported by ISTAT, the National Institute of Statistics, is around 85,000 hectares under almond. However, most traders believe that actual planted area is less than half of the official figure, due to the continued uprooting of the oldest, least productive trees, not offset by new orchards. In view of that, Italian almond production in the long-term is expected to continue to decline. Italian production has decreased down the years. Production during the period 1991-95 averaged about 14,000 tonnes, and represented only 4.2 per cent of the world almond crops. The orchards are very old. In mid-1990s, a few new orchards have been planted with selected varieties such as 'Tuono', 'Ferragnes', 'Filippo Ceo' and 'Falsa Barese'.

Almond production in 2005 recovered to about 15,000 tonnes. Following low crop in 2003. The improvement was due to weather conditions having been relatively favourable in the two leading producing regions (Apulia and Sicily), except for minor damage reported in mid-March due to freezing temperatures in limited areas of Apulia.

For Italy USDA Agriculture Attaché's estimates and FAO data on production of almonds in Italy vary significantly. The two estimates of almond production (shelled basis) for the last four years are given in Table 15.18. FAO production estimates are 75 per cent higher than the USDA ones. There is a need to reconcile these figures.

Table 15.18: Italy: Almond (Shelled basis) Production Estimates

Almond Production (Shelled Basis in Tonnes)	*2002*	*2003*	*2004*	*2005*
USDA	9,000	5,000	12,000	15,000
FAO	26,222	22,850	26,360	26,325

Source: USDA Agriculture Attaches Tree Nut Annual Reports: various years: and FAO STAT Database: March 2006.

Based on the FAO production and trade data, total supply and distribution of almond in Italy, for the last four years worked out by the author, is shown in Table 15.19.

Consumption

Domestic consumption of almond increased from 30,000 tonnes in 1998 to 41,780 tonnes in 2002, but has declined to 37,500 tonnes during the last two years (Table 15.19). Domestic consumption of almond depends partly on prices of imported and domestically produced nuts. As a result of high prices in recent years, domestic almond consumption declined as the Italian confectionery industry reacted to this market situation (as it did in the hazelnut sector), reducing the amount of nuts in recipes for some of their leading products, such as for "pantone", the traditional Christmas cake.

The current EU *ad valorem* customs duty for shelled almonds is 2 per cent, for imports within the EU wide quota of 90,000 tonnes, and 4.7 per cent for imports over the quota. The EU export subsidy for shelled almonds is currently set at 99 lire per kilogram. Table 15.20 shows Italian almond trade during recent years. The conversion factors used from in-shell to a shelled basis in the PS&D are 0.3 per cent for in-shell imports and 0.22 per cent for in-shell exports. The difference in the conversion factors is based on the lower yield (from in-shell into shelled almonds), which applies to the Italian varieties.

Table 15.19: Italy: Almond (Shelled basis) Production, Supply and Distribution

Item	*2002*	*2003*	*2004*	*2005*
Area planted	86,406	86,000	84,441	84,000
Area harvested	86,040	85,500	84,073	86,500
Beginning stocks	6,000	7,440	8,460	9,360
Production	26,220	22,850	26,360	26,325
Imports	20,000	22,000	24,000	20,000
Total supply	52,220	52,290	58,820	55,685
Exports	3,000	2,000	12,000	13,000
Domestic Consumption	41,780	41,830	37,460	37,460
Ending stocks	7,440	8,460	9,360	5,225
Total Distribution	52,220	52,290	58,820	55,685

Note: Area in hectares. Other items are in tonnes.

Trade

Italy had a leading role in the world almond market up until a few decades ago, but in recent years exports have gradually decreased to today's negligible levels. Imports, on the other hand, have been rising to meet the growing demand of the domestic confectionary industry. The extremely low volume of the 1996 domestic crop had caused a dramatic expansion in imports, which in 1997-98 declined only marginally, remaining on the high side. The United States accounted for about 69 per cent of Italy's total imports in 2002-03 and 2003-04, while Spain supplied 21 per cent of total imports in Italy. Total imports of shelled almonds have increased from around 8,690 tonnes in 1995-96 to 25,400 tonnes. Exports have increased from 1,564 tonnes in 1995-96 to 6,538 tonnes in 2003-04 (Table 15.20).

Table 15.20: Italy: Almond Import and Export Matrix
(In Tonnes Shelled Basis)

Import Matrix			*Export Matrix*		
Country	*2002-03*	*2003-04*	*Country*	*2002-03*	*2003-04*
USA	13,964	17,530	Belgium	31	33
Spain	8,878	5,441	Germany	1,299	2,570
Germany	319	432	France	1,203	1,794
France	530	366	Other EU	638	1,520
Greece	177	495	Total EU	3,171	5,917
Other EU	747	755	Other Non-EU	705	621
Total EU	10,651	7,493			
Other non-EU	626	376			
Total	25,241	25,399	Total	3,876	6,538

Source: ISTAT.

Total almond imports in 2004-05 were expected to decline, although slightly, from the 25,000 tonnes annual imports reached in both 2002-03 and 2003-04. Actually, partial trade data (September 2004 through April 2005) indicate a certain increase in imports, especially from the US, but, as said above, the very high prices reported in the recent months have reduced, according to trade sources, imports during the last part of the marketing year. Imports are expected to further decline in 2005-06, due to the larger domestic crop. California almonds, in any case, will continue to represent a large share of domestic almond supplies. Furthermore, a new significant market trend has gained popularity in the most recent years: growing imports from California of in-shell almonds, to be roasted and salted, and sold as snacks in the domestic market. These almonds are of a particular variety, having a very high yield from in-shell into shelled basis (up to 60 to 65 per cent) and a very soft shell, which allow consumers to break them easily by hand.

ALMONDS IN IRAN

According to the FAO data, the Iranian commercial production of almonds in-shell basis increased from about 70,000 tonnes in 1990 to around

112,000 tonnes in 1998 and since then registered a decline trend (Table 15.21). The production is obtained from both orchards and scattered trees. The producing area is practically located in the North-West of Iran, in the Azerbaijan (Tabriz) region, where it plays an important role in the agricultural economy of the region. Nearly all the cultivated almond trees have been obtained from seed and thus show serious problems regarding quality and normalization of the production particular for what concerns the exports requirements.

Table 15.21: Iran: Almond Production, Exports and Quantities available for Domestic Consumption· Selected Years (In Tonnes)

Item	*1990*	*1995*	*1998*	*2001*	*2002*	*2003*
Production (In-shell)	69,866	79,531	111,992	97,144	107,000	80,000
Production (Shelled)	23,289	26,510	31,997	32,381	35,667	26,667
Exports (In-shell)	1,200	2,200	828	879	463	234
Exports (Shelled)	0	0	3,123	5,269	21,549	2,162
Total exports (Shelled basis)	400	733	1,377	2,049	7,337	799
Qty. for domestic consumption (Shelled)	22,889	25,777	36,014	30,332	28,329	25,868
Export value (US$ 1,000)						
Almond In-shell	1,400	7,100	1,293	1,312	792	376
Almond Shelled	0	0	6,852	10,787	37,626	6,213
Total	1,400	7,100	8,145	12,099	38,418	6,583

Source: Based on FAO STAT Database: March, 2006.

Bulk of production is utilized for domestic consumption. Small quantities of almond in-shell and shelled are exported. Exports during the last fifteen years ranged from 400 tonnes to 7,400 tonnes. In terms of production export constituted 3 to 6 per cent. Foreign exchange earnings from almond increased from US$ 1.4 million in 1990 to US$ 38.4 million in 2002.

ALMONDS IN INDIA

For India there are no official data for almond production and consumption. The only source of information is the USDA Agriculture Attaché's Annual Tree Nut reports, which give information on almond and walnut. India's almond crop is rather small ranging from 1,000 to 1,500 tonnes (kernel weight basis). Almonds are grown in the Kashmir Valley, and consumed almost exclusively where produced. The yield ranges from 1000-1500 nuts/tree/year. Shelling rates are 20-25 per cent (hard shell varieties) and 40 per cent (thin-shelled varieties). Almond trees undergo the alternate bearing pattern with better production in up cycle phase. Climatic conditions also have bearing on the output. Table 15.22 shows almond production, supply and distribution for the last few years.

Table 15.22: India: Almond Production, Supply and Distribution: Selected Years: (Area: Hectares; Trees thousand Nos. Production and other data tonnes

Item	*2001*	*2003*	*2004*	*2005*
Area planted	19,00	19,000	19,000	19,000
Area harvested	16,800	16,900	16,900	17,000
Bearing Trees	1,050	1,100	1,100	1,120
Non-bearing Trees	250	200	200	200
Total Trees	1,300	1,300	1,300	1,320
Beginning stocks	4,200	6,700	6,290	6,300
Production	1,000	1,100	1,100	1,000
Imports	26,000	24,900	26,500	22,800
Total supply	31,200	32,600	34,190	30,990
Exports	0	0	0	0
Domestic Consumption	26,000	26,000	27,000	24,000
Ending stocks	5,200	6,600	7,190	6,990
Total Distribution	31,200	32,600	34,190	30,990

Source: USDA Agriculture Attachés Tree Nut Annual Reports: various years.

Consumption

As domestic production is tiny, over 95 per cent of India's consumption requirements are met through imports, with US almonds enjoying an 85-87 per cent market share in recent years. Local consumption has grown sharply, fueled by heavy US exports at attractive prices. Demand has also been supported by the growth in the Indian economy and an expanding middle class. Indian almond consumption is currently estimated at 26,000 tonnes. As US almonds have a dominant share in the Indian market, domestic market prices closely follow US export prices. Table 15.23 shows wholesale almond kernel prices, in Delhi Market during the last four years.

Indian consumers consider almonds a 'high energy' food, especially good for children, recuperating patients, and physically active people. Almonds are consumed as whole nuts and/or used in local desserts, sweets and confectionery products. Due to relatively higher prices of almonds *vis-à-vis* other nuts during the 2004-05 season, according to market sources cashew, pistachios and walnuts partially replaced almonds in traditional Indian dishes, snack foods, and confectionary products. Consumption occurs mostly in the September-January period. Some traditional users (mostly higher income households) prefer Iranian (Mamra/Qumi) and Afghani (Gulbandi/Kagzi) almonds despite premium prices, Cosmetic manufacturers process most of the spoiled/rancid almond kernels for oil.

Table 15.23: Wholesale Almond Kernel Prices (Rs./Kg.), Delhi Market

Type (Origin)	*2004-05*	*2003-04*	*2002-03*	*2001-02*
Californian Almonds	350-465	261-332	243-266	208-270
Mamra Almond (Iran)	600-900	500-650	470-550	420-460
Qumi Almonds (Iran)	350-600	325-450	285-315	280-320
Gulbandi Almonds (Afghan)	325-430	280-325	235-265	250-280

Source: Delhi Market sources.

Trade

Indian almond (Shelled weight) imports currently amount to 24,000 to 26,000 tonnes per annum. Almonds are one of the leading US agricultural exports to India as volumes increased from 6,000 tonnes in 1996-97 to a record 24,150 tonnes in 2002-03 (market share of over 87 per cent). However, almond imports from US in 2003-04 declined to 21,440 tonnes due to comparatively higher export prices *vis-à-vis* those of last year. Imports from Afghanistan have gained in 2003-04 due to the tariff concession (50 per cent of the applicable basic duty) under the Indo-Afghan Preferential Trade Agreement of 2003 (Table 15.24). However, imports from other competing origins, such as Iran, Australia, and Middle East have been stagnant due to comparatively higher prices *vis-à-vis* prices of US almonds. Imports from the US and Australia are mostly in-shell that are hand shelled locally and sold in the market. Imports from other origins are mostly in the form of kernels.

Table 15.24: India: Almond Import Trade Matrix (in tonnes)

Country	*2002*	*2003*	*2004*
US	24,153	21,440	23,530
Iran	1,255	1,180	800
Afghanistan	1,050	1,536	1,900
Australia	845	368	400
UAE	62	50	0
Chile	0	33	150
Total for others	3,212	3,117	3,250
Other not listed	266	33	20
Grand Total	27,631	24,590	26,800

Source: GOI; Foreign Trade Statistics: various issue.

Trade Policy and Marketing Opportunities

While there are no quantitative restrictions on imports of almonds, high tariffs constrain growth in almond imports (Table 15.24). Market sources assess India's import potential at 35-36,000 tonnes of US almonds if tariff levels were "reduced" (i.e., Rs. 15-20/kg *vs.* the existing Rs. 35/kg).

Table 15.25: Imports Tariff for Almond for IFY 2004-05

Commodity code	*Description*	*Import Policy*	*Basic Duty*[2]	*Education cess*	*Total Applicable duty*[4]
HC 0802.11	Almonds In-shell	OGL[1]	Rs. 35/kg.	Exempted[3]	Rs. 35/Kg
HC 0802.12	Almond Shelled	OGL[1]	Rs. 65/kg.	2%	Rs. 66.3/Kg.

[1] OGL (Open General License)—no quantitative restrictions.

[2] Under the IAPTA, a tariff concession of 50 per cent applied on the basic import duty for these goods if imported from Afghanistan.

[3] Almond in-shell are exempted from the education cess.

[4] Methods for computing Total applicable duty:

A: CIF value of good

B: Basic Duty = Basic Duty Rate + A

C: Education Cess (EC) = EC Rate + B

Total Applicable Duty = B+C

Note: India's local food law (Prevention of Food Adulteration Act, 1955) specifies that dry fruits and nuts should not contain more than 5 per cent insect damaged fruits/nuts, by counts.

ALMOND FARMRING IN OTHER COUNTRIES TUNISIA

Almond cultivation in Tunisia dates back to the Punic-Roman period. According to foreign trade industry, the Tunisian production in the last 10 years has been estimated to be about 12,000 tonnes of shelled products. The almond is mostly cultivated in the region of Sfax, around Bon Cape, in the north of the country and also in the pre-desertic area (Kairuan, Kasserine, Feriana, etc.). Each growing area presents particular characteristics. The area of Sfax is characterized by mild winters and low rainfall (200 mm); plant spacing is 12-13 per 12-13 m.

The most important varieties are 'Achaak' and 'Ksontin', as well as 'Mazzetto' (probably 'Tuono') in the new orchards. In the area of Cape Bon, with a rainfall of 500 mm, planting is more intensive (200 trees/ha). The varieties planted are the local 'Heuch Ben Smail', 'Blanco Khooukhi' and 'Abiol de Ras Djebel'. In the flat area and in the hills of the northern part of the country, where the rainfall is about 400-600 mm, the winters are cold and summers hot, the best varieties are 'Tuono', 'Ferragnes', 'Monaco', 'Peerless', 'Fournat de Brezenaud' and 'Desmayo Largueta'. The plant density is about 150 trees/ha. In the northwest area, with a rainfall of about 350-550 mm, 'Ferragnes', 'Ferraduel' and 'Tuono' are cultivated.

According to the FAO data, Tunisia's production of almond in-shell basis, which declined form 52,200 tonnes in 1990 to 44,000 tonnes in 2004, recovered to 57,000 tonnes in 2005. Based on conversion coefficient of 25 per cent from in-shell to shelled almond, the output comes to 13,000 tonnes and 14,000 tonnes. Most of the Tunisian production is locally marketed. Only limited quantities (200 to 350 tonnes) are reported to have been exported in recent years. Unfortunately, almond cultivation in Tunisia is a low-cash product because of the very low production per hectare due to the unfavourable climatic conditions. However, Tunisian production could be attractive to the European market, because of the early ripening of the fruit.

MOROCCO

The commercial production of almond in Morocco is over 70,000 tonnes. It is not possible to quantify the area cultivated in Morocco. The species are also present in the Atlantic forest area. Hence, the production is not homogeneous; it is mixed with bitter almond, and utilized only for processing. In early 1990 an important new plantation rationale has been operated by SODEA, with varieties such as 'Marcona', 'Ne Plus Ultra', 'Ferragnes' and 'Ferraduel'.

PORTUGAL

Portuguese almond production varies considerably. From 1990 to 2005 output ranged 7.2 thousand tonnes in 1995 to 30.9 thousand tonnes in 2002. The almonds are concentrated in two areas, Algarve in the south, and Trasos Montes and Alto Douro in the northeast. The production is not very qualified because of mixed local and traditional cultivars and seedlings used for almond planting.

TURKEY

Almonds are a minor nut crop in Turkey. They are grown throughout the country with production concentrated in the Aegean, Marmara and

Mediterranean regions. The most important producing areas are located in Izmir and in the southeast, near the Syrian border. Most production is grown in orchards for commercial use. Almonds grow naturally in Turkey, but were not cultivated as a commercial crop until recently. Varietal selection during the past 25 years has resulted in improvement of local varieties, which are now grafted to both improved quality and yield as well as to delay blooming, since early frosts are a major problem in Turkey. Other than variations due to weather conditions, almond production in Turkey is relatively stable. Turkish almond production in-shell basis is round 40,000 tonnes, and based on conversion factor of 1:3, in-shelled terms comes to 14,000 tonnes. These quantities are important for the local market. Domestic consumption of almond is estimated at around 15,000 tonnes annually.

Turkey imports almonds around 1500-2000 tonnes annually and these come mostly (around 90 per cent) from the United States. It also exports small quantities to the EU and Middle Eastern countries. Almond trade is mainly restricted to border trade. There is a 44.1 per cent duty on the CIF value of all types of in-shell and shelled tree-nut imports. The duty is 61.8 per cent on processed tree nut product imports.

REFERENCES

1. The above historical excerpts are based on the book, *The Almond People by Gray Allen and Jenni Haas*; Blue Diamond Growers.
2. Townsend, C.C. and Guest, E. (Eds.). (1985): *Flora of Iraq*, Vol. 8, Ministry of Agriculture and Agrarian Reform, Baghdad.
3. Rosengarten, F. (1984) *The Book of Edible Nuts*, Walker and Company, New York.
4. Paramount Farms Almonds (1991): *Paramount Farms*, Bakersfield, California.
5. Rosengarten, 1984; and Paramount Farms Almonds, (1991). *op.cit.*
6. Note: The conversion rate used for almonds, in-shell to shelled is 1 = 0.27. Current exchange rate is approximately 189 pesetas = $1; 1 EURO = $0.8764.
7. *USDA Agricultural Attaché's Tree Nut,* Annual Report for Spain, 2005.

16

WORLD PISTACHIOS ECONOMY

HISTORY OF PISTACHIOS
(*PISTACIA VERA L. ANACARDIACEAE*)

The first provable authentic historical mention of edible nuts refers to pistachios. The first archaeological findings date back to 6760 B.C. in the Paleozoic period—in near settlements in the Neolith—in the territory of the present Jordan. Pistachios were soon considered food for the rich and the chosen. Although pistachio trees have been known for a long time, the place of their origin is uncertain. They probably come from the Middle East, Persia (Iran), and western Asia (eastern Pakistan and India), where they used to grow wildly in high positioned desert regions. The history of pistachio nuts reflects their "royal character", endurance and pride. Especially, fine pistachios are said to have been a favourite delicacy of the Queen of Sheba, who confiscated all Assyrian deliveries for herself and for her royal court. A story goes that lovers used to meet under pistachio trees and listened to the cracking of their nuts below moonlit nights, which was a sign that they would be happy.

History of Iranian Pistachios

Pistachios occupy a special place in the heart of every Iranian. They are a kind of food allowing families to be together, they are in every home, ready as a delicacy for a guest or neighbour who may just drop in to have a cup of tea. They are one of the most popular and delicious snacks Iran has. Pistachio trees have been growing in Iran for centuries, their home being above all in the Kerman province where pistachios are grown on an area exceeding two hundred thousand hectares. Their commercial use began in the 1930s when businessmen from Iran started to export pistachios to Europe and the USA above all, and also to Czechoslovakia before Second World War. At that time they also cleverly allocated individual kinds of pistachios to each market, e.g. Jumbo to the USA, Round to Europe, etc.

After Second World War the actual commercial expansion of Iranian pistachios occurred, and lasted till the 1970s, i.e. the beginning of the Islamic revolution. In the next years all business deals cooled off and the war with Iraq followed. Only after its termination did the modern history of pistachios began again.

Iran is not only a grower of first-class kinds of pistachios but it is also the main producer of this product in the world, with the volume of production reaching 100 to 200 thousand tonnes every year, depending on the period of time. Besides crude oil, carpets and caviar, pistachios belong amongst the main items exported from Iran.

History of Pistachio Growing in the USA

The first pistachios were brought to California around 1854. In the 1930s a team of American experts—botanists started to look for the best material in Iran suitable for cultivation and subsequent growing in the same conditions as those in Iran. This lasted till the 1960s. The commercial growing of pistachios on plantations only started to develop around 1970. Until that time the Americans had been completely dependant on supplies from Iran.

Due to the crisis that followed the incident on the American embassy in Teheran in 1976, and the subsequent interruption of imports as a result of sanctions imposed, pistachios from California appeared in the limelight. Currently nearly the whole of consumption of pistachios in the USA is covered from domestic sources. The production of pistachios in California is one of the industrial branches together with processing of almonds. Production and processing of pistachios and almonds have become a profitable business for a lot of Californian growers. The support provided by the government made a number of growers of almonds extend their growing to pistachios. The first commercially usable crop was harvested in 1976. The production has increased rapidly in recent years.

Pistachios were brought to Europe (in particular to Italy) from Syria during the reign of Tiberius at the beginning of the 1st century AD. Subsequently they were spread to be grown in other Southern European countries (e.g. Greece).

ORIGIN OF PISTACHIO

There are about 11 species of pistachio trees *(Pistacia* spp. L). P. *vera* is the only species grown commercially because it produces fruit of adequate size to be marketed. The pistachio tree is native to western Asia and Asia Minor, from Syria to the Caucasus and Afghanistan. In 1875 a few small pistachio trees, imported from France were planted in Sonoma, Calif.

Turkey, Iran, Afghanistan, Italy, and Syria are the other major pistachio producing countries, outside the United States. Trees are also grown in Pakistan, Greece, India, and Australia. The USDA Plant Introduction Department introduced the tree in California about 1904, but it was not promoted as a commercial crop in California until 1929.

Climate

Pistachio trees thrive on heat; better nut filling and fewer blanks are produced in hot-weather climates. Trees should not be planted above 4,500 feet elevation because cool summer temperatures do not promote good kernel development. Also, temperatures below 10°F can kill the tree, especially young trees. Summer temperatures above 100°F are considered as ideal. However, winters need to be cold enough to complete their dormancy (a rest period during winter). Three-leaflet leaves are produced instead of the normal five-leaflet leaves when cold requirements are not met. About 1,000 accumulated hours of temperatures at 45°F or below are required for pistachio trees to break dormancy, and to start normal growth in the spring.

Soil and Water Requirements

Pistachio trees grow in virtually all soils. However, they grow better in deep, sandy loam soils. Tree density should be increased in poorer soils. This will permit maximum production earlier than in orchards planted with more space between trees, and in about the same time as those planted in good soils. Pistachio trees are long-lived, tap-rooted and can grow to 20-30 feet tall. Like any other fruit or nut tree, well-drained soils are needed for optimum growth. About 2-acre feet of water are required in a mature orchard, including one or two deep irrigations during winter.

Pistachios are drought tolerant, but for commercial crop production there must be adequate soil moisture during late winter, spring and early summer. Within a month after pollination (mid-April to mid-May), pistachio trees grow vegetatively and form flowers for the following year.

Pistachios do not tolerate wet feet. Avoid ponding water around the trees. Pistachio trees are highly tolerant to saline conditions. Trees grow well in some orchards irrigated with water containing 3,000-4,000 ppm of soluble salts.

Adaptation: Pistachios thrive in areas which have winters cool enough to break bud dormancy and hot, long summers.

Flowers: Pistachios are dioecious with male and female flowers on separate trees. Male and female trees must be present for fruit to set, or a branch from a male tree may be grafted on a female tree. Under unfavourable conditions during nut growth, the shells may not split open. Pistachio nuts are rich in oil, with an average content of about 55 per cent. Pistachios tend toward biennial bearing, producing heavy crop one year followed by little or none the next. Production of nuts is also influenced by drought, excessive rain, heat or cold and high winds.

Location: Pistachios should be planted in full sun. The size of the slow growing trees can be further controlled by pruning.

Soil: The trees do best on soils that are deep, friable and well drained but moisture retaining.

Irrigation: Pistachios will tolerate considerable drought but do best with deep, infrequent watering.

Fertilization: Since pistachios grow slowly, they do not require large quantities of nitrogen fertilizer. After initial training, little pruning is needed except to remove interfering branches. Heavy pruning reduces yield.

Propagation: The pistachio is usually propagated by budding or grafting selected scions onto seedling stocks of *P. atlantica, P. terebinthus* and *P. integerrima.*

Pests and Diseases: A number of fungi attack the pistachio. The most serious fungal disease is Verticillium wilt, which can quickly kill trees of varying age. Most pistachios are now grafted to Verticillium resistant *P. integerrima* rootstock. The trees are also sensitive to the oak root fungus, *Armillaria mellea.*

Commercial Varieties Available

All commercial varieties belong to *P. Vera* species. 'Kerman' is the only female variety recommended for commercial plantings. 'Kerman' has higher chilling requirements than other varieties. Two other female varieties, 'Sfax' and 'Joley,' produce a greater number of split shells than 'Kerman'. They also have lower cold requirements than 'Kerman'. 'Sfax', trees produce fewer blanks than 'Kerman', do not go into alternate bearing and the fruit does not have physiological disorders. However, they produce smaller nuts than 'Kerman' trees. 'Peters' is the main male variety available to pollinate 'Kerman'. Pollen shed of 'Peters' trees sometimes does not pollinate some 'Kerman' flowers that become receptive later. Two USDA selections, '2-16' and '2-18', are male trees that release pollen from male flowers later than 'Peters' flowers, especially '2-18'. 'Chico', another male variety sheds pollen earlier than 'Peters'.

Rootstocks

Several studies conducted throughout the years have indicated that pistachio trees produce and grow better with *P. atlantica* rootstock than with *P. terebinthus*, another rootstock. In New Mexico, *P. terebinthus* rootstock has been more cold tolerant than *P. atlantica*. *P. atlantica* not only has a greater per cent take of buds, but trees will grow bigger than those of *P. terebinthus* and will produce earlier.

Spacing and Planting Procedures

Tree spacing varies mostly from 17 feet by 17 feet to 20 feet by 20 feet (few growers plant to 24 feet by 24 feet). Trees planted in fertile soils need to have more space than those planted in poor soils. Some growers use the square system while others use the triangular planting system (also called hexagonal). Growers could also plant on a rectangular system. The triangular system allows planting about 15 per cent more trees per acre while keeping the same spacing between trees.

Preparing land to plant pistachio trees is similar to that followed for other fruit trees. Whenever a hardpan or caliches layer exists in the top 7 feet, it should be broken because pistachio trees are deep rooted and are affected by water-logging.

Pistachio trees form and regenerate roots slowly, and do not lend themselves to being handled bare-rooted. Rootstocks need to be budded with 'Kerman' and 'Peters' budwood to ensure the development of the desired variety (fruit and nut trees do not come-to-true from seed). Budded trees can also be planted but this practice triples tree cost. Seedlings grown in peat pellets will be planted later in special paper pots or paper-mache containers, usually 7-8 inches in diameter and 18 inches long. Containers can be filled with sterilized soil or soil media containing 1/3 peat moss, 1/3 vermiculite and 1/3 perlite. Container-grown plants must be set out in the orchard when roots reach the bottom of the container.

Planting, Budding, Training and Pruning Young Trees

Non-budded trees are usually grown and sold in paper-mache containers. Position the plant so the base of the tree is level with the ground. Trees should be planted about an inch deeper than the depth it was grown in the container. A single, upright seedling trunk, free of lateral shoots, should be developed in the first 18 inches of the seedling's trunk. Established seedlings (3/8 to 1/2 inches in diameter) should be budded in the fall. Depending on planting time and seedling size, seedlings can be budded the same year they are planted for the following year. Buds usually are placed on the windward side. Seedlings (rootstocks) must be growing vigorously to get a good percentage of bud take. Training the bud shoot correctly during the first 5 years in tree's life will develop the desired tree shape, especially when mechanical harvesting is going to be done. Drive the stakes about 6 inches into the ground, about 4 inches away from the young tree, preferably facing the bud and on the upwind side. Two main pruning cuts are done to train pistachio trees: Pinching, this means eliminating only the terminal (end) bud of new shoots, and cutting or heading back, which involves cutting 1/3 to 1/2 of 1 or 2-year branches. In established trees, whole branches are eliminated with what are called thinning cuts.

If trees are not pruned during summer, selection and heading back of the primary scaffolds is done in the second winter. Pistachio trees are trained to grow upward and outward, and develop into a modified open-vase shape. Pistachio trees can sunburn if trees are trained to open vase-shape. The high sunlight may force pistachio growers to limit thinning cuts of secondary branches to prevent sunburn in branches. It also protects trees more when branches are bent down by the weight of the foliage and the nuts. Pistachio trees will probably respond well to the central leader shape used to train pecan trees. Only minor pruning cuts are needed once the tree framework has been established.

Tree Nutrition

Nitrogen needs are similar to other nut trees. Nitrogen fertilizer need not be applied the year trees are planted. One pound of ammonium sulphate per tree should be applied during the second year. During the third year, and if trees are actively growing, 1 pound of ammonium sulfate should be applied in March and 1 pound of ammonium sulfate in June.

The farmers should never apply nitrogen after June to prevent vigorous growth that may delay tree dormancy. Heavy (clayey) soils contain enough potassium to grow trees. However, pistachio trees are usually grown in sandy-to-sandy loam soils, which need potassium to ensure adequate tree growth. Although, research has not been done to learn the best recommended rates, incorporating 150 to 200 lbs of actual potassium, before planting trees, will help tree growing conditions for many years. In established orchards, 2-4 lbs of potassium chloride per tree has helped unthrifty trees grow better. Phosphoric acid (75%), at the rate of 2.5 lbs of actual phosphorus per tree, has been applied through drip irrigation systems in established pistachio orchards with excellent results. Good nutrition levels in pistachio orchards are a must.

Leaf analysis, yields, nut quality, and shoot growth (2 to 2½ feet per year) are some of the factors growers need to observe every year. To get full value of leaf analyses, they should be done every year. There are also some optimum nutritional ranges to look for when conducting leaf analyses in pistachio orchards (Table 16.1).

Harvest

Pistachio trees begin bearing the fourth or fifth year after budding. However, a significant crop is not harvested until the seventh or eighth year. Pistachio nuts are physiologically mature when the hull separates easily from the shell. There are 7 to l0 days when harvesting can be done without shell-staining occurring. Shell staining increases the longer the nuts stay on the tree. However, stained shells usually result when the hull is not removed the same day of harvest. Production of blanks (seedless fruit) is a problem occurring in *P. Vera* 'Kerman' trees sometimes produce 25 per cent. Sometimes nuts grow to normal size without seed. This situation, not associated with tree yield, varies from year to year, from variety to variety and from rootstock to rootstock. Depending upon planting distance and orchard management practices, yields in pistachio orchards could average 2.25 tonnes to 3.35 tonnes per hectare. In the US most harvesting in established pistachio orchards is done mechanically. Pistachio trees are shaken like pecan trees to harvest pistachio nuts. The nuts are harvested when the husk or hull covering the shell becomes fairly loose. A fully mature tree may produce as much as 25 kgs. of dry, hulled nuts.

Biennial Bearing

After an indefinite number of years, pistachios trees ultimately produce relative heavy crops of nuts every other year. They are typically biennial or alternate bearers. During the year of heavy crop, abundant flowers buds are produced, but an excessive bud abscission occurs, leading to lower crops the following year. Vegetative growth is most extensive during the year a heavy crop is produced.

Table 16.1: Nutritional Ranges usually found in Leaf Analyses from Pistachio Trees

	Edible Portion (Per 100 g)			*Minerals and Vitamins (Per 100g).*		*Fatty Acids (Per 100g)*	
	Gram	*(KJ)*	*(Kcal)*		*Grams*		*Grams*
Protein	20.8	387.27	92.56	Potassium	1.020	Palmitic Acid	6.270
Fat	51.6	2007.82	479.88	Phosphorus	5000.000	Myristic Acid	0.100
Carbohydrates	16.4	231.99	50.28	Magnesium	158.000	Luric Acid	0.050
Other	11.2	56.20	18.6	Calcium	136.000	Oliec Acid	36.000
Total	**100**	**2683.28**	**641.32**	sIron	7.300	Linoleic Acid	9.500
				Selenium	0.450	Stearic Acid	0.710
				Nickel	0.080	Palmitoleic Acid	0.290
				Vitamin C	7.000	Linolenic Acid	0.280
				Vitamin E	5.200	Archidic Acid	0.280
				Nicotinamide	1.450	Total Sterol	108.000
				Vitamin B1	0.690	Beta-Sitosterol	90.000
				Vitamin B2	0.200	Stigmasterol	2.000
				Carotene	0.150		
				Folic acid	0.058		

Source: USDA Nutrient Database.

Diseases

Verticillium wilt (*Verticillum dahliae)* has been seriously affecting pistachio orchards in California for years. A large number of trees have died or have developed symptoms since then. This disease affected both *P. atlantica* and *P. terebinthus* rootstocks. The rootstock *P. integerrima* has been recognized as verticillium wilt tolerant, and has been used for planting several thousand acres of pistachios in California. V. wilt is a soil-borne fungus disease. The fungus blocks movement of water and nutrients by occlusion of the tree's vascular system. When rapid wilting occurs, a pistachio tree can die in 1 or 2 weeks. A cross-section of a severely affected pistachio tree shows rings of brown dots, consisting of discoloured vascular tissues. The most recommended way to prevent verticillium wilt is to avoid planting pistachio trees wherever cotton has been planted, and to use verticillium wilt resistant rootstock. Fumigating soil with methyl bromide and chloropicrin before planting helps but is expensive.

Crown Rot (phytophtora parasitica) attacks pistachio trees situated in poorly drained wet areas. Surviving infected trees do not grow well.

Insects

Stinkbug and leaf-footed plant bug are the major insects. Mites also damage pistachio nuts by producing scarlike blotches on stems and hulls. The citrus-flat mite *(Brevipalpus lewisi)* has been identified as the mite affecting pistachio orchards in US and other countries. Browning can eventually cover half of the nut's exterior surface. Nuts affected early in the season will shrivel and drop from the tree. Those affected later may stay on the tree, but kernel development is poor and shells are incompletely developed and discolored.

Pistachio Use

Pistachio nuts are considered one of the prime edible nuts, along with almonds, macadamias and cashews. In the annual average world production of in-shell dessert and Table Nuts of 8.416 million tonnes during 2003-05 pistachio's share was a mere 6.3 per cent. Pistachios are served principally as salted nuts. A large percentage of pistachios are marketed in the shell for snack food. Non-split, filled nuts are used for processing. Pistachio nuts contain 25 per cent amino acids (mainly essential amino acids), 16 per cent carbohydrates (mainly sucrose) and

55 per cent oil (80% unsaturated oil). Pistachios are also an excellent source of dietary fiber, containing 2.8 grams of fiber per ounce.

WORLD PISTACHIO ECONOMY

According to FAO data, pistachios are grown in only 16 countries in the world. The area under pistachio increased from 275,000 hectares in 1990 to about 448,238 hectares in 2005. Production doubled during this period from 273,000 tonnes to about 501,237 tonnes (Table 16.2). Some of the main reasons for this include additional area brought under pistachio, especially in Iran and the USA, the two top producing countries, and effective pest and disease control and the prevention of wastage of the product. In Iran the area under crop has almost doubled, while in the USA 13,000 hectares of new area was added during the period under

Table 16.2: Pistachios Production: 1990-2005 (Tonnes)

	1990	*1995*	*2000*	*2001*	*2002*	*2003*	*2004*	*2005*
World	273,080	394,107	568,838	293,787	517,974	515,310	466,634	501,237
China	22,000	25,000	22,000	26,000	28,000	30,000	32,000	34,000
Cyprus	20	30	15	15	15	15	15	15
Greece	3,439	5,591	9,000	7,500	8,500	9,000	9,500	9,500
Iran	162,831	238,778	303,957	112,432	249,000	275,000	190,000	191,000
Italy	200	2,200	2,768	1,762	1,877	1,993	2,400	2,400
Pakistan	250	200	209	196	200	200	200	200
Syria	13,000	14,538	39,923	37,436	52,840	50,000	40,000	60,000
Tunisia	600	900	1,600	1,100	800	800	800	800
Turkey	14,000	36,000	75,000	30,000	35,000	90,000	30,000	60,000
U.S.A.	54,430	67,130	110,220	73,030	137,440	53,980	157,397	140,000
Uzbekistan		1,000	1,000	1,000	1,000	1,000	1,000	1,000

Source: FAO STAT Database, April 2006.

review. In 2005 Iran accounted for 38 per cent of the world production, while the share of USA was 28 per cent. Syria and Turkey accounting for about 12 per cent each and China about 7 percent followed these countries. The share of most other countries is less than one per cent of the global production. As regards India there are no data on pistachio production either in the FAO database or from the national sources.

In 2005 Iran accounted for 67 per cent global area (Table 16.3). In the USA pistachio area rose from about 22,000 hectares to 35,000 hectares. Its share in global area was around 8 per cent in 2005. The share of area under pistachio in Iran to world total varied from 55 per cent to 68 per cent, while in the USA it ranged from7 per cent to 10 per cent.

World average pistachio yield was 1,182 kg per hectare in 2005. Among major producing countries, the United States with 4,000 kg./ha has the highest yield level. Syria's yield was 2,727 kgs./ha., and China 2,125 kg./ha. Iran yield was only 633 kg./ha. (Table 16.3). The average yield of pistachio in Iran in most of the years was below the world average mainly due to management constraints coupled with drought in some years.

GLOBAL TRADE IN PISTACHIO

World exports of pistachio have increased almost three times during the sixteen years. Quantities exported rose by 116,290 tonnes, from about 92,000 tonnes in 1990 to 268,000 tonnes in 2003, but declined to 235,462 tonnes in 2004 (Table 16.4). Export value went up by 160 per cent from about US$ 368 million to US$ 963 million, but fell to US$ 942 million in 2004 (Table 16.5). Iran's exports rose by 116,290 tonnes, accounting for around 66 per cent of increased quantities of world exports. Quantities supplied by Turkey declined, while exports form Hong Kong increased by five folds. During 1990 to 2004 Iran accounted for over 60 per cent of the global pistachio export quantities in most years. In 2004 Iran with around 139,000 tonnes pistachio exports was the leading exporting country followed by the USA with 35,692 tonnes, Germany with about 15,000 tonnes, Hong Kong with 10,440 tonnes, Netherlands with 7,039 tonnes and Syria with about 2,000 tonnes. Hong Kong and Netherlands, as exporters usually import pistachio from main producing countries and after processing with higher market efficiency re-exports to other countries.

Iran's share in global pistachio exports volume has varied from minimum of 45 per cent to maximum of 76 per cent. The US's share has varied from a minimum of 5 per cent to maximum of 12 per cent in the global market during 1990-2003.

As regards foreign exchange earnings, Iran earned the highest amount (US$ 555 million) from exports of pistachio in 2004. Its share in global value was about 60 per cent. It was followed by the USA (US$ 149 million), Germany (US$ 48 million), Netherlands (US$ 30 million), and Hong Kong (US$ 18 million).

Global imports of pistachio increased from 90,213 tonnes in 1990 to 327 thousand tonnes in 2003, but declined to 272 thousand tonnes in 2004. Hong Kong, Spain, Germany, China, Italy, and France are the major importing countries (Table 16.6). Other countries such as Belgium, Luxemburg, Lebanon and UK import smaller quantities around 6000 - 8000 tonnes each. Table 16.7 shows value of imports of pistachio in selected years.

Table 16.3: Pistachios: Area, Yield and Production in Major Producing Countries: 1990-2004

	Years								Average
	1990	1995	1998	2000	2002	2003	2004	2005	2003-05
Iran									
Area (Hectares)	154,276	218,000	259,431	274,728	295,000	300,000	300,000	300,000	300,000
Production (Tonnes)	162,831	238,778	313,957	303,957	249,000	275,000	275,000	191,000	180,333
Yield (kg./ha)	1,056	1,095	1,210	1,106	844	917	917	633	822
USA									
Area (Hectares)	21,730	24,400	27,880	30,200	33,590	35,610	35,000	35,000	35,203
Production (Tonnes)	54,430	67,130	85,280	110,220	137,440	53,980	158,000	140,000	117,297
Yield (kg./ha)	2,505	2,751	3,059	3,650	4,092	1,516	4,514	4,000	3,343
Syria									
Area (Hectares)	14,900	15,000	20,000	18,500	20,000	20,000	20,000	22,000	20,667
Production (Tonnes)	13,000	14,538	35,684	39,923	52,840	50,000	40,000	60,000	50,000
Yield (kg./ha)	872	969	1,784	2,158	2,642	2,500	2,000	2,727	2,409
China									
Area (Hectares)	16,400	16,600	17,500	12,000	15,000	15,000	15,000	16,000	15,333
Production (Tonnes)	22,000	25,000	26,000	22,000	28,000	30,000	30,000	34,000	31,333
Yield (kg./ha)	1,342	1,506	1,486	1,833	1,867	2,000	2,000	2,125	2,042
World									
Area (Hectares)	275,068	356,246	402,726	407,519	437,652	444,791	443,591	448,238	375,233
Production (Tonnes)	273,080	394,107	511,347	568,838	517,974	515,310	549,837	501,237	418,859
Yield (kg./ha)	993	1,106	1,270	1,396	1,184	1,158	1,240	1,1180	1,112

Source: FAO STAT Database, April 2006

Table 16.4: Pistachio Exports: (Quantities in Tonnes): Selected Years

Exports-Qty (Mt)	Years							Index 2004/1990	% Share in World Total in 2004
	1990	1995	2000	2001	2002	2003	2004		
World	91,862	188,576	164,197	201,013	214,815	268,448	235,462	256.32	100.00
Afghanistan	650	150						0	0
Belgium	0	0	1,688	2,590	3,742	3,969	3,767	0	0
Belgium-Luxem.	1,554	6,545	0	0	0	0	0	0	
China	13	2,154	1,354	1,582	1,919	2,177	3,573	27484.62	1.52
Hong Kong SAR	1,573	9,122	12,869	13,903	10,227	13,860	10,440	663.70	4.43
France	107	229	467	1,094	1,186	571	528	493.46	0.22
Germany	6,302	12,165	12,412	15,726	11,960	12,715	14,986	237.80	6.36
Greece	106	372	122	426	462	317	1,006	949.06	0.43
Iran	68,655	128,000	101,257	115,335	135,314	184,946	138,723	202.06	58.92
Italy	980	1,257	749	906	1,210	936	1,051	107.24	0.45
Luxembourg	0	0	6,654	4,878	5,425	7,334	6,961		2.96
Mexico	783	545	185	2,554	1,153	783	1	0.13	0.00
Netherlands	225	606	578	537	1,622	4,853	7,039	3128.44	2.99
Spain	98	86	947	593	1,060	958	1,989	2029.59	0.84
Syria	1,398	3,868	3,673	9,759	3,050	3,012	1,096	78.40	0.47
Turkey	2,291	1,669	244	4,947	1,936	1,038	757	33.04	0.32
UAE	0	0	0	0	10,551	2,708	992		0.42
United Kingdom	1,413	5,339	2,223	1,421	142	80	173	12.24	0.07
USA	4,227	15,011	15,652	21,592	21,150	23,770	35,692	844.38	15.16

Source: FAO STAT Database, April 2006.

Table 16.5: Pistachio Exports (Value US$ 1,000): Selected Years

Exports (Value US$ 1,000)	*Years*								*% Share in World Total in 2004*
	1990	1995	2000	2001	2002	2003	2004	*Index 2004/1990*	
World	367,576	627,393	536,969	610,831	695,840	963,513	941,565	256.16	100.00
Afghanistan	6,438	350						—	
Belgium	0	0	7,102	9,486	14,623	15,851	15,712	—	1.67
China	48	2,145	1,436	1,560	1,988	3,233	4,803	10006.25	0.51
Hong Kong SAR	3,906	20,955	36,081	32,688	14,928	17,446	18,307	468.69	1.94
France	773	1,348	2,074	4,290	5,560	2,915	3,463	447.99	0.37
Germany	28,354	39,989	46,943	52,424	48,113	47,568	69,516	245.17	7.38
Greece	596	1,345	770	941	1,455	1,075	3,885	651.85	0.41
Iran	259,405	424,700	314,223	358,940	436,553	679,940	555,456	214.13	58.99
Italy	9,786	7,930	5,322	5,730	7,413	6,833	8,709	88.99	0.92
Mexico	877	1,981	1,056	6,890	4,433	2,417	7	0.80	0.00
Netherlands	1,156	2,044	1,889	1,938	5,797	19,893	29,845	2581.75	3.17
Spain	419	381	2,402	1,585	3,696	3,387	8,335	1989.26	0.89
Syria	10,494	17,495	6,416	11,476	4,652	5,065	1,628	15.51	0.17
Turkey	10,107	6,909	1,576	17,028	8,320	6,239	4,834	47.83	0.51
United Kingdom	6,336	18,220	9,044	5,433	699	585	1,226	19.35	0.13
USA	16,082	51,102	63,124	70,976	78,824	91,431	149,339	928.61	15.86

Source: FAO STAT Database, April 2006.

Table: 16.6: Imports of Pistachio: (Quantities in Tonnes): Selected Years

Pistachio Imports - Qty (Mt)	*Years*							*2004/1990 (Index)*	*% Share in World Total*
	1990	1995	2000	2001	2002	2003	2004		
World	90,213	168,500	152,968	177,594	213,810	327,994	271,770	301.25	100.00
Armenia		25	0	750	557	879	1,000		0.37
Australia	514	740	686	749	654	912	1,277	248.44	0.47
Austria	766	1,319	591	199	126	382	340	44.39	0.13
Belgium	0	0	2,879	3,951	4,927	5,449	5,399		1.99
Belgium-Lux.	4,636	10,527	0	0	0	0	0	0.00	0.00
Bulgaria	0	102	82	91	178	322	477		0.18
Canada	2,464	2,557	2,743	3,463	3,331	5,582	3,756	152.44	1.38
China	1,560	7,183	12,370	13,424	11,623	15,964	11,929	764.68	4.39
Hong Kong SAR	3,370	12,179	16,337	18,953	34,142	62,366	37,623	1116.41	13.84
Czech Republic		471	744	1,141	1,089	1,784	1,681		0.62
Egypt	56	237	1,484	656	976	990	454	810.71	0.17
France	5,255	10,165	8,295	9,498	11,533	10,751	14,731	280.32	5.42
Germany	26,377	40,859	25,090	24,965	21,351	21,670	21,722	82.35	7.99
Greece	698	2,552	1,741	1,194	2,546	2,981	3,466	496.56	1.28
Hungary	0	551	808	1,049	1,568	1,405	1,232		0.45
India	867	2,716	4,110	5,680	4,854	8,380	4,972	573.47	1.83
Israel	3,036	3,000	3,282	4,259	2,879	3,831	3,925	129.28	1.44
Italy	6,554	13,381	9,582	11,069	11,869	12,275	13,643	208.16	5.02
Japan	5,391	8,565	2,930	3,466	2,695	2,230	2,347	43.54	0.86
Jordan	590	580	1,599	1,432	1,661	2,137	1,552	263.05	0.57
Kazakhstan		62	65	117	61	118	474		0.17

(Contd.)

Table: 16.6: *(Contd.)*

Pistachio Imports – Qty (Mt)	*Years*							*2004/1990 (Index)*	*% Share in World Total*
	1990	1995	2000	2001	2002	2003	2004		
Korea, Republic	34	781	342	470	445	611	381	1120.59	0.14
Kuwait	597	692	813	549	634	684	677	113.40	0.25
Latvia		25	103	193	272	428	480		0.18
Lebanon	1,300	380	8,403	11,080	8,588	7,346	2,780	213.85	1.02
Lithuania		114	135	493	605	958	955		0.35
Luxembourg	0	0	7,960	7,120	10,968	7,912	11,418		4.20
Malaysia	11	937	281	206	531	634	510	4636.36	0.19
Mexico	4,511	2,166	9,064	13,336	9,316	9,488	7,001	155.20	2.58
Netherlands	1,496	3,660	1,525	1,745	2,469	6,843	6,669	445.79	2.45
Pakistan	1	110	1,089	906	1,041	2,025	3,241		1.19
Philippines	0	271	39	52	59	45	86		0.03
Poland	0	188	556	1,066	1,011	1,240	1,505		0.55
Portugal	490	1,263	412	374	347	385	362	73.88	0.13
Romania	5	44	61	198	281	451	500		0.18
Russian Fed		10,240	1,162	4,490	5,166	5,692	8,912		3.28
Saudi Arabia	3,329	3,738	4,744	4,697	5,376	5,892	1,736	52.15	0.64
Singapore	0	670	490	498	592	470	603		0.22
Slovakia		43	62	301	864	3,771	3,996		1.47
Spain	7,887	10,498	9,422	12,689	15,456	22,359	33,463	424.28	12.31
Syria	464	2,327	1,304	200	1,725	2,733	2,154	464.22	0.79
U.K.	4,881	6,883	5,257	5,902	4,702	7,090	6,511	133.39	2.40
U.S.A.	830	335	226	567	252	375	508	61.20	0.19

Source: Prepared by the author from the FAO STAT Database, April 2006.

Table 16.7: Imports of Pistachio: (Value US$ 1000): Selected Years

Pistachio Imports (Value US$ 1000)	*Years*							*Index (2004/1990)*	*% Share in World Total*
	1990	1995	2000	2001	2002	2003	2004		
World	366,938	560,144	488,704	507,070	643,153	1,038,611	992,302	270.43	100.00
Armenia		101	1	750	331	495	915		
Australia	2,301	3,008	2,769	2,790	2,557	3,481	5,356	232.77	0.54
Austria	3,663	4,778	1,727	935	812	2,050	2,436	66.50	0.25
Belgium	0	0	11,812	14,375	18,820	20,690	23,224		2.34
Belgium-Lux	18,657	34,344	0	0	0	0	0	0.00	0.00
Bulgaria	0	31	36	42	118	184	362		0.04
Canada	8,989	8,422	9,190	11,663	12,478	20,239	15,765	175.38	1.59
China	6,133	12,626	15,419	14,595	16,107	26,724	24,403	397.90	2.46
Hong Kong SAR	10,946	30,275	44,916	49,541	88,011	150,236	112,386	1026.73	11.33
Czech Republic		1,225	2,392	3,369	3,530	4,972	6,335		0.64
Egypt	275	626	3,946	1,504	2,573	1,817	1,057	384.36	0.11
France	23,552	34,327	32,580	33,930	42,017	44,433	55,464	235.50	5.59
Germany	110,750	140,358	97,056	84,550	85,603	89,321	101,409	91.57	10.22
Greece	2,785	8,556	5,848	3,994	9,053	10,111	14,097	506.18	1.42
Hungary	0	1,870	2,566	3,089	5,192	4,003	5,508		0.56
India	1,516	7,110	16,318	22,316	17,946	29,022	21,695	1431.07	2.19
Israel	13,075	9,226	11,763	12,684	8,934	10,735	15,375	117.59	1.55
Italy	26,395	45,352	37,373	38,105	44,958	45,819	58,664	222.25	5.91
Japan	26,580	35,618	15,177	14,606	12,404	11,112	13,290	50.00	1.34
Jordan	2,038	1,989	4,594	3,989	4,626	5,691	3,865	189.65	0.39
Kazakhstan		172	87	181	55	175	2,060		0.21
Korea, Republic	152	2,635	1,351	1,547	1,614	2,141	1,491	980.92	0.15
Kuwait	2,250	2,589	2,868	1,900	2,434	2,897	3,450	153.33	0.35
Latvia		73	488	972	1,521	2,506	1,821		0.18

(Contd.)

Table 16.7: *(Contd.)*

Pistachio Imports (Value US$ 1000)	*Years*							*Index (2004/1990)*	*% Share in World Total*
	1990	1995	2000	2001	2002	2003	2004		
Lebanon	11,000	1,500	25,756	33,459	26,202	22,787	11,047	100.43	1.11
Lithuania		151	410	1,462	2,010	2,728	3,414		0.34
Luxembourg	0	0	25,241	25,235	41,620	38,571	57,272	·	5.77
Malaysia	40	2,134	523	683	1,453	1,390	1,477	3692.50	0.15
Mexico	13,224	4,164	16,192	23,096	9,084	6,317	2,491	18.84	0.25
Netherlands	6,392	12,692	6,780	6,081	8,665	24,421	28,777	450.20	2.90
Pakistan	2	131	759	485	620	1,291	2,190		0.22
Poland	0	556	1,839	3,239	3,193	3,693	5,827		0.59
Portugal	1,972	4,297	1,672	1,473	1,424	1,483	1,737	88.08	0.18
Romania	21	143	162	348	570	1,189	1,841	8766.67	0.19
Russian Federation		31,187	1,702	1,868	2,301	2,506	4,455		0.45
Saudi Arabia	4,813	7,360	8,913	8,570	10,994	10,971	7,903	164.20	0.80
Singapore	0	2,932	1,957	1,797	2,220	1,685	2,330		0.23
Slovakia		175	223	1,039	2,524	5,440	15,831		1.60
South Africa	161	256	331	167	200	271	664	412.42	0.07
Spain	30,994	33,677	32,928	38,653	52,604	69,743	125,032	403.41	12.60
Syria	2,253	30,144	5,470	519	3,572	12,037	4,505	199.96	0.45
U.A.E.	0	0	0	0	59,700	303,322	174,303		17.57
United Kingdom	22,176	23,521	21,341	20,525	16,692	19,081	25,563	115.27	2.58
U.S.A.	2,810	953	1,224	2,100	1,092	1,767	2,319	82.53	0.23

Source: Prepared by the Author based on FAT STAT Database, April 2006.

COUNTRY CASE STUDIES

PISTACHIO IN IRAN

Iran is the world's number one pistachio producing country, accounting for around 50 per cent of the world production and international market. Iran's share as the first producer has varied from minimum of 33 per cent to a maximum of 66 per cent, and that of the USA, as a second top pistachio producing country, has varied from minimum of 11 per cent to maximum of 25 per cent. During 1990-2004 Iran's share as a largest pistachio producer has increased slowly than of the USA in world production.

Kerman province is the main area of pistachio production in Iran and its share in total area harvested and total production was 80 per cent and 83 per cent respectively (Table 16.8). In the US, as discussed below, virtually all of the commercially produced pistachios are grown in California, although farmers in New Mexico have become increasing interested to grow the crop.

Table 16.8: Pistachio Area and Production in different Provinces (2002)

Province/City	*Area (Hectares)*	*% Share in Total Area*	*Production (Tonnes)*	*% Share in Total output*
Markazi	1,684	0.60	2,500	0.83
E.Azarbaijan	63	0.02	127	0.04
Arbedil	1	0.00	0	0.00
Kermanshah	50	0.02	150	0.05
Kerman	224,243	80.09	250,000	83.33
Khorasan	24,943	8.91	15,924	5.31
Isfahan	1,242	0.44	3,420	1.14
Sistan va Baluchetrsan	1,858	0.66	2,585	0.86
Zanjan	65	0.02	702	0.23
Semnan	2,931	1.05	8,252	2.75
Yazd	15,941	5.69	11,490	3.83
Hormozgan	35	0.01	451	0.15
Tehran	804	0.29	103	0.03
Qazvin	2,500	0.89	3,403	1.13
Jiroft and Kahnuj	90	0.03	120	0.04
Total	280,000	100.00	300,000	100.00

Source: Government of Iran: Ministry of Agriculture.

Iran not only produces the finest variety of pistachio, but is also the highest producer of this product with an annual average output of 220,000 tonnes during the last three years. Presently the USA, Turkey, and Syria are the main competitors of Iranian pistachio in the world markets.

A natural snack for health-conscious individuals, Iranian pistachio constitutes an ideal ingredient in the preparation of a variety of dishes and sweets and is served during party receptions and family gatherings. Pistachio has the highest protein content and nutritional value, and is second to none in the world for its high energy content. It contains a high percentage of potassium, phosphorus, calcium, and all the essential amino acids. It is believed that the consumption of pistachio reduces the risk of heart attack and death from coronary diseases. To enjoy its unique taste, the pistachio nuts should be salted, roasted and eaten out of the shell. In the years following the Islamic revolution of Iran, from the viewpoint of job creation and export earnings, pistachio has always been the prime non-oil export product of Iran. Consequently, changes that occur in the international market of this product have a profound effect on the economy of the country.

Future Policies of Iran Regarding Pistachio

- Continuation of the programme for promotion and expansion of market;
- Efforts to reduce pollution and wastage by adoption of ACCP method; and
- Continuation of discussions with European countries; Maintenance and strengthening of sales markets in the European community.

Iran's Pistachio Exports

Iran's export volumes have increased steadily from 1990 to 1996 when records 140,000 tonnes were exported. However, the following year exports fell back to their lowest level 57,900 tonnes, and then registered a continual increase. Exports reached a peak of about 185,000 tonnes in 2003, but declined to 139,000 tonnes in 2004. It is worth mentioning that Iran has a short crop during some years due to huge drought, however, another external challenge is that Iran is not yet WTO member and its accessibility to global markets has slightly decreased from 1996 while some neighbouring countries as WTO members buy pistachio from Iran local markets and export to others.

Exports from the USA also registered steady growth. The US export quantity rose from 4,227 tonnes in 1990 to 10,913 tonnes in 1996 and reached a peak of 35,692 tonnes in 2004, representing more than eight fold increase during the last sixteen years. Iran with exporting 139,000 tonnes of pistachio had 59 per cent and USA with around 36,000 tonnes had only 15 per cent of global pistachio export quantity in 2004 (Table 16.4).

The analysis of exports of pistachios from Iran and the U.S. to the European Union (EU) market reveals that the U.S. share in EU market has increased from 4 per cent in 1992 to 23 per cent in 2004, while that of Iran has decreased from 95 per cent to 70 per cent in the same period. Iran's exports to the EU have declined dramatically from 1997 when only 38 per cent of Iran total export came to Europe, since USA made propagation of aflatoxin percentage against Iran pistachio and interfered in global pistachio market by using opportunity of WTO membership. The reduction of imports to selected European countries was due to the implementation of new European Community regulation on aflatoxin. Although these regulations apply to all tree nuts, but in fact only Iranian pistachios have systematically been subjected to these regulations at the point of entry and often beyond at the supermarket level. After this, Iranian exporters become more active in other markets and less dependent on the EU markets. Iran's exports outside the EU have increased from about 25 per cent until 1987 to 60 per cent in the last three years. The key non-EU markets for Iran are the Far East, South-East Asia, Canada, Russia, Mexico and the Persian Gulf countries.

It is important to note that Turkey's share in the EU market has been increasing since 1997 and now it is the third largest pistachio exporter to EU. Turkey's pistachio market share in the EU from negligible before 1998 has increased to 6 per cent in 2004.

US pistachio export to European markets has been increasing rapidly. During 2000-04, exports to France have increased by 198 per cent. Exports to Belgium-Luxembourg have increased 44 per cent within one year. Germany imported 3722 tonnes of pistachios from the US in 2001; exports to Italy reached 2370 tonnes, up 78 per cent.

According to the US Department of Commerce assessment the future potential markets for the US are considered to be Spain, Czech Republic, Thailand and Columbia. In view of the keen competition from the US it is imperative for Iran to maintain standard of global market and search for new markets to continue safe competition.

Discussion and Conclusions

With proper climate for pistachio cultivation, Iran remains as one of the most important pistachio producing countries in the world. As global data shows currently Iran and the USA are two main rivals in global market for pistachio production and exports.

Iran is the leading pistachio producing and exporting country. It has 67 per cent of global pistachio harvested area, accounts for only about 40 per cent of global pistachio production, and has about 60 per cent of world pistachio export. The USA, Iran's main competitor in the world market, with only 8 per cent of global pistachio harvested area, contributed 28 per cent of global pistachio production in 2004. Its share in world pistachio exports was 15 per cent in 2004. As mentioned above, USA growth rate in global pistachio production registered a faster growth than that of other major producing countries during 1990-2005. Iran yield level remains below world average in most of the years during 1990-2005. However, the US yield level of pistachio seems the highest among all major producer countries and it is more than two-fold of world average (Table 16.3).

The main importers and consumers of world pistachio are European countries, which it shows significant relation between their high income and expenditure. Iran share in European markets has reduced due to strong competition from USA the European Union markets and WTO decisions. Although the USA is the biggest rival of Iran in global war of pistachio production and export, nevertheless its share in the world production quantity was less than half of Iran's share and that of in world export quantity was around 25 per cent of Iran's share.

Despite good capacity for production and marketing of pistachio, Iran faces various internal and external problems in order to retain its better position of pistachio trade. Iran ranks first in terms of pistachio harvested area, production and quality all over the world. However, its yield per hectare is low. Also in volume Iran exports less than half of total output due to internal and external constraints. Internal challenges are mainly management process problems such as: traditional methods in production and harvesting process, misuse of modern technology and pest control, lack of advanced irrigation and preservation system, lack of capital and investment scarcity in marketing processing industries, producers' low literacy and productivity. While external challenges are: lack of marketing advertisement and defective packing system, unfamiliarity with international markets and principles, indirect relation with overseas importers, improper planning for marketing and exporting of surplus pistachio, low accessibility to global markets and non-accession in WTO.

It is worth mentioning that close competition between Iran and the US on world pistachio markets has caused false propaganda in Western *media* on the amount of aflatoxin in Iranian pistachios and the USA attempts to drive Iran out of pistachio trade from global markets. In this regard, the

European Union took the decision to ban Iranian pistachio imports as of September 1997. Three months later on December, the EU lifted the ban for the next 10 months, citing they will only import shipments tagged healthy by the Iranian Health Ministry. Shortly after, a seven-member Iranian delegation met representative from the European Commission and the EU and German health officials in Brussels and Hamburg. The two parties discussed a wide range of issues and agreed on 12 points proposal. Ultimately Iran is committed to prevention of any probable contamination of pistachio with aflatoxin to continue exportation. It also agreed that Iran would do its utmost in ensuring production of uncontaminated pistachio in the coming years. Iran has not been able to become member of WTO up to now since the US and some other countries opposed and rejected Iran's application for WTO membership for 10th time during last 6 years. Iran has also just reciprocated and prohibited USA commodity advertisement and consumption all over the country.

The studies conducted by the Institute for Standard and Industrial Research of Iran show that Iranian pistachios are quite safe and don't contain health hazards according to international standards. However, improper packaging sometimes causes pistachios to absorb moisture when they are carried to ships or stored at warehouse. Moisture increases the amount of aflatoxin in pistachios.[1]

The above analysis indicate that Iran faces two main challenges in production and exporting of agricultural products, particularly that of pistachios in comparison with other major producers, which are:

(a) Inadequate investment in production processing industries, which has caused low yield and productivity of pistachio.
(b) Lack of membership and accession to WTO as a window of global markets, which has caused low quantity and quality of exports.

Last but not least, the USA may defeat Iran in global pistachio markets but it cannot delete that from international markets while it may be concluded that:

1. Considering the USA and Iran yield level gap and world average, it shows that there is capacity for yield level improvement and production increment in Iran.
2. Iran can plan and create adjustment between reductions in domestic consumption and increase in export quantity of pistachio through investment in processing industries and assessing new target markets.

3. Iran would retain its pistachio regional markets and also continue negotiation as a major pistachio producer to enter Word Trade Organization (WTO).

In order to retain competitive power of Iranian pistachio the government needs to provide facilities in pistachio packaging and infrastructures in processing industries. On the other hand, the volume of advertisements for Iranian pistachios would increase as a significant factor for penetrating into foreign markets. Based on research findings fallowing strategies are recommended for better and safe competition in pistachio global market.

Recommendations

- Setup training course for selected pistachio garden owners to improve multipurpose cooperatives for production, distribution and exporting.
- Activate quick transportation and establishment of modernize pistachio processing terminals.
- Development of safe marketing management in all process from farm to warehouses and export ports.
- Investment in processing industries to increase commodity standardization and marketing opportunities.
- Ameliorate advertisement management system in internal and external markets, and standard procedures in respect to quality control with facilitate related research centres.
- Extension of regional markets such as Islamic Common Market (ICM) and Economics Cooperatives Organization (ECO) markets.
- Negotiation for WTO accession along with increment of free trade facilities and mitigation of customs formalities.
- Iran and USA agreement to keep away political conflicts from agricultural exportation challenges in favour of human rights and farmer's welfare.

PISTACHIO IN USA

The US is the second largest pistachio producing country. The Census of Agriculture reported 1,051 farms growing pistachios in the United States in 1992, with 28,000 hectares in orchards. The area under the crop has now increased to 35,000 hectares. The number of farms would also have increased to around 1,350. There are currently approximately 550 pistachio growers in the United States. California accounts for 96 per cent of US pistachio area, and most of the industry's expansion has occurred in that state. The combined acreage of Arizona, New Mexico, Nevada, and Texas accounted for about 4 per cent of all US pistachio acreage.

The bulk of California's production is located in Kern and Madera counties in the San Joaquin Valley. In 1992, Kern county accounted for 40 per cent of the state's pistachio acreage, and Madera county, about 30 per cent. Tulare, Fresno, Merced, and Kings counties (also in the San Joaquin Valley) each reported 2,000 to 5,000 acres. Butte and Glenn counties (in the Sacramento Valley) reported nearly 650 acres each.

Although there are more small farms than large farms producing pistachios, the bulk of production is from large, diversified operations. Nearly a dozen growers have more than a thousand acres and one company (Paramount Farms) has about 15,000 acres of pistachios in western Kern County. Homa Company and Keenan Farms, Inc. are also large operations. However, most pistachio orchards range from 40 to 80 acres (16-32 hectares) in size.

In Kern, Tulare, and Fresno counties, farms with pistachios frequently also grow almonds and citrus fruit. Madera county growers often have a similar number of acres in pistachios and almonds. Other crops produced by pistachio growers throughout the San Joaquin Valley include cotton, wheat, onions, olives, garlic, and lettuce. As discussed earlier, pistachio trees are either male or female, and the trees that produce nuts, consequently, do not produce pollen. Cultivars used as pollinators are called male (or "non-bearing") and those used for nut production are referred to as female (or "bearing").

Bearing Tendency: The aggregate effect of the alternate-bearing pattern is reflected in state-level yields. However, county-average yields reveal additional variations that probably are related to the age of the trees. In Kern County, where some of the first orchards were planted, average yields are 2-4 times higher in "on-years" than in "off-years". Annual yield changes in Madera and Glenn counties are less marked, but follow the same pattern as in Kern county.

The major production perils to pistachio production are excessive rain and humidity, late frosts and hard freezes, warm winters, drought, and various diseases and insect pests. Rain and humidity promote fungal diseases, which have probably contributed more to yield reductions than any other peril. Late-spring frosts, unusually warm winters, and drought may also reduce yields.

Most of the pistachio crop is mechanically harvested in September. The highest-quality nuts are harvested within ten days after maturity. Pistachios are hulled, dried, and sorted soon after harvest, but may be roasted, salted, coloured, and shelled later. There is no marketing order establishing minimum quality standards, but voluntary inspection and grading is widespread. The pistachio industry is well organized, with a state marketing agreement administered by the California Pistachio Commission.

Pistachio production fluctuates widely from year to year, mainly due to the natural tendency of trees to be alternate bearing. However, pistachio nuts can be stored from one season to the next so carryover stocks, and to a lesser extent imports, act to stabilize supplies and prices. Pistachio production increased from 12,227 tonnes in 1980 to a peak of 137,440 tonnes in 2002, declined to 54,100 tonnes in 2003 and recovered to 158,000 tonnes, to decline again to 140,000 tonnes in 2005. The US

Table 16.9: USA: Pistachio Area, Yield, Production, Grower Price and Output Value

Year	Bearing Area Hectares	Yield kg./Hectare	Production Tonnes	Grower Price Cents/kg.	Value 1,000 Dollars
1980	10,931	1,118	12,227	451	55,145
1981	11,376	579	6,591	299	19,759
1982	12,105	1,650	20,000	328	65,560
1983	12,591	953	12,000	310	37,224
1984	12,470	2,302	28,682	215	61,586
1985	13,077	942	12,318	301	37,127
1987	16,599	906	15,045	301	45,347
1988	19,109	2,234	42,727	268	114,680
1989	20,607	860	17,727	359	63,570
1990	21,740	2,504	54,545	224	122,400
1991	22,550	1,549	35,000	275	96,250
1992	22,874	2,919	66,818	227	151,410
1993	23,077	2,998	69,091	235	162,640
1994	23,279	2,515	58,636	203	118,809
1995	24,413	2,751	67,273	240	161,320
1996	26,032	1,830	47,727	255	121,800
1997	26,478	3,088	81,818	249	203,400
1998	27,530	3,099	85,455	227	193,640
1999	28,745	1,942	55,909	293	163,590
2000	30,202	3,660	110,455	222	245,430
2001	31,579	2,313	73,182	222	162,610
2002	33,603	4,098	137,727	242	333,300
2003	35,628	1,516	54,091	266	143,900
2004	35,000	4,514	158,000	215	339,700
2005	35,000	4,000	140,000	220	308,000

Source: USDA: National Agricultural Statistics Service: Fruit and Tree Nut Year Book 2005.

produces roughly 28 per cent of the world's pistachio supply. Time series data derived from the US national resources on Pistachio Area, Yield, Production, Grower's price and total value of production for the period 1980 to 2005 are presented in Table 16.9. The bearing area under the crop increased from 10,931 hectares in 1980 to 35,000 hectares in 2005. Total production rose from 12,227 tonnes to 140,000 tonnes during this period. Yield per hectare, which fluctuates from year to year generally, registered an upward trend. The increase in output was due to larger area brought under the crop and the higher yields. Grower prices have, however, undergone a declining trend during this period. However, with higher output, the total value of pistachio production rose from US$ 55.15 million to over US$ 333 million in 2001, but declined drastically in 2003 to US$ 143.9 million and recovered during the last two years.

Domestic Consumption

Over 40 per cent of tree nuts in the US are eaten in cereals and desserts. Total domestic consumption of pistachio (Shelled basis) has increased from 4,942 tonnes in 1980-81 to 25,696 tonnes, and the per capita annual consumption rose from 0.05 lb to 0.19 lb (Table 16.10). US imports only small quantities, while it exports large quantities. Its exports rose from less than 900 tonnes in 1980-81 to about 16,000 tonnes (Shelled weight). In fact US is the second largest pistachio exporting country in the world. Its pistachio growers benefit from the most modern production technology, while California Pistachio Commission undertakes pistachio marketing abroad.

Imports and Exports

While US pistachio imports have shrunk considerably, the US is the second largest pistachio exporting country in the world, supplying around 15 per cent of the global exports. As California production has grown, new important export markets have been developed in the Far East, notably Japan and Hong Kong, as well as in Germany. Consequently, its exports of pistachio have risen from 836 tonnes in 1980 to around 35,692 tonnes in 2004 (Table 16.4). Top ten pistachio export destinations in 2004 were: Hong Kong (5,845 tonnes), Belgium-Luxembourg (4,615 tonnes), Germany (3,722 tonnes), Canada (2,786 tonnes), France (2,549 tonnes), Italy 2,370 tonnes), Japan (2,300 tonnes), Netherlands (1,752 tonnes), China (1,545 tonnes) and Mexico (1,144 tonnes). The US pistachio growers enjoy benefit of modern technology. Moreover, the US government Market Access Programme Funds has played an important role in the Pistachio export promotion programme.

Table 16.10: USA: Pistachios: Supply and Utilization (Shelled basis): 1980-81 to 2003-04

Year	Marketable Production 4/	Imports 5/	Beginning Stocks 4/	Supply 6/	Ending Stocks 4/	Exports 5/	Domestic consumption Total	Per Capita
				Tonnes			Tonnes	Lbs.
1980/81	5,305	534	2,273	8,112	2,334	836	4,942	0.05
1981/82	2,676	826	2,334	5,836	937	673	4,226	0.04
1982/83	7,721	1,281	937	9,939	2,991	1,476	5,471	0.05
1983/84	5,052	3,038	2,991	11,081	2,262	825	7,994	0.07
1984/85	12,503	3,311	2,262	18,076	5,116	1,254	11,706	0.11
1985/86	5,235	6,761	5,116	17,113	3,346	754	13,013	0.12
1986/87	14,093	2,435	3,346	19,875	6,820	992	12,062	0.11
1987/88	6,627	985	6,820	14,432	2,494	1,577	10,361	0.09
1988/89	20,342	388	2,494	23,224	6,771	2,928	13,525	0.12
1989/90	8,195	965	6,771	15,932	4,566	2,509	8,858	0.08
1990/91	19,112	388	4,566	24,066	7,665	3,946	12,454	0.11
1991/92	11,580	114	7,665	19,359	2,760	7,006	9,593	0.08
1992/93	29,710	180	2,760	32,650	7,998	12,620	12,032	0.1
1993/94	28,141	225	7,998	36,364	11,669	9,575	15,119	0.13
1994/95	23,295	333	11,669	35,297	7,648	11,489	16,161	0.13
1995/96	27,047	192	7,648	34,887	6,270	14,336	14,280	0.12
1996/97	18,375	429	6,270	25,074	3,498	14,637	6,939	0.06
1997/98	34,059	190	3,498	37,747	4,428	16,432	16,886	0.14
1998/99	35,549	250	4,428	40,227	9,665	11,724	18,838	0.15
1999/00	26,401	135	9,665	36,202	4,755	9,001	22,445	0.18
2000/01	51,893	418	4,755	57,067	15,150	14,837	27,080	0.21
2001/02	36,697	242	15,150	52,088	5,648	20,338	26,103	0.2
2002/03	67,960	347	5,648	73,955	25,536	20,204	28,215	0.21
2003/04 7/	26,113	585	25,536	52,234	10,629	15,909	25,696	0.19

= Negligible amounts. 1/ Conversion factor from in-shell to shelled basis varies year to year for production, stocks, and exports and were 0.39 in 1996/97, 0.42 in 1997/98 and in 1998/99, 0.47 in 1999/2000 and in 2000/01, 0.50 in 2001/02, 0.49 in 2002/03, and 0.48 in 2003/04. For imports the conversion factor was a constant 0.40.

2/ Season beginning September 1. 3/ Inedible and noncommercial usage. 4/ California Pistachio Commission. 5/ Bureau of Census, U.S. Department of Commerce.

6/ Marketable production plus imports and beginning stocks. 7/ Preliminary estimates.

Source: USDA: Fruit & Tree Nut yearbook 2005.

PISTACHIO IN ITALY

Production

Italy is one of the small pistachios producing countries, but it imports large quantities each year. Italian production varies considerably from one year to another. During the last five years it ranged from 906 tonnes to about 1,210 tonnes. Pistachios are grown mostly on the slopes of Mount Etna in Sicily, where the growers drastically trim the trees every other year in order to obtain a larger crop in the following season. Total area under pistachios is estimate at 68,500 hectares with most of the area is in bearing stage. The year 2005 which is an "on" year for Italian pistachio, production rose to 2,400 tonnes in 2005 tonnes. Sicilian production is considered to be of superior quality compared to imported nuts from Iran and the US. This is especially true in consideration of their green colour, which is desired by the confectionery and ice cream industry. However, in most recent years Italian traders have started to buy the best quality of in-shell Iranian pistachios, with a green rate higher than local Italian production. These pistachios are then shelled and peeled and mostly re-exported to European destination markets. Local production price in 2005 was quoted at about Euro 6/kg (in-shell), 10 to 11 Euross (shelled) and 11 to 12 Euross (shelled and peeled). According to trade sources, these prices are not competitive with the best quality of the imported Iranian pistachios.

Consumption

Sicilian pistachios are mainly utilized, as stated above, by the confectionery industry, rather than sold for snacks. Overall consumption appears now to be stable, after the drop reported in the late 90s due to aflatoxin problems in Iran. Imported pistachios are mainly consumed as roasted and salted snacks, with a limited share (the best quality, of greener colour) processed by the confectionery industry. Domestic consumption is estimated at 11,500 tonnes.

Trade

EU trade statistics do not separate in shell, shelled and peeled pistachios. In any case in-shell nuts almost exclusively represent imports, while exports consist mainly of shipments of Italian and recently also imported shelled and peeled pistachios. Italy imports annually around 12,000 tonnes of pistachio, valued at US$ 12 million (Tables 16.5 and 16.6). Imports from the US, after the decline reported in 2003-04 have completely recovered in 2004-05, with a volume close to the one reported in 2002-03. As mentioned above, Italy also exports pistachio, though smaller quantities around 1,000 tonnes. Data on Italian imports and export of pistachios during the last two years are shown in Table 16.11.

Table 16.11: Italy: Pistachios Import Export Matrix: 2002-03 and 2003-04 (Tonnes)

Imports	*2002-03*	*2003-04*	*Exports*	*2002-03*	*2003-04*
Greece	42	208	France	87	63
Germany	1,866	2,849	Germany	38	85
Other EU	818	2,995	UK	415	306
Total EU	2,726	6,052	Other EU	134	186
Iran	7,789	5,629	Total EU	674	640
Turkey	198	352	Croatia	60	72
Other non-EU	45	68	Bosnia	11	16
Total	13,653	13,724	Slovenia	14	22
			Switzerland	24	25
			Japan	37	41
			Other non-EU	171	104
Total	13,653	13,724	Total	991	920

PISTACHIOS IN TURKEY

Production

Pistachios are mainly produced in South-eastern Region in Turkey. Gaziantep used to be the major pistachio-growing province (in fact, the Turkish name for pistachios is "Gaziantep Nut"). However, official data indicates continued increase trees in the eastern parts of Southeastern Anatolia, where pistachios are replacing olive production. Sanliurfa Province now has about twice as many trees as Gaziantep. According to the US Agriculture Attaches' estimates there are around 44 million pistachios trees in Turkey, of which 27.5 million are in bearing stage.

In Turkey Pistachio production is highly cyclical and can vary a great deal. Turkish pistachios are thinner and smaller than Iranian pistachios, but are considered to have a better flavour. In recent years, farmers have begun growing a larger pistachio variety in Siirt and neighbouring provinces in southeast Anatolia. Siirt pistachios are similar to Iranian pistachios, except that Iranian pistachios are almost round while Siirt pistachios are oval shaped. Siirt pistachios, about 15 per cent of total Turkish production, are bigger and command higher prices on the local market than the traditional Turkish pistachio. In Turkey, size is directly related to quality: 90 nuts or less per 100 grams are considered first quality, 90-100 nuts are second quality, 100-120 is third quality, and above 120 is fourth quality.

Pistachio production is highly variable due to soil and climatic conditions. There are also cyclical variations from one year to the next. MY 2003 (October-September) was a "good" year for pistachio production. However, rainy and cool weather during the blooming period in April damaged flowers and lowered yields. Despite this production in 2003 reached a peak at 90,000 tonnes (i.e. 45,000 tonnes shelled @ 50 per cent shell rate). For MY 2003 production declined to 30,000 tonnes and recovered from the affect of last year's frosts could increase significantly reaching to about 60,000 MT. This is the theoretical capacity, as long as weather conditions remain optimal. In 2005 GUNEYDOGUBIRLIK, which is the sales cooperative that procures pistachios along with other crops such as red lentils and red peppers, procured 5,290 MT of pistachios and paid YTL 3.00 per kilogram for pistachios with soft red skins.

Consumption

Official estimates of pistachio consumption are not available. In Turkey pistachios are widely used as snack food and in producing confectionery products, especially in deserts and bakery products. Most of the crop is consumed domestically and consumption varies a lot from one year to another according to availability. Total annual domestic consumption is estimated at 43,000 tonnes in-shell basis. In 2005 the retail price for roasted in-shell Gaziantep pistachios was about YTL 15.00 (or about USD 11.00) per kilogram in Ankara. This price was about the same a year ago even though there was 9 per cent inflation during the last twelve months.

Trade

Turkey exports only a small proportion of its production. Primary destinations are the European Union and the United States. According to the US Agriculture Attaché's estimated exports during the last few years ranged from about 4000 tonnes to almost 14,000 tonnes (Table 16.12). However, FAO data for Turkish pistachios exports for recent years are rather low around 1,000-5,000 tonnes. In MY 2004, the average export price for shelled pistachios was about US$ 8,240 per tonnes.

Table 16.12: Turkey Pistachios Export Matrix (In-shell basis) in 2001, 2002 and 2004 (Tonnes)

Country	*2001*	*Country*	*2002*	*Country*	*2004*
US	348	US	733	US	–
France	962	Lebanon	1574	France	141
Germany	923	Germany	1570	Germany	1148
Hong Kong	631	UAE	1444	Italy	207
Italy	623	Saudi Arabia	960	Spain	219
Saudi Arabia	505	Italy	735	Netherlands	244
Lebanon	436	Jordan	669	Greece	155
UAE	316	India	482	Belgium	134
Spain	309	Algeria	451	UK	120
Syria	266	Egypt	402	Romania	56
Egypt	251	Spain	348	Other	620
Others	1833	Others	4333		
Total	7403	Total	13701	Total	3942

Source: US Agriculture Attaché's Turkey Annul Tree Nut Reports: Various issues.

Stocks

Pistachio stocks vary from one year to another depending on supply. There was a relatively large carry over stocks in MY 2005, even though MY 2004 production was very low. This is because of the large quantities Turkey produced in MY 2003.

Policy

The Government of Turkey stopped direct support to pistachio farmers several years ago. GUNEYDOGUBIRLIK, a Union for Sales Cooperatives, only announces procurement prices depending on its financial ability. GUNEYDOGUBIRLIK procured only 5,290 MT of pistachios in MY 2004. There is no subsidy, tax or other restrictions on pistachio exports. Importers pay a 43.2 per cent duty on the CIF value for pistachios and 58.5 per cent duty on processed pistachios.

Marketing

GUNEYDOGUBIRLIK, which is located in Gaziantep Province, is the only exporter union for pistachios. This sales cooperative follows domestic and foreign trade issues, provide information, conduct market research, and sponsor promotional events.

PISTACHIO IN GREECE

Greece has over 5 thousand hectares under pistachios and its current annual production is around 9,000 tonnes. Spring frost, in April does not affect pistachio trees as much as other nut trees because they blossom later. In addition, trees are minimally affected by drought, as all pistachio (and almond) orchards in Greece are irrigated with dripping systems. Reportedly, aging of the trees — coupled with a parasitic diseases, which began on the island of Aigina (south of Athens) and infected other pistachio farms in central Greece—have forced growers to uproot a number of orchards. Due to disease damages, which in 2003 were mostly observed in the prefecture of Fthiotis (Central Greece) and the island of Aigina, pistachio production in Greece, showed a downward tendency. On the other hand, the increase in the cost of labour in recent years has discouraged farmers from replacing orchards and has focused them on managing pistachio orchards in a better way by applying more effective plant protection practices.

In a good year, Greek pistachio harvest can reach almost 10,000 tonnes. New orchards in full production appear in Thessally and the peninsula of Halkidiki in central Macedonia, well managed and free of diseases with a tendency to expand. In these regions, organic tree nut production is occurring, practiced in the framework of relevant EU Directives. Table 16.13 shows the Production, Supply and Distribution of Pistachios in Greece during the last three years.

Table 16.13: Greece: Pistachios Production, Supply and Distribution (In-shell basis): (Area:Hec. Trees: 1000: Other: Tonnes)

Item	*September 2003*	*September 2004*	*September 2005*
Area Planted	5120	5120	5122
Area Harvested	5020	5020	5022
Bearing Trees	1284	1290	1300
Non-Bearing Trees	16	20	15
Total Trees	1300	1310	1315
Beginning Stocks	4440	4140	5480
Production	9000	9500	9500
Imports	3000	2800	3000
Total Supply	16440	16440	15590
Exports	300	350	350
Domestic Consumption	12000	13000	12000
Ending Stocks	4140	3090	3240
Total Distribution	16440	16400	15590

Source: USDA Foreign Agriculture Attaché's Greece Annual Tree Nut Report GR4019.

Prices

Grower prices in 2004 fluctuated between 5.30-5.35 €/kg for the best quality pistachios (delivered with 95 per cent open nuts). However, when large percentage of nuts remain closed, farmers receive a lower price from traders and processors as they have to incur the costs of mechanical shelling, which is then incorporated into the final price paid by the consumer. When this product is finally sold in the retail market as shelled product in snack packages, it fetches a high retail price.

Trade

Imports of pistachios in Greece have increased more than four fold from 1990 to 2004, from 698 tonnes to 3,466 tonnes in 2004. In 2004, imports of pistachios were valued at US$ 14 million compared to US$ 10 million in 2003 and US$ 9 million in 2002, Imports are mostly from Iran and Turkey. Due to shortage of Greek pistachios compared to steadily increasing demand, imports approach 3,000 MT/year compared to less than 2,000 MT a few years back. In CY 2004, only 45 MT of imports are reported from the United States at the value of €109 thousand, although some of the pistachios entering Greece through the EU may have originated in the US.

Exports of pistachio have increased from 698 tonnes in 1990 to 3,466 tonnes in 2004. In CY 2003, exports of Greek pistachios are limited to only 317 tonnes valued at € 955 thousand, compared to 462 MT in CY 2002 valued at €1.27 million. In future exports trade for Greek pistachios will remain of secondary importance, after fulfilling domestic consumption needs, which are of primary importance. Once domestic demand is well covered, then some exports of limited amounts may take place.

Consumption

Domestic consumption since 2002 is estimated at 12,000 MT/annually, which is likely to increase in the next several years, due to the increase of pistachio usage in the confectionary and the ice cream sectors. For 2005, following Athens 2004 Olympics in August and Para-Olympic games in September, there was a slight increase in domestic consumption compared to the previous two years due to a higher demand by the snack and food industry sectors that use pistachios. Greece has a net import balance of pistachios, which are required to meet its domestic demand.

REFERENCE

1. Koshteh, Karim and Erutyan, Vardan E. (2003). *Global Pistachio Production and Marketing Challenges*, A research study carried out by the authors at the University of Guelph, Ontario.

17

WORLD HAZELNUT ECONOMY

Introduction

Historically Hazelnut (or Filbert: Cob; Cory IUS Species, Corylaceae), refers to a nut where the enveloping husk is longer than the nut, "cob" where the husk is as long as the nut and "hazel" where the husk is much shorter than the nut.[1] European hazel: Cory ius avellana is grown throughout Europe and eastward through West Asia to Syria and Iran. It is cultivated in North America for its nuts. Turkish filbert: Coryius maxima, Balkan Peninsula; is grown elsewhere for its nuts.

Description

Hazelnut is a deciduous trees or shrubs; its leaves are alternate, simple, stipules soon falling. Inflorescence monoecious, male flowers in pendent catkins, female flowers in small, bud—like inflorescences. Fruit a large nut is surrounded by more or less tubular involucres.[2]

Cultivation

The European hazel is chiefly cultivated and the Turkish filbert to a lesser extent. The research workers have tried hybridization between the two species and others, both naturally and by breeders. Table 17.1 gives Hazelnut Production Calendar.

New Plantings

Before planting a new orchard serious consideration needs to be given to varieties, orchard design, orchard site (soil and slope suitability), pre-plant soil management, etc. Some varieties are much more sensitive to Eastern Filbert Blight (EFB). One must consider training, sunburn protection, rodent damage, managing soil moisture, blight control, etc.

Table 17.l: Hazelnut Production Calendar

	Jan	Feb	Mar	Apr	May	Jun	Jul	Aug	Sep	Oct	Nov	Dec
Pruning	X	X										
Fertilizing		X	X									
Moss and Lichen			X								X	
Winter Moth			X	X								
Flail			X	X	X	X	X	X				
Cultivate				X	X	X	X	X				
Weed Control			X	X		X					X	
Sucker Control				X	X	X	X	X				
Omnivorous Leaftier				X	X							
Foliar Boron Application					X							
Aphid Control				X	X	X	X					
Leafroller Control				X	X							
Oblique Banded Leafroller						X	X	X	X			
Sun Scald Protection					X							
Filbert Worm							X	X				
Bacterial Blight Control								X	X			
Leaf and Soil Analysis								X				
Pre-Harvest Care								X	X			
Harvesting									X	X		
Management	X	X	X	X	X	X	X	X	X	X	X	X
Eastern Filbert Blight	X	X	X	X	X			X			X	X

Pruning

Hazelnuts will produce some nuts on wood at any vigour; however, unless a pruning and fertilizer programme is used they will fall well short of their yield potential. Because of increasing costs and unavailability of farm labour, mechanical hedging is a practical, economical approach in older, overgrown orchards.

Any method of pruning combined with proper fertilization to produce a six-inch average twig growth is satisfactory. Research on Barcelona (Spain) has shown that twig growth of six inches or less will produce 30 per cent of the total crop while twigs greater than 6 inches in length produce 70 per cent of the crop.

Fertilizing

Mature trees should be fertilized according to leaf analysis and lime applied in the orchard according to a soil test. Take leaves from the mid-shoot of current season's growth. Take enough random samples to represent the whole orchard, and total at least 50 leaves per sample. Both soil and leaf tissue tests are important tools to calibrate fertilizer programme.

Normal requirements for a mature tree are 1½ to 2 lb. of actual nitrogen per tree broadcast (depending on tree densities). Nitrogen fertilizer rate will depend on the age of the orchard. Younger trees obviously need less. Improper fertilizer applications to new trees can kill them. In the US most growers apply nitrogen (1/8 lb. per tree) in the second year. The rates can be gradually increased as the trees age. A normal full rate can be applied to a 12-year old tree. Nitrogen should be applied as urea in March, coincident with bud break.

Potassium required may range from 6 to 10 lb. per tree banded at the drip line. While nitrogen is often an annual need for all orchards, potassium is only occasionally applied, based on leaf and soil analysis results. Trees more than 6 years old may well begin showing a response to boron. Boron, when applied as a soil treatment, is usually applied at a rate of 5 to 7 lb., per acre. In the US most growers apply boron as a foliar spray at the rate of 1 lb. of actual B element content per acre.

Cultivation

It is sometimes desirable to cultivate and level in new orchards for one or two years before using the flail. Cultivation in orchards should start as soon as soil is dry enough to work and cultivate only enough to control weeds and never at a depth of more than 4 inches. Prepare a level and compact orchard floor as early as possible to avoid loss of moisture. Roll the orchard floor firmly prior to harvest.

Weed Control: Weed control is usually associated with the flailing programme where herbicides are banded down the tree row.

Sucker Control: Now chemicals are used to control suckers, these are sprayed when the suckers are six to nine inches tall.

Control of Omnivorous Leaftier and Winter Moth: Leafier larvae hatch from over-wintering eggs in April and May and are carried into orchards by the wind on silken threads. Insecticides are applied when the larvae are very small to protect new plantings. Winter moths hatch in late winter and the light green larvae feed on buds and leaves. These can be controlled by spraying Lorsban early to prevent their damage.

Aphid Control

If natural predators do not keep them under control, insecticides can reduce their numbers. Studies have shown that heavy aphid infestation can reduce crop yield by 8-10 per cent. OSU's IPM programme in hazelnuts calls for aphid sampling to begin April 1. Choose three terminals per tree and count aphids on the newest fully expanded leaf on each terminal. The action threshold for aphids per leaf is as follows: April 20, May 20, June 40, and July 40, with an increasing population.

Leafroller Control

Heavy infestations of Leafroller may result in yield reductions. Spraying is done in late April or early May to control this pest. Orchard should be checked for infestation before applying control materials. Three terminals per tree and three leaf clusters per terminal should be checked. Spray for larvae when there is a 20-25 per cent infestation level.

The tiny larvae feed on developing nuts resulting in stained, misshapen and aborted nuts. Larvae from this hatch are most damaging. A second generation of moths emerges in September.

If an orchard has a history of OBLR damage, pheromone traps are suggested to determine the time of sprays.

Insecticides should be applied soon after traps catch 40 moths per trap per week at the peak of the adult flight and larval damage is detected on the nut clusters.

Use trunk collars or tree paints to protect against sunscald. If paint is used, be sure to paint to the soil line.

Filbert Worm Control

This is the most serious insect problem of hazelnuts in Oregon. Growers should place pheromone traps in the orchards in mid-June. The recommended rate is four traps for the first 10 acres and one for each additional four acres. Thorough application of recommended rates of chemical is usually necessary for control.

Blight Control

Filbert bacterial blight is a serious disease problem seen mostly in young trees up to six years in age. Copper sprays 16 lb. per acre, or Nordox at 4-5 lb. per 100 gallons of water are recommended for application in late August through September but before fall rains begin.

Eastern Filbert Blight

Spores are spread within and between trees via wind and rain. The initial infection occurs on leaf tissue in the spring.

Current control recommendations encourage vigilant scouting for new infections, removal of infected wood, and applications of protestant fungicides.

Pre-Harvest Care

One last flailing just before solid nuts begin to drop in early September will grind up blanks and twigs that have dropped and will put the orchard floor in a proper condition for harvesting.

If orchards are clean cultivated, the final levelling, smoothing, and rolling should be done at this time.

Harvesting

In the USA all commercially grown hazelnuts are harvested mechanically. Sweeping is the first process which cleans the tree row with air blast or mechanical fingers and deposit the nuts in a narrow windrow in the centre of the row. A pickup machine follows which lifts and separates the nuts from the leaves, twigs, etc. and deposits them in a tote box or trailer. A third person follows on a forklift tractor to move tote boxes out of the orchard. This type of operation can harvest around 15 acres of orchard per day. Less sophisticated and less expensive equipment is used in smaller orchards or neighbours work together to increase efficiencies.

WORLD HAZELNUT INDUSTRY

Introduction

According to the FAO data hazelnuts (Filberts) are grown in twenty-six countries in the world. Area under hazelnuts is estimated to have increased from over 457 thousand hectares in 1990 to about 538 thousand hectares in 2005. The main hazelnut producing countries are Turkey, Italy, Spain, USA, Azerbaijan, Iran and China. Although hazelnut is also produced in the Greece, Russian Federation and France, these countries do not have a major input in the world hazelnut trade. Among these Turkey is the leading country that accounted for 67 per cent of the global production in 2005. It was followed by Italy with around 17 per cent, the USA with 3 per cent share, Azerbaijan, Republic, over 2 per cent share and Georgia 0.54 per cent share (Table 17.2).

The world hazelnut production shows fluctuations depending on the climatic conditions from year to year. Overall, world production has increased in parallel with Turkey's production. While Turkey's average in-shell production is 350-400,000 tonnes, this value has crossed 600,000 tonnes in two consecutive years, i.e. 2001 and 2002. The production of Italy and Spain the other important producing countries, varies between 100-140,000 tonnes and 15-25,000 tonnes respectively. The USA consumes most of its own hazelnut production and also imports hazelnut kernel for the industry to meet its home demand. However, it

Table 17.2: Production of Hazelnuts: Selected Years (Tonnes)

Production (Mt)	Years								% Increase 2005/1990	% Share in World Total
	1990	1995	2000	2001	2002	2003	2004	2005		
World	560,761	683,782	679,641	882,604	834,944	686,577	612,793	747,589	133.3	100.00
USSR	10,000									
Azerbaijan		12,000	13,334	15,945	16,120	19,895	5,491	20,000		2.68
Belarus		1,000	1,800	1,800	1,800	1,800	1,800	1,800		0.24
Bulgaria	188	0	0	0	0	0	0	0		0.00
Cameroon	100	100	100	100	100	100	100	100	100.0	0.01
China	8,000	9,000	9,000	11,000	12,000	13,000	13,000	13,500	168.8	1.81
Croatia		80	400	600	400	500	500	500		0.07
Cyprus	50	50	35	50	30	40	40	40	80.0	0.01
France	3,605	3,900	5,113	3,959	5,412	3,710	5,725	6,525	181.0	0.87
Georgia		10,000	14,220	11,375	13,901	14,820	8,800	4,000		0.54
Germany	0	0	0	0	0	0	0	0		0.00
Greece	6,697	4,352	3,000	2,500	2,500	2,500	2,500	2,100	31.4	0.28
Hungary	173	200	225	168	124	127	300	300	173.4	0.04
Iran	4,704	12,000	11,507	11,749	12,000	12,500	13,000	13,000	276.4	1.74
Italy	109,344	118,400	98,540	119,480	119,458	83,292	143,,356	129,259	118.2	17.29
Kyrgyzstan		1,500	785	1,161	1,161	1,100	1,100	1,500		0.20
Moldova		1,000	800	850	800	800	800	800		0.11
Mongolia	0	0	250	300	320	300	300	300		0.04
Portugal	1,900	842	650	573	619	596	502	430	22.6	0.06
Russian Fed.		1,500	2,000	2,000	2,000	2,500	3,000	3,500		0.47
Spain	21,270	15,500	25,188	26,711	26,552	12,559	25,700	22,500	105.8	3.01
Tajikistan		1,000	1,000	1,100	800	1,000	1,000	1,000		0.13
Tunisia	30	40	40	40	40	40	40	40	133.3	0.01
Turkey	375,000	455,000	470,000	625,000	600,000	480,000	350,000	500,000	133.3	66.88
Ukraine		138	44	33	17	18	19	20		0.00
USA	19,700	35,380	20,410	44,910	17,690	34,380	33,570	25,400	128.9	3.40
Uzbekistan		800	1,200	1,200	1,100	1,000	1,000	1,000		0.13

Source: FAO STAT Database, April 2006.

has become a hazelnut exporting country by increasing its production in recent years (33,000 tonnes).

Global hazelnut production (in-shell weight basis) increased from 561,000 tonnes in 1990 to 747,589 tonnes in 2005. It represents a 33 per cent growth in sixteen years. Production has however, varied over the period under review. It peaked in 1998 when production was around 883,000 tonnes, while production in 2005 registered a recovery from the fall during the two earlier years.

International Trade

The world hazelnut exports show fluctuations according to world production. Germany is the most important hazelnut importing country in the world and covers approximately 35 per cent of the total world import. Though Italy is the second largest producing country in the world, it meets an important part of its chocolate industry's demand for hazelnuts with Turkey's production. While Switzerland shows a stable rate of import, France, Austria, Belgium and Luxembourg are noted as countries, which have increased the hazelnut import in recent years.

Hazelnut in-shell and shelled both are traded internationally, though the volume of in-shell hazelnuts is rather small. During the period 1990 to 2004 world export volume of in-shell hazelnut increased from 12,256 tonnes to 27,586 tonnes, representing almost 125 per cent increase over the whole period (Table 17.3). Their exports value went up from US$ 21 million to around US$ 55 million, representing 160 per cent increase (Table 17.4). Higher relative increases in value compared to volume suggest that unit value improved during the review period. The United States is the leading exporting country, which accounted for around 63 per cent of global exports in 2004 and 61 per cent of the value. France exported about 9 per cent of volume and 12 per cent in value terms. Italy shipped 6 per cent of the volume and about 9 per cent in value terms.

However, world export volume of hazelnut shelled remained almost stagnant although they reached a peak in 1995 and again recovered in 2001 and 2002. Global quantities exported were 205,000 tonnes in 1990 and around 203,000 tonnes in 2003, but declined to about 201,209 tonnes in 2004 (Table 17.5). However, there was a marginal increase in the value of global exports from 1990 to 2003. Total foreign exchange earnings rose from US$ 595 million to around US$ 600 million in 2003 but rose sharply to US$ 952 million in 2004 (Table 17.6). For exports of hazelnut shelled Turkey is the leading country, which accounted for around 67 per cent of the global volume and value. It was followed by Italy, which contributed

Table 17.3: Hazelnut In-shell Exports: (Quantities in Tonnes): Selected Years

Hazelnut Export (In Tonnes)	*Years*							*% Increase*	*% Share*
	1990	*1995*	*2000*	*2001*	*2002*	*2003*	*2004*	*2004/1990*	*2004 in World Total*
World	12,256	16,268	27,061	32,608	36,229	28,155	27,586	225.08	100.000
Azerbaijan		379	1,150	338	781	784	135		0.489
Canada	3	521	330	346	261	458	523	17433.33	1.896
Hong Kong SAR	2	81	6,077	6,388	5,525	2,747	3,182		11.535
Croatia		1	233	438	194	345	365		1.323
France	1,403	1,525	2,353	2,161	2,283	1,789	2,375	169.28	8.609
Georgia		0	0	221	757	832	449		1.628
Germany	943	359	268	333	308	130	254	26.94	0.921
Italy	4,933	3,412	2,851	2,718	2,844	2,101	1,614	32.72	5.851
Netherlands	233	40	81	190	85	151	108	46.35	0.392
Spain	119	3	70	135	276	204	120	100.84	0.435
Turkey	326	739	623	675	5,541	3,144	315	96.63	1.142
United Kingdom	44	42	27	37	31	39	30	68.18	0.109
USA	3,627	8,695	12,782	16,765	16,848	14,938	17,387	479.38	63.028

Source: FAO STAT Database, April 2006.

Table 17.4: Hazelnut In-shell Exports: (Value in US$ 1000): Selected Years

Hazelnut Exports Value	*Years*							*% Increase 2004/1990*	*% Share 2004 in World Total*
	1990	*1995*	*2000*	*2001*	*2002*	*2003*	*2004*		
World	21,041	29,076	42,533	45,333	47,888	42,500	54,810	260.49	100.00
Azerbaijan		106	925	198	389	681	93		0.17
Canada	7	539	394	287	287	495	785		1.43
Hong Kong	13	205	9,381	8,888	6,107	1,823	3,754		6.85
Croatia		4	198	410	178	438	626		1.14
France	2,835	3,503	4,432	3,797	4,356	4,054	6,472	228.29	11.81
Georgia		0	0	226	641	959	829		1.51
Germany	1,137	890	585	695	684	348	716	62.97	1.31
Italy	8,681	6,260	4,497	4,143	4,264	4,073	5,006	57.67	9.13
Netherlands	547	134	235	532	214	435	431	78.79	0.79
Spain	341	14	131	235	436	448	364	106.74	0.66
Turkey	535	1,656	1,179	928	5,716	3,640	758	141.68	1.38
UK	154	123	91	113	100	134	175	113.64	0.32
USA	5,882	15,000	20,095	23,352	23,793	24,269	33,691	572.78	61.47

Source: FAO STAT Database, April 2006.

Table 17. 5: Exports of Hazelnut Shelled: 1990-2004: (Tonnes)

Exports— Qty (Mt)	*Years*							*% increase in 2004/90*	*% Share in World Total*
	1990	*1995*	*2000*	*2001*	*2002*	*2003*	*2004*		
World	204,606	212,048	152,571	209,705	210,203	202,799	201,209	98.34	100.00
Austria	111	323	3,730	1,737	518	278	366	329.73	0.18
Azerbaijan, Rep.		304	6,518	4,203	7,131	9,121	3,078		1.53
Belgium	0	0	724	646	1,726	1,252	1,107		0.55
Belgium-Lux.	127	637	0	0	0	0	0		0.00
Hong Kong SAR	1	652	185	618	1,444	681	341	34100.00	0.17
France	609	734	1,147	1,184	2,723	3,806	1,426	234.15	0.71
Georgia		0	0	3,771	3,510	5,219	3,685		1.83
Germany	5,027	6,469	3,257	2,716	3,199	4,875	2,955	58.78	1.47
Greece	1,520	197	110	247	154	423	211	13.88	0.10
Italy	28,045	10,880	14,691	10,938	22,926	26,677	19,513	69.58	9.70
Netherlands	2,611	1,471	984	2,084	2,874	2,937	1,547	59.25	0.77
Spain	3,892	1,755	5,326	3,727	4,022	4,920	3,293	84.61	1.64
Turkey	160,759	185,158	112,129	174,728	157,595	136,648	134,557	83.70	66.87
United Kingdom	168	214	135	62	80	286	169	100.60	0.08
USA	1,525	1,995	2,033	1,533	795	4,086	2,807	184.07	1.40

Source: FAO STAT Database, April 2006.

Table 17.6: Exports of Hazelnut Shelled: Value: 1990 - 2005 : (US$ 1,000).

Exports - Value (1000$)	*Years*							*% Increase 2004/90*	*% Share in World*
	1990	*1995*	*2000*	*2001*	*2002*	*2003*	*2004*		
World	595,444	684,410	497,334	594,033	494,264	599,993	951,955	159.87	100.00
Austria	319	1,243	13,155	5,472	1,637	1,156	2,157	676.18	0.23
Azerbaijan		242	15,000	9,612	13,816	20,436	9,956		1.05
Belgium	0	0	2,757	2,678	4,709	3,724	5,933		0.62
Belgium-Lux.	517	3,169	0	0	0	0	0		0.00
Hong Kong SAR	10	2,577	357	983	1,125	440	489	4890.00	0.05
France	2,211	3,035	3,925	4,003	7,262	10,975	7,071	319.81	0.74
Georgia		0	0	9,569	6,026	11,446	16,792		1.76
Germany	16,270	19,608	11,336	8,802	8,990	16,071	16,849	103.56	1.77
Italy	90,555	41,763	51,251	39,879	64,118	89,437	110,533	122.06	11.61
Netherlands	8,501	4,887	3,619	7,160	7,735	8,368	7,906	93.00	0.83
Spain	11,859	5,983	17,314	9,841	10,341	12,552	17,900	150.94	1.88
Turkey	455,528	589,644	366,737	486,086	361,003	409,229	737,370	161.87	77.46
United Kingdom	540	887	493	265	312	903	999	185.00	0.10
USA	4,196	6,164	5,871	4,112	2,490	9,007	9,972	237.65	1.05

Source: FAO STAT Database, April 2006.

10 per cent in volume and around 12 per cent in value. The share of USA was only 1.4 per cent in volume and 1 per cent in value in 2004 (Tables 17.5 and 17.6).

Imports

Only small quantities of hazelnut in-shell are imported. Quantities imported increased from 17.9 thousand tonnes in 1990 to over 30.5 thousand tonnes in 2003 but declined to 25.8 thousand tonnes in 2004. The major importing countries include Hong Kong, with 11.5 thousands imports accounted for 45 per cent of the world imports in 2004. It was followed by Germany with imports of only 4.2 thousand tonnes and Italy importing 1.5 thousand tonnes in 2004 (Table 17.7). World imports of hazelnut shelled increased from 176 thousand tonnes in 1990 to about 201 thousand tonnes in 2004 (Table 17.8). The overall increase during the last fifteen years comes to 15 per cent. EU is the major importing region of shelled hazelnuts. The largest importing countries in recent years include Germany, Italy, France, Belgium, and Netherlands.

Consumption/Utilization

Among the producing countries, annual per person hazelnut consumption is highest in Italy (0.520 kg kernel/person). According to 2004 data, Greece is second (0.369 kg kernel/person) and Turkey is third (0.250 kg kernel/person). Worldwide, the highest hazelnut consumption per person is in Switzerland (2.096 kg kernel/person), followed by Austria, Belgium, Germany and Luxembourg.

COUNTRY CASE STUDIES

TURKISH FLIBERTS (HAZELNUT) INDUSTRY

Production

Turkey is a bridge between Asia and Europe in the northern hemisphere and has coast on three sides. Hazelnut is one of the most important nut crops in the world and has its origins in the centre of Anatolia. Wild species are found in Anatolia, which have provided the source for today's cultivated varieties. Hazelnut is grown in both the eastern and western regions of Turkey along the Black Sea, in areas where the soil is unsuitable for other crops and on sharply sloping soils (steeps higher than 20 per cent). An additional benefit for hazelnut growing areas with high rainfall is the crop's

Table 17.7: Hazelnut In-shell Imports: (Quantities in Tonnes): Selected Years

Imports (Tonnes)	*Years*							*% Increase 2004/1990*	*% Share in World Total*
	1990	*1995*	*2000*	*2001*	*2002*	*2003*	*2004*		
World	17,892	18,441	25,506	30,760	36,704	30,547	25,751	143.92	100.00
Austria	50	154	332	76	147	52	16	32.00	0.06
Belgium	185	420	85	90	150	102	123	66.49	0.48
Brazil	317	656	387	352	227	240	125	39.43	0.49
Canada	992	971	664	679	920	820	645	65.02	2.50
China	0	82	3,605	5,888	5,731	944	943		3.66
Hong Kong	4	75	8,023	10,823	17,475	16,558	11,540	288500.00	44.81
Denmark	358	419	351	389	356	272	293	81.84	1.14
Egypt	0	473	468	100	719	171	413		1.60
France	1,105	854	1,121	750	383	552	428	38.73	1.66
Germany	5,462	5,062	4,410	3,499	3,708	3,443	4,193	76.77	16.28
Greece	0	49	111	174	81	100	77		0.30
Italy	2,127	1,311	766	1,388	1,090	1,427	1,502	70.62	5.83
Netherlands	436	179	52	263	83	426	203	46.56	0.79
Norway	706	512	484	372	405	334	391	55.38	1.52
Poland	0	913	31	0	185	127	87		0.34
Portugal	129	94	8	55	53	14	22	17.05	0.09
Qatar	0	25	7	24	4	13	12		0.05
Romania	0	921	226	257	256	170	121		0.47
Russian Fed		0	141	349	716	545	421		1.63
Spain	421	1,061	892	970	865	1,094	806	191.45	3.13
Sweden	490	409	306	273	256	256	380	77.55	1.48
Switzerland	119	56	71	34	25	48	23	19.33	0.09
United Kingdom	1,321	991	609	793	650	495	580	43.91	2.25
USA	217	602	354	682	311	607	933	429.95	3.62

Source: FAO STAT Database, April 2006.

Table 17.8: Hazelnut Shelled Imports (Quantities in Tonnes): Selected Years

Quantities (Tonnes)	*Years*							*% Increase 2004/1990*	*% Snare 2004 in World Total*
	1990	*1995*	*2000*	*2001*	*2002*	*2003*	*2004*		
World	176,344	202,631	191,539	222,786	224,729	202,797	201 205	114.09	100.00
USSR	15,046								
Australia	1,090	2,250	1,648	1,990	2,235	2,379	2,261	207.43	1.31
Austria	10,167	6,522	7,367	5,415	3,987	3,828	4,193	41.24	2.43
Belgium	0	0	14,000	13,023	14,817	15,529	14,398		8.34
Belgium-Lux.	7,809	10,269	0	0	0	0	0	0.00	0.00
Brazil	12	652	1,992	1,849	1,870	1,647	2,259	18825.00	1.31
Canada	1,034	684	1,095	1,140	1,200	1,263	1,775	171.66	1.03
Hong Kong SAR	67	825	363	344	574	295	464	692.54	0.27
Croatia		477	471	684	795	626	761		0.44
Czech Rep.		2,066	1,166	1,431	1,833	1,641	1,135		0.66
Denmark	1,916	1,804	1,958	1,985	1,506	1,707	1,420	74.11	0.82
Egypt	745	969	2,001	2,457	2,194	959	1,423	191.01	0.82
France	16,125	16,749	13,528	18,395	20,092	22,582	10,606	65.77	6.14
Germany	68,826	83,420	71,257	82,986	67,889	54,474	47,570	69.12	27.54
Greece	238	2,136	3,645	4,146	3,749	3,808	3;035	1275.21	1.76
Hungary	0	315	707	842	858	814	523		0.30
Israel	1,682	2,000	924	1,362	1,427	968	1,496	88.94	0.87
Italy	8,879	20,906	27,505	28,952	42,058	35,439	24,693	278.11	14.30
Japan	463	480	429	510	725	506	705	152.27	0.41
Latvia		143	352	358	465	544	381		0.22
Lebanon	270	460	405	497	633	361	388	143.70	0.22

(Contd.)

Table 17.8: *(Contd.)*

Quantities (Tonnes)	Years							% Increase 2004/1990	% Share 2004 in World Total
	1990	1995	2000	2001	2002	2003	2004		
Lithuania		381	440	632	806	752	836		0.48
Malaysia	155	153	246	260	220	180	289	186.45	0.17
Mexico	115	149	225	148	208	191	227	197.39	0.13
Netherlands	8,103	6,291	3,183	3,311	4,375	4,299	3,099	38.25	1.79
Norway	1,623	1,265	934	1,094	1,204	1,168	1,272	78.37	0.74
Poland	0	1,422	3,567	5,242	5,434	4,252	5,230		3.03
Romania	0	2,118	228	370	425	490	492		0.28
Russian Fed.		3,000	2,957	5,040	3,989	4,993	8,929		5.17
Saudi Arabia	329	316	56	528	333	160	207		0.12
Serbia and Mont.		150	503	689	939	880	894		0.52
Slovakia		617	593	636	724	813	1,017		0.59
South Africa	684	891	621	699	658	645	456	66.67	0.26
Spain	1,576	4,585	4,234	5,091	5,745	6,020	5,812	368.78	3.37
Sweden	3,336	1,113	716	1,006	884	822	672	20.14	0.39
Switzerland	12,857	12,677	11,848	13,560	11,399	10,899	11,321	88.05	6.56
Syria	1	182	80	199	446	379	343	34300.00	0.20
Tunisia	125	478	213	427	840	740	907	725.60	0.53
Turkey	0	9	419	498	1,924	971	775		0.45
Ukraine		0	0	3,603	2,911	2,677	565		0.33
United Kingdom	4,850	4,909	2,353	2,306	2,444	2,512	2,111	43.53	1.22
USA	3,713	6,263	4,561	5,354	6,309	5,906	4,281	115.30	2.48

Source: FAO STAT Database, April 2006.

ability to prevent soil erosion. Approximately two to three million growers (5 per cent of the Turkey's population) depend on hazelnut growing for their income and it is therefore easy to understand the strategic value of hazelnut production in the social and economic structure of this region.

Turkey is the world's leading hazelnut producer, accounting for about 67 per cent of world supply. Hazelnut production is primarily concentrated along Turkey's Black Sea coast, extending about 25 kilometres inland. The region is divided into three distinct growing areas: (i) the hilly region from Ordu to Trabzon, centered around Giresun, which in a normal year produces about 55 per cent of the crop, (ii) the flatter, mixed farming region west of Ordu to Samsun, which produces about 15 per cent of the crop, and (iii) the area west of Samsun, which produces the remaining 30 per cent. Hazelnuts require relatively little effort to cultivate and therefore inputs are low. Harvesting occurs for several weeks in August and September.

Hazelnut production is the single most important economic enterprise in the Black Sea region. The total number of growers, estimated at about 400,000, is difficult to determine since almost everyone grows at least some hazelnuts for their own consumption. Tied to this problem, crop production and area forecasts are much debated due to the lack of a systematic crop-survey system. Best estimates put total area at about 380,000 hectares. Growers generally have very small plots. Most eastern producers have an orchard size of only 1-2.5 hectares and use hazelnut sales proceeds to supplement other income. Only a few relatively large growers (10 MT or more annually) depend on hazelnut production for the bulk of their incomes. On the other hand, most central and western farmers have 10-15 hectare orchards. Because of the importance of the crop to such a large number of people, hazelnut production policy has important political implications in Turkey.

Current trends show an increase in hazelnut plantation areas and production. Hazelnut productivity in Turkey is lower than in the other main producer countries. Hazelnut yields vary between 700 and 1,500 kilograms per hectare depending upon location and fertility of the land. Yields are lower on hillsides and higher in the valley. Yields are also dependent on the age of the trees, which tend to be older (thus with a lower yield) in the Eastern Black Sea Regions. Kernel or "meat" yield (in-shell to shelled conversion) are not known yet, but are expected to be around 50 per cent in recent years. The number of hazelnut trees has increased in recent years, which should raise production and surplus in the coming years. Production and consumption are increasing. Production is increasing due to good prices for high quality domestic nuts. At the same time, consumption is growing given the availability of inexpensive imported crops.

Production capacity has reached about 500,000 MT in the middle and eastern Black Sea regions and 250,000 MT in the western Black Sea region. For the Marketing Year 2005 production estimates are about 375,000 MT and 135,000 MT, respectively. Turkish hazelnut production increased from 375,000 tonnes in 1990 to 520,000 tonnes in 1992, but declined to 305,000 in 1993, and has since then varied from one year to another (See Table 17.2). According to the assessment by the USDA Agriculture Attaché's in Turkey, in the Marketing years 2006 (September to August) hazelnut production was to reach 600,000 tonnes, depending on weather conditions remaining normal for the remainder of the growing and harvest seasons. This would allow orchards to recover from the last year's frosts. Expanded hazelnut plantings will also contribute to total production capacity, which is currently estimated at about 750,000 MT. This capacity could reach between 800,000 MT and 900,000 MT during the next decade if more plantings continue. It takes seven to ten years for hazelnut orchards to produce at full capacity. Table 17.9 shows Production, Supply Distribution for Hazelnuts in Turkey for selected years.

Table 17.9: Turkey: Hazelnuts (Filberts) Production, Supply Distribution (Trees : Nos: Other items in Tonnes)

Item	*1993*	*2001*	*2002*	*2004*	*2005*
Bearing Trees	270,000	280,000	280,00	300,000	325,000
Non-bearing Trees	18,000	12,000	12,000	14,000	20,000
Total Trees	235,000	292,000	292,000	314,000	345,000
Beginning Stocks	235,000	200,000	235,000	72,000	15,000
Production	300,000	725,000	625,000	380,000	525,000
Imports	12	3,000	3,000	3,500	3,000
Total Supply	535,012	928,000	863,000	455,500	543,000
Exports	265,357	510,000	460,000	400,000	450,000
Domestic Consumption	149,655	183,000	203,000	40,500	50,000
Ending Stocks	120,000	235,000	200,000	15.000	43,000
Total Distribution	535,012	928,000	863,000	455,500	543,000

Source: USDA Agriculture Attachés Tree Nuts Turkey Annual Reports: various years.

Post-Harvest Handling

The handling of hazelnut after harvest consists of two stages. In the first stage, the shell is cracked and the kernel separated. In the second stage, the kernel may undergo a variety of processes, namely: blanching, roasting, slicing, mincing, pulverizing or being made into a paste.

One hundred and sixty processing plants for hazelnut shelling presently operate in Turkey with a capacity of 1,271,250 tonnes per year. The export of processed shelled hazelnut has risen proportionally with the increase in this processing capacity and presently 25-30 per cent of the total exported hazelnut are processed products.

Marketing

Nut quality is determined by type, oil and moisture content, and numbers of broken/shrunken kernels. Turkey produces three types of hazelnuts: Giresun, Levant, and Akcakoca. Giresun hazelnuts (round shape) are reputed to be the highest quality and have the best taste because of their higher oil content. Giresun hazelnuts are used generally in snack foods while Levant hazelnuts are sold as whole kernels or processed. As a rule, Giresun hazelnuts command a five percent premium over Levant varieties. Akcakoca hazelnuts are processed into paste. Kernel size and moisture content are also measures of quality. Standard #1 is 13-15 mm, #2 is 11-13 mm, and #3 is 9-11 mm.

FISKOBIRLIK, which has 50 member cooperatives and about 246,000 member farmers and three sister companies for processing and marketing of processed products, is the most influential organization in the industry. The administration of FISKOBIRLIK, however, is not elected by the members but is appointed by the government. Specifically, the government appoints the Director, who, in turn, appoints, his staff. As a result, FISKOBIRLIK functions more as a quasi-governmental organization than a true cooperative. Since the introduction of the direct income support programme, sales cooperatives, like FISKOBIRLIK, are not allowed to procure commodities at a loss. Procurement is kept separate from processing and marketing to avoid losses. Turkey concentrates its market promotion efforts mainly in the Far East, especially in Japan and China and the United States while planning to start similar promotional efforts in India and Russia. Turkey is making additional efforts to shift its export product mix to processed products as well. Most exporters are represented by an Exporters Union in Turkey and operating under the secretariat of Foreign Trade. Members of the exporters unions are mostly private traders and provide operating capital. There are two hazelnut exporters unions; the largest is the Black Sea Exporters Union, which is located in Giresun, and the other one is in Istanbul.

As a result of past policies especially high support prices, hazelnut production expanded significantly and today the industry is characterized by overproduction, large stocks, and depressed prices. Government policy to address these problems is centered on reducing production incentives while encouraging both exports and domestic consumption.

Historically, the Government of Turkey (GOT) provided FISKOBIRLIK funding to purchase excess production. However, in agreement with the IMF, the GOT agreed to end this support. The World Bank had provided some funds to the GOT to support alternative crops to replace surplus production, including hazelnuts. Hazelnut area could potentially be reduced by 100,000 ha., in five years and total production, especially from valleys, could be reduced 25 per cent by the end of the project.

FISKOBIRLIK supports growers via a support price mechanism. Before the start of the Marketing year, which starts in September, FISKOBIKLIK announces a support price. In 1994 for the first time the support price was indexed to US Dollar. This was because Turkey's then monetary policy was to control the rate of devaluation of the Turkish Lire against the US dollar to well below the rate of inflation, indexing the support price to the dollar established the basis to reduce production incentives in real terms (in line with the monetary policy). As a result, under its monetary policy, indexing ties future production incentives to international prices and encourages both domestic consumption and exports.

FISKOBIRLIK announced the MY 2005 procurement prices on August 15, 2005 with Giresun nut receiving YTL 7.45 (or about US$ 5.50) per kilogram, Levant receiving YTL 7.05 (or about US$ 5.20) per kilogram and Akcakoca receiving YTL 6.90 (or about USD 5.10) per kilogram, in-shell with 50 per cent shelling rate. All these prices are gross (before tax and manipulation cost of FISKOBIRLIK). Producers will be receiving YTL 6.70 (or about USD 4.95) per kilogram for Giresun type, YTL 6.34 (or about USD 4.70) per kilogram for Levant type, and YTL 6.20 (or about USD 4.60) per kilogram for Akcakoca type. The majority of the hazelnuts produced in Turkey are Levant type (about 75 per cent in a normal year). These prices are around 40 per cent higher than the base price announced a year ago (YTL 5.25 per kilogram, YTL 5.05 per kilogram, and YTL 4.75 per kilogram, respectively). The rate of inflation was about 9 per cent during the last twelve months. Many traders feel that the announced prices will reduce exports because international hazelnut buyers will be looking for substitutes, such as almonds and peanuts.

FISKOBIRLIK started procurement on August 22, 2005 and their announced prices was valid for the purchases made between August 22, 2005 and September 30, 2005. After September 2005, FISKOBIRLIK increased the procurement price based on market conditions. FISKOBIRLIK made arrangements to make cash payments at the time of the procurement. Traders were buying Levant type hazelnuts at YTL 5.90 per kilogram before FISKOBIRLIK announced its procurement pricc. Traders have to pay more as FISKOBIRLIK started paying cash. FISKOBIRLIK is not required to procure the entire crop from its members. Instead, by announcing a closing date for buying FISKOBIRLIK can limit the quantity it procures (all prices are in shell). FISKOBIRLIK officials stated that they could buy up to 35,000 MT in 2006.

Consumption

Official data on domestic hazelnut consumption are not available, while the USDA time series data are of doubtful validity, since it indicates a sharp decline from 150,000 tonnes in 1993 to 50,000 tonnes in 2004. Such a decline does not seem plausible. However, Turkey only consumes 10-15 per cent of its domestic production. Processors and traders purchase most hazelnuts. The five largest processors/traders account for over 40 per cent of the consumption, even though there are approximately 350 processors/traders in Turkey. Most of the industry is not vertically integrated. There are approximately 170 hazelnut crackers in Turkey with a total capacity of 1.25 million tonnes (in-shell), while the 20 largest processors have a total capacity of 300,000 MT (in-shell). Most hazelnuts are exported, or processed for export.

Hazelnuts are also a popular snack food in Turkey and the majority is consumed as whole nuts. With the devaluation of the Turkish Lira and availability of large quantities of hazelnuts, comparatively low hazelnut prices encouraged consumption in the past. As a result, domestic consumption was increased to around 80,000 tonnes (in-shell), as both snack food and for confectionery a couple of years ago. FISKOBIRLIK also crushed older crops for oil, which added to consumption. FISKOBIRLIK did not have any stocks to crush for oil since MY 2004. The retail price for shelled roasted hazelnuts in Ankara at the end of 2005 was about YTL 25.00 (about US$ 18.75) per kilogram. A year ago, this price was YTL 18.00 (about US$ 12.20) per kilogram.

Trade

Turkey is the largest exporter of hazelnuts. According to the FAO data, its exports of hazelnut in-shell increased from 326 tonnes in 1990 reached a peak of 5,541 tonnes in 2002, but declined to 3,144 tonnes in 2003 and to 315 tonnes in 2004. Turkey exports much larger quantities of hazelnut shelled, though the volume varies from one year to another. However, there has not been much increase in exports. For instance it exported about 161,000 tonnes in 1990, which peaked at about 185,000 tonnes in 1995, and since then declined to finish at about 134,557 tonnes in 2004. Table 17.10 shows exports of hazelnuts from Turkey for selected years.

Table 17.10: Turkey: Hazelnut Exports for Selected Years

Year	*Hazelnut In-shell*		*Hazelnuts Shelled*		*Total Value US$ 1,000*
	Quantity (Tonnes)	*Value US$ 1,000*	*Quantity (Tonnes)*	*Value US$ 1,000*	
1990	326	535	160,759	455,528	456,063
1995	739	1,656	185,158	589,644	591,300
2000	623	1,179	112,219	366,737	367,916
2001	675	928	174,728	786,086	787,014
2002	5,541	5,716	157,595	361,003	366,719
2003	3,144	3,640	136,648	409,229	412,869
2004	315	758	134,557	737,370	738,128

Source: FAO STAT Database, December 2005.

Based on the USDA Agriculture Attaches report and also the FAO database, in marketing year 2004 Turkey exported lower quantities, but export prices were a record high. Average export prices for whole natural kernels were around US$ 650 per 100 kilogram at the beginning of the season, but continued to increase as the season progressed and reached to around US$ 1,100 per 100 kilogram at the end of the season. Similarly at the end of the season the average export prices of roasted whole kernels were around US$ 1,235 per 100 kilogram; sliced or chopped hazelnuts were about US$ 1,142 per 100 kilogram; and paste, meal, or flour were around US$ 876 per 100 kilogram (all prices are FOB prices). Turkish total export value reached a record US$ 737 million.

Turkish hazelnut exports depend primarily on the EU, especially Germany. About 65 per cent of exports are comprised of raw kernels. Due to the high level of domestic prices in Turkey, hazelnut imports from Azerbaijan and Georgia have increased since 2000. This imbalance in the hazelnut market arises from the current disparity between demand and supply due to excess production. Table 17.11 shows Turkish hazelnut export matrix for 2001 and 2004. Shipping by trucks on a CIF basis has become more popular in recent years with most sales made to traders. About 70 per cent of Turkey's hazelnut exports are raw kernels and remaining processed, including roasted, sliced, chopped, paste, meal, and flour. Very few hazelnuts are exported as finished consumer confectionery items. The trend, however, is to move from raw kernel exports to processed and finished products for additional value added. In addition to a shift in the export product mix, Turkey is also hoping to expand its market presence in the Far East, former Soviet Union, and the United States. Industry representatives in Turkey closely monitor other markets, including the US hazelnut and almond industry.

Aflatoxin is a major industry concern. The Aflatoxin problem for hazelnuts and other crops is primarily stemming from the limits set by the European Union of only 2-ppm. The Hazelnut Promotion Group (HPG) is financing Aflatoxin research for Turkish hazelnuts. The HPG, with representatives from the Black Sea and Istanbul Exporters Union and officials from the Foreign Trade Under Secretariat is responsible for domestic and foreign promotion as well as research and development. Exporters finance HPG activities with funds from sales. Major hazelnut exporters also set up their own laboratories to avoid Aflatoxin problem. The Turkish government started testing all exports and providing export health certificates in 2001. Due to changes in harvesting, there were reported to be no serious problems in MY 2003 and MY 2004. Still only about one per cent of the crop may be returned because the EU found the level slightly higher, such as 2.1 ppm or so, from the samples they take, according to industry sources.

Table 17.11: Turkey: Hazelnut Export Trade Matrix (In-shell basis)

Calendar Year 2001		*Calendar Year 2004*	
Country	Quantity (Tonnes)	Country	Quantity (Tonnes)
US	12,894	US	8,990
Germany	169,996	Germany	126,081
Italy	66,394	Italy	66,935
France	42,602	France	41,892
Belgium	37,486	Belgium	27,034
Netherlands	20,714	Netherlands	22,196
Switzerland	20,259	Switzerland	17,778
United Kingdom	14,684	Spain	13,408
Austria	12,920	Russia	13,275
Spain	11,936	United Kingdom	13,151
Poland	8,009	Austria	11,842
Others	63,845	Others	72,759
Grand Total	481,739	Grand Total	435,301

Source: USDA Agriculture Attaché's Report: Turkey Tree Nut: Various issues.

Policy

In recent years the Turkish Government has not intervened in the hazelnut market, leaving it to operate freely. As a result of this liberalization, hazelnut prices have decreased in both domestic and foreign markets. On the other hand, domestic consumption, as discussed above, is very low in Turkey.

As a result of World Bank programme in the 1990s, the Turkish government promoted alternative crops to decrease hazelnut area. Although 580 hectares of hazelnut orchards were planted with other crops, the area was offset by expansion of hazelnut plantings in other areas. The industry is concerned that these increases will create surpluses and depress prices in the future. According to a Turkish Law, hazelnuts may be grown only in the hilly sides, with a minimum 5 per cent slope, in the Black Sea region. Hazelnut growing areas, however, increased during the last two decades. Current high prices are expected to hamper any efforts to reduce hazelnut acreage and encourage further plantations.

FISKOBIRLIK announced a high price for procurement in MY 2005 as well. Few traders claim that the substitution of almonds and peanuts for hazelnuts will be limited and most companies will be buying hazelnuts even at the high prices. If these industries do seek substitutes in the long term, it will mean fewer exports and larger stocks.

HAZELNUT INDUSTRY IN USA

Introduction

USA is the second largest hazelnut producing country in the world. Two states Oregon and Washington account for the entire US hazelnut production. Oregon has the ideal climate for growing superior hazelnuts: a unique blend of ocean, mountain and river climates unite warm and cold, sun and rain. With some of the richest, most fertile soil in the world, Oregon is prime hazelnut county.

Production

Oregon's Willamette Valley is home to 99 per cent of the US hazelnut industry. The hazelnut was made Oregon's official State Nut in 1989. About 650 farm families grow hazelnuts on 11,500 hectares. Hazelnut bearing area has remained relatively stable over the last ten years.

Hazelnut trees can produce until over 80 years of age, and many Oregon growers are third and fourth generation orchardists. The hazelnut is unique in that it blooms and pollinates in the middle of winter. Wind carries the pollen from yellow catkins to a tiny red flower, where it stays dormant until June, when the nut begins to form. The nuts mature during the summer months, turning from green to shades of hazel nestled in a protective husk, and are harvested in late September or October after they have fallen to the ground. Nuts are mechanically swept into windrows and picked up by harvesters that separate the nuts from twigs and other debris. They are put in tote bins for transport to a facility that cleans, dries, and sells them in the shell or cracks them for kernel use.

Ancient Hazelnut History

According to a manuscript found in China from the year 2838 B.C., the hazelnut (also called a filbert) took its place among the five sacred nourishments God bestowed to human beings. We can assume from this that the cultivation of hazelnuts has been going on for over 4,500 years.

In ancient times, the hazelnut was used as a medicine and tonic. In 200 AD, the Greek physician Dioscorides emphasized the properties of the hazelnut as a medium to cure colds and grow hair. It is speculated by some that the name filbert originated from "full beard," referring to the fact that the husk (or "beard") entirely covers the nut in some varieties. Others believe the name was derived from St. Philibert, as August 22 (a date that corresponds in England to the ripening of the earliest filberts) is dedicated to him.

Local Hazelnut History

In 1858 retired Hudson's Bay Company employee, Sam Strictland planted first cultured hazelnut tree in Oregon. In 1876 David Gernot carried out first significant planting: he planted 50 trees along a fence row (as was customary in the Old County) in the Willamette Valley. In 1885 Barcelona variety (most prominent variety grown today) was developed by Felix Gillet, who emigrated from France in 1952. In 1886 George Steel bought 165 second-generation seedlings from Gillet, and plants them in Portland.

In 1905 George Dorris of Springfield began the first commercial orchard with over 200 Barcelona trees. In 1905-06 Homer Kruse of Wilsonville, Percy Giese of Gresham, NE Britt of Newberg, Thomas Prince of Dundee and John Forbis of Dilley, purchased nursery stock from Gillet, and are considered pioneers in filbert growing. By the end of First World War planting began in earnest. The history of volume of production is given below:

1930	300	Tonnes harvested
1950	5,350	Tonnes harvested
1970	8,750	Tonnes harvested

1990	21,700	Tonnes harvested
1997	49,000	Tonnes harvested, an all-time record crop
2004	37,500	Tonnes harvested

Economics

The hazelnut industry farm gate value (the total value growers received for their crops) has averaged $30,000,000 during the last five years. Using a conservative multiplier, this translates into a total economic impact of $75 million in Oregon. Over half of Oregon's production is exported to countries throughout the world, with the primary markets being China and Germany.

Health Benefits

As a part of the tree nut group, hazelnuts received the first qualified health claim for a food for their positive role in heart health. A low-carb food item can be achieved by replacing a portion of flour with hazelnut flavour. About 80 per cent of the fat in hazelnuts is mono-unsaturated and thus heart healthy.

Hazelnuts are a source of numerous phytochemicals, and the antioxidant vitamin E both, which promote health and prevent chronic disease. Hazelnuts are a source of folic acid, which decreases the risk of birth defects and heart disease. Studies show that including nuts in a weight loss regime will result in greater weight reduction over a longer period of time.

Versatility

Hazelnuts are available in a variety of forms ranging from in-shell to kernels to further processed diced, sliced, butter and paste. Hazelnuts can be added to a wide array of dishes from cereals and breads to soups, salads, yoghurts and main dishes to confections, ice creams and pastries. The hazelnut's unique flavour complements, but does not overpower the flavour of foods with which they are combined. Because hazelnuts must meet Oregon's strict quality standards, Oregon Hazelnuts are the benchmark for hazelnuts around the world.

Time series data on the bearing area, production and yield of hazelnut in US is presented in Table 17.12. Hazelnut bearing area in Oregon increased form 8,745 hectares in 1980 to 11,336 hectares in 2003, registered around 30 per cent rise during twenty-three years period. Bearing area in the second state, which is rather minor has not increased much. Production of hazelnut in-shell basis almost doubled, increasing from 15,420 tonnes to 37,800 tonnes in 2003. Nevertheless, the output fluctuates considerably. It varied from as low as 8,142 tonnes in 1983 to a peak of around 50,000 tonnes in 2001.

Table 17.12: USA Hazelnut Area, Yield and Production

Year	Area (Hectare)	Yield (Tonne/hec.)	Production (Tonnes)
1980	8745	1.73	15120
1981	8745	1.65	14472
1982	8737	2.10	18343
1983	8462	0.94	7942
1984	8745	1.51	13176
1985	9271	2.62	24274
1986	9919	1.51	14945
1987	10283	2.10	21590
1988	10567	1.53	16182
1989	10972	1.16	12737
1990	10931	1.98	21600
1991	11012	2.30	25296
1992	10850	2.54	27604
1993	10810	3.75	40584
1994	11012	1.90	20944
1995	11174	3.46	38640
1996	11417	1.63	18612
1997	11579	4.03	46618
1998	11781	1.31	15423
1999	11660	3.41	39744
2000	11457	1.95	22357
2001	11741	4.22	49590
2002	11822	1.65	19564
2003	11336	3.33	37900
2004	11578	3.19	36800

Source: USDA: Fruit and Tree Nuts Situation and Outlook Yearbook 2005; pp. 125-26.

Domestic Consumption

In the production, supply and distribution estimates, domestic consumption is estimated as a residual of production, plus opening stocks, plus imports, minus exports and minus ending stocks. Based on this method, domestic consumption of hazelnut (shelled weight) in the USA increased from around 5,000 tonnes in 1980-81 to 6,750 tonnes in 2003-04. Total annual consumption varied a lot, ranging from as low as 3,662 tonnes in 1986-87 to around 13,500 tonnes in 2001-02. Per capita consumption remains rather low. For instance the 2003-04 hazelnut season which finished in June 2004, the US per capita consumption declined slight from the previous year to 0.05 pound, despite a large crop. High exports and low imports for the year contributed to the lower consumption. This level was the same as in 1980-81 (Table 17.13).

Table 17.13: USA Hazelnut Production, Supply and Distribution (Shelled basis): 1980-81- 2003-04

Year	Utilized Production	Loss and Exempt	Marketable Production[2]	Imports[3]	Beginning Stocks[4]	Total Supply[5]	Ending Stocks[4]	Exports[3]	Domestic Consumption Total	Consumption Per Capita Lbs.
In Tonnes										
1980-81	5,600	248	5,352	1,819	475	7,646	511	2,150	4,985	0.05
1981-82	5,386	587	4,798	1,797	511	7,106	439	1,795	4,873	0.05
1982-83	6,802	212	6,590	3,081	439	10,109	1,328	1,556	7,225	0.07
1983-84	2,542	184	2,358	3,253	1,328	6,939	292	1,369	5,278	0.05
1984-85	4,288	439	3,849	4,096	292	8,237	247	1,202	6,788	0.06
1985-86	8,722	157	8,565	1,907	247	10,719	570	3,018	7,131	0.07
1986-87	5,216	393	4,823	1,691	570	7,085	181	3,241	3,662	0.03
1987-88	8,185	243	7,942	1,756	181	9,879	431	2,710	6,738	0.06
1988-89	5,970	201	5,769	3,711	431	9,911	312	1,717	7,882	0.07
1989-90	4,727	275	4,452	3,253	312	8,017	263	2,109	5,645	0.05
1990-91	7,062	850	6,213	4,598	263	11,074	499	2,554	8,021	0.07
1991-92	9,030	429	8,601	2,806	499	11,906	1,375	3,733	6,798	0.06
1992-93	10,060	488	9,572	4,004	1,375	14,951	1,343	4,222	9,385	0.08
1993-94	14,756	669	14,088	3,561	1,343	18,993	767	6,524	11,701	0.10
1994-95	7,709	485	7,225	5,584	767	13,539	199	4,738	8,638	0.07
1995-96	13,721	723	12,998	5,083	199	18,279	1,857	6,031	10,391	0.09
1996-97	6,655	381	6,274	1,439	1,857	9,570	181	6,329	3,060	0.02
1997-98	15,516	1233	14,283	3,922	181	18,386	627	9,231	8,527	0.07

(Contd.)

Table 17.13: (*Contd.*)

Year	*Utilized Production*	*Loss and Exempt*	*Marketable Production*[2]	*Imports*[3]	*Beginning Stocks*[4]	*Total Supply*[5]	*Ending Stocks*[4]	*Exports*[3]	*Domestic Consumption Total*	*Consumptior Per Capita Lbs.*
1998-99	5,671	338	5,333	5,666	627	11,627	465	4,622	6,540	0.05
1999-00	14,346	473	13,873	5,779	465	20,117	2,550	5,148	12,419	0.10
2000-01	8,206	290	7,915	5,296	2,550	15,760	635	6,682	8,443	0.07
2001-02	18,000	687	17,313	6,907	635	24,855	1,156	10,241	13,459	0.10
2002-03	7,091	153	6,937	7,449	1,156	15,542	1,112	4,513	9,916	0.08
2003-04 6/	13,738	7	13,731	4,956	1,112	19,799	1,426	11,629	6,745	0.05

l/ Season beginning July l: 2/Utilized production minus loss and exemption.3/ Bureau of Census, Department of Commerce
4/ Hazelnut Marketing Board: 5/ Marketable production plus opening stock plus imports minus exports: 6/Prelimnary.

Source: USDA: Fruit and Tree Nuts Situation and Outlook Yearbook 2005, p. 128.

Trade

The USA is the second largest exporter of hazelnut, though it also imports some quantities. Hazelnuts are the 5th leading US tree nut exports by value. The US exports of hazelnut in-shell increased from 3,627 tonnes in 1990 to around 17,387 tonnes in 2004. The value rose from US$ 5.9 million to US$ 33.7 million in 2004. Exports of hazelnut shelled increased from 1,525 tonnes in 1990 to 4,086 tonnes in 2003, but declined to 2,807 tonnes in 2004.The value increased from US $ 4.2 million to US $10 million. Total export earnings from hazelnut increased more than three folds, from US $10.1 million to US $ 43.7 million. The US is a net exporter of hazelnuts. Its net exports ranged from about 5 - 10,000 tonnes from 1990 to 2004. Its top five export markets (in terms of volume) are China (53% share), Germany (15%), Canada (6 %), Spain (4 %) and others (15 per cent). Other countries include Mexico and in the Middle East Region Israel is the major market for US hazelnuts.

SPANISH HAZELNUT INDUSTRY

Spain ranks fourth in world hazelnut production after Turkey, Italy and the USA. Its 2005 inshell production was 25,700 tonnes. Catalonia, in the nort-east, accounts for some 93 per cent of total Spanish hazelnut areas, with the Tarragona province representing some 88 per cent of the Catalonia total output. Some 60 per cent of Spain's hazelnut orchard area is under irrigation.

Tarragona's orchards topographically can be classified into two groups. Firstly, the orchards of the inland mountain ranges of the province (Priorat), located on hilly slopes, with a low mechanization level, dry farming (around 400 mm of annual rainfall) and low production (500-800 kg/ha) and with a tendency to decrease. Secondly, the flat area orchards of the region called Camp de Tarragona are located near to the Mediterranean coast and are highly mechanized, with high production (2,000-2,500 kg/ha) and modern cultivation techniques. The main commercial hazelnut production is obtained from the second area.

The most important cultivars are native, i.e. 'Negret' (70 per cent), 'Gironell', 'Pauetet', 'Culplà', 'Morell', 'Grifoll', 'Trenet' and Ribet. However, in recent years, in irrigated orchards, 'Pauetet' has been widely used. Some Italian cultivars ('Tonda di Giffoni', 'Tonda Romana' and 'San Giovanni') stand out for their high yields and commercial value.

In Spain hazelnut production has not increased much during the last fifteen years, although it varied from one year to another. Production was 21,270 tonnes in 1990 and 22,500 tonnes in 2005. In 2003 production was as low as 12,559 tonnes, due to severe drought. The 2006-07 harvest is likely to recover, with normal precipitation levels in the spring and summer months of 2006.

Production Policy

Spanish tree nut production takes place within the legal framework set by the EU common fruit and vegetables policy. This policy encourages the constitution of Producer Organizations (POs) to concentrate and market production. POs can apply to EU co-financing of so-called Operational Programmes. These are investment Programmes designed to increase producer competitiveness and marketing efficiency.

Up till 2004, tree nut producers were eligible to a special subsidy paid on a hectare basis, subject to presentation of so-called Improvement Plans on farms. This subsidy was set at € 241.50 per hectare, and was co-financed by the EU, MAPYA and the Autonomy Regions. In addition to almonds, this regime applies to hazelnuts, walnuts, pistachios and carob.

In 2005, new dispositions concerning the tree nut subsidy regime, which were approved under the 2003 CAP Reform, came into force. Level of individual farmer subsidy remained unchanged, and subsidy payments continued to be co-financed by the EU, Spanish Central Government and Autonomies. However, farmers now must apply individually and not through the OP, even if OP membership remains a condition for subsidy access. Further, there is a minimum area restriction for subsidy access, set at 0.2 hectares.

Producers have been complaining at this restriction, especially in the Valencia Community, where tree nuts are produced largely in disadvantaged areas. Farmer sources report that areas in producer subsidy applications in 2005 declined 15 per cent in this region relative to previous year levels on account of this restriction. Same sources report that at national level, out of 16,000 ha under Improvement Plans finalized in 2004, only some 2,200 ha were submitted for subsidy in 2005.

According to Spanish farmer organizations, the new policy could lead to a progressive abandon of tree nuts in less productive regions, and are requesting Spanish authorities to negotiate with the EU a change in this disposition.

Spain has a Maximum Guaranteed Area (MGA) for tree nuts of 568,000 hectares, of which 167,000 ha in the Valenciana Community (800,000 hectares in total EU) in over 252,000 farms. This MGA includes almonds, hazelnuts, walnuts, pistachios and carobs.

Consumption

The bulk of the hazelnut crop is consumed in shelled form. Domestic hazelnut consumption is increasing steadily due to the popularity of the "Mediterranean diet," as well as in tree nut processing activity. Annual consumption is currently around 26,000 tonnes. The confectionery and chocolate industries use about 60 to 70 per cent of domestic supplies. The rest is generally marketed in snack pack. Hazelnut is marketed in Spain throughout the year in competition with almonds, peanuts and other snack foods. In years when almond prices are high, hazelnut demand in the confectionery industry increases. Hazelnut export from Spain is diminishing while import is rising.

Trade

Spain is a net importer of hazelnuts. Spanish imports of hazelnuts increased from about 11,000 tonnes in 1999 to 14,000 tonnes in 2005, while its exports ranged from 6,000 tonnes to 13,300 tonnes. Table 17.14 shows hazelnut production, imports and exports during 1999 to 2005.

Table 17.14: Spain: Hazelnut Production, Imports and Exports (In-Shell weight basis)

MY	1999	2000	2001	2002	2003	2004	2005
Production				*1,000 Tonnes*			
In-shell	29.8	25.2	26.7	2.8	12.6	25.7	18.2
Imports	Tonnes						
In-shell	1,374	927	1,000	884	1,060	1,000	1,400
Shell	9,212	7,682	12,237	12,560	12,736	9,000	12,600
Total	10,586	8,609	13,237	13,444	13,796	10,000	14,400
Exports							
In-Shell	251	72	165	267	215	1,050	600
Shell	13,049	9,435	6,778	10,203	6,943	9,450	5,400
Total	13,300	9,507	6,942	10,470	7,158	10,500	6,000

Note: Converted shelled imports and exports into in-shell basis through the use of 2.03 conversion coefficient.

Source: Global Trade Atlas.

REFERENCES

1. Menninger, E.A. (1977). *Edible Nuts of the World*, Horticultural Books Inc. Stuart, Florida.
2. Tutin, T.G.; Heywood, V.H.; Burges, N.A.; Valentine, D.H.; Walters, S.M. and Webb, D.A. (1964). *Flora Europea*, Vol. I, University Press, Cambridge.
3. Menninger, E.A. (1977): *Edible Nuts of the World*: Horticultural Books Inc. Stuart, Florida.
4. Tutin, T.G.; Heywood V.H.; Burges, N.A.; Valentine, D.H.; Walters, S.M. and Webb, D.A. (1964). *Flora Europea*, Vol. I, University Press, Cambridge.

18

WORLD CHESTNUT ECONOMY

Introduction

Chestnut (*Castanea species, Fagaceae*) is a close relative of oak (Quercus) both belong to the Fagaceae family of the cup-bearing trees. The nut of the chestnut is morphologically similar to the acorn of the oak. The chestnut bur is a vegetative structure comparable to the acorn cup. The Beech (Fagus) also belongs the same family as chestnut and oak.

Chestnut trees have grown in most temperate climate of the world for more than 4,000 years for beauty, fuel and sand shelter. However the food value of the nut has always been of prime importance. Productivity, ease of harvesting, simplicity of preparation for eating and diversity of uses for high and low-income people have been the impelling urge for growing chestnuts.

Ecology and Distribution: American chestnut (*Castanea dentata)* is native to USA, east of the Mississippi River. European chestnut: *Castanea sativa is a native* to southern Europe from Italy to Iran and extending northwards to Hungary, also in North Africa. It is extensively planted and naturalized elsewhere in Europe. Usually it is a calcifuge, in woods on well-drained soils. Chinese chestnut: *Castanea mollissima,* from northern China, was introduced into USA, while Japanese chestnut: *Castanea crenata,* native to Japan; is grown for timber in southern Europe.[1]

Description: Chestnuts are deciduous trees or shrubs. Fruits are 1-3 nuts, brown, coriaceous, in a swollen, spiny capsule which dehisces irregularly by 2-3 valves.[2]

Climate Requirement: Chestnut requires a cool climate and flourishes in the mid-hills at elevations ranging from 1,500 to 2,100 m above sea level. In India, chestnut trees are found in Kashmir, Kulu valley, Shimla hills in Himchal Pradesh and Kumaon hills in Uttrakhand.

Soil Requirement: Chestnut requires a deep fertile loamy soil with good moisture content. Chinese chestnut grows best on a sandy or sandy loam soil that is well drained. The trees will not thrive well on a low ground that is poorly drained.

Propagation/Cultivation: Chestnut trees in India are invariably propagated through seed. Chestnut seeds are planted some time after harvest (a storage treatment of one to two months at 0° to 2.2°C is necessary to the dormancy of chestnut embryos and to ensure uniform germination).

The nuts are usually planted 15 cm apart in rows 90 cm wide to allow for intensive cultivation. Seeds are planted 5 cm to 7.5 cm deep or three times the diameter of the nut. Special methods of propagating chestnuts include the buried-in-arch developed by Jaynes.[3] He also developed a method of rooting cuttings by use of sprouted seeds as nurse plants.[4] Three main essentials to achieve higher success in grafting are (i) good scion wood, (ii) proper training. Nursery grafting is practised for propagating small trees for transplanting. Dormant buds are provided with protective bud scales to prevent water loss.

Cultural Practices: No special cultural treatment is given to chestnut tree. Once established it flourishes without much care. However, the yield under such conditions is not high. To induce heavy cropping, the trees should be given proper cultural treatment as in the case of other fruit trees. Irrigation, if available, should be applied in the dry season. The quantity of organic manure and fertilizers should be applied on the basis of age and growth of the tree. The trees should be trained with a clear stem of about one metre and branches allowed to develop above this height. Pruning consists mainly in removing the crossing and superfluous branches.

Varieties: High-yielding strains belonging to four major groups, viz. *Castanea dentata* (American), C. *mollissima* (Chinese), C. *sativa* (European) and C. *crenata* (Japanese) are being cultivated commercially throughout the world. The principal Chinese cultivars are: "Abundance", "Hemming", "Crane", "Culling", "Nanking", and "Orrin". These have been adopted widely due to their high quality nuts. They require short chilling as compared to European chestnuts. Many hybrids have also been evolved as a natural cross between Chinese and American chestnuts.

In India, no named varieties are under cultivation. New planting invariably consists of seedling trees. In Himachal Pradesh two varieties—Marron de Lizan and Spanish Lady—are under cultivation. In Pithoragarh district in Uttrakhand, superior strains of Japanese chestnut are under cultivation particularly in the Berinag area.

Pollination: The chestnut is a monoecious tree bearing female and male flowers separately on the same tree. The functioning depends upon the proper fertilization of female flowers. Solitary trees sometimes produce no fruits, which show that they require cross-pollination. It is, therefore, necessary that at least three to four seedling trees are planted near each other, and if trees are budded or grafted, they should be of three or four varieties.

Harvesting, Yield and Marketing: Traditionally mature nuts are allowed to fall from the tree and may remain on the ground for several days or longer before gathering by hand. Tree shakers and catchers, which can be used after 4-9 per cent of the ripe nuts have fallen naturally, are being developed, as well as the necessary means of removing the burr.[5]

The average yields of the European chestnut grown in California are 2220 kg/ha. However, new plantations with high-yielding, large nut, grafted cultivars were expected to yield 3,360-4,480 kg/ha. In India, the nuts ripen in October-November. At this time, the bur splits open exposing the nuts inside. The bur still enclosing the nuts are removed by pressing them manually. The yield per tree varies from 10 to 20 kg. The nuts should be marketed soon after harvesting as with long storage, their quality deteriorates as also mentioned earlier. The nuts are roasted on a slow fire before eating.

Post-harvest Treatments: Commercially nuts may be held in refrigerated storage at $0^{\circ}C$ to $-1^{\circ}C$ for several months in ventilated polyethylene liners. Weevil damage may occur during storage and later; unfortunately it is not possible to remove infested nuts by flotation before storage. The risk of incipient fungal infection is increased by the absence of visible moulds on many infected kernels. Unless properly handled, fresh nuts quickly dry out and harden and cannot be roasted or boiled satisfactorily unless regenerated by soaking.[6]

Storage: Chestnut fruits are spoiled during improper storage. The new cultivars-crane and Orrin have been recommended because of excellent keeping qualities of the nuts. However, the chestnut industry is still based mostly upon the planting of seedling trees. Until growers plant improved cultivars with nuts resistant to spoilage, the storage problem will remain. It was formerly considered necessary to cure the nuts before storage. Curing or drying of the nuts is important to prepare them for eating.

Nutritional Value: The nutrient value of chestnuts varies according to species. Respectively, raw American, European and Chinese chestnuts contain approximately 43.7 per cent, 54.9 per cent and 44 per cent water; 4.8 per cent, 2 per cent and 4.2 per cent protein; 1.3 per cent, 1.6 per cent and 1.1 per cent fat; and 48.6 per cent, 40.3 per cent and 49.1 per cent carbohydrates.

Chestnut Uses: Eating quality is best at harvest time. In-shell nuts are roasted and sold as "hot chestnuts"; shelled nuts can be ground to a flour and eaten as chestnut bread or porridge, roasted or boiled they can be eaten as a vegetable or used for stuffing poultry. In France chestnuts are preserved in syrup as maroons glacis and other sweetmeats.

In many European countries, chestnut is looked upon as a staple diet. In France, from the Bay of Biscay to Switzerland, Chestnuts are extensively eaten by human beings and animals. The poor people during autumn and winter often make two meals daily from chestnut. The ordinary way of cooking them is to remove the outside shell, bleach them and put on fire to steam; they are often eaten with salt or milk, mostly as breakfast by working people.

In Japan, great quantities of chestnut are raised, but they are used less for human food than elsewhere. This may account for the poorer quality of the Japanese chestnut. Chestnut has been used in food combination in Asia, Europe and America since recorded history. Chestnut tree timber is durable and rot-resistant, it is used for fencing, furniture, ship masts, telegraph poles, mine props, railway sleepers.

Marketing

The marketing outlook is one of the chief considerations in evaluating a chestnut orchard. Three aspects of a successful marketing programme are as follow:[7]

(i) Development of early maturing cultivars to get a lead over other varieties;
(ii) Development of quality product at a moderate price (this includes grading and storing the nuts to assure a uniform product); and
(iii) Marketing the shelled nuts as clean kernels in polythene bags, both as fresh and frozen products.

The American chestnut provides food for a number of wildlife species also. Recognizing the value of chestnut as food for wildlife officials in several States in the USA began planting Chinese chestnuts on gap preserves 30-40 years ago.

European chestnuts, which are larger but less sweet than the American chestnut, are marketed in-shell for roasting. Chinese chestnuts are smaller and less sweet than the American chestnut but sweeter than the European chestnut. Japanese chestnuts are a variable product with some trees producing huge nuts up to 5 cm in diameter and weighing 30 g or more while others bear smaller nuts; their nuts are also less sweet than those from the Chinese chestnut. Despite the strong demand for chestnuts and chestnut products, the problems of harvesting and storage and the difficulties in obtaining a good, clean nut make chestnut production a difficult venture.[8]

WORLD CHESTNUT PRODUCTION

According to the FAO data, currently chestnuts are produced in more than 35 countries in the world. World harvested area under chestnut has increased from 250 thousand hectares in 1990 to about 335 thousand hectares in 2005, registering 34 per cent growth in sixteen years. Yield has increased from 1,934 kgs. to 3,358 kgs., per hectare Table 18.1 shows production of chestnuts.

The leading countries in chestnut production are China, 73 per cent; Korea Republic, Italy and Turkey over 4 per cent each; Bolivia 3 per cent, Portugal and Japan over 2 per cent each (Table 18.2). These eight countries accounted for over 96 per cent of the world chestnuts production in 2005. Other small producing countries include France, Korea Democratic Republic, Peru, Spain, Russian Federation and the United States, which contributed less than 1 per cent each.

Worldwide chestnut production increased from 484 thousand tonnes in 1990 to about 1,130 thousand tonnes in 2005. The annual growth comes to 8 per cent. China dominates the world production of chestnuts. As a result, China virtually has control of world pricing of chestnuts. Chestnuts produced around the world are viewed by many to be of inferior quality to those that can be produced and distributed in the United States. There are also perceived differences in quality in the varieties currently being produced in the United States. This, coupled with the fact that current production in the United States is so small, means one could reasonably argue US produced chestnuts are not of economic importance.

International Trade

World exports of chestnuts are estimated at around 107 thousand tonnes in 2004. This constitutes about 10 per cent of global production. Exports during the last fifteen years fluctuated in a rather narrow range registering small increase. Value of exports totaled US$ 232 million. Export price per tonne has declined from US$ 2855 in 1995 to US$ 2004 in 2002 and recovered slightly to US$ 2187in 2003, to decline again in 2004 to US $ 1972 per tonne (Table 18.3).

Table 18.1: Chestnuts: Production (Metric Tonnes)

(*Tonnes*)	*Years*								*% Share in World Total*	*Index*
	1990	1995	2000	2001	2002	2003	2004	2005	2005	2005/1990
World	484,276	690,352	954,552	945,506	1,029,462	1,111,650	1,118,972	1,129,173	100.00	233.17
USSR	12,000								0.00	0.00
Albania	0	0	400	400	380	480	480		0.00	
Azerbaijan		500	400	500	500	500	500	500	0.04	
Bolivia	19,708	31,229	34,400	34,500	34,500	35,000	34,670	34,670	3.07	175.92
Bulgaria	21	100	400	300	300	300	300	300	0.03	1428.57
Cameroon	100	100	100	100	100	100	100	100	0.01	100.00
China	115,191	300,000	598,185	599,077	701,684	797,168	805,000	825,000	73.06	716.20
France	13,560	11,016	13,224	13,032	11,223	10,118	12,722	13,000	1.15	95.87
Georgia		0	0	1,000	1,000	1,100	1,200	1,200	0.11	
Greece	10,882	12,053	15,303	14,935	12,000	12,000	12,500	12,300	1.09	113.03
Hungary	869	1,100	1,015	991	580	469	800	850	0.08	97.81
Italy	49,559	71,971	50,000	50,000	50,000	50,000	50,000	52,000	4.61	104.93
Japan	40,200	34,400	26,700	29,000	30,100	25,100	24,000	24,000	2.13	59.70
Korea, DPR	8,000	6,500	8,500	8,700	8,700	9,000	9,000	9,000	0.80	112.50
Korea, Rep.	85,043	93,655	92,844	94,130	72,405	60,017	55,000	50,000	4.43	58.79
Macedonia		300	100	100	300	400	400	400	0.04	
Peru	2,083	2,215	1,990	525	670	759	775	800	0.07	38.41
Poland	0	50	50	50	50	50	50	50	0.00	
Portugal	20,405	23,238	33,317	26,118	31,385	33,267	31,051	24,800	2.20	121.54
Romania	0	1,000	50	50	50	50	47	50	0.00	
Russian Fed.		12,000	16,000	16,000	16,000	17,000	18,000	19,000	1.68	
Serbia & Mont.		1,400	900	700	400	900	900	900	0.08	
Slovenia		200	57	33	33	33	33	33	0.00	
Spain	23,605	10,075	9,230	9,510	9,362	16,821	9,510	10,000	0.89	42.36
Switzerland	0	200	200	200	200	200	200	200	0.02	
Turkey	80,000	77,000	50,000	47,000	47,000	48,000	49,000	49,000	4.34	61.25

Source: FAO STAT Database, April 2006.

Table 18.2: Share in World Chestnut Production: 2000-2005:

(% share)

Percent Share in World Output	*2000*	*2001*	*2002*	*2003*	*2004*	*2005*
1. China	62.67	63.36	68.16	71.71	71.73	73.06
2. Korea Republic	9.73	9.96	7.03	5.40	5.35	4.43
3. Turkey	5.24	4.97	4.56	4.32	4.28	4.34
4. Italy	5.24	5.29	4.86	4.50	4.46	4.61
5. Bolivia	3.60	3.65	3.35	3.14	3.09	3.07
6. Portugal	3.49	2.76	3.05	2.96	2.94	2.20
7. Japan	2.80	3.07	2.92	2.26	2.14	2.13
8. Greece	1.57	1.27	1.17	1.08	1.07	1.09
9. Spain	0.97	1.01	0.91	0.86	0.85	0.89
10. World Production (Tonnes)	954,552	945,506	1,029,462	1,111,650	1,122,244	1,129,173
% share	100.00	100.00	100.00	100.00	100.00	100.00

Source: FAO STAT Database, April 2006.

Table 18.3: World Exports of Chestnuts: 1990-2003

Year	*Quantity (Tonnes)*	*Value (US$ 1,000)*	*Price (US$/Tonne)*
1990	103,795	236,686	2280.3
1991	94,015	231,834	2465.9
1992	92,213	229,623	2490.1
1993	97,335	241,674	2476.7
1994	105,675	304,067	2877.4
1995	96,549	275,688	2855.4
1996	100,220	266,663	2660.8
1997	92,864	234,461	2524.8
1998	102,561	215,080	2097.1
1999	96,909	219,336	2263.3
2000	97,451	223,450	2282.9
2001	97,485	206,089	2114.1
2002	99,631	199,684	2004.2
2003	106,149	232,000	2185.6
2004	107,517	212,070	1972.4

Source: FAO STAT Database, April 2006.

China is the top exporting country, accounting for 37 per cent of the world exports of chestnuts during recent years. It is followed by Italy, whose share declined from 23 per cent in 1999 to 19 per cent in 2004. Korea Republic shipped about 16 per cent of the world exports, Spain 9 per cent, Turkey 7 per cent, Portugal about 6 per cent, while share of Belgium is the lowest 0.07 per cent in 2004 (Table 18.4).

Table 18.4: Chestnuts Exports from Major Countries

(Quantities in Tonnes and % Share in World Total)

Country	1999	2000	2001	2002	2003	2004
1. China	33,731	35,414	31,275	33,412	34,501	39,936
% share	34.81	36.34	32.08	33.54	32.50	37.14
2. Italy	22,332	22,41	23,714	23,469	18,526	20,616
% share	23.04	23.00	24.33	23.56	17.453	19.17
3. Spain	5,710	6,350	7,291	5,552	13,634	10,059
% share	5.89	6.52	7.48	5.57	12.84	9.36
4. Korea Rep.	14,529	14,130	16,007	12,830	12,921	16,123
% share	14.99	14.50	16.42	12.88	12.17	15.00
5. Portugal	8,045	8,553	7,140	6,065	11,095	6,104
% share	8.30	8.78	7.32	6.09	10.45	5.68
6. Turkey	7,835	5,321	6,786	11,665	7,885	7,332
% share	8.083	5.46	6.96	11.71	7.43	6.82
7. France	2,252	2,669	2,711	2,224	2,299	3,240
% share	2.32	2.74	2.78	2.23	2.17	3.01
8. Japan	0	295	33	173	914	582
% share	0.00	0.30	0.03	0.17	0.86	0.54
9. Singapore	619	627	558	458	468	570
% share	0.64	0.64	0.57	0.46	0.44	0.53
10. Belgium	0	104	79	97	407	96
% share	0.00	0.11	0.08	0.10	0.38	0.07
11. Sub-Total	95,039	95,877	95,594	95,945	102,650	104,658
% share	98.07	98.38	98.06	96.30	96.70	93.34
12. World	96,909	97,451	97,485	99,631	106,149	107,517

Source: FAO STAT Database: April, 2006.

World Imports

Japan is the largest importer of chestnuts followed by China, France and Italy. Table 18.5 gives imports of major consuming countries. Japan is a large chestnut producer and consumer as well as the biggest chestnut importer. Approximately one-third of China's chestnut production and approximately 40 per cent of Korea's production is exported to Japan. Japan's domestic production is chilled fresh and consumed throughout the winter, especially around the New Year. Another method is to boil the nuts, cut them in half, and eat the nutmeat with a teaspoon. Japanese chestnut prices range from \$4.00 to \$5.00 per pound for ordinary cultivars. The very best varieties can sell for \$8.00 to \$10.00 per pound. It appears that most of the chestnuts sold to consumers around the world are unshelled. Almost all recipes include steps for shelling the nuts with no mention of the availability of shelled chestnut kernels.

Table 18.5: Chestnut Imports by Major Importing Countries

(Quantities in Tonnes and % Share in World Total)

		1999	2000	2001	2002	2003	2004
1.	Japan	34,726	37,384	31,695	29,073	25,233	25,207
	% share	36.97	37.10	32.45	27.32	23.69	22.07
2.	China	6,083	9,972	9,327	13,571	17,649	21,735
	% share	6.48	9.90	9.55	12.75	16.57	19.03
3.	Italy	2,671	4,892	6,643	8,791	9,629	4.711
	% share	2.84	4.86	6.80	8.26	9.04	4.13
4.	France	9,413	11,232	11,654	9,290	7,766	15,572
	% share	10.02	11.15	11.93	8.73	7.29	13.64
5.	Spain	2,722	2,707	2,749	3,217	5,492	3,831
	% share	2.90	2.69	2.81	3.02	5.16	3.35
6.	USA	4,722	4,428	4,885	4,979	4,551	5,369
	% share	5.03	4.39	5.00	4.68	4.27	4.70
7.	Hungary	2,991	3,020	3,136	3,156	3,202	2,452
	% share	3.18	3.00	3.21	2.97	3.01	2.15
8.	Germany	3,847	3,432	3,246	4,300	2,834	3,542
	% share	4.10	3.41	3.32	4.04	2.66	3.10
9.	Austria	3,377	2,081	2,114	4,029	2,754	2,921
	% share	3.59	2.07	2.16	3.79	2.59	2.56
10.	Switzerland	2,813	2,758	2,773	2,913	2,705	2,570
	% share	2.99	2.74	2.84	2.74	2.54	2.25
11.	Saudi Arabia	1,500	745	548	901	1,268	2,117
	% share	1.60	0.74	0.56	0.85	1.21	1.85
12.	Canada	1,988	1,793	1,834	2,074	2,322	2,174
	% share	2.12	1.78	1.88	1.95	2.18	1.90
13.	Singapore	1,600	1,478	1,398	1,435	1,713	1,213
	% share	1.70	1.47	1.43	1.35	1.61	1.06
14.	Thailand	562	622	741	1,116	1,767	1,808
	% share	0.60	0.62	0.76	1.05	1.66	1.58
15.	UK	2,245	1,914	1,629	2,202	1,573	1,987
	% share	2.39	1.90	1.67	2.07	1.48	1.74
16.	Sub Total	81,344	88,544	84,457	91,130	91,909	97,209
	% share	86.59	87.88	86.47	85.64	86.30	85.12
17.	World	93,940	100,755	97,677	106,415	105,194	114,202

Source: FAO STAT Database: April 2006.

Italy is the world leader in the production of candied nuts, *marrone glacé*, and other processed chestnut products. *Marrone glacé* is a chestnut that has been preserved with sugar liquor to a candied consistency. A box of *marrone glacé* chestnuts is more expensive than a box of fine chocolates. In Italy, the traditional use of dried chestnuts and chestnut flour in cooking is declining but overseas the popularity of these, and similar products, is increasing, especially in the United States. There has been 4 per cent annual increase in the world import demand for chestnut. This trend is likely to continue in the coming decade. Thus the world import demand for chestnut is projected to increase to 170 thousand tonnes by the year 2015. World supply of chestnuts needs to increase *pari passu* to around 1.54 million tonnes by the year 2015, to meet the projected import demand and domestic consumption requirements of the producing countries.

COUNTRY CASE STUDIES

CHESTNUTS IN USA

Introduction

Following the request by the Southeast IOWA Nut Growers Cooperative the University of Nebraska Food Processing Center (FPC) conducted a research study on the market for chestnuts in the USA. The research consisted of:

- Identifying world and US chestnut production and consumption figures, where available.
- Determining current applications for chestnuts.
- Identifying current channels of distribution for chestnuts.
- Market testing three value-added chestnut products in the foodservice market.

The section below discusses the findings of research results of FPC consultant's team. The Team also identified issues and made recommendations on steps required for a successful entry into the various target markets.

Chestnut trees, and consequently chestnuts, were a large part of American culture at the turn of the twentieth century. The American chestnut, which is one of four primary chestnut species—Japanese, European, and Chinese being the other three—was prominent in many parts of the country but particularly, the eastern part of the United States. The wood from the trees was commonly used in furniture making and the chestnuts from the tree were frequently included on ingredient lists from recipes used during that era. To not being familiar with and eat chestnuts then could be likened to not having heard of and eating cheese today. They were a staple in the American diet.

All that changed with the introduction of the chestnut blight fungus from Asia. The fungus was particularly deadly. It was easily spread and killed the trees it infected. The fungus spread quickly through the forests and within a generation, almost all of the chestnut trees in the USA had vanished from the landscape and with them the knowledge and appreciation of the chestnut as an enjoyable food and valuable ingredient. At least two generations exist whose experience with chestnuts amounts to words in a Christmas song—"Chestnuts roasting on an open fire...". Despite the fact the US still imports approximately 5 thousand tonnes of chestnuts annually, US growers and processors of chestnuts face a mostly 'uneducated' market of chestnut consumers and chefs in the USA. The one exception is Asian consumers. Many originate from countries where chestnuts are still a regular part of life and thus they are avid consumers of available chestnuts in the US.

Chestnut Production and Use in USA

The US Department of Agriculture (USDA) does not report separate statistics on the production and consumption of chestnuts in the United States. Chestnuts are included in the other tree nuts category in USDA tree nut statistical reports. Production of chestnuts around the world and the volume exports and imports into major countries including the United States have already been discussed above.

In the United States, chestnut production accounts for less the 1 per cent of total world production. According to the FAO data US annually imports over 4-5 thousand tonnes of chestnuts valued at US$ 10 to 13 million. European in-shell chestnuts primarily from Italy are sold at a retail price of $3 to $4 per lb. Currently, there is a limited amount of processed chestnuts being imported into the US Table 18.6 shows US imports of chestnuts from various countries.

In 2000, price of imported in-shell chestnuts ranged from $1.50 to $3.00 per pound, with an average of $2.10 per pound. Most of the imported in-shell chestnuts come from Italy and Korea Republic. The Italian imports wholesale for approximately $2.00 per pound and are preferred by wholesale buyers because of their consistent quality (large size and easy peeling). Prices of processed, peeled, and frozen chestnut products in the US have reached more than $2.75 per pound. The results from the project's market test of processed, peeled and frozen chestnut products produced in the Midwest indicate a potential for much higher prices ($3.00-$9.00 per pound). Details of the market test are included in a later section of this chapter.

Table 18.6: US Imports of Chestnuts (Fresh or Dried, Whether or Not Shelled or Peeled for Consumption)

Country	1996	1997	1998	1999	2000	2001
			In Tonnes			
Italy	3,003	3,197	3,197	3,182	3,059	2,422
Korea	253	556	1,522	1,098	778	1,561
China	129	171	41	217	280	421
Spain	98	209	115	4	43	207
Portugal	81	108	104	116	139	137
France	21	39	94	52	74	100
Total Imports	3,669	4,337	5,100	4,722	4,428	4,885

Sources: Data in this table has been compiled from tariff and trade data from the US Department of Commerce, the US Treasury and the US International Trade Commission.

There are a number of attributes that determine chestnut quality and thereby impact the price one will receive for chestnuts. The most important quality characteristics are:

- Nut size
- Degree of bur separation from the shell
- Ease of pellicle removal
- Flavour

In the 1990s, large California chestnuts were sold for $3.00 per pound wholesale; organically produced nuts were sold for an even higher price. The wholesale price ranged from $1.20 to $5.00 per pound, depending on the grade, market season, and location. Retailers commonly doubled the wholesale price and paid the best prices for the largest sizes. The size of the individual chestnuts is important in the more choosy fresh markets. Large nuts, 0.5 to 1 ounce (14 to 28 g) each, may well command a premium price as high as $6.00 to $7.00 per pound at retail markets. The most common variety of chestnuts in California is the colossal variety. While larger in size than other varieties, some industry experts believe it produces a chestnut with inferior taste attributes.

Most chestnuts are sold fresh in the shell, but some Italian dealers also sell dried, peeled chestnuts. Ethnic markets are the largest outlets for chestnuts, perhaps as high as 80 per cent in some locations. As evidenced by the large Japanese, Korean, and Chinese role in the world production and consumption of chestnuts, it is not surprising they are willing consumers of the chestnuts available in the US. It appears that the ethnic market is the low ranging fruit for the US chestnut industry. Most of the remaining nuts are sold to upscale consumers for special recipes during the holidays.

In his report, Vossen suggests that chestnuts offer good market potential, given appropriate and sufficient marketing and promotion programmes, "especially since chestnuts are considered a health food that is delectable and can easily be grown organically. These positive aspects appeal to many of today's consumers. Since freshness is a sales factor in chestnut appearance, domestic production has a definite advantage over Europe and Asia due to early ripening."

Chestnut Market Opportunities

The focus of the above mentioned research project was the study of foodservice market; however, the ingredient and retail markets for chestnuts were also explored. Brief results are described below.

A. *Ingredient Market for Chestnuts*

The major market for tree nuts, specifically chestnuts, in prepared foods is a commodity marketplace where supply and demand factors dominate, making price competition extremely important. It is also a marketplace where prices fluctuate a lot. For example, in the case of pecans, a supermarket bakery reported that the price for pecan pieces sometimes will fluctuate as much as $3 per pound depending on the time of year and the supply of pecans.

Given the development of the pecan and other well-known nut industries (almond, walnuts, etc.), the quality of such nuts has a higher likelihood of being uniform and availability is widespread. These are two common characteristics of a commodity marketplace. Chestnuts, however, fall into another category. Both domestic chestnut consumption and production are currently small. Low volume and sparse production can often lead to a larger degree of variability in nut quality. These are characteristics of a specialty marketplace where a supplier who can provide a consistently higher quality product can gain an edge. While price will always be a factor in the ingredient marketplace, chestnuts currently have the advantage of being a speciality item.

Prepared food products are often the last place a new ingredient or flavour will show up in the food supply. The cost of developing new products and the accompanying failure rate of such products means prepared foods manufacturers work hard at minimizing risk when identifying new product opportunities. Chestnuts as an ingredient must mature in the marketplace before a food manufacturer would be likely to develop a product that features chestnuts. The use of value added chestnut products, such as flour, is not uncommon in the gluten-free market; however, they are not widely used in the mainstream market.

Chestnuts are different in composition that many other tree nuts; however, they do offer healthful benefits. In the US the functional food market has been growing quickly in recent years. While determining the nutritional benefits of chestnuts is not covered in the project, the Southeast Iowa Nut Growers should explore and/or promote the healthy aspect of chestnuts.

B. *Retail Markets*

An opportunity exists in the retail grocery market for the growers to sell chestnuts. The Food Processing Centre believes that a market opportunity exists, especially during the holiday season, in the retail grocery market for chestnuts. Initially, the growers should market in-shell bulk chestnuts. As the growers develop value-added chestnut products, they can be introduced to the retail market. The Centre does not believe the consumer market is currently sufficiently developed for chestnuts to be marketed throughout the year. Marketing chestnuts during the holidays must be the starting point.

In Nebraska, the wholesale price (FOB store) paid for chestnuts during the holidays was approximately $2.75 per pound for California chestnuts. This price was obtained from a Midwest grocery distributor. Based upon an informal survey of the Omaha/Lincoln market, the retail selling price was between $4.00-$5.00 per pound during the holidays. These prices are for in-shell, fresh California chestnuts. A nut broker could be used to facilitate the introduction of chestnuts to the retail market.

A nut broker representing the Southeast Iowa Nut Growers would serve as a liaison sandwiched between the growers and their customers (distributors, retail stores, restaurants, and manufacturers) and serve as the grower's sales representative. The broker is paid a commission for their services and, for new products and companies, may have a minimum monthly compensation requirement referred to as a pioneering fee.

C. *Foodservice*

A primary goal of the research was to evaluate white tablecloth restaurants' interest in value-added chestnut products. Determining the market potential of chestnut products in other foodservice outlets was not addressed as part of this project; however, it is likely other foodservice establishments would have limited interest in chestnuts at this stage of the product's reintroduction to the marketplace due to the product's premium price and the limited knowledge of food handlers in utilizing chestnuts in meal preparation.

1. *Project Methodology*

The Food Processing Centre contracted with the Southeast IOWA Nut Growers to develop and process several value-added chestnut products in order to evaluate potential processing technology and conduct a test market of white tablecloth restaurants in the Midwest, using the Omaha/ Lincoln market as the test market area. Approximately 30 restaurants were identified in Nebraska. The first step in the market test was to survey the identified restaurants to determine (1) their existing chestnut purchasing experience, if any, (2) their level of satisfaction with existing chestnut products available to them, (3) the general and chestnut specific attributes they desire, and (4) their level of interest in six potential value-added chestnut products (see Table 18.7).

Table 18.7: Value-Added Chestnut Applications

Product	*Description*	*Uses*
Vacuum packed, frozen-shelled chestnuts	Shelled kernels with the pellicle removed. Ready for preparation in recipes.	Variety of general uses
Vacuum packaged, sugar-cooked frozen kernels	These are frozen whole kernels cooked in syrup (syrup permeated throughout the tissue) with a yellow colour.	Deserts, toppings, etc.
Frozen, sugar-cooked chestnut puree	This is a yellow, not brown, paste that is very sweet.	Sauces, toppings, etc.
Pre-cooked chestnut flour	This would be a dried chestnut puree (not sugar-cooked).	Gravies
Thermally processed, glass-packed chestnuts	Whole-kernel canned chestnuts with a texture similar to a boiled red potato.	Stews, etc.
Thermally processed, glass-packed candied chestnuts	Marron glace	Desert toppings, sauces, etc.

The survey revealed that restaurants in Nebraska were not only not currently purchasing chestnuts but also had insufficient knowledge of chestnuts and chestnut applications to provide meaningful feedback on which of these products they would be most interested in using. This was not totally unexpected as Nebraska currently produces few chestnuts and as a result has not been reintroduced to the product. A decision was made to target restaurants in Iowa as the Southeast Iowa Nut Growers have been promoting and selling their whole, unprocessed chestnuts in the region for some time. Facilitated by the growers, a total of twenty-one restaurants were targeted for participation in the project. Due to time constraints, these restaurants were not given the first survey. They were contacted and expressed interest in participating in the market test and follow up survey.

Three of the six proposed chestnut products were selected for the market test in Iowa-vacuum-packed, frozen, shelled kernels; vacuum-packed, sugar-cooked frozen kernels; and frozen, sugar-cooked chestnut puree. These products were selected based upon their commercial potential and variety of applications.

2. *Processing Results*

One of the goals of the project was to carry out an empirical evaluation of the new shelling technology, Thermal Blast Removal of Peel, Skin or shell. This technology is explained in the following paragraphs:

A new method improves peeling efficiency and reduces wastes. Food processing is often continuous from the time of harvest until the food is cleaned and securely protected from micro organisms and macro organisms. Produce is washed to remove dust, dirt, insect frass, mold spores, plant parts, animal wastes and other filth that may contaminate or affect the flavour, colour or aroma. These cleaning systems must not only clean the produce but also be efficient in energy and water consumption, not erode away usable food or provide refuge for micro-organisms or other pests.

Peeling operations also reduce microbial loads and remove inedible tissues and undesirable defects from the produce. Peeling systems are often problematic because they often have large water demands and generate waste streams, which can attract pests and accumulate microbial loads. In recent years peeling methods have been developed that have reduced water usage, improved energy efficiency of peel removal, and have decreased loss of edible produce. One of these improved peeling methods, Thermal Blast Peeling, was developed in the laboratory of the

University of Nabraska-Lincoln in the USA. Thermal Blast Peeling is applicable to many foods, and has proven to be more efficient than many conventional peeling methods.

The thermal blast process has several operational advantages over caustic and conventional high-pressure steam peeling systems now used in the food industry. Caustic chemicals such as lye are used to peel some food crops, but such peeling requires prolonged exposure to hot caustic solutions and usually results in a softened product with relatively large losses of edible tissue. Processing waste streams, which require subsequent clean up, are also generated in conventional peeling systems.

In conventional high-pressure steam peeling, pressure and time control the peeling. Pressures up to 300 lb. per sq. in. (p.s.i.) are often required to reduce processing times to an acceptable level, making it difficult to process delicate or fragile foods. Apples, for instance, are susceptible to compression bruising. The pressure of the steam compresses apple tissue resulting in tissue damage and bruising that often extends to the core.

In contrast, the thermal blast processing treatments and their effects are controlled in a manner that produces the precise results sought by independently controlling steam temperatures and pressures while maintaining minimal processing times. Temperatures as high as 1000°F may be used while limiting pressures to between 30 and 100 p.s.i. for processing times of 4 to 20 seconds. These lower pressures the most delicate and fragile foods.

The thermal blast process has been proven effective in peeling fruit and vegetable crops, coring of peppers, skinning of onions, shelling of nut crops, skinning of beef and swine tongues, scaling and skinning of fish, and the removal of shells from shellfish. In contrast, conventional peeling processes are generally limited in application to particular types of foods.

Chestnut Processing

Chestnut shelling can be done rapidly and efficiently. The laboratory prototype sheller used in the project shelled essentially all of the good chestnuts while simultaneously removing the pellicle. This sheller will easily shell two eight-pound batches of nuts per minute or 960 pounds of chestnuts per hour. A sheller with four times the capacity could be equally compact and operate at the same cost. At the current time the chestnut-processing bottleneck is separating the shelled kernels from the removed shells and pellicles. This separation operation (removing the shelled kernels from a tank of water after skimming the floating shells and pellicles from the surface of the water) has been done by hand. A new chestnut receiver (catch vessel) has been designed. The receiver is to be built primarily from stainless steel for sanitary operation. Basically this receiver consist of a stainless vessel with a conveyer on the bottom to convey shelled nuts from the vessel to a rod-type washer. The receiver will have a skimmer to simultaneously remove floating shells, etc. A cover providing high volume sprays of recycled water will decelerate and prevent the kernels from overshooting the receiver.

Chestnut Products

Three chestnut products were prepared after the whole, unshelled chestnuts went through the peeling process and a quantity of shelled kernels was available. The three products were vacuum packed, frozen-shelled chestnuts; vacuum packaged, sugar-cooked frozen kernels; and frozen, sugar-cooked chestnut puree. The processing and ingredient information for each of the products was as follows:

Frozen vacuum packaged chestnuts: Shelled chestnuts were washed and pre-frozen with no added ingredients, then vacuum packaged and stored at minus 10°F.

Frozen sugar cooked kernels: Shelled chestnuts were blanched in a sucrose syrup solution containing 0.5 per cent salt and a small quantity of food phosphates to help maintain colour.

Frozen sugar cooked chestnut puree: Contained pureed chestnuts, pieces of cooked chestnut, salt sugar, vanilla bean extract, and food phosphates to help maintain colour.

Market Test Results

The goal of the market test was to evaluate the level of interest of chefs at white tablecloth restaurants in locally produced, value-added chestnut products. The objective in administering the follow-up survey was to provide a framework for the feedback received from the chefs on the chestnut samples. The market test was not intended to provide data that could, using statistical analysis, be generalized to determine the size of the foodservice market for value-added chestnut products; rather, it was designed to assess the potential of such products in individual upscale restaurants. Would the chefs know how to use the products? How would their customers respond to the menu items prepared with chestnuts? How much value would the chefs attach to the value-added chestnuts compared to imported and/or raw, unshelled chestnuts? What criteria do they use when selecting products to use in their restaurants? To aid the chefs in using the various chestnut products, some sample recipes were included with the chestnut samples. The majority of chefs who indicated the dishes they prepared utilized their own recipes in preparing chestnut dishes. The empirical and anecdotal information received on the above mentioned topics provide an interesting and positive insight into the potential of value-added chestnuts in the upscale foodservice market.

Specifically, the survey included questions that sought to identify the attributes chefs deem important when sourcing food products, the perceived value of having a chestnut item on their menu, the quality of the chestnut product samples, and the chef's purchasing intentions should each of the sampled chestnut products become available for sale.

Approximately 450 pounds of chestnut products were produced and packed into one-pound packages. These were hand-delivered to the IOWA restaurants with a cover letter explaining the goals of the project, a compilation of suggested recipes for them to try, and the follow-up survey for them to complete once they had a chance to use and evaluate each of the product samples. Each of the restaurants received approximately 10-15 pounds of samples. The follow-up surveys were collected during April and May 2003. A total of twelve restaurants responded to the survey resulting in a response rate of 67 per cent.

Importance of Product Attributes when Making Product Selection Decisions

The chefs were asked to indicate the relative importance of criteria they use when considering new products for use in their restaurants. Chefs were consistent in their opinions that product taste and quality are still the most important attributes when evaluating a product. An additional survey taken of chefs that are members of the Chef's Collaborative, "a national network of more than 1,000 members of the food community who promote sustainable cuisine...", also identified taste and quality as the most important product attributes. The chefs in the chestnut market test were also in agreement with the Chef's Collaborative members in that products, which are locally grown/produced, are given additional positive consideration.

Interestingly, results from the Chef's Collaborative survey indicate that 94 per cent of chefs say product freshness is either very or extremely important. Consistent product quality was equally important, with 98 per cent indicating it as very or extremely important. The image of a restaurant is dependent upon a patron having a predictable experience each time they come to the restaurant, including the taste and quality of their favourite dishes. These product selection attributes may be especially important for the Southeast Iowa Nut Growers as an alternate, local, fresh source of chestnuts does not readily exist for the restaurants in their region. Product freshness and consistent quality can be an important differentiating factor when marketing their value-added chestnut products.

For the chefs in the chestnut market test, the potential of a product to become a signature item for their restaurant and its ease of preparation were less important. It should be noted that the relative lack of importance of the ease of preparation attribute is likely significantly impacted by the fact the chefs evaluating the samples were well-trained in the culinary arts and working in upscale restaurants. If restaurants further down the value chain were targeted, the ease of preparation issue would likely increase in importance.

Timing of Purchasing Intentions

Since most American consumers who are familiar with chestnuts perceive them as a seasonal item to be consumed around the holidays, chefs were asked about the timing of their purchases. Were they most likely to purchase the chestnut products for which they indicated an interest only during the holidays, mostly during the holidays, or throughout the year?

Six of the eleven restaurants indicated they would likely purchase the chestnuts throughout the year. Another four restaurants indicated that while most of their purchases would probably take place around the holidays, they were also likely to be purchasing them during other times of the year. Only one restaurant indicated that they were likely to purchase chestnuts only during the holidays. This is a very positive response for the growers in that it provides opportunities to increase the volume of chestnuts restaurants consume, as the chefs do not just consider chestnuts to be a holiday item.

Recommendations

The primary objective of the project was to assess the potential of value-added chestnuts in upscale, or white tablecloth, restaurants in the foodservice market. Objectives included identifying value-added chestnut products that have the most potential and evaluating, on an empirical basis, the prospects of a shelling new technology developed. Several insights were gained as a result of this project and serve as the basis for the following recommendations.

According to the Food Processing Center an excellent market opportunity existed for the Southeast Iowa Nut Growers. Chestnuts are a familiar, yet unknown, product for most US consumers and many U.S. chefs. An example of this is people's confusing chestnuts with water chestnuts. The extent of consumer and chef's knowledge of chestnuts is not known. Except for the well-known 'chestnuts roasting on an open fire…' Christmas song, there is little other exposure to chestnuts in today's culture. Nonetheless, the Food Processing Centre believes the product's name familiarity will aid in marketing the product to consumers and chefs. Many consumers probably have some concept of what a chestnut is and may have purchased them during the Christmas holidays. Unfortunately, many of those purchased chestnuts may have been unshelled, poor in quality, and relatively expensive for the quality received. Additionally, it should be noted that most consumers, even though they have heard of chestnuts, probably lack knowledge when it comes to shelling, preparing and eating them. The combination of a potentially poor prior experience and gap in knowledge in knowing how to shell, prepare and eat chestnuts presents a challenge in reaching the consumer market.

This is where the foodservice market, specifically white tablecloth restaurants, can play an important role. It has been believed for many years that the restaurant industry leads the rest of the food industry. New ingredients, ethnic dishes, and exotic flavours are first introduced to the marketplace in a few select restaurants. Other restaurants eventually begin to add similar items to their menus. Consumers experience these new ingredients and flavours in restaurants and try to replicate them at home. As some of these flavours gain in popularity and become more mainstream, prepared food manufacturers begin to develop products that take advantage of the emerging trend. While this pattern has blurred some in recent years as food manufacturers and supermarkets have made efforts to compete more directly with foodservice outlets, it is still the way most consumers are introduced to new ingredients and flavours.

The extent to which upscale restaurants represent a substantial market for chestnut producers was not determined as a result of this project. However, it is clear that the quality of the chestnut samples provided to the chefs were of a superior quality and that the chefs have an interest in utilizing chestnuts in their restaurants on a fairly regular basis. Given the above evolution of ingredient and flavour introduction to mainstream markets, the ability of the Southeast Iowa Nut Growers to market their products to upscale restaurants is an important opportunity.

Seizing and building upon this opportunity requires the coordination and simultaneous pursuit of multiple goals. To achieve these goals the Food Processing Centre has made the following recommendations:

1. *Create an 'Iowa Chestnuts' Brand*: The chestnut industry in the United States is in its early development. No region has clearly established itself or become known as the premier source for chestnuts, although California is moving in that direction. This is potentially the biggest opportunity the Southeast Iowa Nut Growers have in the marketplace. The Southeast Iowa Nut Growers should immediately begin work to establish an "Iowa Chestnuts" brand. Following the example of California Almonds, Idaho Potatoes, Georgia Peach, etc. the Southeast Iowa Nut Growers have an opportunity to establish Iowa State as the source of the best chestnuts in the country.

The growers should work with the Iowa Department of Agriculture, Practical Farmers of Iowa and/or the Leopold Centre on this activity. In Wisconsin, the Wisconsin Department of Agriculture heavily promotes the Wisconsin cheese brand and has firmly established it in the marketplace. These organizations in Iowa could help the growers develop a logo and promotional plan.

2. *Pursue Development of Shelled, Frozen, Vacuum-Packed Chestnut Product*: The shelled, frozen vacuum-packed chestnut kernels were the preferred value-added product of the chefs participating in the market test. One chef summed it up very well, "Chestnuts are high labour if unprepared (i.e. in the shell) so the frozen kernels are ideal." The Southeast Iowa Nut Growers should focus their efforts on processing and marketing this product. While it is the preferred method of the chefs, consumer trends would indicate that consumers would be much more likely to try and eat chestnuts if they were available in a ready-to-use product. Consumers' demand for convenience products is well documented. It continues to evolve and grow with more portable foods and packaging. The growers must strive for a balance between developing an economically feasible product and satisfying the demands of the market. In this case, that means identifying an efficient method for producing a shelled chestnut product.

The volume of chestnuts the chefs indicated they would be interested in purchasing was small; however, it should be kept in mind this is only a starting point. The restaurant that made the soup had customers coming back clamoring for more. Be it a dessert, soup or some other dish, if a restaurant's consumers show great interest in a dish that includes chestnuts, a restaurant's purchases could easily increase. This market test is only a starting point for developing the foodservice market for chestnuts. The growers will need to continue to work with the chefs on recipe development and product specifications. However, the Southeast Iowa Nut Growers should confidently pursue this market as a means of reintroducing chestnuts to consumers.

3. *Explore Shelling Technology Options*: As mentioned above, the shelled, frozen, vacuum-packed chestnuts were the preferred value-added product by the chefs participating in the market test. This product should be the initial product form developed by the Southeast Iowa Nut Growers. In order to produce this, or any other value-added chestnut product, it is necessary for the growers to identify a means of efficiently shelling their raw chestnuts. The technology used in producing the samples for the market test was thermal blast technology. While the efficiency of the shelling for the market test was below par, however the process and technology can be easily enhanced to vastly improve the efficiency.

4. *Educate, Educate, Educate* : Consumers and chefs have a degree of familiarity with chestnuts. They don't, however, know how to shell, prepare, or eat them. The familiarity of chestnuts is a positive, but it also means most people have a pre-conceived image of their usage. Just as the turkey industry has been striving to get people to eat more turkey throughout the year as opposed to just on Thanks giving, so the chestnut industry have to work to change the image of the chestnut from that of a holiday tradition to a tasty food and ingredient that can be used throughout the year. The challenge in accomplishing this hinges on the level of familiarity consumers have with chestnuts and the extent to which chestnuts are perceived as a holiday product.

The growers have several options when it comes to educating both consumers and chefs about chestnut usage. First, they could take advantage of the American image of the chestnut and its association with the Christmas holidays. This leverages most American's image of the product, but reinforces its holiday traditions. Second, the growers could utilize people's familiarity with the chestnut to prompt trial but promote chestnuts in applications such as desserts, soups, or simply as a snack that would likely lead to more year-round usage. Finally, the growers could take advantage of the chestnut's European and Asian heritage and market them as an ethnic food. This would be difficult given the familiarity of the word 'chestnut' in the US as well as potential confusion with water chestnuts.

The Food Processing Centre recommended a combination of the first and second approach. The holiday season is a perfect time to generate trial of chestnut products and dishes. While marketing chestnuts in supermarkets would result in meaningful sales, promoting the use of chestnuts in restaurant dishes during the holiday season will not only achieve broader consumer trial of a chestnut product but also increase the likelihood the experience will be a positive one. While a chestnut stuffing would be an appropriate holiday menu item, the growers should encourage chefs to prepare additional chestnut-based dishes such as desserts, soups, etc. By first encouraging consumer trial of a dish made with chestnuts, the growers have laid the foundation for additional consumer education and usage throughout the rest of the year. Consumers will have a reference point for chestnuts and should potentially be more open and interested in purchasing and consuming them. Educating consumers generally involves sampling. They like to 'try before they buy' and this is especially true with a product with which they have limited experience. This is the start, however, to generating consumer purchases in supermarkets and consumption at home.

5. *Continue and Expand Marketing to Asian Markets in U.S.*: Chestnuts have not only a strong European heritage, but also an Asian one. As seen in the production and import data, most of the world's chestnuts are produced in China and imported into Japan. The US Asian population is currently 4.2 per cent of the US population at 11.9 million people; however, it is growing 5-6 times faster than the overall population. In an informal survey of ethnic Asian restaurants, it was determined there was strong interest in chestnuts. Interestingly, though, the chefs at Asian restaurants were not interested in the chestnuts for their restaurants, but rather for their own personal use. While the Southeast Iowa Nut Growers are identifying and/or refining a technology for shelling the chestnuts for value-added applications, a ready market appears to exist for raw, unshelled domestically produced chestnuts in the Asian population. The growers should pursue this market with their existing crop of chestnuts while the rest of the American market develops.

6. *Focus on Product Quality and Taste*: The chefs involved in the market test, consumers interested in local foods, and chefs from the Chef's Collaboration all indicated that product quality and taste were areas of immense importance when deciding what food products and ingredients to purchase. The Southeast Iowa Nut Growers must

continue to grow and produce a product with superior taste and quality attributes. This is paramount not only when striving to broaden a product's market, but also when attempting to create a brand for that product. Chefs participating in the market test also thought chestnuts were perceived to be unique. Chestnuts could be a marketer's dream-product familiarity combined with perceived product uniqueness. The growers should work hard to promote the chestnuts quality, uniqueness and locally produced heritage.

As stated in the beginning of the recommendations, the Food Processing Centre believes the Southeast Iowa Nut Growers have an excellent market opportunity with value-added chestnut products; however, several issues must be resolved. First, the growers must identify an *economically feasible* method of shelling the chestnuts. This is the key to profitably entering the foodservice market. While the chefs indicated a high degree of satisfaction with the chestnut samples, price will always be an issue. Second, activity A does not always lead to result A. In other words, if chefs begin to use chestnuts on their menu on a regular basis, it is not a guarantee that consumers will automatically follow through with purchasing them from other outlets. The growers likely face a long road in educating the consumer, foodservice and retail markets about the use of chestnuts. This is not a task that can be accomplished overnight, but it is one that the growers must begin immediately.

REFERENCES

1. Rosengarten, F. (1984). *The Book of Edible Nuts*, Walker and Company, New York.
2. Tutin, T.G., Heywood, V.H., Burges, N.A., Valentine, D.H., Walters, S.M. and Webb, D.A. (1964). *Flora Europea*, Vol. 1, University Press, Cambridge.
3. Jaynes, R.A. (1961). *Buried-in-arch Technique for Rooting Chestnut Cutting*, Proc. Nor. Nuth Grow. Assoc., 52, 37-39.
4. Jaynes, R.A. (1964). *Grafting Chestnut without Stock Plants*, Pco. Nor. Nut. Grow. Assoc., 55, 16-20.
5. Menninger, E.A. (1977) and Payne *et al. op. cit.*
6. Ryall, A.L. and Pentzer, W.T. (1974). *Handling, Transportation and Storage of Fruits and Vegetables*, The AVI Publishing Company Inc. Westpoint, Connecticut and Payne *et al.* (1983), *op. cit.*
7. Dewan, M.L., Nautiyal, M.C. and Shah, V.K. (1992). *Nut Fruits for the Himalayas*. Concept Publishing Company, p. 76.
8. Payne, J.A., *et al.*, (1983) and Rosengarten, F. (1984), *op. cit.*

19

WORLD MACADAMIA NUT ECONOMY

Introduction

Macadamia Nuts are dealt with in two chapters. This chapter deals with the general agronomic-production aspects, followed by review of the world macadamia economy and the country case studies for major producing countries. These include Australia, South Africa, Guatemala, Costa Rica and Brazil. The next Chapter analyses Macadamia Production in Hawaii and Southern California in the USA and also assesses the impact of US-Australia Free Trade Agreement on Hawaii's Macadamia Nut Industry.

Distribution and Ecology for Macadamia Nuts

The genus *Macadamia*, a member of the Proteaceae, is native to eastern Australia. Two *Macadamia* species produce edible seeds (*Macadamia integrifolia* and *M. tetraphylla*). Macadamia *integrifolia* is native to the rainforests of south-eastern Queensland, and *M. tetraphylla* occurs farther south in the rainforests of New South Wales. *Macadamia integrifolia* is more tolerant of temperature extremes than *M. tetraphylla*. The flowers are borne in pendulous racemes. Flower colour ranges from white to cream in *M. integrifolia* and cream to beige in *M. tetraphylla*. Hybrid flower colours range from cream to pink. Both species are insect pollinated. Bee pollination is normal in California.

Macadamia tree were introduced to Hawaii in 1880s for growing as windbreaks. The commercial potential as a dessert nut was developed by the University of Hawaii in the 1930s although a plantation had been established in Australia as early as 1888; recent plantations have occurred in California, Florida, Jamaica, Mexico, Guatemala, El Salvador, Costa Rica, Colombia, Venezuela, Brazil, Peru, Ethiopia, Kenya, Tanzania, Malawi, Zimbabwe, South Africa, Thailand, China, Indonesia, Tahiti, Samoa, Fiji, New Caledonia, New Zealand and Israel. The optimum temperature is 25°C; and mature trees are frost tolerant for short periods down to –6°C, longer periods or lower temperatures are fatal. The developing inflorescence is susceptible to frost while the critical temperature above which flowering is suppressed is 20°C. [1]

Description

A spreading, evergreen tree up to 10 m tall; leaves in whorls of 3, simple, entire 10-28 cm long, new leaves pale green (in whorls of 4 and margins serrate with *ca.* 40 per margin, new leaves pink to red in the closely related *M. tetraphylla*). Inflorescence 10-15 cm long with up to 200 creamy white flowers (racemes up to 30 cm long and bearing more than 500 reddish pink flowers in *M. tetraphylla*). Follicles 1-sutured, only 1 out of 2 ovules develops (rarely both, then whole kernel difficult to extract). Fruit borne in hanging clusters of 12 or more, globose, 2-3 cm in diameter, exocarp fleshy, dehiscing on the tree; endocarp very hard, kernels globose.[2]

Cultivation

Macadamia prefers well-drained soils, sheltered from strong winds and a mild, frost-free, sub-tropical climate with a well distributed annual rainfall of at least 1200 mm. Plantations from seed start profitable bearing after 7 years, with productivity peaking after 15 years; the economic life of the tree being 50 years. At full production the yield is from 23 to 70 kg in-shell nuts per tree. Desirable clones may be developed by grafting. The species is cross-pollinated, therefore desirable that at least two cultivars are grown in orchards, preferably in alternate rows. The presence of bees should be encouraged.[3]

Harvesting and Processing

Macadamia nut trees grow best in sub-tropical climates where rainfall is gentle and plentiful during the spring flowering season and early autumn just prior to harvest. Cold climates are not suitable for macadamias as frost can severely damage the root system, which is fairly close to the ground surface.

Most varieties of macadamia trees take approximately 10 years to reach maturity and maximum yields of nut-in-shell. Rootstock is cultivated from nursery seedlings during the first two years then grafted to create specific tree varieties prior to transplanting to the farm in years 3 and 4. Careful attention to good farm management during these formative years is critical if the long wait is to produce good commercial results. Approximately 250-300 trees are planted per hectare, depending on desired spacing, to create the neat and tidy plantations that are the hallmark of the Australian industry. Mature macadamia trees grow to heights of 12-15 metres; they have dark, shiny leaves and bear sprays of long, delicate, sweet smelling white blossoms.

The annual growing cycle takes some 9 months. The first flowering occurs in early spring with nut formation in clusters during early summer. Each spray of 40-50 flowers produces from 4-15 "nutlets" which eventually ripen into nuts. By early autumn large clusters of plump green nuts are very visible and harvesting commences in late autumn and through the winter months.

Macadamia nuts are allowed to fall to the ground naturally as shaking the trees can damage the delicate root system and negatively affect future production. Modern machinery is now used to gather the nuts and the soft outer husk is then removed on the farm before the nuts are placed in storage silos awaiting delivery to the processing plant. The hard, round, nut-in-shell is transported by truck to the factory where they are weighed and samples from each farm are analyzed by the laboratory for quality and moisture content. At a suitable time nuts are moved from storage silos to drying silos where heat is applied to dry them down from 10-15 per cent moisture to 3 per cent moisture in preparation for cracking.

After drying, a specially designed cracker breaks the rock hard shell with minimal damage to the delicate kernel. Both shell fragments and kernel travel along conveyors past an air separation system and through modern, hi-tech, electronic colour sorters, which separate the shell fragment from the kernel. These sorters differentiate between the dark brown colour of shell and the creamy colour of kernel and remove the shell fragments with a burst of compressed air. A final hand sorting inspection is carried out, to remove poor quality kernel, just prior to grading the kernel for packing.

Macadamia kernel is graded into "Styles" numbered from 0 to 8, which represents sizes of the kernel pieces. Style 0 is large whole kernel, style 2 is a mixture of wholes and halves, style 4 is primarily half kernels and higher numbers relate to various sizes of chips and small pieces. Once sorted into styles the kernel is vacuum packed into poly lined, foil bags then into sturdy shipper cartons ready for sale to manufacturers of various value added products such as chocolates, biscuits, snack packs and ice cream.

Post-Harvest Treatments

Freshly harvested nuts contain up to 30 per cent moisture in the husk and 10-25 per cent in the rest and it has to be removed within 24 hours if possible to prevent mould. The husk is removed by husking machines and initially dried to 10 per cent moisture before delivery to the processor. The in-shell nuts are then reduced in stages to about 1.5 per cent water content in drying ovens for long-term storage, efficient cracking and more complete removal of whole kernels. The dried nuts are then shelled in stainless steel drums and the kernels separated by a combination of sieving and air blasting before grading by air or water flotation. The final product is either lightly roasted and salted or packaged raw in vacuum-filled, foil laminate bags.[5]

Table 19.1: Nutritional Value per 100 g of Roasted in Oil and Salted

	Macadamia	*Pistachio*
Water (%)	2.00	4.00
Food energy (kJ)	3,064.00	2,465.00
Protein (g)	7.10	21.40
Fat (g)	78.60	50.00
Fatty acids, saturated (g)	11.40	6.10
Fatty acids, monounsaturated	61.10	33.20
Fatty acids, polyunsaturated	0.14	7.50
Cholesterol (mg)	0.00	0.00
Carbohydrates (g)	14.30	25.00
Ca (mg)	46.40	135.70
P (mg)	203.60	510.70
Fe (mg)	1.80	6.80
K (mg)	332.10	1,107.10
Na (mg)	264.30	–
Mg (mg)	0.12	–
Zn (mg)	1.40	–
Mn (mg)	0.38	–
Cu (mg)	0.33	–
Vitamin A, iu	Trace	250.00
Vitamin A, RE (mg)	Trace	25.00
Thiamin (mg)	0.21	0.82
Riboflavin (mg)	0.11	0.18
Nicotinic acid (mg)	2.14	1.07
Ascorbic acid (mg)	0.00	Trace

Source: Macrae, R., Robinson, R.K. and Sadler, M.J. (1993) *Encyclopaedia of Food Science.*

Food Technology and Nutrition, Vol. 5, Malt-Pesticides and Herbicides. Academic Press, London.

Production and Consumption/Utilization

The optimum requirements for eating and processing are kernels containing at least 72 per cent oil, i.e., specific gravity (SG) <1.0; second grade kernels with SG 1.0-1.025 can be used for low grade production, while third grade kernels with SG >1.025 are commercially unacceptable. The bulk of the macadamia nuts are traditionally roasted in coconut oil and salted although dry roasting is increasing in popularity; also used in confectionery-chocolate coated kernels and nut chocolate, ice cream and baking.[6]

Nutritional Value

Kernels contain more than 75 per cent of oil, the rest being protein and little sugar but no starch.[7] The nutritional value of roasted and salted nuts compared with shelled pistachio nuts are shown in Table 19.1.

By-Products and Other Uses

Macadamia shell may be used as fuel, generating sufficient energy to dry wet in-shell nuts. Kernel oil is suitable for human consumption.[8]

WORLD PRODUCTION AND UTILIZATION

Data on world production of macadamia are rather limited. Australian Bureau of Statistics and USDA have published the data presented in Table 19.2 on world production and utilizations of macadamias in 2003.

Table 19.2: World Production and Utilization of Macadamia for 2003: (Tonnes)

Country/Region	*Production*		*Utilization*	
	NIS	*Kernels*	*Country/Region*	*Kernels (estimated)*
Australia	30,000	9,100	North America	10,880
Hawaii	22,000	5,500	Japan	3,300
Central America	17,000	3,100	Europe	3,050
South Africa	12,500	3,400	H.K./China	1,650
Kenya	8,800	1,000	Australia	1,200
Malawi	4,000	1,000	Exporter-own consumption	1,950
Zimbabwe	900	120	Committee Carry-over	1,200
Total	95,200	23,220	Total	23,220

Source: Australian Macadamia Society: http://macadamias.org/index.php? p=8

In 2003 Australia, the top macadamia-producing county accounted for 31.5 per cent of the world output. Hawaii's share was 23.1 per cent, followed by Central America, with 17.9 per cent share, and South Africa 13 per cent share. As regards the utilization, North America, mainly the USA is the major consumer of macadamia kernels, accounting for 46.8 per cent of global utilization. This was followed by Japan that accounted for 14.2 per cent of the total. Other countries utilized rather limited quantities.

For 2004-05 world output is estimated at approximately 99,000 tonnes. In terms of kernels the output is estimated at equivalent to 23,900 tonnes, of which 50 per cent is consumed in USA. The major exporter is Australia, producing about 35 thousand tonnes of macadamia NIS. USA (Mainly Hawaii), the second largest producer in the world has an annual production of 22,000 tonnes, or near by 26 per cent of the world production. Considered a gourmet delicacy, it is, with pine nuts and pistachios, one of the world's most expensive nuts.[9]

Current world exports of macadamia NIS are around 50 000 tonnes, with Australia accounting for almost half of the global exports. The second largest exporting country is South Africa; supply around 20 per cent of world exports annually. It is followed by Guatemala (with 15 per cent share), Kenya (with 9 per cent share), USA (with 6 per cent share), Costa Rica and Brazil (with 4 and 3 per cent share respectively). The present position and future prospects for each of the major macadamia nut producing countries are discussed in below and in the next chapter.

Future Prospects

World production is increasing at an impressive rate and is expected to increase by more than 50 per cent during the next two decades. There is still only a small demand for this expensive nut and it is a crop that requires considerable initial investment. Nevertheless, the market for macadamia could be expanded considerably into Europe and Asia, where it is still relatively little known. The increase in production can be expected to result in a price reduction.

There are only limited areas in the world where the trees can be grown successfully. To date there have been no successful plantations within *ca.* 15° N and S of the equator and, unlike coffee, a suitable altitude cannot be substituted for latitude when seeking a favourable environment[10]. Obviously there is a need for further exploration for and selection of potential genotypes and a better understanding of the environmental and management factors involved.

COUNTRY CASE STUDIES

MACADAMIA NUT INDUSTRY IN AUSTRALIA

Introduction

The macadamia nut is indigenous to Australia and is sometimes known as the "Australian Bush Nut", the "Queensland Nut", or the "Bauple Nut". The Proteaceae (macadamia) family grows in subtropical climates and requires precise climatic conditions. Macadamia integriflora, the main commercial species accounting for about 98 per cent of total production, naturally occurs within 15 miles of the coast from lower Beechmont to Mt. Bauple, Queensland. Macadamia tetraphylla is native mainly to New South Wales; it has a rougher shell, and is adapted to more temperate conditions. Many hybrids have been developed.

The macadamia nut had its origins in Australia. Allan Cunningham first discovered the "Australian Bush Nut" in 1828. However, it wasn't until the late 1880s that serious cultivation of these trees began. It was only since the 1960s the Australians realized the potential of this indigenous tree nut and began local cultivation. Trees, grafted from successful Hawaiian varieties, were brought to the rolling hills of north-eastern New South Wales and south-eastern Queensland where over one-third of the world's production is now grown. Australian macadamias have developed a worldwide reputation for the finest quality, flavour and texture.[11]

Commercial production has traditionally been centered in northeastern New South Wales with some production in south-eastern Queensland. However, in recent times large areas have been planted in southeastern Queensland, which now accounts for around 40 per cent of production. New South Wales produces over half Australia's production with some small plantings existing in Western Australia. Macadamia trees require rich soils and high annual rainfall or irrigation to produce commercial quantities of nuts. The macadamia nut is harvested as nuts mature and fall during autumn and winter (March to September).

In Australia about 950 farms produce macadamia nuts commercially although this includes "lifestylers" who produce nuts in a non-commercial fashion. Commercial producers are estimated at around 800. Around 730 growers (accounting for around 90 per cent of production) are members of the Australian Macadamia Society Ltd. (AMS), which is the main industry body. The average size of farms is about 40 ha and is believed by industry sources to be increasing slowly.

Most of Australia's macadamia nuts are grown on the east coast of Australia from northern New South Wales to central Queensland. The number of commercially bearing macadamia trees in Australia is estimated at around 5.0 million, covering an area of about 17,000 hectares.

MACADAMIA KERNELS

Australia has been producing macadamia nuts in commercial quantities since 1981, when approximately 4,400 MT were produced. Production has grown steadily over the years, reaching a record 43,900 MT in 2004-05, with exports comprising about 80 per cent of total production. Currently, Australia accounts for around 40 per cent of global macadamia production.

Macadamia nuts are grown in the high rainfall coastal hinterland. Some plantings also exist in Western Australia. Northern NSW has traditionally produced the largest volumes; however, newer areas in central Queensland are increasing the proportion of total production grown in this region (Fig. 19.1).

Crop Area

Area under macadamia has increased from 6,000 hectares in 1990 to over 17,500 hectares in 2005. The average size of farms is about 40 ha, which is significantly larger than the Hawaiian average of 4 ha. A relatively large percentage of macadamia farms in Australia are owned by professional people such as doctors, lawyers, engineers, pilots, accountants and the like.

During the 1970s and early 1980s, a number of macadamia plantations were established as corporate farming ventures. Investors bought shares in schemes that in many instances were managed on a day-to-day basis by management consultants. Absentee owners who are seeking returns on their investments as well as taxation benefits are a significant feature of north coast horticulture in the macadamia, avocado, lychee and low-chill stonefruit industries.

According to industry sources, surveys have identified around 3.0 million trees that were planted prior to 1995 and are now in commercial production. Since then around 200 thousand trees have been planted per annum. The total number of trees was estimated at 5.1 million in 2005. Of the total, bearing trees numbered 4.21 million leaving around 890

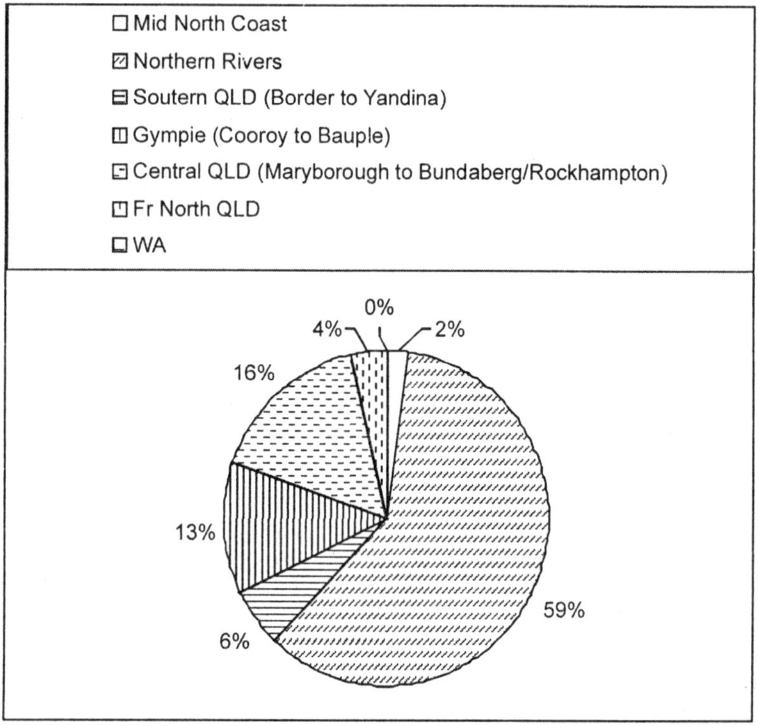

Fig. 19.1: Macadamia Nuts by Region in Australia

thousand trees not yet producing. Industry sources believe that very few of the older trees in production have been removed.

Planted area is estimated at around 17,500 for 2005, based on an historical average planting density of 266 trees per hectare. This figure includes 14,875 ha currently in production and 2,625 ha of trees which are not yet producing. The majority of new plantings is large, mostly occurring in Queensland rather than NSW, continuing the trend of increasing Queensland's share of total production.

The AMS reports that planting density has changed dramatically in the Australian industry over the last 25 years. During the 1970's planting density was around 175 trees per hectare and it increased to over 300 trees per hectare in the late 1980s due to efforts to encourage trees to bear earlier in the season. However, problems associated with over crowding has seen the planting density decrease to around 275 trees per hectare. According to AMS estimates, the industry employs about 1600 people, with 1000 being engaged in nut production, harvesting and consultancy, and the remainder in processing and marketing.

Yield

The AMS reports that mature trees yields between 20 to 30 kg NIS per tree, which is similar to Hawaiian production. However, average Australian yields are reported to be around 15-20 kg/tree NIS. Most Hawaiian trees are already mature and thus achieve a higher yield per tree than in Australia. Nearly half of the macadamia trees planted in Australia are under 10 years and have not reached full production. Average production per producing tree harvested for 2004-05 is estimated at 9.0 kg. Yields are believed to be lower in Australia for a combination of reasons. While the macadamia tree is an Australian native, the varieties selected and grown in Hawaii are not particularly adapted to Australian conditions. These varieties were reintroduced to Australia where they still dominate the older plantations.

Australian varieties are common in all newer plantations. New hybrids and selections are introduced as trials are conducted. Some growers are grafting new varieties on to old rootstock, which halves the time out of production, i.e. normally new trees take around five years to bear, this method means that the reworked older trees take around two years to bear.

Another factor contributing to the lower yields in Australia, and in many other countries outside Hawaii, is the harsher environment. Australia has larger diurnal and seasonal variations in temperature compared with the mild, equitable climate of Hawaii. Australian trees are also subject to greater variations in moisture stress. Yields are likely to increase slowly over the longer term as the average age of trees increases and management practices continue to improve.

Production of Macadamia Nut-in-Shell

There are about 800 macadamia farms in Australia, varying in size from 200 trees to huge plantations with 50,000 trees. At an average of 250 trees per hectare there are over 5 million macadamia trees planted in Australia, of which some 70 per cent are mature, yielding approximately 15 kg of nut-in-shell per tree annually. Table 19.3 provides nut-in-shell production estimates for the period 1987-2005 to demonstrate the growth of the industry over the two and half decades.

Table 19.3: Production of Macadamia Nut-in-Shell: 1987-2005

Year	Production NIS Tonnes at 10% Moisture Content (MC)	NIC Prices—$/kg at 10% MC	Year	Production NIS Tonnes at 10% Moisture Content (MC)	NIC Prices—$/kg at 10% MC
1987	4,400	3.10	1997	25,400	2.70
1988	5,200	3.95	1998	26,500	2.45
1989	6,800	3.65	1999	33,000	2.25
1990	12,000	2.50	2000	29,500	2.12
1991	10,000	1.60	2001	34,800	2.45
1992	13,000	2.03	2002	30,200	2.75
1993	14,500	2.73	2003	29,700	3.20
1994	19,000	2.80	2004	43,900	3.45
1995	17,500	3.00	2005	33,200	3.65
1996	20,500	3.05			

Kernel yields are approximately 30 per cent of the nut in-shell weight. The industry produces a wide range of products, which are sold on both the domestic and overseas markets. Australia currently exports premium grade macadamias to nearly 40 countries. Australia, which has already become the top macadamia nut producing country in the world, is likely to continue to increase its production in the near future. There are 10-12 commercial processors in the industry, however, almost 90 per cent of the processing is done by six major companies, of which the Macadamia Processing Co. Limited is the largest, processing and marketing some 30 per cent of the total Australian crop each year. It is estimated that the current value of the Australian macadamia crop on the domestic and export markets is in excess of $50 million. Supply demand statistics are available only from the USDA Agricultural Attaché's Annual Tree Nuts Reports. Table 19.4 summarizes production, supply and disposal of macadamia inshell nut basis for Australia for selected years.

Quality Assurance

Both the growing and processing sides of the industry are focused on preserving the clean, green and healthy image of Australian macadamias. This is achieved by growers working to a Code of Sound Orchard Practices and by processors adopting Quality Assurance Certification programmes to ISO 9002.

Industry Structure

Until recently the two major horticultural organizations in Australia have

Table 19.4: Australia: Production, Supply and Distribution of Macadamia, in-shell basis (Marketing year beginning March each year shown)

Item	*1992*	*2000*	*2003*	*2004*	*2005*
Area Planted (hectares)	6,020	15,038	17,160	17,500	17,500
Area Harvested (hectares)	6,020	12,030	13,790	14,045	14,326
Bearing Trees (000 Nos.)	900	3,200	4,130	4,210	4,290
Non-Bearing Trees (000 Nos.)	1,100	800	870	890	910
Total Trees (000 Nos.)	2,000	4,000	5,000	5,100	5,200
Beginning Stocks (Tonnes)	763	5,000	425	1,925	2,425
Production (Tonnes)	10,200	35,500	43,900	38,000	43,000
Imports (Tonnes)	0	0	0	0	0
Total Supply (Tonnes)	10,963	36,000	44,325	39,925	45,425
Exports (Tonnes)	8,076	25,500	34,900	29,500	34,275
Domestic Consumption (Tonnes)	2,887	8,500	7,500	8,000	8,250
Ending Stocks (Tonnes)	0	2,000	1,925	2,425	2,900
Total Distribution (Tonnes)	10,963	36,000	44,325	39,925	45,425

Source: USDA Agriculture Attaché's Annual Tree Nuts Reports, various years.

been the Horticultural Research and Development Corporation (HRDC) and the Australian Horticultural Corporation (AHC). The HRDC was responsible for research and development and the AHC was responsible for promotional activities. Both organizations were funded by levies paid by growers and received prorata government funding for specific purposes such as research and development to a maximum of 0.5 per cent of gross value of production. In 2003-04, the total amount of government funding was A$20.2 million.

The Australian Federal Government reviewed the legislation pertaining to these bodies and with industry support has merged both organizations into one. Horticulture Australia Ltd. (HAL) on January 1, 2001. HAL has been established under corporation's law as a not-for-personal-profit company. The focus of the new company is to continue marketing and promoting horticultural products in domestic and export markets as well as exploiting opportunities for uptake and commercialization of new technology.

The Government of Australia (GOA) does not provide subsidies for macadamia nut exports. The GOA provides dollar for dollar funding for research and development activities relating to the macadamia nut industry.

Research and Development

Research and development programmes are undertaken within the industry from two sources. Firstly, most large growers and processors initiate their own private research projects. Secondly, HAL the corporation established in 2001, fund research and development on the basis of equal cost sharing by industry and government up to a maximum level set at 0.5 per cent of the industry's gross level of production. HAL funds are collected from the macadamia industry via a statutory levy on all nuts processed. The Australian Macadamia Society, representing the entire industry, exerts a major influence on how, where and on what projects the HRDC funds are used.

In addition to HAL, the Australian Macadamia Society Limited (AMS), founded in 1974, represents the Australian industry with approximately 830 financial members. It is made up of nursery owner, growers, research, processors marketers, consultants, suppliers and those from a wide range of ancillary support services, as well as 40 overseas members. The AMS offers varied industry services from providing lobby group for industry issues through to research and development information dissemination through a regular news bulletin and this web also coordinates the use of industry levy funds for both research and development and promotion.

Domestic Marketing

Industry activities are funded via a levy applied to all macadamia nuts produced within Australia. This levy is set at a rate of 25.2 c/kg (Australian, kernel basis). Of this, approximately 17.3 c/kg is collected for promotional activities, 7.2 c/kg is collected for research activities, and 0.63 c/kg is collected to fund chemical residue testing.

Price

The price received for macadamia nuts by growers varied considerably. From the peak of A$ 3.95 per kg NIS in 1988, the price declined to A$ 1.60/kg in 1991 and recovered during the next five years. Thereafter for four year in a row price remained low at around A$ 2.20/kg. NIS, about ten per cent lower than in 1996. Once again price recovered sharply rising from A$ 2.12/kg NIS in 2001 to A$ 3.65 in 2005. Industry sources expected prices to remain high in the near future. According to historic industry data, the current projection for prices represents a historically high figure, but remains roughly in line with the higher prices received since CY 2003-04.

Policy

Free Trade Agreements

Australia has Free Trade Agreements (FTAs) with New Zealand and Singapore, and implemented FTAs with Thailand and the United States in 2004-05. Other FTAs are being pursued with the Association of Southeast Asian Nations (ASEAN), Malaysia, China and other countries in the region. Australia completed FTA negotiations with the United States in early 2004, with the agreement taking effect on January 1, 2005. The Australian Minister for Trade has characterized the FTA as "the most important bilateral deal that Australia has ever concluded".

Marketing Macadamia Nut Around the World

Serious marketing of Australian macadamias only began in the late eighties and the quantity produced was small compared to the volume produced in Hawaii. One or two local companies created a range of value added products, principally chocolate coated macadamias, roasted and salted snack nuts and macadamia nut biscuits. These products were marketed through the duty free stores around Australia and eventually they expanded into similar outlets in Japan, Singapore, Hong Kong and some European countries.

At the same time, the largest Australian producer, the Macadamia Processing Co. Limited concentrated on the bulk market for its sales. Everything was packed into 25 lb. cartons and sold to customers in Hawaii who needed nuts for their retail products in the off-season. (Macadamias are harvested at a different time of the year in Hawaii).

1990 was the turning point for the Australian industry. Both Australia and Hawaii had huge crops of macadamias and a glut of product eventuated. During 1991, prices fell as the few mainland USA buyers played one supplier off against the other. Marketing of bulk macadamias to industrial users in the USA had to change, the customer base had to be broadened, more demand had to be created and usage patterns would need to change if prices were to return to realistic levels that would enable both growers and processors to realize a profit from each season's crop.

The macadamia industry has always been unique in its approach to marketing. Unlike the producers of other tree nuts (almonds, walnuts, pistachios, hazelnuts, pecans, and cashews) who sell almost all of their annual production as bulk kernel, the macadamia industry has engaged in value adding and marketing at the processor level Table 19.5 illustrates the extent to which this has developed. Companies who grow and process macadamias market over 60 per cent of all macadamias as branded products.

Table 19.5: Comparative Position of Macadamia Kernel Production of Major Producing Countries

Country	*Kernel Production (Tonnes)*	*Value Added by Processors*		*Bulk Sales (Tonnes)*
		Output (Tonnes)	*% Share in Total Output*	
Australia	6600	3800	57.6	2800
Hawaii	6000	4800	80.0	1200
South Africa	1000	250	25.0	750
Kenya	900	500	55.6	400
Costa Rica	500	100	20.0	400
Guatemala	450	50	11.1	400
Brazil	140	10	7.1	130
Total	15590	9510	61.0	6080 (39.0%)

Note: Figures in brackets are percentage share in the total output.

Exports

In 1991 some 85 per cent of bulk Australian sales of macadamias were exported to the USA. During 1992 the industry focused on Asia, in particular Japan, and Europe to develop awareness of the product as an ingredient in confectionery, bakery products, snack packs and ice cream. Overseas agents and brokers were appointed to develop new business and as the industry grew more nuts the demand was created in overseas markets.

By the end of 1996 macadamia production in Australia had doubled from the 1991 level and the industry only depended on the USA for 35 per cent of its sales. Europe accounted for another 30 per cent while Asia purchased approximately 20 per cent with the rest was sold locally on the domestic market. Since then Australian exports of macadamia have increased considerably. In 2002-03, it exported 4,925 tonnes of macadamia kernels to 35 countries around the world and 6,400 tonnes of macadamia nut-in-shell to some fifteen countries. Its total exports earning from Macadamia kernel and nut-in-shell amounted to A$ 88 million (Table 19.6).

Table 19.6: Macadamia Kernel Exports by Destination: 2000-01 to 2002-03

Destination	2000-01		2001-02		2002-03	
	Volume (Tonnes)	Value (A$ "000)	Volume (Tonnes)	Value (A$ "000)	Volume (Tonnes)	Value (A$ "000)
USA	2,105	24,193	2,096	27,321	1,854	24,454
Japan	1,176	13,762	1,890	25,445	991	11,570
Belgium	555	6,675	995	13,191	671	9,199
Hong Kong	417	1,912	222	2,150	211	2,422
Germany	286	3,703	282	3,865	253	3,615
Netherlands	267	3,167	557	6,254	344	4,182
Taiwan	46	546	90	918	122	1,510
Singapore	43	538	68	892	41	605
Korea Rep.	43	464	113	1,414	52	679
Spain	29	292	18	237	44	719
New Zealand	27	300	40	358	61	871
Malaysia	25	323	36	505	27	470
Kuwait	0	0	16	135	8	123
Lebanon	21	281	56	740	37	551
Canada	17	163	33	403	60	799
Indonesia	16	187	5	66	30	430
Chile	12	85	1	12	0	0
UAE	10	158	15	315	5	85
UK	9	121	30	523	35	612
Philippines	7	90	2	20	6	90
Thailand	5	65	9	113	33	465
Denmark	5	64	1	17	2	35
Saudi Arabia	3	42	8	81	4	28
France	2	13	0.4	4	1	18
India	1	12	0	0	0	0
Switzerland	0	0	4	46	4	76
Vietnam	1	19	0.03	1	0	0
Italy	1	16	3	39	0	0
Turkey	1	20	0	0	0	0
Fiji	1	22	4	56	9	120
Guam	1	8	0.3	5	0.6	12
China	1	10	34	402	14	213
Israel	0	0	5	70	0	0
Bade	1	3	0	0	0	0
Mexico	0	0	0	0	1	15
Brunei	0.5	4	0.4	8	1	21
Samoa	0	1	0	0	0	0
Paraguay	0	0.3	0	0	0	0
Sri Lanka	0	1	0	0	0.08	2
Qatar	0	0	0.15	5	0.04	0.8
Pakistan	0	0	0	0	04	2
Morocco	0	0	0.2	4	0	0
Palestinian	0	0	0.3	5	0	0
Brazil	0	0	0	0	0.01	
NCAL	0	0	0	0	1	0.2
Total	5,132	57,270	6,634	85,622	4,924	64,004

Source: Australian Macadamia Society's Statistics: http://macadamias.org/index.

As regards exports of macadamia nut-in-shell are concerned, China and Hong Kong accounted for 98 per cent of exports each year from 2001-02 to 2002-03. Other major export destinations include Germany, Netherlands, Japan and New Zealand (Table 19.7).

Table 19.7: Macadamia Nut In-shell Exports by Destination: 2000-01 to 2002-03

Destination	*2000-01*		*2001-02*		*2002-03*	
	Volume (Tonnes)	*Value (A$, 1,000)*	*Volume (Tonnes)*	*Value (A$ 1,000)*	*Volume (Tonnes)*	*Value (A$ 1,000)*
China	4,321	9,915	5,104	14,348	6,285	23,364
Hong Kong	2,704	6,330	3,093	8,937	0	0
Netherlands	27	401	49	572	26	176
USA	108	1,316	32	540	0	0
Germany	129	1,612	16	219	31	154
Kuwait	0	0	13	18	0	0
Singapore	<1	2	9	25	1	11
Korea Rep.	4	52	2	53	0	0
Italy	0	0	2	20	5	22
Fiji	0	0	<1	11	0	0
Taiwan	18	113	0	0	0	0
Bahrain	0	0	<1	0.5	0	0
New Zealand	0	0	0	0	2	198
Japan	0	0	0	0	24	137
Malaysia	0	0	0	0	2	27
Philippines	<1	4	0	0	0	0
UAE	1	26	0	0	0	0
Saudi Arabia	1	20	0	0	0	0
UK	<1	0.8	0	0	0	0
Total	7,316	19,791	8,321	24,654	6,400	24,062

Source: Australian Macadamia Society Statistics.

In addition to marketing the tasty macadamia kernel, the industry produces very delicate cold-pressed macadamia oil, which rivals virgin olive oil in its consistency and suitability for salad dressings, sauteeing and baking. The oil is predominately mono-unsaturated and, like all nuts and their by-products, contains no cholesterol. Macadamia oil is also used in a wide range of cosmetic products; skin creams, moisturizers, soaps and massage oils.

In recent years macadamias have also become a favourite addition to many main meals, in particular the popular Asian stir fry dishes, fish dishes, salads and added to cakes and pastries. Many fine restaurants in Australia and overseas are now including a macadamia dish on their menus.

Domestic Consumption

Official up-to-date statistics on macadamia nut consumption is unavailable. Australian macadamia nut consumption, based on the USDA data, is estimated to have increased from about 2,890 tonnes in 1992 to 8,500 tonnes in 2005. Consumption data are derived from production and export numbers.

Future Prospects

The overall international trade volume in macadamia nuts and kernels is rather small compared to other nuts. However, trade sources believe that demand could increase substantially as consumer awareness of this premium nut rises. The macadamia nut is consumed as a snack (roasted and salted nuts) or as nuts in chocolate and ice cream. Promotion, regular supplies and lower prices could result in further openings of macadamia in the main developed country markets. With the economic liberalization policies adopted by several developing countries, several multinational food companies, including the bakery and the ice-cream sectors, are likely to lead to increased demand for nuts including macadamias. Australia, which is the top macadamias producing country, has an added advantage of its well-established infrastructure in the macadamia industry. Its yields per tree and per hectare for macadamia nuts are also high. Excellent growth in markets such as Japan and Europe have seen tonnages to these destinations more than doubled between CY 2000 and CY 2003. These markets are likely to continue to grow relatively in the future. To meet the expected increased domestic and international demand, Australia can boost its production considerably. The production of macadamia NIS, which rose by more than 7 per cent per annum in Australia during the last ten years, are expected to double during the next two decades, to reach around 65,000 tonnes by the year 2025.

MACADAMIA NUT INDUSTRY IN SOUTH AFRICA

Production

South Africa imports more tree nuts than it produces. The fastest growing tree nut industry is Macadamia nuts, with production volume ranking third among the largest world producers. Both Hawaii and Australia are South Africa's major macadamia competitors in European market. Macadamias are mainly grown in four production areas, namely:

1. The Levubu area, which includes the districts of Levubu, Louis Trichardt and Venda.
2. The Tzaneen area, which includes Tzaneen and Duiwelskloof.
3. The Lowveldt, which includes Nelspruit, Baberton, White River, Hazyview and Malelane.
4. Kwazulu Natal, which includes the districts of Port Shepstone and Port Edward.

Total area planted to macadamia nuts increased from 3,830 hectares in 1993 to 7,000 hectares in 2005. The majority of South African macadamia growers (60%) have between 1,000 and 10,000 trees, 7 per cent of the growers have more than 10,000 trees, and the balance, 33 per cent of the growers are farming with less than 1,000 trees. Many of the growers in the last category have other sub-tropical fruit trees, such as avocado, banana, litchi and mango as their primary crop with macadamia as a secondary crop.

South Africa currently accounts for less than 15 per cent of the world macadamia NIS production. Production increased about 85 per cent between 1987 and 2001 as a result of the estimated 300,000 trees planted in the 1980s, which came in full production after 1995. Since 1995 production of macadamia NIS increased further from 2,200 tonnes in 1995 to 17,920 tonnes in 2005. The long-term upward annual trend in macadamia production is continuing. Expansion includes the establishment of about 600 hectares macadamia orchards during 1999 and 2000 in Maclands of the Northern Province by Macadamia Industrial Development Corporation's subsidiary, Sapekoe. New production areas have also been established in Mpumalanga, around White River and Nelspruit and Kwazulu-Natal in the South Coast. It is estimated that 10,300 ha of macadamia trees were planted in 2004, and an additional 4,000 ha were to be planted in 2005. Table 19.8 indicates the estimated number of tree in thousands by age group as of l January, 2003.

Table 19.8: Number of Trees ('000) by age Groups

Age Group in Years	*2000*	*2001*	*2002*	*2003*
0 – 5	1,231	1,464	1,586	1,789
6 – 10	436	528	572	638
11 – 20	250	288	312	348
21 +	106	120	130	145
Total	2,023	2,400	2,600	2,900

Source: USDA Agricultural Attaché's Report, South Africa, Annual Tree Report, 2003.

Table 19.9 shows macadamia production in South Africa from 1998 to 2005. Macadamia kernels output has almost tripled during the last eight years from 1,529 tonnes in 1998 to 4,400 tonnes in 2005. It represents a commendable annual increase of about 25 pcr ccnt. Tablc 19.9 also shows estimated farm gate prices for macadamia in terms of Rand/kg and A$/kg.

Table 19.9: South Africa: Macadamia Production 1998 to 2005

Year	*WIS (Tonnes)*	*DIS (Tonnes)*	*Kernels (Tonnes)*	*Farm Gate Price (Rand/kg.)*	*Farm Gate Price (A$/kg.)*
1998	6,835	6,265	1,529	5.63	2.40
1999	7,353	6,525	1,511	6.00	2.00
2000	10,889	9,742	2,461	6.60	2.15
2001	10,789	9,671	2,530	8.50	2.55
2002	11,463	10,439	2,878	13.00	2.60
2003	15,657	14,091	3,790	n.a.	n.a.
2004	12,800	11,640	4,200	n.a.	n.a.
2005	17,920	16,490	5,000	n.a.	n.a.

Source: USDA Agricultural Attaché's Report, South Africa, Annual Tree Report, 2003.

Macadamia Tree Nut Industry Profile

The South African Macadamia Growers Association (SAMAC) is a dynamic organization, funded and directed by macadamia industry growers, processors and traders. SAMAC membership has grown from 345 in 1997 to a total of 893 in 2003. The industry is export based and has tremendous growth and development potential to increase macadamia nuts production and exports. Its membership is open to anyone interested in macadamias worldwide. In South Africa, non-grower members pay an annual membership fee of $168.63/year. A grower pays an initial joining fee of $163.63 and thereafter pays production levies. International membership rate is US$ 210.00 a year. SAMAC has cooperation with other African macadamia producing countries like Kenya, Malawi and Zimbabwe. In 2001, Zimbabwe Macadamia Producers joined ties with SAMAC as a levy-paying member. SAMAC is a member of the International Tree Nut Council [INC] and hosted their 8th Convention in Cape Town in May 2002, which attracted 233 participants from 26 countries to South Africa.

In 2001, all SA macadamia factories achieved HACCP and ISO 9002 accreditation. Nine processing factories engaged in drying, cracking, sorting, packing and exporting of the nuts support the industry. Four of these factories are located in the Northern Province, with three in Levubu and one in Tzaneen, and the rest in Mpumalanga province.

Da Gama in Nelspruit has been the only macadamia oil processor in the country. Last year Sapekoe bought Zetpro's shares, the oldest and largest macadamia processing factory in Levubu, which processes about two-thirds of South Africa's macadamia production.

Marketing

Macadamia growers deliver their produce after on farm dehusking, as Nut-in-Shell (NIS) at moisture contents varying from 7 to 20 per cent, to any of the five major processing facilities. One of the processing plants is used as a toll cracking facility where producers deliver NIS. to the factory, have them cracked and packed and then market the product themselves. The plant also serves growers on a cooperative basis with the nuts then being marketed by the South African Dried Fruit Cooperative (SAD), which also markets the total production from the Lowveld Cooperative in Nelspruit. Both these plants only produce raw kernels at this stage.

Another company has two processing facilities. These factories purchase NIS on a sliding scale according to the kernel percentage, commonly called the crack out percentage. The factories produce raw and roasted kernels, which they market themselves.

Another factory also buys NIS from growers; to produce only raw kernels, which they market themselves. The final processor produces a wide variety of processed macadamia and other dried nut products, mainly for the domestic market.

Prices

Farm gate prices of macadamia presented in Table 19.9 indicate a sharp increase during the last few years. Macadamia nuts, whole and half, command higher prices in both the domestic and international markets. Only about 20 per cent of total production is of cheaper rejects, i.e. fractured nuts and lower grades, however, they are used for value-adding such as ingredients in baking, nougat making, chocolate coated macadamia nuts, macadamia butter, oil and oil-based soap, skin lotion and salad dressing.

Macadamia oil price in domestic market ranges from about R2/kg to R35/kg for below-premium and premium grades.

The Levubu factory, Royal Macadamia has embarked on a macadamia chips project, earmarking a R5 million for an oil processing plant in partnership with Centre for Scientific and Industrial Research (CSIR) Bio/Chemtek.

Consumption

South African tree nut processors, mainly for macadamia, basically crack and shell the nuts. A small amount of the nuts are value-added, either by in-shell flavouring/seasoning or roasting the nuts. Tree nuts are sold to local retailers/wholesalers packed in small plastic bags as snack foods. Lower graded nuts are crushed for butter and oil, used for salads, cooking and cosmetics, like luxury soaps. However, South Africa does not have enough facilities for oil processing, and the steady increase in production for macadamia nuts will create demand for more value-added products.

Health awareness plays a major role also in local marketing. In 2004, the industry embarked on two promotional programmes targeting health and consumer awareness to term the macadamia nut "The health nut" and "the world's famous nut". The promotion for macadamia oil went well in Durban's outdoor market, as the consumers preferred the macadamia oil to olive oil, even though the price for a 500 ml bottle was R2 higher.

Domestic consumption sales are still a bit of a mystery as there are numerous small growers selling nut in shell and kernels at roadside stalls while the informal hawkers also seem to have a ready supply of nuts in shell available. Annual sales in the domestic market have increased from 75 tonnes in 1996 to 125 tonnes kernels in 2005. However, despite this increase of the total production only about 3.9 per cent of macadamia nuts were sold to the local markets in 2004, while 4.7 per cent is estimated for 2005. Coated nut products (e.g. coconut, honey, sesame, or brown sugar) with retailers are mainly imported products packaged both internationally and locally. The baking industries and confectionary shops use chaffed and cracked macadamia and other tree nuts. Table 19.10 shows demand/supply utilization for macadamias in South Africa for selected years.

Table 19.10: South Africa: Production, Supply and Disable of Macadamia, In-shell Basis (Marketing year Beginning January each year shown)

Item	*1993*	*2000*	*2003*	*2004*	*2005*
Area Planted (hectares)	3,830	6,000	6,900	10,300	14,300
Area Harvested (hectares)	n.a.	2,900	3,100	3,150	3,440
Bearing Trees (000 Nos.)	460	840	1,080	1,100	1,200
Non Bearing Trees (000 Nos.)	305	1,560	1,720	1,800	1,880
Total Trees (000 Nos.)	765	2,400	2,800	1,900	3,080
Beginning Stocks (Tonnes)	n.a.	300	550	567	527
Production (Tonnes)	1,260	9,700	15,567	12,800	17,920
Imports (Tonnes)	0	0	0	0	0
Total Supply (Tonnes)	1,260	10,000	16,207	13,367	18,427
Exports (Tonnes)	684	9,200	15,040	12,240	17,120
Domestic Consumption (Tonnes)	300	500	600	600	700
Ending Stocks (Tonnes)	384	300	567	527	627
Total Distribution (Tonnes)	1,260	10,000	16,207	13,367	18,427

Source: USDA Agriculture Attaché's Annual Tree Nuts Reports, various years.

Export Trade

The South African Macadamia Growers Association (SAMAC) is export oriented with more than 90 per cent of its production sold in international markets annually. According to the US statistics report, South Africa's total exports of tree nuts to the US reached US$ 18.114 million between January to November 2004. This is the highest import level by the U.S. since 1970. South African imports from the US increased to US$ 3.446 million in January to November 2004, also the highest import level since 1970. In CY 2003, imports from the US reached US$ 3.194 million.

No official figures exist for volumes and destinations of exports as Macadamia nuts are not listed separately in the official South African trade statistics, but tariff number 0802.90 apparently consists mainly of macadamia Kernels. According to industry sources the value of exports trebled from R14.7 million in 1995 to R 43 million in 1997, and continued to expand thereafter at a fast pace. Total export volume of macadamia nuts in terms of NIS have risen from 685 tonnes in 1993 to 17,120 tonnes in 2005. Based on an average export price of US$ 12.50/kg. for macadamia kernels export earrings totalled R190.5 million (i.e. US$ 32.12 million) in 2005. USA is the major market accounting for 50 per cent of total kernels exports, followed by Japan, which imports about 12 per cent of the total shipments (Table 19.11).

Table 19.11: South Africa: Macadamia, WIS Exports (Tonnes)

Country	*2000*	*2001*	*2002*	*2003*	*2004*
North America	6,140	5,775	5,720	7,573	6,130
Europe	2,100	2,835	2,640	4,885	3,920
Asia	1,092	1,260		541	490
Japan	(Including in others)		1,650	1,648	1,350
Others	3,194	4,095		7,074	5,760
Other not listed	208	156	990	394	350
Grand Total	9,542	10,026	11,000	15,041	12,240

Source: South African Macadamia Association.

Export prices for 2004 were lower and remained stable in 2005. The 2005 export prices, depending on the size and grades in the markets, increased by 13 per cent from last year. One processor estimated prices for deliveries to have averaged from US$ 12.50–US$ 13.70 a kilogram. Premium grade kernels ranged between US$ 13.25/kg-US$ 13.50/kg, while the price of lowest grade was at around US$ 11.15/kg-11.30/kg. Even though planted area is expected to increase, many farmers are concerned about current land restitution claims.

The macadamia exporters are still fragmented, with individual companies developing customer bases in their export markets, both nationally and internationally. However, the industry association is more concerned about the effect of fragmentation especially on quality and general representation of the South African products to the international markets.

Crop Quality Assurance

Minimum quality standards were implemented in 1994. Each consignment of macadamias sold is tested according to the quality parameters and a certificate detailing the results is issued which is included in the shipment documentation. The minimum quality standards for South African macadamias are as follows:

Moisture content:	Maximum 1.5 per cent
Peroxide value:	Maximum 3 meg/kg.
Free Fatty acids:	Maximum 0.5 per cent
Coliforms:	Maximum 200 per gram
E. Coli:	Maximum 3 per gram

These minimum standards ensure the health and safety aspects of macadamia kernels. Physical quality standards such as size of kernel and percentage whole kernel as described by the word Style' were not described in the minimum standards, as the Style' definition can be specified by the buyer. An example of Style' specifications follow:

Style	*Size Limits*	*Whole Kernel %*
0	Min. 19 mm	Min. 90 %
1	16-19 mm	Min. 90 %
2	14-19 mm	Min. 50 %
3	12-16 mm	Max. 10 %
4	9-14 mm	—
5	6-9 mm	—
6	6-12 mm	—

Policy

There is no clearly stated government policy for fostering the macadamia industry. There are no export incentives or rebates applicable for the export of either roasted or dry kernel; and also as signatory to the General Agreement on Tariffs and Trade, South Africa applies no import tariffs to macadamias, or other dry nuts, except for cashew nuts which carries a 4 cent/kg., duty.

Government assistance to the industry comes in the form of the Agricultural Research Council's commitment to the funding of research, conducted at its Institute for Tropical and Sub-tropical Crops (ITSC) situated at Nelspruit. Research needs for the industry are identified and prioritized annually by the SAMAC research committee, and a large portion of SAMAC's funds, collected from members, is allocated to partially fund the research programme.

MACADAMIA NUTS INDUSTRY IN GUATEMALA

Introduction

Guatemala accounts for 10 per cent of the world macadamia nut production. There are over 350 macadamia producers in the country, ranging from small to large plantations. Most of the macadamia production is intermixed with other crops such as bananas, plantains, beans etc., but according to producers most of it is now being intermixed with coffee as shade for the coffee plant. With the decline of coffee prices farmers have been turning to macadamia production and yield improvements to compensate for the loss in income. Several years ago coffee prices were high and many coffee producers invested in improved agricultural practices in coffee plantations so they have not to invest much more on agricultural inputs to improve macadamia production.

The majority of macadamia plantations in Guatemala are at intermediate elevations along the Pacific slope, in the departments of Sacatepequez, San Marcos, Quetzaltenango, Suchitepequez, Santa Rosa, Huehuetenango, Solola, Alta Verapaz and some in Quiche. Guatemalan macadamia nuts are harvested throughout the year, but peak months are May, June, July and August. Flowering begins between late August and early September but most flowering occurs during the months of October, November and December.

Macadamia Area and Production

Area under macadamia nut has increased from 3220 in 1996 to 4463 hectares in 2005. Harvested area has increased from 1,000 hectares in 1996 to about 2,390 hectares in 2005. According to Ministry Agriculture estimates production rose from 2,270 tonnes in 1996 to a record 7,335 tonnes (wet-in-shell basis) in 2004 but declinced slightly to 6,899 tonnes in 2005 (Table 19.12).The increase in international prices has motivated farmers to plant new macadamia trees and in 2004 alone it was reported that over 30,000 new trees were planted. The largest exporter (Patzulin) planted 25,000 more trees in 2004.

Table 19.12:Guatemala Macadamia In-shell Basis: Production, Supply and Demand Selected Years

Item	*1996*	*2003*	*2004*	*2005*
Area Planted (Hec)	3,200	4,097	4,463	4,463
Area Harvested (Hec)	1,000	2,042	2,390	2,389
Bearing Trees (000 Nos.)	165	349	408	408
Non-Bearing Trees (000 Nos.)	315	380	380	323
Total Trees (000 Nos.)	480	729	788	731
Beginning Stocks Tonnes)	120	50	19	19
Production (Tonnes)	2,272	6,373	7,335	6899
Imports (Tonnes)	70	0	0	0
Total Supply (Tonnes)	2,332	6,423	7,354	9818
Exports (Tonnes)	2,207	6,184	7,060	6844
Domestic Consumption (Tonnes)	15	189	210	55
Ending Stocks (Tonnes)	120	50	17	19
Total Distribution (Tonnes)	2,332	6,423	7,354	6918

Source: USDA Agricultural Attaché's Annual Tree Nut Reports: Various years.

The average output per bearing tree, which was 10 kgs, is estimated to have increased to 12 kgs, in recent years. Some increases in yields are expected in the next couple of years as new plantings begin bearing fruit, new trees are planted and older trees mature.

Inputs

Guatemala's industry is based almost entirely on smooth-shell macadamia (Macadamia Integrifolia), however Tetraphylla variety is also produced. The most popular clones planted are #246, #333, #344, #508, #660, #208, #254, #634. Some plantations have begun experimenting with a new variety called Karo, which has higher yields. Most of Guatemala's land devoted to macadamia nuts is not irrigated. The majority of plantations depend upon the rain. A few growers have attempted to implement irrigation systems but the investment is considered too high for the potential return.

Both the producer/processor/exporter companies provide technical assistance to their producers in the field. Continuously, they are searching for new technology to be applied in the field, to improve plant nutrition, plagues, diseases, flowering, yields, humidity, equipment, etc. There is little to no financing available for producers.

Macadamia nut outer-shells are used as fuel for the boilers in the macadamia processing plants. These nut-shells are also crushed and used as organic matter in gardens and in the fields.

Currently, there is only one significant producer/processor/exporter company in Guatemala, Agronomicas de Guatemala (Patzulin). They purchase macadamia nuts from individual producers for processing and export to other countries. In the past there were two companies, but one (Nueces del Pacifico) had some major financial problems and is no longer a major force. Patzulin has taken advantage of this opening and is buying from most of the small and medium farmers and controls 60-70 per cent of the export market. Macadamia processors divide the shelled nuts according to their size and appearance. The initial grading of kernels for size and colour is done by machine, with a final classification conducted by hand. Classification table follows:

Style 1 - large whole kernels
Style 2 - 90 per cent large kernels 10 per cent halves
Style 3 - 50 per cent whole kernels 50 per cent halves
Style 4 - halves

Style 5 - large to medium nut pieces
Style 6 - medium to small nut pieces
Style 7 - small nut pieces
Style 8- powder

In 2004, about 80 per cent of production was kernels ready-to-eat and 20 per cent other finished goods. For the year 2005 the same trend was expected to continue. In the macadamia industry the diversification trend to finished products such as oils, cosmetics and confectionaries continues but at a slow pace. A local liquor company is also trying to produce an alcoholic beverage from macadamia nuts, but it is in the R & D stage and is using less than 10 Metric tonnes for its research.

Exports

Guatemala's macadamia nuts are exported at 1.0 to 1.5 per cent humidity levels. Macadamia kernels are vacuum packed in 25-pound bags for export. There are no export policies that subsidize or encourage exports. Exports increased from 2,207 tonnes in 1996 to 6,844 tonnes in 2005 (Table 19.13). In 2005 around 4,487 tonnes (i.e. 66 per cent) were exported to the US and the rest were exported to Japan, Hong Kong, Sweden and Norway. Of the total, 25 per cent of exports were on a shelled kernels basis and 75 per cent as finished goods.

The average macadamia kernel export FOB price during 2004 was between US$ 2.38/lb and US$ 2.90/lb. In 2005, the average price remained steady at US$ 2.50. According to the major exporting company, their market efforts for the next five years will be to increase exports, especially to their strongest market, the United States. Producers are receiving technical assistance from the exporting companies in order to improve nut quality.

Table 19.13: Guatemala: Macadamia Exports Trade (In-shell Basis in Tonnes)

Country	*1997*	*2001*	*2003*	*2004*	*2005*
USA	2,029	4,500	5,200	5,208	4487
Japan	239	250	300	300	2
Sweden	n.a.	150	200	300	n.a.
Norway	n.a.	120	137	102	n.a.
Hong Kong	n.a.	200	600	600	870
Others	278	463	380	0	1404
Grand Total	2,546	5,913	6,817	6,510	6,844

Source: USDA Agricultural Attaché's Annual Tree Nut Reports: Various years.

Stocks

Guatemala does not hold large stocks of macadamia nuts in stock because most are exported immediately. Ending stocks for 2004 were 19 MT (wet-in-shell basis), a decrease from the ending stocks for 2003 of 50 MT (wet-in-shell basis). In 2005, ending stocks decreased again to 17 MT (wet-in-shell basis) due to a larger demand for product. In Guatemala the exporter owns Macadamia stock.

Policy

The Guatemalan Government has no policies of subsidies or assistance to producers or exporters. However, the Guatemalan Coffee Association encourages coffee producers to utilize macadamia nut trees as shade for coffee plants to help the environment and at the same time help farmers to diversify their agricultural practices and sources of income. The Guatemalan Coffee Association has provided some technical assistance.

Marketing

The market is experimenting with other finished products such as oils, liquors and cosmetics, but at this time most of the produce is being shipped as ready-to-eat kernels. Locally there are now three different brands on the supermarket shelves, however, according to supermarket executives the product rotation is still slow in comparison to other snack nuts. The brand John Macadamia was not able to survive in the supermarket shelves and was removed from the supermarkets in December 2004.

MACADAMIA NUT INDUSTRY IN COSTA RICA

Introduction

Costa Rica is a very small producer of macadamia nuts. It contributed only 2 per cent of total production by the seven major producing countries in 2001-02. In Costa Rica macadamia is produced in three regions of the country. Of the three areas are shown below, the Atlantic and the North have the largest planted area.

1. Turrialba, Jimenez, Guacimo, siquirres and Pococi, in the Atlantic region,
2. San Carlos, Sarapiqui, Tilaran, Upala and Guatuso in the northern region, and

3. Coto Brus and Perez Zeledon in the southern region.

Varieties

The varieties best suited to the country are HAES 344, HAES 660 and HAES 508. Of these varieties, the HAES 508 is the one that has given the best results. However, many varieties were planted initially, which have not adjusted very well to local conditions. Two new varieties were expected to do well in Costa Rica: Pahala 788 for higher altitudes and Purvis 294 for low areas. These varieties were used to improve earlier plantations.

The Costa Rican macadamia sector is made up of about 700 producers, two large processing plants and several smaller plants. The two larger plants are Macadamia de Costa Rica (with plantations and processing plant located in Turrialba), and Macadamia de Miravalles (which has plantations in Guanacaste and the processing plant in Heredia). There is a smaller plant called Cultivadores de la Costa, located in the Atlantic side of the country, and a company named Agronomicas Costa Rica, which exports macadamia nuts in shell to Guatemala.

Crop Area

The Costa Rican macadamia sector faced a serious crisis that started in the early 1990s when prices declined substantially and affected many producers who partially or totally abandoned their plantations. There are no official estimates of area planted to macadamia nuts in Costa Rica. According to industry sources, however, area planted has declined as a result of abandonment of plantations by producers as well as change of land use. Many producers have decided to switch production to other crops as a result of low prices received and the length of time necessary to reach full production. Industry sources also indicate that there are no plans for new macadamia plantations.

During 1995, several large macadamia plantations were eliminated without new areas being planted. Some large producers (La Francia and Atirro) substituted their macadamia plantations for pineapples and other crops due to financial problems that did not allow them to maintain their macadamia plantations. No new areas are expected to be planted in the short-term as macadamia is a long-term investment and the sector is only coming out of a period of crisis.

The area planted to macadamia nuts has declined from 6,500 hectares in 1993 to 4,250 hectares in 1997 and 3,500 hectares in 2000, the latest year for which the data are available. Of the total area planted in 2000, about 2,250 ha. were currently in production yielding about 0.9 MT of in shell macadamia per hectare. Macadamia production is mainly for export, although the domestic market is growing rapidly.

The number of trees planted per hectare range between 160 and 200 in most of the area planted in the country. Macadamia de Miravalles (about 625 ha.) plants an average of 300 trees/ha. Yield per harvested hectare is around 0.8 to 0.9 tonnes and per bearing tree is barely 4 kg. of macadamia in-sell term.

Inputs

The majority of the macadamia plantations are located in rainy areas, therefore, irrigation is not necessary. However, because of the strong rains during 1995, better drainage was needed in some farms to prevent excessive moisture. Macadamia is harvested by hand in Costa Rica, and other cultural practices are carried out by labourers, including cleaning of the plantations, pruning, and fertilization. Labour supply is adequate in the macadamia plantations (although there are shortages in other agricultural activities) because the work is considered to be "easier" than harvesting coffee or sugar cane and because labourers receive better salaries. However, as coffee prices increased substantially during 1994, coffee workers were paid higher wages and macadamia producers in some areas experienced spot shortages of labourers during the harvest. According to personnel from Macadamia de Costa Rica, independent producers lack sufficient knowledge of some necessary post-harvest activities. The company is working with producers to solve this problem.

Yields

The average yield declined from about 1 ton/ha. in 1994 to 0.9 ton/ha. in 2000. Excessive moisture and lack of adequate care in some plantations are blamed for the lower yield. On the industrial side, the average yield also declined in 1995 from 16 per cent to 14.5 per cent that is 0.145 kilograms of nuts per kilogram of in-shell macadamia. Beside the abandonment of many plantations by producers in the early 1990s (as a result of low prices), chinches (a bug that bores into the nut damaging it) has affected macadamia areas. The bugs attack the nut during a critical period of its development or when the nut is mature. In the latter case, the nut falls off the tree or is damaged, resulting in lower quality. The processing plants are starting a research programme to try to combat the bug using biological controls rather than chemicals. On the industrial side the yields average 16 per cent, that is 0.16 kilogram of nuts per kilogram of in-shell macadamia.

Production

Production which rose from 2,500 tonnes in 1993 to 2,800 tonnes in 1995, declined to 2,000 tonnes of macadamia nuts, wet in-shell in 2000 (Table 19.14). The elimination or abandonment of macadamia areas by producers, including some relatively large farms was the main reason for the decline. In response to the low prices of the past few years, farmers (mostly independent) eliminated macadamia plantations and switched to other crops with faster production cycles. Even Macadamia de Miravalles closed and sold one of the larger farms, formerly owned by Macadamia de Costa Rica because it is located in an area poorly suited for macadamia production. This trend seems to have continued during next few years. There have been no expansion projects or new areas being planted by independent producers or by the larger established companies. Total production seem to have remained stagnant or declined even further, despite the expected yield improvement as a result of favourable weather patterns and good flowerings in some years. Production may have also perhaps increased since 2001 based on the expectation of larger area harvested. The trend towards change of use of areas planted to macadamia could result, however, in even lower production.

Table 19.14: Costa Rica: Macadamia Nut Production, Demand and Supply Balance (Area: Hectares, Tree: Nos. in 1000 and Production etc. in Tonnes)

Item	*1993*	*1997*	*1998*	*1999*	*2000*
Area Planted	6,500	4,250	5,000	4,000	3,500
Area Harvested	2,500	3,500	3,700	2,500	2,250
Bearing Trees	450	750	800	600	500
Non-Bearing Trees	720	475	400	360	340
Total Trees	1,170	1,225	1,200	960	840
Beginning Stocks	246	855	39	530	550
Production	2,40	2,800	2,000	2,000	2,000
Imports	0	0	0	0	0
Total Supply	2,646	3,655	2,039	2,530	2,550
Exports	1,735	3,351	1,244	1,681	1,900
Domestic Consumption	700	265	265	300	330
Ending Stocks	211	39	530	549	320
Total Distribution	2,646	3,655	2,039	2,530	2,550

Source: USDA: Foreign Agriculture Service: Agricultural Attaché's Annual Tree Nut reports for Costa Rica: Various years.

Macadamia production in Costa Rica has consolidated into basically one large producer instead of two. Macadamia de Miravalles purchased Macadamia de Costa Rica and is now the only large producer in the country. There are two much smaller operations in addition to Macadamia de Miravalles. Macadamia de Miravalles decided to close the processing plant formerly owned by Macadamia de Costa Rica to process all production in its plant near San Jose.

Prices

The price received by producers is based on the international price received by the exporter (in Costa Rica the two largest processing plants also export their product). However, the strong competition for product in the domestic market has also influenced prices. During 1995 the average price received by producers was \$6.36/kg of nut as compared to \$5.10/kg during 1994. Since then average prices received by the producer have declined. While prices in 1998 were around \$3.60 per kilogram of shelled macadamia, the average price was about \$3.50 per kilogram in 1999. However, prices rose slightly in 2000. The pricing system remains unchanged, rewarding producers for better quality product and penalizing those who deliver lower quality nuts.

Consumption

Domestic consumption accounts for 25-30 per cent of production and is growing in volume. Most macadamia is consumed as snacks, although it is also used by the candy, ice-cream and confectionery industries. Macadamia de Costa Rica, the largest supplier of the local market had introduced new packaging and products during 1995. No imports of macadamia are made, although the only import restriction is a tariff of 20 per cent and consumption and sales taxes. Market opportunities are limited by good domestic availability of the nut as well as the higher cost of imported product import and transportation costs.

The domestic market is still mainly a bulk market, although sales of consumer ready product are increasing and provide processors with a higher price/margin than bulk product or even than their exportable supply. According to Macadamia de Miravalles, most of their sales are made in supermarkets frequented by higher income consumers. They are also trying to increase sales at hotels (minibars) and other tourist areas. Domestic sales increased from 265 in 1997 to approximately 330 tonnes in 2000 and are expected to continue increasing as the product is sold in more retail outlets.

Quality/Sizing

Exports of macadamia nuts are made according to international standards. Costa Rica exports "Super Macs", "Wholes", "Wholes and Halves", "Cocktail", "Fines", "Bits", "Chips", "Large Diced" and "Tidbits". We are not aware of any special requirements for imported nuts in terms of sizing.

Export Trade

Most of the macadamia produced by Costa Rica is exported. Exports of macadamia nuts increased from 1994 by 21 per cent in 1995 to 2,187 tonnes, wet in-shell basis. The export value of macadamia increased as well during 1995 to $2,665,322, from $2,198,870 in 1994. The composition of macadamia exports is shifting from almost 100 per cent bulk to a mixture of consumer ready and bulk product exports. The consumer ready products exported during 1995 by Costa were Chocolate covered Macadamia, Giant Macadamia, Macadamia Brittle and Salted Macadamia. In the future, the processing plants expect to increase the share of finished product exports and reduce the volume of bulk product export.

According to GOCR trade data for calendar year 1999, Costa Rica exported 3,375 tonnes shelled macadamia, equivalent to 1,681 tonnes of in-shell nuts. Export volume was 2,499 tonnes (shelled) or 1,244 tonnes of in-shell nuts in 1998. The value of exports also increased from $2,025,954 in 1998 to $2,494,973 in 1999. According to Macadamia de Miravalles, it was difficult to sell product overseas during 1999 due to a glut in the international market. Exports were 2,530 tonnes and 2,550 tonnes of in-shell nuts in 2000 and 2001[12]. Macadamia de Miravalles had planned to open marketing office in Florida to sell macadamia nuts as well as other Costa Rican export products.

The United States remain the most important market for Costa Rican macadamia, although exports are also made to Europe and Japan (Table 19.15). The trend, according to the two larger processing plants, is to export more consumer ready product and fewer products in bulk. Both companies are exporting canned macadamia for snacks in different presentations (chocolate covered, giant macadamia, and macadamia brittle).

Table 19.15: Costa Rica: Macadamia Export Trade Matrix: Selected Years (In tonnes)

1993		*1997*		*1998*		*1999*	
Country	*Qty.*	*Country*	*Qty*	*Country*	*Qty.*	*Country*	*Qty.*
US	1,222.7	US	2,536.1	US	899.0	US	1,290.5
Guatemala	258.2	Germany	628.2	France	146.2	France	247.6
Belgium	128.6	Netherlands	59.1	Barbados	5.4	Germany	97.7
Germany	119.4	Peru	14.7	Spain	2.6	Venezuela	20.2
Japan	75.1	Total Others	815.0	Peru	2.5	Spain	9.6
Total Others	375.0	Grand Total	3,351.1	UK	0.4	Total others	375.0
Grand Total	1,804.0			Total Others	345.3	Grand Total	1,681.0
				Grand Total	1,244.3		

Costa Rica does not import macadamia nuts, although there are no quantitative restrictions, minimum import prices or variable levies. The tariff on fresh macadamia nuts is 19 per cent plus 1 per cent fixed tax, no sales tax applies. Dried or processed product pays a 10 per cent selective consumption tax and a 15 per cent sales tax in addition to the tariff and the fixed tax.

Export Incentives

There are no new export incentives. The only GOCR export incentive provided to macadamia exporters is a tax rebate of about 15 per cent of the FOB value of the export ("CATS" are tax rebates provided for non-traditional exports). However, this incentive was eliminated for new exporters by the GOCR in December 1992, and only firms, which had the right to the rebate prior to its elimination, continued to receive it until 1999, when the programme ended.

Stocks

In Costa Rica macadamia stock levels are usually low as the product has a quick turnaround. Also due to the strong competition in the Costa Rican market among the processing plants and because of the production cycle, stocks are usually low at the end of the year and throughout the first months of the year. End season stocks represent about 12 per cent of the annual supplies.

MACADAMIA NUT INDUSTRY IN BRAZIL

Introduction

Macadamia nuts were initially introduced into Brazil in 1955. However, commercial plantings first began in the late 1970s in Bahia and Sao Paulo with seeds imported from Hawaii. All varieties of macadamia nuts cultivated in Brazil originated from Hawaii. The second phase of commercial plantings of macadamia nuts in Brazil occurred between 1982 and 1985 in Espirito Santo, Bahia, Rio de Janeiro and Sao Paulo. The third phase of commercial plantings occurred from 1990 through 1993 in Sao Paulo, Espirito Santo, Bahia, Minas Gerais, Goias, Rio de Janeiro and Parana (Table 19.16). This phased resulted from favourable international prices for macadamia nuts and alternatives to low prices offered for coffee and citrus products. Sao Paulo Macadamia Nuts Growers Association—APROMESP, represents about 80 per cent of all Macadamia nuts growers in Brazil.

Table 19.16: Brazil's Plantings of Macadamia Nuts for Commercial Use

Phase	*Years*	*Number of trees*	*Area in Hectares*
I	1978 - 1990	100,000	800
II	1982 - 1985	150,000	1,200
III	1990 - 2000	840,000	4,500
Total		1,090,000	6,500

Source: The Sao Paulo Association of Macadamia Growers.

In most macadamia orchards, producers intercrop with papaya, passion fruit or coffee. Because the majority of orchards are of recent origin, there are no reports of major disease problem. Flowering occurs in July. Fruit development occurs in August-October. The harvest period is February-April.

Crop Area

The area planted with macadamia trees has increased from 800 hectares to 6,500 hectares in 2000. Of the total 2,950 hectares are in production. Sao Paulo accounts for 35 per cent of Brazil's area planted to Macadamia trees, followed by Bahia, Espirito Santo and Minas Gerais. Approximately 80 per cent of the area planted uses varieties from Hawaii, such as 344, 600, 246, 800, 741, 788 and 506. The remaining 20 per cent of area planted is seeded with varieties developed in Brazil.

Since 1992, the drop in prices for macadamia seedlings from US$10.00 to approximately US$3.00 per tree, favoured new planting. The cost to establish macadamia orchards in Brazil is estimated at US$1,600 per hectare, not including the land. The return on investment is expected after the eight year. The annual cost to maintain a hectare is estimated at US$250 until the sixth year, and after that it increases to about US$ 500 per year.

Table 19.17 shows comparative costs of production between Sao Paulo and Hawaii. Although based on a theoretical study, it implies that macadamia production costs in Sao Paulo with yields between 5,000 kg and 7,000 kg of nuts per hectare, represent only 46 to 50 per cent of the production costs estimated for Hawaii, using manual harvest. These differences are derived basically from the land costs, which in Hawaii are 6.72 times higher than in Sao Paulo, and from labour costs. The labour costs used in the study for Hawaii were US$ 5.00 to US$ 7.00 per hour, while in Sao Paulo they were US$ 0.60 to US$ 1.20 per hour.

Table 19.17: Comparative Production Costs of Macadamia, Sao Paulo and Hawaii.[1]

Sao Paulo[2]		Hawaii[3]	
Yield (kg./ha.)	Cost of Production (US$/kg.)	Yield (kg./ha.)	Cost of Production (US$/kg.)
2,800	1.09	5,828[A]	1.83[B]
3,500	0.87	6,557[A]	1.74
4,000	0.91[B]	7,285	1.40
6,000	0.69	—	—
7,500	0.56	8,742	1.22

Notes: 1. Total costs of production are estimate for orchard in production more than 13 years.
2. Costs of production for Sao Paulo use 1992 as a base and are estimated for a production model of 40 hectares, and a land cost of US$110.38/ha/year.
3. Costs of production for Hawaii use 1989 as a base and are estimated for a production model of 40.47 hectares (100 acres) and a land cost of US$741.30/ha/year (or US$300.00/acre).
A = Manual Harvesting, B= Mechanical Harvesting

Source: Sao Paulo State Secretariat of Agriculture (IEA).

Production

Since the commercial planting of macadamia in the late 1970s, production of macadamia nuts has increased sharply from 10 tonnes to an estimated 2,200 tonnes in 2000. Brazil's area planted with macadamia trees was estimated at 6,600 hectares, of which about 45 per cent were actually in production in 1998-99. The Sao Paulo Macadamia Growers Association estimated that this area should increase only slightly in the next 3 years due to the lack of government support and the lack of overall interest in this type of nuts by the Brazilian snack and bakery industries. A key individual in the industry, however, predicted that in the next 7 years most trees currently standing would enter bearing status, and that by year 2005-06 in-shell production could reach 22,000 metric tonnes. Achievement of this production level would require that yields attain the level of over 4 tonnes per bearing hectare. It seems unrealistic to achieve this production level. However, as more trees entered the bearing phase of their life-cycle, it is highly likely that production continued to increase from 2001-01 to 2005-06, for which no reliable estimates are available.

The major problems affecting production are: (a) non-existence of government support; (b) low growers' price of US$ 0.90 to 1.00 per kilogram (in-shell basis); (c) lack of attractive financing due to the high interest rates in Brazil, poor management of orchards, and occasionally adverse weather conditions. In 1998 a foreign company acquired the largest processor of macadamia nuts in marketing system, this company will pay better prices to them.

Production of Macadamia is reported in 8 Brazilian states, of which four states account for 83.4 per cent of production, with break down shown in Table 19.18. The state of Espirito Santo is now the largest producer of macadamia nuts in Brazil, followed by Sao Paulo and Minas Gerais. States of Espirito Santo and Sao Paulo states accounted for 34.4 and 33.4 per cent of the total macadamia production in 1997-98.

Table 19.18: Macadamia Area, Production by States in 1997-98

State	*Area in Hectares*		*Production (Tonnes)*	*% Share*
	Area Planted	*Bearing Area*		
Espirito Santo	2,250	1,020	550	34.4
Sao Paulo	2,150	990	535	33.4
Bahia	900	300	160	10.0
Rio de Janeiro	200	135	90	5.6
Others	1,000	450	265	16.6
Total	6,500	2,895	1,600	100.0

Source: USDA Agricultural Attaché's Report which based its estimates on interviews with the Sao Paulo Association of Macadamia Growers.

Total processing capacity is nearly 4,000 metric tonnes (in-shell basis), of which about half is utilized due to the current level of production. These plants are mostly located in Sao Paulo, one in Rio de Janeiro and another one in Espirito Santo.

Consumption

Domestic consumption of macadamia nuts is still very small, mostly due to the !ack of consumer awareness of the product. Also, Brazil is a major producer of peanuts, cashew and Brazil nuts, and these nuts have more market penetration and are more reasonably priced. Consumer preference is for imported nuts such as almonds, hazelnuts, pistachios and walnuts. Macadamia nuts are sold only in few places in major cities such as Sao Paulo and Rio, usually together with other imported nuts. Some confectionery and snack food companies are also using macadamia nuts at an increasing rate. Although macadamia nut are normally consumed as snacks, their utilization by the food industry increased in recent years mostly by the ice cream, cookie and chocolate industries. However, according to processors, the lack of awareness of the product and the high consumer price of macadamia nuts are the major constraints to expansion faced by the industry. Domestic consumption in 2000 is estimated at 880 tonnes, representing 35 per cent of the total domestic production of macadamia nut-in-shell basis.

Export Trade

The Brazilian Government does not classify Macadamia nuts under the Harmonized Tariff System as a separate export or import item, so they are in the basket category under "other nuts", which makes it difficult to report any reliable trade data. The HTS number is 0802.90.0000. There are, therefore, no official statistics on Brazil's exports and imports of macadamia nuts. The export sector is not well organized in Brazil and few exporters control exports.

Production of macadamia nuts continued to increase in Brazil as more trees entered into production. Exports became more competitive due to the devaluation of the Brazilian currency. Nevertheless commercial exports are insignificant, although according to the USDA Agricultural Attaché's estimates, which are based on discussions with major producers and traders, quantities shipped from Brazil ranged from 200 to 250 tonnes during the last four years (Table 19.19). The United States accounts for about 50 per cent of the Brazilian export market for Macadamia nuts, followed by the European Union with 15 per cent. Brazil does not import Macadamia nuts. The import tariff for Macadamia nuts is 13 per cent. The trade reports that Brazil does not have sufficient exportable supplies to meet the demand from importers, such as Japan, which wants assurances of at least two containers (22 metric tonnes each) per month. Another problem reported by the trade is that the quality of the Brazilian macadamias is not good enough to meet international standards. However, producers are investing in technology to correct the deficiencies.

Policy

There are no special federal government programmes for macadamia nut production in Brazil. However, the Government of Espirito Santo is very active in providing long-term subsidized financing for establishing macadamia orchards, mostly as an alternative to coffee and as part of a programme to intercrop macadamia with papaya and other fruits. This programme has since been suspended. The removal of the value-added tax (ICMS) on exports of all basic and semi-processed products in 1998-99 represented an additional gain averaging 14 per cent to processors, which growers hoped would be passed on to them.

Table 19.19: Brazil: Macadamia Nut Production and Exports

Year	*Area (Hectare)*	*Production (In-shell basis in Tonnes)*	*Exports (Shelled in Tonnes)*	*Imports (Tonnes)*
1989-90	N.A.	200	0	0
1990-91	N.A.	220	0	0
1991-92	3,200	260	0	0
1992-93	4,500	370	0.	0
1993-94	5,350	580	2	0
1994-95	6,000	780	5	0
1995-96	6,200	950	122	0
1996-97	6,300	1,300	130	
1997-98	6,500	1,600	250	0
1998-99	6,800	1,760	270	0
1999-2000	7,100	2,000	192	0
2000-01	7,300	2,300	211	0

Source: USDA Agriculture Attaché's Reports and author's estimates.

REFERENCES

1. Rosengarten, F. (1984), *The Book of Edible Nuts*, Walker and Company, New York; and ITC (1993): Tropical Tree Nuts. Export opportunities for the Andean Region. International Trade Centre UNCTAD/GATT, Geneva

and Macrae, R., Robinson, R.K. and Sadler, M.J. (1993), *Encyclopaedia of Food Science, Food Technology and Nutrition*, Vol. 5, Malt-Pesticides and Herbicides. Academic Press, London.

2. Menninger, E.A. (1977). *Edible Nuts of the World*, Horticultural Books Inc., Stuart, Florida.
3. Rosengarten, (1984). Macrae *et al.*, 1993.
4. Menninger, (1977). Rosengarten, 1984; and Macrae *et al.*, 1993: *op. cit.*
5. Ryall, A.L. and Pentzer, W.T. (1974). *Handling, Transportation and Storage of Fruits and Vegetables*, The AVI Publishing Company Inc. Westpoint, Connecticut.
6. Rosengarten, 1984; ITC, 1993; Macrae *et al.*, 1993. *op.cit.*
7. *Ibid.*
8. Menninger, 1977; Rosengarten, 1984: *op. cit.*
9. Rosengarten, 1984, *op. cit.*
10. *Ibid.*
11. Art Beavis: *Australian Macadamia Industry Profile*: International Marketing Manager, International Macadamias Ltd., Bruxner Highway, Alphadale via Lismore, NSW, Australia.
12. Trade Statistics in Costa Rica are shown on a shelled basis, the conversion rate used is 6.25 kgs. of in-shell macadamia per kilogram of shelled macadamia.

20

MACADAMIA NUT INDUSTRY IN THE U.S.A.

Introduction

William Purvis introduced the first macadamias into Hawaii in 1881, though the major development of the Hawaiian macadamia industry occurred after 1930. At one time Hawaii produced 90 per cent of the world's supply. Annual macadamia nut production ranged from 21,400 to 22,550 tonnes during the five-year period of 1989 to 1994. Approximately 7,100-7,500 ha of macadamia plantings were harvested during the same period.[1] Most Hawaiian macadamia production is from *Macadamia integrifolia* derived cultivars. The University of Hawaii and Hawaiian macadamia growers have actively engaged in research in macadamia cultivation and in the selection of improved macadamia cultivars. The Hawaiian industry has been diligent and aggressive in marketing and sales.

Hawaiian dominance of world production has been challenged. Australian plantings and production have expanded dramatically during the past 30 years. There are currently 20,000 ha devoted to macadamia plantings. Over 80 per cent of area is in bearing stage, and only 20 per cent is not yet bearing. In 2002 Australia overtook USA in the world production of macadamia nuts. It became the leading macadamia nut producing country. Approximately 32 per cent of world production now comes from Australia. Australian production increased from 4,400 tonnes in 1987 to 43,900 tonnes in 2004, but declined to 32,500 tonnes in 2005 (see Chapter 19). Commercial plantings in Australia were initially based on *Macadamia integrifolia* cultivars developed in Hawaii, but newer selections from Australia are now coming into production. Australia currently has the world's largest macadamia research and selection programme, and their industry is actively seeking new and expanded markets.

Macadamia orchards have also been established in Central America, Brazil, Kenya, Indonesia, Taiwan, and southern Africa.[2] Processed nuts grown in Guatemala are being marketed in the United States by one of the larger Hawaiian macadamia producers and processors. However the total world production of macadamia nuts is quite small, and it constitutes less than 0.5 per cent of the total world nut sales.[3]

This chapter deals with macadamia nut industry in the USA. It consists of three sections. Section I analyzes current position and prospects for macadamias in Hawaii. Section II deals with the macadamia nut production in South California. The final section assesses the likely impact of Australia-USA Free Trade Agreement on Hawaiian macadamia industry.

SECTION I

MACADAMIA NUT INDUSTRY IN HAWAII

Production Performance

The Hawaii Agricultural Statistics Service (HASS) collects data for macadamia nuts based on a season, which begins on 1 July and ends on 30 June of the following year. Acreage under the crop that registered a steady increase upto mid-nineties declined slightly and has stabilized around 18,000 acres (i.e. about 7,200 hectares) in recent years. Almost all the area is now in the bearing stage. Macadamia nut (shelled basis) production increased from 15,180 tonnes in 1980 to about 25,676 tonnes in 2004-05. The increase in output reflects large area brought under macadamia nut, as yield per acre seems to have remained almost stagnant, and in fact declined slightly in recent years. Table 20.1 shows the time series data on macadamia nut acreage; yield, production (in-shell), season average price and value of output from 1980 to 2004.

Production Regions

Currently eight of the 650 farms that produced macadamia nuts in Hawaii occupied 15,507 acres or 86 per cent of the industry's total area. The remaining acreage is comprised of small-scale farms. Seventy-one per cent of farms are smaller than 2.5 hectares (6.1 acres). Ninety-five per cent of the state's production is located on the island of Hawaii. Data on number of farms, acreage, yield, production, price, and value, State of Hawaii for 1996-2005 crop years, are presented in Table 20.2.

Table 20.1: Hawaii: Macadamia Nut Time Series Data: 1980-2003

Year	*Area (Acres)*	*Yield/Acre Lbs.*	*Production (000 lbs)*	*Grower Price Cents/Lbs.*	*Value 1,000 dollars*
1980	10,000	3,339	33,390	72.4	24174
1981	10,000	3,346	33,360	79.3	26454
1982	10,200	3,600	36,720	73.9	27136
1983	10,600	3,440	36,420	65.7	23928
1984	12,000	3,140	37,700	69.2	26,088
1985	13,500	3,110	42,000	72.5	30,405
1986	14,400	3,060	44,000	80.0	35,200
1987	15,600	2,740	42,700	84.0	35,868
1988	16,600	2,740	45,500	90.0	40,950
1989	18,200	2,720	50,500	89.0	44,945
1990	18,400	2,720	50,000	82.0	41,000
1991	18,200	2,720	49,500	70.0	34,650
1992	17,500	2,740	48,000	68.0	32,640
1993	18,500	2,720	48,500	68.0	32,980
1994	18,500	2,740	52,500	69.0	36,225
1995	19,300	2,620	51,000	74.0	37,740
1996	19,200	2,940	56,500	78.0	44,070
1997	19,200	3,020	58,000	75.0	43,500
1998	19,200	2,990	57,500	65.0	37,375
1999	18,900	2,990	56,500	67.0	37,855
2000	17,700	2,820	50,000	59.0	29,500
2001	17,800	3,150	56,000	59.0	33,040
2002	17,800	2,980	53,000	57.0	30,210
2003	17,800	2,980	53,000	61.0	32,330
2004	17,800	3,170	56,500	71.0	40,115

Source: USDA: Fruit and Nut Year Book, 2005. Table 12E.

In 2004-05, the statewide estimate of macadamia nut trees in Hawaii totalled 1.3 million, of which virtually all were of bearing age, 6 years or older. Macadamia nut is the third highest commodity by value in the state. Hawaii was the world's largest producer of macadamia nuts (dried, in-shell) until being overtaken by Australia in 1997. Hawaii produces 99 per cent of the macadamias in the U.S. In 2004, Hawaii produced 23 per cent of the world's macadamia nuts; compared to 40 per cent it produced in 1999.

Farm Price and Value

Farm price for net, wet-in-shell macadamia nuts seems to fluctuate from year to year. The price is influenced by the volume of world supply and

Table 20.2: Macadamia Nuts: Number of Farms, Acreage, Yield, Production, Price, and Value, State of Hawaii, 1996-2005 Crop Years

Crop Year[1]	Farms	Area		Yield	Production[4]		Farm Prices[4]		Farm Value[8]
		In Crop	Harvested[2]	Per Acre[3]	Gross[5]	Net[6]	Gross[7]	Net	US$ 1000 Dollars
	Number	Acres			1,000 Pounds		Cents/Pound		
1996-97	750	20,200	19,200	2.9	63,000	56,500	70	78	44,070
1997-98	800	20,200	19,200	3.0	65,000	58,000	66.9	75	43,500
1998-99	800	20,200	19,200	3.0	66,000	57,500	57	65	37,375
1999-2000	750	19,900	18,900	3.0	64,000	56,500	59.1	67	37,855
2000-01	650	18,400	17,700	2.9	56,000	50,000	52.7	59.0	29,500
2001-02	650	18,400	17,800	3.1	62,000	56,000	53.3	59.0	33,040
2002-03	650	18,400	17,800	3.0	60,000	53,000	50.4	57.0	30,210
2003-04	650	18,400	17,800	3.0	60,000	53,000	53.9	61.0	32,330
2004-05	650	18,400	17,800	2.9	57,000	51,000	54.6	65.0	33,150

1. Season begins July 1st and ends June 30th of the following year
2. Called bearing acreage prior to 1993-94 crop year.
3. Net production per bearing acre.
4. Wet in-shell bases, delivered to processors.
5. Gross pounds delivered for processing.
6. Gross pounds delivered for processing less total spoilage.
7. Farm value divided by gross production.
8. Net production multiplied by net farm price.

Source: Hawaii Agricultural Statistics Service, 2005.

imports from other producing countries. Smaller availability of macadamia nuts on the world in a particular year leads to rise in prices and *vice versa.* The average farm prices during the last two decades and half reached the peak of cents 90 per pound in 1989 and declined to a lowest level of cents 57/lb in 2003. The farm value of macadamia nuts varied from about US$ 45 million in 1989 to US$ 30.2 million in 2002.

Trade

While the United States is a notable exporter of processed macadamias, it is also a leading importer of macadamia products. The United States only exports prepared and processed macadamias while primarily importing shelled macadamias nuts. The USA is a net importer of macadamia nuts. Its exports constitute less than 12 per cent of its domestic production. Table 20.3 shows imports of macadamia nuts from 1995-96 to 1999-2000. US Macadamias exports for the years 1995-96 to 1999-2000 are given in Table 20.4.

Table 20.3: U.S. Imports of Macadamia Nuts: Marketing Years 1995-96-1999-2000

(Metric Tonnes, In-shell equivalent)

Country	*1994*	*1995*	*1996*	*1997*	*1998*	*1999*	*2000*	*2001*	*2002*	*2003*	*2004*
Australia	3534	5044	4712	5666	8808	10419	13091	8654	5744	7418	11701
South Africa	989	1487	1243	1485	2259	4614	6573	6454	6653	8570	7532
Kenya	495	1114	1245	1637	1074	968	65	662	760	2606	5808
China	31	164	127	262	183	88	67	1504	1116	1650	3806
Guatemala	1655	1651	1717	1732	1869	2173	2032	2070	1874	2472	3200
Others	1779	2578	2366	3576	1643	3752	4198	4011	3755	6036	6259
World	8483	12038	11409	14359	15836	22014	26027	23355	19901	28750	38307

During the last twelve years the US imported of macadamia in terms of in-shell nuts increased from 8.5 thousand tonnes in 1994 to more than 38 thousand tonnes in 2004. In recent years South Africa has become the primary US suppliers of macadamias. In 2002 South Africa surpassed Australia to become the primary macadamias supplier to the United States. However, since then Australia have regained its position and continue to be the leading supplier to this market.

As regards the value of imports and exports are concerned latest data are not readily available. The latest year for which the data are available is 2003. Total US imports for CY 2003 totalled US$ 54 million while exports were valued at are record US$ 17 million. Other notable suppliers of macadamia nuts for CT 2003 were Brazil ($ 3.9 million),

Table 20.4: US Exports of Macadamia Nuts: Marketing Years 1995-96–1999-2000

(Metric Tonnes, In-shell Equivalent)

Country	*1995-96*	*1996-97*	*1997-98*	*1998-99*	*1999-2000*
Canada	498	338	343	406	589
China	0	0	35	18	116
European Union	381	206	148	232	205
Hong Kong	580	535	726	138	438
Japan	2,719	2,882	1,400	2,210	2,478
Korea, Rep.	165	193	239	201	219
Lebanon	0	9	13	4	0
Norway	13	22	9	9	13
Philippines	4	22	0	13	22
Singapore	22	35	4	9	58
Switzerland	104	48	100	0	0
Taiwan	281	285	217	121	295
Other countries	5	17	0	54	277
Total	4,797	4,592	3,272	3,351	4,710

Marketing year: July-June.

Note: Shelling ratios for macadamia nuts are from the Hawaii Agricultural Statistics Service (HASS) and are.231.228,.230,.224 and.224 from 1995-96 to 1999-2000 respectively.

Source: U.S. Bureau of Census: HASS.

China ($3.8 million), Malawi ($ 2.7 million), and Costa Rica ($ 2.1 million). The primary markets for U.S. macadamia nuts in CY 2003 were Japan ($ 5.4 million, 32 per cent market share), Hong Kong ($ 1.2 million, 8 per cent) and China ($ 1.2 million, 7 per cent).

Domestic Utilization

As in the case of other countries, domestic utilization of macadamia is derived from production and exports. Domestic consumption of macadamias (NIS term) in the United States is estimated to have increased from 36,630 tonnes in 1997-98 to over 44,000 tonnes in 2003-04, registering 20 per cent increase in six years. However, in its Fruit and Tree Nut Year Book the USDA also gives data on per capita consumption of fruits and tree nuts. Based on the data given in the Year Book 2005, the author has worked out the following Table of total consumption of macadamias shelled and macadamia nuts in shell. Total consumption of macadamias is estimated to have trebled from 1980-81 to 2004-05 (Table 20.5). The use of macadamias in the US is expected to continue to increase at the current rate of 3 per cent per annum in the near future.

Table 20.5: Macadamias: Per Capita and Total Consumption: 1980/81-2004/05

Year	Per Capita Consumption	Total Consumption	
		Macadamia Shelled	Macadamia Nut In-Shell Terms
	Pound/annum	(Metric Tonnes)	
1980-81	0.03	3347.780	14877.532
1981-82	0.03	3349.016	14883.025
1982-83	0.04	3931.163	17470.088
1983-84	0.04	3939.035	17505.073
1984-85	0.04	4324.729	19219.096
1985-86	0.05	4957.876	22032.803
1986-87	0.05	5202.952	23121.919
1987-88	0.05	4946.012	21980.077
1988-89	0.05	5601.684	24893.882
1989-90	0.06	6739.039	29948.288
1990-91	0.06	7189.943	31952.108
1991-92	0.05	5880.143	26131.355
1992-93	0.05	5675.570	25222.235
1993-94	0.05	6223.140	27655.633
1994-95	0.06	6694.442	29750.098
1995-96	0.05	6557.148	29139.964
1996-97	0.06	6858.484	30479.103
1997-98	0.07	8255.353	36686.789
1998-99	0.07	9181.007	40800.395
1999-2000	0.08	9790.384	43508.466
2000-01	0.07	9024.832	40106.356
2001-02	0.07	9634.021	42813.590
2002-03	0.06	8270.653	36754.781
2003-04	0.08	10856.818	48247.700
2004-05	0.09	11965.000	53175.588

Source: USDA: Fruit and Tree Nuts Year Book, 2004.

SECTION II

MACADAMIA PRODUCTION IN SOUTHERN CALIFORNIA[5]

Macadamia seeds were first brought to California from Australia in 1879.[6] A number of seedlings were successfully grown in southern California subsequent to that introduction. However, little interest was shown in commercial macadamia cultivation until the 1950s when several nurserymen began to promote macadamia growing and production. One of these was Cliff Tanner who propagated a number of tropical and sub-tropical fruits and nuts in addition to the macadamia. Another was Colonel Wells Miller. Macadamia enthusiasts formed the California Macadamia

Society in 1953. The Gold Crown Macadamia Association has marketed California grown macadamias for its member growers for over two decades. Macadamia production has not attained the status of an economically important crop in California, despite efforts made by individuals to develop production. Most of the population of the region appears to be unaware that there is any commercial macadamia production in Southern California. Hawaiian and Central American produced nuts dominate the southern California market despite the fact that substantial macadamia production is possible there.

Macadamia trees grow successfully at a number of places in California. Macadamia climatic requirements are similar to Mexican or Guatemalan races of the avocado. Macadamia trees are intolerant of heavy frost. Frost damage begins to occur at -2.8°C (27°F), especially if the period of low temperatures lasts for several hours. Macadamia trees are also intolerant of prolonged periods of high temperatures and low humidity, and this precludes commercial macadamia production in the thermal belts of the San Joaquin Valley or in relatively frost-areas of the Sonoran Desert. Commercial production of macadamias is therefore located in San Diego, Ventura, and Santa Barbara Counties. Climatic conditions are also suitable in Orange and Los Angeles Counties, but those counties are now so intensively urbanized that there is little or no potential land area left for macadamia cultivation. Neither production volumes nor the land area devoted to macadamia production in California are available. There were an estimated 600-800 hectares of macadamia plantings in 1988[7] and 400 hectares were estimated in San Diego County. It appears that the area devoted to macadamia production has probably declined, but there are no accurate figures to indicate how much. Many of the producing trees have been planted to replace avocado trees that have been infected by avocado root rot (*Phytophthora cinnamomi*). Accurate estimates on the land area occupied by macadamia trees that are scattered through avocado groves are not available. Other producing trees have been planted on small plots of land around homes or on the edges of avocado or citrus groves. No one has determined the extent of area planted in macadamias in this manner, yet there is commercial production from these plantings.

Problems

Land is expensive and will become increasingly so as urbanization occurs in those areas best suited for macadamia cultivation. Agricultural land area is being lost due to rapid urbanization, and the average size of all landholdings, including agricultural acreage, is declining. The cost of the labour needed to produce macadamia nuts is higher in California than in other areas. Productivity and return must therefore be quite high to compete successfully with production in other areas of the world. The cost of irrigation water has risen steadily, and it can be expected to increase even more with increasing competition between urban and rural areas of California for finite supplies.

Conclusions

California macadamia growers have both major advantages and disadvantages that confront their industry. They must engage in a major, collective effort if the industry is to expand and be profitable. Decisive leadership and consensus regarding goals for the industry are needed. Those in the macadamia industry must expand their efforts in promotion and marketing. More studies and quantitative data regarding production and marketing are necessary. A long-term University of California research programme needs to be undertaken. More knowledge of cultivation practices, better yielding cultivars, and increased marketing efforts are all prerequisites for increased macadamia production and profitability in California.

SECTION III

LIKELY IMPACT OF US-AUSTRALIA FREE TRADE AGREEMENT ON HAWAII'S MACADAMIA NUT INDUSTRY

The impact of the US-Australia Free Trade Agreement on Hawaii's Macadamia Nut Industry is viewed by the Industry as severely negative. The removal of all the tariffs on the importation of macadamia and macadamia products from Australia is expected to lower the average macadamia kernel price in the US. This will result in a reduced price paid to Hawaii's growers. The long-term impact could be the economic failure of many growers and some of the smaller processors and manufacturers in Hawaii.[8]

Hawaii's economic base is tourist driven. The State depends upon the growth of the agricultural sector to help balance its economy. Agriculture also provides the open space and agro-tourism opportunities that a growing number of younger visitors are looking for. It is, therefore, crucial to the economy of Hawaii to maintain the viability of its agricultural sector. Hawaii's Macadamia Industry believes that the removal of the import tariffs imposed on Australia will severely weaken the industry and its economic contribution to the State.

The Hawaii Macadamia Industry is comprised of 650 growers farming approximately 18,000 acres, producing 25,676 tonnes (in-shell basis), with a farm gate value of $40 million. This does not take into account the value of the industry at the manufacturing and retail sales level estimated to be in excess of $150 million annually. Macadamia ranks fourth in agricultural commodities in Hawaii. Most of Hawaii's macadamia acreage is mature, thus future production is not expected to increase significantly. Hawaii's primary markets are the US and the local Hawaii market aimed at the tourist Trade Secondary markets are Europe and Asia.

Australia exceeds Hawaii in annual production with a significant amount of its planted acreage in the pre-bearing stage. Planting of new acreage continues. Australia's high margin markets are Europe and Asia. The US market is viewed as a high volume market with sales generally to larger importers at lower prices. The Australian Industry is primarily a marketer of bulk kernel. Retail products are sold within the country, but are not the primary mode of export. As Australia's producing acreage continues to grow, the production resulting from this growth is expected to be channelled into the US market, primarily to the low-end retail business.

Hawaii's macadamia producers and manufacturers have spent millions of dollars to develop the US market and spend in excess of $20 million annually to provide the continued market development that is crucial to health and welfare of the industry in Hawaii. The industry has also been responsible for research on the health aspects of macadamia nuts that have had a positive influence on the consuming public, thus increasing the demand. The influx of Australian macadamia kernel and manufactured products will increase the pressure on Hawaii's producers and manufacturers to increase their market development efforts at an increase in the average cost of production for Hawaiian kernel and retail products.

The import tariffs on Australian kernel and manufactured products increases the sales price of the imports thus providing somewhat of a balance in the cost of kernel and manufactured products offered into the US market by both Hawaii and Australia. The elimination of the import tariffs will provide Australia with an unfair economic advantage in the US market.

The President of the Hawaii Macadamia Nut Association (HMNA) in his statement to House of Representatives' Committee on Ways and

Means, requested the committee to consider the severe negative impact of this trade agreement on Hawaii's Macadamia Industry and he appealed that the Committee takes a position against the approval of the US-Australia Free Trade Agreement.

REFERENCES

1. U.S. Department of Agriculture (1993). *Agricultural Statistics*, Government Printing Office, Washington, DC. and Rowley, H.K.; D.A. Martin, and R. Wong (1994). Hawaii macadamia nuts. Final season estimates. California Macadamia Soc. *Yearbook*. 40: pp. 114-21.
2. Arpaia, M.L., 1994, Macadamia Situation for Selected Countries. California Macadamia Soc. *Yearbook*. 40: pp. 27-30.
3. Stapleton, A. 1995: *Australian Macadamia Industry*. Home page of the Australian Macadamia Society. (andrew@nor.com.au) Lismore, New South Wales.
4. Hawaii Agricultural Statistics Service, 2005.
5. This section is based mainly on article by McHargue, L.T. 1996, Macadamia Production in Southern California, pp. 458-62. In: J. Janick (ed.), *Progress in New Crops*. ASHS Press, Arlington, VA.
6. Ferguson, L. and M.L. Arpaia, 1990. New sub-tropical tree crops in California, pp. 331-37. In: J. Janick and J.E. Simon (eds.), *Advances in New Crops*. Timber Press, Portland, OR.
7. Cooper, T.H., 1988. Macadamia: a basic understanding, California Macadamia Soc. *Yearbook*. 34: pp.100-04.
8. This section is based mainly on the Statement given by David, G. Rietow, Hawaii Macadamia Nut Association, Keaau, Hawaii, at the US House of Representatives.

21

WORLD PECAN NUT ECONOMY

Introduction

Pecan (*Carya illinoensis* Juglandaceae) is one of the better-known pecan hickories. It is also called sweet pecan and where Spanish is spoken, as nogal morado or nuez encarcelada. The early settlers who came to America found pecans growing over wide areas. These native pecans were and continue to be highly valued as sources of new varieties and as stock for selected clones. Besides the commercial edible nut that it produces, the pecan provides food for wildlife. Pecans are an excellent multipurpose tree for the home landscape by providing a source of nuts, furniture-grade wood, and of esthetic value.

Habitat

Native Range

Pecan is cultivated in USA, Mexico, Brazil, Australia, South Africa and Israel.[1] In the US it grows principally in the lower Mississippi Valley. Within this region it extends westward to eastern Kansas and central Texas, eastward to western Mississippi and western Tennessee. Sparse occurrence has been reported along the eastern margin of its range from south-western Ohio to Kentucky and Alabama. Pecan also grows locally throughout north-eastern and central Mexico.[2]

Description

Pecan is a large deciduous tree, 50 m or more tall with ascending and outwardly arching branches. Flowers are monoecious with slender male catkins and small erect clusters of female flowers. Fruits are borne in clusters of 4-12, a globose to oblong drupe, angled and narrowly 4 winged at the sutures, 2.5-7 cm × 1.25-2.5 cm, exocarp more or less separating by 4 valves; nut ovoid to ellipsoid, cylindrical or faintly 4-angled; seed solitary, deeply divided longitudinally, somewhat grooved and convoluted, not closely adherent to the shell.

Climate

Pecan grows in a humid climate; the minimum average annual rainfall approximates 760 mm (30 in) and the maximum reaches 2010 mm (79 in). Mean summer temperatures range as high as 27°C (81°F), with extremes of 41° to 46°C (105° to 115°F). Average winter temperatures vary from 10° to -1°C (50° to 30°F), with extremes of -18° to -29°C (0° to -20°F).

Soils and Topography

Sweet pecan grows commonly on well-drained loam soils, which are not subject to prolonged flooding. It rarely grows on low and poorly drained clay flats where it is replaced by water hickory *(Carya aquatica).*[3] Pecan seedlings can survive short periods of flooding.

Cultivation

Pecan orchards are largely planted with grafted and budded trees in the southeast USA, and with seedling trees in the southwest, although there is now a trend towards selected cultivars. Over 300 cultivars have been recognized. Varietal differences range from nuts less than 0.6 cm in diameter to more than 2.5 cm and weighing from over 9 to 18 nuts per kg. Production begins at 6-10 years and can continue profitably for up to 200 years—some native trees are known to be over 1,000 years old. Yields vary from 9-27 kg per tree at 8-10 years rising to 45-68 kg at 16 years or more with exceptional individuals attaining 360 kg under unusually favourable conditions.[4]

Trees prefer a deep, well-drained soil, adequate rainfall or supplementary irrigation and a frost-free growing season of 140-210 days. A cool period is also essential in order to break dormancy; the climatic requirements vary with the variety.

Life History

Reproduction and Early Growth

Flowering and Fruiting: Flowering of pecan takes place from April through May. The specie is monoecious; flowers are borne in staminate and pistillate catkins on the same tree. Staminate flowers appear in slender fascicled, sessile catkins, 8 to 15 cm (3 to 6 in) long. Most pecan cultivars are clones derived from wild trees. Pecan is anemophilous, and excessive rainfall during the flowering period may prevent pollination.

Seed Production and Dissemination: Fruits ripen in September and October and are dispersed from September through December. Pecan fruits are ovoid, globose or pear-shaped nuts, enclosed in husks developed from the floral involucre. The minimum seed-bearing age is 2 to 4 years in some cultivars and up to 20 years for individuals in natural stands. The maximum seed-bearing age also varies considerably; a maximum of 300 years has been reported.[5] The cleaned nuts average about 220 to 350/kg (100 to 160/lb). Good crops are produced at intervals from 1 to 3 years. Seed dispersal is principally by water and animals. The floating nuts can be carried considerable distances by floodwater. Aerial dispersion is mainly by squirrels.[6]

Seedling Development: Seeds can be stored for 3 to 5 years in closed containers at 5°C (41°F) an 90 per cent relative humidity. Seed stratification and germination conditions have been reported by various authors.[7] As with all hickories, germination is hypogeal. Seeds of pecan show delayed germination, since the shell mechanically restricts radicle elongation. To overcome this delay the nuts are stratified at 2° to 5°C (36° to 41°F) for 30 to 90 days, followed by incubation at room temperature.

Under natural conditions, pecan nuts remain dormant until spring when germination starts in early April and extends to early June. Exceptionally dry weather or heavy aerial competition greatly reduces survival. On loamy soils height growth averages about 90 cm (35 in) per year for several years under favourable weather conditions.

Vegetative Reproduction: Rooting experiments with shoot cuttings gave highly variable success rates. The principal variables are time of collection, thickness and origin of cuttings, chemical treatments, and genetic factors. Softwood cuttings are easier to root than hardwood or semi-hardwood cuttings. The time of shoot collection, however, seems most important. Juvenile cuttings, taken about midway of the dormant season and dipped in 10,000 p/m indolebutyric acid, gave 100 per cent rooting; adult wood rooted 85 per cent under these conditions.[8] Commercial cultivators may be propagated by grafting on improved rootstocks.

Sapling and Pole Stages to Maturity

Growth and Yield: On loamy soils, height growth may average 90 cm (35 in) per year for several years.[9] Mature pecan is a medium to very large straight-stemmed tree reaching up to 55 inches in height and occasionally 180 to 210 cm (70 to 83 in) in d.b.h.

Reaction to Competition: Pecan is classed as intolerant of shade but more tolerant than cottonwood and willow. It is a sub-climax species. Pecan responds well to release in all age groups, provided that the trees have good vigour.

Genetics

Population Differences

Studies of variation in natural pecan stands indicated a large genetic diversity within populations. Also, there was a high degree of variation between breeding populations, indicating a close relationship (inbreeding) among trees in small stands. Genotype × environment interaction was highly significant between progeny tests of open pollinated selected trees. Heritability estimates for height growth indicated ample genetic variation to anticipate significant gains in breeding programmes.[10]

Races and Hybrids

More than a hundred horticultural clones have been listed.[11] These were selected primarily for various characteristics concerning commercial nut production. More recently several cultivars have been developed for the same purpose.

Complex hybridized natural populations are common. Natural interspecific hybridization occurs with *Carya aquatica* (C. x *lecontei* Little), C. *cordiformis* (C. x *brownii Sarg.*), C. *laciniosa* (C. x *nussbaumeri Sarg.*), C. *ovata*, and C. *tomentosa* (C. x *schneckii Sarg.*).[12]

Harvesting

Fallen nuts formerly were harvested by hand. Hand harvesting now has largely been replaced by mechanization, including tree or limb shakers, shake and catch harvesters, windrowers, sweepers, vacuum harvesters, conveyers and trash separators.

Post-Harvest Treatments

Pecans harvested mechanically have higher moisture content than nuts that have fallen naturally. Artificial drying is essential in order to reduce moisture to 4.5 per cent as soon as possible in order to prevent mould and discoloration. Dry storage is recommended for 3 weeks at room temperature to cure and reduce moisture in entire nuts to 8.5-9 per cent and to 4.5 per cent for kernels. During curing the free fatty acids and peroxide value of lipids increase and seed coat tannin oxidize to pale or medium brown, the general effect of which is to give the pecan its characteristic appearance, aroma, flavour and texture. Pecans are then stored until required for shelling at temperatures below 2°C and less than 70 per cent relative humidity in order to prevent the development of rancidity and/or insect infestation. Long-term storage should be at *ca.*-80°C in order to maximize freshness and shelf life. Any traces of ammonia during refrigeration, not detectable by odour, can rapidly and permanently blacken the seed coat but not affect the flavour. Storage facilities not using ammonia as a refrigerant are essential. Nuts are shelled using a rotary cracker, which delivers a shock wave to the pecan and explodes the shell without damaging the kernel. Shell fragments are removed using a double flotation system in addition to air separation systems and infrared colour sorting equipment.[13]

Production and Consumption/Utilization

Approximately 85-90 per cent of the crop is shelled prior to marketing, the balance being sold inshell. Shelled pecans are sold to bakeries confectioners, and to retailers, grocery-wholesalers and dairies for ice cream production, etc.

Nutritional Value

Nutritional analyses of pecans are given in Table 21.1.

By-products and Other Uses

Pecan shells are used for gravelling paths, as a fuel and as a garden mulch, stock and poultry litter; ground to a flour for degreasing aero engines, as an ingredient of carpet cleaners and as a filler in feeds, insecticides and fertilizers, soft abrasives in hand soap, non-skid paints and metal polishes, as fillers in plastic wood, adhesives and dynamite, also for veneer and polyesters. An excellent hardwood, the wood and veneer is in high demand for decorative panelling, fine furniture and flooring. The tree is also grown as an ornamental and for shade.[14]

Special Uses

Improved cultivars are extensively grown in the United States and other countries for commercial nut production. Pecan nuts are eaten by a number

Table 21.1: Nutritional Analyses per 100 g Sample of Raw Pecans and Pecans Roasted in Cotton Seed Oil with Butter and Salt

	Raw	*Roasted*
Calories	710.0	740.0
Calories from fat (kJ)	630.0	673.0
Protein (g)	10.0	9.3
Total fat (g)	70.0	74.7
Saturated fat (g)	6.7	9.3
Cholesterol (mg)	0.0	0.0
Carbohydrates (g)	13.3	13.7
Sugars (g)	3.3	3.0
Dietary fibre (g)	6.7	5.7
Ca (mg)	73.0	73.0
P (mg)	603.0	603.0
Fe (mg)	2.4	2.4
K (mg)	603.0	603.0
Na (mg)	0.0	128.0
Mg (mg)	142.0	142.0
Vitamin A (IV)	130.0	120.0
Vitamin C (mg)	2.0	0.0
Thiamin (mg)	0.9	0.9
Riboflavin (mg)	0.1	0.1
Niacin (mg)	0.9	0.9

Source: G. E. Wickens: FAO Edible Nuts: Not-Wood Forest Products No. 5, 1995.

of birds, fox and gray squirrels, opossums, raccoons, and peccaries.[15] The demand for pecan wood has steadily increased in recent decades. It is used for furniture, cabinetry, panelling, pallets, and veneer. The wood has good machining properties, resembling those of true hickories.[16]

WORLD PECAN ECONOMY

Introduction

Pecan is North America's most important native nut tree. It is relatively little known outside America. However, there is certainly a possibility for developing a wider market. The United States is the world's largest producer of pecans. Although exact numbers for world pecan production are not known, it is estimated that the United States produces 75 per cent of total world production followed by Mexico with an estimated 20 per cent. Minor pecan production occurs in countries such as Australia, Israel, Peru and South Africa. Two types of pecans are produced in the US: native or seedling, and improved varieties. Native pecans are varieties that developed under natural conditions. Seedling pecans are produced from seed (the nut) and have not been budded or grafted. Improved pecans are varieties that have been genetically altered through breeding and grafting techniques to produce more nuts, and nuts with a greater percentage of nut meat.

PECAN NUTS INDUSTRY IN USA

Pecan Production and Utilization

Annual pecan production in US varies widely. From 1980 to 2004, 1999 saw the largest pecan crop, totalling almost 184,600 in-shell tonnes, followed by 165,910 tonnes in 1993. The lowest pecan production was about 66,545 in-shell tonnes in 1998. While this production variability exists for both native and improved pecans, improved pecan production ranged from 51per cent (1981) to 77 per cent (1982) of total production from 1980 to 2004. Total pecan production in US has increased from 83.4 thousand tonnes in 1980 to over 128 thousand tonnes in 2003, but declined to 84 thousand tonnes in 2004.

The wide fluctuations create a domestic pecan supply situation which adversely affects the domestic and export market. Wide swings have led to build-up carry-over stocks. Increased international trade helped balance supplies and together with carry-over stocks have tended to off-set the wider production swings of the 1990s (Tables 21.2 and 21.3).

Pecan Prices

The US average price for improved pecans has been consistently above the average native pecan price. In part, this price differential results from quality differences, meat yields, and differences in quantities produced.

From 1980 to 2003, US average pecan prices ranged from a low of 39.6 cents (1993) in-shell pound to a high of $1.12 (1992) per in-shell pound for native pecans, and from 60.1 cents (1987) to $1.54 (1992) pound for improved pecans. During the same period, the price of US improved pecans averaged 89.0 cents per pound, while native or seedling pecans averaged 56.4 cents—an average price difference of 57.9 cents per pound. Differences in prices from state to state reflect national and local difference in supply and demand, as well as differences in quality, nut meats obtained, and market outlets.

The annual gross value of pecans produced from 1980 to 2003 ranged from $134.4 million in 1996 to $330.4 million in 1999, changing dramatically over the year.

Table 21.2: USA Pecan Nut Production, Growers Price and Value of Output

Year	Improved varieties[1]			Native and seedling			All Pecans		
	Production	Price	Value	Production	Price	Value	Production	Price	Value
	Tonnes	Cents/pound	$1,000	Tonnes	Cents/pound	$1,000	Tonnes	Cents/pound	$1,000
1980	58409	84.8	109,015	25000	62.3	34,254	83409	78.1	143,269
1981	79341	64.7	112,987	74795	43.7	71,855	154136	54.5	184,842
1982	76818	72.6	122,776	22545	49.8	24,715	99364	67.5	147,491
1983	76023	67.7	113,199	46705	44.0	45,190	122727	58.7	158,389
1984	76923	68.2	115,406	28714	46.6	29,424	105636	62.3	144,830
1985	69318	79.1	120,582	41773	49.7	45,706	244400	68.0	166,288
1986	83023	79.3	144,765	40932	57.6	51,884	123955	72.1	196,649
1987	81659	60.1	107,953	37523	37.7	31,156	119182	53.1	139,109
1988	84318	62.6	116,210	55773	41.1	50,448	140091	54.1	166,658
1989	73182	78.6	126,491	33273	53.8	39,350	106455	71.5	179,040
1990	65227	128.0	184,135	18750	90.2	37,212	83977	121.0	247,590
1991	74227	114.0	186,917	52273	83.5	95,969	126500	104.0	309,524
1992	47636	154.0	164,333	18682	112.0	46,794	66318	145.0	240,362
1993	107773	62.9	149,189	49636	39.6	43,270	157409	58.6	213,862
1994	54045	115.0	136,945	27091	76.4	45,531	81136	104.0	207,345
1995	79455	112.0	195,216	34909	72.5	55,678	114364	101.0	271,377
1996[3]	75057	68.9	113,749	20170	46.4	20,606	95227	64.1	134,355
1997	92227	93.3	189,226	60045	53.0	69,994	152273	77.4	259,220
1998	50909	135.0	150,908	15636	77.2	26,544	66545	121.0	177,452
1999	99727	101.0	222,647	84864	57.7	107,751	184591	81.4	330,398
2000	72977	126.0	201,575	22409	75.4	37,193	95386	114.0	238,768
2001	112068	66.2	163,204	41795	41.2	37,897	153864	59.4	201,101
2002	59418	107.0	139,597	19173	60.3	25,436	78591	95.5	165,033
2003	92227	110.0	223,547	36000	68.3	54,082	128227	98.4	277,629
2004	63167	1920	267,215	21286	128.0	59,909	84455	170.0	326,924

[1] Budded, grafted, or Topworked varieties.
[2] Includes Arizona, Kansas, Missouri, and Tennessee in 1989-1992; Arizona, Missouri, and Tennessee; in 1993 and 1995; and Arizona, Mississippi, Missouri, and Tennessee in 1994.
[3] Estimates discontinued in 1996 for Missouri and Tennessee.

Source: National Agricultural Statistics Service, USDA. Fruit and Tree Nut year Book, 2005.

Table 21.3: USA: Pecan Nuts Production, Supply and Distribution (Shelled basis): 1980 todate[1]

Season[2]	Utilized Production	Imports[3]	Beginning Stocks	Total Supply[4]	Ending Stocks	Exports[3]	Domestic consumption	
							Total	Per Capita
	←			In Tonnes			→	Pounds
1980-81	38,353	429	21,282	60,064	13,897	2,101	44,065	0.43
1981-82	67,515	382	13,897	81,794	33,066	1,889	46,839	0.45
1982-83	46,280	732	33,066	80,078	25,806	3,287	50,985	0.49
1983-84	55,216	2,608	25,806	83,630	31,403	1,521	50,706	0.48
1984-85	48,888	871	31,403	81,162	22,689	1,225	57,248	0.54
1985-86	49,981	6,441	22,689	79,111	27,005	1,020	51,085	0.47
1986-87	56,505	4,918	27,005	88,429	28,569	1,241	58,619	0.54
1987-88	54,566	5,841	28,569	88,975	28,162	1,772	59,041	0.54
1988-89	60,824	1,224	28,162	90,211	31,885	2,651	55,675	0.50
1989-90	45,941	4,500	31,885	82,326	26,243	4,283	51,800	0.46
1990-91	43,933	13,736	26,243	83,912	20,672	8,015	55,225	0.49
1991-92	53,573	8,435	20,672	82,680	22,335	7,755	52,590	0.46
1992-93	33,399	13,654	22,335	69,389	21,694	7,449	40,246	0.35
1993-94	70,674	10,773	21,694	103,140	34,564	6,831	61,745	0.52
1994-95	38,844	14,690	34,564	88,097	24,791	6,063	57,244	0.48
1995-96	55,041	12,483	24,791	92,314	38,697	7,819	45,798	0.38
1996-97	42,294	12,669	38,697	93,660	26,902	8,815	57,943	0.47
1997-98	66,730	16,395	26,902	110,027	44,156	9,373	56,498	0.46
1998-99	29,505	18,764	44,156	92,425	22,650	8,991	60,784	0.49

(Contd.)

(Contd.)

1999-2000	72,251	12,811	22,650	107,711	49,669	8,493	49,550	0.39
2000-01	41,733	16,621	49,669	108,022	38,776	9,264	59,982	0.47
2001-02	65,576	14,431	38,776	118,784	47,195	10,042	61,548	0.48
2002-03	35,335	18,161	47,195	100,691	30,804	14,208	55,679	0.43
2003-04	52,688	27,142	30,804	110,634	41,622	14,128	54,884	0.42
2004-05[5]	37,186	16,134	41,622	94,942	29,513	15,459	49,969	0.38

[1] Conversion factors from in-shell to shelled basis varies year to year for production, stocks, and exports, and were 0.45 in 1996/97, 0.44 in 1997-98, 0.45 in 1998-99, 0.40 in 1999-2000, 0.44 in 2000-01, 0.43 in 2001-02, 0.45 in 2002-03, 0.42 in 2003-04, and 0.44 in 2004-05. For imports, the conversion factor was a constant 0.50.

[2] Season beginning July 1.

[3] Bureau of Census, U.S. Department of Commerce.

[4] Utilized production plus imports and beginning stocks.

[5] Preliminary estimates.

Source: Economic Research Service, USDA. Fruits and Tree Nut Year Book, 2005.

A review of the supply-price indicates that prices weaken when supplies reach or exceed 181,000 tonnes and strengthen when supplies fall below this level. In the 1990s, except for 1992s record price highs, prices for improved varieties appear to be trending slightly upward while prices for natives and seedlings have been relatively flat. Prices collapsed in 1993, apparently influenced by buyers who felt that they over-paid in 1992 and had to balance their equity in pecans. Prices bottomed again in 1992 and it is interesting to note that while prices fell in 1999, the year of the record high crop, the market did not collapse. Prices for improved varieties have been showing upward resistance at about \$1.13-\$1.30/lb with price bottoms at about \$1.00/lb. Prices for natives and seedlings appear to be swinging around \$0.70/lb average during the past three years.

Pecan Production by States

Depending on the variety, pecan trees require 205-233 frost-free days for the nuts to reach maturity, thus restricting pecan production to southern states. Fourteen states produce pecans commercially. Among these Alabama, Arizona, Arkansas, California, Florida, Georgia, Mississippi, New Mexico, North Carolina, Oklahoma, South Carolina, and Texas are the most important in commercial pecan tree growing (Table 21.4).

Improved varieties production is concentrated in Georgia, New Mexico, and Texas, and native seedling production is greatest in Texas, Oklahoma and Georgia. Average pecan production by state during 2002 to 2004 is shown in Table 21.5. The top five states, in order of native pecan production are Texas, Oklahoma, Louisiana, Georgia, Araknsas. The top five states, in order of improved pecan production from 2002 to 2004, were Georgia, New Mexico, Texas, Arizona, and Lousisiana. When total pecan production is included, Georgia remains the top producer, followed by Texas, New Mexico and Arizona (Table 21.5). Catestraphic

Table 21.4: Average Annual Pecan Production by States During 2002-2004: (Tonnes)

State	Production	State	Production
Georgia	25,000 (25.8)	California	1,667 (1.7)
Texas	22,727 (23.4)	Mississippi	1,667 (1.7)
New Mexico	19,697 (20.3)	Arkansas	1,364 (1.4)
Arizona	7,955 (8.2)	Louisiana	1,015 (1.0)
Oklahoma	6,667 (6.8)	South Carolina	879 (0.9)
Louisiana	5,303 (5.5)	North Carolina	682 ((0.7)
Alabama	3,106 (3.2)	Florida	606 (0.6)
		United States	97,091 (100.0)

Note: Figures in brackets are per cent share to the total output.

Source: USDA: NASS: Agricultural Statistics, Annual Reports Fruits and Nut, October 2004.

Table 21.5: U.S. Pecans: Production, Season Average Price and Value

Variety and State	*Utilized Production*						*Growers price*		*Value of Utilized Production*					
	1997	*1998*	*1999*	*2002*	*2003*	*2004*	*US$/kg.*		*1997*	*1998*	*1999*	*2002*	*2003*	*2004*
	Tonnes						1997[+]	2004	US$ 1,000					
(1)	(2)	(3)	(4)	(5)	(6)	(7)	(8)	(9)	(10)	(11)	(12)	(13)	(14)	(15)
Improved Varieties[1]														
Alabama	3,182	1,591	3,636	1,818	3,182	455	1.67	2.66	5,320	3,339	6,240	2,680	6,580	1,210
Arizona	8,409	5,909	8,864	7,273	10,227	6,364	2.75	4.07	23,125	20,670	24,375	16,480	23,400	25,900
Arkansas	545	136	345	545	636	455	1.65	3.08	900	345	600	720	1,540	1,400
California	1,364	773	1,091	1,727	1,682	1,591	2.90	4.86	3,960	2,822	2,808	4,826	5,254	7,735
Florida	273	91	682	227	227	182	2.20	3.30	600	220	1,500	435	500	600
Georgia	35,000	15,909	36,364	19,091	27,273	19,091	1.99	3.89	69,608	43,400	69,600	42,480	60,000	74,340
Louisiana	909	1,364	1,818	909	1,818	1,136	1.98	3.08	1,800	3,000	3,800	1,780	4,320	3,500
Mississippi	1,182	364	1,364	955	2,182	318	1.86	2.86	2,194	696	3,150	1,995	4,128	910
New Mexico	20,455	14,545	22,727	16,364	25,000	17,727	2.07	5.02	42,300	47,680	50,000	45,000	70,400	88,920
North Carolina	409	682	455	682	1,000	32	2.09	4.40	855	1,500	800	1,425	1,870	140
Oklahoma	1,364	91	1,364	682	682	2,727	1.67	3.52	2,280	244	3,150	900	1,680	9,600
South Carolina	955	364	364	55	1,500	364	1.85	3.96	1,764	992	584	116	2,805	1,440
Texas	18,182	9,091	25,000	9,091	16,818	12,727	1.90	4.05	34,520	26,000	55,550	20,400	41,070	51,520
United States	92,227	50,909	104,073	59,418	92,227	63,168	2.05	4.23	189,226	150,908	222,157	139,597	223,547	267,215

(Contd.)

Table 21.5: *(Contd.)*

(1)	(2)	(3)	(4)	(5)	(6)	(7)	(8)	(9)	(10)	(11)	(12)	(13)	(14)	(15)
Native and Seedling														
Alabama	2,727	682	2,273	455	455	45	1.14	1.85	3,108	1,011	2,400	490	690	84
Arkansas	1,045	114	1,382	227	1,091	318	1.39	2.64	1,449	220	2,128	250	1,728	840
Florida	545	500	636	409	727	45	1.32	2.09	720	825	840	450	960	95
Georgia	10,455	2,273	4,545	1,364	6,818	1,364	1.30	2.73	13,593	5,550	6,500	2,040	9,600	3,720
Kansas	1,909	23	1,591	1,318	909	818	1.47	3.85	2,814	44	3,220	2,175	1,740	3,150
Louisiana	4,545	5,909	6,364	1,818	7,273	3,864	1.06	1.60	4,800	7,800	7,000	2,000	10,880	6,175
Mississippi	636	182	455	409	1,000	136	1.28	1.76	816	264	550	495	1,100	240
North Carolina	273	455	136	182	136	14	1.43	3.30	390	800	180	240	150	45
Oklahoma	14,545	818	14,545	3,864	2,045	10,000	1.21	2.97	17,600	1,224	16,000	4,250	3,600	29,700
South Carolina	636	136	136	36	545	136	1.34	3.08	854	306	204	46	864	420
Texas	22,727	4,545	11,364	9,091	15,000	5,455	1.05	2.79	23,850	8,500	12,500	13,000	22,770	15,240
United States	60,045	11,091	43,382	19,173	36,000	21,286	1.17	2.81	69,994	26,544	51,522	25,436	54,082	59,709

(Contd.)

Table 21.5: (*Contd.*)

(1)	(2)	(3)	(4)	(5)	(6)	(7)	(8)	(9)	(10)	(11)	(12)	(13)	(14)	(15)
Total Pecan														
Alabama	5,909	2,273	5,909	2,727	5,000	1,591	1.43	0.81	8,428	4,350	8,640	3,170	7,270	1,294
Arizona	8,409	5,909	8,864	7,273	10,227	6,364	2.75	4.07	23,125	20,670	24,375	16,480	23,400	25,900
Arkansas	1,591	250	1,727	773	1,727	1,591	1.48	1.41	2,349	565	2,728	970	3,268	2,240
California	1,364	773	1,091	1,727	1,682	1,591	2.90	4.86	3,960	2,822	2,808	4,826	5,254	7,735
Florida	818	591	1,318	636	955	227	1.61	3.06	1,320	1,045	2,340	885	1,460	695
Georgia	45,455	18,182	40,909	20,455	34,091	20,455	1.83	3.82	83,201	48,950	76,100	44,880	69,600	78,060
Kansas	1,909	23	1,591	1,318	909	818	1.47	3.85	2,814	44	3,220	2,175	1,740	3,150
Louisiana	5,455	7,273	8,182	2,727	9,091	4,091	1.21	2.37	6,600	10,800	10,800	3,780	15,200	9,675
Mississippi	1,818	545	1,818	1,364	3,182	455	1.66	2.53	3,010	960	3,700	2,490	5,228	1,150
New Mexico	20,455	14,545	22,727	16,364	25,000	17,727	2.07	5.02	42,300	47,680	50,000	45,000	70,400	88,920
North Carolina	682	1,136	591	864	1,136	45	1.83	4.07	1,245	2,300	980	1,665	2,020	185
Oklahoma	15,909	909	15,909	4,545	2,727	12,727	1.25	3.09	19,880	1,468	19,150	5,150	5,280	39,300
South Carolina	1,591	500	500	91	2,045	500	1.65	3.72	2,618	1,298	788	162	3,669	1,860
Texas	40,909	13,636	36,364	18,182	31,818	18,182	1.43	3.67	58,370	34,500	68,050	33,400	63,840	66,760
United States	152,273	66,364	147,500	78,591	128,227	84,455	1.70	3.87	259,220	177,452	273,679	165,033	277,629	326,924

Source: NASS: USDA: Agriculture Statistics Board.

weather in recent years has destroyed a large number of pecan tree in the US. There is an urgent need to replace the damaged trees.

Consumption and Utilization

In the US while total domestic consumption of pecan nuts increased gradually, per capita consumption remained relatively flat. On an in-shell basis, annual domestic consumption averaged 52,610 tonnes during 1980-90 and 52,270 tonnes during 2000-05. Per capita consumption peaked at about 0.5 lb, shelled basis, during the mid-1980s and weakened during the early 2000s (Table 21.3).

US pecan imports and exports increased substantially since the 1990s. With annual production averaging 52,270 tonnes during early 2000s, and with flat-to-weak per capita consumption, exports have been essential to keep supply and demand in balance. Carry-over stocks, however, have been gradually increasing, also apparently influenced by the wider annual production swings and the record production highs of the 1990s. Carry-in stocks as of September 1, 2000, the start of the marketing year, reached an all time record high of about 50,000 tonnes, but have since declined to around 30,000 tonnes in 2005.

Pecan Imports/Exports

Historically, pecan imports and exports have been only a small portion of total US pecan production. From 1981 to 2003, imports (shelled basis) ranged from a low of 1.1 per cent (1981) of total US production that year, to a high of 51 per cent (2002), while exports reached an all-time high in 2002 with more than 14,300 tonnes (shelled) or about 40 of the total US production. Imports from Mexico and exports to European countries have increased significantly since 1988.

Exports

In 2002, the United States exported 19,875 tonnes of shelled and unshelled pecans. Major US export markets for shelled pecans include: Canada, China, Hong Kong, Mexico, Netherlands and the United Kingdom. Canada and Mexico dominate other countries in terms of US exports, accounting for nearly 43 per cent of all US exports in 2004. Large pecan exports to Mexico (8,519 short tonnes in 2004) are a result, in part, of shipments to Mexican maquiladoras that shell the US pecans and re-export them to the United States. It is estimated that up to one-half of pecans shipped to Mexico from the United States are shipped back to the United States after being shelled. Top export markets for US pecans are shown in Table 21.6.

Table 21.6: Top US Pecan Export Market (Tonnes)

Country	*1998*	*1999*	*2000*	*2001*	*2002*	*5-year Average*	*% of Average*
Mexico	3,657	1,403	2,595	1,820	8,519	3,599	26.7
Canada	3,568	3,860	4,209	4,168	3,476	3,86	28.6
Netherlands	1,770	1,397	1,581	1,574	1,917	1,648	12.2
Hong Kong	26	89	5	3	1,604	345	2.6
UK	1,726	880	1,997	1,680	1,494	1,555	11.5
China	0	20	0	10	849	176	1.3
Others	2,782	1,995	2,430	2,336	2,016	2,312	17.1
World	13,527	9,644	12,818	11,591	19,875	13,491	100.0

Source: USDA Economic Research Service Fruit and Tree Nuts Situation and Outlook Yearbook /FTS-2003/Octoboer 2003.

Imports

Among tree nuts, pecan imports rank third behind coconut meat and cashews. The United States imports both shelled and in-shell pecans primarily from Mexico, which accounted for more than 98 per cent of all pecan imports in 2002. Imports from Mexico totalled 30,008 tonnes in 2002 (Table 21.7).

Table 21.7: Top US Pecan Import Markets (Tonnes)

Country	*1998*	*1999*	*2000*	*2001*	*2002*	*5-year Average*	*% of Average*
Mexico	32,974	22,204	32,294	19,680	30,008	27,432	98.3
South Africa	0	44	0	70	207	64	0.2
Australia	281	528	123	0	78	202	0.7
Peru	0	328	430	125	48	186	0.7
Israel	8	6	7	11	13	9	0.0
Others	0	0	12	31	0	9	0.0
World	33,263	23,110	32,866	19,917	30,335	27,902	100.0

Source: USDA Economic Research Service Fruit and Tree Nuts Situation and Outlook Yearbook/FTS-2003/October 2003.

Other countries that have entered the US market include: Australia, Brazil, Canada, China, Israel, Italy, Peru, Spain, Zimbabwe and South Africa. Imports into the United States from all countries totalled 30,355 tonnes in 2002. Like exports, pecan imports exhibit cyclical behaviour, averaging 27,902 tonnes per year over the years 1998–2002.

Mexico-US Pecan Trade

Since 1992, Mexican imports of US pecans have decreased while exports have remained stable. This can be attributed to new plantings by Mexican growers in the late 1980s and early 1990s in response to high export prices in US markets. Bearing pecan tree stocks in Mexico have increased by 17 per cent since 1993, while production has increased by 36 per cent. Meanwhile Mexican imports of lower quality pecans from the United States have decreased by 64 per cent since 1993. This trend is expected to continue as more non-bearing trees come into production. New production is likely to be channelled toward exports first, whereas domestic consumption gaps will be met with lower quality pecan imports from the United States.

Policy measures that may have affected net trade in pecans between the United States and Mexico over the past decade include phytosanitary issues and the establishment of the North American Free Trade Agreement (NAFTA). In 1991, Mexico began requiring methyl bromide treatment of imported pecans. In 1994, concerned about possible introduction of the pecan weevil, Mexico banned imports of in-shell pecans from Alabama, Arkansas, Florida, Georgia, Louisiana, Mississippi, Oklahoma, South Carolina and Tennessee. It also temporarily requested phytosanitary certificates for imports coming from New Mexico and Texas until these last two states were declared free from pecan weevil later that year.

The passage of NAFTA seems to have had little impact on trade since tariff rates were sufficiently low prior to NAFTA. United States' tariff rates for in-shell pecans from Mexico were set at 5 cents per pound and at 10 cents per pound for shelled pecans. Although Mexico had a higher duty rate of 20 cents per pound on U.S. imports, these were of lower quality than Mexican pecans, and hence lower priced.

MEXICAN PECAN INDUSTRY

Introduction

Pecan nuts are the principal tree nut crop grown in Mexico. Most of Mexico's pecan nuts are grown in northern Mexico states of Chihuahua, Sonora, Coahuila, Nuevo Leon and Durango, where the weather is dry and cold during the winter months. Some plantings also exist in central Mexico. Chihuahua state has traditionally produced the largest volumes; moreover, newer areas in northern Mexico are increasing the proportion of total production grown in this region. According to industry sources the number of pecan growers in Mexico is currently estimated around 900. The number of commercially bearing pecan trees in Mexico is estimated at around 3.4 million, covering an area of about 68,405 hectares.

Mexico is the second largest world producer of pecans. Mexico's pecan production comes primarily from improved varieties. High quality pecans from Mexico are the product of optimal growing conditions including high light intensity, well-drained soil and sufficient water supplies. The main pecan varieties grown are Western and Wichita, which account for 80 per cent of new variety production

Production

The total crop area planted to pecan trees in Mexico has increased from 51,750 hectares in 1998 to 68,405 hectares in 2005. Farmers planted many new trees in the early 1990s, in expectation of continuing attractive export prices for pecans. However, because new trees take around 7 to 10 years to bear fruit, they started to produce in 1997-98. Pecans are harvested in Mexico from October to December.

As a result of attractive export prices, growers have increased input utilization to improve production and yields. Producers generally agree that the most costly inputs in producing pecans are electricity, fertilizers, labour, agro-chemicals and interest on operating capital. Electricity is a major cost because all commercial pecan production is irrigated and approximately 50 per cent of the farms are irrigated by wells.

The average Mexican pecan yield increased from 1.09 tonnes/ hectare in 1997-98 to 1.13 tonnes in 2004-05. A part of the increase is associated with the alternate-bearing crop cycle for pecans. Yields could be further improved with an increase of input utilization and improved tree care.

Area planted to pecan trees has increased considerably in 2004-05 and 2005-06 and is expected to continue increasing in 2006-07. Many farmers throughout northern Mexico suffered from the effects of the drought years, and many fearing a continued drought, reverted to less water intensive crops. Pecan orchards attracted the interest of some of these farmers, because of the favourable yearly prices on the international and domestic market. Therefore, some farmers dedicated part of their land to growing pecans and other crops requiring less water than their traditional crops such as wheat, corn, and cotton. Area planted to pecans for 2006-07 is forecast at 68,700 hectares.

Mexico has been producing pecan nuts in commercial quantities since 1954, when approximately 2,600 tonnes were produced.

Production has grown steadily over the years, reaching 68,222 tonnes in 2005-06, with exports comprising over 75 per cent of total production. Pecan nut production in 2006-07 is expected to reach 69,500 tonnes in-shell basis, up slightly from the 68,222 MT estimate for the previous year. Improved soil moisture conditions associated with the dissipating drought are expected to result in yield increases, with an incremental increase in tree numbers also boosting production Table 21.8 shows Mexico pecan area, production, supply and distribution matrix for selected years.

Table 21.8: Mexico: Pecan Nut Production, Supply, Distribution Matrix: (In-shell Basis)

(Area: Hectares, Trees: No. in 1,000: Production etc. Tonnes)

Item	*1998*	*2000*	*2003*	*2004*	*2005*
Area Planted	51,750	49,500	53,745	61,168	68,405
Area Harvested	41,600	48,500	52,000	58,111	64,800
Bearing Trees	2,850	2,910	3,100	3,250	3,350
Non-Bearing Trees	180	145	125	144	150
Total Trees	3,030	3,055	3,225	3,394	3,500
Beginning Stocks	0	0	0	0	0
Production	45,000	61,900	62,435	68,279	68,222
Imports	3,400	2,677	10,000	14,788	6,650
Total Supply	48,400	64,577	72,435	83,067	74,872
Exports	22,700	36,845	42,398	51,796	54,700
Domestic Consumption	25,700	27,733	30,037	31,271	20,372
Ending Stocks	0	0	0	0	0
Total Distribution	48,400	64,577	72,435	83,067	74,872

Note: Conversion factor used from shelled to in-shell basis: 2.00.

Consumption

Domestic consumption is highly price elastic. Consumption goes up when prices are low. Retail outlets, confectioners, bakeries and food processors are the largest consumers of Mexican grown pecans after the export market. There is also a significant informal market for in-shell pecans, especially during the Christmas holidays. Christmas is the most important consumption season for pecans. Mexican pecan nut consumption has increased from 25,700 tonnes in MY 1997 to around 31,271 tonnes in MY 2004 but declined to 20,400 tonnes in 2005. The decline was due to larger expoters. Official up-to-date statistics on pecan nut consumption are unavailable. Consumption figures are derived from production and export numbers.

Marketing

The grading standards for Mexico's export shelled pecans are the same as the standards in the United States. There are no standards for domestic Mexican pecans. There are not enough cold storage warehouses in Mexico to store pecans throughout the year. Because of this lack of storage, the market for pecans is saturated at production time (October through December) and short of pecans later in the year. Retail distribution to bakeries, food processors, and retail outlets is left to the wholesale market in Mexico, which is also short of storage facilities.

Trade

Exports

Due to increased planted area and new trees that went into production in recent years, total pecan nut exports have increased from 22,700 tonnes in 1997 to 54,700 tonnes in 2005. The increase in production is expected to drive exports in the near future still higher. Excellent growth potential for exports to markets such as Japan and Europe may divert tonnages to these destinations at the expense of the United States, which has been Mexico's traditional market since Mexico began producing pecans commercially.

Imports

Imports of pecan nuts in Mexico have increased from 2,500 tonnes in 1997 to 15,000 tonnes in recent years. The US is the main supplier of total imports of pecan nuts in Mexico. Table 21.9 shows pecan export and import trade matrix for Mexico in recent yeares.

Table 21.9: Trade Pecan Nut Matrix

Year	*Pecan, In-shell*			*Units Metric Tonnes*		
	Exports to			*Imports From*		
	USA	*Others*	*Total*	*USA*	*Others*	*Total*
2000	21,831	82	21,913	20,330	19	20,349
2001	13,684	6	13,690	1,390	15	1,405
2002	19,009	9	19,018	7,252	10	7,262
2003	23,513	5	23,518	8,315	0	8,315
2004	31,468	0	31,468	14,492	0	14,492
2005	25,573	12,561	38,133	5,099	0	5,099

Year	Pecan, Shelled			Units Metric Tonnes		
	Exports to			Imports From		
	USA	Others	Total	USA	Others	Total
2000	7,466	0	7,466	3,210	0	3,210
2001	4,167	0	4,167	262	0	262
2002	8,214	0	8,214	476	70	546
2003	9,442	0	9,442	675	0	675
2004	10,164	0	10,164	148	0	148
2005	14,564	2002	16,566	1552	0	1552

Prices

The price Mexican farmers receive for their pecans is a function of the US market. If supply is tight in the US market, prices are high in the Mexican market. The price the farmer receives from pecan shellers is based on the per cent of kernel of the pecan. Improved varieties such as the Western, which have around 55 per cent kernel, receive a premium price, while native varieties, which have around 40 per cent kernel, receive a lower price. Most of the pecans grown in northern Mexico are of the Western and Wichita varieties. The average price paid for Mexican pecans in 2004-05 was US$2.78/kg., in-shell basis and US$5.08/kg., shelled basis.

Stocks

In most of the years there have been no stocks at the end of the marketing year because the price of pecans was high enough to clear the market. Also, there are not enough cold storage warehouses to store a significant amount of pecans. Because of this lack of storage, as mentioned above the market for pecans is saturated at production time (October through December) and short of pecans later in the year.

REFERENCES

1. Menninger, E.A. (1977). *Edible Nuts of the World*, Horticultural Books Inc. Stuart, Florida. And Prescott-Allen, C. and Prescott-Allen, R. (1986). *The First Resource, Wild Species in the North American Economy*, Yale University Press, New Haven and London.
2. Toole, E. Richard (1965). Pecan [*Carya illinoensis* (Wangenh.) K. Koch]. In *Silvics of Forest Trees of the United States*, pp. 121-23. H.A. Fowells, comp. U.S. Department of Agriculture, *Agriculture Handbook* 271. Washington, DC.
3. Waite, M.D. (1925). Factors Influencing the Setting of Nuts and Fruits. *Proceedings*, National Pecan Growers Association 24:122-24.

4. Amling, H.J. and K.A. Amling (1980). Onset, intensity and dissipation of rest in several pecan cultivars, *Journal of American Society of Horticultural Science* 105(4): 536-40.
5. Vines, Robert A. (1960). *Trees, Shrubs and Vines of the Southwest*, University of Texas, Austin. 1104 p.
6. Nelson, T.C. (1965). *Silvical Characteristics of the Commercial Hickories*, USDA Forest Service, *Hickory Task Force Report 10*, Southeastern Forest Experiment Station, Asheville, NC. 16 p.
7. Adams, J.C. and B.A. Thielges (1978). Seed Treatment for Optimum Pecan Germination, *Tree Planters' Notes* 29(3):1213, 35. Bonner, Frank T. (1976). Storage and stratification recommendations for pecan and shagbark hickory. *Tree Planters Notes* 27(4): 3-5: Dimalla, G. G. and J. van Staden (1977). The effect of temperature on the germination and endogenous cytokinin and gibberellin levels of pecan nuts. Zeitschrift für Pflanzenphysiologie 83(3): 274-80 and Van Staden, J. and G.G. Dimalla (1976). Regulation of germination of pecan, *Carya illinoensis*. Zeitschrift für Pflanzenphysiologie 78: 66-75.
8. Smith, I.E. and others (1974). *Pooting and establishment of pecan (Carya illinoensis)*. Wangenh, K. Koch, stem cuttings, *Agroplantae* 6(2): 21-28.
9. Nelson, T.C. (1965). *Silvical Characteristics of the Commercial Hickories*, USDA Forest Service, *Hickory Task Force Report 10*, Southeastern Forest Experiment Station, Asheville, NC. 16 p.
10. Adams, J.C. (1976). A study of genetic variability in wild populations of pecan (*Carya illinoensis* (Wangenh.) K. Koch). Thesis (Ph.D.), Louisiana State University, Baton Rouge: Rousseau, R.J. (1976). A taxonomic and genetic study of *Carya illinoensis, C. aquatica* and their hybrid C. x *lecontei*. Thesis (M.S.), Louisiana State University, Baton Rouge, LA. and Society of American Foresters, 1980, *Forest cover types of the United States and Canada*. F.H. Eyre, ed., Washington, DC. 148 p.
11. Waite, M.D. (1925). *Factors Influencing the Setting of Nuts and Fruits*, Proceedings, National Pecan Growers Association 24:122-124.
12. Loucks, William L. and Ray, A. Keen (1973). Submersion tolerance of selected seedling trees, *Journal of Forestry* 71(8): 496-97.
13. Ryall, A.L. and Pentzer, W.T. (1974): *Handling, Transportation and Storage of Fruits and Vegetables*: The AVI Publishing Company Inc. Westpoint, Connecticut and Rosengarten, F. (1984), *op. cit.*
14. Menninger, E.A. (1977), *op. cit.* and Rosengarten, F. (1984). *op. cit.*
15. Vines, Robert A. (1960). *Trees, Shrubs and Vines of the Southwest*, University of Texas, Austin. 1104 p.
16. Adams, J.C. and B.A. Thielges (1977). Research underway on pecan timber improvement. *Louisiana Agriculture* 20(2): 14-15. and U Pecan is North America's most important native nut trees. Department of Agriculture, Forest Service. 1974. *Wood Handbook: Wood as an Engineering Material*, pp. 1-9. U.S. Department of Agriculture, Agriculture Handbook 72.

22

WORLD BRAZIL NUT ECONOMY

Introduction

The *Brazil nut* is a South American tree *Bertholletia excelsa in* the family Lecythidaceae. It is the only species in the genus *Bertholletia.* It is native to Guiana, Venezuela, Brazil, eastern Colombia, eastern Peru and eastern Bolivia. It occurs as scattered trees in large forests on the banks of the Amazon, Rio Negro, and the Orinoco.

The Brazil nut tree is a good example of the intricate eco-system of the Amazon, where plants and animals are inexplicably intertwined. Not only is the pollination of this tree so specialized, requiring one particular insect species to produce the fruit, but only one species of animal is capable of chewing through the extremely tough fruit pod to disburse the seeds for new tree growth. The agouti, a rather large rat (up to 10 pounds!) with extremely sharp front teeth, is solely responsible for reseeding the forest with Brazil nuts and ensuring the next generation of trees. In the Amazon rainforest, the tree, bee, and agouti are all dependent on one another for survival.

Brazil Nut Tree

The Brazil nut tree is enormous, frequently attaining the height of 40 to 50 m or more, and it can reach age of 500-800 years old. The tree is called *castanheiro do para* in Brazil and is found throughout the Amazon rainforest in Brazil, Peru, Colombia, Venezuela, and Ecuador. The fruit is a large, round woody capsule or pod, about size of a large grapefruit and weighing up to 2.2 kg. The fruit pods grow at the ends of thick branches, then ripen and fall from the tree from January to June, usually with a loud crashing sound as they fall 150 feet through the canopy like cannon balls. Inside each fruit pod, wedged in like orange segments, are 12 to 25 Brazil nuts, each within its own individual shell. Mature Brazil nut trees can produce approximately 300 or more of these fruit pods annually.

Brazil nut is a large tree, reaching 30-45 m tall and 1-2 m trunk diameter, and these are among the largest trees in the Amazon Rainforests. The stem is straight, and commonly unbranched for well over half the tree's height, with a large emergent crown of long branches above the surrounding canopy of other trees. The bark is grayish and smooth. The leaves are dry-season deciduous, alternate, simple, entire or crenate, oblong, 20-35 cm long and 10-15 cm broad. The flowers are small, greenish-white, in panicles 5-10 cm long; each flower has a two-parted, deciduous calyx, six unequal cream-coloured petals, and numerous stamens united into a broad, hood-shaped mass.

The fruit takes 14 months to mature after pollination of the flowers, and is a large capsule 10-15 cm diameter resembling a coconut in size and weighing up to 2 kg. It has a hard woody shell 8-12 mm thick, and inside contains 8-24 triangular seeds 4-5 cm long (brazil nuts) packed like the segments of an orange; it is not a true nut in the botanical sense. The capsule contains a small hole at one end, which enables large rodents like the Agouti to gnaw open the capsule. They then eat some of the nuts inside, but bury others for later use; some of these are able to germinate to produce new Brazil nut trees.

Despite their name, the most significant exporter of Brazil nuts is not Brazil but Bolivia, where they are called *almendras.* In Brazil, these nuts are called *castanhas-do-Para,* literally "chestnuts from Para". Indigenous. The genus is named after the French chemist Claude Louis Berthollet.

Fig. 22.1: Bnazil Nut Tree

Nutritional Value

Nutritionally, Brazil nuts are an excellent source of selenium and a good source of magnesium and thiamine. They are 14 per cent protein, 11 per cent carbohydrates, and 67 per cent fat. The fat breakdown is roughly 25 per cent saturated 41 per cent monounsaturated, and 34 per cent polyunsaturated. The saturated fat content of Brazil nuts is among the highest of all nuts, surpassing even macadamia nuts. Because of the resulting rich taste, Brazil nuts can often substitute for macadamia nuts or even coconuts in recipes. The high fat content of the nuts results in their not keeping well, and particularly shelled Brazil nuts soon become rancid. The nuts are also pressed for oil; as well as for food use, Brazil nut oil is also used as a lubricant in clocks and for making artists' paints.

Effects of Harvesting

Brazil nuts for international trade come entirely from wild collection rather than from farms. This has been touted as a model for generating income from a tropical forest without destroying it. Analysis of tree ages in areas that are harvested show that moderate and intense gathering takes so many seeds that not enough are left to replace older trees as they die. Sites with light gathering activities had many young trees while sites with intense gathering practices had hardly any young trees.

Statistical tests were done to determine what environmental factors could be contributing to the lack of younger trees. The most consistent effect was found to be the level of gathering activity at a particular site. A computer model predicting the size of trees where people picked all the nuts matched the tree size data that was gathered from physical sites that had heavy harvesting.

Natural History

Taxonomy and Distribution

Serthol/etia excelsa belongs to a pantropical family of trees (Lecythidaceae) that includes approximately 200 species in the Neotropics, distributed from southern Mexico into southern Brazil. The Brazil nut represents a single species in the well-defined genus Bertholletia. Although there is considerable variation in fruit size and shape and number of seeds per fruit, there is no justification for recognizing more than one species of Bertholletia.

The closest relatives of *B. excelsa* are among species of Lecythis commonly referred to in the vernacular as the Jarana group. Other species with edible seeds in the family are *Lecythis pisonis* and its relatives, *L. minor* and *L. ollaria.* The latter two species, however, sometimes cause hair and fingernail loss because of excess selenium accumulation in the seeds. Nevertheless, the differences between *Bertholletia* and *Lecythis* are so great that there is little hope for introducing genetic material from one genus into the other *via* hybridization. Consequently, germ plasma for improvement of Brazil nut production will have to come from the variation found within *B. excelsa,* not from closely related species in other genera.

Bertholletia excelsa is an Amazonian plant that prefers non-flooded forest (terra firma) in the Guianas, Colombia, Venezuela, Peru, Bolivia and Brazil. Brazil nuts are cultivated in tropical botanical gardens far outside its native range, and minor plantations have been established in Kuala Lumpur in Malaysia and Ghana in Africa.

Trees of *Bertholletia excelsa* occur in stands of 50 to 100 individuals that are known as "manchales" in Peru and "castanhais" in Brazil. Density of Brazil nut trees per hectare varies considerably throughout the Amazon. A study of Brazil nut production carried out in 1990 in eastern Brazil found 9 to 26 reproductive trees per hectare, while another study found only one tree over 10 centimetres dbh in a 100-hectare plot in central Amazonian Brazil.

There is some evidence that Brazil nut trees are gap dependent. Moreover, some authors have suggested that stands of the Brazil nut owe their origin to pre-Colombian Indians. An understanding of the development of reproductive individuals from seed is still needed before management of Brazil nuts in natural stands is possible.

Phenology

Flowering of *Bertholletia excelsa* occurs during the dry season and into the wet season. In fact, Brazil nuts grow naturally only in regions with a three-to-five-month dry season. In the eastern part of Amazonian Brazil, flowering begins at the end of the rainy season in September and extends to February. Peak flowering occurs in October, November, and December.

Toward the end of the rainy season, generally in July, the leaves of Brazil nut trees begin to fall. The new growth flushes from directly below the inflorescences of the previous year, and the new inflorescences are produced at the apex of the current growth flush. Large numbers of flowers are produced daily over a relatively long period. The flowers open between 4:30 a.m. and 5:00 a.m. However, the anthers start to dehisce within the bud several hours before the flowers open. The petals and androecia fall in the afternoon of the day that the flowers open.

Fruit development takes longer in B. *excelsa* than in any other species of Lecythidaceae. About 15 months are needed for the fruits to develop after they have been set. Consequently, Brazil nut fruits fall mostly in January and February during the rainy season. Under natural conditions the seeds take 12 to 18 months to germinate.

Pollination

Biology

The flowers of the Brazil nut are zygomorphic, with an androecium that is prolonged on one side into a hood that arches over and is tightly oppressed to the summit of the ovary. In addition the petals are oppressed to the androecium. Consequently, the flowers can only be entered by large-bodied bees with enough strength to pry open the androecial hood to obtain the pollinator reward that is thought to be nectar produced at the apex of the coiled androecial hood. Bees of the genera *Bombusl Centris, Epicharis, Eulaema,* and *Xylocopa* have been captured visiting Brazil nut trees. These bees are non-social or semi-social and therefore, do not lend themselves easily to manipulation by humans such as is the case with the social bees (for example, Apis, Melipona, and Trigona) that can be used to pollinate certain crops by transporting beehives from one plantation to the next.

For the most part, cross-pollination is needed for seed set in Neotropical Lecythidaceae. Therefore, the bees, and to a lesser extent bats, are essential for the pollination and subsequent fruit and seed development of Lecythidaceae. Although a low level of in-breeding may occur in *Bertholletia excelsa,* most seed set in this species is the result of cross-pollination. The development of self-compatible lines of the Brazil nut would facilitate plantation cultivation of this species by eliminating the need for cross-pollination by the difficult to manage bee pollinators.

Bees outside of the native range of the Brazil nut can effect pollination. For example, Brazil nut trees in Sri Lanka, Kuala Lumpur, and Ghana set fruit. However, it is not known if pollinators outside of the native range of the Brazil nut or "weedy" pollinators found in secondary forests are efficient enough to allow for economically viable fruit production.

Dispersal Biology

The fruits and seeds of *B. excelsa* are unique in the Lecythidaceae. At maturity the large, round, woody fruits fall to the ground with the seeds inside. The seeds, which have a bony testa, are removed from the capsules and dispersed by rodents, especially agoutis *(Dasyprocta* spp.*)* Agoutis and squirrels may be the only animals able to efficiently gnaw through the extremely woody pericarps. They eat some of the seeds and cache others for subsequent use. Consequently, the seeds are either eaten or destroyed or they are left in a forgotten cache where they may eventually germinate 12 to 18 months later.

Brazil Nut Harvest

Brazil nuts are harvested almost entirely from wild trees during a five to six month period in the rainy season. The fruits, which weigh from 0.5 to 2.5 kilograms and contain 10 to 25 seeds, are gathered immediately after they fall in order to minimize insect and fungal attack of the seeds, and to control the number of seeds carried away by animals. The number of capsules produced per tree ranges from 63 to 216.

Collection of Brazil nuts has a major impact on local Amazonian economies. Available figures, however, only provide approximations of total production because of the difficulty in obtaining accurate data from the Amazon. Brazilian production has ranged from 3,557 tonnes in 1944 to 104,487 tonnes in 1970. Since 1980, annual production has been around 40,000 tonnes. In the past, the welfare of many Amazonian towns, such as Puerto Maldonado, Peru and Maraba, depended heavily on Brazil nut production. In 1986, the total value of shelled and unshelled Brazil nut seeds exported from Manaus alone was $5,773,228. Most of the seeds are exported to England, France, the United States, and Germany.

The primary value (money paid to the collectors) of Brazil nut is estimated at $97 per hectare in 1990. This value includes an arbitrary 25 per cent discount to allow for seeds left in the stands. The secondary value—in other words, the money received by the exporting company for unshelled nuts by a United States based importing company—was estimated at $ 175.56 per hectare. The tertiary value—the cost of a bag of unshelled nuts in a Florida supermarket—was calculated at $1059.44 per hectare. Shelled and processed nuts are much more valuable. Efforts, such as those by Cultural Survival, to place some of the shelling and some of the processing in the communities of the collectors provide additional incentive for maintaining extractive reserves. Over a ten year period, utilization of a forest for Brazil nut production appears to be more profitable than extracting timber or cutting the forest for pasture. Unfortunately, latest economic data on Brazil nut production are not available.

Brazil Nut Plantations

The methodology for growing Brazil nuts in large plantations has been developed by Muller and his associates of CPATU, Belem, Brazil. As mentioned above, most Brazil nut production is still gathered from wild trees. However, plantations are being developed in various parts of the Amazon. A 12,000 hectare former cattle ranch at Fazenda Aruana, located at kilometre 215 on the Manaus-Itacoatiara Road in Amazons State, Brazil, had been partially converted to Brazil nut plantation in 1980. In 1990 about 318,660 Brazil nut trees were planted on 3,341 hectares. In addition, a large number of individuals have grown Brazil nuts in nearby forests belonging to Fazenda Aruana.

The original intent at Fazenda Aruana was to plant Brazil nut trees in 20 by 20 metre grids and allow cattle grazing between the trees. At first the cattle did not eat the leaves of the trees, but later they did. As a result, the spacing was reduced to 10 by 10 metre grids and the number of cattle was reduced to 300 head. The trees in the Aruana plantation are the result of grafting high yielding clones from the region of Abufari Amazonas where Brazil nuts are known for their large fruits and seeds. An important consideration in the establishment of this and other plantations is the provenance of the seed. Research studies have shown that fruit production as the result of fertilization between trees of the same clone is low. Based on this concept, it has been recommended that buds for grafting should be obtained from at least five different trees. A danger in using so few clones for grafting is that selecting for high fruit yield may also reduce the plantation's ability to resist future attacks of disease and insects.

Rootstock is grown in Fazenda Aruana from seed. The seeds are germinated by softening them in moist sand and subsequently removing the embryo by opening the seed coat along its edges. The embryos, which are treated with a fungicide, germinate in approximately 20 days and the seedlings are grown in plastic bags or cups. When the seedlings are transplanted to the field, about 200 grams of phosphorous is added to the hole in which they are planted. Rootstock is ready for grafting at about 1.5 to 2 years when the young trees have become well established in the field. Better scions are obtained if the leaves are removed from the branches 8 to 10 days before the scion is removed. This promotes the formation of vigorous buds that take better to grafting. Thirty days after the graft has been made, the rootstock is ringed distally to the graft. This allows the scion to gradually outgrow the branches of the root stock. After six years, the trees begin to produce fruit.

The plantation did not appear to have problems resulting from the lack of pollinators. Bixa orellana had been planted to provide pollen as a food source for pollinators. Moreover there is extensive natural forest surrounding the plantation and windrows with natural vegetation transect the plantation. The windrows harbour numerous plants known to be food sources for the pollinators of Brazil nut trees. Although the trees were nearly 10 years old at the time, there was no evidence or history of disease.

The owners of Fazenda Aruana have great expectation for this plantation. At the end of 12 years, they expect yields of 4.8 kilograms per tree and $480 per hectare. At the end of 18 years, they predict 8.5 kilograms per tree and $850 per hectare.

Tribal and Herbal Medicine Uses

The Brazil nut is a three-sided nut with white meat or flesh that consists of 70 per cent fat and 17 per cent protein. For centuries the indigenous tribes of the rainforest have relied on Brazil nuts as an important and significant staple in their diet—so important, that the nuts have even been used as a trade commodity, much like money. Indigenous tribes eat the nuts raw or grate them, mix them into gruels. In the Brazilian Amazon, the nuts are grated with the thorny stilt roots *Socratea* palms into a white mush known as *leite* de *castanha* and then stirred into manioc flour. This food is a valuable source of calories, fat, and protein for much of the Amazon's rural a tribal peoples.

With such a high oil content, fresh Brazil nuts will even burn like miniature candles when lit. The oil is extracted from the nuts and used by indigenous and rural period for cooking oil, lamps, soap, and livestock feed. The empty seed pods, often called "monkey's pots are used to carry around small smoky fires to discourage attacks of black flies, as cups to collect rubber latex from tapped trees, and as drinking cups. The husks of these seed pods have also been used in Brazilian folk medicine to brew into tea to treat stomachaches, and the tree bark is brewed into tea to treat liver ailments.

Plant Chemicals

Brazil nut oil contains mainly palmitic, oleic, and linolenic and alpha linolenic acids and small amounts of myristic and stearic acids and phytosterols. In addition to protein and fat, Brazil nuts provide the highest natural source of selenium. One single Brazil nut exceeds the US Recommended Daily Allowance of selenium use per person. The proteins found in Brazil nuts are very high in sulfur-containing amino acids like cysteine (8%) and methionine (18%) and are also extremely rich in glutamine, glutamic acid, and arginine. The presence of these amino acids (chiefly methionine) enhances the absorption of selenium and other minerals in the nut. In addition to the chemicals discussed above, Brazil nuts contain antimony, cerium, cesium, europium, fatty acids, lanthanum, lutetium, samarium, scandium, selenoprotein, tantalum, tungsten, and ytterbium.

Biological Activities and Ciinical Research

Since the Brazil nut has long been a common food, rather than an herbal remedy, it has not been the subject of any clinical research outside of that concerning its selenium content. Anyone using it "therapeutically" employs the nuts for their high content of natural selenium. Selenium is an essential trace mineral in the human body with antioxidant, anticancer and cancer preventive properties (especially, it seems, for prostate cancer).

Current Practical Uses

Brazil nuts and its oil are mainly used as a food in the United States. Brazil nut oil is clear yellowish oil with a pleasant, sweet smell and taste. It makes wonderful light oil for salad dressings and combining it with raspberry vinegar makes tasty vinaigrette. In addition, Brazil nut oil is often used in soaps, shampoos, and hair conditioning/repair products in South America, and this use catching up in the United States as well. It is a wonderful hair conditioner, bringing shine, silkiness, and softness to hair and renewing dry, lifeless hair and split ends. Brazil nut oil in skin creams helps lubricate and moisturize the skin, provides antioxidant benefits with its high selenium content, helps prevents dryness, and leaves skin soft, smooth, and hydrated.

Production and Utilization

Production of Brazil nut is confined mainly to four countries, viz. Bolivia, Brazil, Cote d'Ivoire and Peru. During the last five years there has been little increase in production at the global level. The substantial growth in Bolivia's output has been offset by a sharp decline in Brazil and Peru.

FAO is the only source of time series statistical information for Brazil nut. FAO compiles data based on national and other sources. Deforestation in the Amazonian rainforest has brought about a reduction in the harvest of Brazil nuts from about 104,000 tonnes in 1970 to only about 50,000 tonnes in 1980. World production from 1990 to 2004 varied in the range of 50,000 tonnes to 75,000 tonnes. Bolivia has become the top Brazil Nut Production, accounting for about 53 per cent of world output in 2004. Brazil's share was 46 per cent (Table 22.1). In-shell Brazil nuts are traditionally for the Christmas market in UK, Germany and USA as "mixed nut in-shell pack". Kernels are used in USA for roasting and salting for inclusion in mixed salted kernel packs. Approximately 60 per cent of the UK market is in kernels for coating with chocolate (enrobing), the remaining 40 per cent are marketed as raw packed kernels. The kernels are used for repacking in Continental Europe.

Table 22.1: Brazil Nut Production by Country, 1970-2004

Year	*Brazil*	*Bolivia*	*Peru*	*Cote d'Ivoire*	*Total*	*Approximate Price FOB*
	←		*ooo tones*		→	
1970	104.5	8.5	1.7	3.0	117.7	£378/ton
1971	67.0	10.5	1.6	3.0	82.1	£487/ton
1972	70.0	11.4	1.2	3.0	85.6	£466/ton
1973	52.1	7.5	1.3	3.0	63.9	US$ 0.63/lb
1974	35.8	10.7	1.4	3.0	50.8	US$ 0.77/lb
1975	51.7	11.8	1.3	3.0	67.9	US$ 0.59/lb
1976	61.0	14.8	1.3	3.0	80.1	US$ 0.76/lb
1977	54.0	11.9	1.2	3.0	70.2	US$ 1.28/lb
1978	40.0	11.4	1.2	3.0	55.6	US$ 1.33/lb
1979	43.2	8.7	1.1	3.0	56.1	US$ 1.04/lb
1980	40.5	9.4	1.2	3.0	54.1	US$ 0.98/lb
1981	36.7	10.4	1.3	3.0	51.4	US$ 1.07/lb
1982	36.8	11.0	1.5	3.0	52.3	US$ 1.63/lb
1983	50.9	13.0	1.5	3.0	68.4	US$ 1.41/lb
1984	40.7	11.5	1.4	3.0	56.6	US$ 0.81/lb
1985	45.0	12.0	1.4	5.0	63.4	US$ 0.82/lb
1986	36.1	15.6	1.5	5.0	58.2	US$ 0.90/lb
1987	36.2	17.8	1.6	5.0	60.6	US$ 1.09/lb
1988	29.4	16.1	1.6	5.0	52.1	US$ 1.18/lb
1989	25.7	17.5	1.6	5.0	49.8	US$ 1.70/lb
1990	51.2	17.0	1.6	5.0	74.8	US$ 1.62/lb
1991	35.8	13.0	1.6	5.0	60.4	US$ 2.24/lb
1992	25.3	18.5	1.6	5.2	50.4	US$ 1.39/lb
1993	26.5	17.5	1.8	5.2	51.0	US$ 1.48/lb
1994	38.9	16.5	1.5	5.2	62.1	US$ 1.61/lb

(*Contd.*)

Table 22.1: (*Contd.*)

Year	Brazil	Bolivia	Peru	Cote d'Ivoire	Total	Approximate Price FOB
1995	40.2	15.4	1.7	5.2	62.5	US$ 1.72/lb
1996	21.5	18.0	1.3	5.2	46.0	US$ 3.50/lb
1997	22.8	23.0	0.5	5.2	51.5	US$ 3.41/lb
1998	23.1	15.4	0.4	5.2	44.1	US$ 0.43/lb
1999	26.9	30.0	0.5	5.2	62.6	US$ 0.32/lb
2000	33.4	36.0	0.5	5.2	75.1	US$ 0.33/lb
2001	38.0	38.0	0.5	5.2	81.7	US$ 0.23/lb
2002	38.0	38.0	0.6	5.2	81.8	US$ 0.22/lb
2003	38.5	38.5	0.6	5.2	82.8	US$ 0.23/lb
2004	37.2	38.2	0.6	5.2	81.2	n.a.

Source: FAO STAT Database; November 2005.

Export Marketing

The world supply of Brazil nuts has varied from as high as 104,000 tonnes to around 72,000 tonnes (Table 22.1). This decrease can be attributed to the destruction of the rainforest. It was formerly second only to rubber as an export crop from Amazonian Brazil and still is a major crop in the overall economy of the region. Nuts are mainly exported to USA, United Kingdom and Germany.

Export is mainly concentrated in north-western Amazonia, Acre State and the Pando/Beni regions of Bolivia. The in-shell nuts are from the generally larger and round nuts from central and lower Amazonia and Pará and the kernels from Acre and Pando/Beni regions. However, over the past decade the demand for in-shell has been decreasing worldwide as traditions have changed and the Food Authorities have become more demanding; the demand for kernels, however, has remained relatively constant. Over 80 per cent of the commercial supply is from Acre where the differences between the Cruzeiro "official" and the Cruzeiro "parallelo" generally favours a contraband traffic between Bolivia, Peru and Brazil. The three influencing factors between production and final usage are the out-turn quality at the shipper's factory, the quality received by the importer at the port of destination and the quality delivered to the consumer, resulting in a rather precarious market. The situation is further complicated by three of the major processing/exporting facilities in Brazil being owned by members of the same family and controlling over 50 per cent of the market.

The importer buys a Fair Average Quality (FAQ) of the crop, which is determined by Combined Edible Nut Trade Association (CENTA) or by the Association of Food Industries, New York (AFI) from time to time during the year. This theoretically allows the market to trade different qualities as determined by the state of the crop at the point or origin. Sale by the importer to the final customer will invariably include guarantees and conditions not covered by the original purchase. Manufacturers have to conform to increasingly tighter legal specifications, particularly with regard to aflatoxin and coli bacteria, especially in Europe where raw or enrobed nuts are eaten. Since much of USA import is rendered sterile by roasting or blanching and detoxification processes, their import regulations tend to be less strict.[1] Blanched grades have been shown to be 99 per cent less contaminated than naturals (shelled but not processed) and are marketed as blanched whole, sliced, diced, slivered, balls, ovals, broken and paste; natural grades are Marketed as natural wholes, sliced and powder.

World exports of Brazil nuts have increased from 9.7 thousand tonnes in 1990 to 25.6 thousand tonnes in 2003 (Table 22.2). Bolivia is the largest supplier to the world market, contributing over 60 per cent of the world exports. It is followed by Peru whose share in 2003 was around 10 per cent and Brazil with 6 percent share. Despite larger volume exported the total value of the Brazil nut exports have declined sharply from about US$ 35 million in 1990 to US$ 13 million in 2003. This is due to a steep fall almost five times in price per unit during this period.

The volume of world imports of Brazil nuts increased form 16.9 thousand tonnes in 1997 to 23.6 thousand tonnes. However, the total value of imports declined from US$ 26 million to US$ 11.8 million. This decline is due to a sharp fall in unit import value. The major import markets are USA, UK and Netherlands (Table 22.3).

Future Prospect for Brazil Nut

Until now Brazil nuts have been gathered mostly from wild trees. In recent years, Brazil nut production has declined because of deforestation, the exodus of Brazil nut gatherers to large metropolitan centres, the flooding of some traditional Brazil nut stands, and perhaps because of disruption of pollinators caused by fires during the dry season when Brazil nut trees are in flower.[2] If traditional methods of Brazil nut production are to be maintained, very large extractive reserves will have to be established in areas of high Brazil nut tree density.

However, those interested in the preservation of tropical nature should be careful not to equate the establishment of extractive reserves with the maintenance of Amazonian biodiversity. Because Brazil nut gatherers and rubber tapers do more than just gather Brazil nuts, they often have a negative impact on plant and animal diversity. Indeed, extractive reserves may become little more than secondary vegetation with economic plants

Table 22.2: Exports of Brazil Nuts: Selected Countries and Years: (Tonnes)

Country	1990	1992	1994	1996	1997	2000	2002	2003
Australia	0	0	0	5	17	4	12	32
Austria	0	0	0	0	5	2	4	5
Belgium	0	0	0	0	0	160	461	295
Bolivia	0	0	0	0	0	13,714	13,968	15,697
Brazil	7,721	5,290	5,603	1,651	2,840	5,362	2,694	1,329
Canada	0	0	0	0	1	45	45	16
Indonesia	0	0	0	0	320	3,696	1,905	1,532
Italy	0	0	0	92	138	164	269	380
Netherlands	0	0	0	1,046	790	666	1,206	1,189
Palestine, Occupied Tr.	0	0	0	57	42	177	110	115
Peru	0	0	0	0	48	1,236	1,898	2,568
United Arab Emirates	0	0	0	0	0	0	3	120
U.K. Kingdom	0	0	0	216	145	126	119	209
U.S.A.	0	0	0	234	308	333	326	351
World Total	9,711	7,282	7,597	5,312	6,662	27,685	25,022	25,841
World Total Value (US$ 1000)	34,589	22,296	26,925	42,021	51,339	20,057	12,226	13,049
Value/per (US$/tonne)	3561.84	3061.80	3544.16	7910.58	7706.24	724.47	488.61	504.97
Value/Lb. (US$)	1.62	1.39	1.61	3.60	3.50	0.33	0.22	0.23

Source: FAO STAT Data Bank, November 2005.

Table 22.3: Brazil Nut Imports by Selected Countries: 1997-2003: (Tonnes)

Country	*Years*						
	1997	*1998*	*1999*	*2000*	*2001*	*2002*	*2003*
Australia	700	620	474	633	765	1,104	1,251
Austria	45	42	32	10	29	25	33
Brazil	50	25	25	50	0	52	57
Canada	616	595	451	775	696	685	615
Colombia	379	451	412	517	517	515	584
Czech Republic	57	99	123	117	157	104	101
Denmark	92	80	81	66	59	14	30
France	178	261	148	260	268	204	281
Germany	1,950	2,078	2,031	1,817	2,002	2,601	1,599
Greece	24	51	17	17	58	63	36
Iran, Islamic Rep of	0	0	0	0	0	0	120
Ireland	27	16	17	21	25	22	54
Israel	0	0	45	95	202	232	133
Italy	243	373	172	359	417	710	599
Japan	17	19	13	20	24	28	19
Netherlands	1,724	1,237	1,000	639	1,576	1,961	1,995
New Zealand	100	141	65	161	137	101	183
Palestine, Occupied Tr.	219	301	268	200	100	110	120
Russian Federation	0	83	54	131	164	488	1,234
Slovakia	70	96	77	29	29	35	39
Slovenia	3	0	10	26	10	13	23
South Africa	151	148	164	169	107	259	160

(Contd.)

Table 22.3: *(Contd.)*

Country	*Years*						
	1997	*1998*	*1999*	*2000*	*2001*	*2002*	*2003*
Spain	312	264	383	336	405	456	503
Switzerland	57	80	73	51	56	84	101
United Kingdom	3,792	3,212	3,963	4,451	4,484	4,545	4,790
United States of America	6,057	5,388	6,410	7,583	8,231	7,740	8,897
World Total	16,863	15,660	16,508	18,533	20,518	22,151	23,557
World Imports Value (US$ 1000)	26,017	21,442	16,024	24,021	11,843	13,253	11,766
Value/Tonne (US$)	1542.85	1369.22	970.68	1296.12	577.20	598.30	499.47

Source: FAO STAT Data Bank: November 2005.

such as Brazil nut and rubber trees scattered here and there. Therefore, the establishment of extractive reserves does not negate the need for well-planned biological reserves.

The future success of Brazil nut plantations is still open to debate. Until now, there have been no examples of economically successful plantations of this Amazonian tree. All attempts at growing tropical trees in plantations that do not naturally grow in nearly monotypic stands have been failures. In their native habitat, Brazil nut trees are distributed more or less scattered in the forest in much the same way that rubber trees grow. The economic disaster of attempting to bring rubber into plantations within its home range has been well documented and there is no reason to believe that Brazil nut plantations in Amazon will not meet the same fate as the Amazonian rubber plantations. Careful observation of the Aruana Plantation over the next decade may help determining if Brazil nut production in plantations is a viable alternative to collection from wild trees. If plantations are viable, then conservationists will have to be prepared to assess the impact that plantations will have on the maintenance of extractive reserves.

Finally, it is important that we do not place too much hope on Brazil nut extraction as an economically viable way to support an ever increasing population in Amazonia. In the first place, world markets may not be able to handle much of an increase in Brazil nut production, and, in the second place, such low intensity use of land is not capable of supporting human populations at the level needed to increase the standard of living demanded by more and more people. If an estimate that hunting-gathering and shifting agriculture can only support one person per 5 square kilometers and one person per square kilometer, respectively, are correct (there is no reason to believe they are not), then extractive reserves will do little to absorb population growth in Amazonian countries. The future of extractive reserves and humanity's ability to preserve a representative sample of Neotropical biodiversity depends on the success of controlling population growth and consumption both inside and outside of the tropics.

REFERENCES

1. Holt (1991) and LaFleur (1992), *op. cit.*
2. Kitampura, P.C., and Müuller, C.H. (1984). Castanhais nativas de Marabà-PA: Fatroes de depredacaoe bases para sua preservacăo. EMBRAPA, Centro de Pesquisa Agropecuãaria do Tropico Ůmido. Documentors 30:1-32 and Morï, S.A., *op. cit.*

APPENDIX

Nutritional Comparison of Edible Nuts and Peanuts

1 Ounce (28 grams)

Nutrient	*Units*	*Walnut*	*Cashew*	*Almonds*	*Pistachios*	*Hazelnuts*	*Chestnuts*	*Macadamias*	*Pecans*	*Brazilnuts*	*Pine Nuts*	*Peanuts*
	kernels/oz	*14 halves*	*18*	*23*	*49*	*21*	*4-5*	*10-12*	*20 halves*	*6-8*	*167*	
1	2	3	4	5	6	7	8	9	10	11	12	13
Calories	kcal	185	163	164	162	178	68	204	196	186	191	161
Protein	g*	4.32	4.34	6.03	6.05	4.24	2	2.21	2.60	4.06	3.88	7.31
Total Fat	g	18.49	13.14	14.36	13.03	17.22	1	21.57	20.4	18.83	19.38	13.96
Saturated Fat	g	1.737	2.596	1.1	1.575	1.266	0	3.387	1.752	4.291	1.389	1.937
Monounsaturated Fat	g	2.533	7.744	9.116	6.865	12.942	n.a	16.804	11.567	6.959	5.320	6.926
Polyunsaturated Fat	g	13.374	2.222	3.463	3.940	2.245	n.a	0.425	6.128	5.824	9.659	4.411
Cholesterol	mg**	0	0	0	0	0	0	0	0	0	0	0
Carbohydrate	g	3.89	9.27	5.6	7.84	4.73	1.179	3.79	3.93	3.48	3.71	4.57
Fiber	g	1.9	0.9	3.3	2.9	2.7	n.a	2.3	2.7	2.1	1	2.4
Calcium	mg	28	13	70	31	32	19	20	20	45	5	26
Iron	mg	0.82	1.70	1.22	1.19	1.33	0.94	0.75	0.72	0.69	1.57	1.30
Magnesium	mg	45	74	78	34	46	0.336	33	34	107	71	48
Phosphorus	mg	98	139	134	137	82	38	56	79	206	163	107
Potassium	mg	125	160	206	295	193	127	103	116	187	169	200
Zinc	mg	0.88	1.59	0.95	0.65	0.69	0.49	0.37	1.28	1.15	1.83	0.93
Copper	mg	0.450	0.629	3.15	0.376	0.489	0.418	0.162	0.340	0.494	0.375	0.324
Manganese	mg	0.968	0.234	0.719	0.361	1.751	0.336	0.861	1.276	0.347	2.495	0.548

(*Contd.*)

1	2	3	4	5	6	7	8	9	10	11	12	13
Thiamin	mg	0.097	0.057	0.068	0.238	0.182	0.144	0.201	0.187	0.175	0.103	0.181
Riboflavin	mg	0.043	0.057	0.230	0.045	0.032	0.016	0.025	0.037	0.010	0.064	0.038
Niacin	mg	0.319	0.397	1.113	0.404	0.510	1.102	0.645	0.331	0.084	1.244	3.421
Pantothenic acid	mg	0.162	0.345	0.099	0.145	0.260	n.a	0.171	0.254	0.052	0.089	0.501
Vitamin B6	mg	0.152	0.073	0.37	0.361	0.160	0.352	0.102	0.060	0.029	0.027	0.099
Foliate	mcg	28	20	8	14	32	58	3	6	6	10	68
Arginine	g	0.646	0.494	0.699	0.598	0.627	n.a	0.391	0.334	0.609	0.684	0.875
Vitamin K	mcg	0.8	9.8	0	3.7	4.0	0	n.a.	1	0	15.3	0
Vitamin E	mg	0.2	0.26	7.33	0.55	4.26	0	0.16	0.4	1.62	2.65	2.36
Total Phytosterols	mg	20	45	34	61	27	n.a	32	29	n.a.	40	62

*g = gram: **mg = milligram: n.a. =Not available.

Note: All of the nuts are unsalted: walnuts, almonds, hazelnuts, chestnuts, pecans, pine nuts and peanuts are unroasted, while cashews, pistachios, and macadamias are dry roasted. Pine nuts and peanuts are not covered in this book.

Source: USDA National Nutrient Database for Standard Reference: Release 18, 2005.

BIBLIOGRAPHY

Abdullah, A. (1994). *Technological Packages for Cashew Development.* Upland Farmer Development Project, Government of Indonesia, Ministry of Agriculture; Directorate of General Estate.

Abt Associates, Inc. (1999): *Assessment of the Status of Competitiveness and Employment in the Cashew Processing Industry in Mozambique*, Betheda, Maryland AIM.

Andrighetti, L. Bassi, G.F. Capella, P. de Logu, A.M. Deolalikar, A.B. Haeusler, G. Malorgio, G.A. Franca, F.M.C. Rivoira, G. Vannini, L. and Deserti,. R. (Editors) (1989): *The World Cashew Economy.* Inchiostroblu, Italy.

Anonymous (2002): *Tanzania Cashew Research Reports for 1994 to 2001.* Agricultural Research Insitute, Naliendele, Mtwara, Tanzania.

Anthony, K., de Groot and Haq, N. (Eds.) (1992): *Underutilized Tropical Fruits in Asia.*

Arpaia, M.L. (1994): *Macadamia Situation for Selected Countries.* California Macadamia Soc. Year Book: pp. 27-30.

Australian Macadamia Society (1995): *Australian Macadamia Industry*: New South Wales.

Bhaskara Rao, E.V.V., (1994): *Cashew Cultivation in Myanmar*, FAO Consultancy Report.

Bhaskara Rao, E.V.V.: *Integrated Production Practices of Cashew in India*: Paper Presented at the FAO Asian Regional Workshop, Bangkok, RAP Publication 198/12.

Bien, P.V. and Binh, N.T. (1997). *Cashew Tree Technical Aspects*: Workshop on Cashew Tree Development in Vietnam, Hanoi.

Bittenbender, H.C. and Hirae, H.H. (1990). *Common Problems of Macadamia Nut*: Hawaii Research Extension Series 112/05, Cooperative Extension Service, College of Tropical Agriculture and Human Resources, University of Hawaii at Manoa, Honolulu.

Brown, R. (1991). *Honduran Cashew Fruit Drying*. Report on Fine Dried Foods.

Burwash, M.D., Tobin, M.E. Woolhouse, A.D. and Sullivan, T.P. (1998). Field Testing Synthetic Predator Odors for roof rats in Hawaiian Macadamia nut orchards: *Journal of Chemical Ecology,* 24(4): pp. 603-630.

Caribbean Technological Consultancy Services (CTCS) Network, (1993): *Information Package on Cultivation, Processing and Marketing of Cashews*: St. Michael, Barbados.

CDI, (1995). Cashew nuts: Potential in Africa. *Partnership*, 18, 6-7.

Charles a. Leslie and Gale: *The Origin of Walnut*. Mcgranahan.

Chemonics/USAID (2002): Cashew Unpublished Document, January, 2002, Abuja – Nigeria.

China National Statistics Bureau: *Year Book of Statistics*.

China State Forestry Administration: *Walnut Total Area and Production*.

Collier's Encyclopedia: Macmillan Educational Company: 1991 Edition, Vol. 23.

Conception A.E. Magboo; (1998): *Integrated Production Practices of Cashew in Philippines*: Paper presented at the FAO Asian Regional Workshop, Bangkok: Rap Publication 198/12.

Cooper, T.H. (1988). *Macadamia: A Basic Understanding*. California Macadamia Soc.

Coulter, J. (1982): *The Market for Cashew Nuts and Cashew Nut Shell Liquid*. London, TDRI Market Note.

Deloitte and Touché ILA (Africa) (1997). *Cashew Marketing Liberalization Impact Study*. Government of Mozambique, Maputo.

Desai, Jaikishan (2001). *Cashew Production and Marketing in the Smallholder Sector in Mozambique*: World Bank Development Report, Vol. 2, No. 2, pp. 172-208.

Dewan, M.L., Nautiyal, M.C. and Shah, V.K. (1992): *Nut Fruits for the Himalayas*: Concept Publishing Company, New Delhi.

Diller, J.D., Clapper, R.B. and Jaynes, R.A. (1964): *Cooperative Test Plot Produce Some Promising Chinese Hybrid Chestnut Trees*: US Foreign Service Research Note NE-25.

Dillon, M. and Griffith, C. (1995). *How to Hazard Analysis Critical Control Point*: An Illustrated Guide MD Associates, Grimsby, UK.

Donafood, (1996): *Cultural Practices for Cashew Trees*. Agric. Services Department of Dongnai Province, China.

Eijnanten, Van L.L.M. (1985). *Development of Cashew in Burma*, FAO Consultancy Report.

Errington, M. and Coulter, J.P. (1989): *The International Market for Cashew Products*. Overseas Development Natural Resources Institute, Chatham, Kent. UK.

Ezeagu, W. (2002): *Nigeria: Assessment of the Situation and Development Prospects for Cashew Nut*: Abuja, Nigeria.

FAO (1982): *Fruit-Bearing Forest Trees*: Forestry Paper No. 34, Rome (Italy).

FAO (1998): *Expert Consultation on Integrated Production Practices in Cashew in Asia*: FAO Regional Office for Asia and the Pacific, Bangkok, RAP Publication 198/12.

FAO STAT Database (2000): *Time Series Data on Production, Exports and Imports*.

FAO STAT Database: (April 2006).

Farrell, O., Blaikie, P. and Chacko, E. (1998). *The New Rural Industries: A Handbook for Farmers and Investors*. Australia, RIRDC.

Fellows, P., Hidellage, V. and Judge, E. (1999): *Making Safe Food*. ITDG Publishing, London.

Ferguson, L. and Arpaia, M.L. (1990): *New Subtropical Tree Crops in California*.

Fernandopulle, M.N. (2000): Fertilizer Use in Cashew. *Cashew Bulletin*, 3(1): 1-6.

Finn Tarp: (1990): Prices in Mozambican Agriculture. *Journal of International Development*, Vol. 2, No. 2, pp. 172-208.,

Global Trade Information Services: *Global Trade Atlas (2005 and 2006)*, USA.

Government of France: *Custom Trade Data*.

Government of Himachal Pradesh: *Human Development Report 2002*.

Government of India, Ministry of Agriculture: Directorate of Economics and Statistics: (2004): *Agriculture Statistics at a Glance*.

Government of India: National Horticulture Board (1997): *Production Year Book 1997*: Vol. IV/97.

Government of India; Directorate of Foreign Trade Statistics: *Foreign Trade: Exports and Imports*.

Government of Iran: Ministry of Agriculture: (2002): *Pistachio Area and Production in Different Provinces*.

Government of Tanzania, Ministry of Agriculture (2000): *Tanzania Agriculture: Performance and Strategies for Sustainable Growth*: Dar-es-Salaam.

Government of Tanzania: Ministry of Agriculture and Cooperatives (1996): *Cashew and Coconut.*

Government of Union of Myanmar, Ministry of Agriculture and Irrigation, Department of Agricultural Planning: *Information Report on Myanmar Agriculture.*

Government of Union of Myanmar: Ministry of Agriculture and Irrigation: *Department of Land Records and Settlement: Area Under Cashew in the Country.*

Government of Union of Myanmar: Ministry of National Planning and Economic Development: *Review of the Financial, Economic and Social Conditions for 1996-97.*

Gray, Allen and Haas, Jenni: *The Almond People Blue Diamond Growers.*

Hall, F.J. (1965): Cashew Nut Processing part II. Trials of Equipment in Western Nigeria. *Tropical Science*, 8(4).

Hanlon, J. (2000): Power Without Responsibility: The World Bank and Mozambican cashew nuts. *Review of African Political Economy*: 27(83).

Hartley, A. (1977): *The Cashew Nut in Papua New Guinea.*

Hawaii Agricultural Statistics Service, (2001): *Data on Macadamia Nuts.*

Hawaii Agricultural Statistics Service. (2005). *Macadamia Nuts: Loss by Cause 1999-2000.*

Holliday, P. (1989): *A Divisionary of Plant Pathology.*

Howes, F.N. (1948): *Nuts. Their Production and Everyday Use.* Faber and Faber, London.

Indian Economic Times, New Delhi Edition: Wholesale Price data for walnut and almonds.

International Trade Centre (1990): *Edible Nuts: A study of the market in the United Kingdom.*

ITDG, (2000). *Cashew nut processing technical brief.* Rugby, United Kingdom.

ITDG: *Cashew Processing*. Project profile. Sri Lanka.

Jaffee, S. and Morton, J. (1995): *Marketing Africa's High Value Foods: Comparative Experiences of Emerging Private Sector*. World Bank, Washington, D.C. USA.

Jain, R.K. and Kumar, S. (1997). Development of a Cashew Nut Sheller. *Journal of Food Engineer*, 32: pp. 339-345.

Janick, J. and Simon, J.E., (Eds.): (1990): *Advances in New Crops*: Timber Press, Portland, USA.

Janick, J. (ed.), (1996): *Progress in New Crops*. ASHS Press, Arlington, VA.

Jaynes, R.A. (1961): *Buried-in-arch Technique for Rooting Chestnut Cutting*. Proc. Nor. Nut Grow Assoc., 52: 37-39.

Jaynes, R.A. (1964): *Grafting Chestnut Without Stock Plants*: Prco. Nor. Nut. Grow. Assoc., 55: 16-20.

Jones, V.P. (1995): *Review of Macadamia IPM in Hawaii*. Proceedings of the Hawaii Macadamia Nut Association: 35: 24-32.

Jones, V.P. (2002). *A Sourcebook for Integrated Pest Management of Insects and Mites Attacking Macadamia Nuts in Hawaii.*

Jones, V.P. and Armstrong, J.W. (1992): *Post Harvest Control Treatments for Tropical Nut.*

Jones, V.P., Delate, K. and Tome, C.H.M. (1992): *Macadamia Nut IPM: Where did All This Damage Come from*? Proceedings of the Hawaii Macadamia Nut Assoc.: 32: 48-56.

Jones, V.P. and Shearer, P.W. (1994): *Advances in the Management of Koa Seedworm and Southern Green Stinking on Macadamia in Hawaii*. Proceedings of the Hawaii Macadamia Nut Assoc: 34: 11-18.

Kangde Liu, Shibang Liang and Deng Suisheng (1998): *Integrated Production Practices for Cashew in China*: Chinese Academy of Tropical Agricultural Science, Danzhou City: Hainan Province, China.

Ko, W.H. and R.K. Kunimoto. (1992). *Fungal pathogens associated with macadamia quick decline*: Proceedings of the First International Macadamia Research Conference, pp. 15-17.

Kokwaro, J.O. (1986): *Flora of Tropical East Africa*: Anacardiaceous. A.A. Balkema, Rotterdam.

Kolinsky, Karen and Blank, Steven, C.: *Practices relevant for the Commercial Walnut Growers in Major Producing Countries.*

Koshteh, Karim and Erutyan, Vardan, E. (2003): *Global Pistachio Production and Marketing Challenges*: Report of the Research Study carried out at the University of Guelph, Ontario, Canada.

Macadamia Nut IPM Multi-Disciplinary Committee (2000). Macadamia nut IPM Protocol Supporting Documentation.

Mathew, A.G. (1994): *Cashew Processing*: FAO Consultancy Report.

Matz, S.A. (Ed.) (1984): *Snack Food Technology*: The AVI Publishing Company Inc. West Point: Connecticut. USA.

Maung Maung Lay: (1998): *Integrated Production Practices in Cashew nuts in Myanmar*: Paper Presented at the FAO Asian Regional Workshop: Rap Publication: 198/12.

Menninger, E.A. (1977): *Edible Nuts of the World*: Horticultural Books Inc. Stuart, Florida.

Nagao, M.A. and Hirae, H.H. (1992): Macadamia: Cultivation and Physiology. *Critical Review in Plant Sciences*: 10(5): pp. 441-470.

Nayar, K.G. (1995): Cashew: A Crop With Unlimited Potential. *The Cashew*: Jan/March, 1995.

Newafrica.com, (2000): *Tanzania Policy for Cashew Processing.*

Obiazu, P.C. (2000): *Quality Requirements for Nigeria Agricultural Products*. Seminar Paper Unpublished.

Ohler, I.G. (1975). *Cashew, Development of Agricultural Research*, Royal Tropical Institute, Amsterdam.

Ohler, J.G. (1979). *Cashew*. Amsterdam, Department of Agricultural Research.

Okafor, J.C. (1978): *Development of Forest Tree Crops for Food Supplies in Nigeria*; Forest Ecology and Management.

Okafor, J.C. (1980): *Edible Indigenous Woody Plants in the Rural Economy in the Nigerian Forest Zone*: Forest Ecology and Management.

Okafor, J.C., and Lamb, A. (1994): Fruit Trees Diversity and Conservation Strategies: in Leakey, R.R.B. and Newton A.C. (Ed.): *Tropical Trees: The Potential for Domestication and Rebuilding of Forest Resources.*

Partnership, (1995): Cashew Nuts: Potential in Africa. *Partnership* 18, March/April.

Payne, J.A., Jaynes, R.A. and Kays, S.J. (1983): Chinese Chestnut Production in the United States: Practices, Problems, and Possible Solutions. *Economic Botany* 37:187-200.

Purseglove, J.W. (1987): *Tropical Crops: Dicotyledons.* Longman Scientific and Technical, Harlow: Essex.

Ranaweera, B: (2000). Management of Tea Mosquito Bug (Helopeltis antonii) in cashew: *Bulletin* 3(1): 21-6.

Rietwo, David G.: *Impact of U.S.-Australia Free Trade Agreement on Hawaii's Macadamia Nut Industry*: Statement given at the US House of Representative.

Rosengarten, F. (1984): *The Book of Edible Nuts*. Walker and Company, New York.

Rowley, H.K., D.A. Martin, and R. Wong. (1994). Hawaii Macadamia Nuts. Final Season Estimates California Macadamia Soc. *Yearbook*: 40: pp. 114-121.

Russell, D.C. (1969): Cashew Nut Processing, *FAO Agricultural Services Bulletin No. 6.* Rome.

Ryall, A.L. and Pentzer, W.T. (1974): *Handling, Transportation and*

Storage of Fruits and Vegetables: The AVI Publishing Company Inc. West Point, Connecticut, USA.

Samuel, R. and Sharma, S.D. (1991): Clonal Propagation of Walnut. *Agric. Sc. Digest*, 11(4): 185-89.

Sharma, S.D. and Chauhan, J.S. (1981): Effect of Shell Thickness on Seed Germination and Growth of Seedlings Obtained from the Nuts of Seedling Nuts. *South India Hort*. 29(2): 87-89.

Sharma, S.D. and Kumar, K. (2000): *Present Status and Problems of Walnut Cultivation in India*: Paper Presented at the IV International Symposium: ACTA Hort. 544, ISHA 2001.

Sijaona, M.E.R.: *Assessment of the Situation and Development Prospects for Cashew Nut*: Ecology and Management.

Singapore Private Limited: (1977): *Myanmar Plantations, Project Report on Development of Southern Green Stinkbug on Macadamia in Hawaii*. Proceedings of the Hawaii Macadamia.

Steven, Jaffee, and Morton, J. (1995): *Marketing Africa's High-Value Foods: Comparative Strategies for Sustainable Growth*. Dar-es Salaam.

Sugano, J.S. and Mau, R.F.L. (2000): *Report on Macadamia Nut Production in Hawaii*.

Suit Chaikiattiyos: (1998): *Integrated Production Practices of Cashew in Thailand*: FAO RAPA Publication: 1998/12.

Surendra, G.B.B. (1998): *Integrated Production Practices for Cashew in Sri Lanka*: RAP Publication 198/12.

Tanzania Cashew Nut Board: *Raw Cashew Nuts Production, Producer Prices and Export Prices*.

Tanzania Marketing Development Bureau: (1993): *Industry Review of Cashew Nuts 1992/93*, Dar-es-Salaam.

Tarp Finn (1990). Prices in Mozambican Agriculture. *Journal of International Studies*.

Tewari, T.N.: CM Uttranchal (2005): Statement on his government achievements: In *Hindustan Times*, 12 April 2005.

Thakur: D.S. (1997): High-Technology Agriculture and Organic Farming in Himachal Pradesh for Higher Production, Income, Sustainable Agriculture and Evergreen Revolution: in *Indian Farming*: Vol. 47, No. 7: October 1997.

The Clipper (1994): US cashew kernel imports remain strong. *The Clipper*, 4.

Tin Saung, U. (1997). *Country Report on Oil Palm Development in Myanmar*.

Tobin, M.E., Kohler, A.E. Kohler and Sugihara, R.T. (1997). Effects of simulated rat damage on yields of macadamia trees: *Crop Protection* 16(3): 203-208.

Topper C.P., Caligari P.D.S., Kullaya A.K., Shomari S.H. Kasuga, L.J., Masawe P.A.L. and Mounami, A.A., (Eds.): *Proceedings of the International Cashew and Coconut Conference Trees for Life*—The Key to Development: Biohybirds International Ltd., Reading, UK.

Townsend, C.C. and Guest, E. (Eds.). (1985): *Flora of Iraq*, Vol. 8. Ministry of Agriculture and Agrarian Reforms: Baghdad.

Tripathi, R.S. and Jagdish Kumar: (1992): *Nut Fruit Production and Marketing in Hills*: G.P. Pant University of Agriculture and Technology: Hil Campus, Ranichauri, Tehri-Garhwal.

Tutin, T.G., Heywood, V.H., Burges, N.A., Valentine, D.H., Walters, S.M. and Webb, D.A. (Eds.) (1964): *Flora Europea*, Vol. L, University Press, Cambridge.

U.S. Department of Agriculture. (1993): *Agricultural Statistics for Macadamia Nuts*. Government Printing Office, Washington, DC.

U.S. International Trade Commission. (1998). *Macadamia Nuts: Economic and Competitive Conditions Affecting the US Industry*.

U.S.A. California (1991): *Paramount Farms Almond Report*, Bakersfield.

University of California: *Walnut Industry*, Fact Sheet.

University of Dar-es-Salaam, Economic Research Bureau, Tanzania: (1980): A Preliminary Analysis of the decline in Cashew Production: 1974-1979: Causes, Possible Remedies and Lessons for Rural Development Policy.

USDA Foreign Agriculture Service: Agricultural Attaché's Chile Tree Nuts Annual Reports.

USDA FAS Agricultural Attaché's Report: PR China Tree Nuts Annual Reports.

USDA Foreign Agriculture Service Agriculture Attaché's China Annual Tree Nut Report: 2005.

USDA Foreign Agriculture Service Agriculture Attaché's India: Tree Nut Annual Reports.

USDA Foreign Agriculture Service Agriculture Attaché's Italy: Tree Nut Annual Reports.

USDA Foreign Agriculture Service Agriculture Attachés France: Tree Nuts Annual Reports.

USDA Fruit and Tree Nut Year Book 2005.

USDA FAS Online: Horticultural and Tropical Products Division: Walnut Situation and Outlook in Selected Countries: 2002/03 Report.

USDA: Foreign Agriculture Service: Agricultural Attaché's Italy Tree Nut Annual Reports.

USDA: Foreign Agriculture Service: Agricultural Attaché's Spain Tree Nut Annual Reports.

USDA: Foreign Agriculture Service: Agriculture Attaché's Turkey Tree Nut Annual Reports.

USDA: National Agricultural Statistics Service: Fruits and Tree Nut: *Annual Year Book.*

Usman Daras: (1998): *Integrated Production Practices of Cashew in Indonesia*: FAO RAP Publication 198/12.

Vaidehi, M.P. and Ray, Babu, R.M. (2000): *Cashew Apple and Nut Recipes with Nutritive Value.* Bangalore, India, Division of Rural Home Science, University of Agricultural Sciences.

Vietnam Cashew Tree Association, (1997): *Present Situation of Cashew Production and Programs.*

Vietnam National Institute of Planning and Projects: (1997): *Orientation for Cashew Tree Development in Vietnam*, Hanoi.

Waithaka, J.H.G.: (2002): *Assessment of the Situation and Development Prospects for the Cashew Nut Sector.*

Wickens, G.E., Haq, N. and Day, P.: (Eds.) (1989): *New Crops for Food and Industry.*

Wickens, G.E. (1995): *Edible Nuts: Non-wood Forest Products.*

Wilson, R. (1975): *The Market for Cashew Nut Kernels and Cashew Nut Shell Liquid.* Tropical Products Institute: London.

Wimalsiri, P., Sinnatamby, A., Samaranayake, S. and Samarasinghe, C.R. (1971): Cashew Apple Wine. *Industry Prospect Report, 44.* Industrial Development Board, Sri Lanka.

World Bank (1995): Tanzania Export Crop Liberalization Review Mission Aide-Memoir.

World Bank (1995) Mozambique: Country Assistance Strategy.

World Crops (UK) (1970): *Cashew Nut Production in Tanzania.*

INDEX